WHERE HAVE ALL THE BIRDS GONE?

PETER MCCANN

All correspondence to the author:
pete.mccann@gmail.com

© Copyright Peter J McCann
First Printed 2023

The right of Peter J McCann to be identified as the author of this work has been asserted by him in accordance with the Copyright, Designs and Patents act.

All rights reserved. No part of this publication may be reproduced, stored in or introduced into a retrieval system, or transmitted, in any form, or by any means (electronic, mechanical, photocopying, recording or otherwise) without the prior written permission of the publisher.

Any person who does any unauthorised act in relation to this publication may be liable to criminal prosecution and civil claims for damages.

This book is sold subject to the condition that it shall not, by way of trade or otherwise, be lent, re-sold, hired out, or otherwise circulated without the publisher's prior consent in any form of binding or cover other than that in which it is published and without a similar condition including this condition being imposed on the subsequent purchaser.

ISBN: 978-0-646-88191-1

Proudly produced by

TheBookStudio

www.thebookstudio.com.au

Cover Image

Peter J McCann is the tall man depicted left on the front cover image. The men alongside him comprised the machine gun group of his platoon section. They were 2 key members of No.1 Section of the Assault Pioneer Platoon which deployed on active service to Vietnam from 17 November 1969 until 12 November 1970 as a Support Company element of 8 Battalion, The Royal Australian Regiment (8 RAR).

The man on the far right, Allan Small, was the primary carrier of the M60 machine gun, while the man in the centre, Des McGrath, was No.2 on the gun. During 8 RAR's deployment to Vietnam, these 2 men shared the carry of their M60 machine gun with occasional assistance from other section members.

On those rare occasions when they weren't out into the field, these 3 men shared rudimentary tent habitation at Nui Dat — the 1st Australian Task Force (1 ATF) base — and became very close mates. Each of them were National Servicemen from the 15th Intake, which fed into the Australian Army on 30 January 1969. They came from quite amazingly diverse civilian backgrounds — public servant, farmer, and carpenter. They resumed and remained in their respective professions for many years after their terms of National Service concluded. Allan Small went on to become Governor of the Coburg Prison Complex — Pentridge Gaol — in Melbourne, Victoria.

When this image was taken, they'd just returned to Nui Dat after completion of one of the battalion's early operations. They are filthy, drenched in sweat and utterly exhausted.

Dedicated to...

LACHLAN MARTIN — 'Signaller Martin L' — the late eldest son of my sister-in-law, Amalia Parke, and Michael Martin, who died in a parachute training accident in Western Australia on 14 May 1996 while serving as a member of 152 Signal Squadron of the Special Air Service Regiment (SASR).

His loving family-focused and effervescent nature, remains very clear in my mind and in those of all my family members. We continue to miss his infectious laughter and mischievous use of black humour. It was an absolute delight to have known him during his short, but hugely well-lived life of only 23 years. Lachlan lived for his Regiment. His horrific death robbed it of a committed and valued member, and his extended family of a wonderful person.

MY WIFE AND CHILDREN who, over many years have somehow managed to put up with a husband and father who has, on balance, been a very difficult person to live and interact with. Nevertheless, each of them has — in quite diverse ways — fully supported me in this telling of my story.

ALL MY ARMY MATES of the Assault Pioneer Platoon, Support Company, 8 Battalion, The Royal Australian Regiment (8 RAR), who served with me in Vietnam and who I have never forgotten and, more generally, to all those more than 60,000 Australian servicemen, servicewomen, and wonderful civilian doctors, nursing, and medical staff, who also served in Vietnam and did their duty for their country.

Acknowledgements

No one can write a tome of this size, telling a very personal story, without a lot of constructive criticism, technical assistance and most importantly of all, ongoing encouragement and support. Fortunately, I received all of that abundantly.

I'd like to formally recognise the very important role that my family played during those many intermittent periods of time when I locked myself away to either write or research aspects of the story I wanted to tell. Without the unwavering tacit support of my lovely wife Elvira (Elvi) — she thought I'd never finish it — this book would never have been written.

For the most part I was a very reluctant author. I didn't want to put too much effort into the writing of this book because I found it really hard work. It wasn't at all easy for me and I am inherently, a lazy person. However, whenever the urge to work on my manuscript became compelling, many aspects of my family life were put on hold as I selfishly brushed aside normality during those relatively short, but frenetically energetic moments. There were long periods of time — several or more years — on at least 5 occasions, when I found it difficult — impossible would be more truthful — to open the embryonic, emerging, and near final manuscript on my computer.

I spent a further couple of years — perhaps even longer — intermittently striving to 'finesse' it by making it as factually and editorially perfect as possible. I was never satisfied with my work until one day when I vaguely recalled the old academic maxim of the 'law of diminishing returns', which I was introduced to at my 'alma mater' back in 1965. After another lengthy period of self-contemplation, I applied the associated principles of that economic theory to what I'd been grappling with for many years, and was able to bring my manuscript to finality.

This public telling of my story hasn't been easy for me because I'm not a particularly gregarious person, and it has brought back into very clear focus what I and my platoon mates experienced together in Vietnam way back in 1969-70. The public disclosure of how these experiences have impacted my subsequent life, and that of my family, hasn't been something I've done without considered and almost agonizing thought. While the jury is still out as to whether this public telling of my story has been personally beneficial for me in a psychological sense, I'm inclined to say, no…it hasn't!

I pondered long and hard as to whether any aspect of my story should be redacted and for the most part, I've not acceded to that very attractive temptation. Those few omissions of factual detail that remain are simply because I concluded that on balance, it's probably better for that not to be publicly recorded. I'm only talking about 2 or 3 happenings or events, and nothing that impacts adversely on me, in particular. I've not sanitised any aspect of my behaviour — some of which was extremely out of character to say the least — during my time in Vietnam.

As part of the reality testing of the operational content of my story, once I completed the early draft of the manuscript I sought feedback, advice, and guidance from a number of people, all of whom energetically responded to my never-ending requests during this very lengthy phase. Some of them had the benefit of reviewing the entire 'bones only' manuscript, while others were only provided with excerpts relating to their particular areas of expertise.

A number of my former platoon mates provided me with invaluable clarification, confirmation, and otherwise, as to events and happenings that took place those many years ago, as well as their unqualified support for the story I wanted to tell. I'm forever indebted to Peter Cousins, John Dolgan, Robin Jagger, Paul Jansen, Terry Lucas, Des McGrath, Denis McNab, Dave Matheson, Bob O'Callaghan, Allan Small, Jeff (JJ) Smith, Fred Vincent (my former section commander) and Peter Wood.

I'd like to formally recognise the very significant contribution that LTCOL Peter J Phillips Retd made. For the most part, he was my commanding officer in Vietnam and I talk about him as honestly as I can recall. While some former commanding officers may well have asked me to revise, edit, or even delete personal references to them that they may have been uncomfortable with, he never did. That's a huge credit to Peter and I thank him for that trust and belief he bestowed on me in this telling of my story. I must also thank him for alerting me — correctly — to my propensity of using double adjectives in descriptive sentences.

Sadly, after a decade or more of declining health, Peter passed away on 25 January 2023, several weeks after the manuscript was signed-off by me for professional production. He was a very good soldier and an even better man. Vale, Peter John Phillips — 'Skipper' — or 'the boss', and my very good friend.

I wouldn't have been able to make my story as detailed and technically accurate and informative as I believe it to be, without the wonderful advice and support I received from Len Avery, Frank Corcoran, Vin Cosgrove, Neil Denham, Derrill de Heer, Robert A Hall, Mick Haxell, John Hewett, Lachlan Irvine, Greg Monteith, Rodney Nott, Noel Payne, Francis (Adrian) Roberts, Pete Ryan, and John Thornton.

Finally, there were a few people who I really must thank. They provided me with the very early encouragement and impetus to tell my story. In this regard, I am exceedingly grateful to Michael Dowsett, Robert A Hall, Steve Lewis, and Graham Walker.

Peter McCann

Contents

Foreword		9
Preface		10
Epigraph		13
Part 1 - Life Before the Army		**15**
Chapter 1	Teenage Years	16
Part 2 - The Australian Army		**33**
Chapter 2	Induction and Enlistment	34
Chapter 3	Recruit Training	37
Part 3 - Infantry and Battalion Training		**71**
Chapter 4	Enoggera Barracks	72
Chapter 5	Infantry Corps Training	74
Chapter 6	Assault Pioneer Platoon Training	81
Chapter 7	Canungra Jungle Warfare Training Centre	91
Chapter 8	Final Exercises	100
Chapter 9	Pre-embarkation Leave	101
Part 4 - Deployment to Vietnam		**105**
Chapter 10	Aboard HMAS *Sydney*	106
Part 5 - Vietnam		**121**
Chapter 11	Phuoc Tuy Province	122
Chapter 12	Climate	125
Chapter 13	Terrain	130
Chapter 14	Mosquitoes and Malaria	133
Chapter 15	Ants and Other Afflictions	136
Chapter 16	1st Australian Task Force (1ATF) Nui Dat	149
Chapter 17	Weapons	178
Chapter 18	Operational Support	200
Chapter 19	Logistics	236
Chapter 20	Assault Pioneer Platoon Demographics	257
Chapter 21	Rules of Engagement	265
Chapter 22	Contact	269
Chapter 23	Operational Tasking	276
Chapter 24	Vung Tau	348
Chapter 25	Behaving Badly	372
Chapter 26	'The Vietnam Game'	378

Part 6 - Returning to Australia		**383**
Chapter 27	The Voyage Home	384
Part 7 - Home Sweet Home		**391**
Chapter 28	Welcome Home	392
Chapter 29	Discharge from the Army	396
Chapter 30	Return to Civilian Life	399
Chapter 31	8 RAR Reunions	408
Part 8 - Reflection		**413**
Chapter 32	Personal Introspection	414
Chapter 33	Vietnam	417
Chapter 34	Conscription	420
Chapter 35	The Australian Army	424
Chapter 36	Agent Orange	428

Epilogue		431
Appendix 1.	Personal Items	432
Appendix 2.	Australian Military Forces 'Guide' to South Vietnam	433
Appendix 3.	Climate data for Vung Tau - Phuoc Tuy Province Vietnam	434
Appendix 4.	Operational Rations	436
Appendix 5.	Equipment and Associated Weights	437
Appendix 6.	Assault Pioneer Platoon Demographics Enhanced	443
Appendix 7.	Assault Pioneer Platoon Activity Matrix	446
Appendix 8.	Enhancing Vietnamese Culture	447
Appendix 9.	US Herbicide Missions Delivered in South Vietnam	449
Abbreviations		450
Bibliography		453

FOREWORD

This book by Peter McCann is an 'in your face' expose and intimate sharing of his experiences as a National Serviceman serving in the Australian Army from 30 January 1969 until 29 January 1971. During that time, he served in Vietnam for 12 months as an infantry soldier with 8 Battalion, The Royal Australian Regiment (8 RAR). The story he tells focuses extensively on that time in his life.

McCann has included a substantial amount of educative material about the life of an infantryman undertaking recruit, corps, and operational training in Australia prior to deployment on active service and soldiering in Vietnam circa 1969-1970. The amount of technical and other detail he has included as background and contextual overlay, is nothing short of astonishing.

He has also managed to inject humour, as well as pathos, into his fascinating story which also broadly tells about related personal issues he has had to deal with after his return to civilian life in Australia. He also raises some of his strongly held views on several issues of continuing interest within many veteran networks and wider community frameworks operating in Australia today.

While parts of his story are confronting, he has told of them in a way which is captivating and real. Given its wide range of scope, detail and personal revelation, his story is an interesting mix. Frankly, it is a compelling and absorbing read. Much of what he tells is extremely informative and his written record of history will prove to be a valuable educational resource for any student or researcher interested in the life of an Australian infantry soldier deployed to the Vietnam conflict.

Those of you who do ponder thoughtfully over his story will understand and appreciate the many word pictures he so aptly describes. They will garner an appreciation of the complex, difficult, and harsh operational life of Australian infantry soldiers deployed to Vietnam. Importantly, they will also understand, to some extent, how operational service in Vietnam has damaged the mental health of many Australian men and women who fought in, or who were otherwise exposed to, that conflict.

The title he has chosen for his book is an interesting and good one. Once having digested the content of his story, it will sit well with most readers. You will have to persevere almost to the end to make that subtle connection.

LTCOL Peter J Phillips Retd
Commander, Assault Pioneer Platoon, Support Company
8 Battalion, The Royal Australian Regiment (8 RAR)
South Vietnam: 5 April - 5 November 1970

PREFACE

This book is an original work which for the most part, tells of my 2 years of service in the Australian Army and my operational deployment to Vietnam — 17 November 1969 until 11 November 1970 — as a member of the Assault Pioneer Platoon, Support Company, 8 Battalion, The Royal Australian Regiment (8 RAR).

In this story, I have relied extensively on my recall of events and happenings that took place decades ago, a few remaining rough handwritten contemporaneous notes — for reasons I now no longer remember — I made at the time, as well as a wide range of other relevant and publicly available information sources.

I interrogated data contained on the 8 RAR Association website, the 8 RAR tour and pictorial books, a number of already published genre-related works, as well as records contained within the Australian War Memorial and the Australian National Archives data bases. I also sought advice from a number of people who, in my view, possessed expertise in infantry field support and in other specific Australian Defence Force (ADF) areas relevant to the Vietnam conflict.

As much as I've been reasonably able to do so, I have clarified and confirmed my recollections — most of which remain remarkably clear to me — with a number of my former platoon mates. Recollections fade over time and can easily become confused and muddled. What I recall about a certain happening or event may be somewhat — or significantly — different to what my platoon mates might now remember. Because of this imbroglio, I've only included detail in relation to significant incidents that I've been able to verify as being factually accurate, as well as some uncorroborated detail that I'm absolutely certain is accurate. This minor filtering of some operational detail in a few parts of my story, hasn't at all been easy for me.

When I first set out to record my recollections of my time in the Australian Army as a conscripted National Serviceman, and the impacts that service has had on my subsequent life, I naively thought that what I have to say might consume around 50 pages or so of random text. Not for one moment did it ever enter my head that the capture and transcription of those recollections would result in the writing of a book, let alone one of this size. The fact that I've written this rather lengthy tome has come as a complete surprise to me.

For most of my married life I've not felt inclined, nor have I ever been pressed to share the experiences of my time in the Australian Army — and Vietnam in particular — with my wife and now 2 adult children. This very private part of my life has remained a complete mystery to them. This reflects badly on me. I know that I should have shared this story with them many years ago and I regret that I haven't done so, until now.

Why did I decide to tell of such an awful time in my life? A time that I had successfully closed off and sealed in the deepest recesses of my mind for these many years? To be perfectly honest, I don't really know. More likely than not, it was because of the gradual cathartic lifting of the over-arching cloak of service denial, so common to Vietnam veterans as they age.

I gradually became far more at ease within myself about my operational military service in Vietnam, including coming to terms with a number of poor personal decisions — or choices — I made back then, which I've never been comfortable with. I also began to realise that it might be useful for my family if I were to set out in writing, in some sort of orderly way, those experiences — good and bad — and try and explain to them how they have impacted, and continue to do so, many aspects of my subsequent life and by logical extension, their lives as well.

Perhaps being an interesting — or perhaps not — story for them to digest, my book might hopefully provide some answers as to why their husband and father is the complex and unpredictable man that he is, always has been, and probably always will be. If I were to achieve that, even in a small way, then the writing of this book will have been a very worthwhile exercise.

My story is also about all those other Australian and New Zealand infantry soldiers who served in Vietnam. Importantly, it also tells in a lot of detail, how they were wonderfully supported operationally in the field by other army elements and by other key units of the wider ADF.

It has been extremely important for me to portray the very significant roles played by the Royal Australian Navy (RAN) — the Senior Service — and the Royal Australian Air Force (RAAF) in their support of the Australian Government's ground commitment — the Royal Australian Army — to the Vietnam conflict. Far too often, those 2 vital roles are almost dismissively pushed aside by many army veterans, almost as if those service arms were incidental to the war in Vietnam. That is far from reality, and I elaborate on each of their key roles extensively.

I apologise to anyone who may be inclined to venture into my very personal world and then curse me for any tedium they might experience. Of course, those of you who don't find my story interesting — I'm sure that there will be a few — have the option of simply glossing over a chapter or two and consigning it to the bookshelf, or worse. Were that to be the case, I wouldn't be offended in the slightest. I've often done the same with many books that I found too hard going, or otherwise simply uninteresting. For example, as often as I've tried, I simply can't cerebrally absorb the following 3 literary masterpieces: 'War and Peace' by Leo Tolstoy, 'Trinity' by Leon Uris, and 'The Gulag Archipelago' by

Alexander Solzhenitsyn.

In telling my story, I've not set out to intentionally impugn the integrity or character of any person. However, there were several individuals who significantly and negatively impacted my life during my time in the Australian Army — particularly the early days — who haven't fared well in my story. However, I have portrayed my recollections of them all those years ago, as accurately as I have been able to do so. I'm sure that if I were to meet these now much older men today, I would find them quite different and would form a far more generous view of them.

If, by any chance, I have omitted to formally include any proper reference, citation, or attribution in relation to any aspect of my story, that's a complete oversight on my part, and one for which I profusely apologise.

EPIGRAPH

'The Appointment in Samarra'
(As retold by W. Somerset Maugham — 1933)

The Speaker is Death

There was a merchant in Baghdad who sent his servant to market to buy provisions and in a little while the servant came back, white and trembling, and said:

> *'Master, just now when I was in the marketplace I was jostled by a woman in the crowd and when I turned, I saw it was Death that jostled me. She looked at me and made a threatening gesture; now lend me your horse, and I will ride away from this city and avoid my fate. I will go to Samarra and there Death will not find me.'*

The merchant lent him his horse, and the servant mounted it, and he dug his spurs in its flanks and as fast as the horse could gallop, he went. Then, the merchant went down to the marketplace, and he saw me standing in the crowd and he came to me and said:

> *'Why did you make a threating gesture to my servant when you saw him this morning?'*

> *'That was not a threatening gesture, I said; it was only a start of surprise. I was astonished to see him in Baghdad, for I have an appointment with him tonight in Samarra.'*

I've included this truly wonderful epigraph leading into my story because I believe it so aptly describes the nature of fate or one's 'karma'. While we may think that we have control over how our lives unfold over time, I believe that to be true only at the narrowest of margins. What's going to happen to us is probably going to anyway, no matter what we do in attempting to ameliorate the end outcome. One's fate is what it is, and it's something that largely can't be changed. There is simply no point in worrying too much about what might be ahead of us. All we can do in life, in each of our various endeavours, is our very best.

While the noted erudite of this new, modern, politically-correct and woke world may not agree with my perhaps contentious interpretation of this famous epigraph, that's really a matter for them to mull over — not me.

I first read this famous literary work in a USA produced 'Playboy' magazine during the first few days — late November 1969 — of my 12-month deployment to Vietnam. I carefully tore out this page from a magazine that had been left behind in my tent at Nui Dat by men from 9 Battalion, The Royal Australian Regiment (9 RAR) — who my battalion replaced — and read and often re-read it during my time in that awful country. I was utterly devastated when a sudden tropical deluge one late afternoon in August 1970 reduced this wonderful page of dog-eared print to pulp. I always carried it with me out in the field.

Whenever I did read this increasingly ragged article, the very clear message it continually delivered to me pretty much shaped the way I approached my operational infantry tasking in Vietnam.

The words and thrust of this ancient Mesopotamian tale, as retold in this wonderful epigraph by W. Somerset Maugham in 1933, are not in any way focused on death. To me, they are all about just getting on with your life and — in the context of my story — soldiering to the very best of your ability without worrying all that much about what might befall you on the battlefield.

Peter McCann

PART 1

LIFE BEFORE THE ARMY

CHAPTER 1

TEENAGE YEARS

ADELAIDE

When I completed my 5 years of secondary school education in Adelaide, South Australia, in late November 1965 at the comparatively young age of 17 years and 4 months, compulsory National Service — or Conscription as it was more commonly known — had been legislated by the government and administratively put in place for a range of obscure political reasons. Perhaps coincidently, at that very same time, Australia was beginning to exponentially ramp-up its military commitment in support of the so-called 'South Vietnam cause' — as a response to the often touted 'Domino Theory'.

Well before then, on 3 August 1962, 30 highly trained military advisors comprising the initial deployment to Vietnam of the Australian Army Training Team Vietnam (AATTV), was in place on the ground. Initially the role of the AATTV was, as its name suggests, the training of elite South Vietnamese — Army of the Republic of Vietnam (ARVN) — troops. In June 1964, that expert role was expanded to include the participation of those training cadre men in ARVN field operations. The first AATTV — and Australian — combat death in Vietnam, Warrant Officer Kevin Conway, occurred on 6 July 1964.

In August 1964, the Royal Australian Air Force (RAAF) deployed 6 Caribou short-landing fixed-wing aircraft from its Transport Flight (35 Squadron) to that conflict along with accompanying support elements. This was later followed by the deployment on 3 June 1965 of infantry — 1 Battalion, the Royal Australian Regiment (1 RAR) — a ground force commitment that quickly grew to 3 battalions comprised of both Regular soldiers and National Servicemen, in about equal numbers. From April 1966 until November 1970, there were always 3 Australian infantry battalions in Vietnam at any one time.

The initial deployment of 1 RAR was the only Australian Army infantry unit where National Servicemen didn't comprise a sizeable proportion of a battalion's posted strength. On this particular deployment, the entire posted strength of 1 RAR comprised only of Regular soldiers — volunteer enlistments. The first battalion to comprise of both Regular soldiers and National Servicemen was 5 RAR, when it first deployed to Vietnam on 1 April 1966.

Australian Army infantry battalions deployed to Vietnam were replaced on a staggered 12-month rotational basis. Apart from 8 RAR and 9 RAR, the other 7 battalions served 2 deployments. 8 RAR replaced 9 RAR after it completed its deployment and, when 8 RAR completed its deployment on 31 October 1970, it wasn't replaced. About 16 months later, on 12 March 1972, the last remaining infantry battalion on the ground in Vietnam, 4 RAR, returned to Australia.

Complete Australian military withdrawal from Vietnam largely occurred on 18 December 1972. This was when 150 residual combat troops from the AATTV, and about the same number from the Australian Army Assistance Group Vietnam (AAAGV) — predominantly an Australian Embassy security unit based in Saigon (Ho Chi Minh City) — departed those foreign shores. A small residual Australian Embassy Guard Platoon of 6 men — as many as 27 strong in late 1972 — primarily resourced from the AAAGV with leadership from the AATTV, was wound down from late March 1973 and formally disbanded at the end of June 1973. It was the last Australian Army unit to have served in Vietnam.

While most Australian soldiers deployed to Vietnam served in that country for a period of 12 months or less, a small number served 2 deployments and, in some rare cases, 3 deployments. Second deployments of infantry battalions were interspersed with periods of service back in Australia, where the bulk of their personnel were changed. For the most part, infantry battalions on their second deployment were of a completely different demographic to that of its first.

Some Regular soldiers served their extended time in Vietnam on almost contiguous postings across infantry battalions, with very short periods of intervening time back in Australia. For example, Lance-corporal Jim Riddle[1] served in Vietnam from 23 December 1968 until 9 March 1972, interspersed with 2 breaks — 42 and 33 days — back home in his country of birth, England. Riddle was on active service in Vietnam for 733 days — say 2 years — and, for the most part, he was on the posted strengths of 4 RAR, 8 RAR, and 9 RAR — all infantry units. Riddle wasn't an Australian citizen and he served in Vietnam as a Regular soldier.

One may well think that a prestigious, enlightened, highly-marketed and expensive Marist Brothers Catholic secondary school education institution, Sacred Heart College Somerton, even as far back as 1965, might have broadly introduced this emerging — even then — historical military tragedy to its avid history students, which included myself. Sadly, that wasn't the case. Pleasingly, I now know that contemporary modern history curricula in most

---

[1] DVA Vietnam War Nominal Roll.

secondary and tertiary education institutions do include significant coverage of Australia's extensive military involvement in the Vietnam War and of more recent Australian Defence Force (ADF) deployments.

While all of this frenetic military activity was going on in the near background of my idyllic teenage life back in the mid-1960s, I was blissfully unaware of any of it. However, communications back in those days were rudimentary to say the least. There were no mobile phones, computers and, ergo, no internet. Television, introduced into Australia in 1956, was prohibitively expensive and only slowly embraced by the consumer market. It was poor quality black and white technology and, in Adelaide, only delivered about 3 or maybe 4 viewing channels with highly regulated and limited reception availability hours.

Then, there were the government-imposed expensive television viewing license fees and legions of deployed secretive inspectors, who preyed on average, struggling, residential ratepayers by creeping up to their homes at night to detect a non-licensed television reception. Talk about State sanctioned 'peeping-toms'! Many residents also reported their neighbours to the authorities. On reflection, this sort of behaviour was abysmal and nothing short of criminal. In fact, it was something right out of the Fascist playbook.

On one balmy summer evening — probably around late 1962 — my entire family was invited to a neighbour's home to watch a 30-minute television episode of the then hugely popular Western serial 'The Rifleman' starring Chuck Connors. Well, what a treat this was for us! Seriously, at that time it really was. My parents didn't acquire a television receiver set until late 1964. Consumers back then usually funded their expensive television receiver sets — and household furniture, along with white goods appliances in many cases — through the agency of long-term rental agreements with associated never-ending fixed monthly payments. Frankly, it was nothing short of government sanctioned usury.

It was around this time when my father spent one weekend working as a casual Electoral Office official for the Federal Government. He was paid an abysmal pittance for his efforts. A very close neighbour — I won't name this long since deceased person — who worked for the Australian Taxation Office (ATO), reported my father to that agency for his later non-declaration of that income in his relevant tax return. My father was subsequently investigated by the ATO and fined a token amount for this petty crime. Frankly, the morals, ethics, and unbridled envy of aspiring middle-class suburbanites in Adelaide in those days, were appalling.

Most family homes didn't have a telephone landline because they were hugely expensive and regarded as a luxury. The only communication tools readily available to us were the wireless — the radio — early morning and late afternoon newspapers, and word of mouth. For example, to find out which football team I'd been selected in for the coming Saturday, and the associated match details, I had to walk down to the men's barber shop on Brighton Road — about a 1km walk each way — to view a handwritten notice attached to the inside of the front window. None of us thought anything of it. While that may sound sort of grossly primitive in the new, enlightened, technological age in which we now live, that's how it was back then.

My seemingly never-ending final year of private secondary school education was notable because of a significant change to my physique. I'd just turned 17 and had lost all of my teenage puppy fat and seriously toned up my stomach, upper body, and arms with hard, lean muscle, along with accompanying strength and balance. This enhanced fitness resulted from spending 30 minutes or so on most weekday afternoons, down in the south-west corner of our backyard — the small ramshackle 'pig-sty' shed with no roof, which was adjacent to the large and often used household 'carbon polluting' incinerator — lifting a range of makeshift weights that comprised of house bricks and lead sheeting, wrapped around hand-held pilfered metal construction rods of various lengths.

While the weights were only moderately heavy, the repetitions were many. I slowly transformed myself into a lean, highly-toned, and incredibly strong young man. I wasn't carrying any fat whatsoever on my body. I don't think that anyone in my class was even remotely aware of this change in my physique because, given the range of relatively low weights — I reckon 65kg maximum — that I lifted almost daily, I'd only bulked-up my upper body and arms to a very latent extent. And we all wore long-sleeve shirts, so it would have been hard to tell anyway. My parents, and even my lovely twin sister, Paula, never commented on my physical transformation either, so I guess that they were also completely deceived.

Well…that's not quite true. One night during dinner, my rather distant and somewhat uncommunicative father told me that he thought I'd lost weight and developed more muscular forearms. I somehow managed to adroitly gloss-over his comment, because the reality was, I hadn't lost any significant amount of weight at all. Rather, I'd pretty much converted all of my former body fat into hard, lean muscle. All the daily walking or bike riding that I was doing at that time, well and truly took care of the lower half of my body. At 17 years of age, I really was in superb physical condition.

Although I never seriously went out of my way to maintain it after I left school, I possessed more than a subtle, embryonic, abdominal 'six-pack' — which even I was in love with! I'd also grown markedly in height to just over 188cm — or 6'2in in the old imperial measure — an aspirational benchmark of sorts for young men back then.

My very late-found and almost driven passion — and very average skill set

— for playing Australian Rules football (now known as AFL), and an increasing obsession in girls, meant that I had no time for, or interest in anything else. I certainly wasn't concerned about what might have been happening in Vietnam.

When I eventually concluded my education and left the cloistered confines of Sacred Heart College for the last time, I was a tall, strong, and fit young man who was well-educated and extremely self-confident. While that last phrase may appear somewhat trite to some, I can assure you that the overwhelming feeling of confidence and inner self-belief that I then held, was extremely important to me. The very significant financial investment my parents invested into my Catholic-based education was now about to pay me a very handsome dividend.

As my final year of schooling drew to a close, I didn't really have a career choice. My father simply decided, without any consultation with me at all, that I would pursue a career with the (now) Australian Public Service. While I more than likely signed a number of pre-completed forms placed in front of me, he just arranged it all. Was that a bad thing? Yes, it most certainly was, but I won't go into that because there's simply no point in doing so.

Within days of finishing school, with a well-rounded package of education, life values, and physical resilience behind me, I was offered, and accepted, a position of employment with the ATO. I commenced work with that government agency in its King William Street, Adelaide office, on 4 January 1966. I was exactly 17 years and 5 months of age.

My first year of employment with the ATO was largely uneventful. I was working in what was then known as the Recovery — or Debt Collection — Section, so my job focused on trying to make people pay overdue income tax assessment debts, that they either didn't want to pay, or couldn't afford to pay. I was routinely exposed to the machinations of many serial well-resourced taxpayers, who contrived to avoid paying their rightful personal income tax obligations. This was my introduction to what is known in Australia as the 'class divide'. That is, the unfortunate, and the more fortunate.

Throughout my life, even though my political leaning has always been slightly right of centre, I've always maintained a strong interest in social fairness, and I'm sure that the roots of this hark back to my time as a base-level clerk in the ATO Adelaide Recovery Section, as well as my very solid Catholic upbringing. I'm not going to comment further on social fairness in contemporary Australian society because, if I were to do so, it would deflect reader focus from my story.

One notable setback in the early days of my ultimately long and successful career with the ATO, was to abysmally fail the 'cashiers-tellers' training course. In addition, I wasn't accepted into any of the prestigious 'assessing' — ATO 101 — training courses. Talk about a disastrous — if not terminally fatal — start to my career! However, I did learn to play a decent hand of lunch-time 'contract bridge', a popular, skilful card game in which I've maintained a strong interest, and still remain a reasonable occasional social player.

Decimal currency was introduced by the government on 14 February 1966, replacing the formerly used United Kingdom (UK) standard of pounds, shillings and pence (£sd). Seriously…how could we have a currency so complicated that 12 pennies (d) equalled one shilling (s), and 20 shillings equalled one pound (£)? And I'm not even going to talk about guineas (21 shillings), florins, crowns, sixpences, threepences, pennies, half-pennies, and farthings. The value of a farthing was one quarter of a penny. Imagine a plumber's invoice for £A2-s4-d2-f1. Something as inane as this, would have occurred regularly back in the late 1950's, and perhaps even into the very early 1960's.

On 'Decimal Currency Day', £A1 converted to its new value of $A2. Because it was so arithmetically simple compared to the former UK standard, decimal currency was readily accepted by the Australian population, which at that time was just over 12 million. The government of the day also funded saturation print media, radio, and television coverage with this very catchy jingle:

'in come the dollars and in come the cents — and out go the pounds, the shilling and the pence.'

This jingle was an absolute winner for the government in terms of explaining what was about to confront the population in relation to the nation's currency conversion.

My mathematically erudite father could rapidly mentally compute the associated math around the array of former non-decimal values. He was simply amazing! His senior insurance company actuarial and underwriting role was focused on currency, numbers, percentages, risk, and profit, so I guess I shouldn't have been all that surprised about his mental numerical proficiency. Even simple calculators hadn't been invented back then, so for the bulk of his working life, my father had to rely on mental or long-form math. I reckon that I inherited much of his mental numerical expertise. For example, I've always been able to easily recall phone numbers of friends and acquaintances — a once rare skill that has now been rendered completely redundant thanks to technology.

My first fortnightly net pay from the ATO after decimal currency conversion was exactly $45.08. From that princely sum — and believe me it was — my lovely mother ever so politely sequestered what I thought was an exorbitant amount of $8.00, in exchange for my full board and keep. While I never explored any reliable metrics on this financial impost, I reckon that she was well and truly right on the money in the context of today's contemporary cost of living prices and norms.

For the 2 relatively short periods of time that I lived at home with my parents — see later in this story — and I was receiving a decent, basic income, I never worried too much about handing over my rightful financial contribution to the family coffers.

My sporting role model back then, Neil Kerley — the South Australian National Football League (SANFL) legend — was coaching, captaining, and playing for my local AFL football team, the Glenelg Tigers. During the winter football season, I used to go along to the nearby Glenelg Oval —about a 4km walk — with a few mates, and watch some afternoon home games. Occasionally we'd get a lift either there or back, in a parent's vehicle, but overall, we did a lot of foot-slogging. We didn't really give it a second thought. Back in those days, walking — otherwise known as 'shanks pony' — was usually our only form of transport. While some lexicon will translate that term for you, you're going to have to look very hard to find it. Although we all had pushbikes, we didn't use them all that much.

There was one time that I was at home on a rather mild May Friday night in 1967 — strangely for me — and one of my mates called around at about 9:30pm to tell me that a certain fellow — who I vaguely knew and didn't particularly like — was at the Brighton Catholic Church Youth Group dance social, apparently giving my sister, Paula, a hard time.

Well, it was about a 1.5km walk for me to convince this guy to voluntarily head-butt his ugly face into my left fist, 3 or 4 times. I'm not too sure if Paula appreciated my help that evening. In fact, I know she didn't! She wasn't happy with me at all and, on reflection, I don't blame her. No matter, I felt chuffed with the outcome of this highly successful mediation meeting.

On the downside though, my left hand didn't fair too well. It was an ugly mess. While the other guy's face was looking pretty ordinary, it was a damn sight better than the state of my hand. Even at this early time in my emerging adult life, I concluded that having people voluntarily head-butt one of your fists, was something to be avoided as much as possible.

After walking about halfway back to my house with my mate, nursing my left hand, I felt an urgent need to urinate. So, as all young men used to do back then, I just ducked into a vacant block abutting the northern side of Sturt Road — a main east-west arterial road of sorts — and blissfully relieved myself against one of the many large gum trees. Next minute, there was a police car with floodlights all over me, and I was accosted by 2 police officers for my exhibition of public urination and wilful indecent exposure. Thankfully, my mate was able to corroborate my need for an urgent 'piss-stop', but that didn't deter the officers from insisting on giving both of us a lift — in their police car — for the last 800m or so back to my house.

My poor parents — and all of the gloating neighbours avidly looking on from their front bedroom windows and front porches — were greeted with the sight of a police car flashing rooftop strobe lights, delivering their son home at around 11:30pm, along with a very audible lecture regarding the irresponsibility of public urination. Talk about socially embarrassing for my parents!

I heard about this misdemeanour for days afterwards and Paula didn't speak to me for at least a week. I couldn't believe it…no one seemed to give a toss about my bruised and swollen left hand! Anyway, eventually the incident all seemed to go away. My hand took much longer to recover and I was unable to play football for quite a while.

My mate on that infamous night — who only lived a street away from me — was a great guy and a former school friend. We often used to drink lots of cheap 'Brandavino' wine — awful stuff, but hugely popular at the time — together on Friday nights as we hunkered-down at any of a number of vacant blocks around the neighbourhood, before staggering home well after midnight…very drunk indeed!

Other alcoholic beverages we'd regularly sample on those hedonistic nights were branded as 'Star-Wine', 'Porphyry Pearl', and a disgusting white wine sold as 'Hock', otherwise colloquially known as cooking vinegar. Although we liked it a lot, beer wasn't often on our buy list. Primarily, this was because back in those days, beer in Adelaide was predominantly available only in long-neck 750mm bottles and, as it had to be consumed cold, we had no refrigeration options available to us. So, cheap fortified wine seemed to be our preferred alcoholic beverage of last resort. How our parents took such a long time to pick up on our regular drunken behaviour, remains a total mystery. But eventually they did, and it was very nasty for both of us.

Back in those days, even when it wasn't fashionable, I often experienced the joys of rough red wine — claret — freely available and encased in a heavy, but easy to carry — by way of an attached glass finger-ring — 2L glass flagon. These flagons were the precursor to present-day 2L and 4L wine casks.

During the early morning Sunday hours after one infamous Saturday night colossal drinking session, I vomited copious globules of foul, red slurry into my bed, and peacefully slumbered — or wallowed — amid it. Seriously, this was a mega-gross event in my life. The next morning, my parents were furious to discover the fetid mess enveloping — and almost drowning — their largely unconscious son. I wasn't quite 19 years of age, so no wonder they were angry with me. The timing of this would have been around June or July 1967.

Even though I was feeling absolutely awful the next morning, my moderately strict father insisted that I still play AFL that afternoon for the Brighton Catholic Church team, as I usually did on most winter Sunday afternoons. I dutifully did as he ordered, but it was a complete and utter waste of time for me, and the team. Ordinarily, I was a reasonable player at this level of football — always managing to kick 4 or more goals from the full-forward or centre-half-forward positions — but I don't think that I garnered more than a few touches of the ball that day. While I did grubber kick a lucky goal from within the goal square, I also projectile vomited residual lumpy, red, claret slurry, all over my full-back opponent. I copped a few vicious punches in the face from him after that, and I guess it was well deserved. It was an ugly game of football for me.

I'd like to think that the bevy of adoring and sex-obsessed young Catholic girls dutifully watching the game that afternoon, were more concerned for my health rather than critical of me for the pathetic physical condition I was in. The very clear lesson I learned from this experience was that excessive drinking of alcohol, and potential sexual liaisons with like-minded and enthusiastic Catholic girls, were mutually exclusive.

My life at that time was wonderful and carefree. The army, let alone what might have been happening in Vietnam, was the very last thing on my mind. In fact, it wasn't on my radar at all. I was far more interested in working for the ATO, improving my bridge game, playing Division 4 AFL for the Brighton Amateur League Football Club on Saturdays, and for the church team on Sundays, drinking lots of alcohol on Friday and Saturday nights, and having as much sex as possible.

On 3 February 1967, at 8am, Ronald Ryan was executed at Melbourne's Pentridge Gaol. His judicial execution — by hanging — was the last conducted in Australia, and the 'death penalty' was formally abolished in 1985. This macabre event in Australian history remains remarkably clear in my recall of my early life. For days, weeks, and even months leading up to, and well after the conclusion of this infamous episode in Australian history, television, radio, newspapers, and word of mouth discourse was seemingly all focused on this event. I've never forgotten that very sad day.

Therefore, I've always been opposed, and remain so today, to capital punishment because it's not a civilized thing to do to any human being, no matter what their particular crime may have been.

CANBERRA

In October 1967, I was offered a transfer within the ATO to Canberra. With the encouragement of my workplace manager in Adelaide, and my parents, I made this very significant move which ultimately set me up for a successful and long-term career with the ATO. I was just 19 years of age.

Work with the ATO in Canberra was vastly different to what I'd been exposed to back in Adelaide. It was varied, less process-driven, more policy-based, and far more interesting. I loved these new challenges. I worked hard and quickly received several promotions that enabled me to easily fund my new, independent lifestyle in Canberra. I also enjoyed my fresh social life, which again comprised playing lower grades football — Rugby Union this time — drinking lots of alcohol on weekends, and having sex whenever possible with the endless smorgasbord of enthusiastic Catholic girls in this rapidly growing national capital.

In 1967, Canberra was home to only around 115,000 people, much smaller in comparison to its dynamic and rapidly growing population of more recent times. For example, as of 10 August 2021, its residential base had grown to 454,499 — 1.78% of the nation's population — reflecting an average annual growth rate since 2011 of 2.72%. A vibrant economy and an urban population density of 588/km² makes it one of the most liveable cities in the world.[2] Government predictions are that the population of Canberra will reach 550,000 around 2032-33.

During my early days in Canberra, I made many good friends and moved into rented group houses with several of them, in the established suburbs of Deakin and Griffith. I also began keeping company with a lovely local girl. Her parents were very welcoming, so I spent many hours in her family home in the inner north suburb of Braddon, hugely enjoying their very stable Christian family environment, and gratefully accepting their generous and almost never-ending hospitality. Her father was directly responsible for introducing me to Rugby Union football, good red wine, and quality cognac. I thank him for that. As was the case when I previously lived in Adelaide, my life at that time was as good as it could possibly be.

NATIONAL SERVICE (CONSCRIPTION)

National Service legislation was enacted on 24 November 1964. It required 20-year-old men, if selected, to serve in the Australian Army for a period of 24 months of continuous full-time service — legislatively reduced to 18 months in 1971 — followed by a 3 year 'on call' commitment to the Australian Army Reserve.

In March 1965, Prime Minister Menzies announced that National Servicemen would be sent to Vietnam to fight in various units of the Australian Army deployed to that conflict. The Defence Act 1903 was amended in May of that year to provide legislative backing for this government policy decision.

The first National Service ballot took place on 10 March 1965, generating

---

[2] Australian Bureau of Statistics (ABS) Census Data for August 2011 and August 2021.

the first intake of National Servicemen into the army some 3 months later. At that time, I was in my final year of secondary school education and the potential likelihood of this legislation ever impacting my life, however remote that may have been, didn't even register in my consciousness. I was completely oblivious to it. I don't recall my parents ever discussing it with me either.

On 24 May, Private Errol Noack — a member of B Company 5 RAR — became the first National Serviceman killed in Vietnam. Noack had been in Vietnam for only 13 days. He was the first Australian fatality from that conflict to be repatriated back to Australia for interment. Until then, 24 of the 25 Australian fatalities in Vietnam had been interred in the Terendak Military Cemetery at Malacca in Malaysia. The other fatality was interred in the Kranji War Cemetery in Singapore. Three Australian soldiers who died while they were deployed to Malaysia — along with 8 deceased dependants (6 spouses and 2 children) of Australian soldiers who served in that country — were also interred in the Terendak Military Cemetery.

With the death of Noack, this arcane practice was discontinued by the government. Following the repatriation of his body back to Australia, all subsequent fatalities of Australian servicemen and servicewomen deployed overseas have been similarly repatriated back to Australia.

In May 2015, the government offered to repatriate the remains of soldiers, and dependants, interred in Malaysia and Singapore. Ultimately, 33 of the affected families accepted that offer and the sacred remains of the country's deceased men and women were returned to Australia on 2 June 2016. One of the 3 deceased Australian veterans whose remains still lay at peace at Terendak, is Major Peter Badcoe VC. Although I now know that Noack's death generated isolated pockets of community angst back in Australia at the time, I was completely unaware of any of that taking place. In hindsight, it seems to me that the Australian community back in those days was either vaguely ambivalent about the country's involvement in the Vietnam War, or was only just beginning to become actively engaged in protesting against conscription and that military intervention.

Around May 1968, whilst happily living and working in Canberra, it suddenly dawned on me that I was legally required to formally register for a National Service ballot, scheduled to take place in several months' time. That did manage to get my attention. In our shared house at Griffith, my 4 house mates were also exposed to this new societal phenomenon of balloted compulsory 2-year military service — known colloquially as the 'call-up' — and each of us reluctantly registered with the, now abolished, Department of Labour and National Service (DLNS) for our respective upcoming ballots. Not one of us was overjoyed at the prospect of potentially being 'press-ganged' into the army. I didn't imagine that there could be anything worse to befall me.

Because I was so concerned about this possible disruption to my life in Canberra and my promising career with the ATO, I formally contacted DLNS and asked for information regarding how the National Service ballot worked. I was attempting to ascertain if there was any available leverage that I might be able to take advantage of. After receiving a very bland response from DLNS, completely dismissive of the focus of my enquiry, I sought the intervention of my father. Through his personal contacts at senior levels within DLNS, I established that there were 2 ballots conducted at 6-monthly intervals each year. They were framed around a predetermined number of National Service enlistments needed for intakes into the army from time to time, usually every 3 months.

DLNS applied broad medical, psychological, and other exclusion rates to the number of eligible males in each ballot — based on compulsory registrations for that ballot — cross referenced against official records of the various Births Deaths and Marriages Registries in each State and Territory. As each birth-dated marble was drawn out of the barrel, DLNS knew how many men were registered against that date and, as marbles were progressively drawn, cumulatively counted the number of registrants 'called-up' until the predetermined number was reached. At that stage, the ballot concluded.

For each 6-monthly —March and September — National Service ballot, out of 181 or 184 birth-dated marbles in the barrel, only as many marbles as required to reach the number predetermined by DLNS were drawn out. It could be many, or only a few. It all depended on the actual number of eligible males born on particular dates in particular years. There were smaller supplementary ballots for those men who'd been out of the country during their registration periods. In his wonderful book, Mark Dapin[3] explores this interesting issue in some detail.

Table 1.

8TH NATIONAL SERVICE BALLOT: 13 SEPTEMBER 1968
(Eligibility Birthdate Range 1 July - 31 December 1948)

MONTH	DATES
July	3 — 21 — 22 — 24 — 30
August	1 — 3 — 16 — 18 — 24 — 26
September	5 — 9 — 12 — 14 — 22 — 23 — 24 — 26
October	3 — 13 — 18
November	5 — 18 — 24 — 28 — 29
December	7 — 12 — 14 — 15 — 19 — 21 — 22 — 26

---

[3] Dapin, M. *Australia's Vietnam - Myth v's History*. New South Publishing, University of New South Wales, 2019. Page 53.

In my case, being eligible for the 8th National Service ballot, drawn on 13 September 1968, which fed into the 15th and 16th National Service intakes into the army in January and April 1969 respectively, required drawing only 35 marbles. See Table 1. In contrast, for the 1st National Service ballot drawn on 10 March 1965, 96 marbles were needed to achieve the required predetermined number of 'called-up' registrants.

Peter Edwards[4], writing for the Australian War Memorial, suggests that while 804,286 men registered for National Service during the years 1965-1972 — when this government policy was in place in its 2nd iteration — only 237,048 of those registrants were actually 'called-up' for 2 years of full-time military service in the Australian Army. This number also includes those who volunteered for National Service — there were quite a few — and those who elected to serve part-time for 6 years in the Citizens Military Forces (CMF), later known as the Army Reserve.

Ultimately, only 63,735 (26.9%) of registrants formally 'called-up', actually enlisted in the army. Of that number, 19,450 served in Vietnam, and 150 served in Borneo. While many others were deployed to Malaysia — in particular — and to Papua New Guinea, and Borneo, the remainder of them served out their National Service obligations in a range of army units based in Australia. Of those who served overseas, 210 died in Vietnam and 5 died in Borneo.

Edwards also says that:

> *'In August 1965, (Prime Minister) Menzies announced that from 1966 the annual (National Service) intake would be maintained at 8,400 (two intakes of 4,200), resulting in a — maintained — army strength of 40,000. He explained that the government's decision had been made...*
>
> *...in the light of the successful introduction of the national service scheme and bearing in mind all the various commitments, at home and abroad, which our forces might be required to undertake...'*

Against that background, the chances of being 'called-up', passing the medical, and other prescriptive tests, enlisting in the army, and serving in Vietnam were very low — something in the order of 2.4%. I ended up being a number in that small percentile.

The ballot process that underpinned the administration of compulsory National Service in Australia during the time of Australia's involvement in the Vietnam War was secretive, selective, and unfair. There was no appeal process

---

[4] Edwards, P. A. *Nation at War: Australian Politics, Society, and Diplomacy during the Vietnam War 1965-1975.* The Official History of Australia's Involvement in Southeast Asian Conflicts 1948–1975. Allen & Unwin with the Australian War Memorial, 1997.

that I was ever made aware of, and failure to register for National Service was an offence for which a custodial sentence was sometimes applied.

When I was in the mix for National Service, some 14 conscientious objectors to compulsory National Service — the random balloted nature of it, and to Australia's military involvement in the Vietnam War — were imprisoned for a time for failing to obey the legislative requirements of a 'call-up' notice. One of those well-known conscientious objectors was the — later — very popular television personality, Simon Townsend, host of 'Simon Townsend's Wonder World'.

For reasons that were never articulated by the government, details of the birthdates drawn in the first 11 National Service ballots weren't made public. Community criticism and loss of confidence in this complete lack of transparency in the process, forced the government to eventually reverse this poor policy decision. The last 5 ballots — from September 1970 — were fully televised and the birthdates drawn in each ballot were widely published.

I quietly tried to figure out how I'd react if I were to be unlucky enough to be 'called-up' and compelled to enter the army. To put it mildly, I was confused and apprehensive. I wasn't at all keen on being in the army for even 1 day, let alone 2 years! Up to that point in time, I hadn't bothered to read one word in the print media, or absorb any radio or television coverage about Vietnam. That suddenly changed overnight. I began to watch television newscasts whenever I could, listened to the Australian Broadcasting Corporation (ABC) and commercial radio morning and evening news broadcasts, and read whatever related print material I could find. I quickly formed the pessimistic view that of the 5 young men in my share house that were eligible for National Service, my birthdate marble would be the one drawn out in our respective upcoming National Service ballots.

We each eagerly checked our mail every day to see if we'd received a notice of 'call-up' or, hopefully, one of deferral or even exemption. Two house mates were granted deferred status because of their ongoing university education, so I began to think that things were turning pear-shaped for me, as they'd received their notices of exemption…and I didn't. My intuition was right.

Around the middle of October 1968, my dreaded 'call-up' notice arrived, along with details of compulsory medical and psychological examinations, which I was required to undertake at the old Canberra Hospital on the Acton Peninsular — now the site of the National Museum.

At that time, there were several hugely popular theories circulating within my broad age cohort as to how one might fail these medical assessments. The more common of these proposed tactics were: to declare that you were gay (not such a clever idea back in 1968); ingest an entire tube of toothpaste to temporarily elevate your blood pressure; swallow silver foil wrappers from cigarette packets to supposedly sabotage chest x-rays; pretend to be intellectually challenged.

Other than perhaps in rare instances, I don't think any of these ruses worked, although the public record failure rate from these medical examinations was exceptionally high, climbing from 37.7% in 1965, to 51.2% in 1971. I reckon that the medical failure rate in 1965 is a high number and, when you think about the much higher failure rate in 1971, any reasonable person may well conclude that there must have been something amiss with medical examinations underpinning the entry of conscripted 20-year-old men into the Australian Army. On the other hand, one might also readily conclude that only the 'crème de la crème' of Australia's male youth were deemed suitable to enter the army, and possibly serve in Vietnam.

Prior to my medical, I was in good health and physically fit in terms of civilian norms of those times. But I was entirely convinced that the extremely poor sight in my right eye — attributable to a congenital birth defect — would easily rule me out of National Service. My right eye never functioned as nature intended. According to optometrists and ophthalmic specialists throughout my life, it has only ever had, at best, a beneficial visual capability of something around 65%. Apparently, I don't use this eye at all! According to those eminent medical professionals, it only serves to provide me with a peripheral perspective to my left-side dominated vision, while markedly assisting in my overall balance. Effectively I am, always have been, and remain so today, a single-eyed or monocular person. That's why, with handwriting being the sole exception — Catholic primary school teaching nun, Sister Mary Regis, please take a bow — I'm chronically left-side focused.

For example, when I played any form of football, I could only kick the ball with my left foot. Playing cricket, I bowled with my left arm, but batted right-handed with my left eye facing the incoming bowler. I'd say that in playing sport, my eyesight shortcoming manifested in issues around being able to quickly assess changing depth, and rapid right-side lateral movement. I was acutely aware of this from a very early age — I wore horrible, thick prescription glasses until I was 13 — and it always affected my confidence in playing ball sports. My often-critical father never understood any of this. So, although always very enthusiastic, I was never all that good at higher level sports. That being said, whenever a club was chasing an average 3rd or 4th grade player, then I was most definitely their man.

My rather lengthy medical examination at Canberra Hospital on 6 November 1968 was an absolute joke, and a complete and utter waste of everyone's time. After being told by an uninterested civilian doctor that my broken right collarbone, incurred playing Rugby Union football some 6 weeks earlier — I really played on that — would be well healed by the following

January, I remember another doctor grasping my balls in his hand, saying, *'Cough please'*, and looking up my arse to see if I had haemorrhoids. I don't know why these so-called genital cough and haemorrhoids tests — so popular among the medical profession at that time — don't appear to be widely used, if at all, in modern-day medical practice.

Amazingly, my eyesight was rated as satisfactory. Even to this day, I remember the optometrist who examined me that night, saying something like:

> *'Although you know your right eye is no good, your bilateral vision meets the standard for Australian military service.'*

I was astounded. No...dumbfounded! I couldn't believe what I'd just heard. Back then, the — later — very well-known Dr Bob Brown, who became a Federal Senator for Tasmania and leader of the Australian Greens Political Party, was undertaking his medical internship training in Canberra. For a time, he was personally involved in medical examinations at Canberra Hospital for the young men 'called-up' for National Service. Anecdotally, he was opposed — perhaps not quite so openly back in those days — to National Service, and to Australia's involvement in the Vietnam War in particular. From what I've since been led to believe, he did his utmost to professionally fail as many potential conscripts as he could. Perhaps doctors like Dr Bob Brown played a role in the increased medical failure rate of these medical examinations over time?

On that very same night, I was formally interviewed and completed some sort of written aptitude test administered by a seriously client-adverse civilian psychologist. I was never told what this test was for, or what my broad results were. And, like all 'called-up' registrants passed as medically and psychologically fit, I later underwent a security and character check — not that I was even remotely aware of this — conducted by the various arms of executive government. Presumably, I passed those checks with flying colours. I also concluded that shooting and killing several of my neighbour's prized homing pigeons with an air rifle when I was 16 — and having that weapon confiscated by the local South Australian police — didn't constitute a major blemish on my character. In today's new-world paradigm, it just might.

Anyway, as it turned out, it was my great misfortune not to have Dr Bob Brown personally conduct my medical examination because, some weeks later, I was advised by letter from DLNS that I'd passed my medical and other tests, and would be formally enlisted into the army on 30 January 1969. I was in a complete state of shock and couldn't believe this was happening.

ADELAIDE

Realising that my lot in life, for the next 2 years, was now firmly established and completely out of my control, I applied to the ATO for a transfer back to Adelaide just prior to Christmas 1968, to spend some quality time with my family. At the same time, I applied to DLNS for permission to enlist in the army from Adelaide, and undertake my recruit training at 2 Recruit Training Battalion (2 RTB) at Puckapunyal near Melbourne, Victoria. Both requests were approved. At my ATO workplace in Canberra, just before returning to Adelaide, I was afforded the courtesy of a short morning tea with the Commissioner of Taxation, Sir Edwin Cain. This was a real honour for a 20-year-old low-level ATO staffer.

Those last 4 or 5 weeks leading up to my formal enlistment into the army were a complete and utter waste of time for me and, I suspect, for the ATO. I was very unsettled and totally obsessed with what was about to happen to me. I don't think my workplace productivity at that time would have been rather high. I have no doubt that the ATO was probably keen to be temporarily rid of me.

On a positive note, those last few weeks back in Adelaide laid down the emerging foundations for my later engaging, and very close relationship with my father. Up until then, it was a respectful but distant one, with little or no paternal interaction of any real substance. That all seemed to change with my upcoming enlistment into the army.

He asked me to join him at the Brighton Hotel — his pub — for a very long drinking session on the last Saturday — 25 January 1969 — before I enlisted. This was a very real honour that he was bestowing on me. Up until that point in my life, we'd hardly spoken to one another — except about sport — in any meaningful way. When I reminded him that I was underage — in South Australia at that time, the legal drinking age was 21 — his response was something like:

> *'You're about to enter the army, and maybe go to Vietnam, so you are old enough to drink with me.'*

And that was it...the real beginning of my relationship with my father, whom I eventually came to love very dearly until he passed away suddenly on 31 July 1988.

PART 2

THE AUSTRALIAN ARMY

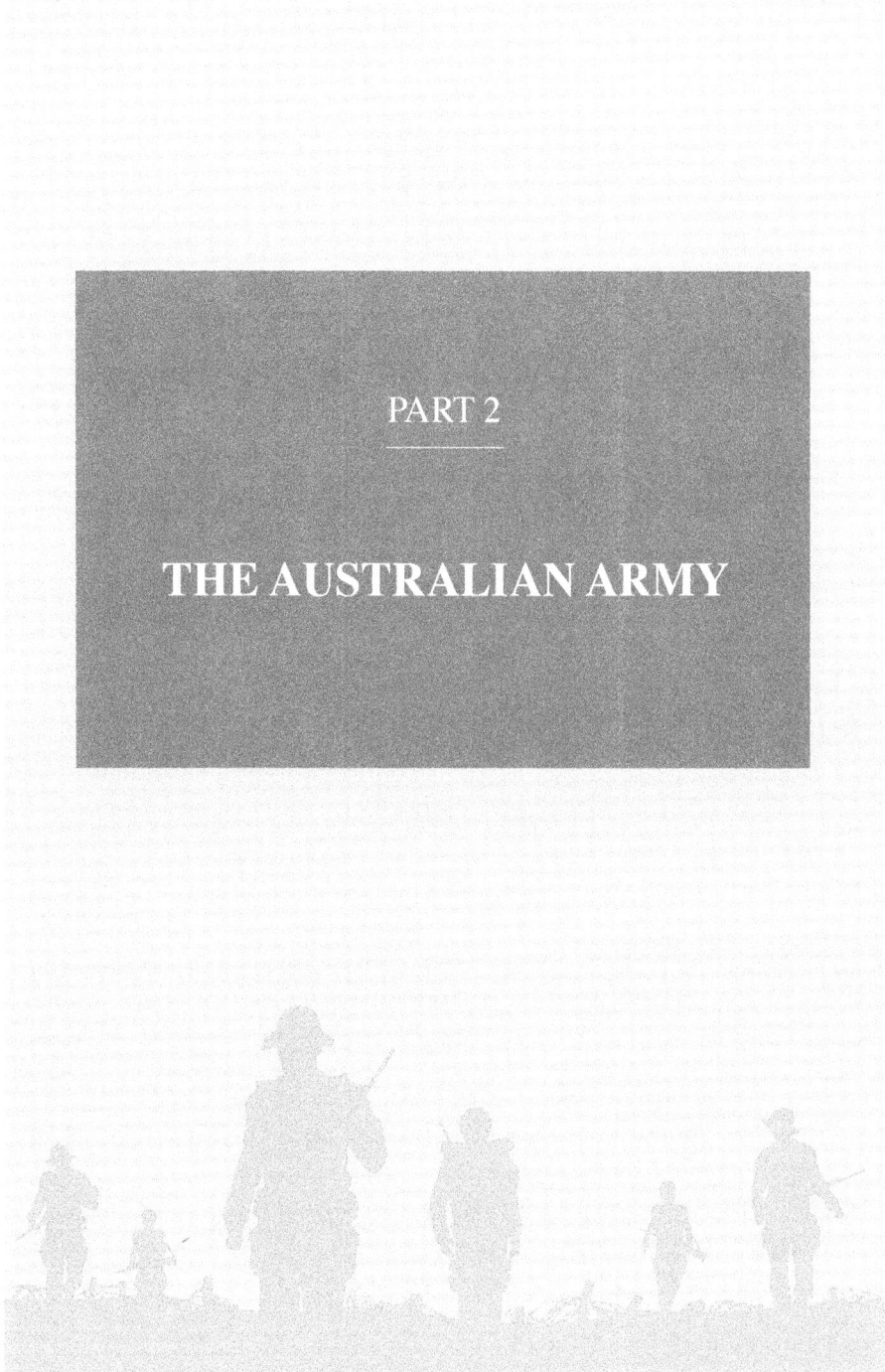

CHAPTER 2

INDUCTION AND ENLISTMENT

The date of my enlistment — 15th National Service Intake — into the Australian Army, was on Thursday 30 January 1969. This was highly unusual because all other intakes of National Servicemen up until then, and even later, took place on a Wednesday. While that might seem to be totally useless data, it does make a lot of sense when you think long and hard about it.[5]

At 7:45am that morning, many confused young men like me assembled at Keswick Barracks on the extreme verge of the south-west outskirts of the Central Business District (CBD) of the city of Adelaide. It was already hot with a forecast maximum temperature that day of 102°F (39°C), which was nothing out of the ordinary for Adelaide at that time of the year. I was in a state of mental stasis and everything seemed to be happening in slow motion. It was so surreal. I now know why cattle, sheep and other food animals submit to abattoir slaughter without too much fuss and bother. They have no idea what's ahead of them. That is exactly how I felt on that morning at Keswick Barracks.

Inside the confines of the barracks, we all mooched around in a rabble looking like lost sheep. I was asked to sign a ridiculous number of unintelligible forms. An army officer casually asked me — almost in passing — if I was feeling well. Afterwards, I learned that this single question was actually my final medical examination prior to enlistment. I kid you not! Many other National Servicemen have reported the same questioning. I think I muttered something like *'Not too bad, mate.'* Talk about being lambs to the slaughter! We had no idea as to the horrors which lay ahead of us.

Anxious family groups of varying sizes mingled outside on the parade ground verges, trying to take advantage of any shade they could find, while the poor unfortunates inside the barracks completed an endless array of formalities. Around mid-morning, we were asked to line up for army bus transportation to Adelaide Airport, where we would be boarding a charter flight to Melbourne before being transported by road to 2 Recruit Training Battalion (2 RTB) at Puckapunyal in regional Victoria. Families were advised that if they independently proceeded to the airport, they would have a final 45 minutes or so with their loved ones before the new recruits boarded an aircraft to depart for their destinies in the army.

---

[5] Blink, Bert. Detachment 131st Divisional Locating Battery. RAA.

Chapter 2 – Induction and Enlistment

Those last few minutes at the airport with my parents were incredibly difficult for me, and I suspect, for them as well. We didn't know what to say to each other. What could I say? What could they say? It was a terrible time for all of us. The only thing that I could really think about was what lay ahead of me. I was only 20-years-old and even though I was physically fit and had lived independently away from home for some 16 months, I wasn't at all prepared for the upcoming physical and mental rigors of military service.

In some respects, it was a huge relief when army movement personnel motioned to us to line up and board the aircraft. As I passed through the departure gate my mother, a lovely woman who I simply adored, said to the magnificently attired Military Police corporal manning the gate:

'Now, you make sure you look after my little boy, won't you?'

Even after all these years I can still recall her words, his beaming smile, and his very polite response to her:

'Yes, Ma'am, we certainly will,' followed by, *'on your way lad, keep moving.'*

The chartered (former) Trans Australian Airlines (TAA) flight, which I thought was transporting us to Melbourne Airport — Essendon, as it was at that time — landed instead at some obscure civil airfield in a desolate place known as Mangalore, which was a diversionary airfield used by Melbourne Airport. While situated in what looked like the middle of nowhere, it wasn't all that far from Puckapunyal. We disembarked the aircraft and pottered around, looking and feeling like stunned mullet. Suddenly, an immaculately dressed sergeant appeared from nowhere and moved amongst us, almost as if he was royalty. He then quietly and ever so politely asked:

'Does anyone here need to take a piss?'

Naturally, many of us replied:

'Yeah mate, where is it?'

This sergeant, who was now literally 'river-dancing', transformed right before our eyes into a psychopathic, raving lunatic. It was like he'd just been extracted from a US Army boot camp movie. With saliva dribbling down both sides of his jutting chin, and his voice almost reaching breaking falsetto heights, the sergeant screamed into our faces as he leeringly pranced amongst us:

'See that shed about seventy metres over there. That's the piss house. You all have three minutes to get there, piss, and get back here. Is that clear?'

'Shit! What's going on here?' I thought. *'What is this?'*

After availing ourselves of the primitive Mangalore Airfield toilets, we boarded army trucks and transported to 2 RTB at Puckapunyal — some 30km distance. I was now almost in the army…perhaps I was right then. That's certainly how I saw it.

During this short road journey to Puckapunyal, the atmosphere was very quiet. I think many of us were in a state of complete shock. Some had already began to appreciate and absorb the awful nature of what might be in store for us. I certainly had, and my worst fears were soon to be realised.

'This is bad, really bad,' I quietly thought to myself.

CHAPTER 3

RECRUIT TRAINING

The awful nature of army recruit training in Australia back in 1969 is probably best summed up in the following address given by an army instructor to a group of recruits:

> '... *At the top of the pile there is the General, then there's the Brigadier, the Full Colonel, Lieutenant Colonel, Major, Captain, Full Lieutenant, Second Lieutenant, Warrant Officers 1 and 2, Staff Sergeant, Sergeant, Corporal, Lance-corporal and Private. Then there are rats and mice, blowflies, and cockroaches. Then there are **you fucking recruits**...*'[6]

THE FIRST DAYS

Over the years, 2 RTB at Puckapunyal, located about a 90-minute drive north-east of Melbourne, has been consistently described by its inhabitants from time to time as:

> '...*the only military establishment in Australia where you can be up to your armpits in mud and get dust in your eyes at the same time...*'

During my 10 weeks of recruit training, there was only one day I recall when it rained consistently heavy and long enough to totally disrupt our training. We all thought it was a wonderful day, our training being relegated to brief, intermittent sessions of indoor lectures. Other than this 24-hour onslaught of biblical deluge, there were only 1 or 2 other days of precipitation worthy of meteorological measurement. On the other hand, I remember the very hot and dusty conditions that mostly prevailed during my time at Puckapunyal. And, when a brutal military basic training regimen was added into the mix, Puckapunyal was nothing short of hell on earth for National Servicemen like myself.

On that hot 30 January day, there were many hundreds of men enlisting in the army. In addition to conscripts from South Australia, the 15th National Service Intake at Puckapunyal also included unfortunate souls from Victoria,

---

[6] Ham, P. *Vietnam, The Australian War*. Harper Collins, Australia, 2007, Page 165.

Western Australia, Tasmania, and the Northern Territory.

Interestingly, during one of our formal parades towards the end of recruit training, one of the men in my company — C Company — paraded with a ribbon bar of the standard 2 Vietnam War service medals across the left breast of his polyester shirt. This recruit was clearly a former soldier who had served in Vietnam for a period in excess of 183 days and was now re-entering the army as either a Regular soldier or a National Service volunteer. I didn't know this recruit and, as he was a member of a different platoon, I never had the chance to speak with him. All of my platoon wondered why this guy had to go through the army recruit training process a second time and noted that during our last weeks at Puckapunyal, he was afforded extraordinary respect by our recruit training staff.

At the same time, when I became inescapably ensconced within 2 RTB at Puckapunyal, comparable frenetic enlistment activity was also taking place at 1 RTB at Kapooka near Wagga Wagga, about a 5-hour drive west of Sydney, and at 3 Training Battalion (3 TB) at Singleton, about a 2.5-hour drive north of Sydney. Other unfortunates from New South Wales, Queensland, and the Australian Capital Territory were being similarly introduced to army life. 3 TB at Singleton was also the traditional venue for infantry corps training which was why it was known as a Training Battalion, reflecting its wider role, as distinct from that of a narrower focused Recruit Training Battalion.

The army's standard recruit training programs were significantly expanded. National Servicemen, volunteers for National Service — there were quite a few — and Regular volunteers were collectively absorbed into those programs. Once recruit training commenced at any location, there was no obvious way of ascertaining one's avenue of entry into the army, not that we cared anyway.

While I only came across a small number of National Service volunteers at Puckapunyal — and became quite friendly with one of them — there certainly would have been quite a few more. During my eventual deployment to Vietnam with 8 RAR, 4 National Service volunteers served time in my platoon.

After arriving at Puckapunyal, we hopped out of the trucks and wandered around in small groups, many of us in a daze. It was around 1:30pm and very hot. Our mass confusion was heightened by rapidly increasing and unpleasant exposure to army discipline, process, and procedure. Unfathomable instructions and orders were shouted and never repeated, so any reasonable questions seeking clarification drew hostile and almost draconian reactions from training staff, whose people skills were, almost without exception, close to zero. We were all quickly learning that our lives had been well and truly turned upside down.

Over the next few hours, we were processed, which included receiving numerous inoculations administered by army medics — generally lance-corporals (trained medics, I was later told) — in something like a human production line. I can't recall how many inoculations we received on that day, or what they were even for, but there were a lot of them. I remember some guys fainting and others vomiting. I guess that would have been a combined reaction to the inoculations and the extreme temperature. As the day went on, it became progressively hotter. Late in the afternoon, someone said that it was well over 106°F (41°C).

As healthy, inoculated, raw recruits, still wearing our civilian clothing, we were then roughly marshalled over to the Quartermaster Store — Q Store — where we were measured for height and weight, photographed, and kitted-out with a range of army clothing and equipment, most of which looked like it had just survived the Great War. With our arms horizontally extended, and heavily laden, we were then directed to a parade ground where we were assigned to various platoons within companies. As I stood there, in a state of utter disbelief, I learned that I, along with 15 others, was a founding member of 15 Platoon C Company 2 RTB. Later that day, we were issued with SLR rifles without any live ammunition.

The 16-man rectangular timber-framed, iron-roofed hut, allocated to 15 Platoon was functional but basic. Personal space, no larger than about 5m², contained a sagging spring bed and a vertical, lockable 2-door cabinet which resembled a government office storage unit from the 1940's. The interior was sectioned with offset side by side banks of these cabinets — 3 sets of 4 quadrants, with half quadrants for 2 recruits at each end of the hut. It was awful. There were no heating or cooling systems in place. I guess we were rather lucky that our recruit training took place during the late summer and early autumn months. During the middle of winter, I reckon it would have been horrendously cold at Puckapunyal.

Typical accommodation hut at 2 RTB Puckapunyal, circa 1969.

I ended up owning the cubicle on the left, just inside the front door to the hut. This was one of the worst locations because it was impossible to hide or look inconspicuous.

We were all exhausted. After a decent evening meal at the C Company mess, and a luxurious long hot steaming shower, we all collapsed into our beds in the newly-shared hut accommodation. Although it was probably no later than 8:30pm, we were physically and mentally trashed. And, to make matters worse, it was still revoltingly hot.

After a substantial breakfast at 7am in the mess next morning, we were treated to an old-fashioned army haircut which took about a minute to complete. There was only one style on offer — 'No.1' all over. In more recent times, such a haircut has been considered fashionable, however, back in these days of the Beatles and the Rolling Stones, the 'mod look' and long hair was all the rage. We thought that we looked disgustingly awful.

After receiving our 'No.1' army haircut, we were then paraded and formally introduced to our Drill Instructors (DIs) whose job it was, over the next 10 weeks, to transform us into recruits suitable to be advanced to the base level of functionality in the army — the rank of private. We were to quickly learn that our army status at that time was rock bottom. Apparently, we had no rights whatsoever and there seemed to me to be no avenue of appeal available for anyone to seek redress against any perceived wrongs perpetrated on us by training staff.

During my 2 years in the army, the concept of personal or employee rights did not appear to exist on any accessible level. I know that is probably not true — it couldn't possibly have been — but that is how it seemed to be at the time. Not that it mattered much anyway. All of us were prepared to play the low value poker hand dealt to us, without upping the 'ante' in a contest which we had no chance of ever winning.

OUR INSTRUCTORS

The Commander of C Company was Capt. Ghost. We rarely saw him, and I guess that is why my overall recollections of him, other than for one event, which I tell of later, are somewhat vague. On the other hand, the Commander of 15 Platoon was 2LT Trainee-Ghost who seemed to be a proper prig and one who consistently exhibited those particular attributes common to a first-class dead shit. While we did not see a lot of Trainee-Ghost, whenever we did, it was always unpleasant. Most of the time when he interacted with us, he seemed to have his head stuck well and truly right up his arse. I reckon that as an early officer role model for us, he failed quite dismally. Frankly, a more enlightened and engaging officer — and I'm not saying soft — would have done wonders for the early collective abject morale of our platoon at Puckapunyal.

Our Platoon Sergeant, Bull-Neck, was an older man who found it hard to be a complete arsehole like Trainee-Ghost and the assortment of other non-commissioned instructors at Puckapunyal. Don't get me wrong, he was as nasty as the best when he wanted to be. But it was a rarity. On balance, I thought he was probably a reasonable sort of guy. Then again, I never had any meaningful personal interactions with him.

Two face-to-face trainers (DIs) who we learned to fear and eventually pathologically hate, were Corporals Rolled-Gold and Knuckle-Dragger. Both of those DIs were top-rated honours graduates, right out of the Spanish Inquisition. Although Knuckle-Dragger mellowed ever so slightly over time, Rolled-Gold remained sadistic, unreasonable, and pretty much totally unapproachable for the entire, utterly miserable 10 weeks of my recruit training.

I have some difficulty in accepting the fact that so many of the DIs at Puckapunyal during my time were infantry Vietnam veterans from 1 RAR, circa 1965-66. Rolled-Gold was one of those. It seems to me that after having been through an infantry deployment to Vietnam, these men should have been far more focused on the skilling of new recruits for possible service in Vietnam, rather than inflicting inane bastardy on them — just because they could do so.

An example of the low regard I held for these people is best illustrated when I was purchasing a new motor vehicle just prior to Christmas 1970, not long after returning home from Vietnam. I literally bumped into Rolled-Gold just outside the front entrance of a Holden vehicle dealership showroom, located at the extreme southern end of the Adelaide CBD. I was completely stunned to see him. Technically, I was still serving in the army, and I assumed that he was as well. I instantly became wary, anxious, and unsettled. Both of us were dressed in civilian attire but that did not detract from the rumblings of repressed vitriol and associated tension which boiled up within me from this sudden and unexpected encounter.

Rolled-Gold recognised me straight away, which was nothing short of amazing, given that it was almost 2 years since we first met at Puckapunyal. He approached me in a very friendly manner. While I knew that I made somewhat of a negative impression on him during my time there, I was quite amazed that I was so indelible. Anyway, my father, who was with me at the time, was absolutely astonished when my slow, measured response to Rolled-Gold's friendly greeting and offered handshake — was declined. Instead, I returned something very much akin to:

'If you don't get out of my way you little prick, I'm going to punch your fucking head in!'

For those of you who continue to read this story, the reasons for my adverse view of Rolled-Gold will become apparent. In the showroom that day, he was rendered speechless at the mouthful of invective I directed at him and didn't hang around. He literally bolted, just like a sewer rat with its tail on the ground after receiving a dab of turpentine on its arse.

Knuckle-Dragger was a nasty piece of work too, but other than one incident, which I describe later, I never really had too much trouble with him. While he was as hard as steel, and very tough on us, he occasionally dropped this veneer. Don't get me wrong, he was still a dead shit, but not quite the complete version of Rolled-Gold.

There was a third DI attached to our platoon and I remember him as the Good Guy. While he drove us mercilessly on physical and basic army skills training, he didn't seem to really enjoy the bastardisation which was relentlessly and so enthusiastically inflicted upon us by Rolled-Gold and Knuckle-Dragger. Although he was party to some minor aspects of it, he always appeared to hang back and not get too involved. After several weeks he became somewhat helpful and eventually our secret confidant. He used to often visit us in our hut at night for a quiet, informal, 'no rank' chat, providing us with encouragement and useful advice.

There was also another DI who interacted with us from time to time but he was not formally attached to our platoon. More likely than not, he was a DI resource used across all C Company platoons. Nevertheless, we saw a lot of him during the second half of our training at Puckapunyal and, whenever we did, it was always unpleasant. This DI was none other than Corporal Beast: the cruellest man to ever serve in any army recruit training establishment...in any world defence force of modern times.

There were 16 recruits in 15 Platoon, the same as for all other training platoons at Puckapunyal. So, with as many as 4 DIs relentlessly hammering us every day and night, and with a sergeant and 2 officers hovering around the fringes, there was simply no escape for any of us. It really was a full-on and very personal 'right in your face' recruit training experience.

We had an aggressive team of very physically fit and experienced DIs whose job it was to promptly turn us into soldiers. The way they were going to do this was to quickly bring us to a peak level of physical fitness, instil in us the very basic elements of army skilling, and attempt to break our mental resilience by exposing us to a concentrated campaign of bastardisation more brutal than one could possibly imagine.

BASTARDISATION

Up until the late 1990's, the ADF consistently denied that bastardisation was institutionalised in its recruit training establishments and, less commonly, within some of its operational units. Public admission finally occurred when several nasty incidents within the Australian Defence Force Academy (ADFA), Duntroon Royal Military College (RMC), and a small number of operational units, were given wide media exposure.

In the contemporary ADF of today, bastardisation may well be mostly stamped out. However, I've ascertained from several incidents reported by the media, and from talking to a number of current serving members, that bastardisation does still exist; it just appears to be in less obvious forms such as deprivation of liberty, social isolation, and unrelenting peer pressure.

I'm not going to comment on the topical issue of sexual abuse in the ADF because I wasn't aware of any incident occurring during my time in the army. And, adverting back to my 5 years of Marist Brothers Catholic secondary school education in Adelaide, I saw no sign of it there either.

However, back in the late 1960's, bastardisation — in the very real sense of the word, was rife in Australian Army recruit training establishments and seemingly sanctioned by the ADF. I cannot accept the fact that it didn't know about this routine occurrence. It was callous, harsh, and often brutal in the way it was applied. No one was able to escape from, or avoid it.

During my time at Puckapunyal I was subjected to, and witnessed behaviours by particular training staff which today, would bring demotion or instant dismissal from the ADF. For some perpetrators, perhaps even criminal charges. While these abject behaviours were the exception rather than the norm, they occurred far too often, and shouldn't have. The supposed justification at that time was that these inappropriate behaviours were only carried out by our instructors, as part of an overall process aimed at making men and soldiers out of us. They consistently removed us from our comfort zones, stretching our mental and physical resilience to breaking point, and in some cases, well beyond that.

As raw army recruits, we were fair game. Some of us were able to deal with it fairly easily, while others struggled for a time. A few simply fell apart under the unrelenting and insidious pressure applied to them by the DIs. I coped with it as well as anyone because very early on, I realised that no matter what these DIs chose to do, they were not allowed to physically touch us. I was also astute enough to realise that there were absolutely no positives to be gained from provoking them. By the time I entered the army, I'd already developed a range of key life survival skills — due to living away from home for a time — so it wasn't as though I was low hanging fruit for the DIs, but some of my platoon mates most certainly were.

Almost from the very first day at Puckapunyal, I decided that the best approach to my upcoming 2 years in the army was not be noticed. While my bed position in the platoon hut sort of compromised this decision to a considerable extent, I decided to go forward with my plan as best as I could.

So, the 'modus operandi' I adopted was to keep a low profile, try and hide or blend into the background as much as possible, never volunteer for anything, never ever complain or show displeasure, and whenever personally targeted by the DIs, just be respectful and broadly smile. The other approach I took, with enormous success, was to spend as much time as possible completing allocated tasks that weren't physically onerous.

There were plenty of occasions when I spent inordinate times at rigid attention, just smiling back at the DIs while they entered my personal space, verbally abusing and attempting to belittle me. It almost drove them crazy because I knew that all they really wanted to do, was punch me in the face. As to be expected, the DIs weren't that stupid. They quickly worked out which guys in the platoon were going to be their primary, secondary, and last resort targets. After a week or so, it was clear to me that I wasn't in the first category but almost certainly in the second. Rolled-Gold took an instant disliking to me for no apparent reason and maintained this stance for the entire 10 weeks of my recruit training.

For example, on one occasion, he made me have — and pay for — two No.1 haircuts, on the same day. Seriously! I should have just ignored his order for the second haircut but, as I hadn't been in the army long enough at the time, I was unsure how to deal with this issue. However, I know that if I was ever to meet Rolled-Gold on more friendly terms — it will never happen — he owes me the cost of a haircut in today's prices, plus interest. For the sake of argument, that would equate to a discounted financial reimbursement of something like $1,200.

DIs screaming and sometimes spitting into our faces, their constant intrusion of our personal space, and publicly demeaning us, while unpleasant, wasn't something I found all that intimidating. Having said that, at times it was very hard to remain composed and put up with their crap, especially when witnessing a fellow recruit melt and collapse under this pressure. It was a very nasty business for some. At the same time, there were other occasions when it was impossible to hold back laughter. I'll give you an example.

On one occasion when my platoon was at the weapons firing range, Rolled-Gold decided to publicly ridicule a platoon mate of mine, Bob Blackmore, in front of us all. Chuckling, he asked Blackmore:

'Recruit Blackmore…have you ever had a flock of starlings (birds) fly out of your arse?'

This was a crude army metaphorical, euphemistic reference to losing one's virginity. Blackmore's slow and measured response from his broad, smiling face was something like:

'No Corporal, not starlings, but can we talk about large black crows?'

Rolled-Gold was rendered completely speechless by this wonderful riposte from Blackmore. He was visibly mortified as the entire platoon, and even the other DIs watching on, broke into paroxysms of uncontrollable laughter. Blackmore copped some obscure punishment detail from Rolled-Gold as a result of this public humiliation but, knowing Blackmore as well as I did, I know that he would have found some way of avoiding it or convincing someone else to do it for him.

As I explain later, Blackmore quickly assumed the moniker of 'Teflon Bob'. Seriously, nothing bad ever stuck to him. At Puckapunyal he just seemed to lead a charmed life. We became great mates and both later served in Vietnam with 8 RAR, just in different platoons. Sadly, he was killed in a car accident on the Pacific Highway, New South Wales, in 2008.

I'll give you another example of the sort of invective often directed towards recruits by their instructors. This, from a later recruit training intake, really appeals to me:

'Well then, don't look at me lad. Keep your fucking eyes to the front. If I see the smallest flicker from your eyes, I'll break your bloody arm off, shove it through your ears, and ride you around the parade ground like a fucking motorbike. Is that clear?'[7]

As far as coping with this unrelenting pressure, it was simply a matter of doing just what we were ordered to do, no matter how idiotic or physically impossible that may be. For example, there wasn't much point agonising over not being able to run a kilometre in under 3 minutes. At the end of the day, all you could do was your best. I never worried too much if that wasn't good enough.

In more recent years, it has been strongly suggested to me by several former senior ADF officers, that perhaps the DIs themselves were also victims of the system that prevailed at that time within army recruit training battalions. Well...I've thought long and hard about that proposition and don't subscribe to it at all. The way in which most DIs at Puckapunyal so enthusiastically embraced the bastardry aspects of their training role, clearly indicates to me that they actually enjoyed what they were doing. As far as I'm concerned, there's no excuse whatsoever for their generally, and almost collective, appalling behaviour back in those times. So, what forms of bastardisation were inflicted on us at Puckapunyal?

Reveille was at 6am each morning. We then had a couple of minutes to marshal ourselves on the parade ground, carrying our bottom bed sheet with us, for the daily roll-call. The reason for the bed sheet stripping was to ensure that we had to make our beds from scratch each morning. This entire process took about 10 minutes.

Breakfast at the mess was at 7am, which gave us around 50 minutes to shower, shave, dress, make our beds to exact army specifications, ensure that our hut and lockers were in pristine condition, and be ready for the dreaded daily hut inspection at 7:30am sharp.

---

[7] Cavanaugh, Ian. *Fun Fear Frivolity - A Tale of the Vietnam War*. Self-Published. Chapter 6, Paragraph 15.

Hut inspections, at any time, provided choice opportunities for the DIs to impose and fine tune the application of their honed art of bastardisation. Stacks of similar clothing items had to be folded exactly in alignment and to precise army specifications. There was to be no trace of dust or grime anywhere, and the bedspread of our freshly-made beds had to be so taut that it was capable of bouncing a dropped coin — one that never bounced.

The daily morning hut inspections were a nightmare for us all. The DIs would barge in, right on 7:30am. The first recruit to notice this intrusion would scream '*Stand fast*', bringing us all to standing, rigid attention by our beds; eyes facing forward, totally unfocused. We all were, to put it mildly, terrified, especially during the first few weeks.

As expected, our hut miserably failed inspection each morning. Invariably, the DIs targeted 1 or 2 recruits in allocating the blame for this failure — a very nasty ploy. During the first week, guys targeted by the DIs each morning, copped it from the rest of us. However, we quickly worked out that hut inspection failures were no one's fault and that they were always going to miss the mark, no matter what.

During a typical hut inspection, a DI would discover invisible dust on top of a personal locker or a windowsill, or notice that locker clothing items were one-tenth of a millimetre out of alignment, or that a bed was poorly made. Any excuse would do, and the DIs had plenty of them.

On one such morning — one of many for me — my personal locker failed inspection. I was ordered to remove my SLR rifle and framed picture of my girlfriend from the locker, and place them on my bed. I was then ordered to use both hands to grasp the top horizontal ledge of the opened locker and, maintaining my grip, walk backwards. Naturally, everything fell out of the locker onto the floor. I was then accused of being a slovenly soldier and given physical duty as punishment. Of course, this had the DIs almost falling over each other because they were laughing so much.

We were all targeted by the DIs this way, on many occasions during our time at Puckapunyal. The inane bastardry of hut inspections was a daily event for about the first 3 weeks of our time there, and somewhat more randomly after that. Rolled-Gold particularly liked hut inspections. He really was a complete piece of shit. I hated him then...and still do, to this very day.

Another nasty ploy orchestrated by the DIs was to summon us onto the C Company parade ground with the bellowed call '*On parade, 15 Platoon*'. This call basically gave us around 2 minutes to line up on the company parade ground in good order and formation. Once on parade and fully accounted for, we were then ordered to return to our hut, change into physical training gear and be back on parade in 3 minutes. This process was repeated several times and, in very quick succession, we paraded in standard greens, physical training gear and formal polyester dress etc. Our hut was an absolute clothing disaster site. The next order conveyed to us was to be ready for a full hut inspection in 3 minutes. This really was the signature work of first-class dead shits, enthusiastically and very ably led by Rolled-Gold. Naturally, the entire hut failed inspection and incomprehensible physical punishments were duly imposed on us all. Knuckle-Dragger really enjoyed this part of his DI role as well.

Sometimes, our DIs liked to interfere in the normal workings of our daily mess queues. Mess mealtimes were 7am, 12pm, and 5:30pm. We usually lined up outside the mess hall about 10 minutes prior. Naturally, because of all the physical activity recruits were undertaking each day, we were always hungry and many of us tried to be in the forefront of the queue. Quite often, just as the mess was opening, the DIs would order us to '*About face*' and enter the mess from the rear of the queue. This really was complete bastardry in my view. It caused lots of problems for the morale of the company, I can tell you. Of course, the DIs thought it was all so very funny.

One of the more difficult things to remember in those early days of our army training at Puckapunyal, was to always salute officers when we were wearing any form of head gear. Just as importantly, we weren't to salute them when we were bare-headed. Recruits who offended in this regard were routinely ordered to stand for 10 minutes in front of the C Company Orderly Room mirror and practice saluting themselves. I thought this was a particularly demeaning punishment because it was in public view of the entire company complement of administrative staff, DIs, and recruits. A very humiliating experience. I felt that this was one of the most unpleasant aspects of recruit training…and I suffered this ordeal more than once.

Running on the parade ground routinely resulted in 20 or more push-ups, as did saluting, or addressing as '*Sir*', anyone below officer rank. A variety of contrived offences, including not remembering one's service number or rifle number, also attracted this seemingly standard punishment. There were a lot of push-ups done at Puckapunyal. I did plenty of them!

Rifle inspections were another one of the DIs favourite obsessions. From almost our first day at Puckapunyal, it was repeatedly rammed home to us that we had to take very good care of our rifles. We were continually cleaning and maintaining them, as we knew that we could face a rifle inspection at any time. On reflection, this was very good training for us because later, when in Vietnam, every man in my platoon made sure that his personal weapon was always in pristine working order. However, at Puckapunyal, how to keep certain integral components of our rifles clean, was never explained. Nor were we ever provided with the proper wherewithal to enable us to do that. In other words, we were set up to fail rifle inspections, and fail them we surely did —

almost every day.

The SLR rifle automatically reloads from a 20-round magazine when a round is fired. The exhaust gases from the expended round operate the self-loading mechanism, which draws up the next round from the magazine into the breach or firing chamber. These exhaust gases are pressure-regulated by a gas plug, located at the forefront of the rifle where the barrel protrudes from the supporting stock.

When the SLR rifle is fired, residual carbon traces progressively accumulate in the arced recess of the gas plug. A build-up of carbon in the gas plug potentially renders the automatic reloading function unreliable. After shooting practice at the weapons firing range, we desperately tried to clean our rifle gas plugs using vinegar and red match heads, or anything else even marginally abrasive that might do the trick. All our efforts were generally in vain, and we routinely failed rifle inspections. This always resulted in a collective physical punishment of some sort. We became obsessive and almost paranoid about cleaning our rifles.

After several weeks or so, late one evening in our hut, the Good Guy told us that if anyone possessed fine steel wool, to ensure that it was never found anywhere near our rifles. He also quietly suggested where we might surreptitiously acquire this item within Puckapunyal. God bless him. Suddenly, our rifles began to pass snap inspections. It's interesting to note that one of the crucial items of SLR rifle maintenance equipment freely available to us in Vietnam, was fine steel wool.

There was one particularly malicious example of bastardisation that I witnessed at Puckapunyal and, even to this day, I can't understand how a DI could allow his personal values to sink so low. One morning, after assembling on parade in company formation, Knuckle-Dragger noticed that a recruit from another C Company platoon hadn't shaved that morning. We all knew this was a mortal sin, however, young men of 20-years-of-age don't all have the same proliferation of facial hair, and this recruit probably didn't need to shave at all, let alone every day.

Anyway, at this awful discovery, Knuckle-Dragger ordered the recruit back to his hut, to collect and return with his army issue Gillette safety razor. Knuckle-Dragger then ordered the recruit to open the razor, remove the blade, and run each edge of the blade over the hard asphalt surface of the parade ground, 2 or 3 times. After inserting the blade back into the razor, the recruit was ordered to dry-shave in front of the assembled company. Naturally, with his razor blade now seriously compromised, it cut his face to pieces. The recruit ended up in tears with blood streaming down his cheeks.

This act was the worst I observed during my recruit training at Puckapunyal. I clearly recall Bull-Neck looking on from the steps of the C

Company Orderly Room, his head bowed, saying nothing. This was one of the few, real nadir moments of my time in the army. On reflection, some of us should have broken ranks and given Knuckle-Dragger a physical hiding. In hindsight, I'm disappointed with myself that I didn't have the courage to do so at the time. Then again, I was only 20-years-of-age and still in awe of the completely misguided and generally misapplied power of our DIs. And, at that time, we were so craven that we mostly submitted to these very poor and utterly lamentable army role models.

There was a low rising knoll, but steep in parts, about 0.4km from the centre of the camp. It could be seen from almost anywhere at Puckapunyal. On top of this knoll was a large, rock cairn inscribed monument. From a distance, the aspect of this knoll somewhat resembled a woman's breast and was colloquially referred to by everyone at Puckapunyal as 'Tit Hill'. A few of us got to know Tit Hill very well because it became the focus of many of our punishment details.

The DIs knew exactly how long it took to run there and back — 10 minutes at worst — and, for even the slightest infraction, they would routinely order recruits to double — run — to Tit Hill, and return and repeat for example, the third word in the second line of the inscription affixed to the monument. There seemed to be no opportunity whatsoever to cheat on this physical impost, which was routinely forced on many of us. However, in hindsight, I wonder if the DIs actually committed the words of the Tit Hill Memorial inscription to memory? Probably not.

Anyway, during my entire time at Puckapunyal, there was a never-ending conga line of recruits from all companies doubling back and forth to Tit Hill. Strangely, I was never given the privilege of doubling to the hill. Given the apparent pathological dislike Rolled-Gold had for me, I find that to be simply amazing. Then again, I performed many hundreds of push-ups for him and the other DIs, so I guess that more than made up for it.

Generally, if a recruit stuffed up, the entire platoon had to pay the price; usually some sort of physical punishment. At times, this was very humiliating. I can recall undertaking drill — marching and formation — practice at 10pm one night. On another occasion, I remember our platoon undertaking night-time drill practice on the parade ground, wearing nothing more than our ceremonial black belt. Most of us found this quite amusing but the more sombre guys in my platoon were mortified.

There was one recruit in our hut who, like all of us, was slowly learning the basic skills of a soldier. But this guy was adjusting to life in the army more slowly than most. For some reason or another, he was always at the forefront of the DIs minds and relentlessly harassed by them. Seriously, it wasn't very nice. To be perfectly honest, given Rolled-Gold's obvious and almost obsessive dislike for me, I'm surprised that I wasn't targeted by the DIs in this way.

Quite late one evening, Rolled-Gold and several other DIs burst into our hut. Rolled-Gold then made the astonishing announcement that he'd discovered why this recruit was continually stuffing up during training...not that any of us knew this was the case. Rolled-Gold's reasoning was that this recruit was a chronic night-time masturbator of the worst kind, and this was adversely impacting his day-time reserves of physical strength and stamina. Yes, this really did happen!

Rolled-Gold's adoring entourage of other DIs were absolutely pissing themselves laughing and totally lost it when Rolled-Gold ordered this recruit to report to the Quartermaster Store next morning and requisition — acquire — a pair of boxing gloves, which he was ordered to wear to bed every night from then on. So, for a few nights, we had to tie boxing gloves onto this recruit's hands, ostensibly to stop him masturbating. After checking on this guy in our hut for a couple of nights, Rolled-Gold seemed to lose interest in masturbation. This hut mate of ours, seemed to manage the public humiliation really well. I recall that he was from regional South Australia. While most of us had some sympathy for him, we were just thankful that he provided such a wonderful distraction for the DIs, away from ourselves.

Routinely, we had to wash, starch, and iron our clothes, acquire the basic elements of army skilling, learn how to work as a team, undertake a lot of formal physical training, and prepare for frequent examinations and practical testing. We quickly developed an elevated level of physical fitness and most of us became very confident and self-assured. By the time we went to bed each night, we were physically and mentally exhausted. During recruit training, my leg and core strength improved significantly. Basically, I was continuously converting most of my inert condition into hard muscle.

Sadly, several recruits couldn't cope with the never-ending and unrelenting pressure that this amalgam of formal training, physical fitness, and bastardisation imposed on them. Some didn't even complete the first stages of recruit training and were quietly removed from Puckapunyal and discharged. I remember another recruit in our hut, also from regional South Australia, crying in bed every night for the first few weeks. None of us were sympathetic to this guy, so we tossed all sorts of paraphernalia at him, just to shut him up. That was very poor of us indeed.

Other guys, who were obviously not coping at all with being in the army, let alone the exigencies of recruit training, resorted to extreme measures to escape from their perceived personal torment. A recruit in D Company cut off one of his fingers with an SLR bayonet. Now that would have been very painful because an SLR bayonet doesn't have a honed cutting edge. It's more of a thrusting weapon. This guy was declared mentally unfit and discharged from the army. Allan Small, one of my eventual 8 RAR platoon mates in Vietnam, who was at Puckapunyal — D Company — at the same time, has confirmed this horrendous event.

A recruit from another company asked the DIs if he could do some additional after-hours training for the upcoming inter-company cross country run. Fortunately, I was somehow able to deftly avoid participating in it. He was given approval to do so and late one afternoon, he just ran away. I really like this guy's style. We never saw him again. What a legend!

However, in fairness to the army at that time, the occurrence and intensity of this bastardisation seemed to abate as our time at Puckapunyal passed. Increasingly, the focus of the DIs was on making sure that we were going to be well-trained base-level soldiers when we marched out of Puckapunyal. Even Rolled-Gold went somewhat lighter on us over the last few weeks, not much, but a bit. The only adjunct instructor who remained a complete 'piece of shit' for the entire 10 weeks of our recruit training, was Corporal Beast.

PHYSICAL TRAINING

We all entered recruit training with varying levels of physical fitness. I wasn't overweight and by civilian norms, in pretty good shape. I didn't see any significantly overweight men at Puckapunyal. Perhaps the pre-enlistment medical examinations did get something right.

The army philosophy for achieving a high level of physical fitness at Puckapunyal was an interesting one. And, I have to say that it worked. Basically, that philosophy seemed to me to be one of perpetual motion. This concept did in fact form the basis of a number of weight-reducing regimens which were extremely popular in the late 1990's and early 2000's.

From early morning until the time our DIs tired from making our lives utterly miserable, we were continually on the move. Rarely were we allowed to sit or relax unless attending formal lectures, participating in a particular skills activity, at the weapons firing range, or at the mess. There isn't much point in asking someone to shoot their rifle at a target if they're gasping for breath!

Every day we had a formal physical training session of about 40 minutes, led by instructors who drove us very hard indeed. In the army of those times, all physical training (PT) in any infantry unit was provided and overseen by bombardiers (corporals) from the Artillery Corps – our physical training instructors (PTIs).

We were put through a continuous raft of variable exercises such as rope climbing, gymnastic equipment activities, sit-ups, chin-ups etc and — of course — the almost ridiculous number of push-ups. On many days we went for a 5km run whilst singing inane songs — covering the ground in column formation, that is, in ranks of 3. It was all quite varied and as time progressed, I enjoyed it immensely.

Recruits who were regarded as 'slackers' or not trying hard enough, were given a very bad time by our PTIs and routinely ordered to '*Double to Tit Hill*'. While examples were made of those recruits with poor attitudes, I have to say that the physical part of my recruit training was pretty good and generally without any semblance of bastardisation. It was, after all, only ever about fitness. Of course, there were some more difficult aspects to our physical training.

One of these was a time trial where we had to run 1.6km — about a mile in the old imperial measure — in under 6 minutes, or fail recruit training. Failing this time trial didn't mean an escape from the horrible world in which we were living, because if that were the case, I suspect many recruits would have intentionally failed. Rather, failing meant an extension of recruit training. At least that was the implied threat. The dreaded thought of being 'back-squadded' was something every recruit always had in the back of his mind.

During the time trial for my platoon, I made sure that I kept just ahead of the PTIs who were setting the benchmark pace for this test. Distance running, running in general — or any other form of physical exertion for that matter — were never ever my strong points. I and all of my mates in 15 Platoon managed to pass this test on the first attempt. In fact, I thought that it was a bit of a snack. Without any doubt at all, my physical fitness had already improved significantly during my time at Puckapunyal.

The most difficult physical task I had to undertake at recruit training was the 20-mile (32km) route march in company strength. We had to complete this task in full gear including our rifles and loaded backpacks in less than 6 hours. It wasn't easy. I'm guessing that our packs weighed around 15kg.

The route for this march was the dirt ring road around Puckapunyal. As we passed the halfway mark — there were numerous distance markers — we noticed Salvation Army (Salvos) water stands. Bloody hell…did we need that! At around the 20km checkpoint, some of us began to exhibit signs of physical distress. Did that matter? Not for one moment. If a recruit was lagging, another more capable recruit was ordered by our DIs to take over his backpack, but never his rifle. Army thinking was always focused on teamwork and helping each other. We had to finish this torturous task as a composite group.

With some 5km to go, we were all totally exhausted and well behind time. Was there any relief for us? Not at all. Before this route march I thought that I was very fit, but alas, I was struggling. As we covered the final kilometre or so into the main confines of Puckapunyal, our DIs relentlessly urged us on. They were continuously running up and down the side of our column trying to get us into some sort of proper order for our final approach to the barracks. In some cases, they were literally screaming at laggards like myself. It was surreal. I was dead. This was simply not happening. I was stumbling forward in a daze. I just wanted to die. I hated everyone. I especially hated myself for not being able to find a way to escape the physical misery of my life in the army. But most of all, I particularly hated Rolled-Gold. He ran up and down alongside us throughout the entire march and still seemed so sprightly that he could possibly have done it all over again. Begrudgingly, I'll give this awful man some rare credit, as he really could 'walk the talk' when he had to.

Then, in the distance, we saw the gate leading into the barracks. As we approached, the DIs were literally screaming at us, trying to get us into some decent sort of order and formation to enter the barracks precinct. Unbelievably, we were ordered to salute the Battalion Commandant with an '*eyes right*'. I don't think I did. I was finished.

At our company parade ground, we collapsed. For the first time at recruit training, we weren't harassed by the DIs. We were left alone for a time to recover with medical orderlies and Salvos administering first aid, water, and comfort. Some recruits were vomiting and several were taken to the Regimental Aid Post (RAP) for medical attention. It really was horrible. The DIs knew that we were too physically and mentally exhausted to respond to any more of their absurd bullshit, so they didn't hassle us at all.

Apart from the seemingly tireless Rolled-Gold, I don't think any of them were too good either. After all, they'd completed the march just like the rest of us, with the exception of carrying a weapon or a heavy, loaded backpack. But, in fairness to them, they did do a considerable amount of back and forth running alongside the platoon, relentlessly urging us on. During this route march, I reckon the DIs would have probably covered 5km more than the rest of us. I've never forgotten that.

During my 2 years in the army, I did another 2 route marches similar to this one — during my infantry training with 8 RAR at Greenbank in June, and again in August at the Canungra Jungle Warfare Training Centre — both in south-east Queensland. Neither of these later route marches seemed to be anywhere near as physically demanding as the original one at Puckapunyal, even though we were told that the distances were about the same. The truth of the matter is that we were so much more physically fit by then.

I never really saw any objective rationale for this sort of bastardry other than the resultant engendering of a common spirit and bonding among fellow recruits. What did it prove? Not a lot, I'd say. It all seemed pointless to me. Even during my time at Puckapunyal, I knew that the nature of the ground war in Vietnam didn't lend itself to this kind of operational physical activity. In Vietnam, we were never going to be tasked with trekking long distances in relatively short periods of time or, if we were, it wasn't going to be too far or very often. My intuition was later proven to be completely accurate.

Then, there were the endless drill exercises, otherwise known as 'formation marching' — on the company parade ground — practicing for parades. We practised drill until we were marching sheep in our sleep at night. Although drill was reasonably slow-paced, over a medium to lengthy period of time it became physically debilitating and utterly exhausting. Drill wasn't nice at all. In fact, it was a lot worse than that...just plain horrific! I never liked drill and I was always looking for any excuse to avoid it.

Drill was always performed carrying an unloaded SLR rifle that weighed 4.25kg and, after a time, it really did become heavy. Drill is very clever army psychology in that every member of the squad must perform to the required standard or the drill movement fails. So, whenever a recruit stuffed up a drill movement, the entire platoon had to suffer the consequences, whatever they may be. Often it was a physical punishment of some sort, for example, a run down to the creek and back — say a 200m return trip — or a series of push-ups. It was very tiring. For the first month or so at Puckapunyal, we ended most of our training days dead beat. I managed to stuff up a lot of drill movements. We all did a lot of running and push-ups at Puckapunyal because of me.

Aside from the physical fitness, disciplinary, and ceremonial aspects of it, drill was a complete waste of time in my view. My total disinterest and lack of any associated expertise in drill was clear to all the DIs and I was ultimately excluded from our recruit training graduation marching-out parade, because of it. Was I concerned or upset about this? Not for one moment. Let all those other poor suckers sweat their dumb arses off while they march around the battalion parade ground like mindless sheep! A healthy number of us, including myself, failed the drill marching standard at Puckapunyal. And guess what? Not one of us cared.

I was simply amazed at how important drill seemed to be to the DIs and especially to the Regimental Sergeant Major (RSM). During graduation marching-out parade rehearsals, he used to strut around with a swagger stick under his crooked arm, screaming out almost unintelligent comments like:

'That horrible man is fucking up my parade. Get him out of my sight now!'

Boxing was a compulsory sporting activity at recruit training. The weight-graded elimination competition was run along company lines with trained and highly competent pugilists being very carefully seeded. My company had a guy, Terry McClure, who boxed really well and was, for several years, the Victorian Golden Gloves boxing champion for his weight division. I reckon he would probably have been around light middleweight. He wasn't a big man by any measure, but he wasn't small either. Terry ended up easily winning his weight division at Puckapunyal. He also later served with 8 RAR in Vietnam, as a member of B Company.

In one of the early elimination rounds of the heavyweight category, I managed to draw a massively-built Tasmanian guy from D Company as my first opponent. How I managed to be graded in that weight category still astounds me. I was certainly not a heavyweight. Why boxing weight categories are so carefully and incrementally managed until the heavyweight category, escapes me. Here I was, at maybe 88kg, about to box for 3 rounds with a guy who was at least 25kg heavier than me, and very much taller. Seriously, he was a giant and not at all overweight. He was just a very big, fit man. He seemed to be almost twice my size and I knew that he was going to kill me. Is there any wonder I had serious concerns about this physical mismatch?

Cunningly, as we were having our boxing gloves tied on, I casually asked him if he knew anything about boxing. His negative response overjoyed me immensely. We conspired to do a bit of shadow and feint boxing — nothing too serious. He seemed to be as enthusiastic about this plan as I was.

After the first 2 rounds went according to our agreed plan, I had a complete brain snap. I formed the view that, because he was so lead-footed and slow when moving around the ring, I could actually beat this guy. As the final round began, I feinted, moved in, and belted him with 2 seriously hard shoulder-thrown left hooks to his jaw.

Back in those days, I could throw a decent left-hand punch, so they must have stunned him. Most recipients of these blows would have fallen to the canvas semi-conscious...not this guy. I looked on in absolute disbelief as he staggered backwards and reeled against the ropes behind him, shook his head, looked at me, staggered forward, and proceeded to belt the shit out of me. The fight was mercifully stopped and I was dragged out of the ring. I received no sympathy whatsoever from the DIs or PTIs for my bruised ribs, bleeding nose, or very sore head, because they had worked out what happened. I later became quite good friends with this genial Tasmanian giant, but lost touch with him after we finished our recruit training.

Gradually we attained peak levels of fitness. When I underwent my medical for enlistment into the army in Canberra on 6 November 1968, I weighed 90kg. I was 188cm tall and of broad frame. I wasn't at all overweight. I'd put on a couple of kilograms of condition over the 1968 Christmas and January 1969 period, due to all the home-cooked food and beer I consumed after my return to Adelaide. However, by the end of my 10 weeks of recruit training, I had fined down to a superb weight of 88kg and felt so fit and invincible, except of course in the boxing ring.

It was during inter-company sporting contests, such as boxing, that I came across Royce Hart, the (later) legendary former AFL player from Victoria. Hart was a really good guy and his huge hands and long fingers were obviously part of the secret to his powerful overhead marking of the ball across the front of packs as the star centre-half-forward for Richmond in the Victorian Football League (VFL). He could also spin a cricket ball quite prodigiously. Though we were in different platoons of C Company, he and I became reasonably friendly at Puckapunyal, because of our common interest, and participation in all sports on offer.

I was a little taken back by his height. I'd always imagined him to be an extraordinarily tall man, but at 188cm, I was exactly 1cm taller than him. On the other hand, Hart wasn't what I would describe as 'heavy below the waist'. His body was lithely built, which obviously generated his explosive speed over short distances, and his leaping ability, both of which served him so well during his wonderful VFL and AFL careers.

Hart was in no doubt whatsoever that after completing his recruit training, he would be posted to a capital city where AFL was played. He would then be able to continue his emerging football career without any real interference from the army. He almost bored me shitless with his repetitive and endless talking about his future-blessed career in the army, and my most likely miserable destiny as an infantry soldier in Vietnam. And guess what? He was correct on both counts. That is exactly how it turned out for both of us.

After recruit training, Hart was initially stationed at the School of Artillery at North Head, Sydney, and later at the 16th Light Anti-Aircraft Regiment at Woodside near Adelaide. He flew to Melbourne every weekend to play for Richmond in the VFL competition. Although not playing in the SANFL, Hart regularly trained with my beloved Glenelg Tigers and when they made the Grand Final against Sturt in late September 1969, he was allowed to play for them under some bizarre VFL-SANFL sanctioned leasing arrangement between Richmond and Genelg. Amazingly, even his wonderful contribution of 24 penetrating kicks from centre-half-forward wasn't enough to get my team over the line that day.

Anyway, good luck to Hart because he was a decent sort of guy. Nevertheless, it still makes me angry how, in those days, the rules were sometimes bent to provide favourable treatment for a select few.

I also came across another well-credentialed AFL player from the Sturt SANFL club. This recruit was Brenton Meils, a fantastic player who was as well-known in AFL circles in South Australia, as Royce Hart in Victoria. Unlike the garrulous and rambunctious Hart, Meils was a very shy and retiring sort of guy — not at all verbose. While we often crossed paths at Puckapunyal, I was rarely able to engage him in meaningful conversation. Whenever I did, I have to say that he always seemed to be totally disconsolate about his lot in life. He wasn't at all happy about being in the army, and I could certainly relate to that. I have no idea as to the detail of his eventual 2-year tenure in the army.

Meils ended up playing 202 games for the Sturt Club and passed away in October 1997 at the very young age of 49. He was 183cm tall and weighed 76kg. Meils possessed a rare but wonderful athletic attribute of sheer blistering pace, and an amazing in, out, and away swerve. He also had an extraordinarily long kick and was a fantastic wing player back in those days, which just goes to show that size doesn't matter. Hart and Meils constantly sympathised and consoled each other about their bad luck in terms of their 2 years of compulsory military service in the Australian Army. Whenever I chatted with them, it was always the same self-serving bullshit, particularly from Hart.

To his credit, the legendary musician and entertainer Normie Rowe didn't seek or receive any special treatment during his time in the army as a National Serviceman. He served in Vietnam as an armoured personnel carrier (APC) driver with A Squadron, 3rd Cavalry Regiment, Royal Australian Armoured Corps (RAAC). I never met Normie Rowe, but as far as I've been able to ascertain, he was a good soldier who did his job well and, for those 2 years of his life, basically shelved his career as a musician and got on with life in the army. Normie Rowe certainly did his bit for our country.

Drivers of APCs in Vietnam were engaged in a high-risk line of work, as they were always vulnerable to front-on enemy rocket-propelled grenade (RPG) and landmine attack. Well done, Normie Rowe.

BASIC SKILLING

At Puckapunyal we were taught how to fire and maintain personal weapons; predominantly the SLR 7.62mm rifle —and there's a lot more to it than one may think. For example, SLR rifles had to be zeroed, which meant adjusting the forward and rear sights of the rifle for each individual user. This task took time and required some serious concentration.

At our first zeroing rifle shoot at the weapons firing range, all my rounds were grouping left and high on the target at about 100m distance. Using a special grub-screw tool, the rear sight could be moved slightly left or right and the front sight could be moved slightly higher or lower. It was a trial-and-error process but, as soon as the fall of shot was grouping in the centre of the target, both sights were firmly fixed into position by the grub-screw tool. Strangely, if another soldier used my zeroed rifle, he would need to make minor adjustments for his particular line of sight through the rear aperture sight.

After joining 8 RAR, and during our training in north-eastern Australia, we zeroed our rifles a number of times. The last was just before we deployed to Vietnam. Interestingly, during my 12 months of operational service in Vietnam, we only occasionally checked the zeroing of our rifles. Engagements with the enemy were always up close and personal. Precision accuracy over relatively long distances wasn't paramount in that conflict. Rather, it was only about concentrated firepower into the near killing ground.

The gas plug — or gas regulator — at the forefront of the stock of the SLR rifle, regulated the volume of spent gases needed to operate the automatic reloading mechanism. It had numbered settings from 1 to 7, half settings in-between, and we were trained to set the gas regulator between settings 4 to 5, so there would be less wear and tear on the rifle's working parts, thereby extending its useful life.

Going forward somewhat, early on the morning we arrived in Vung Tau, Vietnam, a sergeant who I'd never seen before ordered us to change the gas plug setting on our rifles to zero. In other words, he didn't want any of us having an operational gas stoppage and, if that meant more wear and tear on our rifles, he wasn't personally worried. Nor was I. Gas plug setting zero was a 'no-brainer' as far as l was concerned. There was one downside though. The lower the gas plug setting, the larger the recoil back into one's shoulder when firing the weapon. But, knowing that our personal weapon wasn't going to fail us in battle, we'd take that all the time.

We were also taught how to completely disassemble a range of personal weapons quickly and even when blindfolded, simulating a night-time emergency. We practised these actions endlessly and became very proficient. Thankfully, during my time in Vietnam, I was never called on to exercise this skill under enemy fire. However, it's worth noting that during the Battle of Long Tan — a late afternoon and early evening engagement with the enemy amid torrential rain — on 18 August 1966, there are recorded accounts of at least one damaged M60 machine gun being made serviceable by men from D Company, 6 RAR, using salvageable parts stripped from another damaged weapon. In hindsight, I can see the rationale behind the army's obsession with immediate weapons actions training at Puckapunyal. While our weapons training was mainly confined to the SLR rifle, we were also briefly exposed to the F1 9mm light sub-machine gun, and introduced to the M60 7.62mm machine gun.

The F1 9mm light sub-machine gun was never used in Vietnam during my time there, so I have no idea why it formed part of our recruit training skilling. Although it was of a high calibre, I thought it was a low performance weapon. There was a story circulating around Puckapunyal when I was there, to the effect that very early on in Australia's involvement in Vietnam, an enemy soldier was hit across the back by a swathe of rounds from a burst of fire from an F1 9mm light sub-machine gun. It didn't even slow him down as he fled into the dense jungle. While I did find this story somewhat hard to believe, not one of our instructors ever said anything to the contrary.

This particular weapon had a kinetic energy payload of about 510 J at muzzle velocity, significantly less than 3,226 J for the SLR rifle, and 1,872 J for the M16 Armalite rifle, both of which my platoon extensively used during its time in Vietnam. No wonder raw recruits like myself were able to work out so quickly that the F1 9mm light sub-machine gun was a very poor weapon. Amazingly, it remained in production at the Lithgow Small Arms Factory in New South Wales, until 1991. I talk more about the relative ballistic properties of some weapons used by Australian soldiers in Vietnam later in the story.

One time at the firing range, some loud-mouthed sergeant placed the butt of an M60 machine gun in the crease where his right thigh joined his hip, and fired about 30 rounds. I cursed him and hoped that he'd fractured his pelvic bone or ruptured his prostate. No such luck it seemed.

On the same day, another instructor fired a round from an SLR rifle into a 44-gallon (200L) drum full of water, placed about 25m away. The results of this demonstration were simply staggering. The entry hole into the drum was slightly larger than the 7.62mm diameter of the round. However, when the round exited the opposite side of the drum, it tore the metal casing outwards, leaving a jagged hole of about 5cm in diameter. That was when I first realised the enormous hitting and stopping power of a low velocity 7.62mm round.

We were introduced to map reading, an important and vital infantry skill that I never really mastered. While some took to it more readily than I, my poor aptitude for, and lack of interest in this discipline, never really improved after I joined 8 RAR or during my time in Vietnam.

Quite early on in my army career, I decided that being promoted, even to lance-corporal, wasn't for me. Because I'd already determined that rank meant more responsibility and, even worse, more work, I certainly didn't aspire to any rank promotion. While I've always been a very responsible sort of person, for as long as I was in the army, work and I were going to be mutually exclusive to the maximum extent possible. And my ongoing and highly successful preoccupation regarding 'not being noticed' was always going to be a major promotional drawback.

So, rather than stress about my skill limitations in map reading, I managed to find solace in relation to this aspect of my infantry skilling by simply deciding to trust others to know where we were at any given point in time. When deployed operationally in Vietnam, other than a broad awareness of the geographical scope and range of each operation, I usually had no idea where we were. I almost always enthusiastically agreed with anyone in my platoon who professed to having that particular on-ground knowledge. All humour aside, this deficiency is an important infantry skilling discipline and in difficult, adverse operational circumstances, could possibly have proven disastrous for myself and my platoon mates. I really should have paid far more attention to this part of my infantry training.

On reflection, the infantry skilling provided to us at recruit training was very rudimentary indeed. I guess that's understandable, given that the focus of our training was an introduction to service life, fitness, discipline, and exposure to the very basic skills required of an infantry soldier. Recruit training was only over 10 weeks, and I have to say that the army did achieve what it set out to do. We were very well-trained for advancement to the rank of private. We were also physically fit. And, without any doubt whatsoever, the 16 of us in 15 Platoon, C Company, pathologically hated Rolled-Gold and his offsider Knuckle-Dragger.

CAREER PLANNING

At around week 7 of our recruit training, each of us in my platoon were individually paraded, in the C Company Orderly Room, before a sombre panel comprised of Ghost, Trainee-Ghost, and Bull-Neck.

Although these meetings were supposed to be free and open bi-lateral discussions about our future careers in the army, once we'd completed recruit training, they were anything but that. In my case, I felt like I was at an extreme disadvantage. To be perfectly honest, I was almost shitting myself with fear and trepidation as I stood *'at ease'* — knees slightly trembling — before the panel.

By this time, I'd well and truly worked out that being an infantry soldier wasn't a career path for me. Prior to this meeting, I had very carefully rehearsed my presentation to the panel and, when asked by Ghost, informed him that my choices of corps, in order, were Armoured Corps, Artillery Corps, and Intelligence Corps. I then explained how and why I decided on these preferences and the respective rankings of each.

Although I didn't convey this to the panel, I was by this time, very much aware that walking for days and weeks across difficult terrains, carrying very heavy loads, digging holes, and getting rained on a lot, wasn't what men in those Corps generally endured. I thought that the very strong arguments I presented to the panel in support of my choices of career corps placement were very persuasive indeed. I couldn't see any reason why I would not be allocated to one of my corps of preference.

Before responding to my presentation, Ghost — who I'd never previously spoken a word to — became almost paternal. He leaned forward over his desk and, with a very kind expression on his face, looked up at me and quietly asked what I thought about Australia's military involvement in the Vietnam War. I no longer recall exactly what I said to him, but I clearly remember the thrust of his next question, which was something like:

Chapter 3 – Recruit Training

'Now, Recruit McCann, if you were posted on operational service to Vietnam, would you have any strong objection?'

Well, that's putting it right out there, isn't it? Over previous weeks, as we all chatted together in our hut at night, a number of us had concluded that if we were going to be in the army for the next 2 years, we may as well do something other than simply serve time in Australia at some boring army base. Many of us thought that going to Vietnam would be an experience. Little did we know! Nevertheless, with that vague thought in the back of my mind, I responded in terms something like:

'No Sir. No objection at all.'

At that juncture, Ghost leaned back in his chair, drew a deep breath, exhaled slowly, placed both hands flat on his desk, smiled broadly at me — no, he literally beamed, just like the Cheshire cat of literary fame — looked sideways at the other 2 members of the panel, and asked Bull-Neck what his thoughts were on my previously-stated corps preferences. Unbelievably, Bull-Neck responded in word-perfect recall:

'Sir, in my opinion, Recruit McCann would make an excellent infantry soldier.'

A still beaming Ghost leaned forward over his immaculate desk with, I presume, only my personal file on it, looked me in the eye, and informed me that subsequent approval of Infantry Corps as my chosen career path in the army would be a formality. He then congratulated me on being successful with my first preference.

Why didn't he place the 'black hat' on his head? I was gob-smacked and immediately thought '*is that it?*' That indeed was it. The infantry. I couldn't believe it! I was well and truly up shit creek now. There I was, a young lad of 20 with quite a few smarts, being 'press-ganged' into the infantry which, as far as I was concerned, was the worst possible outcome for me. What could I do? Absolutely nothing whatsoever. I remained standing at ease, in a state of complete shock and disbelief, until ordered by Bull-Neck — the rotten bastard — to '*attention*', salute both Ghost and Trainee-Ghost, '*about face*', and march out of the C Company Orderly Room.

These many decades later, I still clearly recall this discussion with Ghost and his panel members, almost as if it was yesterday. Its significance has grown on me in later years because I'm now firmly of the view that had I informed him of my strong objection to serving in Vietnam, I would have remained in Australia for my entire 2-year period of National Service. In his wonderful, but to some controversial book, Paul Ham states:

'... Many conscripts do not recall being asked to sign a form but in practice they were all offered (at the very least) a verbal exit (from serving in Vietnam). Very few withdrew, the vast majority went to Vietnam enthusiastically, for the sake of their mates, out of a sense of duty, or simply for the excitement and adventure...' [8]

My personal experience as a National Serviceman in the ADF at that time, totally supports what Ham says. Despite what some may think about his book, I reckon he absolutely nailed this issue. Robert A. Hall says that one 8 RAR veteran he spoke to, remembered:

'... there was a battalion parade about six to eight weeks before we went over (to Vietnam) *and we were told that if we did not want to go, we should report to our platoon commander after the parade and they would have you replaced...'* [9]

I have no recollection at all of any such question ever being asked of me, at any 8 RAR parade I may have participated in, noting of course that I was usually deftly able to avoid participating in most of these time-wasting ceremonial interludes. Anyway, within my eventual 8 RAR platoon, which was heavily weighted with National Servicemen, there was never any talk whatsoever about not wanting to be deployed to Vietnam with the battalion.

By early 1969, Australia's involvement in the Vietnam War was becoming very unpopular within the general community, as was the government's policy of conscription. The government was under increasing pressure to withdraw its troops from the Vietnam War and end conscription. The last thing the government and the army wanted was for conscripts to be sent to Vietnam against their will, and then perhaps be killed or badly wounded. Potentially, it made for very bad press. Politically, it was an absolute 'no-brainer' for them.

I've always said, and maintain today, that I was offered a choice to be sent to Vietnam, or not. At the same time, I also believe that it is entirely plausible that others, particularly Regular soldiers, may not have had a choice at all, in terms of their deployments.

Within a week or so, our postings were made available to us. It came as no surprise to discover that I'd been posted to 8 RAR, which was in the process of returning to Brisbane from Malaysia, and tasked with undertaking work-up exercises in North Queensland before deploying to Vietnam in November 1969. It seemed that anyone being posted to the Infantry Corps — and there were quite a few of us — were being sent straight to Enoggera Barracks in Brisbane, where 8 RAR was based.

---

[8] Ham, Paul. *Vietnam, The Australian War*. Harper Collins, Australia, 2007, Pages 170-171.
[9] Hall, Robert A. *Combat Battalion*. Allen and Unwin, 2000, Page 12.

Chapter 3 — Recruit Training

This was interesting because as I've already mentioned, most infantry soldiers undertook their corps training at 3 TB at Singleton, New South Wales. We were going to do our infantry corps training with the battalion, an experience which I've no doubt engendered into all of us, the real spirit of 8 RAR, the 'Grey Eight'.

A FEW LAUGHS

Despite the harshness of our recruit training, we did manage to have a lot of fun at the same time. Twenty-year-olds always find a way to get up to no good, or otherwise amuse themselves.

In any large group of young men, you'll find a few bad eggs. It was with some dismay that my good mate Bob Blackmore, glumly informed us one night in our hut that all of his freshly-washed clothes had been stolen from the C Company communal clotheslines. Was Blackmore concerned about this for too long? Not at all. He simply visited D Company's clotheslines, which were adjacent to ours, late one night and helped himself to the smorgasbord of clothing freely available there.

Having said that, stealing from your mates — I'm talking about cash and valuables — simply wasn't on and, in the army, there was an informal code of conduct that everyone knew about. If you were caught stealing from your mates, the physical beating you were going to receive would ensure that you never did it again. And there was no way you would remain in your unit, because you could no longer be trusted to live up to the old axiom of 'mates looking after mates'.

Not long before 8 RAR deployed to Vietnam, a Support Company thief was apprehended in our lines at Enoggera Barracks in Brisbane. Apparently, he was paraded before assembled elements of the company — I wasn't present because of my increasing ability to avoid participation in any sort of formal parade — and told *'you'll be formally dealt with, after you're discharged from hospital'*.

This unfortunate comment, if it was ever made, was said to have been uttered by a senior non-commissioned officer. I will leave the rest up to your imagination. As to whether this member of the battalion ever received a physical beating from his former mates in Support Company, I don't know. There were some choice stories circulating around the company that suggested this may well have been the case. Thankfully, he wasn't a member of my platoon. I never saw him again.

Towards the end of our time at Puckapunyal, one of the so-called highlights of our drill training was the Commandant's Parade, where selected recruits representing each platoon, were on show and had to display their 'stuff' before the Commandant. The recruit unlucky enough to be chosen by us, his peers, to represent 15 Platoon on this parade was, no great surprise, Bob Blackmore. Part of the deal was that the rest of us had to help him achieve a first-class dress presentation.

So, each evening leading up to this parade, while Blackmore lay on his bed endlessly smoking cigarettes — most of which he obtained from platoon mates — we spent many hours cleaning his SLR rifle, spit-polishing his boots — until they could be used as mirrors — gaiters, black belt, rifle sling, polishing the associated brass fittings, and meticulously prepared his green trousers and shirt. Blackmore simply gloried in all of this adulation and attention. Frankly, this guy could have walked into any royal family and been right at home. It would have been a seamless transition for him. He was incredible.

Eventually, Blackmore's big day arrived. He now had to repay our collective platoon investment in him. The wooden components of his rifle were so highly polished that they resembled veneered rosewood. His brass fittings were gleaming. We had starched and re-starched his greens until they took on a grey, pallor tone. His boots and gaiters shone like the sun.

The Commandant's Parade was scheduled for 4:30pm in the afternoon and we were allowed to finish training early that day to help Blackmore get dressed and ensure that he looked the part. As we all vehemently hated drill and formation marching, it was simply amazing that we put so much collective effort into making him look so good. Army psychology, I guess. Make the bastards work as a team. It was a very effective strategy.

Blackmore's greens were so highly starched that the trousers actually stood up on their own. I kid you not...they really did! To get into his trousers, he climbed up onto the shoulders of several guys and they carefully lowered him into them. Then, with Blackmore assuming the pose of a crucifix, we dressed him. He looked like a million dollars. Initially, we had no doubt that he would be the winning recruit on the Commandant's Parade, bringing glory and fame to 15 Platoon of the 15th National Service intake at 2 RTB. He looked magnificent...a modern-day Greek Adonis and Spartan mix.

Suddenly, we all realised that Blackmore had a major problem. There was so much starch in his trousers that as soon as he bent his knees, he was going to crease them. We instructed him to walk stiff-legged to the main parade ground, hoping that his body heat might subtly melt some of the starch. So, off went 'Teflon Bob', lumbering down the road to the main parade ground with a sailor's rolling gait, looking like a robot.

Within less than half an hour, Blackmore was back with us. Apparently, he was kicked off the parade and given several punishment details because of his disgraceful presentation. Because there was so much starch in his trousers, as soon as the first drill order, '*Attention*' was given, Bob's automatic physical

Chapter 3 — Recruit Training

drill response resulted in his right trouser leg riding high up on his thigh and remaining there. As he said, it felt ridiculous and would have looked equally so. We all told him that it was about time he shared in the shit we were getting from the army. Up until then, 'Teflon' Bob Blackmore seemed to lead a charmed life. Later, we all had a good laugh about it, including Blackmore himself.

It will come as no surprise when I say that Blackmore's associated punishment details were performed by others — not me — in our hut, on his behalf. I simply don't understand how this man was able to so easily off-load disciplinary penalties allocated to him. It was incredible. Even though Bob and I were very good mates at Puckapunyal, and later in 8 RAR, I was never 'that good' of a mate. Perhaps this is why our friendship was so long lasting.

While food in the company mess was plentiful and varied — and I'm sure balanced and nutritious — it was still a product of bulk cooking. Pretty difficult to fry, poach, or scramble many hundreds of eggs, have them ready for breakfast consumption, and not have them taste ordinary. At breakfast one morning, a very brave recruit nailed a fried egg through its albumen to the mess notice board to demonstrate its rubbery and chewy consistency. The egg just hung there. The sergeant cook in charge of the mess wasn't amused and went after this recruit with a meat cleaver. It was hilarious.

One evening, a day or so after our 32km route march, Trainee-Ghost along with his bevy of accompanying sycophantic DIs, regally barged into our hut. Rolled-Gold literally screamed at us to line up by our beds, with our pants around our ankles, for an arsehole inspection. I kid you not!

Rolled-Gold then informed us that extreme physical exertion like the route march we had just undertaken, can induce haemorrhoids. For some reason that totally escapes me, it appears that the army of 1969 was keen to ensure that its soldiers had pristine arseholes! At this time of our recruit training, we weren't raw recruits and far from being 'fair game'. So, as we quite happily dropped our pants, bent over, and spread our arse cheeks, we all tried to fart. Many of us were successful in this endeavour. Trainee-Ghost — who was an officer in the Infantry Corps — was far from amused.

To this day, I'm still confused as to whether it was military protocol that allowed recruit training platoon commanders and DIs to check recruits for haemorrhoids — or if they were just perverted men who got their 'rocks off' looking up young men's arses for personal pleasure. While I didn't think too much of it at the time, on reflection, it really was another low point in terms of core values displayed by our training staff at Puckapunyal.

While there was a boozer at Puckapunyal, it was out of bounds to us for much of the time. That didn't really concern us, because we were too exhausted on most nights to even consider going for a few cheap beers. I only recall going to the boozer twice during my entire time at Puckapunyal. However, as resourceful young men, we managed to acquire and smuggle occasional supplies of long-neck 750mm bottles of beer into our hut. How we managed to accomplish that, I can now no longer remember. Our DIs used to tell us that they knew all the alcohol smuggling tricks, and not to waste their time. They were quite right. The empties were invariably discovered under the floorboards and up in the ceiling, and then all hell would break loose for a day or so. It was interesting that hut searches by the DIs for beer bottle empties, didn't seem to occur towards the end of our recruit training. On balance though, we never gave alcohol a real nudge at Puckapunyal.

There was one guy in our platoon who was different, to say the least. He was an extra-ordinarily massive, but very physically fit young man, again from regional South Australia. For other more subtle reasons, we openly and affectionately referred to this guy as 'Lurch'. Well, Lurch wasn't only a huge man, but he was also a really good mate. All we had to say to him was *'Lurch, kill'* and point towards an intended victim. He would then lumber away with arms stretched forward, just like Lurch from 'The Munsters' 1964-1966 television series, as he closed in on his unsuspecting target. Lurch provided all of us with a lot of fun and a few physical scuffles as well, as we sometimes had to rescue him from over-reacting recipients of his robotic death embrace. I have no idea what happened to Lurch after recruit training at Puckapunyal, but I hope that his subsequent time in the army was as interesting and as busy as mine.

SOME TIME OFF FROM TRAINING

After about 4 weeks of training, we were given a weekend off. Most of us descended on downtown Melbourne for a 24-hour hedonistic drinking session. Because my group got so shit-faced, we bombed out badly in terms of getting city girls to be nice to us. Although it was a good break from our training, most of us felt like crap when all the army bullshit resumed back at Puckapunyal at 6am the following Monday morning.

About 2 weeks before our recruit training ended, we were given a 4-day leave pass. Along with another guy from my platoon, Tony Porter, I managed to get a lift with one of the Puckapunyal staff to Canberra, and spent those days with my girlfriend. It was a good break for me and we had a terrific time together. The rest allowed my body to absorb and consolidate the fitness levels I'd been continuously building from the very first day I was inducted into the army. I didn't catch up with Porter over this period, so I guess he had similar personal issues to address.

After our short leave period expired, my girlfriend drove us both to Yass, after which we hitch-hiked back to Puckapunyal. We managed to jag a lift within our first hour of foot-slogging up the Hume Highway. Our well-dressed 'Good Samaritan' dropped us off at the front guard gates of Puckapunyal at around 5pm. What a champion! When we arrived, we both realised that we were now entering the home stretch, so to speak. Strangely, and although the bastardisation was still to continue — although in much lesser ways — recruit training no longer held any real concerns for any of us.

Porter and I had both worked for the ATO in Adelaide prior to being 'called-up' and enlisting in the army and, although we'd never formally met each other in that government workplace, we were quite friendly at Puckapunyal. Amazingly, while both of us eventually resumed our careers with the ATO — myself in Canberra, and Porter in Adelaide — our paths never crossed again during the almost 4 subsequent decades working for the same Federal Government agency.

Porter served in Vietnam from August 1969 with the 1st Australian Reinforcement Unit (1 ARU) and 6 RAR for relatively short periods of time (94 days in total). As far as I've been able to ascertain, his tenure in that awful country was significantly curtailed due to personal issues back home that he had to deal with, and concluded around the time mine began.

I'm also aware that he passed away in Adelaide on 5 May 2015. That saddens me because although I never really knew him that well, I can clearly recall him being a nice guy and a fellow 'crow-eater' to boot. Again, the lexicon aficionados may struggle to properly identify that descriptive adjective of a South Australian.

PASSING OUT (MARCHING OUT) PARADE — GRADUATION

Our graduation from recruit training took the form of a 'passing out' parade to which parents, other family members, and relationship partners were invited to attend. Both my parents from Adelaide, and my girlfriend from Canberra, came to Puckapunyal for this formal event — signifying my advancement to the illustrious rank of Private.

Our graduation formalities consisted of a battalion parade and demonstration of marching and formation drill. As expected, I was excluded from this event because of my failure to display any expertise in marching. Did I care? Not at all. The last thing I wanted to do was spend an hour or so getting all hot and bothered from marching around a parade ground, just to give the RSM a raging erection.

Anyway, after the parade I was able to spend a few enjoyable hours sharing a light meal and quite a few beers in the boozer with my parents and girlfriend. It was a strange time for me. Although it was a relief to be finishing recruit training, I knew that early the next morning I'd be travelling by army bus convoy up to Brisbane to join 8 RAR. My emotions were in overdrive. I was pretty much overwhelmed by it all.

CORPORAL BEAST

During recruit training, our DIs were utter bastards, particularly for the first 6 weeks or thereabouts. Over the last few weeks, even Rolled-Gold eased off on us a little. Don't get me wrong now…he still remained a nasty piece of work. There was another DI to whom we were exposed from time to time, and who remained a complete and utter arsehole for the entire 10 weeks of recruit training. This DI was none other than Corporal Beast, a man whose impact on me was so significant and indelible in my memories, that I've never forgotten him. Although I saw a lot more of Rolled-Gold during my time at Puckapunyal, the 'Beast' left far more of a negative impression on my psyche compared to Rolled-Gold…and that's really saying something!

The Beast was born in the Netherlands and my military history research leads me to conclude that the Dutch are only surpassed in battlefield cruelty by South Koreans, who were also militarily deployed to Vietnam. So, perhaps his behaviour at Puckapunyal was entirely in line with that of his inherited genetic disposition.

While I was able to rationalise my recruit training experiences and realise that the DIs were performing a necessary job — which a small proportion of them probably had no real heart for — I'm convinced that the Beast got his jollies by just being himself. He took any opportunity to impose himself on us and cut no slack whatsoever. I have no doubt that he thoroughly enjoyed what he did to us at Puckapunyal. While other DIs also seemed to be entertained by aspects of recruit training bastardisation, no one relished in it more than the Beast. An example is reflected in the following, very accurate public scenario:

Corporal Beast:
'Recruit McCann, down for 20 (push-ups)*'*.
*'Now, recruit McCann, am I a c**t?'*

Recruit McCann:
*'No Corporal, you are not a c**t.'*

Corporal Beast:
'Recruit McCann, down for 20 for lying to me'.
*'Now, recruit McCann, am I a c**t?'*

Recruit McCann:
*'Yes Corporal, you are a c**t'* (really meaning it too).

Chapter 3 – Recruit Training

Corporal Beast:
'Recruit McCann, down for 20 for insubordination'.

This was the sort of game that hugely amused the Beast, and one that was a 'no win' situation for recruits like me, who basically had no rights whatsoever. The Beast could have you doing push-ups for as long as he wished. Five or more push-up quotas were par for the course, whenever he decided to take a disliking to you at any time of the day or night. I wasn't the only recruit who the Beast tormented at Puckapunyal. There were plenty of us who suffered because of him.

As our recruit training marching out day ended, large numbers of civilian spectators formed up around the various company parade grounds to observe some final close order drill by the graduating recruits. As C Company platoons were forming up, I was, for some reason, a tardy arrival and made the unforgivable mistake of running on the parade ground. Parade grounds are for drill, not for running. So, this was a gross infraction on my part, against the strict rules in place at Puckapunyal. I was spotted by the Beast who, in full view of the gathering public throng, subjected me to a tirade of verbal abuse, as well as a series of push-up quotas. Any reasonable DI at that time would have either overlooked this infraction, or dealt with it after the public dispersed. Not the Beast. He simply had to make himself look the big man.

My parents and girlfriend, who observed all of this, were absolutely appalled. Apparently my father had to be physically restrained by other parents from accosting the Beast and giving him a public hiding. The Beast was extremely fortunate because it would have been no contest.

Without an integral component — that being the bolt — an SLR rifle is rendered inoperable. So, at recruit training, we were required to sign our rifle bolts into the armoury each afternoon after completing our training. However, on recruit training marching out day, because of the very late finish to the associated formalities, I think the DIs forgot about this army standard operating procedure in force at recruit training establishments.

First thing next morning — our last few remaining hours at Puckapunyal — we were ordered to sign in our rifle bolts before separately signing in our SLR rifles. Back in my hut, I routinely removed the bolt from my rifle and casually tossed it onto my bed — you know, the one that was never capable of bouncing a tossed coin — whereupon it immediately disintegrated into several component parts. As rifle bolts are spring loaded, there was simply no way that I could repair it. That was now a job for the armourer.

As my turn came to sign in my rifle bolt, I casually rolled the various pieces of it over the Beast's bolt register for 15 Platoon C Company. He looked up and me and said:

'Recruit McCann, I don't believe it!'

My extremely loud retort to him, knowing that I was boarding an army bus for Brisbane in an hour or so, was something like:

'Corporal, why don't you go and stick your head right up your arse!'

Well, did that get a reaction. The Beast was apoplectic with rage. And being the bully he was, he instinctively lurched to his feet. We stood face to face for a few tense moments. Although the Beast was a solidly-built man, some years older than me, I was very much taller than him, and I reckon any physical confrontation between us would have been interesting to say the least. However, given my imminent departure from Puckapunyal, he knew that there was little he could do and said nothing as I walked away from him. Sometime later, he was still red in the face when I signed over my SLR rifle. He simply ignored my broadly smiling visage as I bade him farewell.

This was one of my most enjoyable days in the army, though there were very few of them. Soldiers like the Beast aren't good for the army because they diminish respect for rank. I was very pleased to leave him at Puckapunyal, where I hoped that his army career would rot and wither on the vine. I'm not even remotely interested in trying to find out what eventually happened to him. I simply don't care.

PART 3

INFANTRY AND BATTALION TRAINING

CHAPTER 4

ENOGGERA BARRACKS

According to my official ADF records, I was formally posted to 8 RAR on 8 April 1969, and left Puckapunyal on or around that date.

The home for 8 RAR was Enoggera Barracks, located in the leafy inner western suburbs of the sub-tropical city of Brisbane. In those days, Queensland's capital was an emerging, vibrant metropolis with a population of around a million people. The large, modern army barracks was also home to other army units of various corps.

After leaving Puckapunyal the day after recruit training graduation, and waving goodbye to the Beast, making sure that we collectively gave him the 'one finger salute' — yes, he waved us off — we travelled by army bus convoy to Enoggera Barracks. It was one hell of a trip. Other than for several food and toilet stops, we drove all day and night and arrived, completely exhausted, at the barracks early the following afternoon. On arrival, we were logged-in by a formal roll-call conducted by a couple of indifferent looking types, and allocated to our living quarters.

Our 3-storey, brick constructed living quarters at the barracks were luxurious compared to what we had at Puckapunyal. Four men shared a comparatively spacious room divided into semi-partitioned quadrants, which provided some small degree of privacy. Communal toilet and shower blocks were located on each floor. I ended up sharing a room on the second level of my accommodation block with Des McGrath, Allan Small, and Peter Wood; all good men.

Later that afternoon, a short but solidly-built man entered our room and informed us that he was Corporal Fred Vincent, our Section Commander, and that each of us was now a member of No.1 Section, Assault Pioneer Platoon, Support Company, 8 RAR. We didn't have the slightest idea what that meant of course. Nevertheless, Vincent seemed to be an alright sort of guy and left us alone that night to familiarise ourselves with the barracks, catch a meal at the mess and have a few quiet beers, and take a long, hot shower before collapsing into the sack. The following morning was the start of my time in the real Australian Army.

Over the next couple of days, as we were fully kitted-out in the latest army issue gear, we couldn't believe it. The quality was first-class, not like the ancient issue items we'd been wearing at recruit training. And to be provided with a pair of the then legendary General Purpose (GP) boots, was nothing short of amazing. (See Appendix 1).

Around the time I entered the army, a protracted debate began within the ADF as to appropriate footwear for its deployed service men and women. Incredibly, more than 5 decades later, this debate has still not concluded. There have been recorded instances of soldiers deployed to Iraq and Afghanistan, personally purchasing their operational footwear. This could only ever happen in the Australian Army.

From my perspective, the army issue GP boot, circa 1969-70, was nothing short of top quality. It was relatively lightweight, extremely comfortable, durable, and provided very good ankle support and half-calf high protection from snakes and other low level environmental nasties. The low level eyelets drained water quickly and the boots were made of such high quality soft pliable leather, that they could be worn comfortably without socks. All of that, coupled with the thin, steel plate embedded into the thick rubber sole, made it a boot to die for, as far as I'm concerned. I don't know of anyone in my platoon who was unhappy with their footwear during our time in Vietnam. More to the point, many of us managed to conceal at least 1 pristine pair of these GP boots, as well as some other 'not so legitimate' items, in our locked, personal trunks, which were shipped back to Australia by the army on our departure from Vietnam.

By this time, the main body of 8 RAR was gradually returning from Malaysia and proceeding on leave. Only the advance party had arrived back at Enoggera Barracks. The Assault Pioneer Platoon was nowhere near full strength, as its National Servicemen from the 15th National Service Intake — newly advanced to the rank of private — waited to be bolstered by the battalion's larger complement of Regular soldiers and National Servicemen from earlier intakes, along with full lines of command and control.

CHAPTER 5

INFANTRY CORPS TRAINING

During our first weeks at Enoggera Barracks, we spent time settling in, working hard on our fitness and a wide range of instructional base-level technical skilling infantry-related activities, most of which are now difficult for me to recall with any clarity. Whatever we were doing, it couldn't have been too exciting, because I'm sure I would remember at least some of that detail. It was probably the only time of my army life, where it was all a bit too boring for me. Anyway, it was only for about 2 weeks and after that everything changed.

On 6 May 1969, we relocated to an almost desolate bush base camp known as Greenbank. This camp was about a 1-hour army bus or truck drive — 44km — almost due south of Brisbane, or a 1-hour drive — 77km — north-west of the Gold Coast. To complete this lesson in triangulated geography, Canungra, an army locale infamous in the memories of most Vietnam Veterans, was about 44km south of Greenbank.

Greenbank was a huge tract of government owned land used by the army and it was to be our home for the next 6 weeks. Here we underwent concentrated infantry training provided by seasoned 8 RAR Regular soldiers — all Malaysia veterans. A fair number of them were Vietnam veterans as well.

Facilities at Greenbank were basic to say the least, significantly more so than those at Puckapunyal. I don't remember any substantial, permanent building structures at Greenbank. It was basically a tented environment. We were accommodated in roomy 6-man tents and slept on camp stretchers placed on top of concrete slabs. Thank God we were in south-east Queensland with its friendly climate. Toileting and showering facilities, while rudimentary, were more than adequate and messing was provided by a well-resourced, tented kitchen and dining complex.

Given the Spartan-like conditions, the meals served by the mess were of a surprisingly high quality. And, as was usual for the army in any static base, quantity was never an issue. No one ever went hungry in the army, unless you were reliant on rations out in the field.

I don't know how many of us were at Greenbank, but I imagine that the entire complement of those 148 National Servicemen from the 15th National Service intake who'd just augmented the battalion, would have been there.[10]

---

[10] Hall, Robert A. *Combat Battalion*. Allen and Unwin, 2000, Page 5.

There were also a number of men from earlier intakes, veterans from Malaysia, who functioned as the demonstration platoon. They performed the role of 'mock-enemy' in the many training simulations we were exposed to, as part of our infantry training. Collectively, when considering the number of instructors and other support personnel, there would have been something well in excess of 200 men at Greenbank during the tenure of our infantry corps training.

Our daily activities covered a wide range. We worked on our physical fitness and spent many hours repeatedly undertaking immediate action infantry responses. Much of my infantry training at Greenbank was provided under the leadership and guidance of Corporal John Smigowski (1 RAR Vietnam 1965-66) from B Company, who was a hard but very fair task master. Day after day, Smigowski drove us to near exhaustion, until we knew instinctively what to do if we were ever to have contact with the enemy in Vietnam. All these years later, I can still clearly recall one of the very important mindsets that he indelibly drilled into every one of us:

'Contact left — gun (M60 machine gun) *right to the high ground'*.

The reason for this particular immediate contact action is to bring to bear enfilading, or lateral fire on advancing or static enemy strength. The rational for this operational tactic should be obvious. And, of course, the high ground was always a major advantage in any contact with the enemy. Unfortunately, there wasn't a lot of high ground in the Vietnamese province where Australian infantry troops were deployed.

We learned the basics on how to stealthily move forward, either as a platoon or as a section in formation, understanding that there were several ways to do this, depending on the prevailing terrain and tactics decided upon by the Platoon and Section Commanders. Although all of this training was physically very hard work — something like 9 or more hours each day — it was interesting and, for the most part, relatively enjoyable because of the absence of any of the inane bastardisation that highlighted much of our time at Puckapunyal.

We were also exposed to the nuances of each of the roles performed by individual members of a 10-man section — one of 3 — of a full-strength infantry rifle platoon. There were the 2 forward scouts, the section commander — a corporal — the machine gunner and his number 2, a lance-corporal, and 4 riflemen; one of whom had the interesting job of being tail-end-charlie. Each of these roles within the section were different and we spent countless hours simulating the various patrolling modes and learning how each of us should react and interact, when in contact with the enemy. This training, a fair amount of which was nothing more than 'rote' learning or 'immediate action responses', was to stand us in very good stead during our eventual time in

Vietnam.

Because it seemed to be a very dangerous position, the role of tail-end-charlie didn't appeal to me in the slightest. I'm still in awe of Peter Cousins, who quite happily opted to take on this position during our entire 12 months in Vietnam. Cousins was a first-class infantry soldier and a great guy as well. At the same time, he did have a few rather strange idiosyncrasies, which provided us all with a lot of amusement. Cousins was a good man to have near you in any hot, operational moment. I'll talk more about him later in the story.

At Puckapunyal we spent hours at the weapons firing range, zeroing our rifles, and practising marksmanship. We continued this activity at Greenbank. I quite liked weapons firing range activity and became an extremely accurate marksman with the SLR rifle. Eventually, from the prone position, I could consistently hit a man-sized target at a distance of 300m, which even I have to say, is no mean feat. Unfortunately, precision long distance accuracy was totally irrelevant in Vietnam. Fire fights, usually at a range of 40m or less, do not require perfection. What they do require though, is concentrated fire power into the killing ground. You will notice that I often make this point at various times throughout my story. Reason being, it's important for anyone reading this book to understand that Australian infantry ground combat in Vietnam was mostly at extremely close range and generally at night. For an infantry soldier, it was a terrible conflict.

We were also introduced to the M16 Armalite fully-automatic rifle — the precursor to the modern day M4 carbine — and reintroduced, in a much more meaningful way, to the M60 machine gun. As was the case at recruit training, we spent countless hours stripping and cleaning each of these weapons, as well as our SLR rifles, until we could quickly do it blind-folded — replicating a night-time weapons malfunction repair — without even thinking about it.

Importantly, we were taught how to adjust our webbing shoulder supports so that they supported the webbing belt and everything attached to it. This ensured the flow of blood through our hips and legs wasn't constricted by a belt that was too tight or dragging. We also learned how to adjust the harness and straps on our backpacks so they sat high up on the shoulders, with our upper backs taking the majority of the weight. It was much easier to carry a heavy backpack that way.

With a properly adjusted backpack, if you leaned slightly forward, there was little, or no weight drag down your back. This way, you could carry quite enormous weight loads. The only real problem was standing up from a prone or seated position, and we learned techniques for doing that. Unfortunately, even all of this first-class infantry training at Greenbank never quite prepared me for the incredible amount of weight we were ultimately required to carry out in the field. Again, I talk much more about this later on.

At Greenbank, we were again exposed to map reading and I continued to struggle with this discipline. During a particular night-time exercise, using a map, compass, and a pencil torch, I almost couldn't find my way back to the main camp. Even with a lot of training in this discipline at Greenbank, my map reading skills remained generally poor. However, I did manage to develop one — and only one — particular and vital map reading skill.

Military maps are grid-based and if I knew exactly where our position was in terms of a grid reference — someone would have to tell me exactly what that reference was — my map understanding proficiency was quite good. I would have been able to radio back to Battalion Headquarters (BHQ) and provide it with the approximate distance and line of sight, or reverse compass bearing, that would confirm the platoon's ground position. This information for BHQ was crucial if mortar, artillery, or other field support were ever to be required by the platoon. As it turned out, I was never called on in Vietnam to display this singular, but important, map reading skill…which I did possess.

At Greenbank, we went for an early morning 8km run every day. However, that wasn't as easy as it may sound. We wore our boots, green trousers, and no shirt. We ran, in columns of 3, singing idiotic songs, 1 of which was rather aptly titled, 'Green Clad Jungle Killers'. The front rank of 3 men carried a 2.4m long oak timber railway sleeper, that weighed around 45kg. Every 2 or 3 minutes, the rear rank would sprint up to the front and take over the lead rank of the column, along with the carrying of the railway sleeper, from what now became the second rank. This was the routine for the entire run and it was seriously tough indeed. Have a quiet think about that…certainly not for the faint-hearted, I can assure you.

These daily platoon runs weren't for the athletic purists either, as they didn't focus on individual performance. Some men in my platoon who were used to running competitively, or running in an unfettered way, found them to be very physically debilitating. The reason for this was that they were never allowed to run to their full potential, so their athletic performance was always significantly constrained. The only easy analogy that comes to mind is that of trotters compared to racehorses.

While these runs were always about fitness, overall teamwork was a much more important army consideration. Running in step in a column of like-minded men, does have several advantages. Firstly, while the pace is not slow, it's regular and never frenetic. It's controlled and provides a rhythm which, within a very short space of time, subliminally intoxicates the entire column. Secondly, it was almost impossible to drop out of one of these runs because the dynamic of being a member of a column — a team — under physical stress, discouraged anyone from letting down his mates. I can't recall a single man ever dropping out of one of these gruelling runs. At worst, our instructors may have sometimes subtly slowed the pace of a run, where they perceived it to have become too fast for some members of the column.

Moreover, because we were all so supremely fit by this stage, within a few minutes of completing a testing run, we were already physically recovered. During these runs, our training staff ran alongside us all the way, moving up and down the sides of the column — encouraging and urging us on — just like the US Army boot camp movies. Like us, they were very fit men too.

Of course, in true army tradition, the entire Greenbank training complement had to undertake a 32km route march in full field kit. This march was almost as tough as the one I undertook at Puckapunyal several months earlier. However, as we were now much fitter, we finished this march inside the prescribed time of 6 hours and with minimal physical collateral damage. That's not to say that some of us weren't completely exhausted. I certainly was.

One lighter aspect of this route march was to see a very short, overweight sergeant — the only poor role model I'd come across since joining 8 RAR — struggle back to the camp some hours after the rest of us completed it. Quite unkindly, we really took the piss out of him as he painfully limped into the camp, passing our tent lines, with the aid of some helpers. He received medical attention, showered, and after a few too many drinks in the Sergeant's Mess, (bearing in mind that those of us in infantry training had no boozer, or access to alcohol) approached our tent lines and challenged any of us to a machete fight in a forlorn effort to restore his so-called honour.

He was very drunk and physically wrecked so, treating him as a joke, we completely ignored him. In the end he was left doing machete air swings and arguing with himself. It was quite sad really. I don't think this poor sergeant toured Vietnam with 8 RAR. While I'm not certain about that, I'm pretty sure that I'm right, because I never came across him again after training at Greenbank.

There were also some frivolous training sessions like a course formally described as 'elements of sand-bagging'. How hard is it to fill a woven cloth or nylon bag with sand or soil, twist and wrap down the loose end, and pack it into an emerging wall or defensive barrier? By this time, it was beginning to dawn on me that the army seemed to be preoccupied with a range of manual activities involving earth moving. Sand-bagging completely lost my attention. Given that the average dry weight of a full sandbag was around 27kg, I quickly realised that this task was to be avoided as much as possible. Sand-bagging exertions for my personal protection were fine…but for anything else, forget it. Then there was training in 'hole-digging'. While I had, by this time, realised that infantry soldiers sometimes do have to dig-in for their own self-protection, training in digging holes or shell scrapes to fit a prone body, was an even greater waste of time and energy. This was another skill I never mastered. My view was that if I really needed to dig-in, I would. Otherwise, not on!

Even at this very early time in my army career, the army's view of infantry life compared to my own, was definitely on a different wavelength. My negative thoughts on sand-bagging and hole-digging were later confirmed in Vietnam, when on only 2 occasions I was required to dig-in: once fully, and once 'sort of'. Any other shell scrape that I may have dug — I really can't remember any of material substance — would have been very shallow indeed. To me, it was always very much a line-ball decision: dig-in or possibly die. Each event seemed to be equally as bad as the other. While I was never bothered all that much with the amount of weight I carried out in the field in Vietnam, just the thought of having to pick up a shovel or entrenching tool made me feel immediately wan and lethargic.

During my time in the army, I always did my utmost to avoid being caught up in any earth moving activity. As I often say in my story, one of the best army skills I well and truly mastered was that of not being noticed. And, as for raising my hand when volunteers were called for, that never happened. It really was a no-brainer.

On the other hand, I never once minded being deployed out into the field on combat operations. That is, when I was tasked with doing my 'real' infantry job; one that I was well trained and well-armed for, and one that I absolutely loved. Like all of us in the platoon, I couldn't wait to actually get out there and do my job. I didn't ever really care how much weight I carried operationally.

All that aside, I'm able to confidently say that, discounting the necessary and inescapable heavy-duty machine-assisted earth moving by the platoon in establishing 2 fire support bases, and improving another fire support base and 2 night defensive positions, of all the Australian infantry soldiers who served in Vietnam, I was, without any doubt whatsoever, the soldier who actually disturbed the least amount of soil in that awful country. This is a historical fact and one that has been indelibly etched into my consciousness. I'm incredibly comfortable with, and extremely proud of this admission.

After finishing our training at Greenbank, around mid-June, we returned to Enoggera Barracks. However, we went back to Greenbank repeatedly for short periods of specialised training, such as re-zeroing rifles, weapons firing range shooting, familiarity with explosives, and training in mines and booby traps deactivation. Greenbank was sort of like our second home after Enoggera. I didn't mind it too much at all. I loved the open-air 'camp living style' environment and all of the physical activity that accompanied it.

After Greenbank, we felt as though we were a real part of 8 RAR and recognised that most of its Regular complement and National Servicemen from earlier intakes, returned from Malaysia as well-seasoned soldiers. While there was much more training ahead of us before we could claim equal bragging rights, so to speak, not one of us was in any doubt that we were as good as, if not better than those more experienced members of the battalion.

CHAPTER 6

ASSAULT PIONEER PLATOON TRAINING

When we returned to Enoggera Barracks after completing our infantry corps training at Greenbank, the main 8 RAR party had arrived back from Malaysia. Its posted personnel had largely returned from leave, so in no time at all, the Assault Pioneer Platoon was at near-full strength, comprising predominantly of National Servicemen at its base level rank of private soldier.

I'm sure that some of the specialised Assault Pioneer training we were about to undertake was second nature to some of the Malaysia veterans. But, if that was the case, they never let on and became as involved as anyone in this very important phase of our training. Importantly, even at this early stage of our integration into the battalion, there was never any mention of our National Service status, not that it was of any material significance anyway. As far as I could tell, no one in our platoon really cared.

During training at Enoggera and Greenbank, I began to form some idea as to the specialised role of an Assault Pioneer Platoon within an infantry battalion. And, I can't say that I was overwhelmed with joy. In fact, I was utterly dismayed. Essentially, men of an Assault Pioneer Platoon are the first response engineer resource of an infantry battalion. They also provide protective support for deployed elements of battalion headquarters in fire support bases and in night defensive positions. Overarching each of those important roles, they are also just another deployable infantry platoon resource of the battalion.

Fire support bases were heavily defended out-posted battalion positions, established with artillery capability when the operations of the battalion were out of range of supporting artillery fire from Nui Dat. By way of contrast, night defensive positions were usually smaller, and didn't generally contain artillery support — some form of mortar support was always in place. They were established to protect specific military initiatives such as quarry mining and road building. As Bruce Picken[11] so expertly explains in his wonderful book 'Fire Support Bases, Vietnam':

'... the fire support base was a rapidly constructed fortified artillery base position (gun area), usually sited near the centre of an area of operation

---

[11] Picken, Bruce. *Fire Support Bases, Vietnam*. Big Sky Publishing, 2012, Pages 8-9.

(AO) and used as a support base for Task Force, Battalion or Company operations. The role of the fire support base was to bring artillery and mortar fire within range of friendly forces operating in depth...'

Picken goes on to say:

'... another vital factor to consider was the location of other friendly artillery units which could be operating in the same AO or adjoining AOs. An unequivocal Task Force rule stipulated that ground troops must operate within range of the guns (or mortars) which, in the case of Australian artillery units equipped with 105mm Howitzer field guns, meant within a range of 9,000m of the gun position. Only on rare occasions did Allied forces in Vietnam operate beyond the range of friendly artillery and, on those occasions, the units involved were supported by armoured units from 3 Cavalry Regiment (APCs) including a section of armoured mortar carriers (AMCs) and/or 1 Armoured Regiment (Centurion tanks) and air support...'

Picken also says:

'... Fire Support Bases were sited so that they could fire in support of one another as well as cover their own AO, rather than set apart at (absolute) maximum gun range of 11,000m (Aus. 105mm Howitzer field guns)...'

While the Assault Pioneer Platoon performed pretty much the same role as that of other infantry rifle platoons of the battalion, its primary tasks were — as required — to establish (build) fire support bases and night defensive positions and ensure that the deployed elements of battalion headquarters and those static sites themselves, were very well defended.

At 2 fire support bases, we were required to dig-in the battalion command post. That meant digging a hole 2.5m deep and about 56m^2 (about 8m x 7m) — that works out to about 140m^3 — a task for which I wasn't well suited, given my total lack of interest in sand-bagging and hole-digging techniques during training. A 140m^3 hole is very large indeed!

This subterranean battalion command post also had to be protected above ground level with a sand-bagged roof of around 6 layers (900mm), surrounded by offset sand-bagged perimeter fortifications on all 4 sides. All up, this meant a hell of a lot of earth moving. After being 'press ganged' into the infantry, this isn't how I wanted to spend my time in the army.

Seriously, I reckon the worst job in an infantry battalion is that of an Assault Pioneer. Before any operational tasking, which I knew was going to involve a lot of initial earth moving, my underling depressive mental state always became more fragile. I turned to even more alcohol to deaden these earth moving nightmares I was exposed to from time to time. However, in the event, it wasn't so depressing for me.

With a full platoon working on the task and the availability of heavy duty, handheld earth moving machinery, we could dig-in a battalion command post and put in place the necessary barbed-wire perimeter defence systems of a fire support base, in about 3 days. During my time in Vietnam with 8 RAR, the Assault Pioneer Platoon only had to completely dig-in command posts at Fire Support Bases Peggy, and Bond, and improve a number of other fire support bases and night defensive positions. However, even when located at either fire support bases or night defensive positions, our operational roles were quite varied and often mirrored those of the battalion's main line rifle company platoons.

For example, after digging-in the battalion command post at Fire Support Base Peggy during our first operation and putting in place barbed-wire and other perimeter defensive barriers, we tended to operate more-or-less in exactly the same way as a normal rifle company platoon. This meant that I was often trudging around, carrying very heavy loads, amid stifling heat and suffocating humidity. My underlying depression brought on by being in the army, trained as an infantryman and exacerbated by being an indentured member of 'Assault Pioneer Platoon Earthmoving Pty Ltd', became almost permanently chronic after a very short time.

Assault Pioneers were also tasked with demolishing enemy bunker systems and, when engineers weren't available, disarming booby traps and anti-personnel mines. So, our platoon played a key role in Vietnam and our specialised Assault Pioneer training over many weeks was designed to provide us with skills in all of these disciplines.

We learned the intricacies of how to use explosives, namely Dynamite and C4 plastic. Both explosives work in very much the same way, in that they're classed as 'high' because of their detonation velocity of over 8,000mp/s. Because of this particular property, the explosive shock waves move stuff close to it, at very high speed, and completely shatter and lift whatever they are applied to. However, C4 plastic has a specific and highly attractive property. Because it's malleable — soft, with a texture more-or-less like that of plasticine — it can be 'shaped', meaning its kinetic energy charge release can be directed as required.

Detonation of explosives was initiated by electrical impulses or fuses, so we had to learn all about primers, detonators, detonation cord linking explosive charges — and M18 Claymore anti-personnel directional mines — how to fix and shape C4 plastic to tree trunks, fuses, and their rates of burn. With any bunker system demolition, we had to make sure that all explosive charges were initiated simultaneously. It was all very interesting and I enjoyed this part of my Assault Pioneer training immensely.

When I discovered that C4 plastic could also be very effectively used out in the field to provide instant high heat for cooking and water heating purposes, I was overjoyed. During my entire time in Vietnam, I never ran out of this form of cooking heat for my operational food rations or brews of coffee and tea.

However, I wasn't nearly as enthused about being exposed to the intricacies of disarming enemy booby traps and anti-personnel mines. Those activities seemed highly dangerous to me. So, for the first time in my relatively short army career, my full attention was acutely focused on this aspect of training. By its conclusion, I reckon I was 'up to speed' on these vital field techniques. For example, I was confident that if I was tasked with disarming an M16 anti-personnel mine, I'd be able to do just that...even though I'd be completely scared shitless during the entire process.

Very early during its involvement in Vietnam, the 1st Australian Task Force (1 ATF) laid down a defensive barrier minefield. As Greg Lockhart has shown in his published history of that field, it comprised 22,592 M16 anti-personnel mines, 12,700 of which were underpinned with anti-lifting devices — basically modified M26 hand grenades and anti-lifting pressure release switches[12] — laid from Fire Support Base Horseshoe near the town of Dat Do, running south-east to the coast near Lang Phuoc Hai (See map - Chapter 11). This barrier minefield was 11km long, 100m wide, and contained on each side by 2 adjacent parallel barriers of barbed-wire, each roughly 2m high and 2m wide. However, for very complicated reasons (which Greg Lockhart elaborates on) security and defence of this minefield by Allied Forces soldiers — mainly South Vietnamese Army of the Republic of Vietnam (ARVN) soldiers — was very poor.

The Viet Cong — despite many associated deaths — learned how to breach this minefield and, over time, removed thousands of them along with the associated, modified hand grenades and anti-lifting devices. In doing so, they acquired a very nasty weapon that they used against Australian soldiers — the dreaded M16 'Jumping Jack' anti-personnel mine. During my time in Vietnam, this minefield was more commonly known by everyone as 'Charlie's Ordinance Depot'.

M16 Anti-Personnel Mine.

The M16 anti-personnel mine comprised of a cylindrical steel casing that housed moulded cast iron, both of which fragmented and dispersed laterally at extremely high velocity on detonation. The mine was about 19cm high, had a diameter of 10cm and weighed 3.8kg. It had about 0.5kg of TNT as its main explosive charge.

---

[12] Lockhart, G. *The Minefield, an Australian Tragedy in Vietnam*. Allen and Unwin, 2007, Page 237.

The activation of most anti-personnel mines at that time was initiated either by stepping onto prongs raised slightly above ground level, stepping onto a pressure plate, or walking into an attached, low-level trip wire, at which juncture the mine detonated. While still highly effective, in terms of fatal or injurious outcomes, much of the resultant explosive blast — fragmentation and dispersal of metal elements — all at very high speed, was absorbed by the earth that surrounded and camouflaged the placement of these mines. However, the M16 anti-personnel mine was designed to operate in a more unique way. It was a devastating weapon.

The M16 mine had 2 detonation systems. Once initiated, the first, smaller directional explosive charge propelled the entire internal contents of the mine vertically to an above ground height of about 1m — which we colloquially referred to as 'balls height' — at which juncture the main explosive charge detonated with the resultant shrapnel being mainly expelled horizontally at extremely high velocity.

As Greg Lockhart states:

'... the mine was usually lethal within a 25m radius, was known to have killed at 75m and was dangerous to 200m...' [13]

It was a horrific weapon and the Viet Cong used these mines — our mines for God's sake — against Australian soldiers, including 8 RAR, with devastating effect. According to Lockhart, M16 anti-personnel mines accounted for the deaths of 55 Australian and New Zealand soldiers in Vietnam, and inflicted horrendous wounds to about 250 men. He also says that M16 anti-personnel mines caused approximately 11% of all Australian deaths in this war and 8% of all harmful wounds.[14] A later study suggests that M16 anti-personnel mines killed 61 and wounded 272 Australian and New Zealand soldiers in Vietnam.[15]

8 RAR was to experience the devastating effect of this (enemy?) weapon when, on 28 February 1970, they encountered the worst M16 anti-personnel mine incident during Australia's entire military involvement in Vietnam.[16] During the ordeal, 2 of these mines detonated, killing 9 men — 8 from No.1 Platoon, A Company, and an engineer — as well as seriously wounding 15 others. Apart from the Battle of Long Tan on 18 August 1966, and on 13 May 1968 during the Battles of Coral and Balmoral, these fatalities represented the greatest loss of Australian soldiers in Vietnam, on any single day.

We all knew that as members of an Assault Pioneer Platoon we may very

---

[13] Lockhart, G. *The Minefield, an Australian Tragedy in Vietnam*. Allen and Unwin, 2007, Page 74.
[14] Lockhart, G. *The Minefield, an Australian Tragedy in Vietnam*. Allen and Unwin, 2007, Page 238.
[15] Ross, Andrew. *Mine Warfare, 1st Australian Task Force's struggle for South Vietnam*. Big Sky Publishing, 2021, Page 68.
[16] Lockhart, Greg. The Minefield, an Australian Tragedy in Vietnam. Allen and Unwin, 2007, Page 209.

well be called on to disarm these sorts of mines. I can say that our training on disarming M16 anti-personnel mines and booby traps never bored me. In fact, I was completely fixated on what I was being trained for.

In more recent times, Australian soldiers deployed to both Iraq and Afghanistan were confronted almost daily with the possibility of Improvised Explosive Device (IED) attack. A number of these brave soldiers were either killed or very seriously wounded by these assaults and I see a real parallel between what they had to cope with in battle, compared to what Vietnam veterans had to contend with decades ago. Anyone who says that 'participating in battle for the sake of it is glorious', is quite simply mentally challenged.

We also learned how to use trip flares, how to set trip wires attached to banks of M18 Claymore anti-personnel directional mines, how to set poppers (early warning alarms), how to use flame throwers for assaults on enemy bunker systems and, of course, how to use a range of heavy duty, handheld, earth moving equipment.

During this specialised period of Assault Pioneer training, we returned to Greenbank many times for repetitive practical training, which I enjoyed immensely. And, as I've already said, on those occasions I also loved the increased physical training aspects of it, which dropped off slightly whenever we were back at Enoggera Barracks.

By this time, our platoon sergeant Montague (Monty) White, had joined the platoon and on one occasion at Greenbank, he took us by army trucks to some obscure bush pub for a night out on the beer. Bloody hell, did we give it a lashing. Back in those days, I'd always thought that Monty was much older than all of us. How wrong can one be? I now know that he was only 28 during his time in Vietnam with our platoon. Seriously though, he looked like he was about 40! Monty was ex-Special Air Service Regiment (SASR) and he was built like a racing greyhound. I didn't like him much at all and my intuition was later proven to be spot on.

Next morning at 5:30am as we lay on our camp stretchers, heads pounding, and suffering from colossal hangovers, Monty loudly roused us with his booming call '*on parade pioneer platoon*' and then announced that we were going to go for an 8km run in 3 minutes time. Seriously, this wasn't good news at all. After a few minutes or so into this run, Monty, who was basically jogging backwards at the same rate as our forward pace, and not sweating a bit, lit up a cigarette and said:

'*Gentlemen, smoke if you wish.*'

I remember Ray Salmon vomiting over guys close to him, including me, and others vomiting near to me as well. While I wouldn't describe this particular early morning run as 'bastardisation' in the true sense of the word, it was very nasty.

After we finished, in great disorder, Monty spent a few minutes bouncing around on the balls of his feet as he preened himself like a peacock, still without any semblance of perspiration on his ugly visage. Strangely, there seemed to be no carry-over of any angst towards Monty afterwards either. I reckon we were too bilious to worry about it. And, unlike many of our related experiences at recruit training, I think we were all aware that sometimes in the battalion these sorts of nasty happenings occur from time to time.

When based at Enoggera Barracks we had the weekends to ourselves. Friday night for most of us was usually dinner in the mess, a few quiet beers, and then relatively early to bed. Saturday morning was always spent doing our laundry. Various groups then ventured into downtown Brisbane later that afternoon for marathon drinking sessions and mostly futile attempts to pick up local girls. I guess the ambient environment of downtown Brisbane was like a magnet to us, and we quite happily paid the asking alcohol prices. Some of us had a faint, almost forlorn hope, that we might get lucky with a lovely lady.

On at least 4 consecutive Saturdays, some us set out with the firm intention of watching the afternoon screening of Gregory Peck's latest hit western movie 'McKenna's Gold'. On each occasion, our decision to have a couple of quiet drinks before the movie started, totally ambushed us. I still haven't seen that movie and now probably never will.

My serious downtown Brisbane drinking group, the other core members consisting of Bob Blackmore (8 Platoon, C Company), Des McGrath, Steve Middlemo (Mortar Platoon, Support Company), Mick O'Shea, Allan Small, and Peter Wood, used to congregate at Lennon's Bar in the city at around 2pm. Often, many hours later, some of us would move on to the Treasury Hotel and try to pick up girls who we thought may have loose moral standards. As I've already alluded to, that endeavour was usually a complete and utter waste of time because the young girls of Brisbane were well aware of the antics and intentions of the army's wild young men out on the grog. Sadly, we usually ended up getting a taxi back to Enoggera Barracks on Sunday morning, where we staggered to bed and slept until about midday.

On one such evening — or early morning, more likely — Mick O'Shea, Allan Small, and I ended up at some sleazy tattoo enterprise in Fortitude Valley — back in those days it was the equivalent of Sydney's former, vibrant Kings Cross — where we each drunkenly agreed, as brothers in arms, to get our blood group tattooed on the high deltoid muscle area of our arm. Talk about being heroes! Anyway, I was the poor bastard who volunteered to be the first victim and, for the princely sum of $0.50, emerged with a very bloody upper left arm. Allan Small followed suit and at that stage, O'Shea decided that he wasn't that stupid and forwent his tattoo. Then, on the taxi ride back to the barracks, he kept telling us what idiots we were. Although I later agreed with him, I never really gave it another thought. I have certainly never regretted it. And, to the best of my knowledge, neither has Allan.

Steve Kaliczinsky used to regularly arrive back at the barracks much later than most of us, usually so drunk that he could hardly walk, loudly and repetitively singing a famous phrase from Charles Dickens' 'Oliver': *'Please Sir, I want some more food'*. After this, he usually proceeded to regurgitate about 1kg of semi-digested prawn slurry into a hand basin in the shower block. He repeated this disgusting performance time and again. Whenever Kaliczinsky did some serious drinking, he became very difficult to reason with, and often became rather nasty. Mostly though, he was a likeable sort of guy but one who was almost impossible to get close to in any personal sense. He never once told me anything about his family or life, prior to his enlistment in the army. He was a Regular soldier.

After a lazy Sunday morning in bed, recovering from our massive alcohol intake the previous day, we spent the afternoon relaxing and cleaning our quarters, including the shower and toilet blocks. We insisted that Kaliczinsky somehow get rid of his usual marinating prawn slurry in the bench bowls. After an evening meal at the mess and a few quiet beers, we were usually in bed relatively early on Sunday nights.

While we always had an accommodation block inspection at 7:30am on Monday mornings, they were nothing like the opportunities for bastardisation that accompanied hut inspections at Puckapunyal. If the block was clean, neat, and tidy, there were generally no issues for us to deal with. I can only remember one occasion at Enoggera when Sergeant Monty White seemed to be irrationally preoccupied with personal locker management. It was only a minor irritation for us though, and he was nowhere near as good at it compared to those assholes at Puckapunyal. So, Corporals Rolled-Gold and Knuckle Dragger, please take a bow. You are legendary!

On a rotational basis, elements of all units based at the barracks had to provide men for the 'front gate weekend guard detail'. As far as I was concerned, to be allocated guard duty was about the worst thing that could possibly happen to me at Enoggera Barracks. I was sucked into this senseless army activity once, and once only.

From what I can recall, a front gate weekend guard detail at Enoggera comprised 16 private soldiers, a junior commanding officer, and perhaps a senior corporal. I can't quite remember. This 48-hour guard detail commenced at 4pm on a Friday afternoon and concluded at 4pm the following Sunday afternoon, at which time a more relaxed rotating guard arrangement was put in place for the following 5 days.

While their overriding responsibility was base security, guard detail members were required to mount sentry over various areas adjacent to the front gate, which led into the barracks. For example, this meant mounting guard over the water heater hardware servicing the guard house, several locked doors, and some garbage bins, etc. It was a regime of 4 hours on, and 4 hours off, for the entire 48 hours. It was shit-boring, exceedingly tiring and utterly pointless. Only the army could dream up something as foolish and soul destroying as this.

From time to time, the guard commander would check each of the guard points to ensure that we weren't asleep, smoking a cigarette, or otherwise doing anything we weren't supposed to be doing — so basically nothing except standing still, looking moronic, and guarding low value items of no strategic or intrinsic importance whatsoever. After about 12 hours of this bullshit, I was almost going crazy…and only another 36 miserable hours to go. I thought being in the infantry, particularly as a member of an Assault Pioneer Platoon, was bad enough. However, I have to say, guard duty was almost on par with Assault Pioneer Platoon earthmoving tasks. In terms of ranking each of these 2 activities, it would be a close-run contest I can tell you. As for the poor officer of the guard…well, God bless him, the poor bastard. That's what he gets for being a junior officer, I guess.

After my first and only guard detail, which I somehow managed to survive, I cleverly worked out how to avoid being selected for any further duty. Because I didn't want every other soldier at Enoggera adopting my clever 'avoidance plan', I only ever shared this subterfuge with my very good drinking mate, Steve Middlemo, from Mortar Platoon.

On those subsequent, but rare Friday afternoons whenever our company, Support Company, was selected to provide the weekend guard detail at the barracks, we paraded in full No.1 dress at around 3:30pm. The army mentality behind this, was that 16 of the best-dressed soldiers would be chosen for the guard detail commencing at 4pm.

Accordingly, I always paraded on those Friday afternoons looking like a complete bucket of shit. And, while I may have been given a few hour-long chores for being a slovenly soldier, I was always rejected for guard detail. Steve Middlemo was never selected for guard detail either. The dumb-arsed officers running the show at Enoggera never worked this out. Steve and I always celebrated those Friday evenings with more than a few quiet beers.

On reflection though, most of my Assault Pioneer training was enjoyable. And, more importantly, we were very well trained for what might lay ahead of us. As it turned out, this specialised training —which was honed into us —was rarely put into practice after our first few months in Vietnam. We more-or-less operated in very much the same way as a normal rifle platoon for much of our time out in the field. However, I can say that we did use fairly massive amounts of C4 plastic for cooking purposes.

The mix of men who made up my platoon, Regular soldiers, and National Servicemen alike, all seemed to get along very well. As I've already said, no one really seemed all that bothered as to what enlistment type anyone else was. We quickly developed a strong-bonded ethos within the platoon where, as a matter of course, we looked after and trusted each other. As far as I'm concerned, the strong solidarity that our platoon consistently displayed during its time in Vietnam was born at Greenbank, during our Infantry Corps training, and inured during our specialised Assault Pioneer training. If there was any light-hearted repertoire at times within the platoon, then it only focused on what National Service Intake initiated one's enlistment into the army.

CHAPTER 7

CANUNGRA JUNGLE WARFARE TRAINING CENTRE

By the time we completed specialised Assault Pioneer training it was around the middle of July 1969. We proceeded almost immediately to the Canungra Jungle Warfare Training Centre (JTC) for 3 weeks of intense, specialised training in close quarter jungle warfare. Canungra was located in the elevated lush hinterland about an hour's drive inland, almost due west from the Gold Coast in south-east Queensland.

I recall the timing of my training at Canungra almost exactly because I was lying on my camp stretcher in a freezing cold tent late one evening, wondering why God had forsaken me. I was also listening to a wireless — radio — broadcast of Neil Armstrong setting foot on the moon. I don't remember if I was hearing live coverage of this iconic event that took place on 20 July, or a replayed broadcast. It doesn't really matter anyway. I also marked my 21st birthday in Canungra...yet it was hardly call for celebration.

We passed our time here by undertaking what was known as the 'battle efficiency course', the successful completion of which was generally mandatory for all soldiers deploying to Vietnam. After completing 3 weeks of intensive training, we immediately relocated to the adjacent Wiangaree State Forest for a 1-week exercise in larger scale infantry tactics and integrated battalion exercises.

Canungra was the second most difficult period of my 2 years in the army. I didn't think too much of it at all. While my time in Vietnam was far more physically demanding and mentally taxing, our operational tasking when out in the field wasn't usually impacted by the ever-present and unrealistic element of urgency, which seemed to overlay much of what we did each day at Canungra.

There was basically no rank for those undergoing the battle efficiency course. We were all sort of lumped in together, in a number of small groups, and subjected to a wide range of training regimens and disciplines led by hard-nosed JTC instructors. It was a very tough place, designed to ascertain if soldiers earmarked for Vietnam had the physical and mental resilience to survive and operate effectively as members of a team in that very harsh and hostile environment.

The 2 key principles rammed home to us by our instructors — day in and day out — were never to give up, and always help each other. So, even when we were struggling with a particular physical task, we simply had to keep trying to complete it. We could never admit defeat. To do so, may have meant failing Canungra and possibly being posted out of 8 RAR. Several men, fortunately no one from my platoon, failed to complete the course during my time there. Once they were removed, we never saw them again.

The beds on which we sparingly slept were camp stretchers layered on concrete slabs within 6-man tents. It was very much like Greenbank except the temperature was a lot colder at night because of its elevated altitude. It was also the middle of winter. Because of this, constant weapons cleaning became a new and very real priority for us — due to their propensity to accumulate surface rust in the overnight cold, and damp day-time climate.

Our daily routine during the 3 weeks — no time off at all — was nothing short of exhausting. Each morning we were out of bed at 4:45am and went for an 8km run in boots, trousers, and no shirt. Once we returned, we had to shower, shave, and clean our tented living areas and weapons prior to breakfast at 6:30am. By 7:15am we were out training and didn't return to our lines in the camp until around 5:15pm. After a shower, followed by dinner in the mess at 6pm, we attended evening lectures across a broad range of relevant military topics. This didn't allow us to crash into bed until well after 10pm. The next day we had to do it all over again. It was just like the 1993 USA movie 'Groundhog Day', starring Bill Murray.

Each morning after breakfast, several lunch sandwiches and a fruit pack was either provided to us as we left the mess, or delivered by army jeep out in the field. Lunch brought some short respite from the ordeals of Canungra, but not for long. Only about 30 minutes as I recall. Much of our time each day was spent consolidating the infantry training we were provided at Greenbank, having regard to what we might shortly be confronted with in Vietnam. There was a concentrated focus on close quarter engagements with the enemy and night-time ambushing.

Although there was no overt bastardisation like that we'd been subjected to as raw recruits at Puckapunyal, it did manifest itself in the unrelenting physical brutality of what we were required to do each day. Back in 1969, Canungra wasn't a place where any sane person would want to be. It really was physically and mentally testing, and a hard day's work was exactly that, every day. At the same time, not one of us wanted to fail this ordeal either. Getting through it was akin to an aspirational badge of honour. And, at that time, surviving Canungra was mandatory for an army deployment to Vietnam.

We were exposed to several live firing simulation exercises where we had to strategically negotiate something like a 100m smoke-covered tract of land, with live rounds zipping over our heads with targeted explosions, and associated diversions such as smoke grenades. This created all sorts of confusion in our ranks, and to further complicate matters, there were JTC instructors moving amongst us, urging us on and screaming for us to either get down or move more quickly. It was frightening stuff. It certainly got my adrenalin pumping and accelerated my heart rate.

There was one infamous day when an army jeep delivered boxes full of steaming hot meat casserole for lunch, a meal that looked and smelled a lot more appealing than the sandwiches and fruit we were accustomed to. We got stuck into this feast with real gusto and, for one rare time in my army career, I didn't see what was coming. I fell for the 3-card trick, just like the rest of my platoon mates. What I failed to notice was that our JTC instructors, while urging all of us to have second helpings of this marvellous fare, weren't eating at all. So, there we were, with bloated stomachs, totally unaware of what was shortly about to befall us.

As soon the jeep departed with the empty boxes, our instructors informed us that we were now going to run to the hand grenade range for live throwing practice. The problem for us was that the range was located on a small plateau at an elevation something around 60m higher than our current position. The run to this elevated range — while probably no longer than 0.5km — took a circuitous route, inexorably climbing higher and higher. And, we were in full gear, not just greens and boots. I nearly blacked out as I reached the plateau abutting the range. Some guys vomited up the contents of their recently-ingested lunches, amusing the JTC instructors no end. This was my only exposure at Canungra to what might possibly be regarded as classic, low-level army bastardisation. The lesson I learned from this nasty experience was to always expect the unexpected. It was a lesson well-learned.

The hand grenade range experience was interesting. At first, it was very serious business. Each of us were provided with live M26 high-explosive fragmentation hand grenades, which we had to throw under strict supervision from our instructors. Individually, we would run in full gear and personal weapon, from throwing point to throwing point. With a JTC instructor closely watching our every move, we were required to pull the safety pins and then lob the grenades forward towards certain targets. I think we each threw 6 hand grenades in something like 2 minutes. For obvious reasons, our adrenalin levels were exploding. It was very exhilarating stuff and we soon forgot about the horrendous run leading up to this important training exercise. This part of our training at Canungra seemed to go off without any problem though.

One of the trickier aspects of this particular exercise was an associated test, designed to focus our minds on both weapons' safety and operational awareness. Prior to commencement, we were informed that our instructors would closely mentor each soldier during the throwing of his quota of hand grenades, and check to make sure that the safety on our rifles was always on. What we weren't told however, was that at some of the throwing points, as we laid our rifles down by our side to pull and remove the safety pin and throw the grenade, the JTC instructor would deliberately move the safety of our rifles to the 'off' position.

I was almost fanatical about having the safety of my rifle on, and remained that way during my entire time in Vietnam. That said, during my initial experience in this hand grenade throwing exercise, there were several occasions when I had to re-engage the safety of my rifle to the on position. In other words, the JTC instructor mentoring me at these throwing points had interfered with my rifle. At the time, had I noticed any instructor doing that, I would have been hard-pressed not to belt him — and if I did so — I reckon that I would have gotten away with it. Interfering with a soldier's weapon is something akin to sexual assault in my view. While the law of averages suggests that some of my platoon mates would have been caught with their safety off, I don't recall any associated ramifications for anyone. Perhaps we were all switched-on soldiers by then.

Fairly close to the administrative hub of the large JTC facility, there was a low-arched pedestrian bridge traversing a small creek or rivulet of the adjacent Coomera River. The bridge was wide enough for 4 people to comfortably walk across, side by side. From point to point, the bridge span was about 75m. The intended mechanical design of the bridge was such that it was extremely susceptible to pulsating vibrations. Accordingly, if soldiers like a platoon moved across it in columns of 3, in step, and in time, it would absorb those synchronised kinetic energies and gradually start to vertically buckle in a small ripple or wave effect. Eventually, this would throw those soldiers off their feet and perhaps over the low side-railings, into the freezing water below. Once or twice, we were ordered to cross this bridge in the recommended way, but we always refused to do so by breaking step. We had heard about this bridge before coming to Canungra and weren't keen on being dumped into the murky water below. There were never any issues from our JTC instructors in terms of the way our platoon traversed this bridge, in direct contravention of quite opposite formal orders.

The confidence — also known as the obstacle — course, was another legendary and physical challenge. This course track, which extended for about 500m, was largely constructed over flat ground, interspersed with several minor water crossings and other marsh-type ground features. It contained a number of obstacles of varying degrees of difficulty.

The benchmark for passing this course was that we had to make the start to finish run, negotiating all the obstacles, in less than 8 minutes. That was a tough ask and, to top it all off, at the end point of this challenging course, there was a compulsory jump — the last obstacle — from a 10m tower into the Coomera River. Given that it was July, the water in the river was very cold indeed.

It didn't matter if you couldn't swim, you still had to take this tower jump. There were no exceptions. It was simply not possible to avoid this final test of the confidence course. I remember when it came my turn to jump, the JTC instructor — an officer — supervising the top of the tower platform, asked me if I could swim. When I said '*yes, Sir*', he loudly relayed my affirmative response to the 2 men in wetsuits in the river below. What this meant, of course, was that I was going to be left to my own devices to struggle out of the river onto the nearby bank. As soon as non-swimmers plunged into the river, they were assisted over to the bank by these 2 guys. It must have been a frightening experience for those who couldn't swim.

Confidence Course 10m water tower jump at Canungra Jungle Warfare Training Centre.

The obstacles we had to negotiate on the confidence course were devices such as heavy, tied-down wet cargo nets (semi-taut 40mm woven ropes), moving pathways, ropes to climb, a flying fox over a shallow water course, and horizontal ladders which had to be traversed hand over hand. Other than the wet cargo nets — one of the early obstacles — most of it wasn't too physically difficult. However, every obstacle slowed you up. As we progressively made our way through each of the obstacles, we held the mantra 'only 8 minutes' constantly in the back of our minds.

The only obstacle I didn't really like was one known as the 'bear pit'. It comprised a 2m high wall, constructed from horizontally-tiered logs, on the other side of which was a very deep pit full of liquid slop and other assorted crap.

Confidence Course 'Bear Pit' at Canungra Jungle Warfare Training Centre.

This pit was rank, and it absolutely stank. You often see this sort of obstacle in US Army boot camp movies. As a JTC instructor showed us each obstacle in turn, while we walked the course in reverse order back to the start point, he demonstrated how fetid and vile this pit was, by openly pissing in it, right in front of us. The pit was sufficiently deep, wide, and long enough for it to be impossible for anyone to avoid going right into it and fully submerging, once you'd successfully negotiated the wall. At that point, there was only one directional option…and that was down!

Fortunately, I managed to complete my first and only attempt at this course within the required 8 minutes, and after fully submerging myself in the foul, human urine-tainted slop of the bear pit, I welcomed the cleansing water jump at the end. The very few guys in my group who failed to complete the course in less than 8 minutes had to attempt it again over succeeding days, after training, until they were able to do so. Only one guy in my group ultimately failed to pass this course and it had nothing at all to do with the 8-minute time limit.

This soldier was a cook from Admin Company and, for some strange reason or other, he was attached to my group during our time at Canungra. After indicating to the JTC instructor supervising the top of the tower platform that he was a non-swimmer, he directly refused to take the water tower jump and prevaricated on the tower platform for quite some time. Although I can't be certain, I think he may have eventually been nudged over the edge of the platform by the supervising JTC instructor. I came to this conclusion because the soldier made a hell of a lot of hysterical noise on his descent, and entered the water horizontally instead of vertically. As he was assisted by the 2 men in wetsuits to the bank of the river, he looked like a bedraggled half-drowned water rat.

Because of the protracted delay in relocating this man from the tower platform to the Coomera River, we were gathered on the riverbank below and hurled torrents of abuse at him, denigrating the soldier over his sheer terror and panic. We all thought it was terribly funny at the time, but on reflection, our behaviour that day was ordinary to say the least. This man was quite clearly scared out of his mind. And, I wonder how we would have reacted if it were one of our platoon mates in his place. Quite differently I suspect. This soldier managed to last slightly longer at Canungra but, after a disastrous — for him — night-time ambush simulation exercise, he was removed from the course, never to be seen again.

As expected, we had to undertake another 32km route march in full gear and, although this was my third such march during my time in the army, it still seemed like hard work. Even as supremely fit as we all were by then, to march that distance in full gear, in under 6 hours, was no mean feat. And Canungra had a very nasty landscape feature known as 'Heartbreak Hill'. We often wondered why it was given this strange name but, when we realised that it was part of the final leg of the route march back into the main facility area, we had our answer. It was an absolute killer, and nicely topped-off another shitty day in the army for me.

However, what I did notice was how this route march differed so markedly to the previous 2 I'd undertaken. Our recovery time after this march was much more rapid, so we suffered no real physical, collateral damage. Next morning, when we climbed out of bed at 4:45am for another 8km run, we were all pretty much in good shape. Compared to when we first entered the army back in January, we were now so unbelievably fit and inured to physical stresses on our bodies. Just after our time at Canungra concluded, we would often say *'we're so fit that we could eat bricks for breakfast'*. We had a few other associated sayings as well, but I don't think I should repeat them here in my story. At that time, I really was in the best physical condition of my entire life even though, as I later discovered, I had slightly dropped my weight down to 85kg. Seriously, I wasn't carrying even one gram of fat on my body.

While I can't be certain, I'd be absolutely flabbergasted if today's contemporary Australian Army infantry units include 32km route marches as part of their training and fitness regimes. I'm pretty sure that OH&S legislative requirements would prohibit it. Perhaps the ADF Special Forces and Commando elements still use this iconic physical torture as part of their field testing protocols, but that would probably be the extent of it in my view.

I participated in, and completed 3 of these 32km ordeals during my time in the army. I still don't know that they achieved anything other than to make me vehemently hate the army even more than I already did. Anyway, moving right along...

We performed one memorable night-time ambush simulation exercise that was extremely useful in terms of demonstrating some of the difficulties associated with springing an ambush in the dead of a pitch-black night. We were told that this type of ambush was often the norm for infantry units deployed to Vietnam.

After springing — initiating — this simulated night-time ambush on enemy (JTC instructors) moving through the designated killing ground, other instructors — who were positioned with us in our ambush ground position that night — ordered members of the ambush party to move out and deal with the 'pretend' dead and wounded enemy. Several other guys (remember...I never volunteer) obediently obliged and immediately became lost and completely caught up in the stringy 'wait-a-while' tendrils endemic amongst the semi-jungle terrain landscape that inundated many parts of Canungra. These fronded tendrils were so named by much earlier Canungra inhabitants, because their barbs were like fishing hooks, and the tendrils so long and numerous that you simply couldn't move forward without stopping and disentangling yourself from them. Hence, the very accurate and apt name of 'wait-a while'.

The soldier who refused to take the water tower jump on the confidence course some days earlier, was one candidate who eagerly moved out into the demonstration killing ground. Almost immediately he became caught up in strand-after-strand of 'wait-a-while' tendrils. And, the more he struggled, the more he became cocooned. I remember him whimpering and crying like a child as it ultimately immobilised him. It was very sad in some respects, because he seemed to be ill-suited for the infantry and probably even the army itself. Strangely though, he was a Regular soldier and not a National Serviceman like many of us. Next morning, as dawn broke, we rescued our immobilised mate from his 'wait-a-while' cocoon. It was clear that he was mentally broken. He was removed from our group that same day, never to be seen again.

What this exercise did teach us, was not to move from our defensive ground position after springing a night-time ambush. It was far too dangerous. During my eventual 12 months in Vietnam, apart from the initial set up of the cordons, and searches of 3 civilian centres, I only moved at night on one occasion — 8 January 1970 — and that was when my platoon, supported by APCs, reinforced another 8 RAR ambush party under sustained, heavy fire from a large enemy force. Basically, we never moved at night after contact with the enemy. We always waited until dawn to see what the lie of the land held for us.

There was one occasion during 8 RAR's time in Vietnam when Sergeant Chad Sherrin moved a C Company 8 Platoon night-time ambush, so as to be better able to engage the enemy when they moved out of the village that they were previously observed entering. This relocated ambush, when sprung some hours later, was devastatingly effective in terms of the number of enemy killed and wounded. But I have to say that it was a very high-risk manoeuvre and if it were to have become ugly for the platoon, Sergeant Sherrin would, more likely than not, have been in a lot of serious trouble.

Some of the evening lectures we attended at Canungra were interesting to say the least. There were a series of presentations on health, which dealt with personal hygiene in the field, battlefield wounds and how to treat them, along with one particular...amazingly detailed and descriptive — colour slides and all — presentation of what your penis might look like if you were unlucky enough to contract any of the insidious venereal diseases supposedly carried by many bar girls in Vung Tau, which would be our R&C (rest-in-country) venue.

Were we worried by any of this graphic material? Not for one moment. Nearly all the questions following this very popular presentation focused on the availability at the RAP — our 8 RAR GP — of medications to cure these diseases once contracted. This training session saw the presenters overwhelmed with questions that they were simply unable to respond to, and it was quickly closed in true, military fashion.

After 3 weeks of non-stop frenetic physical activity and jungle warfare

Chapter 7 — Canungra Jungle Warfare Training Centre

training, we concluded our time at Canungra. Although I wasn't sad to leave it behind, I've always felt that our time here instilled in each of us the common bond of true mateship, the real spirit of what army mates are all about. We had been through a very difficult time and simply had to rely on each other to get through it all, and we did.

As I said earlier, we immediately relocated from Canungra to the nearby Wiangaree State Forest for a 1-week exercise in infantry tactics and associated battalion exercises. I don't remember too much about that now, other than it was my first experience in learning how to defecate into pits with 'grunting poles' embedded at each end — no privacy whatsoever — and the copperhead snakes and other assorted nasties that used to crawl around and sometimes over us at night. I can't remember anything else about that week.

After completing the Wiangaree exercise, we returned to Enoggera Barracks and were given a 4-day leave pass. I managed to bum a lift with one of my platoon mates, Peter Wood, who was from Goulburn, and travelled down to Canberra for some quality time with my girlfriend. Unfortunately, I don't think I was able to fully relax with her. I was becoming increasingly focused on my rapidly approaching departure for our tour of duty in Vietnam. But it was still a very welcome break for me.

I'll never ever forget this round trip to Canberra as a passenger in a very small car, driven by a guy who was clearly training for the International Grand Prix circuit. It was frightening stuff. The highways back then were nowhere near as good as they are now. Anyway, somehow we managed to get back to Enoggera in one piece. Sadly, another very popular member of our platoon, Alan Howie, died in a car accident during this 4-day period.

CHAPTER 8

FINAL EXERCISES

Returning to Enoggera following our break in mid-August, we immediately moved into an almost continual phase of field exercises, leading up to our departure for Vietnam. We spent very little time at the barracks, as our training activities were concentrated in testing landscapes many hundreds of kilometres north of Brisbane.

During these exercises, we were exposed to infantry and armour — tanks and APCs — integration training at Wide Bay, a desolate part of coastal Queensland where the sandflies are massive and literally eat you alive. I hated Wide Bay. This was followed up with helicopter insertion and extraction familiarisation training, which we were told was going to be crucial in terms of our operational role in Vietnam. And indeed, it was. The Vietnam War was the first military conflict where helicopters were used extensively in support of ground troops. And, I have to say that was the case during my time there with 8 RAR. Although always terrified of riding in helicopters, I absolutely loved them because of what they provided us in terms of re-supplies and operational relocations.

Beginning around early September, the first full battalion strength exercise was undertaken in the Mount Byron State Forest area, followed up by final exercises at Shoalwater Bay later that month, where we were re-introduced to those damn sandflies. I hated Shoalwater Bay too. During these exercises, we were extensively trained in reconnaissance in force tactics, how to attack and counter-attack an enemy ground force, how to assault fortified positions such as bunkers, and the techniques we might need to employ in the cordon and search of civilian centres. It was extremely varied training with a continual emphasis on jungle conditions and guerrilla warfare — unrelenting and utterly exhausting!

We were now a very fit and highly-trained professional infantry platoon, equipped with the latest personal weapons, armaments, and other military hardware of the day. We were certainly well-prepared for what was to later confront us in Vietnam.

CHAPTER 9

PRE-EMBARKATION LEAVE

The battalion officially proceeded on pre-embarkation leave on 15 October 1969. I think that we were all given a 7-day leave pass, plus several extra days for travelling time, or something like that. It was quite generous. My personal service records indicate that I was granted leave from 13-22 October.

We were provided with airline or other fully paid travel options to our respective home States or Territories. I returned to Adelaide to be with my parents. I was sorely tempted to spend my pre-embarkation leave in Canberra and spend quality time with my girlfriend but, in the end, my very strong family ties swayed me otherwise.

On reflection, that decision was probably the first stage of failure of my long-term relationship with my girlfriend. After I returned to Australia in December 1970, the chemistry between us just wasn't there anymore. I have to say this though…she was a lovely woman, whom I loved at the time, and I really appreciated the many letters of support she sent me during my entire time in Vietnam. Our paths still sometimes cross in Canberra and, pleasingly, we have remained on very good terms. I recently attended her father's funeral and chatted pleasantly for a time with both her and her husband of many years.

For the 7 days of my leave in Adelaide, my father – a WWII RAAF veteran, took time off from his busy executive job with a large insurance company to be present and provide paternal, moral support for what lay ahead of me. But instead, no overt assistance or encouragement was offered. That just wasn't my father. And to be honest, it probably wasn't the way I wanted it to be anyway. His proud recognition of me as a soldier of the wider McCann ex-service family, who was about to experience active war service as an infantry soldier, was only ever subliminally implied, if that makes any sense. It certainly does to me.

My father had always been somewhat of a distant figure whom I respected, but one who never went out of his way to foster a proper, or any, father-son relationship. For example, he only ever watched me play one quarter — 25 minutes — of one game of AFL junior football, and that wasn't until I was playing Under 17's for the Brighton Amateur League Football Club in 1965. And, after that match, he publicly criticised me for not being aggressive enough in my contested field play.

While I've never forgotten this, I also realise that his detached relationship with me — not sure about my sister, Paula — wasn't entirely his fault. Though he had a well-paid job, he also worked a second job on Saturdays, for about 7 years, to help pay the expensive private school tuition fees for us both. He didn't have a lot of spare time on Saturdays. That aside, during my later teenage years, he was often critical of me and I felt much of that criticism was totally unwarranted. To be perfectly honest, I never understood any of it at all.

Some 8 or 9 months previously, when I was about to enter the army, we began to forge the basis of a proper father-son relationship down at his pub. But it was only with a very large degree of caution that I allowed him to enter my personal world at this time. It didn't take long to realise, without any doubt whatsoever, that my father was delighted by what I had achieved in my short career with the ATO. He was also pleased with, but concerned about my upcoming deployment to Vietnam as an infantry soldier.

My father was a proud RAAF veteran, so active military service was a status symbol to him, almost a badge of honour if you like. At the same time, he was anxious that I, his only son, wouldn't come to any harm in achieving this veteran status, which he valued so highly. Although he was never able to articulate these related thoughts and feelings to me, I was acutely aware that my deployment to Vietnam as an infantry soldier was a major dilemma for him.

So, we did what most men would do in those exact same circumstances. We went to the Brighton Hotel on each of those 7 days and consumed far too many beers together, without talking much at all. Anyway, the good relationship we had tentatively established earlier that year, eventually developed into a strong and loving one…which we both built on, and maintained, until the day he died — 31 July 1988.

My mother was a lovely woman who simply worked her backside off in maintaining the family home and providing wonderful home-cooked meals for the family — and the many unexpected drop-in friends of both my sister and I during our teenage years — each evening. I was very close to her back in 1969 and remained so over the ensuing years, until dementia finally overtook her mental capacity around 2010, leading to her eventual passing in 2013.

One morning, as I lay half asleep in my bed, my mother walked into the room and noticed the tattoo high up on the deltoid muscle of my left shoulder. Literally, she almost had a heart attack. She must have told my father because, as I was taking a shower later that morning, he came into the bathroom, pulled aside the shower curtain, looked at the tattoo, said, '*Bloody idiot*', and walked out. Neither of them ever mentioned it again. Many years later when my own son proudly displayed his tattoos to me, I had no choice…I had to be totally relaxed about it.

Chapter 9 – Pre-embarkation Leave

On the last evening before I returned to Enoggera, my parents put on some sort of family-and-neighbour barbeque for me. It was all very nice and well-intentioned. But the pointless, repeated question, '*How do you feel about going to Vietnam?*' almost drove me crazy. I very quickly became bored with this gathering, just wanting it to be over, and probably wasn't good company for anyone. As I recall, I wasn't drinking much alcohol either — very strange for me at that time of my life. I was returning to my army home, and my mates the next morning, so I was just anxious to get there and ready myself for Vietnam. The following day, when I departed Adelaide airport for Brisbane, I was a very relieved young man.

In the 4 weeks leading up to our embarkation for Vietnam on HMAS *Sydney*, we were fully occupied on maintaining our fitness and making sure that our personal and collective platoon equipment was in first-class condition. We completed a final zeroing of our rifles at Greenbank, packed our heavy, specialised platoon equipment into crates and otherwise made sure that we were fully squared away for 17 November — the official day of departure from Australia for Vietnam.

During this time, we also attended formal education sessions which, again, dealt with issues such as the medical and health aspects of our upcoming service. In addition, just prior to our pre-embarkation leave, we attended a detailed presentation by officials from the Red Cross, which focused on the requirements of the Geneva Convention; particularly those concerning the proper handling of prisoners of war.

It was a very busy time for us and, before we knew it, we were boarding army buses heading to Hamilton Wharf on the Brisbane River before boarding HMAS *Sydney*, the aircraft carrier that had been converted into a fast troop and material carrier, to transport us to Vietnam.

I remember the crowds of people lining the roads adjacent to Enoggera Barracks that morning, cheering and waving to us as our buses headed for Hamilton Wharf, not too far north-east of downtown Brisbane. The families of many of the Regular army complement of 8 RAR lived in the western suburbs of Brisbane and there were, literally, many hundreds of people at the wharf to see us off. It was around midday on 17 November when 551 officers and other rank men of 8 RAR boarded *Sydney* and departed Brisbane for an 11-day voyage — her 15th — to Vietnam. *Sydney's* crew comprised 686 officers and other rank sailors. Collectively, some 1,237 souls were aboard.

That day there were 26 men from the Assault Pioneer Platoon who were eager to meet up with their other 3 members, due to later depart Australia by air as part of the Advance and Rear Parties. As you will see later, even from the time we left the shores of Australia, the platoon was well short of its prescribed posted strength of 34 men.

Anecdotally, it seems that there were numerous members of the Fourth Estate — the Press — at Hamilton Wharf that morning. They were very keen to talk to the many agitated National Servicemen who were being sent to Vietnam, allegedly against their wishes. From what I understand, the commanding officer of the battalion, LTCOL Keith O'Neill, offered the Press free and unhindered access onto the *Sydney*, to speak with any disaffected National Service member of the battalion. Apparently, as hard as they tried, the Press couldn't even find one conscript willing to talk to them.

The advance party of some 150 men, followed some days later by the rear party of 46 men, flew out the following day to formally take over the battalion's Task Force responsibility from 9 RAR, to plan its first operation and greet the main party when it arrived at Nui Dat on the morning of 28 November.

PART 4

DEPLOYMENT TO VIETNAM

CHAPTER 10

ABOARD HMAS *SYDNEY*

HMAS *Sydney*, laid down in 1943 as HMS *Terrible*, was one of 6 Majestic Class light fleet aircraft carriers built by the British Government for its Royal Navy (RN). However, her final construction, along with that of her sister ship HMS *Magnificent*, was placed on hold until the end of WWII. After the cessation of those hostilities, the Australian Government purchased both vessels from the British Government.

When her construction and fit-out was finally completed, HMS *Terrible* was commissioned — on 15 December 1949 — into the Royal Australian Navy (RAN) as HMAS *Sydney*. She was the last vessel to be commissioned into the RAN as 'His' Majesty's Australian Ship. After the death of King George VI on 6 February 1952 and the subsequent coronation of Queen Elizabeth II as monarch of the United Kingdom on 2 June 1953, all subsequent RAN commissioned ships became known as 'Her' Majesty's Australian Ship. Following the death of Queen Elizabeth II on 8 September 2022, all RAN commissioned ships will now be known once again as 'His' Majesty's Australian Ship in deference to the new reigning Monarch, King Charles III.

HMS *Magnificent* was commissioned — on 28 October 1955 — into the RAN as HMAS *Melbourne*, and was to later achieve worldwide notoriety on 2 occasions. First, on 10 February 1964, when on naval exercises just off Jervis Bay — some 106nm (190km) south of Sydney — she collided with the Daring class destroyer HMAS *Voyager*, cutting that ship in half with a subsequent loss of 84 sailors of its crew complement of 314. Some years later — 3 June 1969 — during South East Asia Treaty Organisation (SEATO) exercises in the South China Sea, she collided with USS *Frank E Evans*, also cutting that ship in half with the loss of 74 sailors.

Sydney was a highly effective light fleet aircraft carrier and saw active service in that key operational role during the Malayan Emergency (1948-60), the Korean War (1951-53), and during the Indonesian Confrontation (1963-66). With the advent of Australia's involvement in Vietnam, *Sydney* underwent a major refit as Australia built up its commitment to that conflict and was converted into a fast troop and materials carrier.

Sydney made 25 return trips to Vietnam and was affectionately referred to by her RAN crew and army passengers alike as the 'Vung Tau Ferry'.

Sydney was a magnificent naval resource and, along with her escort destroyers, frigates, logistical supply ships, and fuel replenishment tankers, contributed enormously to Australia's war effort in Vietnam.

During those voyages, spanning a 7-year period (May 1965 - February 1972), *Sydney* transported 8,129 Australian troops — predominately infantry — to Vietnam. Her return voyages safely brought home some 7,490 of those exhausted and traumatised men. She also transported — both ways — around 5,561 short tons — a USA measure — or 4,289 tons in the imperial measure used by Australia now, and at that time. Of that gross cargo weight, a significant amount was military hardware such as APCs, tanks, and aircraft. Overall, *Sydney* transported 2,301 vehicles to, or from Vietnam. By any measure, *Sydney's* importance to the ADF at that time and the absolute effectiveness that she consistently displayed in her new and vital role, should never be underestimated.

Sydney was decommissioned on 12 November 1973 after steaming 711,549nm (1,317,077km) overall, and some 395,591nm (732,239km) as a fast troop and materials carrier. On 28 October 1975, she was sold by the Australian Government to a South Korean steel-milling company as scrap metal for $A673,516 ($A3,717,808 in 2022 prices) and left Sydney under tow on 23 December that year. Personally, I reckon that was a sad end for such a lovely lady of the sea.

HMAS *Sydney*.

In her troop and materials carrying role, *Sydney* had a crew complement of 700, a lot less than the 1,300 she needed in her former capacity. Even though the ship had an overall length of 213m and a beam of 24m, the addition of 551 soldiers from 8 RAR made it a very crowded place below deck.

The average speed of the ship was logged each day at around 24kts or 44km/h. That might not sound too fast but when a ship moves at that speed, or even approaches it, every hour — for 24 hours a day, every day — the distance to the end destination becomes inexorably smaller. For example, in a 24-hour period, *Sydney* would have steamed some 1,080km.

Putting this into some perspective, if *Sydney* departed Brisbane at say 8am, she would arrive at her namesake city sometime after 4am the following morning. Although driving from Brisbane to Sydney during the day would have taken much less time, travellers using both forms of transport would have been in Sydney for early business meetings or private activities, early the very next day.

Our living quarters aboard *Sydney* were nothing short of abysmal. She was designed for service by the RN, primarily in the North Atlantic Sea. Accordingly, she was fitted with a limited ventilation system, completely inadequate for service in tropical waters. Not only was the sleeping area allocated to my platoon minuscule by any reasonable standards, it had no air-conditioning whatsoever. In all other areas of the ship, which I frequented from time to time, there was no observable air-conditioning of any sort.

With so many soldiers, along with all the sailors, crammed into confined below deck rudimentary living spaces, it was very unpleasant and, with the ship's course heading almost due north, I knew that it was going to get hotter, more humid, and much more unbearable in the days and nights ahead. It has been suggested to me that below deck temperatures were often nudging 50°C as the ship relentlessly steamed north. And, to make matters worse, try as I did during our first night at sea, I simply couldn't sleep in a hammock. I became very despondent relatively quickly.

So, I decided not to use my hammock each night in the prescribed way. Instead, I dismantled it and affixed the support ropes at each end to interlace the horizontal tiers of coiled-wire side railings that ran alongside one of the higher decks, alongside and underneath — as I recall — the ship's most forward starboard or right-side lifeboat. This allowed me to sleep on the deck on the seaward side of the lifeboat, without any chance of falling overboard. If, for any reason, the lower and upper support mountings of the lifeboat hovering next to, and above me, were to have failed, I would have been crushed to death. However, that unlikely occurrence never once entered my head.

I also managed to scrounge up some scrubby and very dubious-looking thin mattress bedding — probably infested with legions of microscopic critters. My new sleeping arrangements were still uncomfortable, but it was much cooler and more spacious than trying to sleep inside the cramped and suffocatingly hot lower decks of the ship. I also had ample freedom to stretch and move around. Because of the relentless forward momentum of the ship, there was always some sort of prevailing breeze. I slept reasonably well each night, even though I was always wide awake well before 4am each morning. I was a confirmed cigarette smoker at that time, so I was able to pass the quiet pre-dawn hours by improving my nicotine habit.

As soon as dawn broke each morning, I interfered with the robust canvas protective covering of my lifeboat and was able to cram-in and secure my modest bedding, in readiness for the next night. Mind you, I was always at my lifeboat just after dinner each evening, checking that no one could invoke squatter's rights over me. Amazingly, I was never challenged for my unique sleeping locale, and I even reclaimed this position on my return voyage home to Australia some 12 months later. How's that for good luck?

Just after dawn one morning I became very lazy and, with a full bladder, pissed over the side of the ship. This ended up being a stupid decision. Without going into further detail, not that I think I really need to, it all became quite embarrassingly messy for me. RAN sailors don't piss over the sides of ships when they are under full steam...for good reason!

As you can imagine, showering facilities on the ship were totally inadequate for the number of sailors and soldiers aboard, and potable — some fresh, but mostly desalinated — water, while not strictly rationed in the very real sense, was only ever used sparingly. As far as I was able to observe, it appeared that the sailors aboard *Sydney* were inured to this ship discipline and they never abused their well-understood and accepted Spartan-like water privileges. During the prescribed shower time limit — 1 minute — they were able to wash their hair, scrub their armpits, arse, genitals, and that was about it. There was no time for any loitering in the showers with guys backed-up in the queues. I have no recollection of any sailor shaving in my presence, not that it was a prescribed condition of naval service.

So, after my first 1-minute shower — which cost me around 40 minutes in wait time — I opted to avoid these long and endless queues. Instead, I either didn't shower at all, or took the occasional saltwater pressure-hose shower in an open area located in the forward part of the ship. Although a saltwater shower left me feeling sort of starched, it was much better than lining up and waiting in a long queue for just a 1-minute rinse. I don't think I showered more than 4 times during our 11-day voyage to Vietnam.

I pretty much got used to this minimal attention to personal hygiene, though I probably smelled quite rank to my platoon mates for much of the time. I seem to recall most of them weren't too fresh themselves. This personal body odour was a precursor for what we were to later experience in Vietnam and it was something that ultimately never really bothered any of us. Going forward somewhat, there was one period in Vietnam when I was deployed operationally for 119 days with only a 9-day break in the middle. During this long and arduous period of 16 weeks or so, we lived on rations, rarely showered or changed clothes, occasionally took off our boots, and lived what

I would describe as a very squalid life. While not one of us was all that happy about it, the Greek Spartans of times long ago would have been very proud of us.

Mealtimes — particularly breakfast — were usually an absolute nightmare for us. For the most part, we were so hungry each morning that we could have, quite literally, *'eaten the arse out of a rag doll'* to quote my brother-in-law, good friend, and fellow Vietnam Veteran, James Francis (Frank) Corcoran (12 Field Regiment, RAA and 4 RAR W Company, attached). Though the quantity and quality of food for its army and naval contingents was very good, hanging around waiting for a spare seat in one of the allocated messes — or galleys as they are known in the navy — was time consuming and frustrating. Galleys were also confined — no elbow room at all — hot and very humid areas. And I simply didn't like, and never have, endless queues and humidity. So, I was forced to improvise.

For breakfast, I decided not to partake of anything other than 3 or 4 slices — I'm talking about a thickness of 2.5cm or more — of warm, freshly baked bread, topped with generous lashings of butter and spreads from a range of various jams, vegemite, or peanut butter, washed down with several large mugs of steaming hot tea or coffee. I was usually able to acquire this continental feast within minutes at around 5:30am, well before the galley queues started to form up.

The moronic queues were for the more substantial meals that were available each morning for anyone who wanted a cooked breakfast. If you wanted 2, 3, or 4 fried eggs, bacon, ham, tomato, baked beans, onion — lots of onion — and a molten cheese-laden potato au gratin, topped with some tasty diced green herbs etc, then that was all there for you. You could proffer your plate to the serving personnel for as much as you wanted. There was also a massive array of cereal, fresh fruit, and fruit juice options on offer. Water, coffee, and tea were a given, of course.

All of that breakfast largess wasn't for me. I only tried it once — on the first morning after our departure from Brisbane — and after queuing up for an intolerable time, I nearly vomited in the sauna-like galley shortly afterwards. Breakfast was always the main problem for me, and I solved that quite easily, as did several of my platoon mates.

I spent some time each day in one of the ship's galleys, peeling potatoes. When I first heard that I'd been allocated this ship duty, I became terribly depressed, imagining endless hours of painstaking work using a paring knife on individual potatoes. While still a shit-boring task, my misery abated considerably when I discovered that all I had to do was repetitively load, operate, and unload some sort of vertical, cylindrical, centrifugal contraption that spun the loaded potatoes at very high speed, thereby peeling them via the

Chapter 10 – Aboard HMAS Sydney

straightforward process of side wall abrasion. The ship's crew and its army passengers on that outbound voyage to Vietnam ate a lot of potatoes...many peeled by me. There were also a few other allocated galley chores that I usually managed to deftly avoid or, if they weren't particularly onerous, take as much time as possible in doing.

Working in the galley also gave me the opportunity to steal plenty of choice food items and get in early for lunch, if I was still hungry. At dinner time, I used to wander into the galley about 10 minutes before it closed, and 'cherry pick' from the residual food items still available. Mostly, it was still a reasonable selection — certainly more than enough for me. And, no waiting.

I didn't really mind galley duty all that much and I made a point of becoming friendly with all the sailors who worked in my galley. Anyway, it was only for 3 hours a day, at most. I'm pretty sure my duty hours were something like 11:30am to 2:30pm each day, but it could have been an hour or so either way. I really can't remember now.

The only other ship duty I really aspired to, was working in the laundry — located way down in the extreme bowels of the ship. Because it was so hot in the laundry, those rostered shifts were relatively short and interspersed with frequent above deck rotations. Men assigned to laundry duty also received a double beer ration each day, for working in those stifling and almost inhumane conditions. Peter Cousins, one of my platoon mates, was one of those fortunate few, but the beer was completely wasted on him because he was a confirmed non-drinker at that time. Obviously, many of us were really nice to Cousins. I was particularly nice to him.

Each day at 4pm we were provided with a very welcome beer ration. The beer ration pipe — tune — over the ship's public address system, was the signal for almost mass hysteria, as most of us did all that we could to be first in the various beer queues. The daily beer ration consisted of one 750ml can per man, which cost the princely sum of $0.20 ($1.43 in 2022 prices). A few guys in my platoon, other than Cousins, didn't drink alcohol either, so most afternoons I managed to consume 2 of these cans, or at least a good share of a second. I recall on one memorable occasion, managing to even get a share of a third can. Mind you, it may have only been a mouthful at most.

On the ship's black market — yes, there was a thriving one — 750ml cans of beer were being traded for quite enormous sums of money. However, I never paid more than the standard $0.20 a can. I wasn't that desperate for alcohol. Well, not then anyway.

Sydney's flight deck was 213m long and, even though a lot of it was randomly cluttered with heavy cargo, we were subjected to a tough running and exercise regimen every day. Given the substantial number of soldiers aboard the ship, and the variable timings of their allocated ship duties, this must have taken some unbelievable co-ordination by the PTIs — Artillery Corps bombardiers (corporals) — who were temporarily attached to the battalion for the purpose of maintaining our fitness levels during our voyage to Vietnam.

On one of *Sydney's* prior voyages to Vietnam, the late Bob Fulton, a Manly and later Australian Kangaroos Rugby League player, was one of these training instructors (Trip 12, transporting 9 RAR to Vietnam in November 1968). I personally confirmed this fact with him by both email and telephone, and with data contained on the Department of Veterans' Affairs (DVA) Nominal Roll. I doubt that many people would be aware of his contribution as a former National Serviceman to Australia's commitment to the Vietnam War.

On quite a few days, we spent time on the flight deck at the stern of the ship, undertaking rifle shooting target practice at coloured balloons, partially filled with water. As these bobbing targets rapidly diminished in size and floated on the undulating ocean, they became progressively harder to hit. While it was useful rifle shooting practice for us, it also gave us something to do afterwards; cleaning and maintaining our weapons...and I was never averse to doing that. It also occurred to me during the first time I was exposed to this activity, that if I was ever again minded to piss over the side of the ship, then the stern was the only viable place to do so. Even then, it was still going to be highly problematic.

My girlfriend's father — A WWII navy veteran — was well connected in naval circles in Canberra and he personally knew Captain D H A (Nobby) Clarke of *Sydney*. On my voyage to Vietnam, he made the Captain aware of my presence. Though her father had previously told me that he was going to do this, I thought that nothing would ever come of it. By the way, in the RAN of that time, all ships Captains with the surname Clarke, were known as 'Nobby'. I doubt much has changed since then.

Anyway, over several days, some of my platoon mates kept telling me that they were hearing public address announcements ordering me — Private McCann — to report to the ship's Master-at-Arms (MAA), the RAN equivalent of RSM. While I never actually heard any of these announcements, I eventually made myself known to the MAA and was severely castigated by him for not doing so much earlier. I didn't think much of this guy and I'm absolutely certain that he thought a hell of a lot less of me.

After conferring with the Captain, the MAA came back to where he had left me waiting and escorted me to the Captain's quarters. I was very warmly greeted and invited to join him for a few quiet beers. For well over an hour — completely out of my comfort zone — I avidly drank every glass of ice-cold beer he offered. And to make the most of this tricky situation, I subtly indicated when my glass was empty, to which he would kindly oblige by refilling it. During our heavily-loaded one-way conversation, I agreed with absolutely everything he said to me. I mean, who was I to disagree with the ship's Captain while he was providing me with all of this free, cold beer in a frosted glass? By the way, the Captain didn't seem too averse to quaffing the good stuff either!

There was one other naval member who joined us in this convivial drinking session. He was very young — probably not that much older than me. I vaguely recall him being the Captain's son — attired in pristine 'whites' just like his father. This was later confirmed as factual, so the Captain's son was aboard the *Sydney* in some formal RAN role, or perhaps just having a 'jolly' at the taxpayer's expense. Not that I cared a toss about that anyway. Having someone more-or-less my age accompanying me, certainly made the experience a less stressful one.

I have no idea what the MAA thought about all of this, as he basically ignored me while I was being escorted back to my platoon quarters. He probably noticed that I was somewhat drunk — and I was — with the day's beer ration yet to come. It was very nice of the Captain to be my generous host and bartender for a time, and I later wrote to my girlfriend's father to thank him for arranging this very pleasant meeting. My platoon mates were unbelievably pissed-off that I didn't manage to get them free beer as well.

Seasickness affected many soldiers aboard *Sydney*. Amazingly, I wasn't stricken with this very nasty affliction. However, many guys in my platoon became really ill, vomiting into many of the ship's internal toilet bowls, as well as over the sides of the ship when caught short. Now that would have been very hideous indeed!

The day we boarded *Sydney*, a very young sailor — he would have been no older than 16 or 17 — who'd been allocated to my platoon as a 'ship-daddy', advised me that if the seas ever became rough, to keep a few pieces of dry bread crusts in my pocket, and if I ever felt queasy, to eat them slowly. I followed his advice and I reckon that it was my salvation. I would say that over 70% of my platoon mates were struck down with seasickness, particularly on one occasion when, not all that far from Vietnam, we had to weather a rather nasty storm with associated high seas and swells, for well over 24 hours.

My personal observation is that seasickness is a particularly horrendous illness to contract. But, for as long as many of my platoon mates were laid low with this affliction, I happily imbibed my share of their daily beer ration. I was very comfortable with that. As sick as a platoon mate may have been, we still made him line up for his daily beer ration — and pay for it — which we then avidly consumed on his behalf. I didn't care if these guys suffered from seasickness all the way to Vietnam!

Because of its navy class type, and its operational role during the Vietnam War in particular, *Sydney* was very lightly — or hardly — armed, carrying only 4, single, Swedish-manufactured 40mm Bofors anti-aircraft guns as its entire defence armament capability. Accordingly, *Sydney* was always protected by escort ships when entering and departing Vietnamese waters. The vessels that carried out this vital role for *Sydney* at various times were destroyers HMAS *Anzac*, *Duchess*, *Vampire*, and *Vendetta*, as well as frigates HMAS *Derwent*, *Parramatta*, *Stuart*, *Swan*, *Torrens*, and *Yarra*, along with the Fleet flagship HMAS *Melbourne* which, strangely, was still tasked as an active operational light fleet aircraft carrier. Collectively, the escort ships steamed 404,000nm (744,102km) in this key capacity from 1965 to 1972.

On my voyage, Sydney was escorted by HMAS *Duchess*: a heavily-armed Daring Class destroyer capable of some 30kts, or around 56km/h. *Duchess* carried 2,500 high-explosive rounds for her six 4.5in (105mm) guns, and many thousands of rounds of other ammunition for her smaller calibre guns. Collectively, the three 4.5in twin gun turrets of *Duchess* were capable of firing high-explosive rounds weighing 24.9kg at a rate of 100rp/m, very accurately out to a range of over 18km. *Duchess* had a crew of 300 sailors and more than half of them were required to man the ship's guns whenever she went to 'action stations'. *Duchess* also had six 40mm Bofors anti- aircraft guns — 4 mounted in twin turrets — and one anti-submarine 'squid' mortar: a 3-offset barrelled 305mm weapon that fired 177kg depth charges out to a distance of some 250m.

When I was undertaking some early research for my story, I was pleasantly surprised to discover that the Captain of *Duchess* at that time was Commodore Harry Adams. This man became very well-known to me in more recent years by virtue of his good work on several DVA sponsored ex-service committees, an activity that also occupied much of my time during the early years of the new millennium. He was well aware that I had deployed to Vietnam with 8 RAR on *Sydney* in November 1969, but had never mentioned that he captained *Duchess* on that voyage.

On 24 November 1969, *Duchess* went to simulated 'action stations' and conducted a rapid open-fire exercise with all guns, to demonstrate her firepower capabilities to the 8 RAR soldiers aboard *Sydney*. For this demonstration, *Duchess* fired 3 rounds of squid and 15 rounds of 4.5in high-explosive rounds in 20 seconds. While this wasn't anywhere near approaching the ship's maximum rate of gunfire offensive power, it was a very impressive demonstration for its army passengers to observe. It certainly focused my attention.

It was comforting to know that *Duchess* was always close by, particularly when shortly after this wonderful demonstration of her firepower — some 4 days out from Vietnam — it was rumoured that *Sydney* might be menaced by a Russian submarine. While this was no doubt fanciful scuttlebutt, it certainly seemed plausible to most of us at that time. Back in 1969, the Cold War was certainly not becoming any warmer and, in our view, anything was possible. Both Russia and China were openly assisting North Vietnam in its war effort against South Vietnam and its allies.

It was about this time when *Sydney* went into blackout mode, known in naval parlance as 'darken ship', during the night-time hours. All personnel aboard *Sydney*, both navy and army, became somewhat more tense and apprehensive. We were all in a heightened state of alertness from this time onwards.

Decades later, when discussing this so-called Russian submarine incident with LTCMDR Rodney Nott Retd[17], who was Gunnery Officer aboard *Duchess* at that time, I began to appreciate more precisely what actually occurred in terms of this perceived threat to *Sydney*.

HMAS *Duchess*.

According to Nott, shortly after the rapid open-fire exercise demonstration by *Duchess* on 24 November concluded, and as both ships were making fast passage along the south coast of Java, the Electronic Warfare Office in *Duchess* detected 2 Russian naval radar (signature) transmissions coming from a bearing astern of the 2 ships. Immediately, both ships closed-up. *Duchess* moved to a defensive position close to, but still astern of *Sydney*, and prepared her six 4.5in guns.

Apparently, one of these identified non-friendly radar types was the Styx missile control and guidance radar used on the 12 OSA Class missile patrol boats, which the Indonesian Navy had at that time. Potentially, this was an extremely serious development and one which posed a very real threat to the security of *Sydney* and the safety of all soldiers and sailors aboard. This is why *Sydney* and *Duchess* reacted swiftly and adopted overt defensive postures.

Nott went on to say in his paper that the political situation with Indonesia at that time was delicate, as not all of its military officers had accepted the political expediency that concluded the hostilities between Indonesia and Malaya — a confrontation which, for several years, heavily involved the British and Australian Defence Forces — and included both *Sydney* and *Duchess* in active operational roles.

Since 1964, Indonesia had from time to time, attempted to impede British, Australian, and New Zealand naval ships from exercising their right of free passage through the Sunda, Lombok, and Gasper Straits. Sabre-rattling on both sides eventually resulted in an agreement whereby Indonesia was advised in advance of the transit of foreign warships through these Straits and the

---

[17] Nott, Rodney LTCMDR. *Northbound for Vietnam*. A paper.

Java Sea, even though every other country considered these routes to be open, international waterways.

Posturing about these specific international waterways was never considered anything other than territorial aggrandisement by the Indonesians but, because of their unpredictability, RAN ships always adopted appropriate defensive precautions whenever they were in those confined waters.

Both *Sydney* and *Duchess* were hopeful that now wasn't the time for some junior Indonesian naval officer to make a big name for himself by ordering the firing of a Styx missile at either ship. Fortunately, at around 8am on 25 November, these intrusive radar transmissions ceased. *Duchess* immediately further closed-up to a position about 900m astern of *Sydney* and, by midday, both ships were safely through the Sunda Straits.

Later that evening, *Sydney* maintained its position ahead of *Duchess* for a fast transit of the Gaspar Straits. There was no radar interference from the Indonesians on this occasion and, after both ships were safely through, ahead lay an unimpeded stretch to Vung Tau harbour (Cap St Jacques) in South Vietnam.

Two days after rendezvousing with *Sydney* on 18 November, *Duchess* was re-supplied with fuel from *Sydney*. This was an extremely interesting procedure and many of us watched for the entire time it took to complete. I was simply amazed at the skill of the sailors aboard both ships as *Sydney* and *Duchess* were side by side, at a minimum speed of some 14kts (26km/h), for the duration of this refuelling procedure, which took about an hour or so. *Duchess* seemed to be less than 30m alongside *Sydney* throughout this entire manoeuvre. For such relatively large ships, the refuelling process wasn't anywhere near as simple as the 'lock and load' procedure that we were accustomed to. There was a very high degree of risk involved and the engrossed 8 RAR audience recognised that. The transfer and connection of the fuel hose between both ships was no easy task either, and once established, this connection had to be maintained. That seemed to me to be a very tricky operation.

The transfer of a sailor from *Duchess* to *Sydney* was facilitated by some sort of contraption that I later found to be known as a 'jackstay'. Clearly, the idea was that the 2 ships didn't move too close together and dump this transiting sailor into the water below, or move too far apart and risk snapping the cable, which would cause the same result. The main difference with the latter scenario would be a significantly greater degree of danger for everyone looking on, not to mention the sailor, with a 7.5cm thick manila rope flying around at great speed. Naturally, we were all hoping that the sailor would get a dumping into the sea. Alas, we were extremely disappointed when that didn't happen. The return trip for this sailor was just as uneventful, so we all booed and jeered him, and why not? It was all wholesome fun. Even the navy guys around us seemed to join in with the spirit of the event. My already high opinion of the professionalism of Australian Naval Servicemen was confirmed by this wonderful display of precision sailing and operational performance.

Almost immediately after refuelling that day, *Duchess* detached from *Sydney* for a high-speed run to Darwin, to collect mail and urgently needed supplies. *Duchess* regained contact with *Sydney* on 22 November and was again immediately re-supplied with fuel.

On 26 November, 2 days out from Vietnam, both ships rendezvoused with the RN auxiliary ship HMS *Tidepool*, a fuel tanker, and replenished their tanks. While this at-sea interaction and co-operation between RN fuel tanker support and RAN warships occurred on a regular basis, it was kept well away from the media because the British weren't overtly involved in the Vietnam conflict.

Nevertheless, the RAN would say that it was indeed fortunate for *Sydney* and its escort destroyers and frigates that the RN — for almost 7 years — always seemed to have a fuel tanker located in waters within the vicinity of South Vietnam. It was available to refuel those ships either before they arrived at Vung Tau harbour, or soon after their departure from port.

When *Sydney* and *Duchess* entered what was known in naval parlance as the 'Market Time' area, defined as 100nm (185km) from a hostile coast — South Vietnam — they both went to 'Defence Stations' as the ships' second stage of readiness or 'preparedness' as it was termed. It was around midnight when this occurred. I was wide awake because I knew full well that we were only hours from Vietnam. I didn't sleep a wink that night. Don't think that many of us did. I was both excited and apprehensive about what lay ahead and my intuitive defence mechanisms for personal survival had already come into play.

That night, as I lay on my scrubby mattress bedding, under a lifeboat, surreptitiously smoking cigarettes, it suddenly hit home that all of us aboard *Sydney* and *Duchess* — soldiers and sailors alike — were in this together. We were now in very dangerous waters indeed. Soldiers like myself, and the rest of the 8 RAR contingent, needed to be delivered safely to an unpredictable war zone and the sailors aboard both ships were going to do exactly that.

With *Sydney* remaining at 'Defence Stations', *Duchess*, who had gone to 'Action Stations' several hours earlier, preceded *Sydney* and entered Vung Tau harbour at 5:35am on the morning of 28 November. *Sydney* followed some 16 minutes later and anchored at berth B12, about 1.85km offshore from Pt. Ganh Rai in 7 fathoms (13m) of water. *Duchess* anchored 0.3km from *Sydney's* berth point and downgraded her alert status to that of 'Defence Stations'. Sunrise that day was about an hour later — 6:55am — and as the new day dawned, it occurred to me that my life was about to be changed forever.

HMAS *Sydney* In Vung Tau harbour.
(*Courtesy of Defence Australia*)

Just after 8am, and with a basic issue of 60 rounds of ammunition for each of our personal weapons, we were organised — corralled I'd say — to progressively disembark *Sydney* onto six LCM6 Mk 2 landing craft, each of which carried around 90 soldiers.

As some 8 RAR officers and other key personnel were relocated from *Sydney* to Vung Tau by helicopter, it was possible to cram the entire 8 RAR contingent into these landing craft. I don't recall any second transfer landings. It was just like what you see in those old USA WWII movies. Talk about melodramatic! Anyway, that's exactly the way it was. We hit the beach — figuratively speaking — with our hearts in our mouths, and were somewhat disappointed that we didn't encounter enemy fire. In hindsight, thank goodness for that! We had no idea what to expect that morning, and we certainly weren't properly briefed as to the nature and scope of the highly secure defence systems in place, supporting our arrival at the harbour, or our landing at the secure beach.

By around 9am we were mobilised into 2 separate convoys of trucks for the 40-minute road trip north, up Route 15, and then north-north-east up Route 2 to the 1 ATF base at Nui Dat. We were replacing 9 RAR, and joining 5 RAR and 6 RAR, each of whom were later replaced during our time in Vietnam by 2 RAR and 7 RAR, respectively.

There was, however, some significant delay in our departure for Nui Dat that morning. We had to dove-tail our movements to coincide with the late arrival of 9 RAR soldiers from Nui Dat in army trucks, and their embarkation onto *Sydney* for return to Australia later that day. As you might imagine, I'm perhaps talking about an overall mix — or melee as it seemed to me — of around 1,100 soldiers. It was a very confused harbour precinct for quite some time.

As we boarded the trucks, an officer, who I'd never seen before, ordered those of us with SLR rifles to set our gas plug setting to 'zero'. As we were all acutely aware of the importance of this order, we didn't need any urging at all. I wasn't even remotely interested in preserving the long-term functional life of my SLR rifle. I simply didn't ever want to experience an automatic reloading malfunction, because of a high gas plug setting. I was more than happy to manage the greater recoil into my left shoulder when firing. During my entire time in Vietnam, my SLR rifle gas plug was always set at zero...and it never failed me.

Travelling on Route 15, heading north from Vung Tau to Ba Ria, we very quickly passed over 3 bridges that were protected by South Vietnamese Regional Forces soldiers. The adjacent landscape was predominantly one of rancid-smelling mudflats — probably because it was low tide — and mangrove swamps interspersed with many small, residential hamlets. After leaving Ba Ria and heading along Route 2 towards Nui Dat, the landscape quickly changed to one of small rice paddy fields, unworked rubber copses set well back from the road, and a few areas of low scrub, similar in some ways to the low mulga vegetation that abounds in outback Australia. The land was very flat and uninspiring. The only significant residential centre we came across on this route was the relatively large town of Hoa Long, a place which was to later feature in many of the future operational activities of the battalion.

We arrived at Nui Dat — 11:15am — and were re-acquainted with Assault Pioneer Platoon elements of the Advance Party and Rear Party. They had flown to Vietnam sometime earlier courtesy of Qantas Airlines, affectionately known back in those days as 'Skippy Squadron' — 'Skippy, the red kangaroo'.

Allied ships anchored in Vung Tau harbour didn't want to remain there any longer than absolutely necessary. Even though the tidal influences in Vung Tau harbour were severe — making any underwater enemy attack highly unlikely — ships at anchor, even though they might be the best part of 1km or more offshore, were always a potential target for the enemy. I can well understand the mental stress suffered by Australian sailors as they waited out their time at anchor in Vung Tau harbour. Navy clearance divers were continually deployed underwater to check for any compromise to the safety of the ship. That must have been an exhausting task indeed, given the extremely strong tidal currents that prevailed in this harbour. The benign high and low tide influences were only fleeting.

By noon that day, *Sydney* had embarked all 9 RAR soldiers departing Vietnam and, preceded by *Duchess* some 10 minutes earlier, left Vung Tau harbour, steaming back to Australia. Both ships' transit time in Vung Tau harbour on this occasion was only 6 hours.

During *Sydney's* first voyages to Vietnam, transit times while anchored in Vung Tau harbour had taken as long as 6 days. Clearly, substantial efficiencies had been achieved by *Sydney's* crew, along with the on-shore army and navy elements at Vung Tau, so as to vastly reduce that transit time in our case.

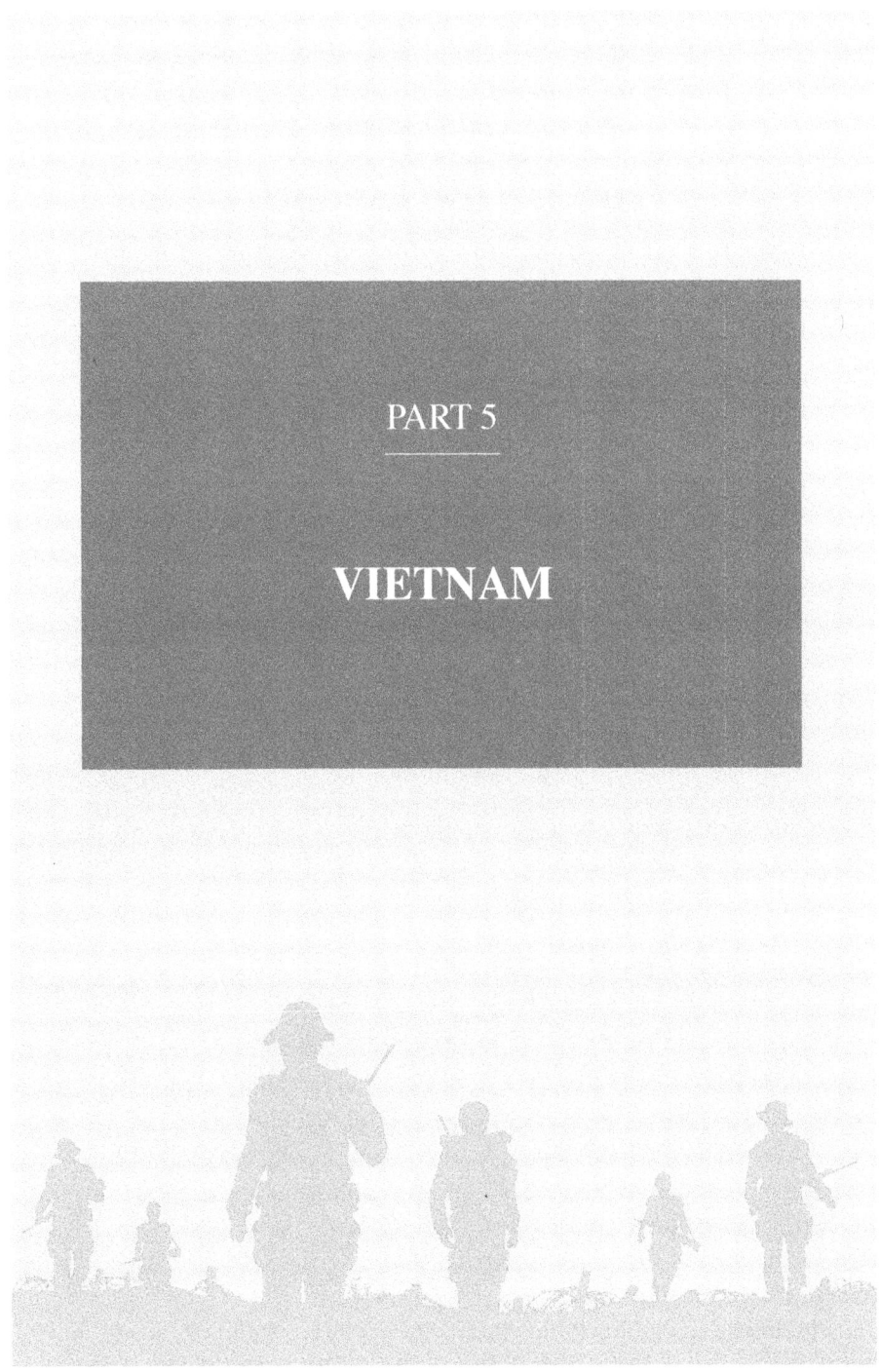

PART 5

VIETNAM

CHAPTER 11

PHUOC TUY PROVINCE

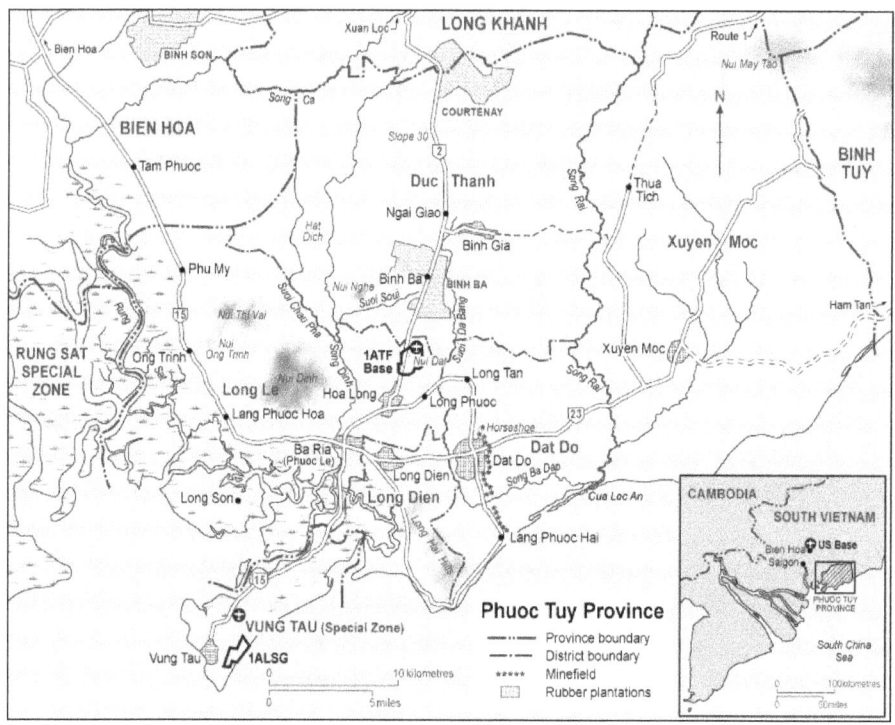

Map of Phuoc Tuy Province 1969-70.
Courtesy of the Department of Veterans' Affairs (DVA)

During my time in Vietnam with 8 RAR, 1 ATF military operations were generally contained within Phuoc Tuy Province — a relatively small south-eastern coastal area about 73km east-south-east of Saigon (Ho Chi Minh City) — which shared land borders with Long Khanh Province in the north, Bien Hoa Province in the north-west, Gia Dinh Province in the west, and Binh Tuy Province in the east. The southern and south-eastern provincial border was the coastline of the South China Sea.

Interestingly, the Assault Pioneer Platoon was deployed, along with a troop of 4 Centurion tanks from A Squadron 1st Armoured Regiment (RAAC), into the southern reaches of Long Khan Province for 2 separate, short periods of time. I don't think that many other platoons of the battalion would have been deployed in concert with tanks, other than perhaps C Company, in the Long Hai Hills area around February 1970. The AATTV was deployed over a number of provinces including Phuoc Tuy, and the SASR probably was as well, though I have no idea about their operational tasking in Vietnam.

Of an irregular square shape, Phuoc Tuy Province was about 2,000km^2 in area, slightly smaller in size than the confines of the Australian Capital Territory (ACT). The province extended approximately 50km north to south, and some 40km east to west. It wasn't a large area at all. The province had around 35 towns, more than 100 hamlets, as well as numerous small, inhabited enclaves. The more significant civilian population centres of the province were the comparatively highly-populated port city and commercial metropolis of Vung Tau, the provincial capital of Ba Ria, Long Dien, Dat Do, Hoa Long, Binh Ba, Binh Gia, and Xuyen Moc. There were also a few smaller towns such as Ap Nui Nhon and Ap Suoi Nghe etc.

Much of the provincial landscape was uninhabitable and not at all suitable for the commercial production of rice. In late 1969, it was thought that about 106,000 people resided, worked, subsisted, or otherwise tried to eke out some sort of existence in Phuoc Tuy Province. Vietnam is known today as 'the rice bowl of Asia', but that certainly wasn't the case in Phuoc Tuy Province back then.

Most provincial residents lived close to the 1 ATF base at Nui Dat, and generally along or near to the main arterial corridors of Routes 2, 15, 23, and 44. While Vung Tau had a densely-compacted population of around 35,000, the residual population of the province was very modest compared to that of other southern provinces.

Phuoc Tuy Province is famous in the annals of Australian military history because of the events that took place on 18 August 1966, during the Battle of Long Tan. Although it was impossible to accurately determine, active enemy numbers in the province in 1969-70 were estimated to fluctuate between 3,500 and 5,000.

What is probably not widely known is that the province is also famous within Vietnamese military folklore, due to the outcome of the Battle of Binh Gia that played out over the period 28 December 1964 to 1 January 1965. Binh Gia is north of Binh Ba and about 16km north of where Nui Dat would later be established in 1966.

Towards the end of 1964, the North Vietnamese Army (NVA) and Viet Cong commenced a series of large-scale military operations against the southern ARVN. As part of that offensive, the Viet Cong unleashed its newly created 9th Division against the ARVN forces at Binh Gia, fighting a large set-piece battle for the first time. Over a period of 4 days, the Viet Cong 9th Division held its ground and savagely mauled the best Ranger units that the ARVN could send against them, only breaking from contact after intense attacks on their ground positions by US Air Force (USAF) bombers and fighter aircraft.

While the ARVN — along with the help of USAF air support — eventually overcame this determined NVA and Viet Cong southern assault, their casualties were very high and, to some extent, mirrored those that occurred during the Battle of Long Tan some 18 months later. However, on this occasion, the scales of balance were completely reversed.

Over 200 ARVN soldiers and 5 — at least — US Army advisors were killed. Some 300 ARVN soldiers were wounded or simply went missing. There were only 32 confirmed Viet Cong soldiers killed. No wonder the Viet Cong regaled this outcome as a major victory, and it encouraged them to become more aggressive in their infiltration into the deep southern provinces of Vietnam.

It was against this historical background that the Australian Government, in June 1965, committed ground troops to the Vietnam conflict and to Phuoc Tuy Province in particular.

CHAPTER 12

CLIMATE

While Vietnam is a country that extends north to south for some 1,650km, its meandering coastline runs for nearly double that distance. Geographically, the central latitudinal third of the country is not very wide and, at its narrowest part, only 48km separate its neighbouring country of Laos from the grey, tepid, and uninviting waters of the South China Sea.

The climate in the north of the country tends to be classically monsoonal with 4 somewhat distinct seasons, but in the south it's tropically monsoonal. The lower reaches of southern Vietnam aren't all that far north of the equator. This fact probably explains why the prevailing climate that Australian soldiers had to endure and cope with in Vietnam, was so brutal.

Southern Vietnam has 2 distinct climatic seasons: the dry and the wet. The on-ground effects of these respective meteorological weather systems are very dissimilar. See Appendix 3. The dry season runs from around November to March, and the wet season extends from April to October. The arrival of 8 RAR in Vietnam on 28 November 1969 coincided with the onset of the dry — but still very humid — season.

Phuoc Tuy Province is very near to the massive Mekong Delta and abuts the South China Sea, both of which provide vast surface areas for the water evaporation that continuously feeds the energy-sapping and physically debilitating extreme humidity levels, which were a constant part of our lives during our time in that God forsaken country.

On early morning of 28 November, as I stepped ashore from the LCM6 MK 2 landing craft that disembarked us from *Sydney* onto the gritty, dirty sands of the totally uninspiring flat South Vietnamese coastline adjacent to the eastern precincts of Vung Tau, I simply couldn't believe the prevailing heat and humidity. And this was the early dry season. It just about knocked me over and almost left me gasping for breath. I also couldn't comprehend the foul stench of filth, decay, and raw sewage. It was virtually overpowering. Although we eventually got used to the gross rankness of it, this ever present foul stench permeated throughout most of the inhabited parts of Phuoc Tuy Province. We should all thank those earlier engineers for the modern drainage and sewage infrastructure systems that we enjoy in Australia today.

Throughout both the dry and wet seasons, average temperatures in the province ranged from a low of 29°C — at night — and routinely as high as 35°C during the day. Occasionally, day-time temperatures approached 40°C. There wasn't all that much variation in temperatures across the 2 seasons: perhaps only a degree or two. Strangely, while I thought that the humidity level would have changed quite measurably over the course of a 12-month period — because of the sheer volume of rain that fell from May to October and even during parts of April and November — it remained constant at an extremely health-depleting level of 85% or perhaps even slightly higher. The dew point reading remained disgustingly high at around 23°C. See Appendix 3. So, perhaps more recent meteorological data for Vung Tau regarding humidity — on which I'm relying — may have been 'smoothed' for a range of reasons associated with tourism. I'd like to think that this isn't the case, but I can come to no other logical conclusion.

Perhaps that sort of humidity might be sufferable today — as a tourist visiting this economically emerging country? But, for infantry soldiers and associated field support elements, the prevailing climate was nothing short of horrendous. We used to refer to the Vietnamese climate, jokingly, as 'slimy balls' weather...for quite obvious reasons.

During my entire time in Vietnam, it was very rare not to feel hot and sweaty. I never felt physically comfortable there. At the same time, and probably the only positive observation I can make about the climate, was that I was never ever cold either, even when lying on the ground in sodden clothing in night-time ambushes or when engaged on other operational activities amid torrential rain.

Well, that isn't quite correct. One night, while we were laying on the ground in an ambush, it rained heavily — I'm talking about rain of almost Biblical proportions — for the entire night. Just before dawn the next morning, I actually started shivering for about 30 minutes or so until the sun rose, and the humidity vigorously kicked in again.

I can't explain why I felt so cold that early morning — even completely saturated as I was — because I was in such a hot country. All that I can now remember is that we were situated in a very heavily vegetated and forested area — not rubber — amid some old USAF B-52 bomb craters. I suspect that we were in the far north of the province, west of Route 2, just south of the De Courtenay rubber plantation, and somewhere near the ground position of the (then) closed former Fire Support Base Peggy. So, my best guess as to the timing of this infamous night is around mid-August 1970.

Whenever we were back at Nui Dat, we usually took the opportunity to have tepid or cold showers for a few minutes every morning and afternoon, just to feel almost human, before profusely perspiring again. Although there wasn't really much point in showering more than once a day — if at all for that matter

— most of us tended to do so because our next operational tasking away from Nui Dat might be anything from 5 days to 6 weeks, or even longer. We never knew the planned timings of our next operational tasking until about a day or so before we re-deployed out into the field. What we did know, was that Nui Dat was our secure home base, but we weren't going to spend too much time there. And that was how it turned out for us.

Because of the unrelenting heat and humidity, and our relatively poor field hygiene, many of us developed a skin condition known colloquially as 'prickly heat'. This very nasty affliction manifested itself in the form of many hundreds of tiny, itchy, pimple-like eruptions over our shoulders, backs, chests, and stomachs. Prickly heat didn't seem to afflict our arses or our genitals — probably because of a lack of exposure to light. Thank God for that! Stomach itching was considerably far worse than that of other affected body areas. Scratching just seemed to make it worse, so the constant itching and scratching almost drove some of us crazy.

We all seemed to contract this condition to varying degrees not long after arriving in Vietnam. Fortunately, I never suffered all that badly from 'prickly heat'. After a time, and for some inexplicable reason, the problem seemed to just disappear for many of us. Either that, or we simply got used to the constant itching and managed to ignore it. However, some of my platoon mates suffered badly from this irritating physical condition during their entire time in Vietnam. My platoon mate, Peter Wood, seemed to have an extreme ongoing problem with 'prickly heat'. For a time, I tried to avoid going anywhere near him because it looked like he may have contracted leprosy. While I intuitively knew that wasn't the case, I was just being cautious because leprosy was, after all, a prevalent disease in Vietnam at that time and one that we'd been seriously alerted to during our time at Canungra.

Other unpleasant physical side effects of the constant heat, humidity, and generally wet landscape were tinea on our feet, and a range of fungal groin rashes. The groin rashes were commonly referred to as 'ball rot'. We used a purple lotion medication, provided by the RAP on our feet, and genitals. All that the application of this prescribed remedial lotion seemed to do was make those body parts very colourful.

I've since ascertained that this lotion, known back then as 'Blue Gentian', was actually Methyl Violet 10B, a supposed anti-bacterial and anti-fungal compound medication that's no longer prescribed in current day medical practice. Well, no wonder...because that medication was absolutely useless in terms of treating our groin and foot ailments. God only knows what its active ingredients might have been!

Two of my platoon mates, Lance-corporals Ron Goubareff and Bob O'Callaghan, both experienced Vietnam veterans — 1 RAR 1965-66 — told us to regularly piss on our feet and let it dry, because that would kill any emerging tinea fungus. I dutifully followed their sage advice during my time in Vietnam and I have to say that it worked.

In the first decade or so after I returned home from Vietnam, I occasionally developed a recurrence of tinea. Naturally, much to my wife's disgust, I used to walk out onto the back lawn and piss on my feet, sit back on a plastic chair with a can of Green VB beer in my hand, and let it dry. Nevertheless, it always seemed to work for me, and it fertilised the lawn at the same time. My former tinea problem hasn't recurred for many years.

I'm aware that present day medical science in relation to this gross — to some — practice suggests that it provided no measurable therapeutic benefit, given that prescribed medications for tinea contain the compound urea — H_2NCONH_2 — in a concentration 40 times of that contained in human urine. Well, while that may be clinically and chemically accurate, I can only say again that pissing on our feet certainly worked for all of us in Vietnam. And that's an absolute fact. So, there you go!

At the end of the day, the generally adopted solution for our common foot and groin afflictions was to forgo the wearing of socks and jocks. Our feet melded into the comfortable fit of our soft leather, high quality, well-draining, half calf-high GP boots. The 'free-balling' and the pissing on our feet seemed to do the trick as well. While this commonly adopted personal health regimen was probably not really the most hygienic, it certainly seemed to solve the problems for most of us.

During the horrendously oppressive wet season, it rained every afternoon from around 1:30pm until about 5:30pm, and frequently during the early morning hours of the next day as well. You could just about set your watch to the regularity of these downpours which were, often, nothing short of torrential. Try and imagine up to 50mm of rain falling on you while you're just trying to get on with your job as an infantry soldier out in the field. On some other rare occasions, steady light rain set in all day or all night and sometimes even both.

Historically, something like 90% of the average annual rainfall of 3,100mm (124in) that plummets in the far south of the country, including Phuoc Tuy Province, occurs during the 7-month wet season. Seriously, unless you've lived it, no one would be able to comprehend what it was really like to be rained on, to that extent, while engaging in operational infantry tasking. By way of contrast, where I now live in Canberra, the long-term average annual rainfall is something less than 600mm. In Darwin — the most northern and wettest Australian capital city — the average annual precipitation is in the order of 1,900mm. I don't think this comparison requires any further comment.

It was probably fortunate for 8 RAR that its men arrived in Vietnam during the early onset of the dry season, as the humidity levels had probably dropped

Chapter 12 – Climate

slightly from those that prevailed during previous months. With the arrival of the next wet season in April 1970, we were far more acclimatised and able to better cope with the wet and more oppressive aspects that accompanied it. I really pity those many Australian soldiers who would have arrived in Vietnam during the height of the wet season.

Whenever we were away from Nui Dat out in the field, and not located at fire support bases or night defensive positions, we had no protection whatsoever from the elements and became saturated in no time whenever it rained. Even when temporarily domiciled within a static site — other than Nui Dat — trying to keep dry was never easy, and coping with the ever present glue-like red mud was a very real and constant challenge for us. On the other hand, it was common for us to sometimes just stand naked amid the pelting rain, washing our hair, shaving, and rudimentarily washing our clothes.

Whenever we were outside of fire support bases and night defensive positions, we often had no option other than to be completely saturated for many hours and then drip dry later with the assistance of the prevailing hot temperatures, suffocating humidity, and our own body heat. While that drying process was nothing short of stifling in itself, it never seemed to take too long at all. At least it gave our filthy clothes some sort of a heavy cleansing rinse, but at the same time, it made our never ending task of weapons maintenance just that much more difficult.

I know that Australian soldiers of historical large scale military conflicts, and those of more recent deployments, have had to cope with unbelievably harsh environmental conditions as well. The trench warfare and mud in France during the Great War; the privations of Kokoda in New Guinea during WWII; the cold and snow of Korea; the extremes of temperature and the sands of Iraq and Afghanistan, are examples that readily come to mind. However, I have to say that the heat, humidity, and rainfall of Vietnam, given our military role as infantry soldiers, were something that had to be experienced to be believed. It really was nothing short of horrendous.

So, there we were in a strange country with a disgustingly oppressive climate, facing enemy who were already well and truly adapted to their country's climatic conditions.

CHAPTER 13

TERRAIN

The southern third of Vietnam is predominantly a large plain, dominated by the vast Mekong Delta and confluences of the Saigon and Dong Nai rivers. Apart from several small, low-rising mountain ranges, the area is relatively flat and, during the wet season, large tracts of it are completely inundated. The south-western part of this delta region is heavily forested and extensive mangrove and mud flats abound in the coastal areas. In the centre of this delta region, there are large, marshy areas covered with tall reeds and scrub trees. Much of southern Vietnam is significantly covered with dense jungle and high-level canopy cover. Phuoc Tuy Province was typical of that.

By way of contrast, the landscape of central northern Australia is literally inundated with medium-height spindly trees — significantly eaten away by termites — along with very sparse and stunted low-level ground vegetation that struggles to grow out of inert, ochre-coloured shale-like soil. There are few areas of significant rainforest. The much-vaunted Kakadu National Park is mostly a barren area, much like what I've just described, interspersed with some truly magnificent gorges and other watercourses — which are only really worth experiencing during the wet season — and several other natural arid wonders, unique to Australia. However, it's nothing at all like a tropical wonderland...far from it!

Considering their almost corresponding latitudes either side of the equator, there couldn't be 2 more totally dissimilar landscapes. Ho Chi Minh City — 73km west-north-west of Vung Tau — is only 182km closer to the equator than Darwin, at 1,387km. The difference in average annual rainfall and soil composition in these 2 geographical areas is probably the main reason for their entirely different landscapes.

For such a relatively small land area, the topography of Phuoc Tuy Province varied enormously. Typically, it was flat with about somewhere between half and three quarters of it comprising of almost impenetrable jungle, rainforest, other heavy afforestation — where the tree canopy and dense ground vegetation had completely taken over — or variable grasslands. Abundant and inaccessible thorny-bamboo thickets were particularly plentiful along the banks of many of the numerous watercourses such as creek lines. Throughout its south-eastern and southern coastal areas there were large tracts

Chapter 13 – Terrain

of flat, low lying, sandy and rocky land areas, almost totally devoid of any significant vegetation. A totally uninspiring vista, very similar in appearance to the coastal areas of Wide Bay and Tin Can Bay in South East Queensland. Many parts of the coastal countryside became inundated and swampy during the wet season.

Sitting astride the main road north from Ba Ria — Route 2 — were 2 commercial rubber plantations. Binh Ba, located centrally in the province, and De Courtenay, which straddled the northern provincial border. These working rubber plantations were quite large and we frequented them from time to time. Numerous smaller plantations and unworked rubber-treed areas, were randomly dotted throughout the province.

A few large tracts of land were farmed for rice production and local consumption. Other agricultural crops grown throughout the south of the province were bananas, peanuts, coffee, tobacco, pepper, and a range of assorted vegetables and tropical fruits. Major commercial activities were few and, other than rubber, seemed to be limited to timber milling, fishing, and seafood processing.

We also often had to cope with several low-rising, but quite rugged mountain ranges, such as the Long Hai Hills in the far south of the province, and the Nui Dinh and the Nui Thi Vai Mountains west-south-west of Nui Dat. Fortunately, we were never exposed to the more imposing Nui May Tao Mountains in the far north-east.

The Long Hai Hills feature significantly — for all the wrong reasons — in the annals of 8 RAR operational history in Vietnam. Each year, on 28 February, 8 RAR veterans solemnly observe what is known by them as 'Long Hai Day' — the sad anniversary of 2 disastrous contiguous M16 mine incidents in 1970, when 8 men from 8 RAR — and an engineer — lost their lives, with 15 others being seriously wounded.

And then there was the ubiquitous red dirt. It just got into everything and made our lives even more miserable. It was like very fine dust and, when wet, had the consistency of Clag glue. It certainly made weapons cleaning a more frequent and much more onerous task.

The red dirt at Fire Support Base Pat. Peter McCann is sitting on top of a 7.62mm ammunition box, with Peter Cousins to his left. *(Note the clean weapons and the M79 Grenade Launcher to the author's right)*

Overall, the terrain of Phuoc Tuy Province was a challenge

because we always had varied ground conditions confronting us. From one operation to the next, sometimes from one day to the next, we never knew what terrain or landscape we were going to encounter. On several occasions we were relocated — at very short notice — by Iroquois helicopters or APCs, to other locations that had markedly differing terrains. We never seemed to be doing it easy. While no Australian soldier, no matter what his or her role was in Vietnam, did it easy…infantry soldiers and their attached field elements found it much harder than most. I'm absolutely certain that no one is going to argue with that proposition.

The terrain of Phuoc Tuy Province was harsh, unforgiving, and extremely variable. From my perspective, as an infantry soldier, it was a totally forgettable landscape — even more so, considering the prevailing climate.

CHAPTER 14

MOSQUITOES AND MALARIA

The Vietnamese climate, typified by its temperature, humidity, and the ever-present wet terrain, was an ideal breeding environment for mosquitoes. Many varieties of these insects were known to carry one or more of the various strains of parasitic malaria infection. The last thing any operational military force wanted was for its soldiers to be struck down by an epidemic of malaria. For that reason, 8 RAR was very particular about how it managed this potential threat to its operational capability.

At Nui Dat, decent quality mosquito nets were provided to everyone. Their use was mandatory at night, and they were certainly used by us whenever we were living there — even during the day, if we were taking an afternoon nap. Although we eventually got used to it, the pulsating rhythmic drone of the multitudinous mosquito attack-squadrons, as they futilely tried to breach the silk netting defences of our bed spaces to reach the warm blood circulating within our bodies, was almost deafening.

We were also provided with liberal — literally as many as you wanted — small plastic bottles of liquid mosquito and insect repellent, which we frequently rubbed over our exposed skin whenever we were out in the field or at Nui Dat. I don't think any of us needed much encouragement to do that. I reckon this repellent was reasonably effective, and we would have done almost anything to abate the physical afflictions imposed on us from the mosquito and insect plagues that infested southern Vietnam. Many of these small — around 50ml — green bottles eventually became very useful containers for the fine-grade oil we used to clean and maintain our weapons.

Mosquitoes were most active after the sun went down and, because of this, we weren't allowed to shower at Nui Dat before 6:30am or after 6:30pm. Vietnam seemed to be pretty much like 'mosquito heaven'. While we were supposed to wear a shirt — and allowed to roll the sleeves up — between those hours, most of us were bare from the waist up during the day at Nui Dat. Many of the men (myself included) used to take a second daily shower around 3:30pm, after which we usually put on a clean shirt — again with sleeves rolled up (in total contravention of battalion standing orders) — and enjoyed ourselves immensely at the boozer.

Two days before we departed Australia for Vietnam, we started taking the anti-malaria tablets 'Paludrine'; a practice we continued twice a day for the best part of the next 12 months. Once we arrived in Vietnam, we took another tablet 'Dapsone', each morning as well. Twice every day, at dawn and at dusk, whether we were at Nui Dat or out in the field, my section commander personally handed out these so-called anti-malaria tablets and watched us swallow them, recording that fact in his notebook.

Corporal Fred Vincent never exhibited any attribute particular to an anal-retentive person, so his pedantic preoccupation surrounding this record keeping must have been directly related to battalion standard operating procedures. I don't think we ever worried too much about these anti-malaria tablets during our rare, short stints in Vung Tau on an R&C break. We may have, I just don't remember. On balance, I'd say not.

No matter what precautions we took, some mosquitoes were always going to find their target and probably infect a few of us with various parasitic malaria infections. Apparently, from what I was told at the time, and have subsequently been able to vaguely confirm, the underlying function of both Dapsone and Paludrine was to inhibit the development of malaria in host bodies — our bodies. In other words, these drugs that we ingested daily were only suppressants that rendered the infection temporarily dormant in instances where we were in fact infected.

Fourteen days prior to our departure from Vietnam, the requirement for us to take Dapsone was discontinued, but the administration of Paludrine was maintained. At the same time, we were provided with 2 new tablets: 'Chloroquine' and 'Primaquine', taken in varying daily doses over that period. These latter tablets were colloquially referred to by us as 'RTA (Return to Australia)' tablets. We were told that these tablets apparently provided the knock-out punch to any parasitic malaria infection that may have been lying dormant for many months in some of our body systems.

We were also informed that it wasn't operationally possible to provide Australian soldiers with these RTA tablets throughout their time in Vietnam because of the extremely high likelihood of undesirable, physical side effects. This certainly seemed plausible to me. I noticed that some of the men in my company reacted very poorly to RTA tablets during our last days in Vietnam. Fortunately, I wasn't one of them.

As far as I'm aware, the long-term Dapsone and Paludrine cocktail option — experimental as it probably was at the time — generally worked well for most 8 RAR soldiers because, as far as I can recall, there were very few reported instances of anyone in the battalion contracting malaria. Certainly, no one that I knew, and I don't recall hearing about anyone in my Company contracting it either. However, I do know that my brother-in-law who deployed to Vietnam about 12 months or so before me, was stricken with malaria and still occasionally suffers from minor relapses.

Whenever we were out in the field, our shirt sleeves were always rolled down for camouflage security reasons and, as most of our operations lasted for weeks — or more — at a time, we became absolutely filthy — our skin was ingrained with dirt, dried sweat, and congealed mosquito and insect repellent. We noticed that after several days of these squalid living conditions, mosquitoes had difficulty penetrating the layers of our personal grime with their proboscises. So, in effect, we were generating our own personal defence mechanism of sorts, against the dreaded Vietnamese mosquito strains, of which there were many.

CHAPTER 15

ANTS AND OTHER AFFLICTIONS

In Vietnam, not only were we confronting a clever, highly organised, well-armed, well-trained, and vicious enemy, we were also constantly exposed to a seemingly endless array of environmental distractions, some of which still haunt me to this day. While the naive might suggest that snakes were our worst nightmare whenever we were out in the field, they would be completely wrong.

By far, the most dreadful environmental challenge I experienced was the diverse species of ants that proliferated throughout the country. I don't have fond memories of Vietnamese ants and admit that their impact on me during this 12-month period of my life generated a psychosis of sorts in my mind. I don't like ants of any variety and never will!

Around late February 1970, while we were laying up overnight in an ambush on an elevated, densely-treed and heavily vegetated position along a ridge line in the Nui Dinh Mountains, I finally succumbed to an impacted wisdom tooth that had been troubling me on and off for several days. That night, the pain was so intense that along with the associated toxins running through my body, it brought on near delirium. I was suffering from a raging temperature and an unquenchable thirst. I wasn't well enough for anything, let alone soldiering. Thankfully, my section commander recognised this. Arrangements were made for my medical evacuation early the next morning by helicopter back to Nui Dat for medical and dental treatment.

However, all that long night I had to endure the pain and associated fever from my tooth, as well as unrelenting attacks from a class of horrible critters known as 'chomper ants', which made my already miserable life at that time, even more miserable. Chomper ants had a relatively sturdy body and they weren't small. They were probably about 1.5cm long and possessed incredibly powerful jaws, encased in a wide, elongated head, comprising about one third of their length. The jaws of these ants could score steel...I kid you not! And once they latched onto your flesh, you could attempt to kill them, but it would all be to no avail. Mostly, their jaws remained firmly locked in place, while their venom glands continued to inject poisons into you. They weren't nice at all.

For the entire night, these ants feasted on my overheated, temperature-racked body and, in my semi-delirious state, it almost drove me crazy. After a

Chapter 15 – Ants and Other Afflictions

time, I was so unwell that I became oblivious to it. I had several platoon mates that night who were pissing on the ground around me to deter them. This only partially worked. Without any doubt whatsoever, it was the worst night of my entire time in Vietnam. I was a very sick soldier. I have no recall whatsoever as to what, if anything, may have occurred that night in terms of our ambush.

Early next morning, when I was medevac'd out of the field back to Nui Dat by a Bell Sioux helicopter from the Army Aviation Unit — 161 Independent Reconnaissance Flight (161 Recce Flight) — I was so sick, exhausted, and covered in wounds from ant bites, that I don't remember all that much about the short flight, subsequent medical treatment, or extraction of the offending wisdom tooth. What I do vaguely recall though, is that when the short medevac flight landed at Luscombe Field — not Kanga Pad — at Nui Dat, I was met by a team comprised of a doctor, several medics, and 2 stretcher bearers from 8 Field Ambulance. They had clearly been expecting the arrival of a battlefield casualty, not a soldier with a very serious dental problem.

After the extraction of this errant tooth, I quickly recovered and re-joined my platoon back out in the field within a couple of days, courtesy of an Iroquois helicopter from 9 Squadron RAAF. From that moment on, my concern and respect for ants was on an equal ranking with my apprehension about confronting the enemy.

Late on the afternoon before I re-joined my platoon back in the field — some 2 days later — I was ordered by a Support Company sergeant, who I'd never seen before, to acquire 2 cans of soft drink per man in my platoon — let's say 60 cans — from the Support Company boozer, chill them overnight, and take them with me the next morning. I had no problem with any of this, did what I was ordered to do, sorted out the issue of chilling the soft drinks, and promised to pay the boozer functionary at a later time…which I never did.

Anyway, try and imagine this…I'm a soldier, who is now only marginally well, and about to re-join my platoon out in the field. I have all of my personal weapons and gear to carry — say the best part of 67kg — as well as 60 cans of ice-cold soft drink — another 22kg — contained in 5 or 6 sandbags. I'm then ordered to present myself at Kanga Pad, probably at least an 800m distance, at 6am.

I said to this sergeant:

'No sergeant, I simply can't do this. I'm not a pack horse and I'm still not at all well.'

Thankfully, he could clearly see my predicament, didn't charge me for my insubordination, and quickly solved my problem. Next morning, he arranged for Gary Piper — the Support Company driver — to pick me up, along with my weapons, all of my field equipment, and the soft drinks, and deliver me to Kanga Pad for insertion back into the field by Iroquois helicopter from 9 Squadron. When I re-joined my platoon after a 10-minute flight, there was almost mass hysteria brought on by the delivery of the soft drink, which was distributed amongst the men by the sergeant and section commanders.

During the 2 days and 2 nights that I was back at Nui Dat convalescing after my dental issue was resolved, Arthur Koo, our platoon storeman at that time, did a truly magnificent job — worthy of being awarded a medal for 'the most invisible man'. Seriously, I never saw him at all, not once. I can honestly say that I didn't even catch a distant glimpse of Koo, or his shadow. Then again, it's a well-recognised fact that ghosts don't leave shadows. He must have spent all that time within the confines of the platoon store, doing God knows what. I always thought that I was good at not being noticed, but I reckon Koo managed to elevate this very desirable army skill to an art form. I'm possibly being somewhat hard on Koo because, during my brief time back at Nui Dat, all I did was sleep and contend with our platoon pet, Rachel. There's a lot more about her later in my story.

In heavily-treed and canopied areas — and we spent many days operating in those landscapes — an extremely nasty species of red ant resided. These ants were somewhat larger than common Australian black bull ants, and they were pastel-reddish or dark ochre-like in colour. They particularly frequented rubber trees and must have been extremely intelligent. Either that, or I exuded an odour that suggested 'come and eat me'. Without fail, whenever we quietly and carefully moved through these treed areas, murderous cohorts of these ants would drop onto my neck, crawl down over my shoulders and back under my shirt, and proceed to eat me alive. If you've ever watched the USA production of the 1986 Vietnam era war movie, 'Platoon', you'll understand what I'm talking about. Actor, Charlie Sheen, knows all about Vietnamese ants.

I could understand being attacked by these ants if I leaned against a tree or laid on the ground amongst them. However, these red ants must have been fully fledged members of the US Army 101st Airborne Division, the 'Screaming Eagles'. In waves, they often strategically dropped down onto me, crawled under my shirt, and harassed me as if they were in a frenzy. Their bites were excruciatingly painful. To put it mildly, they drove me nuts — almost as bad as the chomper ants.

There was another class of Vietnamese ant that also never ceased tormenting me. Unlike the 2 former varieties, these nasty guys were tiny. You could hardly see the little fuckers and yet, their bites were exceedingly painful. And there seemed to be large colonies of them, no matter where we were in Phuoc Tuy Province.

I don't know why this was the case but, during my time out in the field, ants seemed to find me more appealing than any other member of my platoon.

Chapter 15 — Ants and Other Afflictions

Most of my mates found this extremely funny, especially on evenings when we laid down an ambush. I always pissed all around my ground position and asked them to do the same, to create a barrier between myself and local ants, or any other nasty crawlies surely headed my way during the night.

For quite some weeks before the onset of the wet season in late April, Lance-corporal Ron Goubareff — who was on his second tour of Vietnam — kept repeatedly warning me about the flies that would appear when the wet season rains arrived. He was very much aware of my obsession and preoccupation with ants, so I just thought he was having some fun at my expense. Anyway, at the end of the day, he was correct.

Just like a Biblical prophecy, it happened exactly as Goubareff had foretold. Daily, immediately after each torrential afternoon downpour, tens upon tens of thousands of flies would descend on each and every one of us then attach themselves to the saltiest parts of our clothing and packs. We were literally covered in flies which, while harmless enough, was nothing short of a damn nuisance. Walking around with our backs, shoulders, arms, and legs covered in flies, looking like a mobile swarm of bees, wasn't my idea of having a fun time. Flies simply drove me crackers and, every so often, Goubareff would turn around and look back at me with a huge smile — revealing his filthy, yellow, rotten teeth — and his own ugly visage covered in flies. I really hated him on those occasions.

We didn't spend too much time operating on coastal rocky shale, sand flats, or mangrove swamps...and thank goodness for that. On the few occasions that we were very close to the coastline, sandflies literally ate me alive. These guys are related to those occupying coastal areas of north Queensland, but they are much bigger and far more aggressive.

Throughout most of the province — particularly the totally inhospitable coastal areas — there were plagues of ticks and, when we returned to Nui Dat after each operation, we would routinely have our mates perform a tick inspection of our shoulders and backs whilst in the showers. To the best of my knowledge, the many varieties of ticks common to Vietnam didn't carry the bacterial-based debilitating Lyme disease that some European varieties did, and still do. Anyway, I have at least a score of deep scars on my back and shoulders where ticks were removed — or dug out to be more accurate — by my sadistic but well-meaning platoon mates. Mick O'Shea really enjoyed carrying out this procedure, by trying to inflict as much pain on me as possible. As I now know, removing ticks in this way is not recommended practice because it invariably results in the injection of additional venom into its hosts — our bodies.

On those rare occasions when we operated on the coastal, rocky shale and sand flats, we wore flak jackets and metal helmets as protection against enemy-laid pilfered M16 anti-personnel mines. A flak jacket consisted of a sleeveless vest, made up of numerous layers of Kevlar. It was about 3cm thick and weighed in at around 4.25kg. Helmets were something in the order of 1.4kg. Because of the climatic conditions and the nature of 1ATF ground operations in Vietnam, flak jackets and helmets were generally unsuitable for extended infantry operations. With the combination of heat, humidity, extremely hot and heavy flak jackets and helmets, massive sandflies, ticks, and the ever-present legions of well-organised mosquitoes, along with all of the other weight we carried, there were times when suicide almost seemed like an attractive option to me.

As a completely different landscape, we often operated in very wet areas such as dense jungle — ideal territory for leeches. Although they were quite harmless compared to many other environmental challenges we faced, it was the visual effect of their feeding on the blood of our bodies that turned our stomachs.

Leeches were very unpleasant, mainly because we didn't notice them until they had engorged themselves on our blood, and swollen to something like 10 times their original body size. After they attached to our bodies and breached the skin with their acerbic mouths, the anaesthetising enzyme in their saliva ensured that as they fed, we didn't feel any pain or other physical sensation. Unless we looked for, and found leeches attached to our body parts, we generally weren't aware that we'd suffered leech attack.

We often checked each other for leeches, particularly if we'd crossed a watercourse or taken a rest break in, or moved through dark, damp, wet, canopy-covered areas. On one such occasion, Ron Goubareff dropped his trousers to discover several fully engorged leeches attached to his balls, and one on the shaft of his penis. We helped him remove them by applying salt, and lit matches to them. That did the trick. The last thing any of us wanted was to find a leech intruding into the meatus or opening of our penis. If that happened, it surely meant big trouble for the poor unfortunate guy, and the entire platoon. Anyway, that leech attack certainly quietened Goubareff down for a few hours. I was really happy about that.

Although I suffered a few instances of sporadic leech attack, they seemed to leave me pretty much alone. I think this may be because I was always very fastidious about how I utilised our extra-long boot laces to tie the bottoms of my trousers to my boots. Getting past that barrier was always going to be difficult.

Strangely, spiders weren't all that much of a problem for us. However, the 2 species I did see a lot were massive and by virtue of their size — relative to the spiders I came across at home — were quite frightening. In terms of their venom potency and danger to humans, they were nowhere near as sinister as the Australian Funnel Web or Red Back spiders. They just looked a lot bigger

Chapter 15 – Ants and Other Afflictions

and a lot nastier. Then again, a female Funnel Web spider rearing up on her back legs with her enormous venom-dripping fangs exposed, was an imposing sight. You definitely wouldn't go out of your way to upset her.

The Assault Pioneer Platoon lines at Nui Dat were home to numerous colonies of easy-going Tarantula spiders, who largely kept to themselves. That is, until an idiotic platoon mate — Peter Cousins — decided one afternoon to pour a volatile petroleum-based highly-flammable solvent, known as 'range fuel', down a humungous spider burrow between our tents. He then lit it, just to see what would happen. Well, what did he expect?

Spiders, just like humans, need oxygen to breathe, so as this supply in their deep underground tunnels began to deplete, and the range fuel burned fiercely, scores of them came charging to the surface — rearing up on their legs with fangs exposed — all fit to kill. That is, kill poor bastards like me. Talk about panic! These angry arachnoids were seriously massive. I'm talking about very pissed-off spiders with bodies of 5cm or more in diameter. My platoon mates and I took off like startled gazelles and, as I ran, I fervently prayed that Cousins would be caught and eaten by them. That night, we made sure that our beds were clear of any spiders who may have been lurking around to seek revenge on us.

Often in rubber plantations we saw massive spiders living in webs that were vertically interlocked at about head height, between the perpendicular trunks of the low-level, branchless trees. These spiders were extremely colourful and quite easy to see in the early morning and late afternoon, as the dew from humidity and condensation caused their webs to shimmer. In turn, their iridescently-hued bodies reflected the dim waves of light that somehow penetrated the ambient gloom of the rubber forest.

The central and southern parts of Vietnam are infested with snakes, most of whom are highly venomous. I can't comment on the north of the country, but I imagine that it would be the same. In my view, as it was for mosquitoes, Vietnam was also 'snake heaven'. They always seemed to be in abundant numbers, no matter where we were. I clearly remember that, during our voyage to Vietnam, we were told that something like 15,000 Vietnamese people died every year from snake bite. While I didn't ever rate snakes in the same category as the nastiness of ants, they certainly deserved some respect and kept us on our toes during our time in Vietnam.

Snakes of the adder variety abounded in dense, thorny-bamboo thickets, and were commonly referred to by the local Vietnamese as '3-5-7-minute bamboo snakes'. Their name apparently reflected how much time you had to live, if you were bitten by one. Being a very tall man, I didn't like thorny-bamboo thickets because I found them quite difficult to navigate and manoeuvre through, so I always tried to avoid them like the plague. On a few occasions in late January and through February, we spent considerable time intermittently moving through these sorts of dense bamboo thickets, and my eyes were in constant motion, I can tell you. Not for sign of any enemy, but for snakes.

One time, my platoon was taking a short rest in a sunken, half-dry wadi bed, when Mick O'Shea noticed a bone-coloured, tapered stick, protruding from the side bank undergrowth. He decided to play a prank on us all by grabbing it and walking amongst us whispering *'snake!'* The problem for O'Shea was that on this occasion it was, in fact a snake. An even bigger problem was that it was a seriously massive Cobra. Talk about panic in the ranks! The entire platoon instantly evacuated the wadi bed at great speed and in complete and utter disorder. O'Shea was well and truly in the shit with our platoon commander for being a complete dickhead. Talk about a very lucky guy. A bite from a Cobra of any variety in Vietnam was invariably fatal without immediate medical intervention.

Within the multitudinous jungle areas, particularly near watercourses, there lived several species of snakes known collectively as Kraits. These generally dull-coloured black and grey reptiles, some with white bands, were of varying sizes but not overly large. The ones I came across from time to time were probably less than 1.5m long and reasonably slender. Although not seemingly aggressive, this snake — of which there are many interrelated species — also infests southern parts of India and south-east Asia. We'd been told that a bite from a Krait was always going to be fatal. Naturally, we kept well clear of them and I'm sure that they tried to keep away from us. As a general rule, snake bites — by and large — only occur if you accidentally step on, or otherwise go out of your way to aggravate one. Humans aren't natural prey for snakes.

Late one afternoon, prior to harbouring-up for the night in an ambush amid dense ground vegetation abutting a small, low-depth watercourse crossing, I stealthily moved out to relieve Steve Kaliczinsky, who was situated about 40m forward of our main platoon party in a listening post sentry position. As I carefully approached him, Kaliczinsky noticed my presence and indicated for me to be quiet. When I got closer to him, I saw that he was holding a thin piece of wire that had been threaded through the eyes of several juvenile Kraits. Talk about being stark raving mad! Rather than intently watching and listening for any likely enemy movement, he'd been quietly occupying himself by collecting inquisitive young Kraits — risking a quick and reportedly painful death — to create a snake necklace.

As I relieved him, he smiled at me and asked that I keep adding to his necklace. No way! I spent the next 40 minutes or so absolutely terrified, as I kept a close watch out for any similar reptile intruders. If there was any enemy movement close by, I wouldn't have noticed. My eyes never stopped continuously scanning my ground position for Kraits. For quite some time leading up to this point, I viewed Kaliczinsky as being somewhat mentally deranged, and I now knew that to be completely true.

One evening, sometime after midnight, as we harboured-up on a very steep, rocky ridge line near Night Defensive Position Isa, Peter Wood, who was on sentry duty on one of the platoon's M60 machine gun positions, came over to where I was lightly sleeping. He woke me up and shone a pencil torch onto his lower forearm, where I could see 2 pin-pricks of blood with raised swelling around them. I knew he was experiencing some pain as he asked me what I thought had bitten him. I — encouragingly — answered straight away, *'A snake of course, what else?'*

Naturally, Wood's big worry was how toxic the snake's venom might be. I reassured him no end that most snakes in Vietnam were highly venomous, and that he would probably die within a very short period of time if he didn't get immediate medical treatment. Although I was trying to use humour to relieve his obvious concern, what I was actually saying was probably not all that far from the truth.

With Wood experiencing an immediate and serious health issue, Corporal Bob O'Callaghan radioed for a night-time emergency medevac helicopter to pick him up and transport him to 1st Australian Field Hospital (1 AFH) at Vung Tau. There was no moon to speak of that night — it was as black as hades — and there was little, if any, flat ground adjacent to the rising ridge line where we were located. It was going to be a tricky, maybe even suicidal landing for a very brave helicopter pilot. More to the point, there were going to be some significant problems in finding a helicopter pilot who was even prepared to attempt this extremely dangerous evacuation.

I can still remember O'Callaghan literally screaming into the radio handset:

'No, we can't wait until morning to carry him down to the base of the ridge line, because he may well be fucking dead by then!'

This was the one and only occasion that I saw O'Callaghan lose his ever-present cool and calm composure. Anyway, his insistence on an immediate night-time emergency evacuation of Wood must have been compelling. Some short time later, with a number of men from my platoon located at 4 points of a tiny-squared but still sloping ground area, barely big enough for an Iroquois helicopter, the pilot — with obviously no fear of death and great trust in his load master onboard, combined with his fellow Australian soldiers on the ground, guiding him down over the radio and shining their torches vertically up into the sky — actually managed to land his aircraft. Thank God for that! We were getting very concerned for Wood, who seemed to have taken a turn for the worst.

Wood was promptly transported to 1 AFH at Vung Tau where he was diagnosed as suffering a probable bite from a snake of unknown species. He returned to us after a few days, a bit paler, but raring to get back into it. It's true that most snakes in Vietnam are highly venomous, so this must have been one of the few friendly snakes that fancied him. That all said and done, he was a very lucky man.

On another occasion, Peter Cousins — the platoon's failed arachnoid expert — used one of the platoon's flame-throwers to annoy several snakes, again of unknown species, who were happily minding their own business amid the denser vegetation in the outer limits of our platoon lines area at Nui Dat. This was probably just as idiotic as his previous attempt to barbeque tarantulas! One very pissed-off large snake reared-up and chased him for a time. Snakes can move very quickly over short distances and believe me, so can Cousins. He really was a fabulous guy; a very good soldier who often provided us with a lot of laughs. At other times though, we just simply shook our heads, as we did almost every other day with another serial platoon pest, Mick O'Shea.

Scorpions were very nasty creatures that could be found almost anywhere throughout Vietnam and in abundant numbers. We kept a constant look out for them. Although the venom from their tail stinger wasn't usually fatal, we'd been told that it was exceedingly painful if it was deeply injected into the body. And there was always the possibility of anyone being stung by a scorpion to experience a life-threatening anaphylactic shock reaction, something that wasn't treatable at all out in the field.

Only 3 platoon members were unlucky enough to be stung by scorpions. And it comes as no surprise that one of them happened to be my very good mate, Mick O'Shea. Whenever we were out in the field, if something was happening in our platoon, Mick O'Shea always seemed to be in the middle of it. On the other hand, if we were back at Nui Dat, Peter Cousins was usually the culprit.

Anyway, one day out in the field, as we were taking a rare, short break from our operational tasking, O'Shea lay back on the ground to rest. A scorpion crawled up under one of the rolled-down, unbuttoned sleeves of his shirt and, when he scratched the irritation, the arachnid sank its tail stinger into the underside of his forearm. Because we were good mates, I was sitting next to him, quietly chatting, so I saw his immediate reaction. At first, he used the ball of his opposite hand to smash and crush the scorpion, not that he knew what it was at the time. He soon knew all right! Then, all he could do was lay back and wait out the waves of agonising pain that coursed through his arm. It must have been incredibly intense because, although he was a tough sort of guy, O'Shea was reduced to tears and deep, guttural sobs for about 30 minutes or so. Talk about making a lot of noise. I decided there and then to give scorpions far more respect than I had previously.

Chapter 15 — Ants and Other Afflictions

I'd also concluded that other than drinking enormous amounts of beer together in the boozer at Nui Dat, or at Vung Tau, I should largely avoid O'Shea — he just seemed to be a magnet for trouble. That very thought was to later haunt me, after a nasty incident involving both of us in Vung Tau. I tell of this incident a little later.

The other platoon members who were bitten by scorpions include Jeff (JJ) Smith, and Arthur Koo. Smith was a tough sort of guy — as you'd expect from a man who later became a fully-badged 'biker' — so that scorpion probably came off second best. On the other hand, Koo's body reacted very badly to the venom and he spent 10 days under medical care at 1 AFH at Vung Tau. When he was discharged at the end of May, or thereabouts, he was seconded to the 1st Australian Civil Affairs Unit (1 ACAU). I'm guessing this was due to his civil engineering background. Although he — strangely — remained on its posted strength, Koo never returned to the platoon. I re-engaged with Koo at a battalion reunion in Adelaide in 2010, and again in Canberra in 2017. He still remains the very smart and lovable guy I first met way back in May 1969.

Not only did Vietnam have aerial environmental challenges, such as mosquitoes and flies for us to contend with, it also had its fair share of hornets. They used to build their humungous mud nests high up on the sides of large, tall trees. My section of the platoon — No.1 Section — meant that for some inexplicable reason — which no one was ever able to logically explain to me — we were always the lead section; whether on foot, onboard APCs, or aboard helicopters. Anyway, either Steve Kaliczinsky or Peter Wood, our section's 2 forward scouts, would invariably spot these elevated nests of hornets and guide the platoon on a wide detour around and away from their defended, elevated territory.

On one afternoon, as we were quietly and slowly moving towards a likely enemy bunker complex, word was whispered back to us that we had to detour around a large hornet nest. That seemed to me to be a perfectly good idea and, as we slowly proceeded forward again, giving a particular tree about 40m away to my right a very wide berth, I glanced across, looked up, and saw the massive mud-formed fortress attached high up on the trunk.

Then, for some unaccountable reason, a stray hornet, one that was either leaving or returning to its fortress, saw me and reasoned that I represented danger to either it, or the wider colony. Having formed this totally unreasonable viewpoint, the hornet went into attack mode and buried its venom-loaded stinger behind my right ear. I didn't even see the hornet. I only heard the whirring of its supersonically-beating wings for about one tenth of a second, as it lined up my ear on its high-speed approach.

Though I didn't see this hornet coming for me, I certainly felt what it delivered to the soft, delicate flesh behind my earlobe. The pain was just unimaginable. I've never experienced anything quite like it in my entire life. I immediately jettisoned my backpack, let go of my rifle, and dropped to the ground in extreme pain. My platoon mates later informed me that I also made a hell of a lot of noise. It seemed to take ages for the pain to even start to subside. This wasn't one of my fun days in Vietnam.

As you would appreciate, my platoon commander was completely pissed-off with me because I'd totally compromised the security of the entire platoon. While that was true, as far as I was concerned, with the area behind my ear now swollen to the size of a golf ball, I didn't really give a toss what the platoon commander thought.

Of course, all of my platoon mates found this extremely funny and took the piss out of me for days afterwards. Anyway, I seem to recall that after a quiet 30-minute break or thereabouts, while I sort of recovered, we moved on in line with our operational tasking for that day. Did any of my platoon mates offer me any sympathy? Not at all. For a time, Ron Goubareff kept looking back at me with his broad grin. As I've said before, he was a great guy but, at times, I just loathed him.

Late one afternoon we ended up right on the coast at a sandy beach area very near to a small, local hamlet. We were hot, filthy, and utterly exhausted. The grey waters of the South China Sea looked so tempting and someone asked our platoon commander if we could have a quick swim.

Now, I have to say that this was an extremely difficult conundrum for him. While our security was paramount, he was very much aware of our need to chill out, even if only for a few minutes, after an extended time out in the field. Some considered thought and consultation with the platoon sergeant and section commanders took place, and in the end, he reluctantly agreed, provided that we briefly wallowed in the water in a number of small, sequential groups of about 4 or 5. This ensured that the major part of the platoon was at full operational readiness, if by chance enemy soldiers were to come across us.

Seriously, this was a very high-risk decision for our platoon commander, and one for which I applaud him. However, consider this? If it were to have all turned to shit for the platoon — with some of its members having a languid swim in the ocean — you might easily conjure up a range of ugly disciplinary outcomes for him, following a Court Marshal hearing.

Mr Phillips was a conservative commander and in making this decision, he really went out on a thin limb for the men under his command. I'm not sure that I would have made the same decision. I admire him for his courage that afternoon.

Anyway, never one to hang around waiting, I managed to get naked in time to enter the water as part of the first group. Not surprisingly, Peter Wood beat us all to it. Watching on from no more than about 30m or so away, were

Chapter 15 – Ants and Other Afflictions

several variously-aged female residents of the hamlet. They were all tittering and laughing at what we assumed was our nakedness. How wrong we were.

Around 5 or 6 of us quickly waded out in the water to about waist deep, luxuriating in the relative coolness of the murky water. The southern waters of the South China Sea weren't pristine like back in Australia. Suddenly, we knew exactly why these locals were laughing their heads off. Wave after wave of sea lice began to strike us, inflicting massive, raised, purple welts all over our bodies. The welts were so severe that, in some cases, they almost drew blood. As we struggled out of the water, with hands cupped around our genitals, the locals almost collapsed in hysterical laughter. Talk about being set up! They knew full well what was coming our way. Platoon members who were still fully-dressed and operationally-alert, quickly decided they were no longer interested in taking a dip. And who could blame them?

There was one other time, quite late in the day, when BHQ tasked the platoon with moving rapidly to a different ground position that was some good distance away. Now, given the timing, this was highly unusual. With daylight about to disappear in less than an hour, the asking distance — given the terrain — was going to be a real stretch for us physically and, even if we were to attempt to do so, we would have to deliberately degrade our operational security because of the need for speed. I clearly remember hearing Mr Phillips advising BHQ over the field radio that his men were just too exhausted to be able to do that. We didn't end up moving to the new position and, alternatively, set up an overnight ambush where we were. I'm unaware if there were any later ramifications for our platoon commander. Again, I admire him for that decision.

These 2 events clearly illustrate Mr Phillips' almost obsessive focus on the safety and well-being of the men under his command. He was an excellent platoon commander. When I dissect the reasons why he went out on a limb for his men, on each of these occasions, it only boils down to the fact that he recognised his platoon was utterly exhausted.

Apparently, there was also a reasonably large orange and white coloured spider, or beetle-crawly that, as described to me, was about 7cm long with furry legs — I never actually saw one — known by us as the 'RTA (Return To Australia) beetle'. Although it was a very rare species, rampant hearsay at the time was that if you managed to get bitten by one of them, you were well and truly on your way back to Australia for long-term medical treatment. I seem to vaguely recall that at least one 8 RAR soldier — an officer from another company — was repatriated back home due to RTA beetle attack.

The large feral monkeys that we encountered from time to time at various natural watercourses, were always potentially dangerous. Because of the never-ending extremes of heat and humidity, water was a daily imperative for all land-based life forms in Vietnam — not just humans. Territorial monkeys, while wary, didn't appear to be afraid of us. We'd been told that they could be exceedingly aggressive, particularly in any confrontational situation. And because of their large, razor-sharp teeth — and 2 imposing, oversized upper incisors that were generally festooned with rotting food and other fetid debris — monkeys were able to inflict a very nasty bite and quite possibly infect you with one or both of the insidious diseases they often carried: Rabies and Leptospirosis. We made sure that we kept well away from monkeys. I was very surprised that Cousins, our resident platoon naturalist, didn't try to befriend them.

Vietnam had enough environmental challenges to keep me totally stressed-out of my mind for the entire time spent in that awful country. Having to overcome a vicious and cunning enemy added significantly to those stress levels. During my entire 12 months in Vietnam, I was rarely able to relax or let down my guard. I don't really think anyone could. The closer we came to the end of our time in Vietnam, the more anxious, obsessive, and innately nastier we all seemed to become.

CHAPTER 16

1ST AUSTRALIAN TASK FORCE (1 ATF) - NUI DAT

1 ATF was the Australian and New Zealand brigade-sized combined arms military force that was formally attached — although it operated independently — to the US Army 2nd Field Force Vietnam from 1966-72.

Nui Dat was its large, pivotal fire support base from which all Australian ground based operations in Vietnam emanated. It was the key resource of 1 ATF and played a vital role during the time of Australia's military involvement in the Vietnam War. Many Australian Vietnam veterans will remember it as their home, whenever they weren't otherwise deployed on operational tasking out in the field. For most of us in infantry battalions it was very welcome, though only a transitory locale.

LOCATION

Nui Dat — known locally as 'small hill' or 'clay hill', depending on who you want to believe — abutted Route 2 and was situated about 30km north-north-east of the comparatively large port-based civilian centre of Vung Tau, and was about 5km south-west of the geographical centre of Phuoc Tuy Province.

Infantry and other supporting elements — Armour, Artillery, Army Aviation, Civil Affairs (some), Engineers, Intelligence, Logistics (some), Signals, etc — were based at Nui Dat. A wide range of other supporting elements were located at the 1st Australian Logistic Support Group (1 ALSG) on the southern coastal peninsula adjacent to Vung Tau, slightly to the north-east of its large deep-water port.

The primary role of 1 ALSG was to provide logistical support necessary to keep 1 ATF and its 3 battalions of infantry soldiers, associated field support, and other extraneous task force elements, fully operational at all times. It also provided very occasional R&C facilities for soldiers based at 1 ATF and 1 ALSG and superior medical and hospital services for any allied serviceman or servicewoman killed, wounded, injured, or otherwise seriously ill.

The supporting arm of Australia's military involvement in Vietnam, based within 1 ALSG at Vung Tau, was a very large, collective, and diverse contingent. The fact that there were such large numbers of support soldiers, sailors, airmen, doctors, and nurses reinforcing 1 ATF field operations in

Vietnam, should come as no surprise to anyone. The need for extensive support for combat field elements has been a constant feature of all major wars and lesser conflicts. Vietnam was no different.

Once 1 ATF was fully established — with 3 infantry battalions in place at any one time — about 3,000 combat field soldiers were based at Nui Dat, along with around 2,000 men in direct support. Some 3,000 other supporting men and women were based at 1 ALSG. At the height of Australia's commitment to the Vietnam War, as many as 8,000 Australian servicemen and servicewomen were deployed to that conflict at any given time. This was certainly the case during my time in Vietnam with 8 RAR, circa 1969-70.

The 5:3 ratio between the direct combat, associated supporting personnel elements, and other indirect supporting elements of Australia's war effort in Vietnam, was extremely efficient compared to ratios of previous larger-scale conflicts in which Australia was involved. That's a telling testament indeed as to how well organised and committed those support elements based at Vung Tau were, and how well they performed their vital support roles. By way of illustration, although 9 Squadron RAAF was based at I ALSG for quite obvious reasons, it was a superb supporting combat resource for 1 ATF.

In the late 1960's, the overall strength of the ADF was said to have been around 40,000. While recognising that significant elements of the RAAF and the RAN were also a crucial part of Australia's military commitment to the Vietnam conflict, the army's contribution consumed something like 25% or more of its available manpower strength when rotational pre-deployment training was factored into the equation...a huge military commitment by Australia in support of its USA and South Vietnamese allies.

Nui Dat was located 8km north-east of Ba Ria. Because of its generally central location, it was ideally located for 1 ATF to launch military operations almost anywhere within the province. I imagine that's exactly why the site was first chosen back in the early 1960's. This somewhat elevated site was formerly a large, disused rubber plantation, so it was very attractive in terms of the shade and canopy cover it provided to the soldiers based there from time to time.

Below and across to the right of the water dam on the left side of this image (opposite page), there's a substantial open area. Just below that, across a dirt road, is a small, but just discernible area surrounded by dense vegetation, foliage, and canopy. This vague area was much larger than it appears to be in the image shown. It is here, in and around this region, that the 8 RAR Assault Pioneer Platoon lines were located.

Worth noting...all potable water used within Nui Dat was hauled in by army road transport from other sources. For obvious reasons, it was far too risky for 1 ATF to rely on accessing water from the adjacent dam.

Chapter 16 – 1st Australian Task Force (1 ATF) - Nui Dat

An aerial view of Nui Dat (North is at 1600 hours).
Kanga Pad (left) and Luscombe Field (right).

Historian, Brian Ross[18] says:

'... Phuoc Tuy (Province) *was chosen because there was a reasonable amount of enemy activity, no risk of border violations in the pursuit of enemy and it had excellent air and sea access ensuring adequate supplies and an assured evacuation route. The terrain was not dissimilar from that often encountered by Australians in Malaysia and Borneo. In addition to this, the pacification of Phuoc Tuy was essential to the Republic of Vietnam because of its wealth and to the MACV* (Military Assistance Council, Vietnam) *because of the significance of Vung Tau port and the supply line* (Route 15) *to Saigon and Bien Hoa* (Province).

The exact placement of the Task Force was to be Nui Dat, a hill on Route 2 heading north through the centre of the province and was an obvious challenge to the NLF (National Liberation Front) *and NVA* (North Vietnamese Army) *forces in the area. The logistics and supply group* (1 ALSG) *were to be situated in Vung Tau where it was hoped that it would be somewhat safer from large scale attack...'*

---

[18] Ross, B. A paper; *Australia's Military Involvement in the Vietnam War*. 1995.

DEFENCE AND SECURITY

By the time 8 RAR arrived in Vietnam, Nui Dat was a large and fully operational military base. Its irregular defensive perimeter extended for some 13km and housed within it the Australian infantry battalions operating in Phuoc Tuy Province at any one time. The skewed rectangular average ground diameter of Nui Dat was about 3.8km — much longer north-south compared to east-west, and it occupied a significant ground area of about 14.5km^2.

Nui Dat had a fully functioning 884m tarmac runway — Luscombe Field — for short landing fixed-wing aircraft such as DHC 4A Caribou from 35 Squadron RAAF, and twin-engine C123 Fairchild Hercules from 36 and 37 Squadrons RAAF, as well as a separate tarmac — Kangaroo (Kanga) Pad — for Iroquois helicopter aircraft from 9 Squadron RAAF and US Army Chinook rotary aircraft. All of that air support was either based at 1 ALSG at Vung Tau or at a number of nearby US Army bases. The Australian Army aviation unit — 161 Independent Reconnaissance Flight (161 Recce Flight) — based at Nui Dat, was equipped with both fixed-wing and rotary aircraft, and predominantly used Luscombe Field for its operations.

Near the main entry point, known colloquially as the 'Pearly Gates' leading into Nui Dat, adjacent to the short bypass road linking Nui Dat with north-south running Route 2, and located high on a plateau — the only significantly elevated feature within Nui Dat — there was always a Squadron from the SASR. Three SASR Squadrons were deployed to Vietnam on a rotational basis. We rarely, if ever, saw SASR soldiers, and heard almost next to nothing about their operational tasking, other than the fact that they were largely engaged on reconnaissance and intelligence gathering. While that may have been their primary role, they were certainly involved in many contacts with the enemy, suffered a surprisingly low casualty rate — only 1 man was actually killed in action — and achieved significant positive outcomes in terms of the number of enemy killed, and the value of real-time intelligence gathered by them for the Task Force. For obvious reasons, we commonly referred to the knoll on which they were located as 'SAS Hill'. From what we were told, elements of the SASR provided expert intelligence assistance to 8 RAR on several occasions during its time in Vietnam.

During the early construction and development of Nui Dat in April 1966, by both 5 RAR and 6 RAR, the initial perimeter defence systems were doubtful at best, and it would be some time before I ATF were to become viably established. There is ample evidence to suggest that when D Company 6 RAR became embroiled in the Battle of Long Tan on 18 August 1966, NVA Main Force and Viet Cong Provincial Units had massed in strength as a prelude to a likely major ground attack on the emerging base. Reliable estimates suggest that as many as 2,500 enemy were in place on the ground late on the afternoon when 105 men from D Company 6 RAR, and 3 attached Royal New Zealand Army (RNZA) forward artillery observers, rudely interrupted their preparations. Fortunately, the remarkable successful outcome of that now famous battle, prevented any such attack on Nui Dat. This event very quickly precipitated significantly improved perimeter defences.

By the time we arrived in late 1969, the entire perimeter of Nui Dat was extremely well defended with substantial barbed and other significant offset wire barriers in place, augmented by a series of well-guarded M60 machine gun bunkers or redoubts, many of which were manned 24 hours a day. The lines of fire from each M60 machine gun intersected with those of its adjacent weapons, and were capable of a high degree of enfilading firepower. There were no dead areas and no blind spots. At night, all defensive M60 machine guns on the perimeter of Nui Dat were manned.

Extending out some 500m from the heavily-wired perimeter was a flat, defoliated, barren area. This replication of what 'no man's land' — a phrase coined during the Great War — may have looked like, was also saturated with further irregularly-aligned barbed-wire defences, M18 Claymore anti-personnel directional mines, and trip flares. The constantly defended perimeter of Nui Dat would have been impossible to breach without the enemy being seen by men manning its defences. Any enemy force attempting to penetrate the perimeter defences of Nui Dat in a ground attack, totally exposed as they would have been and, because of all the defence systems in place — with absolutely no forward momentum whatsoever — would have suffered quite horrendous casualties. Simply put, it would have been carnage.

In addition, extending 5km beyond the perimeter defence systems of Nui Dat was an area that had been cleared of all civilians. There were 2 large towns situated just outside of this so-called exclusion zone: Binh Ba to the north, and Hoa Long to the south. The former civilian populations of the villages of Long Phuoc and Long Tan, both of which were once located within this exclusion zone, had been compulsorily resettled some time earlier to Hoa Long, Dat Do, and Long Dien.

Shortly after the resettlement of these 4,000 civilians, the entire village of Long Tan was burnt to the ground by 5 RAR. However, Long Phuoc, although no longer inhabited by civilians, remained a fortified enemy stronghold for a time, and was later completely destroyed by 6 RAR. No allied financial compensation arrangements accompanied these 2 resettlement programs, so perhaps that's why the town of Hoa Long — in particular — remained so openly hostile to the presence of 1 ATF at Nui Dat.

In his paper, Historian Brian Ross also says:

'... The base at Nui Dat ... was not cleared as were American bases and few ARVN (Army of the Republic of Vietnam) *personnel and no Indigenous Vietnamese were allowed into the base. This meant that ... security was excellent...'* [19]

During its time at Nui Dat, 8 RAR and 1st Australian Reinforcement Unit (1 ARU) were responsible for the defence of Sector 7 of the perimeter; the south-east corner. 1 ARU came under the command of 8 RAR for the purposes of base defence. Sector 7 defences included 25 piquet — or sentry points — on the perimeter wire. Of these, 21 were always manned continuously at night, whereas only 13 were manned during the day.

Each day, when the battalion was back at Nui Dat, one third of all men from each rifle company were required to 'stand to' on the perimeter wire between 5:30am and 6:15am, and again between 6:30pm and 7:15pm. These timings may have changed slightly on occasions, depending on minor seasonal variations in the onset of sunrise and sunset. In conjunction with each of these twice-daily periods of 'stand to', regular clearing patrols were sent out beyond the perimeter wire defences to confirm, or otherwise, the security of Sector 7 of Nui Dat's defensive perimeter. It was a very intense base security protocol.

As 8 RAR's Support Company was located more centrally than the 4 rifle companies of the battalion — and with both 1 ARU and D&E (Defence and Employment) platoon positioned between it, and the defensive perimeter of Sector 7 — the requirement for early morning and evening 'stand to' didn't often apply to men of its platoons. Men from the Assault Pioneer Platoon were rarely required to participate in piquet duties on the perimeter defensive systems at Nui Dat. When 8 RAR was away on field operations, the defence of its perimeter responsibility for Sector 7 was undertaken by its residual battalion elements and men from 1 ARU and D&E Platoon.

From my personal point of view, and probably because of my highly successful propensity to not easily be noticed, I only participated in one 4-hour night-time piquet duty, and no day-time piquet duty on the perimeter wire, during my entire time in Vietnam. And I reckon the only reason I was fingered for piquet duty on that single night was because I had to return to Nui Dat for the removal of that bloody wisdom tooth! With the remainder of the battalion still deployed out in the field on Operation Keperra, numbers to man the Sector 7 perimeter night-time piquet points that evening, must have been at a premium.

Although it was potentially vulnerable to artillery, mortar, or rocket attack,

---

[19] Ross, B. A paper; *Australia's Military Involvement in the Vietnam War*. 1995.

I'd say that Nui Dat was completely impenetrable to any enemy ground attack during the time I was there. The enemy were not resourced with aircraft or artillery of any sort, so these were complications we didn't have to deal with.

PERSONAL WEAPONS WITHIN NUI DAT

Although Nui Dat was, by and large, a relatively safe environment for Australian soldiers, there were several weaponry prescripts that every man was required to observe. My recollections are that strict observation of these prescripts — or standing orders — became second nature for us all.

Upon returning to Nui Dat after any operation, all weapons, armaments, and pyrotechnics, other than personal SLR and M16 Armalite rifles and associated magazines and ammunition, were cleaned, oiled, and locked away in the platoon arsenal. When machine gunners secured their prime weapon — the M60 machine gun — they immediately withdrew their own personal SLR rifle and its ammunition from the arsenal. Whenever we were back at Nui Dat our loaded weapons were with us in our tents at all times.

Within the defined Assault Pioneer Platoon lines and the shared Support Company areas such as the mess and the boozer, we weren't required to carry rifles with us. My tented accommodation was only about 75m from each of these facilities. However, if we left these relatively small areas for any reason — for example to visit the RAP or wander down to the open-air movies area at the eastern end of Luscombe Field — we always had to carry our loaded, personal weapons with us.

As far as I can recall, there were no accidental weapons discharges within the Assault Pioneer Platoon lines or the wider Support Company areas, or any other improper use of weapons during my time in Vietnam. That's not to say that there weren't any breaches of 8 RAR's prescribed weapons safety regimen within Support Company, or other companies of the battalion, but if there were, I'm completely unaware of them.

The high level of weapons training and associated regimens of safety that were drilled into us repeatedly back in Australia, and often reinforced in Vietnam, were why we all conscientiously observed weapons safety responsibility for our collective wellbeing. For example, when out in the field with my platoon, I always carried my SLR rifle in such a way that I could almost instantly disengage the safety switch if we were to ever encounter the enemy. In other words, my safety was always on, and I used to check, almost obsessively, to ensure that it was. If I ever happened to trip and fall over — and that occurred reasonably often (hence my nickname 'Stumbles') — my rifle wasn't going to discharge. I also followed this good practice whenever we were back at Nui Dat. As far as I can now recall, all of my platoon mates were acutely conscious of weapons safety.

Realistically, large numbers of men in possession of loaded weapons in relatively secure environments such as Nui Dat, might be regarded as an elevated risk. As far as I'm concerned that view never entered our thinking, nor that of the battalion command group, during the major part of my time in Vietnam. Other than one isolated operational incident with an M79 grenade launcher — not me — it never became an issue for anyone in my platoon.

However, I will say this…as our tour of Vietnam neared its end, whenever we were back at Nui Dat there seemed to be an increased focus by command elements of Support Company on weapons safety. I can completely understand that because I have to admit, by October 1970, I don't believe that some of us were anywhere near as mentally robust as when we first arrived on the putrid, sandy shores of Vung Tau, some 12 months prior. Recorded history tells, as the operational Vietnam tenure of previous deployments wound down, there were some incidents concerning the improper use of weapons within Nui Dat by men of other battalions, which shouldn't have occurred.

For example, on 23 November 1969, a few days before 8 RAR replaced 9 RAR in Vietnam, LT Robert Thomas Convery from 9 RAR was killed by a 20-year-old Regular soldier. Private Peter Denzil Allen placed an initiated, live hand grenade next to Convery's bed in his tent at Nui Dat. Private Allen was charged with murder and early in 1970, he was tried at 1 ALSG by an ADF General Court Marshal (Military Court), found guilty, and sentenced to life imprisonment with hard labour. He was later released from Risdon Prison in Tasmania after serving 10 years and 8 months of that sentence.

I initially thought he got off far too lightly. But, then again, who am I to pass judgement on the mental health of a young, disaffected infantry veteran, nearing the end of his 12-month deployment to Vietnam? And there is much more history around the long-term personal interactions between Convery and Allen, which I won't delve into at this time. However, those of you still reading and hopefully absorbing my story, may find it fascinating if they were to do so. All that detail is contained on the public record.

OUR LIVING QUARTERS — OR LINES

As mentioned earlier, Nui Dat was situated within what was once a wild rubber forest, as opposed to a working rubber plantation. When it was first established, much of the prevailing foliage and trees were retained and the rudimentary living quarters for soldiers based there were mostly, but not always, situated around the plentiful, shady, treed areas.

Through the 'luck of the draw' in allocation of accommodation for my platoon, the tent that I shared with Des McGrath and Allan Small had no shade

Chapter 16 — 1st Australian Task Force (1 ATF) - Nui Dat

cover whatsoever. As you're now aware, I don't recall a single day in Vietnam when I wasn't feeling hot, sweaty, very thirsty, and constantly scratching my balls and arse.

In addition to the backdrop of wild rubber trees scattered around and amid the Assault Pioneer Platoon lines, there were variably-sized patches of banana, mango, breadfruit (jackfruit) and mangosteen trees, as well as a plethora of other local non-fruiting flora. I don't pretend that any of this greenery or overhead canopy in many parts, did anything to lessen the ever-present heat and humidity. However, it certainly provided welcome shade for some, and comforting visual respite for others, whenever we returned to our lines at Nui Dat for short periods of rest between operations.

Each unit based within Nui Dat — 8 RAR for example — had its own allocated space within which discrete areas were set aside for respective companies. Within company areas, each platoon had its own separate, tented habitation lines with core facilities — such as the mess and the boozer — shared with other platoons of that particular company.

While the Assault Pioneer Platoon shared core Support Company facilities with Anti-Tank and Tracker, Mortar and Signal Platoons, as well as Company Headquarters, we never really interacted with men from those elements — except randomly out in the field, or the rare occasions when we were back at Nui Dat at the same time, either eating together in the mess or imbibing massive amounts of beer in the boozer.

Accommodation at Nui Dat was in the form of large waterproof tents of indeterminate age. These tents, which provided something like 25m^2 of living space, were generally shared by 3 men, rarely if ever 4, and occasionally only 2. Officers had tents of comparable size for their sole use, and I can't remember if sergeants shared tents with other members of the platoon. I suspect they at least shared with a senior platoon corporal.

Surprisingly, these tented accommodations were relatively roomy for our modest needs and I guess that's the main reason we never seemed to get on each other's nerves. There was ample space for our 3 beds, plus a shared, vertical, steel storage cabinet, and a small roughly-constructed timber table and 2-chair setting. Individual lockable steel trunks were stored under our sagging, sprung beds. We also had 3 or 4 fold-up chairs, which we would use when relaxing outside the confines of our rudimentary home, or when — rarely — watching new movie releases or sporting replays at the walk-up and sit-down movie theatre at Luscombe Field.

I shared a tent with Des McGrath and Allan Small, the gun group of my section of the platoon and, although we must have annoyed each other from time to time, we never had a physical altercation between us — as far as I can remember — or ever came close to it. The fact that we weren't actually living together in these confined environments for extended periods of time, probably helped in that regard.

Assault Pioneer Platoon Lines at Nui Dat.
Peter McCann's tent - His bed space was right rear.
(Note the empty ammunition boxes atop the front sandbag wall)

Assault Pioneer Platoon Lines at Nui Dat - Peter McCann's tent.
(Note the complete lack of canopy shade cover)

Chapter 16 — 1st Australian Task Force (1 ATF) - Nui Dat

Because of the tropical climate, the timber floorboards of our tented homes were raised about 250mm off the ground. Each tent was protected from artillery, mortar, or rocket attack by sand-bagged, off-set wall barriers on all 4 sides. Most tents were set a reasonable distance apart. Overall, it wasn't too bad. Not one of us really gave it a second thought. We didn't spend too much time in Nui Dat anyway, so it didn't really matter much to us.

While our living conditions were extremely basic, they were certainty more than satisfactory. The oppressive tropical climate readily leant itself to our environmentally air-conditioned tents. Our army issue basic sprung beds were draped overhead with decent-quality mosquito netting and most nights when reposed, I was able to at least rest and sleep reasonably well, naked and protected from aerial nasties hovering outside the netting barrier. For much of its time in Vietnam, the Assault Pioneer Platoon wasn't based at Nui Dat. The platoon was an integral component of an infantry battalion, after all. Mostly, it was deployed on various operational activities out in the field.

A full 12-month Vietnam tour of duty for the majority of 8 RAR members has been officially recorded as 361 days. That's what my official service record reflects. However, transportation by HMAS *Sydney* to and from Vietnam, actually counted as operational service and was 23 days in total. So, my actual time physically spent in Vietnam was 338 days. Those who were part of the Advance and Rear Parties, at both ends of the battalion's deployment, may have spent slightly more or less time in the country.

I called Nui Dat home for only 76 days during that 12 months. Something like 55% of those were at the front and back ends of my time in Vietnam. See Appendix 7. I can remember on several occasions, we only had a couple of days to rest at Nui Dat before going out into the field again for a further 4, 5, or more weeks. During the last few weeks, we were tasked with singular night-time ambushes on alternate nights, successive, and occasionally multiple nights. The point I'm trying to make here is that although Nui Dat was supposedly our base home in Vietnam — a bush barracks if you like — we were never there long enough to really get to know it, let alone get used to it.

The longest time the platoon spent away from Nui Dat was 67 days. And, after a 9-day rest period, the platoon was back out in the field again for a further 52 days. All up, we were tasked with 119 days of operational activity — from 8 May until 12 September 1970. Admittedly, there were intermittent periods when we were based at fire support bases or night defensive positions.

Through very little interaction with other 8 RAR elements or 1 ATF units, I guess to a large extent we led what might best be described as an unhealthy, closeted way of life. So, while we were all very good mates within our platoon, we were closer mates within sections, and even closer to those with whom we shared tents.

From left: Peter Wood, Peter McCann, Des McGrath and Allan Small.

From left: Allan Small and Des McGrath.

From left: Peter Cousins, Peter Wood, Des McGrath, Allan Small and Peter McCormick.

Aside from my platoon mates, and perhaps 10 men from other Support Company elements, I'm hard-pressed to name another 10 men in 8 RAR. At any one time, I probably only knew 6% of the battalion's prescribed posted strength of 795 men. That was simply the nature of our time as infantry soldiers. It really was so very internal. When you think about this, any sensible person might reasonably conclude that Nui Dat wasn't a healthy environment for anyone, let alone physically and mentally exhausted soldiers who always had loaded weapons in their possession. I couldn't agree more. And, when you consider operational experiences as well…how most of us emerged from Vietnam relatively normal, for a time, defies rational thinking.

ABLUTIONS AT NUI DAT

The communal showers for my platoon were never heated and that wasn't a problem because of the prevailing climate. In any case, the water was always tepid and couldn't even remotely be described as 'cold'. Our platoon storeman, who remained at Nui Dat — but not always — while the rest of the platoon was out in the field, was tasked with having hot showers available for us on the day of our return. He generally failed miserably in this regard. I seem to recall only having one warm

— one notch above tepid — shower at Nui Dat. In fairness to the storeman, the reasons why hot water wasn't usually available in our platoon lines, were mostly beyond his control. Overall, our platoon shower block was quite reasonable, and showers of any water temperature were very welcome indeed after extended periods of time out in the field.

There were also several very basic public urinals, otherwise known as 'piss-a-phones', strategically positioned throughout our lines. I have to say that the real-time usage of these urinals seemed to work efficiently. Our more elaborate platoon toileting area was a communal row of 4 'thunder boxes', the main feature of which was the complete lack of any privacy whatsoever. Guys seated next to each other usually conversed amongst themselves while reading pornographic or other material — particularly inane trash-western and military short story comics — as they conducted their serious toileting business. I know that several of the more prudish guys initially found this lack of privacy very difficult to cope with.

Personally, I had no problem whatsoever with toileting facilities at Nui Dat. Whenever we were out in the field, we had to basically conduct our personal ablution business maybe 15m out in front of our defensive perimeter, with our mates looking on at all times for obvious security reasons. Not much different to Nui Dat. The reality of natural bodily functions took on a very basic meaning for me during my time in the army…and Vietnam in particular.

Scattered randomly throughout our lines were many open infantry defensive gun pits, which sometimes became an occupational hazard after drinking at the boozer. Having said that, while several guys did sometimes fall into them, I was lucky enough not to be one of them. I can still remember Peter Wood — completely drunk at the time — plunging into one, after a particularly long afternoon precipitation deluge. He then emerged from it as a vivid and disgusting example of why soldiers shouldn't consume vast amounts of beer.

MESS FOOD

The Support Company mess served up reasonable meals and I had no complaints. Although there was always plenty of food available, the variety wasn't great. Pretty much all of the meat — cheap steak, lamb chops, and fatty sausages — provided as the main ingredient of our meals, was barbequed.

I can no longer remember if the Support Company mess gave us bread, but my best guess is that it probably did on occasions. In saying that, I'm also certain that there was no bread-making facility. While there was plenty of fresh bread baked daily by the local populace in Vung Tau, and elsewhere within the province, I appreciate the health concerns of 1 ATF in acquiring local food products for our consumption. So, on balance, I'd say that any form of bread that may have been available to us at Nui Dat, would have been imported from Australia by RAAF Hercules C130 aircraft — though I could be completely wrong about this. The other downside was the general absence of fresh milk and eggs, leaving us to mostly make do with powered products.

In total contrast to the somewhat bland culinary rating of 'Hotel Nui Dat', I was raised by my parents on a high protein diet of lamb, chicken, tripe, and rabbit — grills, roasts, stews, and casseroles — along with frequent glutinous feasts of freshwater yabbies and crayfish (marron), accompanied by plenty of vegetables, salads, and fruits. To augment this already hugely varied carnivorous fare, my family also ate regular servings of self-caught — by me — seasonal saltwater seafood delights such as sand and blue swimmer crabs, squid (calamari), tommy ruffs, garfish, mullet, and small but very succulent skate (similar to flounder). And, although there were never prawns, from time to time there were plenty of octopus around the nearby rocky Seacliff and Marino areas. This free seafood repast largesse was available for garnering within easy walking distance from my modest, coastal family home in Adelaide.

Depending on the timing and heights of the St. Vincent Gulf tides, my mother would often ask me to go down to the beach in the afternoons after school, or very early on weekend mornings, and bring back some mullet or tommy ruffs for dinner that night. Between the ages of (say) 8-18, I was a regular provider of substantial amounts of freshly-caught seafood for the family. I really enjoyed my youthful fishing escapades down at the Brighton Jetty — the adjacent northern and southern beaches — and I became quite adept in hooking and reeling-in the family dinner.

While all of this background commentary is interesting, food was never a major issue for most of us in my platoon. And, I say that for very good reason. The main problem in relation to food during our time in Vietnam was that our stomach cavities were constantly shrinking because of the limited, low-volume, high protein rations we had to exist on, whenever out in the field. This was exacerbated by climatic extremes and the massive amounts of weight we had to carry on a daily basis.

After a very short time in Vietnam, most of us couldn't eat large meals at the Support Company mess anyway. Our eyes were always much bigger than our stomachs. Even half of an average-sized meal, consumed slowly, often tested the majority of us. Putting that into a Support Company mess BBQ dinner context: 1 sausage and 1 small 150gm piece of steak, or 2 medium-sized lamb chops, were usually more than enough for me. Strangely, we were still able to imbibe quite enormous — and I say again, enormous — quantities of beer. I've often wondered about this digestive conundrum.

It was strongly rumoured that to lower our ever-present youthful and surging sexual urges, the mess staff secreted Bromide — reputedly a libido-inhibiting chemical or compound — into our food whenever we were based at Nui Dat. I didn't know if this was true or not, but at the time, I strongly suspected it was. Usually, none of this talk bothered us and we didn't really give it a second thought.

However, on the 2 or 3 occasions that my platoon was about to deploy to Vung Tau for a 40-hour period of R&C leave, we wanted our 'junk' in proper working order for the bar girls, who we knew would lead us astray. In the mess on the night before those rare occasions, we desperately tried to find out which food item contained Bromide, if any. One evening, some idiotic guy with a death wish, made a loud public announcement:

'It's in the peas!'

No one ate peas that night. As we were leaving the mess, this very same guy then yelled out:

'Sorry guys, I made a mistake, it was in the mashed potato.'

What an arsehole! He was probably just having a bit of fun but I can tell you, this really was a serious issue. Some of us belted the living shit out of him.

As it turns out, Bromide — or more correctly, Potassium Bromide — was never added to our meals and beverages at Nui Dat. It would appear that this long-held military myth has been legendary since the time of the Great War. However, duped as we surely were, we certainly felt strongly about what we suspected was being done to our youthful and vital manly body parts at that time.

DRINKING – ALCOHOL

There seems to be a widely held community view that most Vietnam veterans are alcoholics, and that drinking was a top priority during their deployment to Vietnam. While I can't comment on the generality of that view, I can talk about the interaction between alcohol and men of the 8 RAR Assault Pioneer Platoon during 1969-1970.

8 RAR was a classic infantry unit, so for the majority of time in Vietnam its various elements were out in the field; ergo, no alcohol. In relation to the Assault Pioneer Platoon, Appendix 7 sets out a time profile of the platoon's tasking in very clear detail. The platoon was only based at Nui Dat for 76 days. During the period of February-August 1970, it only spent 29 days at Nui Dat. On each of those days, and during the longer periods at the start and end of our time in Vietnam, we really did give the alcohol a nudge. Our short stints (collectively 4-6 days) in Vung Tau were hedonistic alcoholic —and sexual — interludes for many.

So, in regard to the wider definition of classic 'binge drinking', this should not adversely define veterans of my platoon because the frequency of this behaviour was only contained to relatively short periods of time. In my view, to characterise Vietnam veterans as 'drunken sots' is an abomination. However, to say that many of them once were, or may still be addicted to alcohol, is probably a reasonable proposition to put forward. On the other hand, my life experiences suggest that most Vietnam veterans consume alcohol daily, just as I do, but usually within controlled limits.

For obvious reasons, the Support Company boozer was our favourite hangout whenever we were based at Nui Dat. Because of the appalling climate, and for other good reasons, our boozer didn't open until 4:30pm and final drinks were served at 10pm. That gave us 5 hours or more to drink and relax over numerous icy cold cans of the good stuff.

Because 8 RAR was a Brisbane based unit, Fourex (XXXX) and USA brands such as Budweiser, Schlitz, and Blue Label, were the only beers available to us. Worse still, while they were served cold from the large and continuously-restocked boozer refrigerators, the cans were always opened. This ensured that hoarding for drinking back in our lines wasn't even remotely possible. How do you hoard an open-canned beer for later consumption in a climate like that of Vietnam? Well, the very simple answer to that question is…you can't.

Drinking alcohol outside of the confines of the boozer precinct was strictly banned. Doing so was considered a 'prevalent offence' and usually attracted a very severe punishment. This was largely accepted as a reasonable and inescapable fact of service life. And, for the most part, we observed this reasonable restriction on when and where we were permitted to consume alcohol. Beer and soft drinks were the only beverages available to us at the boozer.

The prescribed beer ration for those of us based at Nui Dat from time to time was 2 full strength 375ml cans per man, per day. However, as our beer ration accumulated — apparently — when we were out in the field, and because we had a small number of non-drinkers and some very light drinkers in our company, we always had an inexhaustible collective supply of beer available for the princely sum of $US0.10 per can.

During our entire time in Vietnam, we were paid in a form of substitute currency called 'Military Payment Certificates', the various denominations of which had a face value identical to that of the $US. I later talk much more about this ersatz currency, and how it, and the hard $US, significantly and generously impacted our lives.

According to the Reserve Bank of Australia (RBA), the average exchange rate of $A to $US during my time in Vietnam was consistently in the order of 0.81. So $US1.00 was worth $A1.23. Although this exchange rate wasn't the sole driver, our beer was incredibly cheap. By way of illustration, the Australian Bureau of Statistics (ABS) suggest that the cost — $A0.08 — for a can of beer in Vietnam, was about one quarter of the average cost — $A0.33 — of what was being paid back in Australia at the same time. And our generous, warlike operational service pay loading, combined with an all-encompassing Australian income tax exemption, resulted in a very healthy net income for us.

In addition, there were always large quantities of beer available for which we didn't have to pay for at all. The reasons for this are rather impossible to explain and I'm not even going to attempt to do so. But suffice to say, it was fairly easy, and inexpensive, to get absolutely shit-faced at the boozer, which most of us did on some occasions. And many did so over successive nights when we were back at Nui Dat. Some men — like me — did exactly this, on most nights. Those of us who were hardened drinkers — again, including myself — often used to forgo eating dinner at the mess because it intruded on our precious drinking time. Although the boozer didn't serve beer during evening mess time, we easily overcame this problem by acquiring 2 or 3 opened cans to last us during the temporary bar closure of about 45 minutes.

Usually the first night back at Nui Dat after an operation, was a time when we really gave the boozer a solid workout. We almost celebrated our sheer relief to be alive, relatively safe for a time, getting back to some form of functional normality, and being able to relax somewhat.

When deployed on any battalion operation, the level of concentration required, continual mental alertness, an almost complete absence of conversational interaction, a debilitating climate, filthy living conditions, a very poor diet, and the awareness that we may engage with the enemy at any time, collectively contributed to our extreme stress levels. Excessive drinking whenever we were back at Nui Dat, and even more so during those times we visited Vung Tau on 40-hour R&C withdrawals from operations, appeared to be a perfectly acceptable way to deal with this stress or anxiety; insidious mental conditions that seemed to significantly impact many of us, the longer we were in Vietnam.

At Nui Dat, there were a number of inducements — some subtle, others not so discreet — or pressures to drink alcohol. For example, it was tradition that you shouted the platoon on your birthday, or as close as possible to it, depending on what your platoon was doing in an operational sense at that particular time. You were also expected to get rollicking drunk. And, if your wife or girlfriend sent you a 'Dear John' letter — *'it's over, I'm leaving you. I've met someone else'* — you were made to pin that letter to the boozer notice board for everyone to read, just so they could take the piss out of you and make you feel even more miserable. You were also required to shout the platoon upon receipt of one of these demoralising letters of personal rejection. Observation of these boozer rules was mandatory and not negotiable.

A mate of mine in Anti-Tank and Tracker Platoon received a 'Dear John' letter from his mother. Apparently, he inadvertently sent her graphic, photographic colour slides, depicting close-up images of him having strange sex with a Vung Tau bar girl. I'm sorely tempted to state his name for the official record, but have decided not to do so. After he pinned that famous letter to the boozer notice board, we all read it and publicly belittled him. Hilarious for us at the time...poor bastard. Although he was a legend, what an idiot!

It was strongly rumoured that there was a beer reward provided to platoons by their commanders, for each confirmed enemy killed, and that some platoons maintained formal scorecards. I don't know if there's any truth to that rumour or not. However, I can confidently say that my 2 respective platoon commanders didn't for one moment engage in that sort of inappropriate behaviour, but there appeared to be very strong opinions amongst us that perhaps a couple of other commanders in the battalion did. None of my mates in other company platoons ever confirmed, or denied this rumour. I'd like to think this was baseless speculation but, at the time, the stories circulating in the 8 RAR Support Company boozer — even allowing for the flawed wisdom of alcohol — were very compelling indeed.

Apart from sex, sport, music, and motor vehicles, boozer talk at Nui Dat was occasionally centred around nasty operational happenings. Sometimes it was basic, gross talk indeed, and very uncivilised. I must admit that although I happily entered and participated in some of these obscene drunken conversations, I always felt somewhat uneasy about this open chattering. However, I'm certain that it occurred, to a greater or lesser degree, amongst the platoons of all allied infantry battalions in Vietnam. I do know that many of the US Army infantry commanders were completely obsessed with body count metrics. Their misguided reasoning was based on this sort of spurious logic:

> *'If we kill 100 enemy and lose only 35 men in the process, then we have won that contest. And, if we keep doing that every day, then we will eventually win this war'.*

There were a few guys in Support Company who were budding musicians and they'd acquired several stringed instruments and a couple of harmonicas. There may have been a few kettle drums as well...I can't remember now. A couple of these men were pretty good vocalists. I used to seriously urge them to play and sing my favourite song — and it still is — 'The Midnight Special' by USA band Creedence Clearwater Revival.[20] When I was pleasantly inebriated, absorbing renditions of this musical work of art always ameliorated another

---

[20] Released by Fantasy Records in November 1969. Album: *Willy and the Poor Boys*.

difficult day for me…in shit-hole Vietnam. It's probably not the band's highest rating song but, at that time in my life, it was an absolute winner for me. All these decades later, I still access the song on YouTube about once a month, and listening to it always takes me back to my life as an infantry soldier in that wretched place.

A week or so after ANZAC Day 1970 — about 4 May — when we were back at Nui Dat for a couple of days of rest between operations, I was roughly woken from a deep sleep just before dawn — 6am — by my platoon sergeant, Monty White. He was lugging around a seriously large stainless-steel container full of a mix of steaming-hot black coffee and rum, in about equal proportions — for us to partake of — and belatedly celebrate the iconic Australian national day of veteran observance. Well, that was worth waking up for!

Along with my tent mates, McGrath, and Small, I avidly devoured this alcoholic breakfast — that Monty generously ladled several times over — into our operational 600mm aluminium field mugs. What a fantastic way to start the day. I've never since consumed that much concentrated alcohol at this early hour. But I do have to say that it was a well-appreciated gesture of comradeship by Monty, and recognition by him, and ourselves, of our veteran forebears.

Along with most of my platoon mates, I never understood Monty or became anywhere near 'close' to him. He was a very difficult man to get to know. Although early morning hot rum and coffee on ANZAC Day was a long-standing army tradition, his attempt to break down the barriers between us was as close as I ever got to him in a personal sense. I'm sure that many of my platoon mates would agree with me. I used to go out of my way to avoid any interaction with him. Indeed, many of us shunned him, almost as if he had the plague or leprosy.

By the end of our 12 months in Vietnam, very few of us were what any reasonably civilised person might regard as 'normal'. We were a nervous and testy bunch of guys, many of whom appeared to be addicted to alcohol — to some degree or another — whether it be intermittent, short periods of drinking, or longer sessions of consistent, slower alcohol consumption. I have no doubt whatsoever that I was a founding member of both of those cohorts, and I was easily able to transition between them.

When we returned to Australia, I'd say that a fair number of us were probably not in any proper mental state to re-engage with the Australian community, or re-enter the general workforce. In reality, some of us were nothing short of dangerous. Did we think that we were like that? Of course not!

It seemed perfectly clear to me that the army recognised alcohol consumption as an acceptable way for its combat soldiers to unwind and de-stress after an operation. Other than on one disastrous, very short-lived and never repeated occasion — 8 August 1970 — whilst celebrating the birthday of the battalion — the 8 RAR command group didn't ever attempt to seriously moderate the consumption of alcohol by its Support Company soldiers. And that was probably the same for the other companies of the battalion as well. I'm sure some of you may find that to be very unfair criticism of the 8 RAR command group. Well, I'm sorry, but that's how it appeared to me at the time, and my view on this has never changed.

Having said that, not one of us was concerned by this. As soldiers, and as supremely fit young men, we all thought that drinking huge volumes of cheap beer was a wonderful way to de-stress and relax without ever thinking — not even for one moment — about the long-term adverse health and social implications that have affected so many Vietnam veterans in their later lives.

While I generally subscribe to the proposition that *'all men are masters of their own destiny'* — often uttered by my very erudite father — I have no doubt that the consumption of massive amounts of alcohol, over short periods of time, was instrumental in large numbers of Vietnam veterans becoming variably dependent on alcohol. The fact that alcohol was so readily available and so cheap in Vietnam, simply made the eventual problem far more acute for many of us.

I returned home to Australia as a confirmed drinker and alcohol is an irritating addiction that I've lived with, and constantly struggled against, for much of my subsequent life. Although I don't fully blame the army for this, I don't absolve it from its major and complicit responsibility either.

DVA recognised many decades ago that alcohol addiction is a major factor in terms of the comparatively poor medium and long-term health of many Vietnam veterans.

SLEEPING

Whenever we were based at Nui Dat, we spent a large amount of our time sleeping, or at least trying to. In Vietnam, noting very minor seasonal variations, the sun rose at around 6am and set at about 6pm. Every day we were up and about, showered, and ready for breakfast at the Support Company mess at 7am. From around 8am until lunch at noon, we were engrossed in a range of activities such as weapons and equipment maintenance, firing-off obsolete ammunition, maintenance of the landscapes surrounding our lines, and a range of other mundane tasks — some understandable, and others utterly pointless. Mostly though, we seemed to have the afternoons to ourselves. So, what did we do when we had time on our hands?

Well, we retired to our shared tents and took a nap — probably from around 1:30-3pm. And, even if we were giving the alcohol a touch-up in the boozer before and after dinner at the Support Company mess, we were still getting 8 or so hours sleep during the night. Many of us were racking-up 10 hours or more, in every 24-hour day. So, why did we sleep so much at Nui Dat? I'll tell you why.

When out in the field, sleep became a rare and precious commodity. When based at fire support bases or night defensive positions there was always the need to man all perimeter defences from just before sunset until after dawn. This task was often undertaken in pairs and occasionally singularly. Sentry shifts could be as short as 2.5 hours, or as long as 4 hours. The number of men available determined the length of the sentry schedules. Throughout the day, the manning of sentry points was much less intense, but still a constant imposition on our time and mental health.

When we weren't based in fire support bases or night defensive positions, night-time ambushing was always put in place and 3-hour sentry shifts on the M60 machine guns were routine. I vividly recall that on a couple of occasions, my sentry shifts were 4 hours. And, to make matters worse, because of the revolting climatic conditions, it was almost impossible to doze off before 11pm. So, if you were allocated the 12pm-3am shift, the chances of catching more than a couple hours of sleep that night weren't good. Many of us became chronically sleep deprived. So, Nui Dat really did become a sleep haven for many of us.

Numerous infantry veterans have suffered from varying degrees of insomnia since their time in Vietnam. On a personal note, this health issue is one that I've consistently dealt with for all of my post-military service life. To this very day, no matter what time I retire to bed, I still wake up just before 5am. I don't need an alarm clock.

BREAKING, ENTERING AND STEALING

The Assault Pioneer Platoon had a secure store facility, which — from around mid-May 1970 — was managed, and lived-in, by our platoon storeman, Mark Smith. Although he was a regular sort of guy, I didn't become all that friendly with him. Nevertheless, his very important job as our platoon storeman was to maintain our lines whenever we were out in the field, send out our mail, replacement clothing, ammunition, water, rations, and anything else we needed on scheduled, or otherwise emergent re-supplies. His job was an extremely important and necessary one for the entire platoon. In reality, it was a vital platoon role.

At Nui Dat one night I decided towards the looming end of a marathon drinking session at the boozer, to break into the platoon store — making sure of course that Smith was preoccupied back at the boozer — and pilfer some 1L bottles of spirits. We knew there was a stash he'd been acquiring from the

US PBX Store at Nui Dat, and hoarding for later shipment back to Australia. I had no trouble whatsoever in recruiting a couple of very good mates of mine to help me in this clandestine endeavour. While I was the actual architect and prime felon, my eager partners in crime — in terms of receiving and disposing of the liquid proceeds that night — were Des McGrath and — who else — Mick O'Shea.

With precision planning and relative quietness — quite remarkable given my already grossly-drunken state — along with McGrath and O'Shea riding 'shotgun' for me, I easily breached the locked door of the store and gathered up 3 or 4 — I really can't remember — bottles of Bacardi rum and Johnny Walker whisky. Carrying my ill-gotten gains, I staggered — perhaps 80m — amid torrential rain to the banana copse, adjacent to our lines, and was met shortly afterwards by McGrath and O'Shea who, in the interim, had acquired half a carton of opened soft drink cans for mixers, as well as three 600ml aluminium mugs. We were all set to go! Seriously...even decades later, the reality of this infamous night still horrifies me.

So, before settling in for this hedonistic drinking session, we slowly slid down the slimy banks into the watercourse below — about waist deep and steadily rising. It was, in fact, a rudimentary but fully-functioning stormwater drain that ran through our lines and the adjacent banana copse. Did we care? Not at all. What could be better than sitting with your mates in a deceptively dangerous, fast flowing, turbid drain, amid a constant precipitation deluge of some magnitude, while drinking spirits and warm soft drink in a mix of about 1:1? Was drowning a possibility? Well, on reflection now...it almost certainly was.

There we were, 3 pathetically drunk young men, drinking ourselves into an even greater alcoholic stupor. I vaguely remember passing out once or twice, then waking and profusely vomiting several times. It's a wonder I didn't die that night from alcohol poisoning or, more likely, from drowning.

Anyway, we must have been making a noise that only inebriated young men make, because at about 12:30am we were rudely — thankfully, I'd now say — disturbed by our platoon commander, 2LT Peter Phillips, and our platoon sergeant, Cliff Grant. Upon hearing our raucous voices — or perhaps we were reported missing, I'll never know — with torches in hand, they finally located us. We were indeed busted!

Anyway, Mr Phillips ordered us to go straight to the shower block, undress, shower, and to leave our red, mud-sodden clothes on the floor. After showering, vomiting, showering, and then vomiting again — it was around 1am or thereabouts — McGrath, O'Shea and I staggered, and at times crawled — completely naked — back to our tents under the almost paternal guidance of Sergeant Grant. We then collapsed into our beds, fully expecting to be formally charged by Mr Phillips the following morning. O'Shea's tent was only a short distance from McGrath's and mine.

Within 8 RAR, drinking alcohol in the lines, effectively outside the confines of the official company boozer, was a 'prevalent offence' — something that we were all very much aware of — and one that attracted severe punishment. Serious offenses of this sort were usually dealt with by the company commander and sometimes even by the battalion commander. It was conceivable that the 3 of us might receive a custodial sentence of incarceration in the 1 ALSG military prison in Vung Tau.

Custodial sentences at this prison were usually for 7 days minimum. So, by my drunken mental reckoning, we were going to get at least 7 days of hard labour — if not more — in the 'slammer' at Vung Tau, where we'd be engaged in a never-ending process of relocating wet sand from point A to point B, then back to point A. Or we may be included in a 'chain gang' production line, where we'd spend each day doing nothing other than filling, emptying, then refilling 27kg capacity sandbags with wet sand. All of this likely physical punishment activity was focused on nothing other than endless earthmoving. And, as you know, this was something that I wasn't remotely interested in, or good at. As drunk as McGrath and I were, while being helped into our beds by our tent mate Allan Small, my subconscious awareness already vaguely alerted me to what earthmoving horrors might be about to befall me.

At 8am next morning, the entire platoon was paraded in 2 ranks in front of the Assault Pioneer Platoon store. This was our usual morning form-up point after breakfast at the Support Company mess. McGrath, O'Shea, and I — after giving breakfast a miss — were ordered to stand together by ourselves in a third rank, in front of the formed-up platoon. Sergeant Grant then informed the assembled platoon that on the previous night, the platoon store was broken into and many bottles of spirits were stolen. What did he mean by 'many'? I knew that it was probably only 3 bottles at most, not that I really knew how many I actually pilfered. Realistically, I couldn't have carried more than 3 bottles anyway. Sergeant Grant then ordered the perpetrators of this break and enter, and subsequent theft, to step forward. Not one of us in the parade moved at all.

Sergeant Grant then asked, in turn, for McGrath, O'Shea, and myself to take one step forward from the 3-member front rank — because he knew damn well that we were the culprits — and individually asked each of us what we knew about this robbery. While I can't speak for McGrath or O'Shea, I was still completely drunk at the time and feeling awful. I was hardly capable of standing upright, let alone thinking lucidly and logically. Anyway, each of us denied any knowledge of the break and enter robbery.

While this cursory interrogation by Sergeant Grant seemed to be going nowhere, I was suddenly startled when I saw our platoon commander, Mr

Phillips, casually leaning against a tree near his tent, observing all of this. Even though he was also well aware of the fact that we were the perpetrators, he never said a word, or otherwise intervened in Sergeant Grant's interrogation of us.

As I was somehow just managing to suppress the overwhelming urge to projectile vomit all over Sergeant Grant's ugly, scowling visage, it suddenly dawned on me that if Mr Phillips were to have been presented with a 'fait accompli' — in terms of admissions or dependable independent witness' testimony to this break, enter, and robbery — then he would have had no option other than to deal with it according to army standard operating procedures of the day. I quickly realised that perhaps my good luck had just arrived, because it was now clear that Mr Phillips wasn't going to personally intervene in Sergeant Grant's interrogation of us, unless he had no alternative. Anyway, that was my theory on that infamous morning. Suddenly, I liked Mr Phillips a hell of a lot more than I had previously. Anyway, end result, we continued to profess our innocence and without any admissions, all the angst surrounding this break and enter robbery seemed to swiftly disappear.

However, while my personal observations at the time seemed to accord with my naïve understanding of army discipline, there was a far more important reason why McGrath, O'Shea, and I didn't end up being charged that morning, because undoubtedly, we should have been. Admissions by us weren't necessary. We'd been well and truly caught 'red-handed' by Mr Phillips and Sergeant Grant, with much of the 'not yet imbibed stolen goods' still in our possession. That was ample evidence for a conviction on any associated charge.

When talking about this incident with my former platoon commander, Mr Phillips, in very recent times, I discovered that the reason we weren't charged that morning was simply due to the very low complement of available personnel in the Assault Pioneer Platoon at that time. Apparently, the platoon was down to something like 23 or 24 men available for operations, which meant he couldn't afford to be deprived of 3 more men — doing hard labour in the Vung Tau 'slammer' for a minimum of 7 days — when the platoon was ready to deploy from Nui Dat in a day or so, on a new and important operation.

Although this robbery issue was never officially solved, I made sure that Smith knew I was the ringleader. There was no need for secrecy because everyone else in the platoon, including Smith, knew who the culprits were anyway.

Smith was probably a pretty good guy, but for some reason or another, he and I just didn't connect. Having said that, he contacted me by phone when I was back in Canberra some 3 years later and we had an interesting and pleasant conversation for an hour or so. Hopefully, I'll meet up with him again one day. I'm sure that I'll like him a lot.

OTHER DRUNKEN EVENTS

On one very rare occasion when I was at Nui Dat, I decided not to go to the boozer after dinner at the mess. Instead, I had an early night after coming back from the open-air movies. At around 10pm or so, not long after the boozer closed, I was rudely woken by my good mate Mick O'Shea. He was holding up the mosquito net over my bed and pissing all over me, while I lay there gasping for breath amid the stifling ambience. This display of real 'mateship' between O'Shea and I quickly developed into a full-blown fist fight just outside my tent, with 4 or 5 of our communal mates urging us on. It was a very unfair contest because O'Shea was completely drunk, whereas I, amazingly, wasn't totally consumed by alcohol. And, as I always slept naked at Nui Dat — as did most of us — I'm not even sure if I was wearing any boxer shorts or undies during this physical altercation. I hope I was!

Anyway, after a few minutes of trading maybe 20 or 30 decent blows to our heads and bodies, our mates managed to calm us down and we ended this ridiculous brawl. O'Shea and I must have heads made of steel because during this very serious joust, we each received several thunderous blows from one another. Next morning, my left hand wasn't in great shape so I knew that it must have been one hell of a punch-up. I never liked fist-fighting because my hands weren't well-designed for that sort of physical contest. They always ended up as collateral damage.

O'Shea and I never, ever, discussed this incident afterwards — seriously — and we remained firm, rock-solid, good friends. Although in different sections of the platoon, we'd become very close after an ugly incident in Vung Tau one night — which I talk about later — and we particularly enjoyed our marathon drinking sessions together in this dangerous Vietnamese city.

ENTERTAINMENT

Though it was for the most part, Nui Dat wasn't only a binge-drinking beer fest. It had an open-air movie venue — a natural amphitheatre if you like — at the eastern end of the Luscombe Field airstrip. We could wander down at night, take along a fold-up chair and our personal weapons, and watch recent movie releases and occasional replays of recent sporting events held back in Australia. It was very much like the hugely popular drive-in movies of those times, just without the cars and, worse still, without the girls. From the Assault Pioneer Platoon lines, it was a trek of about 600m.

Once or twice I took in a movie instead of drinking at the Support Company boozer and remember watching a replay of the 1970 VFL — now AFL — grand final where Carlton — in front of 121,696 fans at the MCG (Melbourne Cricket Ground) — came back from a half-time deficit of 44 points to defeat

Collingwood in the last quarter by 10 points. Ted Hopkins, a 68kg fringe player, came on at half-time for Carlton and kicked 4 goals in that famous game — 3 within the first 15 minutes of the 3rd quarter — which was otherwise notable for the most renowned leaping overhead mark of all time, by one of Carlton's iconic heroes, Alex Jesaulenko.

Amazingly, Hopkins played just one further game for Carlton. In total, he only played 29 games of VFL football and kicked an overall total of 10 goals during his very short career. He retired from football before he was 22-years-of-age to pursue other personal and business interests. What an enigma! How good is that? It's called doing things on your own terms.

Adjacent to our open-air movies venue on the southern perimeter of the eastern end of Luscombe Field, 1 Field Squadron, Royal Australian Engineers (RAE), constructed an elaborate stage for the hosting of entertainer concert parties. Interestingly, one of my very good neighbours in the townhouse complex where I now live, Brig (then Capt.) Grahame Hellyer Retd, oversaw the structural design of this stage, which later become known as Luscombe Bowl. Unfortunately, he was severely injured in a Bell Sioux helicopter hard-landing crash on 2 June 1967, and was medevac'd back to Australia before it was constructed. The first concert party held at Luscombe Bowl took place in October that year. Grahame is a really nice guy and we interact socially from time to time.

There were several civilian entertainer concerts held at Luscombe Bowl during my time in Vietnam. I have to say that I didn't see any of them. I don't know if I decided not to attend any of these concerts because they would have interfered with my imbibing in the boozer, or because we happened to be out in the field on operations whenever they were held. I suspect the answer is that we weren't there when they were held, otherwise I'm sure that I would have attended at least one of them. However, as some of my former platoon mates do recall attending at least one of these concert parties, I guess I must have been more interested in drinking beer at the boozer than watching quality, live entertainment.

Nevertheless, these concerts were hugely popular and the various entertainers and those who made tours to Vietnam, have the undying admiration of Vietnam veterans. All told, some 364 Australian entertainers toured Vietnam and performed at Nui Dat and other locations. Many of these entertainers toured the country on multiple occasions.

Interestingly, it's a recorded historical fact that as the Battle of Long Tan unfolded in the late afternoon on 18 August 1966, such a concert featuring 'Little Patty' and 'Col Joy and the Joy Boys' was in full swing at Nui Dat. Understandably this concert was quickly aborted and the performers were swiftly relocated by Iroquois helicopters to a much safer location at Vung Tau.

DISCARDED AMMUNITION

We frequently replaced the ammunition and magazines for our personal weapons for all sorts of reasons; rust being the main concern I'd suggest. Within our lines at Nui Dat we had a large, lockable, walk-in, heavy-duty steel container that — along with the platoon's M60 machine guns, M18 Claymore anti-personnel directional mines, large quantities of ammunition, slabs of C4 plastic explosive, and a range of other assorted pyrotechnics — was also full of rusty ammunition and plenty of unusable ordinance. This secure container served as the platoon's arsenal and was sort of like a combined refrigerator and trash can.

One afternoon towards the very end of my time in Vietnam, probably around late October 1970, I was half asleep in my tent at Nui Dat, almost comatose from the heat and humidity that was enveloping me. Then, I was woken by a loud summons from Sergeant Grant, to meet him at the platoon arsenal. Joining me there was Peter Wood. This was a very rare occasion when my practice of 'not being noticed' failed dismally.

The sergeant ordered us both to dig a 4m² hole, 0.5m deep. While we did this, he chose items from the vast array of rusty ammunition and other obsolete pieces ensconced in the platoon arsenal. As experienced and very compliant infantry soldiers, Wood and I followed Sergeant Grant's orders without question. As you're aware, earthmoving wasn't one of my military strengths and this hole — as small as it appears — was still a large hole. Well, to me it was.

Wood and I, given the soft, pliable nature of the soil, completed this task in about 45 minutes. I then ambled back to my tent. Within a few minutes, Wood and I were again summoned by Sergeant Grant and ordered to reclaim the ammunition and other ordinance that we had just placed in the hole.

Apparently, our platoon commander decided that he would prefer the contents be destroyed by explosives. That was fine with me. I liked working with explosives anyway. However, nothing was ever that simple in the Australian Army in 1970. Over the next few hours, Sergeant Grant had Wood and I burying, reclaiming, burying, and reclaiming this rusty ammunition and other obsolete ordinance, as he and the platoon commander disagreed over how to dispose of it. Eventually, Wood and I both told Sergeant Grant that he could do what he liked with it...and suggested that perhaps he could even consider sticking it right up his arse!

Amazingly, I wasn't charged for this overt display of insubordination. Nor was my accomplice, Wood. Not that we were too worried about it anyway. Given the circumstances, I think it would have been extremely difficult for my platoon commander to impose anything more than a token penalty on us.

During my time in the army, the lack of common sense at its most basic level, sometimes defied reason and logic. In any event, the very next day Wood and I destroyed this rusty ammunition and other obsolete ordinance with the use of explosives, which was always the most sensible way of disposing of it.

ASSAULT PIONEER PLATOON PET — 'RACHEL'

Almost from our first days at Nui Dat, the 8 RAR Assault Pioneer Platoon had a pet — or mascot — that lived with us for a time. She was cared for by our platoon storeman whenever we were out in the field on operations. Or, if the storeman was out in the field with the rest of the platoon, which he was from time to time, she had to fend for herself. It's a wonder she never left the confines of our lines.

This pet, Rachel, was a female baby bear of unknown origin and unknown species. While there was a broad consensus amongst us that she was likely a honey bear, none of us really had any idea. I have some sort of vague recollection that we inherited Rachel shortly after we replaced the 9 RAR Assault Pioneer Platoon in late November 1969, but some of my platoon mates think that she was left abandoned in the field — after an early night-time ambush by another 8 RAR element, during which her mother was accidentally killed — and eventually found her way to our lines at Nui Dat. How we ended up 'owning' her doesn't really matter. She was our platoon pet…our baby bear, and we all loved her.

Rachel was about the size of a small koala bear and, for a time, equally as cuddly. She used to faithfully follow us to the boozer and once there, paw at our legs to encourage us to pick her up and cuddle her. She was incredibly friendly and lovable. Naturally we introduced Rachel to beer, and poured cans of it down her throat. My good friend Bob Simpson was the main culprit here. Nevertheless, it was all in playful fun. Rachel never seemed to complain, even on occasions when she was almost too drunk to walk, as she followed us back to our lines. During the early weeks of her life with us, Rachel loved us, and we certainly loved her. However, this 'love-match made in heaven' didn't last. When we inherited her, she was just a baby. And like all babies, Rachel rapidly grew in size. She quickly developed her innate, cunning instincts and soon became an absolute pest and a destructive presence within our living areas at Nui Dat.

Her transition from a small cuddly animal, whom we'd routinely pick up and cuddle, into a relatively large, very clever, uncontrollable, and insatiably-gluttonous scavenger with large claws and powerful crushing teeth, that she would use efficiently when ransacking our tents in search of food, didn't take too long at all. She even managed to inflict a rather nasty bite on Peter Cousins,

Chapter 16 – 1st Australian Task Force (1 ATF) - Nui Dat

and I was really happy about that. Knowing Cousins, he would have deserved it. Also, Rachel defecated, literally, wherever she was at the time, whenever she felt the need to do so, and that was pretty much all the time. She left her copious mounds of excrement everywhere throughout our lines, and often on the floors of our tented living quarters.

Around late February 1970 back at Nui Dat — after medical evacuation from the field, and following the extraction of my wisdom tooth — Rachel almost drove me crazy. At that time, she probably weighed something like 30kg. She was still a very friendly and social animal, and as the rest of my platoon was still out in the field, she must have been lonely. Now, I have to ask…what was Arthur Koo — our storeman — doing at that time? In our absence from Nui Dat, he was supposed to be her official keeper.

Over these 2 days, Rachel couldn't enter the fully-enclosed platoon store where Koo lived and slept, so she made herself at home in my tent, socialising with me, completely shredding my mosquito net, and shitting copiously all over the floor. She was a complete and utter pest. As I still wasn't feeling on top of the world after my dental surgery, I was in no mood to deal with her. At the same time, her large and expressive eyes reflected complete animal innocence. It was impossible not to like Rachel.

However, at the end of the day, as she continued to grow in size, keeping her as a pet became completely untenable. We couldn't properly feed her, let alone care for her. Even the invisible man, Arthur Koo, could no longer manage her. When we eventually traded Rachel to a US Army unit for about 20 cases of beer — delivered by a USAF Iroquois helicopter to the open green area some 200m from our lines — she weighed something like 45kg. She was no longer the cuddly bear that we first inherited…she had turned into a monster!

On balance, it was a very good trade for those of us who have no conscience. On the downside though, Rachel's long-term chances of survival were probably quite low, and we were all sad when she left Nui Dat. Seriously, there were some tears as we waved goodbye to her, and I reckon I was the one who probably cried the most.

CHAPTER 17

WEAPONS

During my time in Vietnam, Australian infantry soldiers were equipped with a range of personal weapons and other armaments that — for the most part — reflected innovative military weapons technology of the day.

SLR L1 A1 RIFLE

While the US Army may have waxed lyrically about the M16 Armalite rifle, which did have some attractive features — and was standard issue for its infantry units — and, in limited numbers made available to Australian infantry units, it wasn't a patch on the SLR rifle generally used by most Australian infantry soldiers in Vietnam, as their primary personal weapon. For example, within the 8 RAR Assault Pioneer Platoon, there would have been no more than 8 or 9 Armalite rifles on issue. In my section there were only 2.

The SLR rifle was an Australian[21] version of the Belgian FN FAL rifle originally developed, manufactured, and marketed in that country by the Fabrique Nationale Company. Over time, this wonderful weapon was widely brought into operational service by the military forces of more than 70 countries and manufactured locally under licence by quite a number of them as well, including Australia. It still remains in use throughout some emerging 3rd World countries of today, because it really is that good a weapon.

Aside from being highly dependable it was a hard-hitting, semi-automatic, magazine-fed, gas-operated, air-cooled rifle capable of firing rapid, accurate, single shots of 7.62mm x 51mm (7.62mm long) 147 grain NATO rounds from quick-changing, bottom-fed, 20-round magazines. The rifle weighed 4.45kg unloaded, and 5.18kg when loaded with a full magazine. Although comparatively heavy, it was such a well-balanced weapon that it was very easy to carry. Even though it had an optional shoulder sling, we only used it on ceremonial occasions. It also had a carry handle — positioned at the 'sweet spot' — that was never used out in the field. With a highly accurate range of well over 600m, it had an effective, sustainable rate of fire of 20rpm.

---

[21] Small Arms Factory Lithgow, NSW.

Chapter 17 — Weapons

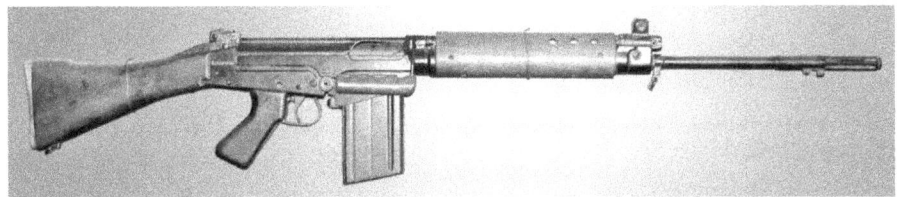

SLR L1 A1 Rifle.

Spent rounds casings, along with gas and powder residue, were ejected from the right side of the rifle making it — so it was said — potentially difficult for left-handed soldiers to use. However, even though I'm chronically left-handed, I had no problem whatsoever using the SLR rifle.

The one difficulty I experienced was in cocking it. That is, when drawing up an initial round from the attached magazine into the breech or firing chamber, or when clearing a round with the magazine removed. The rifle had to be cocked each time a new magazine was clipped in place underneath. The cocking lever was positioned on the left side of the rifle, as you would expect for right-handed users. So, when holding it in the firing position with my left hand grasped around the rear, backwards-sloping under handgrip, and with my right hand supporting the horizontal forward stock, I had to release my right hand and turn the weapon upside down with my left hand, to then cock it with my free, right hand.

Although this practice would have undoubtedly offended the purists, it wasn't a problem for me at all. As the trajectory of the spent rounds casings and other firing residue ejection was at almost 90° to the right side of the rifle, there was no issue there either. By the time I embarked for Vietnam, this personal adaptation of the cocking procedure for my rifle had become second nature. I didn't even have to think about what I was doing; it simply became an automatic action…almost an embedded component of my military DNA genome.

During our utterly pointless drill exercises at Puckapunyal and those occasional formal parades with 8 RAR, which I couldn't deftly avoid, I always performed as a right-handed soldier. I didn't have any other choice. For example, how could I *'for inspection, port arms'* in any way other than that observed by a right-handed soldier? The answer is, I couldn't. Although my serious left-handedness would have been blatantly evident at the various weapons firing ranges, the DIs at Recruit Training, the 8 RAR training cadre, and all members of my platoon never said anything about it. Seriously, not even once!

The SLR rifle was a particularly easy weapon to aim over any distance. The rear aperture sight was a hinged, vertical, oblong tab of metal, about 2.25cm high and 1cm wide, located on the rear, uppermost part of the rifle, behind the breach and other working components. This metal tab could be quickly lowered or raised. Towards the top of this metal tab was a centrally-located hollow circle, the diameter of which was slightly more than about half the width of the tab. When the rifle was brought to bear, with the stock hard up against the shoulder, the rear sight was very close to the user's aiming eye — the left eye in my case.

When aiming the rifle, the idea was to position the profile of the top of the vertical front post sight — positioned on the uppermost forward part of the protruding rifle stock — in the exact centre of the hole of the rear sight. With a properly zeroed rifle this would make the aiming true. After a while we became quite adept at being able to quickly bring our rifles to bear, that is, correctly aimed. However, as I've said before…and I'm sure I will say over and again, precision accuracy in Vietnam wasn't what that conflict was all about. Mostly, it was about concentrated fire into the killing ground and always over very short distances – generally 40m maximum.

As the primary personal weapon of Australian infantry soldiers in Vietnam, the SLR rifle was generally carried by 5 or 6 men in each 10-man section (3) of a rifle platoon. The remaining members of each section carried either a fully-automatic M16 Armalite rifle or the M60 machine gun as their primary weapons, augmented by one M79 40mm grenade launcher for each section. The bearer of this latter weapon also had to carry his personal weapon — an SLR rifle — as well.

The SLR rifle had a relatively low muzzle velocity of 840m/s but, given the large round it fired, it delivered what was called 'stopping power'. In other words, if you were hit in the head or the body — particularly centre mass — by a 7.62mm round, fired from either the SLR rifle or M60 machine gun, you were going to be in a lot of serious trouble. Because of its size and low muzzle velocity, the round didn't deflect when it hit bone — it just kept going right through whatever it encountered, causing an enormous cavitation-effect along the way. It didn't generally inflict flesh wounds. If the round didn't kill you outright, it basically delivered horrific and often fatal injuries, accompanied by horrendous exit wounds. And there were always exit wounds from a low muzzle velocity 7.62mm round. If you hit an enemy soldier with this round, then he was most definitely out of the fight.

In many Hollywood western movies of decades past, there's often a headline scene depicting a gunfighter being hit by a round, fired from a high-calibre low muzzle velocity pistol at close range — say 15m — then he clutches his chest and falls forward onto the ground. With the SLR rifle, this simply didn't happen. The kinetic energy contained within a just-fired 7.62mm round, which transferred on impact with a human body at close range, was so powerful that the recipient was always thrown backwards. And, more likely than not, the target would be blown completely off his feet, particularly if the impact was at centre mass. I talk about the respective kinetic energy properties of some weapons commonly used by Australian infantry soldiers in Vietnam, later in this story.

Anecdotally, Australian infantry soldiers were universally feared by their Vietnamese enemy. In addition to their military professionalism and bravery, consistently displayed by them in Vietnam over an extended period, our enemy combatants also had to contend with a personal weapon that delivered a devastating punch — in concert with its even more effective partner, the M60 machine gun. After one particular 8 RAR contact with the enemy, retrieved documents confirmed a clear reflection of the high esteem that our enemy bestowed on the battalion's fighting men.

Each of the 3 sections of the Assault Pioneer Platoon had 2 forward scouts or, in US army jargon, 'men on point'. In my section of the platoon — No.1 Section — Steve Kaliczinski always carried an M16 Armalite rifle. Peter Wood, our other forward scout, only ever carried an SLR rifle. As far as I'm aware, their weapon types were based on personal preference.

The SLR rifle was an extremely effective and reliable weapon that Australian soldiers liked. I always maintained mine in pristine condition. When out in the field, it was common for me to clean and oil it 3 times a day, or more. Let's face it…in any potentially nasty moment, I didn't want it to ever fail me. And it never did. Weapons maintenance only took a few minutes on each occasion anyway.

M16 ARMALITE RIFLE

The M16 Armalite rifle — an upgraded military version of the Colt Armalite AR 15 rifle — was standard US Army issue for its infantry soldiers. It was a fully-automatic, magazine-fed, gas-operated, air-cooled rifle that allowed a soldier to fire continuous bursts, or rapid accurate single shots of 5.56mm x 45mm (5.56mm) 62 grain rounds from quick-changing, bottom-fed, 20-round magazines. It weighed 2.89kg unloaded, and 3.24kg when loaded with a full 20-round magazine. It had an effective, accurate range of greater than 550m.

Late during the Vietnam conflict, a 30-round magazine was introduced by the US Army for this fine weapon. However, only 1,000 magazines of this type were ever manufactured, and I imagine that most of that arsenal would have been directed towards its combat elements. If some of these magazines were provided to 1 ATF units, it almost certainly would only have been to the AATTV or the SASR.

Spent round casings, along with gas and powder residue, were ejected backwards from the right side of this rifle at an angle more acute than 45°.

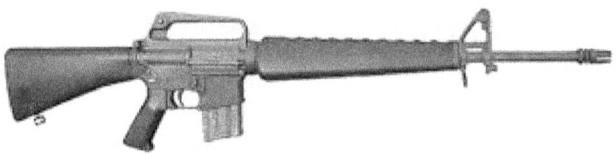

M16 Armalite Rifle.

This made it very difficult for left-handed soldiers to use. I always experienced problems when using this weapon during infantry corps training, due to this extreme backwards trajectory of the spent rounds casings ejection. For example, during range shooting practice, the hot, spent rounds casings would invariably eject onto my right cheek. Ergo, I never carried this rifle in Vietnam.

Compared to the SLR rifle and the M60 machine gun, the M16 Armalite rifle had a relatively high muzzle velocity of around 950m/s but, with its much smaller round, it didn't deliver anywhere near as much stopping power. In other words, if you were hit in the body by a 5.56mm round from an M16 Armalite rifle, it was probably going to be very nasty for you, but not necessarily fatal. Because of its relatively small size, and high muzzle velocity, the round often fragmented when hitting bone, so flesh wounds were common. The round had to hit vital organs to be fatal, and this often occurred when the round or fragments of it moved with very high speed throughout the target's body. It was all quite variable. Significant exit wounds from a high velocity 5.56mm round were uncommon.

On balance though, it was an effective personal weapon...just not one that I ever aspired to carry. However, what the M16 Armalite rifle lacked in stopping power, compared to the SLR rifle, it made up for in its fully-automatic capability, and its far lighter weight. Officers, sergeants, section commanders, and most forward scouts usually carried this weapon.

PLATOON CAPABILITY AND FIREPOWER

In Vietnam, an Australian infantry platoon at full operational strength consisted of 3 sections of 10 men: a storeman, and a headquarters or command group comprising the platoon commander (LT), a sergeant, a signaller, and sometimes a batman (personal assistant for the platoon commander). All up, that was 34 men. For all sorts of reasons, the 8 RAR Assault Pioneer Platoon was never at full strength during its entire time in Vietnam, not even when it departed Brisbane on HMAS *Sydney*. Some of its sections routinely operated with 8 or less men. My section only ever comprised 9 men, and even as few as 8 for some periods of time. Collectively, the platoon never operated with more than 29 men, and this included the platoon headquarters (PHQ) contingent of 3 (later 4) and the storeman.

Chapter 17 — Weapons

Shortly after he took over command of the platoon on 5 April 1970, 2LT Peter Phillips called me aside one morning at Nui Dat and in a private conversation said that he'd like me to become his 'batman'. This would entail collaborating very closely with him, within PHQ. I politely declined his offer and lived in dread — desperately hiding from him for a few days — very much aware of the fact that he could have simply ordered me to assume this role within the platoon.

I had no genuine issues regarding the role of batman, and there were certainly some attractions in terms of being a member of PHQ and working closely with him out in the field. My overriding concern was that in an operational context it would take me away from my mates in No.1 section, and from my close tent mates Des McGrath and Allan Small in particular. Other than that, I may well have agreed to this meaningful change in my role within the platoon. I guess if platoon numbers had been anywhere near full strength at the time, it may well have been a different — compulsory — outcome for me.

Mr Phillips also unsuccessfully tried to recruit John Dolgan to this role. In the event, Terry Lucas, who joined the platoon on 3 July 1969 as a reinforcement, became Mr Phillips' batman and as I recall, quite liked this role within PHQ. On reflection, I probably made a poor decision when I was offered this opportunity.

Given that our average platoon numbers were always well below standard operating strength, was there any firepower leverage available to offset this manpower shortage? Well, yes, there certainly was. And that came in the form of the M60 machine gun, one of which was carried by each of the platoon's 3 sections, and 2 of which were carried by each half-platoon squad — typically comprising 12-14 men. The heavy firepower that a platoon, or half-platoon squad could bring to bear on the enemy, came from these M60 machine guns. They were big, heavy brutes that weighed 10.5kg.

US Army infantry referred to this weapon as the 'Pig' or 'Hog' because according to them, when it was fired, its report sounded like the grunt of a barnyard hog. I'm not so sure that I can make that connection. Nevertheless, the name stuck and Australian infantry adopted this name as well. My recollection is that we called it the 'Pig', because of its weight.

M60 MACHINE GUN

The M60 machine gun was a fully-automatic gas-operated, air-cooled, belt-fed weapon that fired 7.62mm x 51mm (7.62mm long) 147 grain rounds. The standard ammunition mix for this gun was 4 ball-type (M80) rounds for each tracer (M62) round. The 4:1 ammunition mix allowed a gunner to adjust his fire at night by observing the fall of shot.

M60 Machine Gun.

The M60 machine gun had a muzzle velocity of 860m/s and its rate of continuous fire was around 600rpm from disintegrating, metallic, split-link belts. Because of its high rate of fire, its longer-range accuracy — effective out to only 1,100m — was significantly less than that of SLR and M16 Armalite rifles. Even at much shorter distances, its initial accuracy was somewhat problematic.

However, this wonderful weapon wasn't designed for precision accuracy. Its primary purpose was to deliver comparatively high-calibre, low muzzle velocity rounds onto a designated target, in either repetitive short bursts, or as a greater concentrated rate of fire. In other words its effectiveness was in the delivery of either suppressing defensive firepower or devastating offensive firepower.

Each belt of ammunition for the M60 machine gun contained 100 rounds and weighed 2.95kg. It was a heavy weapon and rather difficult to accurately aim without barrel ground support. For this reason it was generally fired from the prone position, using a forward bipod rest, in short repetitive bursts of 5 to 7 rounds.

The M60 machine gun, just like the SLR rifle, fired 7.62mm rounds. With a low muzzle velocity, large round, and its potential high rate of fire, it delivered enormous stopping power. In other words, if you were hit in the body by a swathe of 7.62mm rounds from the M60 machine gun, more likely than not, you were going to be literally cut in half. The M60 machine gun was a highly effective weapon. Although many of us sometimes complained about having to carry the heavy belts of ammunition for it, we really wouldn't have had it any other way.

It had an iron sighting line consisting of a non-adjustable post front sight, and an adjustable, flip-up rear graduated sight with an open notch. If it was placed in a fixed vice and fired at a target about 100m distant, the spread of strike of the rounds on the target would disperse over an elliptical circle of around a 1m diameter. This wasn't a fault of the weapon…it was simply designed to operate that way.

Aiming of the M60 machine gun didn't require too much precision. The idea was to aim just short of the target, determine the fall of shot from the dust, soil, and other debris being disturbed on the ground by the initial rounds fired, and then bring the barrel of the weapon up to bear on the target. In a close-range combat scenario, as was the norm in Vietnam, it was a devastating weapon indeed.

Chapter 17 — Weapons

Because the barrel of the M60 machine gun often became heated when rounds were fired in long bursts — or even fired in regular short bursts over an extended period — a spare barrel that weighed 3.74kg was carried by the No.2 on the gun. Barrels could be quickly changed.

The No.2 on the gun was an important member of the group and he carried belts of ammunition for the gun, as did most other section members. He also assisted with the interlocking of belts of ammunition and the feeding of them into the breach or firing chamber of the gun whenever it was used in any engagement with the enemy. The No.2 on the gun also carried his own SLR rifle, along with its ammunition. From time to time he also carried and operated the M60 machine gun. Gun groups worked as a team and their members usually became close mates. The section 2nd in command — a lance-corporal — was always very strongly associated with the gun group.

The M60 machine gun remains in operational service today, many decades after its extensive use in Vietnam, and is used by military forces in numerous 3rd World conflicts. The reason for this is simple. This weapon is no longer expensive and it's a dependable, very hard-hitting piece of infantry hardware.

During the second half of my time in Vietnam, the Assault Pioneer Platoon often operated as 2 discrete half-platoon squads, each of which comprised of between 12 and 14 men, rather than the classic 3 section platoon structure. In these instances, one squad was commanded by the platoon commander and the other by the platoon sergeant or, sometimes, by a senior section commander. Whenever we operated in this smaller capacity, a fourth M60 machine gun was always introduced into our armament capability: 2 guns for each squad.

On a disastrous 14-man night-time ambush on 12 January 1970, we had three M60 machine guns with us. I later describe this infamous ambush in more detail. The Assault Pioneer Platoon and other elements of the battalion, when operating in half-platoon strength, possessed enormous firepower for such small, self-contained operational units. While half-platoon night-time ambushes weren't common for the 4 rifle platoons, they almost became the norm for the Assault Pioneer Platoon after April 1970. On several occasions, Assault Pioneer Platoon night-time ambush parties of only 12 men engaged enemy forces of much greater numerical strength.

US Army infantry units, that only ever operated in significantly larger numbers — variously between 80 and 150 men — viewed Australian soldiers as nothing short of crazy for engaging the enemy in such small numbers. As we occasionally shared more than a few beers with them in Vung Tau, they would say to us '*You guys are just nuts!*'. Perhaps we were, but this thought never entered our heads. We were just doing the job we were asked to do. And, I'm relaxed to say that we were all particularly good at it. The M60 machine guns of the Assault Pioneer Platoon provided us with a large amount of leverage.

M79 GRENADE LAUNCHER

The M79 grenade launcher was intended to be a close support weapon for the infantry and designed to bridge the gap between the maximum throw of a M26 high-explosive fragmentation hand grenade and the closest range of initial supporting mortar fire — a distance range said to have been somewhere between 40m and 300m.

This weapon, which weighed 2.7kg, closely resembled a large-bore single-barrel sawn-off shotgun. It was a single-shot, shoulder-fired, break-barrel loading weapon that fired a spherical 40mm high-explosive grenade, and several other round types. Its effective rate of fire was something like 6.0rp/m although for short periods of time, it could be higher, particularly when needed for illumination over the battlefield after the initiation of a night-time ambush.

The 40mm high-explosive round fired from the M79 grenade launcher had a muzzle velocity of 75mp/s and a keen eye could visually sight and track its trajectory if it was fired up and over open clear ground. The same could also be said of any incoming enemy rocket-propelled grenades — RGP 7's in particular. However, because so much was happening down at ground level when in contact with the enemy, whenever a M79 grenade launcher was fired no one was trying to visually track its trajectory and flight path. Of much more interest to us was where it landed and detonated.

The day-time ammunition type most commonly used in this weapon — high-explosive contained within a steel casing — had propellant that gave it a maximum range of about 400m. While the sights were incredibly true, its accuracy was doubtful beyond 350m. Upon detonation it produced over 300 steel fragments, dispersing at a velocity of 1,524mp/s and lethal out to a radius of up to 5.0m, imposing a measured casualty radius out to as far as 130m. However, confrontation with the enemy in Vietnam was always up close so the long range accuracy of this weapon wasn't a major issue for us and was never seriously tested by those in my platoon who carried this weapon.

Interestingly, while the M79 grenade launcher was no longer manufactured after 1971 — the US Army only produced 350,000 units — it was still being used by elements of the US Army Ranger and US Navy Seal teams decades later when they were deployed to the conflicts in Afghanistan and Iraq. I doubt that there would have been any modification to this weapon from my time in Vietnam other than for its ammunition types and lethality.

In addition to its primary armament of high-explosive rounds — each of which weighed 230gm — the M79 grenade launcher also fired illumination flares (220gm) that were often used during night-time ambushes, buckshot — 20 shotgun pellets collectively weighing 156gm — and other types of rounds such as fleshette and smoke.

Fleshette was an ammunition comprised of 45 flighted barbed darts, collectively weighing 65gm and it had a much deeper penetration capability into a target centre mass at close range than that of buckshot. On the other hand, buckshot was regarded by many as a much more effective round than fleshette, because of its blast effect to the head or centre mass of a target. In other words, if you were going to be hit at close range in the upper body or head by a round of buckshot, you were certainly going to lose complete interest in continuing to do whatever it was that you were just previously doing. Buckshot was effective out to about 15m. With both buckshot and flechette, the propelled contents of the rounds dispersed upon leaving the muzzle of the weapon.

In the image below, the high-explosive round is shown second from the left in the top row and far right. The illumination round, which was more commonly used by the Assault Pioneer Platoon, is adjacent, second from the right in the top row between the two high-explosive rounds.

Whenever I carried this weapon, which was often, I only ever toted high-explosive and illumination rounds. While buckshot rounds were devastatingly effective at extreme short range, I'd rather have a high-explosive round heading an enemy's way compared to a lot of relatively small shotgun pellets. Nevertheless,

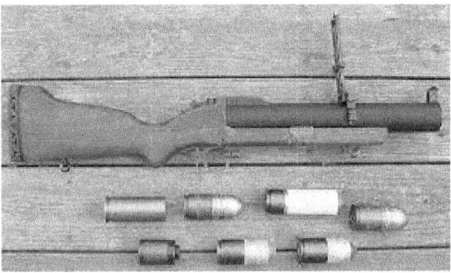

M79 Grenade Launcher and its ammunition types.

other carriers of this weapon in my platoon sometimes loaded it with buckshot during the day-time and swore by their reliance on that round type. Anecdotally, Major Mal Peck Ret'd — former commander of D Company, 8 RAR — was very fond of the M79 grenade launcher and its buckshot ammunition.

When fired, the flare of an illumination round descended to the ground via the agency of a small deployed parachute, at a rate of 2.1mp/s. The flare itself was designed to burn for 40 seconds. Each of these flares produced a large amount of light — 90,000 candlepower (or 1,145K lumens) — which made them indispensable in the initial stages of a sprung night-time ambush. This amount of dispersed light from each illumination flare was about the same as what would have been produced by 714 — now obsolete — 100-watt incandescent light bulbs. These illumination flares provided a lot of light and accompanying visual awareness over the battlefield.

The M79 grenade launcher weighed 2.95kg when loaded with a high-explosive round and was extensively used by Australian infantry soldiers in Vietnam. My platoon always carried three M79 grenade launchers and the carry of each of these weapons and its ammunition was often shared between 2 men in each section. Strangely, some guys loved this weapon and wouldn't readily give it up. Others vehemently hated it. Anyone carrying the M79 grenade launcher also had to carry his own rifle and its ammunition as well. In the US Army it was completely different because that allied force had an infantry role designation of grenadier, and those men only carried the M79 grenade launcher.

The high-explosive rounds fired from this weapon were designed not to arm — or become lethal — until they travelled about 30m. When the weapon was fired, the 'rifling' inside the barrel ensured that the round left its muzzle spinning at extremely high speed — 3,700rp/m — which not only provided stability for its flight path but also initiated the internal arming mechanism of the round.

During my time in Vietnam there were several reported instances of an M79 grenade launcher being fired at extreme close range at an enemy soldier, if not by 8 RAR soldiers then by soldiers of other Australian infantry battalions or supporting field elements. Anecdotally, several enemy soldiers were hit in the body by a high-explosive round from a M79 grenade launcher before it travelled a distance sufficient for it to arm. With 230gm of high-explosive — and unknown armed status — partially embedded in their bodies, it was problematic as to how they were dealt with as wounded enemy soldiers. I did hear some interesting stories. As to whether those stories were true, I can only speculate.

There was one infamous event within my platoon when Mick O'Shea — again, it was always Mick O'Shea when out in the field — was carrying an M79 grenade launcher with it slung over his backpack, barrel facing upwards which was, of course, good field practice. We were moving through a very densely foliated area and somehow a thin branch or vine tendril — or something like that — snagged the trigger and all of a sudden we heard the unmistakable sound of a high-explosive round being fired. O'Shea had been carrying his M79 grenade launcher with a high-explosive round already loaded in the breach of the weapon, as I always did whenever I carried it. However, on this occasion he'd obviously not properly engaged the safety switch of his weapon, or it may have been dislodged by errant features of the dense vegetation. This was a serious moment for all of us. Someone quietly muttered:

'Fuck! Where is that going to land?'

I've confirmed with Lance-corporal Jeff Smith (JJ) that he was the man who uttered those few words of abject despair. Other than that one salutary comment from JJ, the rest of us were mute and just stood motionless. There was no point in anyone moving or saying anything because we had no idea whatsoever as to the downwards trajectory of that high-explosive round. So we just stood there for those tense seconds, looking at one another, hoping that its trajectory wasn't precisely vertical, waiting for it to land and detonate — which it did quite harmlessly a short, yet far too close distance away from our ground position. O'Shea was well and truly in the shit with our platoon commander over that incident. And we were all pretty angry with O'Shea as well.

The M79 grenade launcher was an extremely useful and highly effective infantry weapon. I carried this high value weapon for No.1 Section of the Assault Pioneer Platoon with occasional assistance from Peter McCormack, after April 1970, during my 12 months in Vietnam.

M72 A2 LIGHT ANTI-TANK WEAPON (LAW)

The M72 A2 LAW was a lightweight self-contained anti-tank weapon that fired a 66mm high-explosive, amour-piercing round with a muzzle velocity of 145mp/s. The round became armed after a flight distance of 10m, weighed 1kg, and had an effective range of about 200m. Its terminal range was something less than 1km.

It was a portable, once only, throw away weapon that could be fired from either shoulder in standing, seated, kneeling, or prone positions. The complete unit weighed 2.2kg. It was a much lighter equivalent of the immensely popular Bazooka weapon used extensively during WWII by US Army forces.

The M72 was an open-chambered weapon and therefore had little, if any, recoil. However, its back blast potentially extended as far as 40m and all personnel, equipment, and flammable material had to be clear of this area. If M72's were going to be used within the platoon in any contact with the enemy, it was crucial that everyone knew exactly what was going on. Anyone hit at close range by a fired launcher's back blast wasn't going to be happy with his lot in life at that very moment.

While the round was capable of penetrating 300mm of rolled homogeneous amour (RHA), it wasn't overly effective in terms of breaching other target types such as densely packed earth or reinforced concrete and steel. While the penetration was still reasonable, there was limited resultant fragmentation. However, against heavy timber structures, free of earthen buttressing, it was an effective weapon.

Over short to medium distances this weapon was extremely accurate and, although it was designed to be used against light armored tanks and vehicles, it was used extensively in Vietnam — but with limited overall success I'd say — against less imposing but much harder to destroy targets such as earth buttressed bunker systems.

Although my platoon always carried a number of these weapons as part of its overall armament capability, I don't think that any were ever actually fired during any of our engagements with the enemy. Given the operational conditions that prevailed in Vietnam, I thought it was an extremely poor weapon and, because of its bulkiness, did my very utmost to avoid carrying one. Nevertheless, while I loathed it, others in my platoon readily carried it.

M18 CLAYMORE ANTI-PERSONAL DIRECTIONAL MINE

The M18 Claymore anti-personnel directional mine was oblong in shape and had a slightly backward curved face. Its dimensions were 12.4cm high, 21.6cm wide, and 3.8cm deep. It weighed 1.6kg. As for its lethality, this mine contained 700 steel ball bearings, 3.2mm in diameter, encased in a shaped charge — hence the curved face — of C4 plastic explosive.

The mine was detonated electronically from a manually operated, battery charged firing device that was connected using a 30m electrical firing cable to the mine's blasting cap assembly. While it was also possible for the mine to be detonated via the agency of a trip-wire and other activating mechanism types, manual operation was the common method adopted by my platoon and by platoons of the battalion more generally.

M18 Claymore Anti-Personnel Directional Mine.

M18 Claymore Anti-Personnel Directional Mines, in series. An 8 RAR Assault Pioneer Platoon night-time ambush.

M18 Claymore anti-personnel directional mines were connected serially by detonation cord, thereby enabling us to manually detonate banks of these mines simultaneously. The M18 Claymore anti-personnel directional mine was a very popular allied weapon and they were used extensively in Vietnam by Australian soldiers.

For example, my platoon always carried somewhere between 20 and 30 of these mines as either defensive systems or, more usually, as a first strike night-time ambush armament. Whenever we laid down an ambush — day or night — we'd always set up left and right banks of these mines, each facing directly into the chosen killing ground. Each bank comprised 8 or more mines that were serially connected by detonation cord. A similar bank of these mines was always put in place out in front of the rear protection party as well.

When detonated by the 0.75kg layer of shaped C4 plastic explosive, 80J of kinetic energy was produced which completely fragmented the mine and propelled forward — at a velocity of 1,200mp/s — a fan-shaped swathe of steel ball bearings in a 60° horizontal arc. The mine had an effective killing range of 50m and a measured casualty range out to as far as 100m. Aimed properly, the mine projected outwards a lethal spray of dispersed steel ball bearings that was 2m high and 50m wide, at a range of 50m. At that distance, there was a reasonably high probability of enemy casualties, if not fatalities. If you happened to be in the very close, direct path of that array of steel headed your way, it wasn't going to be a good outcome for you. We always set the aiming level of these mines for direct effectiveness, commonly known by us as 'balls' height. This meant that it was always our intention to only detonate the mines when the enemy was almost on top of us.

Most night-time ambushes were sprung by the detonation of these serially connected banks of M18 Claymore anti-personnel directional mines, with the desired effect to kill, maim, or otherwise confuse any enemy who'd ventured into the killing ground. Detonation of these mines — the noise was simply deafening — was immediately followed up by concentrated rifle and M60 machine gun fire into the killing ground, assisted initially and later with illumination provided by M79 grenade launchers. The M18 Claymore anti-personnel directional mine was a very effective weapon.

M26 HAND GRENADE

The M26 high-explosive fragmentation hand grenade carried in Vietnam by Australian soldiers was, from my personal observations, a marginal weapon with limited operational effectiveness. I didn't think that it was all that suitable for use in Vietnam. As a safety measure, mainly due to the rust conducive climate of Vietnam, and the somewhat so-called risky design of the safety pin feature, we used to wrap black electrical tape several times laterally around each hand grenade, further constraining their initiation safety release levers.

An M26 high-explosive fragmentation hand grenade was 99mm in height, 57mm in diameter, and weighed 0.45kg. Most men could lob it from a semi-prone or kneeling position, no further than about 40m. However, for such a small weapon, its effective killing radius of 5m and casualty radius of 15m made it an attractive armament option for

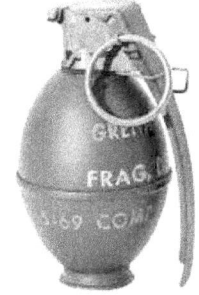

M26 Hand Grenade.

some. And when closer than that range, there was also the devastating impact on a target mass of the blasting lethality on detonation — particularly in confined spaces, which certainly wasn't the case in Vietnam unless you were dropping them down into inhabited enemy bunkers.

Once the firing mechanism was initiated by pulling and removing the safety pin, and with the safety lever releasing after the grenade was thrown, there was a built-in 4.5 second delay before the grenade detonated. So, in other words, you needed to be very much aware of what you were doing when using the M26 hand grenade in any hot moment. And God help anyone who pulled the pin and dropped the grenade, thereby releasing the safety lever! It did happen from time to time but only in training situations back in Australia. While the M26 hand grenade wasn't particularly large or overly heavy, it certainly could deliver a real punch to the enemy in some engagement scenarios.

On the detonation of a M26 hand grenade, 86J of kinetic energy was produced, dispersing around 1,250 cast iron fragments of shrapnel, each weighing about 200mg, at a saturation coverage of something like 3.7 fragments per 1m². The explosive content of a M26 hand grenade was 'Composition B': a 60:40 mix of RDX (detonation velocity of 8,750mp/s) and TNT (detonation velocity of 6,900mp/s). The addition of RDX into the explosive mix made the blasting effect on detonation much more pronounced.

I eventually concluded that hand grenades were nothing other than a constant irritation for me. My reasoning was that although they weren't all that heavy, they were bulky and almost impossible to efficiently pack in my operational equipment. I used to carry them in my backpack, and after a time, I couldn't see much sense in that. In addition, the terrain and landscape that prevailed in Phuoc Tuy Province didn't seem to be at all conducive to tactical warfare weapons like hand grenades which, quite clearly, would have been far more effectively used on flat, open, and dry landscapes, or in house-to-house fighting. I got rid of the 2 that I'd been carrying after my second operation, preferring instead to carry additional ammunition for my rifle and much more water.

I'm not sure if hand grenades were a prescribed personal weapon or not within the Assault Pioneer Platoon. They probably were. Anyway, I never advertised the fact to anyone in my platoon that I was no longer carrying them whenever I was out in the field. And I don't recall anyone ever asking me the question either!

However, I do know that most, if not all other members of my platoon carried one or more hand grenades with them on each of our operations, and some of them were used on several occasions. I still clearly recall the resonant voices of Bob Simpson and John Dolgan as they shouted *'Grenade!'* whilst throwing their collective 4 grenades — maybe more — on 29 May 1970.

It was during a fierce night-time half-platoon ambush engagement south of Night Defensive Position Isa, on the low rice paddy fields abutting the northern slopes of the Long Hai Hills. Although the grenades made a lot of noise, I don't remember them being overly effective. Lobbing hand grenades into rice paddy fields doesn't seem to make a lot of sense to me, I'm afraid. Maybe I'm being a bit harsh here.

BAYONETS

The SLR bayonet, which weighed 0.5kg, was a solid piece of blued steel of very robust manufacture, the blade of which was about 20cm long. While the blade wasn't honed and had no useful cutting edge, if it was ever used as a lunging weapon, the bayonet was more than capable of inflicting serious or fatal injuries. A slightly smaller but probably more effective bayonet — because of its more defined and keener cutting edge — accompanied the M16 Armalite rifle.

Though I was never required to fix bayonets in the military sense often depicted in old movies of past conflicts, I did carry this weapon in Vietnam for quite some time by getting rid of my bayonet belt frog and somehow attaching the bayonet to my machete scabbard. I found that carrying it using a standard bayonet frog attached to my webbed belt had become a real nuisance for me.

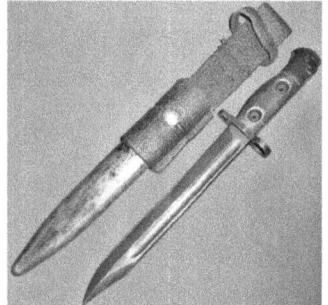
SLR Bayonet.

I eventually discarded it because I concluded that I'd never have to use it in any close quarter combat with the enemy. And the way in which the Assault Pioneer Platoon tended to operate after March 1970 made it highly unlikely that I'd ever need to use it in any anti-personnel mine clearing task. This was a significant risk on my part I guess, but that's just how it was at the time.

Almost from the time of our first operation, the amount of weight we carried with us out in the field was an issue that obsessed most of us. It

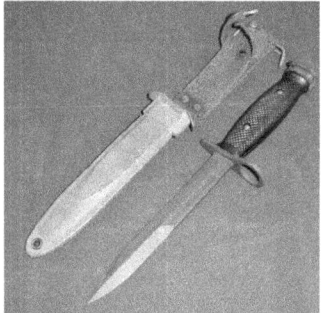
M16 Bayonet.

certainly became an obsession for me. I was always looking at ways to lessen my overall weight carry load while maintaining my water and ammunition holdings.

Eventually, getting rid of my bayonet wasn't a decision that I agonised over for too long at all. Having said that, I do know that most other members of my platoon carried their bayonets for the entire time we were deployed to Vietnam.

MACHETE

Machetes issued to Australian soldiers in Vietnam were of high quality, perfect weight — 0.7kg — and manufactured from high-grade, quality tempered steel. Its overall length was 46cm. The blade, acutely honed, was 33cm long and it was never dulled because of our constant attention to this item of weapons maintenance. It was also very well balanced and therefore not overly heavy in the hand. While not a large machete, it really was a superb piece of craftsmanship.

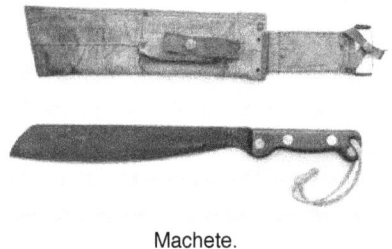

Machete.

Although it may have been a handy personal weapon under dire circumstances, it was more of a useful tool rather than an operational armament. Given the variable prevailing dense jungle terrains which we often had to negotiate, it was carried and used by all members of my platoon. I always carried a machete and I used to spend a lot of time when out in the field, and back at Nui Dat, honing its blade and keeping its cutting edge acute as possible.

Anyone trying to purchase one of these now rarely available iconic Vietnam era 'Golok' machetes today, is going to have to be prepared to part with at least $250 (in 2022 prices).

EXPLOSIVES

As an Assault Pioneer Platoon, one of our core roles was the demolition of enemy bunker systems and, when engineers weren't available, the disarming or destruction of booby traps and anti-personnel mines. Now in these latter situations, I may have very well needed my bayonet. But that's another story altogether. Nonetheless, we had been very well trained back in Australia for these highly specialised and dangerous roles.

In demolishing enemy bunker systems we used 2 types of high-explosives: TNT and C4 plastic. One of the main properties of both explosive types was that of instant detonation which manifested in the form of a very high velocity bursting charge. In other words, the resultant detonation from either explosive moved stuff near it at very high speed. For example, the bursting charge velocity of C4 plastic was 8,092mp/s while that of TNT was 6,900mp/s. TNT was a stable explosive, but it was still somewhat sensitive to heat, shock, and

Chapter 17 — Weapons

friction. On the other hand, C4 plastic was basically a very inert compound and largely insensitive to all of those factors.

When used in demolishing an enemy bunker system, TNT tended to lift, shatter, and then drop any impacted material down onto the residue below. In other words, it imploded bunker systems making them totally unusable and not easily repairable.

On the other hand, C4 plastic was highly malleable (it was somewhat like plasticine) and capable of being shaped to direct the bursting charge more acutely upon detonation. So when affixed at opposite sides, but at different heights to a large tree trunk, it literally severed the tree. In Vietnam we used C4 plastic to drop trees across already imploded bunker systems, adding to the already significant devastation caused by the TNT, making the overall damage to those bunkers absolutely total.

However, as we often operated more-or-less in the same way as a normal infantry rifle company did for much of our time in Vietnam, our explosive and demolition talents weren't called upon much at all after March 1970. After that, while still carrying substantial amounts of C4 plastic with us whenever we were out in the field, it was rarely used by us for operational purposes. Mind you, during the first 3 months of our time in Vietnam, the Assault Pioneer Platoon destroyed many hundreds of enemy bunkers using both TNT and C4 plastic explosives.

So why did our platoon use vast, if not massive quantities of C4 plastic when we were no longer routinely engaged in demolishing bunker systems? The answer is very simple. All of us routinely used plenty of the 570gm slabs of it to heat up our rations food and boil water for coffee and tea.

During my time in Vietnam, the army issue cooking heat agent for operational purposes was a slow-burning, low-heat compound known as hexamine. This substance took ages to even half-warm food and never came close to properly heating a mug of water for tea or coffee. The resourceful members of the Assault Pioneer Platoon never used this low-heat, time poor resource. Instead we used thumb-sized lumps of C4 plastic to boil a large field mug of water in 30 seconds or less. In addition, the warming of canned rations deposited in the mug only required the addition of an experienced based measure of water, constant stirring, and a close attention to the process because of the propensity of the food to burn due to the high heat source temperature. Generally it took it no time at all, and we became quite expert at 'cooking' with this resource. We used quite enormous quantities of C4 plastic during our time in Vietnam. It was 'government funds very well spent' as far as we were concerned. Strangely, we were never challenged as to the quantum of our operational use of this commodity.

C4 plastic was quite stable. When small amounts of it were ignited with a match or cigarette lighter, it burned ferociously, and slowly, with an intense white heat. It basically needed to be impacted by an electrical impulse for it to explode. In saying that, I've since learned that it's probably not a clever idea to ignite large quantities of C4 plastic. As it aged, it engendered significant sweating which, thankfully, seemed to be totally inert when compared to the nitro-glycerine end product — the result of sweating of other explosive products such as TNT. God only knows what poisons my platoon mates and I may have absorbed into our bodies from handling lots of sweaty C4 plastic and TNT explosives. I guess we'll never know. Maybe our children and grandchildren will find out one day!

Whenever we were out in the field I regarded C4 plastic as an essential commodity and I didn't care about its weight. A slab of C4 plastic weighed 570gm, and its dimensions were 28cm long, 5.1cm wide, and 3.8cm deep. I used to carry plenty of it with me, and just like water, cigarettes, and ammunition, I never ever ran out of it.

OTHER ARMAMENTS AND OPERATIONAL AIDS

In addition to these main operational field armaments, we had access to a variety of other useful armament types, each of which had their own particular uses.

For example, there were M49 trip flares which were sometimes used at night as early warning devices to detect and illuminate enemy movement in ambush situations. However, the Assault Pioneer Platoon tended to rely more on M79 grenade launchers for illumination and not M49 trip flares.

Smoke grenades —an assortment of colours — were extensively used by my platoon to indicate our ground position to air support, generally in the form of Iroquois helicopters from 9 Squadron. Helicopters wouldn't land — to evacuate wounded soldiers or to deliver a re-supply of rations, clothing, ammunition, mail, and other equipment, or to relocate the platoon — until a smoke grenade was thrown with the pilot indicating to the men on the ground the colour of the smoke, and having that indication confirmed from the ground. This was a basic governance protocol and seemed to work quite well. Having said that, it was always a high risk time for the crews of the helicopters and we, as soldiers, always understood that.

Some of us also carried phosphorous grenades for incendiary purposes. Why we carried these grenades with us out in the field, I can no longer remember. Back in Nui Dat, we often used them to fumigate the open pit latrines in our lines very effectively.

As far as I can recall, there seemed to be no real restriction as to what additional personal weaponry a soldier could carry with him out in the field,

Chapter 17 – Weapons

as long as he was armed with his standard army issue personal weapon, ammunition for it, ammunition for the M60 machine gun, as well as a number of M18 Claymore anti-personnel directional mines etc. Several guys in my platoon were walking arsenals. Others, like me, were far more measured. It was very much a personal choice.

I was happy with my SLR rifle and carried a lot of ammunition for it, as well as — for much of the time — the M79 grenade launcher and its ammunition. Whenever I wasn't carrying the M79 grenade launcher, I was always loaded up with a few 100-round belts of 7.62mm rounds for the section's M60 machine gun and a few M18 Claymore anti-personnel directional mines.

UNARMED COMBAT

Unarmed combat, or hand-to-hand engagement with the enemy, was never part of our training regimen. I clearly remember asking my section commander back in Australia why this was so, and his response was something like:

> *'I'll tell you this McCann — he never ever called me Peter[22] — if it gets down to that in any contact which we might have with the enemy, then we're going to be in a shit-load of very serious trouble.'*

I've never forgotten those words by Fred Vincent and, in much later years, I've often wondered how we would have fared if we had ever been overrun by the enemy and forced to confront them in hand-to-hand combat. Thankfully, I'll never know. However, in that context, I do take solace in the events of the battles of Long Tan, Coral, Balmoral, and Binh Ba in particular, where vastly superior enemy forces were repelled and defeated by very well trained, well-led and determined brave Australian and New Zealand soldiers.

During the extended battle of Fire Support Base Coral, some of the fighting did indeed get down to hand-to-hand combat when, not long after 3:30am on 13 May 1968, the enemy briefly overran the 1 RAR Mortar Platoon and captured — for a brief time — one of 102 Field Battery's 105mm artillery gun emplacements. Sadly, in the 1 RAR Mortar Platoon that night, 5 men were killed and 13 were wounded, some very seriously.

WEAPONS MAINTENANCE

Southern Vietnam is a very hot, humid, wet, and exceedingly nasty part of the world. During the long 7-month wet season, it rained on most afternoons between 1:30pm and 5:30pm and usually for somewhat shorter periods during

---

[22] Probably because there were 4 men named 'Peter' in my section of the platoon.

the night as well. These downpours of rain were often torrential. While not anywhere near as heavy, it sometimes rained during the dry season as well. These conditions were ideal for generating rust on weapons and otherwise causing operational weapon malfunctions.

Because the metal components of our weapons were blued[23], they were pretty much resistant to rusting in these sorts of conditions as long as we kept them well-oiled. When out in the field, we routinely cleaned our weapons several times a day, liberally dousing them with generous coatings of a very fine protective oil and lubricating the insides of barrels. In fact, during my entire time in Vietnam, we were always cleaning and oiling our weapons whether we were out in the field or back at Nui Dat. On my return home to Australia, the large calluses on the outside of my rifle-cocking right index finger — remember I'm left handed — were deeply ingrained with oil. It took a long time for these unsightly calluses to fully wear away.

When we returned to Nui Dat after each operation, and even before we had our first shower in many weeks, we completely disassembled our personal weapons and thoroughly cleaned them in upturned, cut in half, 200L drums containing range fuel. Range fuel was a volatile solvent and strong astringent. It completely stripped the metal working parts of our weapons of any grime or grit and permeated into the minute crevices of those parts, highlighting any semblance of emerging rust, making it relatively easy for us to bring our weapons up to pristine condition quickly. Liberal coatings of fine oil had our weapons back in first-class condition and ready for use again in no time. After that, we were then able to luxuriate in a mostly tepid shower while our mates dug ticks out of our shoulders and backs.

While cleaning weapons and personal hygiene are mutually exclusive, it was simply not possible for us to accomplish that in any strict order. However, for some inexplicable reason, whenever we returned to Nui Dat after the conclusion of any operation, Peter Wood was always the first platoon member, personal weapon cleaned, squared away and freshly showered, who then used to gloatingly strut around with towel around his waist casually smoking cigarettes very near to quantities of uncontained and highly flammable range fuel while the rest of us were still immersed in the cleaning of our weapons. He was absolutely incredible.

Between operations we'd routinely strip rounds from our rifle magazines, replacing them with new, clean ammunition. We often replaced magazines as well because their spring loading mechanisms for raising rounds to the top

---

[23] A chemical solution applied during manufacture, created a thin (2.5 micrometres) protective layer that was partially resistant to rust. The end product is a black to dark blue colouring of a treated weapon's relevant components.

Chapter 17 — Weapons

Cleaning weapons at Nui Dat after an operation.
Steve Kaliczinsky, Ron Goubareff, 2LT Peter Phillips, Sergeant Cliff Grant,
Ray Salmon, and the serial exhibitionist - Peter Wood.

were potentially subject to malfunction due to rust and other accumulated crud. We couldn't afford a weapon stoppage in an enemy contact because of a malfunctioning magazine. Belts of M60 machine gun ammunition were also frequently replaced due to occasional rusting of the links between the belted rounds. Discarded ammunition became a routine problem for the platoon.

While we spent a lot of time maintaining our weapons, both out in the field and back at Nui Dat, we never needed to be told to do so. We all wanted weapons on which we could rely. As far as I can recall, my personal weapon was inspected for cleanliness on only one occasion during my time in Vietnam. It easily passed inspection. I think that it was simply understood by us all that we'd properly maintain our weapons. And we did.

When I really think about it, this 'second nature' care of our weapons, and observance of weapons safety that we religiously adhered to during our entire time in Vietnam, was probably a productive and lasting carry over from our recruit training — where random rifle inspections made our lives so utterly miserable. To that extent at least, recruit training did have a very positive and long-lasting impact on our professionalism as infantry soldiers.

As a very close-knit group, each of us in my platoon expected others to do the right thing in maintaining their weapons. As far as I can recall, not one man ever let the platoon down. If anything, our weapons were obsessively cleaned. They certainly were in my case. And that was no terrible thing.

CHAPTER 18

OPERATIONAL SUPPORT

There were several main types of operational support available to Australian infantry soldiers out in the field in Vietnam. Without this assistance, field operations in Vietnam would have been completely untenable.

For example, the Battle of Long Tan on 18 August 1966 would almost certainly have ended badly for D Company, 6 RAR, were it not for the incredible support provided by 2 Iroquois helicopters from 9 Squadron RAAF. Under heavy ground fire from below, these helicopters delivered a desperately needed ammunition re-supply to those embattled and grossly outnumbered Australian and New Zealand soldiers on the ground. In addition, the medium field guns of 1st Field Regiment, RAA — and 161 Field Battery, Royal New Zealand Artillery, RNZA — and the heavier field guns of the US Army A Battery, 2nd Battalion, 35th Field Artillery Regiment — at Nui Dat, some 5km away, were crucial to the positive outcome of this fierce battle. So too were the 12 APCs from the 1st Armoured Personnel Carrier Squadron — which later became A Squadron, 3rd Cavalry Regiment, RAAC — that ultimately delivered blistering offensive firepower and infantry reinforcements from A Company of 6 RAR, to the battlefield.

Against this background, I believe it would be useful in terms of contextual overlay for my story if I were to describe the associated capabilities and major features of the wide range of support generally available to Australian infantry soldiers out in the field, during my time in Vietnam.

ARTILLERY

REGIMENT OF AUSTRALIAN ARTILLERY (RAA)
1st, 4th, and 12th Field Regiments: 105mm medium field guns

ROYAL NEW ZEALAND ARTILLERY (RNZA)
161 Field Battery: 105mm medium field guns

US ARMY 35TH FIELD ARTILLERY REGIMENT
A Battery, 2nd Battalion: 155mm heavy field guns

A key infantry support element of 1 ATF at Nui Dat was its artillery capability, variously provided by medium field batteries from the 1st, 4th, and 12th

M2A2 105mm Artillery Howitzer.
(Courtesy of Neil Denham)

Field Regiments, RAA. Each of these Australian Field Regiments deployed 2 medium field batteries from its overall strength of 3, to Vietnam in staggered 12-monthly rotating cycles. They were augmented by one attached RNZA medium field battery.

161 Field Battery, RNZA, was permanently deployed to Vietnam from June 1965 until May 1971 and regularly rotated men through its posted strength complement, as did the US Army A Battery, 2nd Battalion /35th Field Artillery Regiment. The vital Detachment 131st Divisional Locating Battery (131 Div Loc Battery), RAA, was permanently deployed to Vietnam from May 1966 until July 1971 and also regularly rotated its posted strength complement.

131 Div Loc Battery was a radar-based enemy locating resource, capable of rapidly triangulating and accurately identifying the firing position of enemy mortar rounds. It would then relay those map grid references to the artillery network at 1 ATF for subsequent offensive fire missions. There are recorded instances of enemy mortar crews abandoning their mortar base plates and tubes, as soon as they heard 105mm guns at Nui Dat fire in response to a barrage of mortar rounds they'd fired earlier. 131 Div Loc Battery was a highly effective unit and a constant feature of available artillery support capability for any 1 ATF element coming under enemy mortar and other fire.

All up, there were always 3 ANZAC medium field batteries in place at Nui Dat — 18 guns in total. A section of three 105mm guns from one of the batteries was sometimes located at the permanent Fire Support Base Horseshoe — 'the Horseshoe' — which was about 8km south-east of Nui Dat. This base overlooked the enemy-friendly town of Dat Do, on Route 23, from its superbly elevated and relatively easily-defendable position.

Occasionally, a section of 3 guns from US Army A Battery, 2nd Battalion,

35th Field Artillery Regiment was also deployed to the Horseshoe. Generally, there was always an understrength infantry company — let's say 80 men — and sometimes a section of 3 mortar tubes from one of the 3 infantry battalions, as base defence for the Horseshoe.

The Horseshoe was a very dynamic fire support base in terms of its composition of personnel, and one that I never had the pleasure, or otherwise, of being deployed to. Veterans with whom I've spoken, share mixed recollections of their time at the Horseshoe.

Table 2.

AUSTRALIAN AND NEW ZEALAND ARTILLERY SUPPORT AVAILABLE TO 1 ATF DURING 8 RAR'S DEPLOYMENT TO VIETNAM

Nov 69 - May 70	May 70 - Nov 70	Nov 69 - Nov 70	Nov 69 - Nov 70
1st Field Regiment RAA 101 & 105 Batteries	4th Field Regiment RAA 106 & 107 Batteries	RNZA 161 Battery	Det 131st Divisional Locating Battery RAA

There was also the formidable firepower capability — six M109 155mm guns — of the permanently attached US Army A Battery, 2nd Battalion/35th Field Artillery Regiment, which I later talk about in much more detail.

For the most part, each of the infantry battalions of 1 ATF had either an Australian or New Zealand artillery battery allocated to it — in direct support, which meant that fire from this battery's six M2A2 105mm guns was always guaranteed for that battalion — 24/7 — in all but the most exceptional of circumstances.

To deliver this guaranteed fire support, infantry battalions were assigned small groups — around 3 men — of artillery personnel, known as forward observer parties (FOP). These parties were attached to each rifle company headquarters (CHQ). The battery commander's party (BCP) was attached to BHQ. Both attached artillery elements provided specialised advice, communications, and artillery fire control skills to those respective elements of the battalion.

In 8 RAR's case, we were provided with direct artillery fire support by 161 Battery RNZA. This battery was always our main artillery support resource. US Army Chinook helicopters were capable of transporting the battery's 105mm guns, as slung loads, from Nui Dat to defended fire support bases very quickly.

The M2A2 105mm towed artillery howitzer was a robust and highly effective medium field gun and one which served Australian infantry soldiers extremely well in Vietnam. It was capable of a sustained rate of fire of high-explosive rounds — either on known enemy positions or as harassment and interdiction fire into areas of suspected enemy activity — of 3 rpm. In the case of a major heavy engagement with the enemy, and for only very short periods of time, each of the 6 guns of an artillery battery was capable of a firing rate of up to 6 rpm.

M2A2 105mm Artillery Howitzer.
(Courtesy of Neil Denham)

Each gun was served by a crew of 7 men, although with rostered R&R leave, occasional illness and random secondments etc, 5 detachment members for each gun, was about the usual resourcing. This meant there was often only 1 gunner effectively clearing spent shell casings from its breech, and loading live rounds into the gun during a fire mission:

- No.1   Gun Sergeant - in charge of the gun;
- No.2   Gunner - elevation of the gun;
- No.3   Gunner - direction and bearing of the gun;
- No.4   Gunner - loading/unloading/preparation of ammunition;
- No.5   Gunner - loading/unloading/preparation of ammunition;
- No.6   Gunner - loading/unloading/preparation of ammunition;
- No.7   Bombardier - 2IC - preparation of the ammunition.

While the 105mm artillery high-explosive round weighed 19kg, the actual projectile itself weighed 15kg. Its blast and fragmentation effect on detonation was generated by a high-explosive charge of TNT weighing 2.2kg. The propellant for each round consisted of a base charge — charge 1 — with up to a further 6 charge bag options available for longer distance fire missions. The muzzle velocity, at maximum charge 7, of a high-explosive 105mm round was 465m/s. High-explosive rounds could be fused to burst in the air above target areas, on impact with the ground — which was usual — or after a slight delay following impact with the ground, so that the round effectively buried itself for bunker-busting purposes.

In addition to high-explosive rounds, these medium field guns also fired smoke, white phosphorus, illumination, and anti-personnel rounds. The latter, known as 'splintex' and 'beehive' were designed to detonate just outside the muzzle of the gun, in a direct fire role. They projected outwards a broad swathe of thousands of tiny arrow-headed flechette darts in a giant shotgun effect. On some rare occasions in Vietnam, Australian 105mm artillery howitzers were used in this direct fire role. For example, during the battles of Coral, and Balmoral — fought variously over the period 12 May-6 June 1968 — against enemy infantry attacking in strength. I don't recall them being used in that way during my time in Vietnam with 8 RAR.

High-explosive round and charge bag for M2A2 105mm Artillery Howitzers.
(Courtesy of Neil Denham)

The maximum range of these very dependable and highly accurate medium field guns was a little over 11km and at that distance, latitudinal accuracy was no worse than 40m, with a longitudinal accuracy no worse than 10m. The lethal killing radius of a 105mm high-explosive artillery round, on flat, open terrain, was something in the order of 35m. The casualty radius could often be more than double that. Although terrain and vegetation significantly retarded its killing effectiveness, the M2A2 105mm howitzer was a good close-support medium field gun for any infantry soldiers who required supporting artillery fire — either when they felt overly threatened by the enemy, or needed assistance in driving the enemy towards established ambush killing grounds, particularly at night.

In a worst-case scenario or in very desperate times, the six 105mm guns of 161 Battery were able to provide artillery support to 8 RAR of 36 rpm for up to 5 minutes, and a variable sustained rate of fire of 18 rpm thereafter. If the situation on the ground ever became exceedingly grim, or if operational tasking called for more intense artillery support, the 2 Australian 105mm batteries — another 12 guns — and perhaps even the US Army A Battery, 2nd Battalion /35th Field Artillery Regiment — six 155mm guns — could also be called on to provide supporting fire.

During the Battle of Long Tan, with all 3 ANZAC 105mm batteries — 18 guns — firing in support of D Company 6 RAR, that rate of fire was, for short periods of time, something in the order of 108 rpm. 161 Battery was tasked with providing 6 RAR with on-call artillery fire support, and whenever that level of support required was deemed 'Fire Mission Battery' or 'Fire Mission Regiment', 161 Battery responded. The 2 Australian batteries and occasionally the US Army A Battery, 2nd Battalion/35th Field Artillery Regiment, only responded during calls for 'Fire Mission Regiment'.

For the time of that famous and now legendary battle, 24 artillery guns at Nui Dat fired 3,284 high-explosive rounds — 3,129 (105mm) and 155 (155mm) high-explosive rounds — in support of D Company 6 RAR, over a 3.5-hour period. I can't comprehend how those magnificent gunners were able to maintain that artillery gunfire support for such an extended period.

Spent artillery shell casings are hot, bulky, and eventually would have become a logistical problem around each of the gun platforms. Not only that, the main repositories of 'yet to be prepared' live rounds for each field battery, weren't too easily accessible, so the supply of that ammunition to the gun platforms also became a major problem as frantic fire missions continued almost unabated.

It would have been 'all hands to the deck' back at the gun platforms, with men from each battery headquarters — and from anywhere else I imagine — being press-ganged into the gun emplacements as untrained gun labour. While I don't really know for sure, I reckon this must have been what occurred on that late afternoon and early evening of 18 August 1966. Commentary contained on the 103 Field Battery Association website seems to confirm that this was indeed the case. Don't forget that an 'about to be loaded' 105mm high-explosive round weighed 19kg.

At times, each of the eighteen 105mm ANZAC guns delivered artillery support well in excess of 3 rpm in support of D Company 6 RAR. Even recognising that there would have been some intense peaks, lesser troughs, and even lulls in that extraordinary rate of gunfire support, it almost defies belief. All of this energetic and frantic activity at Nui Dat was undertaken against a backdrop of late torrential rain and skyrocketing humidity levels. The surrounds of the gun platforms would have resembled Irish bogs littered with piles of discarded shell casings, by the time the battle concluded.

It was a magnificent effort and one that I'm sure D Company 6 RAR were incredibly thankful for. Without that wonderful artillery support, they most likely would have been over-run and wiped out to a man. And, 1 ATF at Nui Dat may well have subsequently been confronted with a massive attack by a well-resourced and energetically-buoyed enemy. As it was, the enemy copped an almighty 'hiding' which, according to many historians, the government and military command of Vietnam still can't comprehend.

For the gunners back at Nui Dat, the fatigue factor would have become an issue, the longer the battle went on. Fatigue can easily result in poor decision making. For example, it may have been disastrous for D Company 6 RAR if there had been a charge bag, gun elevation, or direction and bearing miscalculation in relation to one or more of the rounds fired during that battle.

So, against that historical background, the collective artillery support available to 8 RAR was just as deadly a resource, and one that thankfully wasn't required during its time in Vietnam. Having said that, 161 Battery was called on to support 8 RAR troops in the field on many occasions, and a couple of times, naval guns provided that support as well, particularly during the early operations of the battalion. Once in a while, particularly during the initial stages of an operation, the 2 Australian artillery batteries at Nui Dat also provided supporting fire to 8 RAR.

US Army self-propelled howitzers — with M109 155mm guns — were able to provide very effective artillery support when necessary. Just like Australian and New Zealand field batteries, US Army field batteries comprised 6 guns. Their heavier field batteries usually only had 4 guns and they were deployed elsewhere in South Vietnam — equipped with 175mm guns and 8in howitzers.

Compared to the 105mm howitzers of the Australian and New Zealand medium field guns, their 155mm counterpart had a much longer range at well over 14km. The high-explosive rounds these larger guns fired, weighed in at 43kg, almost 3 times the weight of equivalent rounds fired by the 105mm howitzers of the medium field batteries of the 1st, 4th, and 12th Field Regiments, RAA, and by 161 Field Battery, RNZA. The lethal killing radius of a 155mm high-explosive round, on flat, open terrain, was something in the order of 50m. Its casualty radius was often more than double that.

US Army Field Artillery M109 155mm Self-Propelled Howitzers.

A US Army field artillery battery of six M109 155mm self-propelled howitzers could provide supporting fire at a rate of 24 rpm — the intense rate for a few minutes at most — and a sustained rate of 12 rpm after that.

What the US Army M109 155mm heavy field artillery guns lacked in their rate of delivery of high-explosive rounds to a designated grid reference target area, they made up for with their significantly greater blast, fragmentation impact on detonation, and larger killing radius. It was rare for these M109 155mm field artillery guns to be called upon to support 8 RAR soldiers in Vietnam.

While the 105mm medium field artillery guns of the Australian and New Zealand artillery batteries at Nui Dat were highly precise, the US Army 155mm guns, even at maximum range, were said to be so accurate that they could land a round on a US1 coin.

DIRECT BATTALION FIELD SUPPORT

F29 81mm Mortar

An integral element of Support Company during my time with 8 RAR was its Mortar Platoon, which served a battery of six F29 81mm mortar tubes. Like the artillery support provided to the battalion by 161 Battery, the Mortar Platoon was an essential component in the support of 8 RAR soldiers in the field and, indeed in the wider defence of both Nui Dat and, as required, defended fire support bases and night defensive positions.

The F29 81mm mortar was a smooth-bore, muzzle-loading, drop-fed, light artillery piece that mainly fired high-explosive rounds at a muzzle velocity — at maximum propellant charge — of 225m/s over short to medium distances. Unlike the heavier artillery guns, mortars were capable of high-arching ballistic trajectories and were extremely accurate, light field weapons.

Like the much heavier artillery weapons of the day, the targeting of a mortar tube was focused on a sighting equation considering the direction, bearing, elevation, and the required amount of propellant charge in the form of bagged explosive ringlets — a base charge, plus 6 optional incremental charges — wrapped around the slender tail of the mortar round, immediately above its stabilising fin. Artillery and mortar fire missions weren't simple 'lock and load' procedures, which those of us in the infantry rifle platoons of the battalion were routinely familiar with.

The maximum effective range of the 81mm mortar was a little over 5km and each mortar tube could sustain an intense rate of fire of 20 rpm for rather short periods, and something like 12 rpm for extended periods. With all 6 mortar tubes in operation, the delivery of 72 rpm was very concentrated light artillery support for soldiers in the field, or for tactical defensive purposes.

F29 81mm Mortar.

The F29 81mm mortar was predominantly an anti-personnel weapon, crewed by a minimum of 3 men. For the most part, it fired high-explosive rounds weighing 4.5kg which, when detonated by an explosive charge of 1kg of TNT, delivered significant fragmentation and blast to nearby enemy combatants. It was a highly accurate weapon, lethal to within 35m, and highly dangerous as far as 150m. Other round types that were less commonly fired by mortars were illumination and smoke. Mortars were a relatively simple, easy to operate, light artillery piece. Medium sized mortars like the F29 81mm version used by Australian soldiers in Vietnam, were also easily transportable — the barrel, bipod support, base plate, and sights, collectively weighed only 36kg — and were used extensively in fire support bases and night defensive positions.

The main advantage that mortar armament had over artillery, was its relatively smaller size and therefore its mobility. Mortars could be relocated quickly and fired from almost anywhere. The battalion's 81mm mortars were excellent infantry support weapons. They weren't burdened by extensive logistical support, which was always required for the heavier guns of 1st and 4th Field Regiments (RAA), 161 Battery (RNZA), and the US Army A Battery, 2nd Battalion/35th Field Artillery Regiment.

ARMOUR

ROYAL AUSTRALIAN ARMOURED CORPS (RAAC)

B Squadron 3rd Cavalry Regiment: M113 A1 Armoured Personnel Carriers

One of the most welcome and distinctive sounds we heard out in the field was that of the 275hp 6V53T-V6 Detroit two-stroke diesel engines (5,210cm^3) that powered M113 A1 APCs — known colloquially as 'tracks' — from B Squadron, 3rd Cavalry Regiment, RAAC, as they approached our ground position. These tracks were also known as armoured cavalry assault vehicles.

The recognisable drone of the undulating, high-revving engines of this wonderful form of armoured support meant that we were soon to receive either a re-supply of food, water, equipment, maybe a mail delivery, or that we were being transported to a new ground position or — ever hopefully — back to Nui Dat. Whatever the reason, we were very pleased to meet up with APCs and their crews.

APCs weighed 12.3t and could move across flat, open ground and sealed roads at a speed of something like 66km/h. Also, being diesel powered, they could travel about 300km before needing to refuel.

The armour plating of these 'tracks' consisted of pressed aluminium; a thickness varying between 12–38mm (0.45in–1.5in). Because of the relatively light weight of this armour they were air-transportable by US Army Chinook helicopters. A number of them were fitted with 600kg of belly armour as a defence against enemy land mines that became a problem from time to time.

Overall, the armour of these tracks provided fairly good protection against small arms fire and, for the most part, rocket-propelled grenades and recoilless rifles. The only real weakness they had was a susceptibility — for the driver — to front-on attack from those weapons and land mines. Did the Viet Cong know about this? Too right they did!

APCs were versatile, highly manoeuvrable all-terrain, moderately amphibious, tracked, and reasonably fast light armoured vehicles. Each track was crewed by 2 men — a driver and a commander. The latter operated the track's turret armament. They mostly operated in discrete sections comprising 3 tracks. A sergeant usually commanded one track, and held overall command of the entire section. Sometimes the section commander was a Lieutenant. Often, there was a seventh crew member for each section of 3 tracks. While I don't remember his particular role, I'm guessing that it primarily related to communications between section tracks within the entire troop, and perhaps even back to 1 ATF at Nui Dat.

An APC troop comprised 3 sections of 3 tracks, as well as 2 command and support tracks: generally 11 tracks in total. Three troops along with a headquarters of 6 tracks (39 tracks in all) generally comprised an APC squadron. From time to time the odd 1 or 2 extraneous special purpose tracks may have been attached to a troop or a squadron.

During Australia's military commitment to the Vietnam conflict, 178 M113 A1 APCs were deployed, 75 of which suffered significant battle damage — 21 were unrepairable — from land mines, recoilless rifles, and rocket-propelled grenades. Sadly, 20 crew members were killed in action and 115 were wounded; some very badly. If you were a member of the 1st APC Troop — or the 1st APC Squadron and either A and B Squadrons 3rd Cavalry Regiment, RAAC, during the nearly 7 years that they shared deployments to Vietnam — then your chances of becoming a battlefield casualty — killed or wounded — were about 1:7...not great odds! Then again, just like our cavalry mates, none of us ever knew what might be about to befall us on any given day or night. To be perfectly honest, we never worried much about it anyway. We were always far too busy for that.

The prime offensive armament of each APC was either a top-mounted

Browning M2 fully-automatic, air-cooled, heavy machine gun — that fired devastating 50cal 290 grain rounds — or 2 top-mounted Browning M1919 machine guns, each of which fired 30cal 150 grain rounds.

The rate of continuous fire for the Browning M2 50cal machine gun was 550 rpm, from disintegrating metallic split-link belts fed from below. It had a high muzzle velocity of 920m/s and a killing range said to be as far as 1.5km. It was an extremely effective weapon, as evidenced by the concluding hostilities at the Battle of Long Tan in August 1966. The rate of continuous fire for the above-mentioned Browning M1919 30cal machine guns, also from disintegrating metallic split-links belt fed from below, was 600 rpm. The Browning M1919 30cal machine guns mounted on APCs had significantly more 'grunt' than infantry M60 machine guns.

Visually, rounds fired from our personal weapons weren't what I'd in any way describe as overly large. It's all relative I guess, but that's how it initially seemed to me at recruit training. Well, how wrong was I? While the 7.62mm round — universally regarded as a complete brute — is noticeably larger than a 5.56mm round, it doesn't take your breath away unless, of course, you're actually hit by it.

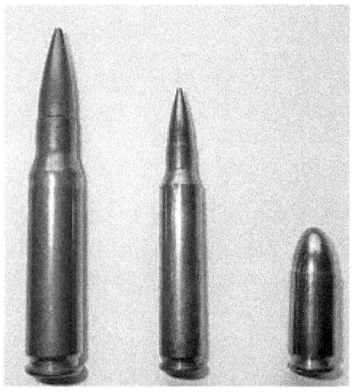

7.62mm   5.56mm   9mm   7.62mm 5.56mm   AA Battery

With that said, the 50cal round is an absolute monster and will seriously focus your mind on its size. This round can be fired very accurately over long distances, which has been proven in more recent times in both Iraq and Afghanistan. It really is very nasty.

US Army, Marine, Ranger, Delta Force, and Seal sniper teams deployed to these conflicts, often using 50cal weaponry equipped with telescopic sights, had to inject wind factors into the sighting equation as well as applying an estimate as to the flight path drop of the round over the distance to the target enemy. Some of these snipers have been known to register a number of 'high value' enemy kills at distances greater than 2.5km. Simply amazing!

Although modern day military snipers are usually assisted by a spotter — a number 2 — a range finder, plus a wind measuring device, as well as pre-calculated sighting matrices, at the end of the day, the distance to the target always injects a significant element of guesswork into the sighting equation. This was very clearly demonstrated in the wonderful movie 'American Sniper' released in the USA in December 2014.

Anyone unlucky enough to be hit with even one 50cal round is, more likely than not, going to be simply blown apart. By way of illustration, a 50cal projectile is about 58.8mm long and 12.7mm in diameter, recognising that the 7.62mm round fired from SLR rifles and M60 machine guns, is about half that overall mass. The 50cal round is a huge, very serious lump of lead. If headed your way at 920m/s, it's going to be bad news.

By way of further illustration, the projectile of a 50cal round weighs 290 grains, with one grain equalling 64.8mg. In terms more easily understood by the general community, a 5.56mm round weighs 4.15gm; a 7.62mm round weighs 9.525gm; and the 50cal round weighs in at a whopping 18.792gm!

Although rounds only weigh a relatively small number of grams, they impact on a target at a variable, yet high velocity, transferring a large amount of kinetic energy when they do so, particularly at close range. This kinetic energy has to be absorbed by something and it always transfers to the benign kinetic energy of the surrounding tissues of the target, usually shredding it as it does so, as well as producing a devastating cavitation effect, along with the dispersal of residual heat. In the case of higher amounts of transferred kinetic energy associated with larger rounds, much of this energy is usually dissipated in the creation of destructive exit wounds. The table below sets out the muzzle velocities and kinetic energy attributes of the rounds of some of the weapons I've discussed.

Table 3.

MUZZLE VELOCITY KINETIC ENERGY VALUES OF WEAPONS USED BY AUSTRALIAN SOLDIERS IN VIETNAM

WEAPON	ROUND	KINETIC ENERGY (J) /MUZZLE VELOCITY (m/s)
SLR Rifle	7.62mm	3,226 / 840
M16 Armalite Rifle	5.56mm	1,872 / 950
M60 Machine Gun	7.62mm	3,226 / 840
Browning M2 50cal Machine Gun	12.7mm	7,610 / 920
Browning M1919 30cal Machine Gun	7.82mm	4,030 / 870
F1 Sub Machine Gun	9mm	533 / 380
Pistol – Browning	9mm	533 / 380

By way of contrast, the most common personal weapon, other than shoulder-fired rocket-propelled grenades — predominantly RPG 7 — used by the enemy in Vietnam was the AK 47 Kalashnikov 7.62mm rifle. It produced 1,991J of kinetic energy at a muzzle velocity of 710m/s, only slightly greater than that of the much smaller calibre M16 Armalite rifle. Although its kinetic energy payload was much less than that of both the 7.62mm calibre SLR rifle and M60 machine gun — a direct result of the smaller length projectile (39mm compared to 51mm) and its propellant load — it was nevertheless an effective weapon because of its fully-automatic functionality. It was also extremely reliable and not often impacted by operational malfunctions.

The M16 Armalite rifle, while a very useful weapon in close quarter combat, wasn't a patch on the SLR rifle in terms of stopping power. Then again, as evidenced by the data in Table 3, the Browning M2 50cal machine gun round adds a whole new dimension to that term.

A 9mm round weighs 7.5gm and has a very low muzzle velocity of 380m/s, compared to say that of a 7.62mm round which weighs somewhat more — narrower, but much longer — at 9.5gm and has a significantly greater muzzle velocity of 840m/s. The comparative kinetic energy values generated at muzzle velocity of these 2 rounds, as reflected in Table 3, is nothing short of incredible. No wonder we thought the F1 sub-machine gun, which we were introduced to during recruit training, was such a poor weapon.

Commonly used modern day military (Sig Sauer) and police (Glock) pistols are also 9mm weapons and, given the very large calibre and reasonably-weighted round fired from them, a low muzzle velocity is absolutely essential to reduce the recoil when fired.

Even then, in an adrenalin-charged moment, pistols are only marginally accurate out to some 10m at best. In a close-up street gang fight they might be a pretty useful weapon, but I reckon that's going to be highly problematic anyway. However, if someone's going to shoot you with a 9mm pistol at close range, and actually hits you in the head or centre mass, it's going to be very nasty...so don't lose sight of that. Excluding my reservations in regard to the effectiveness of 9mm pistols, they probably do play an effective role in community policing.

While I thought 9mm pistols were a poor combat weapon, they seemed to be popular among some of the battalion's officer cadre and even by some men within my platoon. I recall that 2 of my platoon mates sometimes carried Browning 9mm pistols as part of their personal operational armaments; namely Steve Kaliczinsky — one of the forward scouts of my section of the platoon — and Dave Matheson — the platoon medic. I'm not sure if that was even technically allowable under the battalion's standard operating procedures of the day, and I have no idea how these men were issued with the weapons anyway. I was never remotely interested in doing the same. I had more than enough weight to carry with my SLR rifle and — usually — the M79 grenade launcher, along with a shit-load of very heavy ammunition for both weapons.

The average kinetic energy values reflected in the data contained in Table 3 are at muzzle velocity and degrade exponentially over the flight path of a propelled projectile. That scientific fact, of course, generates a whole new area of conjecture surrounding relative ballistics...which I won't enter into, because I don't understand any of it and, more importantly, don't ever want to. Moreover, any discussion concerning this would only be applicable to long range sniper scenarios in any case. Because Australian soldiers in Vietnam were always engaging with the enemy at very close quarters, this stopping power degradation over flight distance, wasn't of any importance to us at all. So I'll move on from all of this technical ballistic data, however, I know that some readers taking in my story may have found this information useful.

In the following images, regarding one of the APCs that supported my platoon in Vietnam, it's very interesting to note how the turret armament of this particular track was altered so as to position its second Browning M1919 30cal machine gun well above the standard turret mounting position, adjacent to the other Browning M1919 30cal machine gun.

M113 A1 Armoured Personnel Carrier at the foothills of the Long Hai Hills.

Although I don't really know for sure, it seemed to me that this weaponry adaption gave the commander of the track more firepower options — exposed as he was above the armour protection of the turret — as well as the ability to lay down far more accurate fire on enemy positions. I don't recall any commander of any track I was inside, or on top of, hunkering down below the turret armour protection. They were always up in the turret performing their very dangerous task.

The only time this wasn't the case, happened to be on 8 January 1970.

M113 A1 Armoured Personnel Carrier at a fire support base.

That evening, a section of APCs transported the Assault Pioneer Platoon to reinforce a composite 8 RAR Support Company ambush party under sustained heavy fire from a large enemy force. When we arrived at the battle site, the incoming enemy fire from medium and small arms was so intense that, initially, the commander of our track decided that it was impossible for us to safely disembark...and he wasn't even sticking his head above the turret. I'll talk more about this incident later.

Because we were never at full strength, a section of 3 APCs was always able to relocate our platoon as one composite unit. Although the interior of each track was large enough to cram in 9 or maybe 10 men, along with all of their personal weapons and equipment, most Australian infantry soldiers usually preferred to sit on top with their personal weapons, leaving their backpacks in the main body of the track. This may appear to be potentially more dangerous than remaining inside the track, but many of us believed it was a more preferable place to be, should an APC ever be blown up by a land mine. And this did happen on a number of occasions to other elements of 8 RAR. Whilst being transported by APCs, there was always a risk of land mines, front-on rocket-propelled grenade, and recoilless rifle attack from the enemy.

As you know, I was a member of No.1 Section of the Assault Pioneer Platoon and we always seemed to be sitting up on top of the lead track. Why my section always had this dubious honour, totally mystified me. Why wasn't there some section rotation? Always being on the lead track significantly raised the chances of men from my section suffering the consequences of our track detonating a land mine or being the recipients of an enemy attack. Fortunately, that never happened...so it's all a bit academic now I suppose.

APCs were targets highly prized by the enemy and many of them were significantly damaged by land mines and shoulder-fired rocket-propelled grenades. The drivers of these carriers — positioned left low front, inside the tracks — were always vulnerable to direct attack and a number of those brave men lost their lives in Vietnam. Many who survived lost one, or both of their legs in this horrific way.

On more than a few occasions, a section — 3 — APCs harboured with us at night when we laid an ambush. Sections of APCs were numbered serially and they had those numbers and nicknames screenprinted on their side panels. The APC section that always seemed to be supporting the Assault Pioneer Platoon out in the field comprised tracks serially numbered 86A, 86B, and 86C, otherwise known — only because of their emblazoned side panel printing — as 'The Good', 'The Bad', and 'The Ugly', after the popular Clint Eastwood spaghetti western movie released in the USA in 1966. The track that always interacted with my section of the platoon was 86A — 'The Bad'. Strangely enough, somehow the naming sequence — or the screenprinting — was out of order.

M113 A1 Armoured Personnel Carrier (back door lowered).

I have always been, and remain so today, an unabashed fan of Clint Eastwood spaghetti western movies, and of that movie in particular. Not only is it a great movie, whenever I view it, I always remember back to those awful times in Vietnam when 'The Good', 'The Bad', and 'The Ugly' provided my platoon with a number of very welcome short periods of relative operational safety and the delivery of eagerly awaited re-supplies of food, water, equipment, and mail to us out in the field.

The soldiers who crewed APCs were interesting to say the least. They were a breed apart, as you'd expect, given that in former times they were what would have been known as the cavalry. Remember the US Army General Custer and the Battle of the Little Big Horn in June 1876? Or perhaps the fearsome and utterly ruthless mounted British Dragoons of the American War of Independence about 100 years earlier?

These guys in our army were the modern day descendants of those horse-mounted, sabre-wielding shock troops. To a casual observer, they gloried in this elite role. For the most part they seemed to be totally indifferent to the appalling conditions that we, as infantry soldiers, were exposed to and continually confronted with out in the field. I know this wasn't the case but that's the aura they exuded whenever we interacted with them operationally.

For example, on the side panels inside the body of each of the three 86 series tracks that supported my platoon, there were large signs that read something like this:

'Grunts (infantry soldiers), wipe your fucking feet and don't steal any of our food or porno mags!'

Well, what did they expect us to do? Pilfering was the name of the game if you were an infantry soldier and, I have to say, all of us in the Assault Pioneer Platoon were pretty good at it. While Peter Wood was our section's pilfering expert, most of us weren't too far behind him. I don't recall any of us significantly appropriating their rations, but any pornographic magazine was immediately snaffled-up as an absolute treasure.

Generally speaking, the APC guys were pretty good. They always gave us plenty of water and, occasionally, surplus rations. Their combat role, while nowhere near as physically debilitating as ours, was very dangerous indeed. Coming under attack was a risk they faced every time they were deployed into the field in support of infantry ground forces. All of us knew full well the respective dangers particular to each of our different operational roles. So, after always trading the usual light-hearted, half-nasty inter-corps banter whenever we interacted with them in the field, we always bonded with them as Australian soldiers engaged in a common cause — a terrible war in a foreign country that we really knew very little about, and an enemy who we knew even less about.

A SQUADRON 1ST ARMOURED REGIMENT

Centurion Mk (5/1) Tanks

The other heavier element of armoured support for 8 RAR in Vietnam was provided by Centurion tanks from A Squadron, 1st Armoured Regiment. Operated by a 4-man crew which comprised of the commander, gunner, driver, and operator-loader, these all-terrain tracked tanks were fearsome.

Centurion tanks weighed 52t and with their Rolls-Royce Meteor petrol 650hp engines (27,000cm^3), only had an off-road range of 90km. This necessitated the installation of additional armour-protected fuel carrying capacity — nearly doubling that range — during their deployment to Vietnam. They could travel over flat, open ground at something like 35km/h.

The main tank armament was an extremely accurate 105mm L7 rifled gun, augmented by one range finding Browning M2 50cal machine gun, as well as two Browning M1919 30cal co-axial machine guns. Each tank carried 62 rounds for its gun: 4,000 0.5in calibre rounds and 9,000 0.3in calibre rounds.[24]

The armour plating of these tanks was pressed steel with a thickness varying between 51-152mm (2-6in). Overall, it was pretty good protection against small arms and machine gun fire, rocket-propelled grenades, and

---

[24] Ham, Paul. *Vietnam, The Australian War.* Harper Collins, Australia, 2007, Page 379.

recoilless rifles. The main weakness of these tanks was a major susceptibility — in terms of tracks being blown-off, thereby immobilising them — by land mines.

A Squadron, 1st Armoured Regiment, RAAC, when deployed to Vietnam was comprised of 18 battle tanks, 2 command and support tanks (HQ), 4 dozer tanks, and 4 bridge building tanks, as well as several recovery tanks — 28 tanks in all. During Australia's military commitment to the conflict in Vietnam, 58 Centurion tanks saw operational service — 42 of which suffered battle damage — with 6 of those unrepairable. Sadly, 2 tank crewmen were killed in action in Vietnam.

Unlike tanks of earlier conflicts, Centurion tanks were able to fire their main cannon gun while moving. This made them an attractive and highly potent armament resource indeed. Unfortunately, that incredible field advantage was negated significantly in Vietnam because of the terrain and the particular nature of the conflict in Phuoc Tuy Province. Tanks of earlier major conflicts always had to stop for a time to fire their cannons at enemy targets. Clearly, that in turn made them a fixed target with often disastrous results.

Although capable of firing quite destructive armour-piercing rounds, the main type of round used in Vietnam by Centurion tanks was a 9.1kg high-explosive round — muzzle velocity of 430m/s — that was highly accurate out to a distance of something like 6.6km. This range wasn't too important in any close quarter engagement with the enemy, which typified the nature of the usual type of contact confronting Australian infantry soldiers in Phuoc Tuy Province. Centurion tanks also fired canister rounds — muzzle velocity of 650m/s — which were highly effective out to a range of about 200m.

Canister fired by tanks, operates in very much the same way as a shotgun, by dispersing the contained desiccated shrapnel in the round as it leaves the barrel. It was very effective against attacking enemy infantry and was utilised this way during the Battles of Fire Support Bases Coral, and Balmoral, fought variously between 12 May to 6 June 1968. Canister was not dissimilar to splintex or beehive, which was sometimes used in Vietnam by Australian artillery batteries.

Although extremely practical when used in operations over flat, cleared ground, in attacking bunker systems, massed enemy soldiers, and as defensive armaments in static ground positions such as fire support bases, the types of operations that my platoon was engaged in, made them almost obsolete from a tactical and practical viewpoint. Generally, our day-time movement in either platoon or half-platoon strength was deliberate, slow, and very quiet. Tanks were relatively slow moving, very noisy, and destroyed our operational security whenever they were attached to us.

Nevertheless, while tanks were often used quite extensively in support of other 8 RAR elements, particularly in assaults against large bunker systems and in operations around the Long Hai Hills and the flat, sparsely forested Xuyen Moc areas, there were only 2 occasions when the Assault Pioneer Platoon operated in concert with tanks.

One of these instances was quite early during my time in Vietnam. We were in dense, almost impenetrable jungle in the far north of the province, and much later for over a week in areas north of the De Courtenay rubber plantation, well over the provincial border and some distance into Long Khanh Province. Tanks were attached to our platoon for this latter period while we operated as a northern blocking force for other battalion operations.

Just like the occasions when we ambushed at night in the company of APCs, it was pleasing to know that we had this additional form of firepower during those spasmodic days and nights out in the field. While soldiers from other elements of 8 RAR may have often travelled sitting on top of APCs, not too many of my 8 RAR peers would have done the same.

Tanks were certainly used by other elements of 8 RAR to clear routes through parts of the Long Hai Hills, thereby enabling APCs to follow in their tracks without too much of a threat from land mines.

I can also appreciate how tanks in Vietnam were used as mobile perimeter defence systems for fire support bases or night defensive positions, as they certainly were in the large Battles of Coral, and Balmoral, when they fired canister at point blank range at attacking enemy infantry. Tanks also performed an outstanding and vital role in the battle of Binh Ba.

However, overall, I'm not a great fan of tanks given that the jungle, rubber, and most other landscapes typical to Southern Vietnam, wasn't conducive to tank warfare. Having said that, the A Squadron, 1st Armoured Regiment soldiers that I encountered during my time in Vietnam were well-trained and brave men, doing a very dangerous job.

ROYAL AUSTRALIAN AIR FORCE (RAAF)

9 SQUADRON

Bell UH-1H Iroquois Helicopters (Huey)

Another very welcome sight, along with the distinctive 'thwack, thwack, thwack' sound we heard many times out in the field in Vietnam was that of Iroquois helicopters, usually from 9 Squadron — Call-sign 'Albatross' — approaching and then descending to our ground position.

The Vietnam War was the first major military conflict where helicopters played such a crucial and effective role in supporting ground troops. It precipitated the impetus for a quantum leap forward in the review and development of military strategy and infantry tactics of those times.

This wonderful form of air support meant that we were about to be provided with either aerial firepower support, rations, water, equipment, delivery of mail, or that we were going to be transported to a new location or, again, ever hopefully — back to Nui Dat.

9 Squadron RAAF (Bell UH-1H) Iroquois Helicopter (Huey) at Nui Dat.

Such superb air support also meant that a wounded, injured, or deceased soldier could be air lifted from the battlefield and transported back to the US Army 36 Evacuation Hospital, 1 AFH at Vung Tau, or more rarely, 8 Field Ambulance at Nui Dat, very quickly indeed. Usually within 20 minutes or less. Having said that, Phuoc Tuy Province wasn't a significant ground area. It only occupied 2,000km² (approximately 50km x 40km).

While Iroquois helicopters reached a maximum speed of 110kts (204km/h), they generally cruised at around 97kts or (180km/h). The stock standard (slick) Iroquois helicopter had 2 pilots as well as a crewman, and a side gunner, both of whom operated a single side-mounted M60 7.62mm machine gun, belt-fed from drums below. The side doors were never closed and although there were 5 seats across the back, they were always folded up or not even there in many cases. No seat belts were ever fitted because of their propensity to tangle and impede quick entry into, and egress out of the aircraft. Effectively, the area behind the pilots was usually just an open void into which poor infantry cannon fodder, like myself, were sometimes crammed into.

Depending on the number of men on board a particular aircraft at any one time, some of us sat on the edge of each side door opening, with legs dangling over the sides and mates holding onto our waist belts…in case there was any tendency to fall out. Generally, although it was a real squeeze, 3 or sometimes 4 Iroquois helicopters were able to relocate an entire infantry platoon. In terms of relocating one entire infantry company in one airlift, I reckon that a minimum of 14 aircraft would have been required. So, it might have been 2 airlifts. I don't really know.

Quite frankly, to travel operationally in an Iroquois helicopter in Vietnam was nothing short of absolutely terrifying. We were often told that when the helicopter banked, or turned at speed, the associated centrifugal generated 'G' forces that came into play, would ensure that no one could actually fall out. Did

9 Squadron RAAF (Bell UH-1H) Iroquois Helicopters (Huey) at Nui Dat.

I ever believe that sort of dubious advice? Not for a minute!

One of my very good Vietnam veteran mates, the late Pete Ryan, once told me that the 'G' forces applied to my body during those tight turns meant that I effectively weighed 2 to 3 times my actual body weight, and therefore couldn't have fallen out of the aircraft even if I wanted to. At the time, I treated this information, and still do, with a great deal of scepticism. Would a RAAF'ie tell me a pork pie? Well, yeah, I think he would...especially Pete Ryan!

Pete Ryan was a leading aircraftsman airframe fitter in 9 Squadron who, like most of us, served only one 12-month deployment to Vietnam. However, I'm not aware of any other Vietnam veteran who knew so much detail regarding the 10-plus years of Australia's involvement in that conflict, or who personally knew, and had access to so many influential veterans and notable persons whom he was able to draw upon in his efforts to help any Vietnam veteran in dire financial, medical, or social need. Frankly, his endless energies in this area never ceased to amaze me.

From the time we first met in late 1996, he continuously bored me almost shitless with his unlimited, but mostly accurate recall of events in Vietnam, along with his somewhat myopic views on some veteran happenings and associated internal political wrangling in Australia since those times. Nevertheless, even though we lived in quite different, but somewhat parallel universes, he was a very genuine guy and remained a firm friend of mine until his premature death on 6 April 2017. No matter what anyone ever thought of him, he really was a veteran's friend, and we are all much poorer for his passing. Vale, Pete Ryan.

Whenever my legs were dangling over the side of an Iroquois helicopter I made damn sure that the guys behind me had a very firm grip — I actually used to check to make sure — on my webbing waist belt. And I almost instantly learned to lean back heavily, with one hand tightly gripping whoever or whatever I could latch onto behind me. To put it mildly, I was terrified of falling out, and I could never overcome this horrible phobia. The fact that I was repeatedly told that no-one had ever fallen out of an Iroquois helicopter made absolutely no difference whatsoever to my inured mindset regarding this awful experience.

For obvious reasons Iroquois helicopter crews, when out in the field, didn't want to spend any more time on the ground than was absolutely necessary. When boarding these aircraft out in the field, it was always a mad scramble to get airborne as quickly as possible. Conversely, when dropping us off at a location out in the field, these aircraft didn't generally land at all. They usually hovered a short distance above the ground and once we were off-loaded, they were able to drop their nose and quickly gain forward momentum, speed, and altitude. My personal observations were that it took some serious seconds of time for a 'landed' Iroquois helicopter to actually disengage from the ground and do this.

Quite clearly, helicopters on the ground were 'sitting ducks' for enemy rocket-propelled grenades, mortar, recoilless rifle, and even small arms targeting. I always fully understood the almost obsessive preoccupation of their crews in relation to the speed and efficiency of our embarking and disembarking.

US Marine Corps (USMC) Vietnam veteran, Mike Ryerson, penned a wonderful poem in 1986 titled 'The Man in the Doorway'.[25] I have reproduced the first 2 short paragraphs here:

> *'... They came in low and hot, close to the trees and dropped their tail in a flare, rocked forward and we raced for the open doorways. This was always the worst for us, we couldn't hear anything, and our backs were turned to the tree line. The best you could hope for was a sign on the face of the man in the doorway, leaning out waiting to help with a tug or to lay down some lead.*
>
> *Sometimes you could glance quickly at his face and pick up a clue as to what was about to happen* (behind us at the tree line). *We would pitch ourselves in headfirst and tumble against the scuffed riveted aluminum* (aluminium), *grab for a handhold and will that son-of-a-bitch into the air...'*

The reason I've included these riveting words is because they so accurately describe what it was like to board an Iroquois helicopter out in the field.

The horrendous pulsating, collective noise from the powerful Lycoming T53-L-13 turbine engines — each generating 1,400 shaft hp — and the rotor blades of 3 or more Iroquois helicopters on the ground at one time, was simply deafening. We couldn't hear what anyone was saying — even if they were yelling — and we were doing everything at breakneck speed in terms of getting

---

[25] Ryerson, Mike USMC. *The Man in the Doorway*. 1986.

on or off the aircraft. And for the most part, we couldn't see properly either, as clumps of loose vegetation, leaves, other debris, and more often than not that disgusting fine red dust, usually enveloped us. This was always a time of confusion, great stress, and potentially extreme vulnerability for us, as well as the aircraft crews.

Fortunately, I never had to disembark from, or board an Iroquois helicopter in a 'hot zone'. Having to cope with incoming enemy fire would have added significant complication to an already highly stressful period of long seconds for us. As it was, our adrenalin levels were quite literally surging anyway.

Although I'm applying some considered 'vague' memory guesswork here, when picking up an infantry platoon out in the field, Iroquois helicopters would have been on the ground for no longer than perhaps 20 seconds, if that. Even then, I'm quite certain that the crews of those aircraft probably felt that was about 10 seconds too long. Dropping us off in the field wouldn't have taken as much time, probably no more than around 12 seconds.

Those timings don't seem very long, do they? But, in reality they are. Try counting to 20, or even 12, while watching the progression of the second hand of a clock. Tic...toc...tic...toc! They're both long periods of time for a helicopter crew to be sitting in their grounded — or almost grounded — aircraft, pretty much defenceless against any potential incoming enemy fire.

We utilised Iroquois helicopters occasionally and, to make matters worse, I was usually one of the poor bastards courting death — so it seemed to me — by testing the laws of physics in relation to the properties of centrifugal forces. In addition, I often felt that I wasn't even properly on board the aircraft when it lifted off from a pickup point out in the field. Sometimes I was half-dragged into the void behind the pilots by platoon mates as it was already beginning to lift off. These experiences weren't nice at all.

Leaving aside the emotional and diametrically opposed mix of relief and sheer terror I invariably experienced whenever I was in an Iroquois helicopter, I have to say that there was no way that I wasn't going to board one at any chance I had. While I may have gradually become somewhat mentally deranged during my time in Vietnam, I was never that cerebrally unbalanced. Well, that isn't completely true...there were some occasions when my fragile mental health led me to make several very poor personal choices that I've never forgotten, and very much regret making to this very day. I'll elaborate on this a bit later.

By the time 8 RAR arrived in Vietnam, 9 Squadron comprised 16 Bell UH-1H aircraft, along with about 170 personnel, and a substantial ramping-up of its earlier capability of 6 Bell UH-1B aircraft prior to late 1967. Four of these modern rotary aircraft had been converted into Bushranger gunships.

During their service in Vietnam, of the 33 Iroquois helicopters collectively

Chapter 18 – Operational Support

deployed by 9 Squadron, 7 were shot down, crashed, or otherwise destroyed. A further 23 suffered major battle damage from enemy ground fire. Six squadron members were killed on operations, as well as another member from No.1 Support Unit who was attached to the squadron at that time. Also, 8 members were wounded by enemy ground fire or as a direct result of that fire.

Bell UH-1H Iroquois Helicopters (Bushranger Gunships)

As well as transporting and re-supplying troops in the field, evacuating wounded and deceased soldiers from the battlefield, and undertaking special operations with the AATTV and the SASR, 4 Iroquois helicopters from 9 Squadron provided direct aerial fire support for ground troops in their converted role as heavily armed attack helicopters, otherwise known as 'Bushranger gunships'.

9 Squadron Bushranger Gunship at Nui Dat.

Bushranger gunships had a crew of 2 pilots and 2 side gunners, who each operated twin-mounted M60 7.62mm machine guns, belt-fed from drums below. In addition they were equipped with 2 side-mounted rocket pods, each containing seven 2.75in (70mm) rockets. These rockets were able to be fitted with either high-explosive or white phosphorus rounds. They were also armed with two 7.62mm mini guns, with a rate of fire something in the vicinity of 4,500 rpm. On some of these aircraft, mini guns were 'tweaked-up' to be capable of firing 6,000 rpm. Bushranger gunships were able to provide handy air support for Australian infantry on the ground, and did so on many occasions during the Vietnam War.

Because of its very significant armaments, the Bushranger gunships were much heavier than standard slick Iroquois helicopters. Accordingly, they had reduced maximum and cruising speeds, and decreased overall time in the air before necessary refuelling. Nevertheless, Bushranger gunships were called on to support 8 RAR in the field on many occasions and, whenever they did so, provided concentrated aerial supporting fire for soldiers on the ground.

During its deployment to Vietnam — 2,000 days including 900 of these with Bushranger gunships in operation — 9 Squadron flew 237,806 sorties, carried over 414,000 passengers, and medically or casualty evacuated 4,357 soldiers. In addition, the quantum of ammunition expended by its aircraft in support of 1 ATF ground troops during that period was extraordinarily high: 2.75in (70mm) rockets - Total 29,285 and 7.62mm rounds - Total 15,512,361.

9 Squadron Bushranger Gunship at Nui Dat.

2 SQUADRON

GAF Canberra Mk.20 Tactical Bombers

In April 1967, the RAAF deployed 2 Squadron — Call-sign 'Magpie' — Canberra MK 20 tactical bombers to Vietnam. These aircraft were built under license in Australia by the United Kingdom based Government Aircraft Factories (GAF), and were powered by Rolls-Royce 3,400kg thrust Avon Mk 109 turbojet engines. The Canberra cruised at 379kts (703km/h) and reached a top speed of 503kts (933km/h).

The squadron was attached to the US 7th Air Force, under the operational command of its 35th Tactical Fighter Wing. They operated out of the large USAF Phan Rang base in Ninh Thuan Province, located on the east coast of Vietnam, about 290km north-east of Vung Tau. Flying around 5% of the 35th Tactical Fighter Wing sorties during its attachment, 2 Squadron was credited with 16% of the resultant — and later confirmed — aggregate Wing bomb damage assessment.

During its lengthy deployment to Vietnam and attachment to the US 7th Air Force, the squadron achieved an aircraft serviceability rate of 97%. I reckon that given the squadron's workload over more than 5 years, that was nothing short of amazing. It really is worth having a quiet think about this sustained performance level. I wonder if the squadron's ground crews were ever formally recognised for their extraordinary effort. My guess is, probably not.

Canberra bombers were versatile aircraft and very well suited to low level sorties. They often delivered their bomb payloads from altitudes well below 1,000m. On a number of occasions these aircraft released their bombs from as low as 245m, followed by a rapid power climb to a height above the resultant blast and fragmentation envelope. However, a number of these aircraft were damaged by their own bomb fragments — shrapnel — and some navigators suffered minor injuries as a result. Frankly, I wonder why their bombs weren't the 'Hi-Drag' type, which were commonly used by the USAF McDonnell Douglas F-4 Phantom jets. See later in this chapter.

During the deployment of 2 Squadron to Vietnam, 8 Canberra bombers, each of which were flown by a crew of 2, consistently conducted 8, and sometimes 9 sorties a day, 7 days a week, every week. The squadron — which operated in all 4 Corps Tactical Zones — flew 11,963 combat missions and dropped 76,389 bombs. A typical bomb payload for each aircraft during a paired sortie was six 341kg bombs: 4 in the bomb bay, and one under each wing tip. From time to time these highly effective strike aircraft supported I ATF field elements including 8 RAR.

The squadron was credited with 786 confirmed enemy kills, 3,390 estimated enemy kills, and the destruction of 15,568 bunkers, 1,267 sampans, 74 bridges, and 8,637 other structures.

During their service in Vietnam, of the 13 Canberra bombers collectively deployed by 2 Squadron, 2 were shot down, crashed, or otherwise destroyed. One other aircraft suffered minor damage from ground fire.

A particular aircraft — A84-231 — which was shot down on 3 November 1970, was crewed by Flying Officer Michael Herbert. He attended Marist Brothers Sacred Heart College in Adelaide, my old 'alma mater'. While I didn't know Herbert at all during our school days — he was 2 years older than me — I sometimes think about our loose 'Vietnam' connection, particularly after his remains and those of his flight navigator partner, Pilot Officer Robert Carver, were located in northern Vietnam, extracted, and repatriated back to Australia on 31 August 2009. Herbert now rests peacefully, close to where both my parents repose, in the military section — Derrick Gardens — of Centennial Park Cemetery in Adelaide.

The other aircraft — A84-228 — was shot down on 14 March 1971 in the Khe Sanh area. The crew, Wing Commander John Downing and Flight Lieutenant Allan Pinches, ejected from the aircraft and following their rescue the next day by a US Army rescue UH-1H Iroquois helicopter, confirmed that they'd been hit by a SA-2 surface to air missile, which completely blew their right wing off.

The squadron's last operational sortie in Vietnam was on 31 May 1971 and it departed the USAF Phan Rang air base on 4 June 1971, arriving back at the RAAF Amberley air base in Queensland the next day.

35 SQUADRON

DHC – 4A Caribou

An Australian workhorse in Vietnam was the De Havilland Canadian DHC-4A Caribou aircraft from 35 Squadron, 6 of which were first deployed to Vietnam on 6 August 1965. These aircraft were integrated into the South-East Asia Airlift System — operated by the USAF — and initially became part of the USAF 315th Troop Carrier Group (Assault), which later became the USAF 315th Air Commando Wing. Operational control of the squadron passed to the 834th Air Division of the US 7th Air Force.

The Caribou's operational tasking was a varied and heavy workload, and covered much of the air space above Corps Tactical Zone 3, which included Phuoc Tuy Province. The squadron routinely transported personnel and equipment into some 115 airfields of varying surfaces and dimensions throughout southern Vietnam. The Caribou also carried livestock, mail, fuel drums, and from time to time even peasant workers. The squadron — call sign 'Wallaby' — quickly became known as 'Wallaby Airlines'.

These versatile aircraft were vital to the movement of troops and materials in both operational and non-operational spheres. As well as its crew of 2, and a variable number of load handling personnel, a single Caribou was capable of carrying up to 32 field soldiers, along with all of their operational equipment. In other words, a full-strength platoon. Caribou aircraft reached a top cruising speed of 207kts (384km/h) but generally flew at a more fuel economical speed of 158kts (293km/h).

The Caribou was a particularly useful aircraft due to its rear loading facility, and its short take-off and landing capability. It only required a runway length of 365m for takeoff and it could power down to taxi speed within 80m after touchdown on the tarmac. These features allowed it to easily operate in and out of Luscombe Field at Nui Dat, as well as the majority of rough 'bush' airstrips dotted throughout South Vietnam. Caribou aircraft were also the usual mode of transport for soldiers needing to get from Nui Dat and Vung Tau to Tan Son Nhut — renamed Tan Son Nhat — airport at Saigon — now known as Ho Chi Minh City — and return when proceeding on, and returning from R&R leave.

After its initial deployment to Vietnam, 35 Squadron eventually operated 7 Caribou aircraft. Of the 13 aircraft that collectively served, 3 were shot down, crashed, or otherwise destroyed. A further 7 suffered major battle damage from enemy ground fire. One aircraft (A4-193) was hit by enemy ground fire on 6 separate occasions.

Caribou aircraft flew 80,000 sorties — 47,000 hours of flying time — during the deployment of 35 Squadron to Vietnam. Overall they carried 677,000 passengers, 36mkg of freight, and 5mkg of mail.

36 AND 37 SQUADRONS

Hercules Lockheed C130A and C130E

Lockheed Hercules C130A aircraft from 36 Squadron and Lockheed Hercules C130E aircraft from 37 Squadron were the other 2 workhorses in support of Australian troops in Vietnam. C130E aircraft had a longer range and greater load carrying capability than that of the C130A. These lumbering, but utterly reliable aircraft, performed courier runs to and from Australia 3 times a week, carting mail and essential supplies from Australia to 1 ALSG.

The main distinction between these 'Hercules' squadrons was their respective roles. 36 Squadron operated solely as a cargo carrier, whereas 37 Squadron was also used for medical evacuation flights. The Monday flight each week was the 'medevac' flight, which transported wounded or seriously ill soldiers back home. On Tuesdays and Saturdays, caskets containing the bodies of deceased soldiers were transported back to Australia. RNZAF Bristol Freighters also performed regular transport and freight courier runs to and from New Zealand in support of our Kiwi allies.

AUSTRALIAN ARMY AVIATION UNIT

161st (Independent) Reconnaissance Flight

I must confess that when I was searching the obscure recesses of my mind, and otherwise undertaking research for my story, the very important role of 161st (Independent) Reconnaissance Flight — the Flight — in Vietnam almost passed me by. This is hardly surprising given that during my time in Vietnam, not only was I at the bottom end of the infantry information chain, I was also extremely preoccupied with not being noticed (as you know). Therefore, I never questioned or sought clarification on anything that didn't directly relate to my current operational tasking. Asking questions superfluous to that, was a very unwise decision in my mind, because it always meant that someone of higher rank might notice me.

The Flight — call sign 'Possum' — wasn't part of any RAAF deployment to Vietnam. I can tell you that veterans of the Flight would be mortified and highly insulted if anyone were to ever associate them with the RAAF. It was an army aviation unit, pure and simple.

As the Flight's call sign suggests, the various aircraft that this army unit employed in Vietnam were extensively used for low-level ground surveillance. This usually meant flying at low speed, and because of this, the Flight's aircraft — both rotary and fixed-wing — were highly susceptible to being shot down or otherwise damaged by enemy ground fire.

In Vietnam, circa 1970, the Flight comprised 6 Bell 47G-3B-1 Sioux light observation helicopters and 4 Pilatus PC-6 Turbo Porter fixed-wing aircraft. Interestingly, when 8 RAR deployed to Vietnam on HMAS *Sydney*, the ship delivered 3 of these fixed-wing aircraft to the Flight.

While its primary role was reconnaissance for Task Force Headquarters (TFHQ), the daily operational tasking of this army aviation unit based at Nui Dat — not 1 ALSG at Vung Tau, as per 9 Squadron — was quite varied. During 1970, a substantial and very significant operational commitment of the Flight was for it to provide dedicated helicopter support daily to each of the 3 Australian infantry battalions. Not surprisingly, each battalion made full use of this operational support.

For example, its day-to-day operational tasking in support of 8 RAR routinely involved liaison, aerial reconnaissance, artillery fire adjustment — all pilots of the Flight were qualified to provide range-adjusting instructions, based on the fall of shot of artillery and mortar fire — spotting for naval gunfire support, re-supply, casualty evacuation, and radio transmission relay.

Tasking often involved taking the Commanding Officer of 8 RAR out to meet with his Company Commanders in the field or, more rarely, Company Commanders to meet with their deployed Platoon Commanders. Aerial reconnaissance tasks usually involved looking for signs of enemy on the ground, providing information on terrain features, and assisting ground troops with navigation advice in the more impenetrable jungle areas.

At first light each day, the Flight conducted an aerial reconnaissance of Phuoc Tuy Province, usually by fixed-wing aircraft. At the same time, rotary-wing aircraft conducted document runs to all Australian liaison officers located with outlying South Vietnam military detachments. These early morning flights also doubled as reconnaissance missions, as Phuoc Tuy Province wasn't a large ground area.

Another major operational tasking of the Flight was target marking for USAF or RAAF air strikes. When engaged on this extremely dangerous task, unarmed Sioux helicopters — Possums — would swoop down and drop white phosphorus grenades on target positions and then quickly withdraw. After the

Chapter 18 — Operational Support

subsequent air strikes, the Possums would dive in low over bombed target areas whilst their pilots visually conducted a detailed damage assessment report for TFHQ back at Nui Dat.

The aircraft employed in these air strikes were usually USAF F4-E Phantom jets and occasionally, RAAF GAF Canberra MK20 bombers, or South Vietnamese Sky Raiders. On some rare occasions, USAF B-52 and F100 Super Sabre aircraft from Bien Hoa Province and Tan Son Nhut (Saigon) airbases, were used in support of 1 ATF field elements.

Although it used 2 aircraft types in its highly specialised, dangerous, and very effective role, the workhorse of the Flight during my time with 8 RAR was the Bell 47G-3B-1 Sioux helicopter — the Possum.

The Sioux helicopter was a small, relatively slow, but very maneuverable light observation aircraft. Although Possums were unarmed, some of them did fly a small number of day-time sorties with an M60 7.62mm machine gun mounted on their right side. A ground based crew member performed the role of side gunner. Possums were rarely, if ever, tasked with night-time sorties.

161 (Independent) Reconnaissance Flight Bell 47G-3B-1 Sioux Helicopter.
(Courtesy of the Australian War Memorial)

When 1 Platoon, A Company of 8 RAR was impacted by 2 contiguous and disastrous M16 anti-personnel mine incidents on 28 February 1970 — with a resultant large number of fatalities and other casualties — a Possum, piloted by 2LT Malcolm R Smith, played a significant role in quickly delivering an engineer to the battlefield, followed up on subsequent sorties with medical staff and further engineers, as well as undertaking 4 urgent casualty evacuations. 2LT Smith was later awarded the Distinguished Flying Cross (DFC) for his bravery that day over a 5-hour period. I don't know how the remaining deceased and wounded were repatriated from the battlefield on this infamous day in 8 RAR history.

On a personal note, when I was medically evacuated from the Nui Dinh Mountains for that urgent dental surgery in late February 1970, it was a marvelous Possum that took me back to Nui Dat. It generally cruised at 75kts (138km/h) and, for defensive purposes, usually at treetop level.

Between September 1965 and September 1971, 37 Possums saw service in Vietnam. Eight of them were either shot down by enemy ground fire, or otherwise written-off as irreparable due to battle damage. Some 13 of them served a second tour of Vietnam. Collectively, Sioux helicopters flew a total of 43,911 hours and conducted 66,069 sorties during operations in Vietnam.

The other aircraft type of the Flight — Pilatus PC-6 Turbo Porter fixed-wing aircraft (Porters) — in early 1970, replaced the 3 Cessna 180A aircraft that had been used previously. While the Porters had a maximum speed of 150kts (280km/h), they usually cruised at around 118kts (219 km/h).

The Porters performed daily early morning reconnaissance of Phuoc Tuy Province and were often engaged on a range of operational tasking including night-time battlefield illumination, rocket ground attack and target marking for artillery, mortars, and naval gunfire support, as well as some more routine functions like leaflet drops, radio relay, voice and sniffer missions, and electronic surveillance tasks with 547 Signal Troop. In terms of their armament, the Porters were equipped with either 7 or 19 pod 2.75in (70mm) high-explosive rockets when providing top cover for Sioux aircraft.

The 161 (Independent) Reconnaissance Flight was an integral component of necessary air support provided to 1 ATF field elements, and complemented the wider and more conventional air support provided by the RAAF and the USAF. While the Flight was the main reconnaissance and target marking resource for 1 ATF, it was also supported in this role by USAF Forward Air Controllers — Call sign 'Jade' — using Cessna O-1 Bird Dog, Cessna 02 Skymaster, and Rockwell OV-10A Bronco fixed-wing aircraft that operated out of Vung Tau. Some of these Forward Air Controllers were RAAF fighter pilots attached to the USAF and a number of them were formally decorated by the US Government.

ROYAL AUSTRALIAN NAVY (RAN)

RAN warships provided naval gunfire support for allied units in Vietnam from March 1967 until September 1971. During this time HMAS *Brisbane*, *Hobart*, and *Perth* were attached for rotating 6-monthly attachments to the US Navy (USN) 7th Fleet, which patrolled the waters off the east coast of South Vietnam, as part of what was known as the 'gun-line'. HMAS *Vendetta* was attached to the gun-line for one 6-month period only. The gun-line usually comprised 7 ships, a variable mix from the USN and the RAN.

HMAS *Hobart* and *Perth* actively participated in 'Operation Sea Dragon' — the bombardment of North Vietnamese military targets and the interdiction of supply routes and logistical craft along the coast of North Vietnam from the Demilitarised Zone (DMZ) to the Red River Delta — during the period of April 1967 to November 1968.

The RAN gun-line ships during my time with 8 RAR were the Daring Class destroyer HMAS *Vendetta* and the Charles F Adams Class guided missile (DDG) destroyers HMAS *Hobart* and *Perth*. HMAS *Brisbane*, another DDG destroyer, didn't serve on the gun-line during my time in Vietnam.

HMAS *Hobart*. Charles F Adams Class destroyer escort and 'gun-line' ship.
(Imagery courtesy of Defence Australia)

HMAS *Vendetta*. Daring Class destroyer escort and 'gun-line' ship.
(Imagery courtesy of Defence Australia)

During her gun-line deployment from September 1969 to April 1970, *Vendetta* fired 13,265 high-explosive rounds from her 4.5in guns, as well as 414 rounds of 40mm ammunition from her bofors guns. *Hobart* fired 16,901 and *Perth* 9,712 high-explosive rounds from their 5in guns respectively, during their period of deployment from March 1970 to April 1971.

The guided missile armament on the DDG destroyers was basically an anti-air warfare capability. It wasn't used during their service in Vietnam, other than for training exercises. However, the guided missile armaments could have been used by both of these ships at very short notice.

HMAS *Hobart*, *Perth*, and *Brisbane*, in addition to their guided missile armaments, could fire their two 5in guns at a sustained rate of fire of 40 rpm to a highly accurate range of over 22km. This rate of fire for each gun was sustainable for lengthy periods of time due to the loading mechanisms for the extremely heavy 35kg high-explosive rounds being fully automated. They were manoeuvrable ships capable of reaching 35kts (65km/h).

During the Vietnam War, South Vietnam was divided into 4 military command zones below the DMZ. This DMZ was just on the 17th parallel north of earth's equatorial plane, and 100km north of the eastern coastal city of Hue. Australian military personnel operated almost exclusively in part of what was known as Corps Tactical Zone 3. Besides supporting 1 ATF field elements in Phuoc Tuy Province, all gun-line ships — whether USN or RAN warships — were rotated through all 4 Corps Tactical Zones, otherwise known as Military Regions after July 1970.

The main roles of these ships were surveillance of the extremely long and meandering coastline south of the DMZ, patrolling of the associated 'Market Time' areas, interdiction and suppressing of enemy water-borne logistic craft movement, the bombardment of enemy military targets in South Vietnam, gunfire in support of allied ground forces and, in the case of the RAN DDG destroyers, provision of air defence capability for USN aircraft carriers on station off the coast of South Vietnam.

When RAN gun-line ships were in range to support 1 ATF field elements, they did so. Reliable statistics indicate that the vast majority of their firings were visually spotted, accurate, and greatly feared by the enemy. Many gun firings by the ships in support of 1 ATF field elements were very effective in close support of those ground forces.

During the 5 years that the RAN saw service in Vietnam on the gun-line, these 4 warships collectively steamed over 397,000nm or 735,244km, and fired about 102,546 high-explosive rounds from their guns.

Although not widely known, the RAN also provided direct air support for the allied war effort in Vietnam in the form of its Iroquois UH-1 Helicopter Flight — Call sign 'Emu' — which was attached to the US Army 135th Assault Helicopter Company. They operated variously out of Vung Tau, Blackhawk Fire Support Base in Long Khanh Province, Bearcat Fire Support Base in Bien Hoa Province, and at Dong Tam in the Mekong Delta region south of Saigon.

The US Army 135th Assault Helicopter Company flew Iroquois helicopters and provided for the tactical movement of combat troops, supplies, and equipment. They often assisted in large troop airlifts for 1 ATF.

US ARMY AIR SUPPORT

Cobra (AH-1G) Attack Helicopters

The Cobra was a US Army high performance attack helicopter specifically designed to provide top cover for troop carrying helicopters such as Chinooks and fire support for troops on the ground. As a very much scaled-down and redesigned Iroquois helicopter, it was capable of relatively high speed at around 170kts (306km/h) and, because of its much lighter weight, it could remain airborne over the battlefield for much longer than Bushranger gunships.

Its armament was like that of Bushranger gunships in that it comprised a single 7.62mm mini gun and 2 side-mounted pods (7 or 19 tubes) for 2.75in (70mm) rockets.

CH 47 Chinook Helicopters

The US Army Chinook was a twin-engine, tandem-rotor, heavy-lift, medium transport helicopter. The Chinook's primary mission was moving personnel, artillery, ammunition, and other supplies to and from the battlefield. It was a very lightly-armed helicopter and often required air support. The Chinook's maximum airspeed was 170kts (320km/h) with a normal cruising speed of 130kts (240km/h).

The Chinook had a crew of 2 pilots, at least 1 load master, and could transport between 30 and 40 soldiers, depending on the amount of equipment they were carrying. Australian infantry units in Vietnam, including 8 RAR, used these heavy load carrying helicopters on some occasions, particularly when establishing fire support bases and more elaborate night defensive positions.

US AIR FORCE (USAF) AIR SUPPORT

There were also USAF McDonnell Douglas AC-47D/DC-3 gunships that were affectionately known as 'Puff the Magic Dragon' — Call Sign 'Spooky'. These large, slow, low-flying aircraft were very deceptive because they could 'hang-around' circling for many hours while providing suppressing fire in support of infantry on the ground. They were equipped with 3 General Electric 7.62mm mini guns, each of which very accurately fired at selected rates of either 50 rps or 100 rps. These guns could be used intermittently — while cruising at 120kts (220km/h) in an overhead, anti-clockwise orbit, at an altitude of 900m over the target — for hours, or as long as its 45 flares and 24,000 round loads of ammunition held out. Bursts of directed and accurate fire from 'Spooky' were usually short and sharp and certainly much less than 3 seconds.

During my time in Vietnam, the USAF replaced 'Spooky' with upgraded Fairchild AC-119G and AC-119K gunships, known as 'Shadow' and 'Stinger' respectively. The Fairchild AC-119 series saw service in the Vietnam War (1962-1975) and fulfilled a dual-role capability based on the model types.

Although both aircraft were similar in many respects, 'Shadow' served in close support of ground troops and airbase defence roles, whereas 'Stinger' fulfilled more aggressive search-and-destroy sorties. While the AC-119K Stinger models were sometimes used in direct support of US Army ground troops, its targets were usually road transport and other enemy infrastructure located far north of Phuoc Tuy Province.

Each of these later aircraft types were powered by 2 Wright R-3350-85 'Duplex Cyclone' radial piston engines, each one generating 4,500 drive hp. Stinger was also equipped with 2 under-wing J85-GE-17 turbojets. For both aircraft types, the maximum speed was around 335km/h, with an economical cruising speed of 240km/h. They had a range of 3,100km and a maximum operational ceiling of 7,100m.

Armament varied between the 2 models. While the AC-119G (Shadow) aircraft carried four 7.62mm SUU-11A/1A Gatling mini guns — as did the AC-119K (Stinger) — the latter aircraft also carried an additional two 20mm M61 Vulcan six-barreled Gatling guns. Each aircraft carried 50,000 rounds of 7.62mm ammunition, as well as 60 Mk 24 flares fired from an LAU-74/A series launcher. The AC-119K (Stinger) also carried 4,500 rounds of 20mm ammunition.

With just one 3-second burst from its mini guns, 'Spooky' was capable of laying a round in every 2.2m^2 across an elliptical area 50m in diameter. 'Shadow' could lay a round in every 1m^2 of a football field sized area, with a similar burst of supporting gunfire.

'Puff the Magic Dragon' ('Spooky') and 'Shadow' were used extensively in Vietnam by the USAF for close ground support in and around Phuoc Tuy Province. There were also occasions when elements of 8 RAR, including my own platoon, were provided with this wonderful form of targeted and concentrated air support.

I personally received the benefit of that fire support on 8 January 1970, during a 9-hour night-time engagement with the enemy. 'Shadow' provided my platoon — and other Support Company and armoured elements — with direct air support during that engagement. It delivered in excess of 48,000 rounds of concentrated fire from its high performance 7.62mm Gatling mini guns, onto the positions of enemy soldiers persistently testing our defensive perimeter that night. I guess the USAF may have chosen the name 'Shadow'

Chapter 18 – Operational Support

to reflect the dense swathe of 7.62mm rounds that this devastating air support was capable of delivering with great accuracy.

Another much less common form of USAF air support available to 8 RAR in the field was in the form of huge Boeing B-52 Stratofortress bombers. These aircraft were known affectionately as 'BUFF' (Big Ugly Fat Fellow, or more colloquially, Big Ugly Fat Fucker). 8 RAR was provided with B-52 air support only once — during Operation Hammersley in February 1970.

Boeing B-52 Stratofortress bombers (56m wingspan), powered by 8 Pratt & Whitney TF33-P-3/103 turbofan engines, usually delivered their huge high-explosive payloads — weighing as much as 32,000kg (35tn) — from very high altitudes. They had an operational ceiling altitude of some 15km and a range of about 14,000km. These payloads wrought total devastation on the ground wherever the huge bombs landed and exploded. Paul Ham suggests that these large aircraft usually carried up to 84 bombs internally, each weighing 227kg, and 24 bombs under each wing, weighing in at a hefty 341kg each.[26] As recently as 2020, 76 of these aircraft were still engaged in USAF active service; admittedly with many significant upgrades to their operational performance.

The residual ground crater from a B-52 bomb was extraordinary and simply had to be seen to be believed. My platoon came across these craters from time to time in the north of the province and they were certainly massive land features.

Although rarely used by 1 ATF in Vietnam, USAF air support in the form of McDonnell Douglas F-4 Phantom jets was also available. The Phantom was a supersonic, long-range, all-weather fighter-bomber that was equipped with a wide range of state-of-the-art weaponry. Paul Ham, in his wonderful book 'Vietnam, The Australian War' says that the Phantoms were armed with 2 external cannons and typically carried 12 MK 82 'Hi-Drag' bombs, each weighing 227kg, 4 Sparrow radar missiles, 4 Sidewinder missiles, and several napalm canisters.[27] The finned-drag feature — which activated on the release of the MK 82 bombs — slowed their forward momentum relative to the aircraft that released them, which in turn allowed for much lower and safer low-level bombing. F-4 Phantoms also dropped white phosphorus incendiary bombs, anti-personnel cluster bombs, and 'area denial' chemicals — otherwise known as defoliants. Occasionally, they carried massive high-explosive 900kg bombs.[28]

---

[26] Ham, Paul. *Vietnam, The Australian War*. Harper Collins, Australia, 2007. Page 393.
[27] Ham, Paul. *Vietnam, The Australian War*. Harper Collins, Australia, 2007, Page 390.
[28] Ham, Paul. *Vietnam, The Australian War*. Harper Collins, Australia, 2007, Page 390.

CHAPTER 19

LOGISTICS

AMMUNITION

While I can no longer recall whether there was a minimum requirement for the amount of personal ammunition we were expected to carry out in the field, there would have been a battalion standard operating procedure in place for us to observe. I vaguely recall that we were required to carry at least 7 or 8 20-round magazines for the SLR rifle.

That would make sense because at the Battle of Long Tan, recorded history tells that each SLR rifleman in that battle carried 3 magazines (60 rounds); 1 on their weapon, and 2 in their webbing ammunition pouches. While that ammunition load many have been sufficient for relatively short contacts with small enemy forces, it was grossly deficient in terms of larger and longer contacts, such as this famous battle. There has been some conjecture that the men involved carried additional 'boxed' — not 'magazine-loaded' — rounds in their backpacks.

At the end of the day, it was really left up to each man in the platoon to decide on the balance of weight he carried out in the field, with a priority placed on ammunition and water. Although I'm certain that he would have done so, I can't actually remember my section commander ever physically checking the amount of ammunition I was carrying for my SLR rifle.

I always carried 12 spare magazines plus another one fixed in place under the weapon, with a round already sitting in the breech or firing chamber, safety on. That gave me 260 rounds of ammunition. I don't think that anyone else in my platoon carried more ammunition for their SLR rifle than I did! Somehow, I was able to cram 6 or 7 magazines into the ammunition pouches attached to my webbing belt, and secure the remaining magazines inside my bumpack. Each fully loaded 20-round magazine weighed 0.73kg. A few platoon members opted to carry some non-magazine loaded ammunition encased in soft bandoliers in their packs, thereby reducing their overall weight carry load by some margin. I never considered doing the same.

Those men using M16 Armalite rifles carried as many as 20 magazines — 400 (smaller) rounds. Each M60 machine gun group carried around 600 linked rounds (6 belts) with another 10 belts dispersed throughout each section of the platoon. Each belt weighed 2.95kg. I've already mentioned the significant additional weight that each section's M79 carrier was also loaded up with.

OPERATIONAL FOOD/RATIONS

Prior to any operational tasking, the field rations available to us were the same as the C Rations provided to US Army units. Sporadically, we were also given the option of selecting items from a very limited range of ADF Australian manufactured canned food items, most of which I thought were better quality.

On one occasion we were provided with assorted samples of freeze-dried and vacuum-sealed NZA ration sachets. Although this — at the time — innovative army ration type was extremely lightweight and easy to cram into our backpacks, once reconstituted with near-boiling water, they tasted incredibly awful. Thankfully, it was only an experimental ration type option and not a prescribed one. However, in today's contemporary ADF, ration provisions of this type have been significantly improved are now standard fare for its men and women out in the field.

I sampled one of these experimental NZA ration sachets that day. It was a meat-based meal of some kind, possibly hogget but — more likely than not — mutton. Our comrades from 'over the ditch' loved mutton and nothing else, other than beer of course! This particular NZA meal was seriously nasty. Try and imagine a chewy mutton meal, infused with cheap gravy thickener, and garnished with crunchy granules of desiccated mutton gristle, globules of fat, dried onion flakes, tomato seeds, long-cut stringy green celery and tasteless tendrils of some other almost inedible tuber-type foods particular only to New Zealand — and there you have it. Gross! Whilst this may not be exactly what I sampled that afternoon at Nui Dat, this was more or less what it looked like, and how it tasted to me. However, on a positive note, I reckon that this meal would have been an excellent bowel purgative prior to any medical colonoscopy. Unbelievably, our New Zealand mates, particularly those of Maori heritage, loved this sort of rations food.

I opted never to take any of these repulsive NZA food items out into the field, and given my obsession regarding the amount of weight I carried out there…that's really saying something! There was one instance, sometime later, that I ruefully regretted this hasty decision.

In our lines at Nui Dat on the afternoon before each operation, as we spent time cleaning our weapons, checking ammunition, the associated magazines, and getting our equipment squared away, there was always plenty of rations food items for us to choose from. We always knew how many days before our first scheduled re-supply out in the field — usually 5 days, but sometimes 7 — and decided on the quantity and type of rations to pack, according to those time frames.

Generally, there was no restriction as to the food items in terms of both volume and type. The only limiting factors were that we had to be able to actually fit them into our backpacks and bum-packs and, more importantly, be physically able to carry this weight along with the weight of everything else. Now this wasn't as easy as it sounds. The overwhelming bulk of our rations were contained in 'late 1960's era' heavy cans — tin plate or tin-coated steel — not the lightweight aluminium ring-pull containers of more modern times.

In determining the overall weight load before any operation, my strict order of priority was as follows: ammunition, water, cigarettes, anything else that was compact, lightweight and may be useful — then food. While personal hydration, cigarettes, my daily ablution regime, and trying to moderate my horrid facial acne affliction were daily imperatives for me...food certainly wasn't.

The US Army C Rations presented a very wide range of items in optional can sizes. They included meat-based meals, a variety of preserved fruits, breads, cakes, snacks etc. There were also numerous sachets of par-boiled freeze-dried rice to provide the basis for a quick, hot, tasty curried meal when mixed with the contents of a small meat-based can. I always carried plenty of this rice option with me because it weighed next to nothing and was very easy to pack. While its energy content was low, its high fibre was a positive feature.

There were also many sachets of salt, pepper, tea, coffee, sugar, powdered milk, and small tinned containers of jam, crackers, cheese etc. While the powdered milk was very ordinary indeed, the tubes of long-life condensed milk — which many of us were sent by family members back in Australia — were far too sweet for me. I rarely used the ones sent by my mother and instead gave them to other platoon members.

From the vast range of canned food item types, I was more focused on the small meat and medium-sized fruit meals. Amazingly, some of my platoon mates were indelibly wedded to other food types that I placed into a 'never to pack' category. Simply amazing!

From what I managed to discover decades later, it seems that the 3 platoons of one of the battalion's rifle companies were required to exist on near-starvation rations out in the field, and they were always eaten cold. While I understand the tactical thinking behind that very poor command decision, I offer my deepest sympathies to my 8 RAR peers of those affected platoons.

The US Army calculated that the average infantry soldier in the field in Vietnam needed to consume 15,100kj (3,600cal) per day, just to maintain his body weight of (say) 83kg. The US Army C Rations provided to us well and truly offered a potential daily feast approaching more than twice that magnitude. There was, however, a major downside to all this available largesse. The average daily weight of these US Army C Rations packs was a little over 2kg

Chapter 19 – Logistics

per man. Ergo, none of us ever packed rations with a collective energy content that came anywhere near approaching the US Army prescript of 15,100kj per day.

This US Army prescript was almost twice the average daily energy requirement — 8,700kj — recommended for the average-sized Australian male, some 50 years later. This very clearly reflects what the Allied Forces Command in Vietnam expected their infantry soldiers to do in terms of physical exertion when they were out in the field, bearing in mind the weight carry load asked of them. Being an infantry soldier was really arduous work, if not an utter slog. It wasn't for the faint hearted.

After a very short time, the average daily rations I carried generally weighed no more than 0.8kg, and even less as my time in Vietnam passed. I only ever took a minimal amount of food. When I say 'minimal', I'm talking about an almost Spartan-like quantity. No wonder many of us lost a significant amount of lean body weight. I never made allowances for an overdue rations re-supply. After a time, I got used to living on nothing more than a daily energy intake grossly insufficient for my body's needs — basal metabolic rate — let alone satisfying the significant energy demands imposed on my body due to my role as an infantry soldier.

When I returned home from Vietnam in November 1970, I weighed 76kg which, for a tall, large-framed and fit young man, was relatively underweight. This simply reflected my poor diet and the climatic and physical operational deprivations that I and my platoon mates were exposed to during the preceding 12 months.

By way of comparison, when I completed my 4 weeks of battle efficiency training at Canungra in late August 1969, I was in the best physical condition of my entire life. At that time, I weighed exactly 85kg and wasn't carrying even one gram of fat on my body. During 12 months in Vietnam, I lost 9kg of lean body mass. Weight loss of this magnitude was common for infantry soldiers deployed to Vietnam. For example, Gerald Windsor wrote:

> '... it was certainly Norris' (8 Platoon, C Company, 7 RAR 1967-68) view that... the men were run down and exhausted. He was 66.5kg when he went to Vietnam and 54kg when he returned...' [29]

The images on the following page were taken at Night Defensive Position Isa, probably around late July 1970. They speak volumes in terms of my generally poor physical condition at that time.

My daily food intake out in the field generally consisted of a small 5.5oz (160gm) can of a meat-based meal and a small 2.75oz (80gm) can of crackers

---

[29] Windsor, Gerald. *All Day Long the Noise of Battle*. Pier 9, Murdock Books Australia, 2011. Page 37.

and cheese for breakfast; later followed by a larger 12oz (340gm) can of a meat-based meal or an 8.75oz (250gm) can of preserved, diced fruit-meal for dinner. These evening meals were sometimes augmented with about half a mug of curried rice. We didn't ever eat lunch. See Appendix 4.

Peter McCann - Early morning at Night Defensive Position Isa.

Peter McCann with Des McGrath to his right.
Early morning at Night Defensive Position Isa.

Chapter 19 — Logistics

By the end of our first 32-day operation in the field, even breakfast almost became a non-event for me. However, on most early mornings I did try to eat something small, immediately after '*stand to*', if only to nudge my lower alimentary tract into doing what it was supposed to do. For the most part, I didn't eat anything else until late afternoon.

As my platoon used C4 plastic explosive to heat our food and boil water, none of us ever carried the standard army issue collapsible aluminium cooking stove. Unlike the stove's associated low value heating agent — hexamine — the intense burning heat from a small piece of C4 plastic would have just melted it. As far as I was concerned, the seemingly unlimited availability of C4 plastic for cooking and water heating purposes was the one and only benefit of being a member of the battalion's Assault Pioneer Platoon.

We improvised in terms of how we cooked out in the field by scraping a very shallow 30cm^2 hole in the ground to contain the small 15cm^3 knob (large-sized marble) of C4 plastic. We then ignited it with a match or Zippo cigarette lighter. The next step was to hold an aluminium mug — by its handle — over the white-hot furiously burning C4 plastic and — when it contained solid food with a measured amount of added water — vigorously and continuously stir its contents with either a lightweight army issue aluminium spoon or, sometimes, a firm piece of dried vegetation — a clean twig or stick — and variously raise and lower the mug above the heat source to inhibit the burning of its contents. Because we always used C4 plastic for cooking, the warming-up of food didn't take long at all. In terms of water, we were able to bring 500ml to the boil in about 30 seconds or less.

Given the oppressive climate and the daily physical demands imposed on us — moving at a very slow pace while carrying a heavy load — my food intake was grossly inadequate. But, frankly, because of its weight and a lack of packing space, it just wasn't physically possible for me to carry more food than I did. By the beginning of March 1970, I'd pretty much lost the desire to eat solid food anyway, even when I was back at Nui Dat.

By around early April — remembering that I carried plenty of lightweight par-boiled and freeze-dried rice sachets and curry powder — my minimal rations allowance for the first 5 days at the start of any operation, generally weighed no more than 3.5kg. On the other hand, the amount of water I carried often weighed as much as 10kg in its intrinsic form, which added to the dilemma of what I was physically capable of carrying out in the field.

On reflection, the US Army C rations were pretty average at best, and only tolerable long-term with the addition of curry powder and the occasional inclusion of canned food items sent by family back in Australia. To quote Corporal Bob O'Callaghan — overheard by my good friend Lance-corporal JJ

Smith — as he ate a can of meat-type rations:

'... like angels with feathered feet, flitting across my taste buds...'

In other words, whilst facing adversity he was making the best of a bad lot with his brand of 'grunt' humour. After a time, most of us couldn't consume substantial amounts of food because our stomach cavities had shrunk — and were constantly shrinking — as a direct result of our poor diet and operational deprivations. Apart from several rare exceptions — including Steve Kaliczinsky, Denis McNab, and Mick O'Shea — very few of us were ever hungry, even when we were back at Nui Dat.

However, I can recall one time, operationally, when I was completely out of rations and I became — strangely for me — absolutely ravenous. This occurred sometime during Operation Keperra in February 1970. At that time, our scheduled field re-supply was overdue by several days.

Because I'd already existed for a number of days on limited rations and had made no provision whatsoever for a delayed re-supply, I opened and ate the entire contents of my vacuum-sealed tin of concentrated dark energy chocolate — which was only ever to be consumed in emergency situations — thereby pissing-off my section commander no end. He told me that he was going to charge me over this blatant breach of battalion standard operating procedure. The fact that our rations re-supply was significantly overdue and constituted a 'first and last' food emergency to me, didn't seem to matter to him at all.

I liked Corporal Vincent and, as I was ultimately not charged by him for this incident, it never became an ongoing issue between us. That all being said and done, I resolved never to test him this way again. When I think long and hard about it, I don't remember ever being able to replace that highly valuable chocolate item anyway.

One afternoon at Nui Dat, before going out into the field on a new operation — and knowing that our first re-supply was due, unusually, in 7 days — I grossly miscounted the number of food items I packed. Once out in the field, it didn't take long for this awful mistake to dawn on me. So, I had no alternative other than to 'man up' and make something like 2 days' supply of frugal rations last for the next 5 days. God wasn't going to be kind to me if that re-supply was significantly delayed.

I had well and truly stuffed up! And I had no one to blame except myself. I was always obsessively meticulous with my personal preparations before each operation and I can't explain what happened on this occasion. I can tell you this though...it never happened again. This was the one and only occasion that I seriously regretted not cramming several of those inedible NZA dehydrated ration sachets inside my backpack and bum-pack.

This miscalculation on my part created a very serious problem for me.

Chapter 19 – Logistics

There's a base-line minimum daily energy requirement that I needed just to maintain my body weight, let alone provide the wherewithal for my physical exertions on any given day. And I had nowhere near enough energy resources to satisfy that basal requirement, even remotely, over the next 5 days. While I'm aware that some modern contemporary weight loss regimes are based on periods of fasting, devotees of those regimes will not be doing — in terms of physical exertion — what we were doing in Vietnam. There's simply no comparison between the 2 scenarios.

Although a couple of platoon mates eventually became aware of my predicament, I was certainly not going to advertise it. They weren't forthcoming in sharing any of their meagre rations with me...and I wasn't in the business of asking them for help either. I think that I may have been tossed a couple of sachets of rice, but that was about the extent of it. I actually thought this was very generous of them. As I discuss later, my obsession regarding water made me a total miser in terms of that precious commodity, so I fully understood their indifferent attitude towards my relatively short term, but very significant energy intake problem.

Strangely, during those 5 days leading up to our eventual scheduled field re-supply — I'm guessing my average daily energy intake would have been something less than 1,000kj — I didn't ever feel hungry, even though our daily operational tasking activities were, as usual, nothing short of exhausting.

On the contrary, I felt well-energised, clear-headed and totally focused on what I was doing out in the field. And I thoroughly enjoyed my morning and evening meals of small portions of curried rice accompanied with coffee, tea or water, and cigarettes. Incredibly, there seemed to be no impact whatsoever on my early morning ablution regime either...I still produced something substantial each morning from almost nothing! Now that's a mystery, and one which has always confounded me.

In his wonderful book on the post conflict health of Vietnam veterans, Peter Yule states that chronic constipation and associated haemorrhoids were problems that affected many infantry soldiers when they were in the field, because of the high protein and low carbohydrate nature of the US Army C Rations they were consuming; exacerbated by the limited availability of drinking water.[30] While I agree with that, the low volume of those C Rations would have also been a contributing factor. Strangely, those adverse physical complications referred to by Yule, never once affected me. This may be due to my high consumption of water out in the field, and my reliance on rice as an energy roughage staple.

Each day's available rations largesse included 3 USA packets of 4 premium

---
[30] Yule, Peter. *The Long Shadow*. New South Publishing, Sydney. 2020. Page 60.

brand cigarettes — 12 sticks in total — per man. I never had a problem snaffling 24 cigarettes or more a day from the vast array of discarded ration packs. Nevertheless, I always carried one carton — 10 packets — of Benson and Hedges Gold cigarettes (200 sticks) carefully wrapped in waterproof oil-skin cloth. I don't recall ever having to resort to using that reserve of premium brand cigarettes out in the field — other than on one occasion — but I was just ensuring that I could always feed my — then — insatiable nicotine habit. I never ran out of cigarettes and returned home to Australia as a committed, heavy chain-smoker; a horrible addiction that I finally overcame on Monday 22 September 1986.

On that memorable day, I arrived at my workplace around 7:45am and by 12:30pm, had depleted the last 13 sticks remaining in my overnight packet…I didn't waste one of them. I then went into a mentally committed 'cold turkey quit smoking' mode. Frankly, it was a horrendous nightmare for me and, after somehow managing to survive the first week of indescribable mental nicotine withdrawal challenges, I was able to successfully extricate myself — permanently — from this very unhealthy addiction. I never once faltered in my resolve to overcome this insidious habit and haven't smoked a cigarette since that day. Strangely, while the smell of cigarette smoke remains marginally intoxicating — certainly not unpleasant — I've never once felt the urge to re-engage with that former unhealthy habit.

Over the years I've been told by several Canberra-based medical general practitioners that long-term nicotine addiction is often harder to overcome than entrenched heroin addiction. Well, there you go! In my view, overcoming an addiction to any substance is all about a determined mind-set and just toughing out the testing mental and physical challenges as, and when, they inevitably arrive. I know that this is really very hard for some. Personally, I was one of the lucky ones, because I didn't experience any significant physical withdrawal symptoms whatsoever. In my case, it was all mental. Once I was determined to jettison the habit, I just stuck with it…but it wasn't at all easy.

Several of my platoon mates — Terry Lucas and Paul Jansen — only smoked 'Kool' brand menthol flavoured cigarettes. As these cigarettes weren't popular within the platoon, they had no trouble in garnering as many free packets as they wanted from the piles of rations discarded by us before any operation. I don't think they ever had to purchase one cigarette during their time in Vietnam.

Sergeant Cliff Grant also had a preoccupation with menthol flavoured cigarettes. This directly related to the thriving Vung Tau black market economy, and the addiction of the local Vietnamese in some small civilian centres near Nui Dat, to menthol flavoured cigarettes — it had nothing at all to do with his personal choice of cigarette type.

Chapter 19 — Logistics

Whenever I was back at Nui Dat, I purchased many cartons of premium brand cigarettes from the US Army Post Exchange Store (PX) for the princely sum of $US1 ($A0.81) for a carton of 10 packets (200 sticks). I then sent them back home to Australia for later consumption. At that time, the cost for a carton of the very popular Craven A, Marlboro, and Peter Stuyvesant brand cigarettes back in Australia, was around $A3.80. So, the cost of these bulk cigarettes I was purchasing at the PX was less than a quarter of the Australian price. And this was pretty much the same with comparative beer prices in Vietnam, compared to the price back home in Australia. Because most men in my platoon became confirmed smokers, it's no wonder we repatriated such vast quantities of cigarettes.

When I arrived back home in late November 1970, my father went out of his way to vigorously shake my hand, slap me on the back, and effusively thank me for the thousands of 'free' cigarettes I'd sent him from Vietnam. He'd avidly consumed them at a rate of around 50 a day…and didn't even leave one packet for me. Not one miserable stick! I couldn't believe it. And there was absolutely nothing I could really say to him either, so there was no point in even attempting to do so.

The PX at Nui Dat was something like a large Aldi Store in Australia. Their main aisle shelves were crammed full of mountains of current USA released electrical and photographical hardware products, premium brand cigarettes, and a broad range of spirit alcohol encased in 1L bottles. There were many other items for sale, but I can no longer remember the content of that diverse range. The prices — in $US — for all items on sale in the PX were inexpensive in the context of the beneficial exchange value of our $A currency, the comparative pay rates of Australian and US servicemen, and commercial prices back in Australia. However, other than a Panasonic radio — now a very valuable collector's item that I still use — a Yoshika Minister D SLR camera — since sold to a collector — reels of film for it, a great many cartons of cigarettes, a large number of bottles of spirit alcohol, and several Seiko wrist watches, I didn't buy much else at the PX.

Getting back to my father. Thankfully he was a committed and lifelong beer drinker, so he didn't raid any of the bottles of spirit alcohol that I'd also sent back home for later consumption. All of these commodities were transported back to Australia — free of any Australian postage cost or Australian customs duty — tightly packed with green army towelling and lengths of loose-weave netting, inside heavy-duty cylindrical cardboard packing of expended 105mm artillery rounds. While I don't know how much customs duty I managed to avoid during my time in Vietnam, it would have been a largish sum indeed.

Every 6 or 7 weeks, my lovely mother would send me a food parcel containing wonderful items like Keen's curry powder; course ground black pepper; course ground salt; Lea and Perrins Worcestershire black sauce; vegemite; tubes of condensed milk; a variety of preserved jams, chutneys, and pickles; small tins of processed cured meats such as Camp Pie and Spam; cured fish and meat based pastes; as well as a variety of other canned foods, condiments and old-style boiled lollies that were commercially available in Australia in 1970. They were all very gratefully received by me. Anything that was long-lasting, tasty, compact, and light, was highly valued.

While the tastier of these treats were consumed by myself, Des McGrath, and Allan Small, the remainder, known colloquially within the infantry as 'jack' rations, were always shared among my platoon section and, of course, with that serial 'platoon pest' and very good mate of mine from another section, Mick O'Shea. Most of this largesse from home was consumed operationally, not back at Nui Dat.

On a more delicate matter, but one that I do have to talk about, the US Army C rations provided to us before each operation included very limited quantities of inferior quality toilet paper. Yes, granted, we were out in the field, in a very dangerous war zone, but that shouldn't interfere with the basic complexities associated with one's daily, normal body functions. Should it?

Anyway, try to conjure up a visual image of the following daily ablution scenario facing each and every one of us whenever we were out in the field. A standard one-man US Army C ration day pack only provided 3 sheets of wafer-thin, largely non-absorbent, and almost grease-proof paper — I'm talking about $100cm^2$ sized sheets — the unwritten user instructions of which, according to Ron Goubareff, and attested to by my very good friend JJ Smith, were:

'One up, one down, and one for the polish.'

All good humour aside, I think you'll easily work out the problem we faced early each morning and at other odd times as well. For obvious reasons, not that they were ever available to us anyway, we simply couldn't carry bulky commercial toilet paper rolls out into the field. Therefore, we had no option other than to improvise. So, what did we do?

Well, this is what I did, and I suspect it was exactly the same for all members of the platoon. We never spoke amongst ourselves about this personal hygiene matter, other than to say something like:

'I'm going just out in front of our perimeter (machine gun position) *to take a shit. Keep a watch out for me and please don't shoot me as I come back, okay?'*

After every serious call of nature during the steamy, half-dark, misty-gloom dawn each morning, I carefully used several of the minuscule sheets of non-absorbent, matter-dispersing toilet paper — in exactly the way recommended by Ron Goubareff — and then finalised this process using soil and leaves scooped up from the surrounding ground area.

Soil, leaves, and lush dew or overnight rain-laden vegetation provided rudimentary hand cleaning materials, following the burial of the tell-tale signs of our presence. Given the prevailing climate of southern Vietnam, particularly during the wet season, there would have been little, if any indication of our former presence in the area within a day or so. Were we able to wash our hands in the true meaning of that in today's contemporary society? Sadly, no. But that's simply how it was. Interestingly, our Viet Cong enemy never buried their faecal waste, so that was often a dead giveaway as to their former or likely near presence.

While this basic hygiene practice may seem primitive to some — and I accept that it was — we had no alternative. Dirt, leaves, and ground cover — and I really mean that — provided a very hygienic toileting solution for us. Later in my story, I also talk about using soil and leaves to clean my operational eating utensils. If you take a deep breath and think long and hard about it, soil is variously granular, absorbent, and an excellent natural abrasive. And, probably surprisingly to some, in its pristine state, it's generally a totally inert and very clean substance.

Adverting back to the fact that we always moved forward, directly ahead of one of the M60 machine gun positions on our perimeter line to take a shit, this was an extremely vulnerable time for us. Picture a man — maybe 15m or more forward of his section's perimeter — in sight, but by himself, with his trousers around his ankles in the squat position, still holding his rifle and constantly scanning his eyes left, right, and centre. At this moment, he's in an entirely compromised position should he be confronted by an enemy soldier. And, maybe even worse, on his measured return to the wider platoon area, he had to rely on the keen visual observation, hearing, and awareness of the sentries manning the perimeter M60 machine guns. This was always a very stressful time for each one of us, every day.

During its time in Vietnam, 8 RAR suffered 4 fatalities from internal friendly fire[31] — 2 of which occurred during night-time ambushes — so our daily personal ablution safety was something always in the forefront of our minds.

Because the battalion's 4 rifle companies were generally deployed in platoon or greater strength, the serious early morning toileting of those particular men was often more safely conducted in a communal pit, inside their defensive perimeters. However, as the Assault Pioneer Platoon was mostly deployed as 2 under-strength half-platoon squads when outside of fire support bases and

---

[31] Hall, Robert A. *Combat Battalion*. Allen and Unwin, Sydney. 2000. Pages 183-185.

night defensive positions, it adopted the riskier toileting arrangement that I've described.

Amazingly, besides a very nasty impacted wisdom tooth, and an uncountable number of monumental hangovers, I never became ill during my entire time in Vietnam. I also don't recall any of my platoon mates ever being seriously sick or unwell either, except for a few nasty bite reactions from several scorpions, one snake, and a hornet.

However, I did arrive back in Australia with a seriously damaged, and very painful, lower left rib cartilage — number 8 — inflicted by a platoon mate who viciously kicked me during a drunken disagreement one night, just prior to our departure from Vietnam. That, of course, is another story that I'm not sure I'll elaborate on. I might…we'll wait and see. He and I have remained great friends and have never spoken about this unfortunate incident. It was just one of those things that happens from time to time between mates, particularly when they're both physically and mentally trashed and loaded up on alcohol.

PERSONAL HYDRATION — WATER

Southern Vietnam is always hot and seasonally very wet. During the 7-month wet season from mid-March to mid-October, and even during the 5-month dry season for the most part, humidity levels are nothing short of extreme. I very quickly realised that I was going to need a lot of water to survive out in the field. And, from the initial day — 10 December 1969 — of our first battalion operation, I was preoccupied, and most probably irrationally obsessive with the amount of water available for my personal consumption at any given point in time.

Whenever we were out in the field, I seem to recall that we were required to carry at least 4 water bottles, each with a capacity of 1L. Some of the men in my platoon carried 6 water bottles. I always carried 8, and occasionally as many as 10. To put this into an operational context, 1L of water weighs exactly 1kg. The bottle itself and the webbing carrier adds another 0.56kg. So, the gross weight carry load of 1L of water was something in the order of 1.56kg. In my case, 4 water bottles were attached to my webbed waist belt, supported by an extremely efficient webbing shoulder harness arrangement; the remaining 4, and sometimes 6 bottles, somehow affixed to my backpack and bum-packs. I have to admit that when going out on any operation, I didn't look anything like an organised infantryman.

Being a relatively tall man made me prominent and, as I frequently carried the M79 grenade launcher, as well as my SLR rifle and lots of ammunition for both weapons, I was often told by my section commander that I looked like a *'complete bucket of shit'*. Well, that was just fine with me. As far as I was concerned, if anyone was going to even attempt to reign in my obsession regarding water, then there would be trouble. Limiting the amount of water that I was prepared to carry into the field was simply not an option…ever!

As often as I could, I refilled my empty, half-empty, or even slightly-empty bottles from local catchments. I never ran out of water because I didn't waste any of it, and I never missed an opportunity to replenish my water holdings.

On a related issue, whenever I was out in the field, after my post '*stand to*' early morning ablutions, I rarely felt the urge to urinate again until very late in the afternoon. Even though I was constantly imbibing mouthfuls of water throughout the day, I guess that the unrelenting stream of perspiration emanating from my body must have been depleting my fluid waste.

Eventually, when the urge to urinate became compelling it was generally a strong, dark colour, and sometimes caused me a great deal of discomfort. To put it more crudely, when I took a late afternoon piss, it often stung really badly. I'm no urologist, but I reckon that my particular metabolic body type required a lot of fluid intake, given the climate in Vietnam. This might explain my total obsession for water whenever I was out in the field.

The availability of water around my personal consumption was constantly in the near foreground of my mind. Because it was so oppressive, I was always incredibly thirsty and mentally preoccupied about not having enough water to drink. At any given moment I intuitively knew, almost exactly, how much water remained in my collective water holdings. If I was ever to have been assessed on this, I reckon my answer would have been accurate to at least 90%.

While I was never asked —other than on one occasion — to share my water holdings with another platoon member, I really don't know how I would have responded to any regular requests. Most likely I would have begrudgingly obliged, just as I did on that rare occasion, but I also know that I was very angry with this particular platoon mate for allowing his personal water management protocol to fail him so badly.

Routinely we were issued with sterilising tablets that were supposed to be used when garnering water from local catchments. I never ever used them and, more to the point, never even carried them with me. However, I only gathered water from catchments that were shallow — 1m or less — and relatively fast-flowing over a sandy or gravelly type base. In other words, only from classical side verges of relatively clean water systems. During our time at Canungra, we were told that such water was generally potable and, somehow, that random piece of useful information managed to cement itself in the recesses of my mind.

I steered well clear of any stagnant or slow-moving water, or water that ran over a muddy or sludgy base, and always kept in mind the old adage that if local fauna — more often than not troops of large and utterly fearless feral monkeys — were inhabiting a watercourse, then it was probably potable for humans as well. Interestingly, I never became ill from not using the water sterilising tablets, which was probably more 'luck' than good field practice on my part.

After a time, I became quite ingenious in terms of the ways I conserved water. Firstly, other than my daily personal consumption regime, I tried to use water very sparingly. When I occasionally shaved or cleaned my teeth, I only ever used the dregs of my early morning mug of tea or coffee. If we were moving through rubber-treed areas and stopped for a short rest, I used to gather the seasonal rainwater that had collected in the ceramic rubber-sap collection saucers — attached to the trees — by tipping it into either one of my water bottles, or directly into my mouth. While it tasted rather ordinary, it was still very potable water.

My all-purpose eating, drinking, and shaving vessel was an aluminium field mug with a collapsible handle. This mug could be fitted to the base of one of my water bottles, before being inserted back into one of the carry pouches attached to my webbed belt. I carried 2 of these mugs. See Appendix 1.

Rather than waste precious water on cleaning my mug after a meal, I usually used soil and leaves to scour the inside of it and, occasionally, a piece of mesh netting to wipe off any residual grime. I seldom used water to clean my mug. Whenever I did use precious water for that purpose, it was no more than perhaps 100ml for a rare, semi-proper clean.

I do have to confess that whenever we were about a day out from a scheduled field re-supply of rations and water, diversion to a fire support base, night defensive position, or a return to Nui Dat, I used to relent — ever so slightly — in terms of my strict adherence to my personal water management protocol. Having said that, it was probably much more of a mental relaxation rather than any significant departure from my stringent routine out in the field.

Although daily shaving out in the field wasn't mandatory, a few of us did make some sort of effort every 4 or 5 days or so, to shave and clean our teeth, if for no reason other than to restore some semblance of humanity to our almost primeval existence. Given my terrible facial acne, shaving out in the field was a nightmare. On the other hand, something as civilised as combing our hair, never even seemed to enter our minds. Most of us kept our hair very short anyway. I certainly did, courtesy of our 'in-house' barber, Corporal Fred Vincent, and occasionally Frank Balcombe from Mortar Platoon.

As a final comment on my obsession around personal hydration out in the field, it was common for me to return to Nui Dat with as many as half of my water bottles still full. I reckon that says it all!

Whenever we were out in the field, we increasingly became very different people compared to who we were when based at Nui Dat. Although we didn't think too much about it at the time, our quality of life out in the field was really horrible. And the associated subliminal, but insidious degradation of our mental health, became far more entrenched the more time we spent in that awful country. Of course, none of us were even remotely aware of this.

EQUIPMENT

Our army issue operational clothing — 'greens' — comprised of a jungle-green shirt with sleeves always rolled down, and jungle-green trousers. While there was no modern-day camouflage feature to this clothing, the fabric was of decent quality and very durable. More than half of the men in my platoon — including myself — didn't tuck our shirts inside our trousers, preferring instead to leave them hanging loose outside. Because the climate readily nurtured rashes and other nasty skin afflictions, not one of us ever wore underwear or socks.

A thick webbed waist belt supported by a shoulder strap harness — otherwise known as 'webbing' — was worn over our greens. This waist belt didn't actually support too much weight at all. Its main purpose was to provide anchor points for other items to attach to it. It was the shoulder straps of our webbing harness that took the majority of the weight hanging from our waist belt. Ammunition pouches, machete, bayonet, water bottles, a bum-pack, and other extraneous items were attached to this waist belt.

As we'd all learned during our infantry training at Greenbank, the shoulder straps of our webbing harness needed to be painstakingly adjusted to exactly fit our individual body shapes, in order to provide maximum support and load carrying comfort. We always made sure that our shoulders were taking all of the weight, not our hips. The rationale behind this practice was that having one's hips constricted by a lot of weight was probably going to impede blood flow into and from our legs, thereby inducing lactic acid build-up and fatigue far more quickly.

Our backpacks and bum-packs carried a myriad of items. See Appendix 5. My packs contained minimal food rations to last anywhere from 5 to 7 days — until it gradually ran down, leading up to the next operational re-supply out in the field — spare magazines of SLR rifle ammunition; a rifle cleaning kit; a container of various grades of 'illegal' steel-wool; containers of very fine oil for cleaning weapons; plenty of C4 plastic explosive for cooking purposes; a compass; a plastic navigational extender-arm protractor; several pilfered waterproof provincial grid maps — even though you know I wasn't good at map reading — several boxes of waterproof Greenlight matches; letter writing materials; plenty of cigarettes, all protected by waterproof oilskin wrapping; curry powder; spices; sauces and other non-prescribed food condiments; an army issue spoon — no knife and fork — and anything else that I thought might possibly be useful.

For example, I always carried 2 very sharp-bladed standard sized folding pocket knives; 2 sturdy, high quality US manufactured stainless steel hand knives with acutely honed 15cm and 12cm blades; several pairs of different sized scissors; an army issue sewing kit, otherwise known by us as a 'housewife'; a shaving kit; a toothbrush (no toothpaste); soap (one very small container); a large army issue torch; several pencil torches and spare batteries for all of them; plenty of mosquito, tick and other insect repellent; foot powder; boot polish and brushes; plus a number of other personal items that I now can't recall. All up, it was a shit-load of stuff! One member of my platoon routinely carried a pornographic magazine with him. Another member, on at least one occasion, packed a 1L bottle of spirit alcohol. Seriously, can you believe it?

Now, speaking of boot polish…as strange as this may seem to some, we spent a lot of time whenever we were back at Nui Dat, or out in the field, fastidiously cleaning and applying thick layers of polish to our boots. Why did we do this? The answer is because if our boots were to ever fail us out in the field, then we had a major problem, not just for the individual concerned, but for the entire platoon. Our boots were mostly sodden or damp and none of us needed any encouragement to keep them in good and proper working order. We weren't all that fussed about shine, or a lack thereof on our boots. It was only ever about trying to preserve the leather and having footwear that was durable, supple, extremely comfortable, and reliable.

These 'GP' boots were made from high-quality leather and they were relatively lightweight, providing us with plenty of foot, ankle, and lower calf support. They also had a thin stainless-steel plate embedded into the sole, ostensibly for protection from concealed punji sticks — I never saw one — covered with either snake venom or human faeces. They were sometimes put in place by our enemy in camouflaged, shallow, subterranean pits as booby traps.

I wore out 4 pairs of GP boots during my time in Vietnam and managed to make sure that the fifth pair — which I wore back home to Australia — were in reasonably good condition. I also pilfered a pristine pair that I safely secured inside my locked, steel trunk, which followed me back home sometime later. On balance, a pair of boots only lasted about 3 months at most, predominantly because they were always wet or damp.

Napoleon Bonaparte of France, and Frederick the Great of Prussia — now part of modern-day Germany — have both been quoted as saying '*an army marches on its stomach*' or words to that effect. Well, I have to say while that may have been the case in the 18th and early 19th centuries, this view doesn't resonate with me at all. Take it from me, when out in the field in Vietnam, reliable footwear — along with water — was far more of an imperative for us than food.

Chapter 19 – Logistics

Each afternoon prior to a new operation, we loaded our backpacks and bum-packs very precisely — and this always took some time — ensuring that plenty of waterproofing material covered items like cigarettes and letter writing materials. We spent ages getting the balance of weight in our backpacks just right. We couldn't afford for the weight to be lopsided. In addition, we set the harness and straps of our backpacks so that they rode as high up on our shoulders as possible, thereby reducing the drag and strain on our backs. The front of each shoulder strap of our backpacks had quick-release pull tags, so we could jettison or get rid of them almost instantly in the case of any contact with the enemy.

And we wore our comfortable and very durable GP boots. We used the extraordinarily long boot laces to tie the bottoms of our trousers to the lower calf-high segment of our boots, as a defence of sorts against leeches and other environmental challenges we encountered out in the field.

Like almost any infantryman's rite of passage, we also had a 1.5m length of loose-weaved netted towelling layered around our necks, as protection from the heat of the generally muted sun — bright, sunny days were an absolute rarity — and to absorb some of the continual flow of perspiration that cascaded over our shoulders and streamed down our backs and stomachs. Some of the men in my platoon wore this netted towelling wrapped around their heads in a cross between a turban and a sweat band.

Our final item of clothing was an optional, green floppy hat. Most of us used to wear them regularly, if only to mop up the salty perspiration that would otherwise stream into our eyes. The hat was an extremely useful piece of equipment. Not only did it provide a small degree of protection from the prevailing elements during the day-time, it also became a very useful item during night-time ambushes.

The smokers in my platoon invariably cut out one of the breathing eyelets in their hats — leaving a ragged-edged hole that was just large enough for us to surreptitiously poke through — to smoke a few cigarettes during night-time ambushes. The hat kept any lit cigarette covered, and only the filter poked up through the eyelet hole. For very good reason, regarding operational security, we were absolutely forbidden to do this, but in reality, it occurred quite frequently, especially during the latter part of our time in Vietnam. I confess to being a serial operational night-time ambush smoking offender!

On every morning of each operation — and late in the evening on every night-time ambush — we layered black and dark green camouflage paint on our faces, necks, and on the backs of our hands. After a week or so, we became increasingly more dishevelled looking. We must have been a frightening sight to the local populace, whom we very occasionally came across. I'll never forget Ray Salmon, a guy of very swarthy complexion. To be perfectly honest, after a week or so out in the field, he almost looked like a demonic monster. God only knows what the enemy and the local villagers thought of him!

We routinely re-applied camouflage paint each morning, without any real complaint. The compulsory use of this product — which had the consistency of tacky motor vehicle grease — and the complete absence of any real personal hygiene out in the field, eventually resulted in my 'already ugly visage' developing a shocking case of disfiguring acne vulgaris. Seriously, when I returned home from Vietnam, it was disgustingly awful.

However, thanks to the persistent advocacy of my dear mother, the Repatriation Department (renamed as the Department of Veterans' Affairs in 1976) accepted my disfiguring facial acne as a war-caused disability from as early as 26 August 1971. In 2023 prices, the quantum of associated Disability Compensation that the government has paid me for this physical disfigurement since that date, is now something in excess of $A75,000. This example clearly reflects that the cost of war for any government extends well beyond the period of its involvement in any military conflict.

While some may say '*so what?*' to this acne problem, in my case, it was such a severe affliction that it took some years for it to abate, and for me to overcome the associated negative impacts on my psyche and innate nature, following my discharge from the army. While this may seem a relatively minor matter to many, it was certainly a major issue for me in my early twenties, I can tell you. Fortunately, in May 1972, I was blessed with a lovely wife whose constant attention to my skin condition eventually resulted in almost magical improvement, and it's now more or less resolved.

As infantry soldiers we were issued with excellent, high quality equipment to support us out in the field on operations. However, while some of that equipment, such as hutchies — small, lightweight, interlocking tent halves — and mosquito nets were very occasionally used when we were located at static sites, for all sorts of reasons we didn't carry any of that hardware when we were away from those fire support bases, or night defensive positions, which was more often the case.

While weight was always an issue for concern, the main consideration regarding the use of this sort of equipment was really one of security. All of those 'niceties' made noise and reflected light, especially during the wet season, and more importantly, they would have taken up valuable packing space in our backpacks and could never be used in a night-time ambush.

When I now think about it, I didn't carry much supporting field equipment with me at all. In fact, the more time I spent in Vietnam, the less personal equipment I carried. I always seemed to be shedding equipment along with my personal body weight.

In terms of supporting field equipment, I generally carried nothing more than a sleeping bag liner — or inner — which we referred to as a 'silk' because it resembled a very lightweight, closely-woven aerated half-blanket, and a few pieces of army towelling and netting. The silk only weighed a few grams at most and could be folded and compressed into a very small package. I still have my Vietnam era silk secured in my garage.

So, during those rare few hours of precious rostered sleep, which I was sometimes able to take during night-time ambushes, my backpack, bum-pack, webbing, and silk became my pillow, and the ground my bed. If it rained at night, which it did an awful lot from April to October, we just got wet. We all became pretty accustomed to a drip-dry existence whenever we were out in the field.

The weight carry load of a typical 8 RAR Assault Pioneer Platoon infantry soldier at the beginning of an operation — with a typical 5-day scheduled re-supply — would have been something in the order of 67kg. The 2 men in each of the M60 machine gun groups, the carriers of M79 grenade launchers, and the platoon signaller, had to cope with a much heavier weight carry load. See Appendix 5. Here I have also included data relating to the horrendous weight of the explosives and other associated materials that we also carried whenever we were tasked with demolishing an enemy bunker system.

Gerald Windsor says that:

'... *Out in the bush, men* (C Company, 7 RAR, 1967-68) *could be carrying up to 45kg of equipment, twice as much as their predecessors in the Second World War...*'[32]

Windsor's estimate of the amount of weight carried by infantry soldiers out in the field in Vietnam is undoubtedly based on what he was told by 7 RAR veterans. On the other hand, my significantly larger estimate is based on extensive research in relation to actual weights and measures and known quantities, as well as my own very clear recollections. While I accept that my metrics may be somewhat on the higher side for some of the men in the 8 RAR Assault Pioneer Platoon during 1969-70, I'm also certain that Windsor's number is short by at least 15kg.

Moving operationally while carrying all of this weight wasn't really a major problem for us because, for the most part, we were never required to cover vast distances on any given day, or to move very quickly. On an average day, we moved slowly and probably covered no more than perhaps 3km at most. There were only a handful of occasions when we were tasked with rapidly relocating to another ground position or moving a long distance, or both.

For obvious reasons, whenever we had one of our frequent rest breaks, we

---

[32] Windsor, Gerald. *All Day Long, the Noise of Battle*. Pier 9, Murdoch Books Australia. 2011. Page 38.

Nui Dat - Kanga Pad. Relocating out into the field by helicopter insertion. Peter McCann is right of centre, with a M79 grenade launcher across his backpack, seemingly sleeping. Others in this image who are clearly identifiable: Des McGrath (forward sloping hat), Cliff Grant, Brian Taylor, Steve Kaliczinsky, and Ron Goubareff.

didn't drop all of our gear. It would have taken far too long to re-set it all again. The effort of standing upright from a seated position placed enormous stress on our knees and hips, particularly for very tall men like me. I quickly learned that the best way to do this was to get on my hands and knees and try to use a tree or other vegetation to draw myself to a standing position. Once I was upright, I was able to manage the weight load relatively easily. Mates helped mates anyway, as a matter of course.

During our first operational deployment in Vietnam — Operation Atherton — one of the lessons learned by the battalion, in order to better maintain operational security, was to preferably move on foot as much as possible and to keep re-supplies by either Iroquois helicopters or APCs to an absolute minimum. This sometimes meant carrying rations to last 7 days, as well as always garnering potable water from local catchments.

Whenever the Assault Pioneer Platoon was engaged on bunker demolition tasking, the overall weight load that its men carried was simply enormous.

CHAPTER 20

ASSAULT PIONEER PLATOON DEMOGRAPHICS

SERVICE TYPES - REGULAR AND NATIONAL SERVICE

When 8 RAR deployed to Vietnam it comprised of approximately 50% Regular soldiers and 50% National Servicemen from the 15th and earlier National Service intakes.[33]

Within the battalion's Assault Pioneer Platoon, there were 2 Regular soldiers and 4 National Servicemen whose terms of enlistment were due to expire part way through their deployments. From very early on, it seemed clear to me that there was going to be some degree of churn within our platoon over the next 12 months. Turned out, this was indeed the case, as it probably was for all other elements of the battalion.

8 RAR Assault Pioneer Platoon Logo.

Aside from changes in senior platoon leadership roles, which I talk about later, the Assault Pioneer Platoon had those 6 men return to Australia part way through the term of its deployment to Vietnam. Two other men — 1 Regular soldier and 1 National Serviceman — were seconded to the 1st Australian Civil Affairs Unit (1 ACAU) on a long-term basis and 2 other men — again 1 Regular soldier and 1 National Serviceman — were similarly seconded to 1 ACAU for relatively short periods of time. During the terms of their secondments, these 4 men weren't available for operational deployment with the platoon but, inexplicably, remained on its posted strength. Over time, the platoon was reinforced by 6 National Servicemen, 1 Regular soldier from 1 ARU, and 1 internal transfer — a National Service volunteer — from D Company.

Robert A Hall says that whereas the maximum prescribed posted strength

---

[33] Hall, Robert A. *Combat Battalion*. Allen, and Unwin. Sydney. 2000. Page 5.

of the battalion was around 795, some 1,163 men served in 8 RAR during its deployment to Vietnam. Tracker dogs Janus and Julian were also integral members of the battalion's Support Company Tracker and Anti-Tank Platoon. Hall also suggests that 55.4% (644) of all those who did serve with 8 RAR in Vietnam were National Servicemen.[34] Extrapolating that data, as its time in Vietnam progressed, the battalion was reinforced by twice as many National Servicemen than Regular soldiers. Given the seemingly endless production line of National Servicemen who were entering the army at that time, courtesy of the government's policy of National Service, that's not surprising.

Collectively, 38 men served with the 8 RAR Assault Pioneer Platoon during its time in Vietnam. Of that number, 23 were National Servicemen, 60.5% of the platoon's average posted strength, a significantly higher percentage when compared to that of the overall battalion. Only 20 men — including myself — were on the posted strength of the platoon for the entire time of its deployment to Vietnam. Of its aggregate complement of 27 men at the base level rank of private, only 5 weren't National Servicemen. Interestingly, 3 of the platoon's National Servicemen were volunteers.

Aside from the 23 National Servicemen in the platoon, 4 other members were former National Servicemen who had extended their terms of enlistment in the army, thereby becoming Regular soldiers. Two of those men — 2LT Ken Jones and 2LT Peter Phillips — both did so to accept Officer Commissions. The other 2 men — John Floyd and Jeff (JJ) Smith — did so to facilitate a deployment to Vietnam with the battalion.

The average age of the men — all ranks — who collectively served in the platoon in Vietnam was 22.7 years. Discounting the 3 older members, the average age was significantly lower at 21.9 years. Table 4 below illustrates this demographic.

Table 4.

AGE PROFILE OF THE 8 RAR ASSAULT PIONEER PLATOON

Age	19	20	21	22	23	24	25	28	33	36	Total
No.	2	2	11	10	5	2	3	1	1	1	38

Sergeant Monty White was 28 years of age. Corporal (later Sergeant) Cliff Grant was the oldest member of the platoon at 36, while Lance-corporal Bob Whiley was 33. Lance-corporal John Dolgan and Arthur Walsh were only 19 years of age.

---

[34] Hall, Robert A. *Combat Battalion*. Allen and Unwin. Sydney. 2000. Pages 5 and 241.

A PLATOON

In 1969-70, a platoon was the base level element of the standard ADF infantry structure. Over the decades since, while the size, composition, and operational nature of a classic ADF infantry platoon has changed somewhat, the concept of a platoon and its inherent overarching structure has, arguably, remained the same. So, how was the 8 RAR Assault Pioneer Platoon structured?

At full posted strength — this was never the case — it would have comprised 34 men: 3 sections of 10, a PHQ of 3, and a reliable and important man taking on the indispensable and vital role of base storeman at Nui Dat.

I can't emphasise enough how important this latter man's role was. During the platoon's time in Vietnam, its base storeman was occasionally deployed to fire support bases and night defensive positions, along with the rest of the platoon…and he sometimes participated in other aspects of its operational tasking. However, his key role at Nui Dat was to logistically support the platoon whenever it was out in the field.

He was responsible for sending supplies out into the field, either by Iroquois helicopters or APCs. Supplies included replacement weapons (rarely), ammunition, rations, water, clothing, mail, and anything else deemed to be useful or otherwise called-for by the platoon.

For about 6 months the platoon also had the part-time service of a Support Company driver — plus army jeep — who was attached to the platoon in a very general 'as required' role. This fabulous man — Private Gary Piper — wasn't part of the platoon's posted strength and never deployed operationally with it. Nevertheless, his part-time support role back at Nui Dat was a very necessary and important one for the platoon.

When the platoon arrived in Vietnam, its posted strength was only 29 men. Its resourcing never exceeded that number and, at times, dropped well below. During its entire time in Vietnam, the operational capability of the platoon was seriously compromised.

Because of secondments out of the platoon — Les Lupuljev (long term after 10 January 1970), Arthur Koo (long term after 3 July 1970), John Dolgan, and Des Lock (both short term around late January and early February 1970) — occasional illness, and irregular R&R leave, the platoon often only had 24 and sometimes even less men available for operational deployment, particularly in June and July 1970. Table 5 on the following page reflects the average gross monthly posted resourcing of the platoon during its time in Vietnam.

The data contained in this table reflects a stable — but significantly understrength — average manpower resource of 29 men. However, that number includes the PHQ element of 3, the base storeman, and 2 long-term secondments out of the platoon. That left 23 men and sometimes less, to

Table 5.

**MONTHLY RESOURCING:
ALL RANKS OF THE 8 RAR ASSAULT PIONEER PLATOON**

Mth	Nov 69	Dec 69	Jan 70	Feb 70	Mar 70	Apr 70	May 70	Jun 70	Jul 70	Aug 70	Sep 70	Oct 70	Nov 70
No.	29	29	29	29	29	29	29	27	26	29	28	25	25

be shared between each of its 3 sections. A further reduction in its effective operational sectional resourcing was exacerbated later by the filling of the batman role within PHQ (increasing it to 4 men) by Terry Lucas, who joined the platoon as a reinforcement on 3 July 1970. The months of June and July were very difficult times for the platoon, its commander, and section commanders.

While the battalion may have ceased major operational tasking on 4 October 1970, the majority of its platoons were — for several weeks or more — engaged on irregular and singular night-time ambushing at locales near Nui Dat. In my view, the resourcing of the platoon during October and November 1970 was more than adequate for that sort of tasking.

On 3 October 1970, 3 reinforcements who joined the platoon on 22 July 1970, along with another man who joined the platoon on 7 August 1970, were transferred to other 1 ATF infantry units or HQ 1 ALSG. It was around this time that one of the long-term secondments to 1 ACAU, Les Lupuljev, returned to the platoon. The other long-term 1 ACAU secondment, Arthur Koo, never did return.

Table 6.

8 RAR ASSAULT PIONEER PLATOON

Platoon HQ (PHQ)	Sections (3)	No.1 Section
2LT (Commander) Ken Jones/Peter Phillips	Corporal (Commander)	Fred Vincent
Sergeant Monty White/Cliff Grant	Lance-corporal (2IC)	Ron Goubareff/ John Dolgan
Private (Signaller) Paul Jansen	Private (Forward Scouts or men on point)	Steve Kaliczinsky Peter Wood
Private (Batman) Terry Lucas from 3 July 70	Private (Machine Gunner) Private (No.2 on the gun)	Allan Small Des McGrath
	Private (Rifleman)	Peter McCann
Private (Storeman) Arthur Koo/Mark Smith	Private (Rifleman)	John Dolgan/Vacant/ Peter McCormick
	Private (Rifleman)	Peter Cousins
	Private (Rifleman)	Vacant

At full posted strength, the 8 RAR Assault Pioneer Platoon was formally structured as per Table 6. I have included actual No.1 Section resourcing data as reality context, because I know it's accurate. Unfortunately, I've not been able to reconstruct the broad variable personnel compositions of No.2 and No.3 Sections of the platoon. My memory is just not that good.

No.1 Section only ever had a complement of 9 men. After the battalion's first operational tasking concluded on 10 January 1970, that number was reduced to 8 for a lengthy time with the secondment of John Dolgan to 1 ACAU duties external to the battalion. Although Dolgan returned to the platoon sometime around early March 1970, it wasn't to No.1 Section. He was eventually replaced within No.1 Section by Adrian (Peter) McCormick on 25 March 1970. When Lance-corporal Ron Goubareff was promoted to corporal — and commander of one of the other platoon sections — towards the end of June 1970, he was replaced as lance-corporal within No.1 Section by John Dolgan, a former member of that section. No.2 and No.3 Sections only ever had 8 men on strength, and on some occasions in June and July 1970 it would have been even less. Because of this imbalance of relative section manpower capability, I'm sure that's why the platoon — particularly from April 1970 — often operated as 2 discrete half-platoon squads, each comprising of 12 men or thereabouts, and to bolster their undermanned firepower: 2 M60 machine guns.

I'm sure that many of you who are reading my story will have seen the classic Vietnam era USA war movie 'Platoon' starring Charlie Sheen, Tom Berenger, Willem Dafoe, and Forest Whitaker, to name a few. If you haven't seen this wonderful movie, then you should, because if will literally scare the shit out of you!

'Platoon' was the first movie to truly depict the horror of the close-quarter combat nature of the Vietnam War, amid an appalling climate played out against a backdrop of an even more unfriendly range of landscape types. One graphic scene quite early in this movie depicts Charlie Sheen being tormented by ants amid a night-time tropical precipitation deluge. I can relate to that. During my time in Vietnam, ants became my psychological nemesis or, more to the point, my recurring nightmare to this very day.

The story that this fascinating movie portrays is one of a totally dysfunctional US Army infantry platoon where leadership, professionalism, mateship, and trust were sadly lacking. By way of contrast, the 8 RAR Assault Pioneer Platoon was a highly trained, professional, and for the most part, tightly-knit unit that was very well led by its commanders at every level. Whenever out in the field, all members of the platoon completely trusted and relied on each other without question. I have no doubt at all that if the platoon ever found itself embroiled in an impossible situation in a hot moment, each and every one of us would have placed our lives on the line for the others. I say that without any reservation or qualification whatsoever. As a well-trained infantry platoon, we were tightly bonded and indelibly inured to always supporting and helping each other.

While we may not have universally liked each other — to be expected among an aggregate group of 38 men — that was always completely put aside as soon as we were out in the field on operations. Other than for a couple of operational events or happenings, one of which I talk about later, right up until the end of our time in Vietnam, we pretty much remained a very tight unit in full control of itself.

Having said that, had anyone in the platoon been killed or even badly wounded, particularly late in our time in Vietnam, I can't really say for certain how some of us may have reacted. I do know that emotions would have reflected disbelief, anger, despair, and fear; all exacerbated and magnified by the associated increased levels of adrenalin and cortisol surging throughout our bodies. Thankfully, that's a scenario we didn't have to contend with.

LEADERSHIP

During the platoon's deployment to Vietnam there were key leadership changes at platoon commander level, platoon sergeant, section commander — corporal — and lance-corporal ranks. I remember thinking at the time, and my view on this hasn't changed over the decades since, that the 8 RAR Assault Pioneer Platoon was very well served during its time in Vietnam by its leadership overlay. I'm not sure that men of many other infantry platoons that served in Vietnam would be able to attest to that.

For the first 4 months, 2LT Ken Jones commanded the platoon. I had little, if any, personal contact with him and therefore didn't really know him at all. However, from my distant and detached perspective, he seemed to be a decent sort of person. I was told that he was approachable and he certainly didn't appear to be one of those 'in your face' type officers who are often depicted in USA war movies. If anything, he seemed to have a very laid-back attitude. I can't ever recall seeing him angry, morose, or acting aggressively towards anyone in the platoon. On those few occasions when I simply couldn't avoid personal interaction with him, he seemed to be a mentally sharp, reasonable person. I was comfortable with him as my platoon commander.

As his leadership of the platoon during its first few operations in Vietnam seemed to be very professional, I have to say that I really didn't give Mr Jones a second thought. Mind you, he would have had no idea whatsoever that he was another innocent victim of my hugely successful approach to not being noticed. Even so, it came as a complete surprise to me when on 1 April 1970, he was suddenly posted out of the platoon to HQ 1 ALSG at Vung Tau.

Chapter 20 — Assault Pioneer Platoon Demographics

Mr Jones' replacement as Platoon Commander on 5 April 1970 was 2LT Peter Phillips, a former volunteer National Servicemen who signed-on for service beyond his 2-year National Service obligatory term, and later graduated from Officer Cadet School (OCS) Scheyville. Mr Phillips was only 3 months older than me, and though I didn't ever go out of my way to seek his company, I ended up having much more personal interaction with him —mostly out in the field — compared to the little I had with Mr Jones. I ended up liking Mr Phillips a lot. Mr Jones was also a former National Serviceman.

Compared to Mr Jones, Mr Phillips was a completely different person. He was much more intense, initially very shy, and somewhat introverted. While I didn't know it at the time, Mr Phillips' Officer Commission — and presumably that of Mr Jones as well — was only probationary, so he knew full well that if he stuffed up badly in the field, he'd possibly be demoted back to the rank of corporal. Although probably a hollow threat, perhaps that might explain his overt and obsessive concern regarding the safety and welfare of the men under his command. It was a very noble personal trait and one that he steadfastly displayed during the entire time he commanded the platoon in Vietnam. On balance, I thought he was a very good, but ultra-conservative, infantry platoon commander. I talk about him a lot more later on.

Quite obviously, there is — and always has been — a clear divide between officers and other ranks in terms of responsibility and respect. Accordingly, the thought of perhaps wandering down to Mr Philips' tent at Nui Dat for a friendly chat never — not even once — entered my head. For a start, that would have meant being noticed by him. And, as far as I was concerned, Mr Phillips was the 'boss' and I was just one man under his command. I didn't want him to notice me. That was my mindset anyway. However, whenever we were out in the field, there was simply nowhere for me to hide, so I had no choice other than to personally engage and interact with him. For some strange reason, that seemed to occur quite frequently.

Over recent years, he has told me that during our short periods at Nui Dat between operations, he yearned for informal interaction with the men in his platoon — he was our average age after all — and was utterly dismayed that it occurred so rarely. His lottery of service life in Vietnam as an infantry platoon commander was a responsible, but very lonely one. To be perfectly honest, I'm pretty sure that nothing much has changed in the contemporary ADF, even all these decades later.

Having said that, there was one momentous occasion, around the time of the battalion's birthday — 8 August 1970 — when he drank with us in the other ranks' Support Company boozer after we returned from a long and exhausting operation. We all ended up getting absolutely drunk — Mr Phillips included. Yes, he had to be invited by us to our boozer.

Initially, the platoon sergeant was Montague (Monty) White, a relatively quiet man with a service background in the SASR. On 28 June 1970, Monty was suddenly posted out of the platoon to 1 ARU and replaced as platoon sergeant by Corporal Cliff Grant from within the platoon. The almost secretive transactional nature of this change in personnel of a key leadership position within the platoon, seemed to be even stranger than the replacement of Mr Jones by Mr Phillips some 2 months earlier. Decades later, I became aware of the associated detail behind Monty's posting out of the platoon. However, as much as I'd like to, I've chosen not to tell of that interesting hearsay.

I have a somewhat fleeting and very neutral recollection of Monty because I never initiated any conversation with him...and did my very utmost to keep out of his way. I just didn't like the man at all. What was surprising though was this. While I was a fully-fledged long-term member of the platoon (May 1969), I was never told of the reasons for, or circumstances behind, these sudden changes in senior platoon leadership roles. Even more surprising was the fact that I don't recall anyone — and that includes me — ever asking for a proper explanation either. To this day, while I've heard some very vaguely related chatter, I still don't really know why 2LT Jones was replaced as platoon commander.

The platoon was well served by its corporals and lance-corporals, and I say that with very real meaning. The vital core of the platoon's non-commissioned officer strength was largely comprised of experienced Regular soldiers. Corporals Fred Vincent (1 RAR and 6 RAR), Bob O'Callaghan (1 RAR), and Lance-corporal — later Corporal — Ron Goubareff (1 RAR), had previously served in Vietnam. In addition, Corporal — later Sergeant — Cliff Grant, and Private — later Lance-corporal — Bob Whiley, were seasoned Regular soldiers and a decade or so older than most of the men in the platoon. Sergeant Cliff Grant had actually seen 358 days of active service in Korea with 2 RAR, during the period 17 March 1953 – 6 April 1954.

One of the platoon's National Servicemen, Dave Matheson — the 'medic' — was promoted to the rank of lance-corporal. The platoon also had two 19-year-old members. The youngest of those, John Dolgan — a Regular soldier — was also promoted to lance-corporal. More detailed demographics of the Assault Pioneer Platoon are contained in Appendix 6.

CHAPTER 21

RULES OF ENGAGEMENT

In all modern and not-so-modern military conflicts, Rules of Engagement are a prescribed set of conditions underpinned by the Rules of War — the satisfaction of which provides sufficient justification for opening fire on likely enemy. The Rules of War, or International Humanitarian Law (as they are more formally known), set out what can and cannot be done during armed conflict. The main purpose of the Rules of War is to maintain humanity, save lives, and reduce suffering.

Rules of Engagement, framed against the overarching Rules of War and in strict accordance with the Geneva Convention, provide field commanders with legitimacy in terms of men under their command engaging — opening fire on — enemy, while at the same time providing a necessary responsibility protocol that must always be administered by those field commanders and strictly observed by the men under their command. They help to ensure that anger in warfare is controlled as much as humanly possible. It would be difficult, if not impossible for a lay person to understand the anger and frustration felt by soldiers when they witness their mates being killed or wounded by well-concealed anti-personnel mines planted by an unseen enemy, as was often the case in Vietnam.

Without such a set of rules, the local civilian population and perhaps even allied forces soldiers as well, may have been at some personal risk. I would also guess that there may have been a very remote possibility of questionable incidents taking place which involved Australian soldiers. That last comment is simply a reflection of what the reality of war is all about. In any significant military conflict there are always going to be incidents or events that probably shouldn't have happened. Rules of Engagement put in place an operational protocol aimed at ensuring that questionable incidents don't occur, or at the very least, significantly reduce that likelihood.

At the end of the day, the Rules of Engagement for Australian soldiers in Vietnam were integral in reducing the risk to civilians and friendly forces and, if anything ever did go badly wrong, responsibility and discipline could be sheeted home to the perpetrators. In all wars and military conflicts a field commander's worst nightmare is — or should be — firing on civilians...and equally as bad, firing on friendly troops. Vietnam was no different.

The massacre of civilian residents of the Song My village at My Lai, a cluster of hamlets in the coastal lowlands of 1 Corps Tactical Zone — the most northern sector of Vietnam, south of the Demilitarised Zone (DMZ) — by US Army soldiers on 16 March 1968, is a well-documented event during which the Rules of Engagement — if there even were any — were simply ignored.

However, it's worth noting that encapsulated within this particularly ugly historical incident, there were other forces at play such as poor leadership, low morale, and below-standard rudimentary skill levels of the US Army soldiers involved. At My Lai, ignoring Rules of Engagement was really an outcome, rather than a primary cause for this unforgivable massacre of unarmed civilians: predominantly elderly men, women, children, and even babies. Estimates of the number of innocent civilians killed — and many women of all ages raped — during this infamous atrocity range between 300 and 500. Graphic detail surrounding this horrible incident is abundantly available on the public record.

The Rules of Engagement imposed on 8 RAR soldiers were frequently reinforced during our first week or so in Vietnam, and more broadly before each operation by respective platoon section commanders. Whether we actually absorbed and fully understood them is another question entirely. To be perfectly honest, I don't think I took too much notice at all.

When I started to write this section of my story, it became clear that my recollections of the official Rules of Engagement under which the Assault Pioneer Platoon operated in Vietnam, were somewhat vague. So, I sought specific advice and views from several 8 RAR veterans, including a few former field commanders and, of course, my former platoon commander, LTCOL Peter Phillips Retd.

It seems that during 1 ATF operations in Vietnam, circa 1969-70, persons weren't to be engaged — fired on — unless they were positively identified as enemy; opened fire first; failed to stop when challenged; were otherwise not obviously friendly; or approached a friendly ground position at night, in which case they were quite clearly not friendly. During the day-time, the onus of responsibility for the positive identification of likely enemy before the initiation of any fire on them, was on the respective field commanders.

In Phuoc Tuy Province, the larger local villages and hamlets were surrounded by high wire fences. At around nightfall each evening, there was a curfew in place that required the villagers to be ensconced inside the perimeter of those barriers. After nightfall, anyone detected in areas outside these villages was assumed to be enemy.

During the day-time villagers worked in the surrounding paddy fields, in the commercially operated rubber plantations, and in various light industrial and agricultural commercial enterprises, but weren't permitted to stray into the jungle areas. Even so, during the day-time, anyone encountered in those jungle and other supposedly uninhabited areas away from the paddy fields, rubber plantations, and other employment locales, couldn't be routinely fired on. They first had to be identified as enemy, which basically meant observing that they were carrying a weapon. Even then, it was regarded as very good field practice to be absolutely certain that they were indeed carrying a weapon, and that they weren't friendly.

These broad rules, regardless of curfew timings — day or night — were applied in and within a 1km range from a number of designated areas such as Nui Dat, US Army and other allied fire support bases, civilian access areas, permanent areas of operation assigned to sub sectors of the Phuoc Tuy Province, villages, South Vietnamese Regional Forces, and Provincial Forces posts.

Outside of these specified areas, no friendly forces or civilians were deemed to be in an assigned area of operation (AO) and any movement other than by 1 ATF field elements was considered as hostile. If there was any doubt, then the Rules of Engagement were to be applied by the on-ground field commanders. The most important implication of this was: 'If in doubt, don't fire!'

Now, all of this was rather confusing to poor 'grunts' like me, down at the bottom end of the battalion information chain. So, field commanders conveyed these rules in a far simpler day-to-day operational protocol. For example, in my platoon there was a set of more basic rules that we always did our very best to observe. Broadly, they were:

RESTRICTED FIRE ZONES

- Generally located near inhabited or commercial areas.
  For example, the Binh Ba and De Courtenay rubber plantations;

- During the day-time, platoon members needed to be certain that the likely target was enemy, was armed, or was otherwise exhibiting hostile behaviour before firing on them;

- At night-time, any person encountered was automatically deemed to be hostile and would be immediately fired on.

UNRESTRICTED (OR FREE) FIRE ZONES

- Largely, designated uninhabited areas;

- During the day-time, platoon members had very liberal discretion in terms of engaging likely enemy. Persons encountered during the day-time were at very high risk of being fired on without warning;

- At night-time, any person encountered was automatically deemed to be hostile and would be immediately fired on.

In practice, the Assault Pioneer Platoon fired on anyone it encountered at night-time in an ambush situation. In addition, anyone it encountered during the day-time was always regarded as hostile and fired on, unless they were quite clearly civilians or were otherwise friendly.

Even though proper Rules of Engagement were put in place for Australian soldiers in Vietnam, anecdotally, it seemed that there was a degree of pressure placed on some field commanders to achieve enemy kills — the so-called 'kill count', which was a combat statistic so incredibly important to US Army commanders — as a formal performance measure of some kind. While there will almost certainly not be any official record of this, it's probably true and may well have impacted upon the dynamics of some field leaderships. My 2 respective platoon commanders 2LT Ken Jones, and 2LT Peter Phillips, weren't at all obsessed with enemy kill counts. To me, they were very responsible, measured, and sensible commanders, both of whom I respected.

While we were all vaguely aware that if we badly contravened the terms of the Rules of Engagement under which our operations in Vietnam were conducted, we were going to be in a shit-load of serious trouble, we never really gave that a second thought. To be perfectly honest, we were so conditioned by our training and inured army culture that by the time we arrived in Vietnam, we regarded the enemy as totally worthless and eminently expendable. Our individual security and that of our platoon mates was sacrosanct. And, we would have done anything to maintain that. Seriously!

While I'm certain that it occurred from time to time — and probably far more often than what might be regarded as unfortunate — I'm personally unaware of any 8 RAR soldiers significantly contravening the Rules of Engagement under which we all operated back in those horrible times. If there were occasions when those rules were not properly observed to the maximum extent, then, as far as I'm aware, those events were never officially reported and ergo, never actually occurred.

CHAPTER 22

CONTACT

The classic role of the army infantry is — and always has been — to seek out and close with the enemy, kill or capture them, seize, hold ground, and repel attack — by day or night — regardless of the season, weather, or terrain. It's not a very attractive job description.

In commonly accepted infantry parlance, the word 'contact' has a very clear and specific meaning. If you're in a 'contact' it means that you have closed with the enemy — or maybe they have closed with you — and each individual is now trying desperately hard to kill the other. Being in a contact with the enemy is not a nice experience!

A contact might be something as large as the Battle of Long Tan on 18 August 1966 when 105 men from D Company 6 RAR, and an attached RNZA forward artillery observer party of 3, successfully engaged in a fierce late afternoon and early evening defensive battle in a rubber plantation — amid relentless and torrential sheeting rain — against a 2,500-strong well-armed, highly-trained and organised enemy force for the best part of 3.5 hours. The enemy, as it's now reliably known, had secretly massed in strength over previous weeks and were quietly preparing to assault the emerging — but yet to be adequately defended — 1 ATF base at Nui Dat, some 5km due west of D Company's ground position.

On the other hand, a contact might be as insignificant and brief as the following incident — sometime around the third week in December 1969 — when at Fire Support Base Peggy, I fired my SLR rifle at, and probably missed — a subsequent section sweep of the area failed to locate a body, only managing to detect a fresh, minor blood trail of somewhat dubious significance — a solitary armed enemy combatant at an embarrassingly drop-dead distance of about 80m. I'll elaborate on this very personal experience later in the story. In the context of Australia's military ground involvement in the Vietnam War, both of these instances — at the extreme opposite ends of the infantry engagement scale — are examples of what was known as a contact.

In any contact with the enemy, there were always 3 common and ever-present features. In order, they are: noise, confusion, and anxiety or mental stress experienced by all men involved in that contact. And it was completely different for each and every contact, depending on who initiated the engagement;

what the opposing numbers were; how long the engagement lasted; the relative firepower capabilities; ground positions of the opposing forces — height being a significant advantage — and whether it occurred during the day or night.

During the day, 8 RAR elements were seldom engaged in ambushing. Most of their day-time tasking centred on slow and measured reconnaissance in force, search, and destroy activities; demolition of discovered enemy bunker systems; and occasional cordon and search of suspected hostile civilian centres, etc. So, day-time contacts with the enemy were generally quite surprising. Well, that's my take on it anyway. Surviving members of No.1 Platoon A Company — and C Company more generally — may well have a completely different view on this because of their tasking during Operation Hammersley. And given the awful events of 28 February 1970, that's entirely understandable.

At night-time — and many 8 RAR contacts with the enemy were at night — it was completely different. Whenever the Assault Pioneer Platoon was out in the field, outside of a fire support base or a night defensive position, we were always ambushing likely enemy transit routes into villages or hamlets at night and sometimes during the day as well. At night, we were laying prone on the ground, M18 Claymore anti-personnel directional mines in place, waiting for any enemy to enter the chosen killing ground before springing the ambush. Now this may seem to be a much safer position to be in, compared to the uncertainty of a typical day-time scenario. And yes, I do agree, but only up to a point.

During the day we could at least see 'something', though it did rain torrentially for 4 or more hours on most afternoons from April to October. Even during these precipitation deluges — see Appendix 4 — we could still scan, listen, hear, see, detect enemy movement, evaluate, and hopefully make good decisions for ourselves and our platoon mates.

On the other hand, once a night-time ambush was sprung, there was always so much noise, confusion, smoke, seasonal rain, rising ground mist, poor or no visibility, and variable amounts of incoming enemy small and medium arms fire — sometimes a lot, sometimes not too much, and often none at all — that it was very hard to work out what was actually happening. And, more importantly, if the enemy that we engaged with decided to take us on for a time and fight hard on the battlefield, this was an outcome we weren't all that enthusiastic about.

The initial confusion during any contact always gave rise to an evaluation of the state of play, and amid all the noise of battle, what had to be done was done. I have to say that there was always a fair amount of 'hugging the ground' in the very first instance in any day-time contact. At night, we were already in that prone position on the ground.

In any contact with the enemy, there was always a lot of noise, and I do mean a hell of a lot of noise! It was simply incredible. At times there was so much noise — particularly during the initial stages of a contact — that it was virtually impossible to communicate with one another effectively. That's just how it was.

When in contact with the enemy, no matter how long or fleeting, a man's anxiety and stress levels elevated astronomically. They simply skyrocketed right off the scale. It was nothing short of astonishing. Adrenaline was the neurotransmitter that was rapidly released into the bloodstream to help prepare those men on the ground to cope with the personal crisis they were experiencing. This Adrenaline geared them up to meet the 'life or death' challenge head on. At those stressful times, there were 3 subliminal options facing them: fight, flight, or passively blend-in by not vigorously engaging with the enemy.

While flight was never an issue among Australian infantry soldiers in Vietnam, 'passively blending-in' means that sometimes a man's stress levels are so high when he's under enemy fire that it renders him incapable of any level of operational functionality. When this occurs, he often loses his aggressive nature for varying periods of time. In Vietnam, I'd like to think this would have only been a transitory glitch — if one at all — in any Australian infantry soldier's operational effectiveness. Robert A Hall explores this conundrum further in his wonderful book.[35]

During the Great War, WWII, and in Korea, there are recorded instances of soldiers not firing their weapons at adversaries, or if they did, aiming randomly high over their heads. For Australian infantry soldiers in Vietnam, while there may well have been similar instances of this occurring, I'd be surprised if that were the case. But I just don't really know.

LTCOL Dave Grossman (US Army) Retd[36] has written a fascinating account of the psychological cost of killing in war and society: 'On Killing'. Significantly, Grossman quotes from a number of academic studies which suggest that:

> '... a 90% to 95% firing rate was attained in Vietnam ... This contrasts with ... a 'firing rate of 15% to 20% of US soldiers in World War II' ... and ... a firing rate of 55% in Korea...'[37]

While the firing rate in the Great War was even lower than that of WWII, the dynamics of the completely different natures of infantry ground combat in those earlier conflicts make any useful conclusions almost impossible to derive. So, why have I ventured into this difficult and highly contentious area?

---

[35] Hall, Robert A. *Combat Battalion*. Allen and Unwin. Sydney. 2000. Page 137.
[36] Grossman, Dave LTCOL. *On Killing*. Back Bay Books/Little, Brown, and Company. New York/Boston. 1995.
[37] Grossman, Dave LTCOL. *On Killing*. Back Bay Books/Little, Brown, and Company New York/Boston. 1995. Page 35.

According to Grossman, allied infantry soldiers in Vietnam were so highly trained and exposed to ground combat — actually or potentially — for such prolonged periods of time, without any significant withdrawals from that hostile environment, that they increasingly became conditioned to actively participating in any contact with the enemy. For most of them, shooting at, and trying to kill the enemy, was simply not a problem. Now, that's not surprising.

While many of those pre-Korean War combat infantry veterans may have been deployed overseas for 3 or even 4 years, many of them only experienced actual or potential combat for perhaps 25% or even less of that time, interspersed with exceptionally long intermittent periods of non-combat related tasking. On the other hand, in Vietnam it was continuous operational tasking — with very few minimal periods (days) of respite — for 12 solid months. When infantry soldiers returned home to Australia after a deployment to Vietnam, they were physically and mentally spent. I certainly was.

This might explain why the Australian Vietnam infantry veteran cohort has such poor, long-term mental health, compared to that of infantry veterans from earlier conflicts. Grossman explores this issue in some detail, but I will leave it for others to make up their own minds on that. For those of you still reading on, it might be worth your while to purchase a copy of Grossman's wonderful book and ponder over its enlightening and thought-provoking content.

The key effects of surging adrenaline levels on the human body include a rapidly increased and maintained heart rate, elevated blood pressure, expansion of the air passages of the lungs, enlarging of the eye pupils, a redistribution of blood flow from the benign body mass parts to the muscles, and an altering of the body's metabolic function to maximise blood glucose levels (primarily for brain function).

During times of anxiety and stress, the adrenal gland also releases copious amounts of cortisol, another hormone that's otherwise produced very gradually by the body. Ordinarily, cortisol has many therapeutic impacts including its beneficial effect on the liver to accelerate the removal of unwanted toxins. It also heightens short-term memory and tends to significantly help reduce any form of inflammation in the body.

However, surging levels of cortisol aren't at all useful. They overburden stress levels that may be already impacting infantry soldiers on the ground. Symptomatic of Cushing's disease in both humans and small — terrier sized — canines, is a permanent and extremely elevated level of cortisol in the body. Some may well ask...*'what's the point of this largely uninformed layman medical expose of the likely impacts on the body and mind of an infantry soldier under stress?'*

Well, this illustrates that in any 'hot' combat situation, an infantry soldier on the ground is not himself. Not by any measure at all. He instantly becomes

Chapter 22 — Contact

a completely different person. He enters a surreal world where his later recall is invariably that of either very high clarity, or one of a rather vague, slow-motion event. Much later, after a contact with the enemy — and it varied quite significantly — some men became violently ill, particularly if it had been an intense or protracted engagement.

Over the early years after returning home from Vietnam, I was asked numerous times by well-meaning but totally unthinking people, if I was ever scared or frightened during my time in that awful country. While I always deflected that line of inappropriate questioning to something not quite so personal, it would have been untruthful of me to answer *'No, I was never scared.'* Of course I was! And almost completely shitless on several occasions. I've never forgotten being mentally disturbed and physically unwell for many days after 7 or 8 incidents during my time in Vietnam. I touch briefly on 2 such occasions in this part of the story and cover them, and other incidents, a little later.

The term 'scared' isn't about being cravenly cowered and whimpering. It's really just being taken — extraordinarily — out of one's comfort zone to a place where, subliminally, they don't want to be. In a military context, it's all about doing a job that you may not like at that particular moment in time, but getting on with it regardless, as best you can. Sometimes, I found this really hard to do.

My very clear recollections are that in any contact with the enemy, or exposure to any other highly stressful operational event, men in my platoon just did — without question — what we were told to do by the 'on the ground' chain of command — usually our section commander. If that direction wasn't immediately forthcoming, we just did what we felt was the best thing by utilising our infantry training routines. And, when initial confusion was usually the order of the day — or night — that action may have been to do nothing for maybe 30 seconds or so, but definitely not much longer than that. During this variable, brief interlude, every man on the ground was in a very different world to where he really wanted to be…and completely consumed by a shit-load of mental anguish.

After contact with the enemy or involvement in any other traumatic operational event, the nausea, agitation, tremors, and soul-searching, always presented themselves much later and affected individuals quite differently. For one man, he might appear to be completely unaffected, while another may be unable to stop talking about the experience. Some men became morose, almost mute and sullen for days and sometimes for much longer. For others, like myself, it wasn't only battlefield contacts with the enemy that caused psychological grief later on.

On 19 April 1970 during a battalion-sized cordon and search of a large, well known hostile civilian residential area near Nui Dat, I came within a hair's breadth — it was that damn close — of shooting and killing an unarmed but seriously aggressive young civilian woman, as she physically assaulted me — hard slaps to my face and violent pushes to my right shoulder, whilst my SLR rifle barrel forcibly pressed into her sternum, trying to keep her at bay — and relentlessly hectored me in her vile, high-pitched screaming tirade of invective...of which I didn't understand a single word. This horrible confrontation lasted for at least 20 seconds. For a personal standoff situation like this, in a hostile locale in a highly dangerous war zone, that was a long time. At that moment, I knew that I really wanted to shoot and kill this crazy woman. Thankfully, I didn't do so. But it really was a 'line-ball' decision on my part. I've never forgotten it.

On another occasion, mid-morning on 30 May 1970, I was helping inter 2 enemy who were killed by the platoon on the previous evening or early morning, perhaps 10 hours earlier. When interring these bodies — placing them in the very shallow grave that 3 of us had just dug — I became very nauseated and copiously vomited a short distance away from this rudimentary burial site. By way of contrast, the other 2 men — Lance-corporal Ron Goubareff and Peter Wood — who were helping me, appeared to be nonchalant about what we were doing that morning. I'm not passing any judgment at all on those 2 fine men. Both were very good soldiers and firm friends of mine. It's just how it was for me on that particular morning.

I've never forgotten these 2 awful moments in my life, and I know that I never will. While most members of my platoon seemingly dealt with these sorts of operational happenings easily, or perhaps even routinely, I never did. I always thought that I was a good infantry soldier. I liked my role within my section of the platoon and I also liked being out in the field on operations — that was my job after all, and one for which I was well-trained and well-armed. I always did whatever I was operationally tasked with doing 'almost' without question and to the best of my ability.

During my entire 12 months as an infantry soldier in a very difficult and utterly confused conflict like Vietnam, I know that — for the most part — I never lost sight of the value and sanctity of human life. Mind you, if you were trying to kill me, then I most certainly was trying even harder to kill you first. That, of course, was a 'no-brainer'. But it never became a personal issue for me, as it did for several men in my platoon and, from what I've been told, others within wider elements of the battalion.

Interaction with civilians was an operational dynamic that sometimes gave rise to experiences I never enjoyed. I vehemently loathed and utterly detested any contact with civilians out in the field, and always did my absolute utmost to avoid it. Unfortunately, that wasn't always possible, particularly during the first 5 months of my time in Vietnam.

Finally, to place some contextual overlay around this part of my story, the average age of the 38 men who collectively served in the 8 RAR Assault Pioneer Platoon in Vietnam during 1969-1970 was 22.7 years. I was very much one of its younger members at 21.

While we were all incredibly physically fit, highly-trained, exceedingly well-armed and professionally led infantry soldiers, we were still very young men. If you think long and hard about these indisputable facts, you may well conclude, '*those poor young men*'.

CHAPTER 23

OPERATIONAL TASKING

GENERAL OVERVIEW

Call-sign 62 was the common field radio identifier of Assault Pioneer Platoons of infantry battalions in Vietnam. 5 RAR was slightly different in that it adopted the call-sign of Tiger 62; reflecting the nickname of the battalion in deference to its mascot — a real male Bengal tiger quietly living at the Taronga Park Zoo in Sydney — who gloried in the ancient Latin name of 'Quintus'. For a time, 5 RAR contributed to the cost of his upkeep at the zoo. A very young lion cub was made available by the zoo for a number of formal 5 RAR parades prior to deploying to Vietnam on its second tour in February 1969.

While I don't recall any official 8 RAR mascot, D Company did have one for a time: a huge python, dubiously known as 'Private Sneed', who travelled to Vietnam with the battalion on HMAS *Sydney*. I have no idea what became of Private Sneed.

During the first 2 months of its time in Vietnam, the 8 RAR Assault Pioneer Platoon also had a mascot: a beer guzzling, food pilfering, constantly defecating, tent trashing, very young female bear who responded to her adopted name of Rachel, and more avidly, to her numerous beer treats. Can you believe it? A bear that loved beer! I've spoken a lot more about her earlier in the story.

During its 12-month deployment to Vietnam with 8 RAR, the Assault Pioneer Platoon — call-sign 62, or call-signs 62 Alpha and 62 Bravo when operating in half-platoon or less strength — probably saw more combat action than some of the battalion's rifle platoons, and certainly less than most. I'm entirely comfortable with that analogy.

The specialised role of the Assault Pioneer Platoon and the battalion's accelerated adoption after March 1970 of the 1 ATF strategy of pacification, were 2 of the reasons why that was the case. The third, and probably main reason, was nothing other than damn good luck.

No one in their right mind would want to have been engaged in any more contacts with the enemy than what the Assault Pioneer Platoon experienced. Having someone shooting at you — generally at close range and mostly at night — trying very hard to kill you, isn't a pleasant experience. It's certainly not one that I'm keen to revisit anytime soon. War is a very nasty business and although a small number of men in my platoon — and undoubtedly others in 8

Chapter 23 — Operational Tasking

RAR more generally — and also within the wider ADF may have revelled in their combat experiences during their time in Vietnam, the vast majority of us certainly didn't.

I remember a section orders group briefing — 'O Group' — in the platoon lines adjacent to my tented living quarters at Nui Dat, just after dawn on the morning of 10 December 1969 by my section commander Corporal Fred Vincent. This was the start day of our first field operation in Vietnam: Operation Atherton. He gathered those of us in No.1 Section of the platoon into a close-knit huddle as he addressed us, emphasising that over the next 12 months there were 3 things that each of us had to do to the very best of our ability. In order, they were to:

- Do anything and absolutely everything we were tasked with doing, in terms of our operational activity;
- Always look after ourselves and our mates in the platoon, not only when we were out in the field but also back at Nui Dat and, in particular, during those rare periods of time at Vung Tau on R&C breaks;
- Ensure that each and every one of us returned safely home to Australia after our deployment to Vietnam ended.

This short homily from Fred Vincent that morning, certainly got my adrenalin surging. Over the decades since, I've often thought about Fred Vincent because he was, after all, my immediate boss in Vietnam and for the best part of my 2 years in the army. In my considered view, I'd say that he was the epitome of a first-class infantry platoon section commander (tough but fair, and always approachable). I reckon he was just that good at his job. He had my complete confidence and I always obeyed his operational orders and directions without too much question.

Two former platoon members, whom I've spoken with in more recent times, have a somewhat less favourable view of him and that's entirely a matter for them. After hearing and digesting potted versions of their vague and unsubstantiated criticisms, I declined to further debate the issue. I was a member of Vincent's section for my entire time in Vietnam and they weren't. I got to know him very well and I reckon that I've nailed his military competence accurately, even though he only ever addressed me by my surname. He never, not even once, called me Peter.

I haven't forgotten Vincent, or those riveting words he delivered to us that morning. As far as I'm concerned, men can talk all they like about officers and sergeants but, whenever it was getting hot on the ground, it was the section commanders who really made a difference — particularly in the early stages of contact with the enemy. In my view, Vincent was one of these commanders.

Others who have written about the Vietnam War, talk about the platoon and the sectional nature of the internal cohesion within infantry battalions. I can attest to that. Although I knew every man in my platoon well, I was far more emotionally attached to the men in my section; particularly Des McGrath and Allan Small, its machine gun group, both of whom also shared my rudimentary tented habitation at Nui Dat. Mick O'Shea from No.3 Section was another very close platoon mate of mine.

During its 12-month deployment to Vietnam, 8 RAR accounted for the officially recorded deaths — confirmed body count — of 173 enemy; officially wounded more than 80; and captured a very small number of enemy.[38] The Assault Pioneer Platoon was directly responsible for the deaths of 4 of those enemy, and the capture of 1.

On the debit side of the ledger, 18 men from 8 RAR were killed and 107 were wounded.[39] Seven of those fatalities were National Servicemen. Given that the average posted strength of the battalion was said to have been around 795 men, those numbers equate to a fatality rate of 2.3% and an overall casualty rate of 15.8%. The Assault Pioneer Platoon was extremely fortunate and suffered no fatalities with only one man lightly wounded. How lucky is that? Extremely, I would say.

Over the 10-year period of Australia's active military involvement in the Vietnam conflict, 521 men were killed and 3,129 were wounded. Significantly, of those fatalities, 210 were National Servicemen, as were 1,279 of those wounded.

Table 7.

AUSTRALIAN CASUALTY DATA:
8 RAR AND ALL BATTALIONS OF THE ROYAL AUSTRALIAN REGIMENT, THE VIETNAM WAR AND PREVIOUS MAJOR CONFLICTS

Casualties	8 RAR		All RAR		Vietnam		WWII		Korea	
Killed	18	2.3%	330	2.6%	521	0.9%	27073	2.7%	340	2.0%
Wounded	107	13.5%	1757	13.8%	3129	5.2%	23477	2.4%	1216	7.2%
TOTAL	125	15.8%	2087	16.4%	3650	6.1%	50550	5.1%	1556	9.2%

The collective casualty rate of The Royal Australian Regiment was 16.4%.[40] The data for 8 RAR is pretty much in line with that number, as well

---
[38] Hall, Robert A. *Combat Battalion*. Allen and Unwin. Sydney. 2000. Page 105.
[39] Hall, Robert A. *Combat Battalion*. Allen and Unwin. Sydney. 2000. Page 111.
[40] Various publicly available sources.

Chapter 23 — Operational Tasking

as the overall category split for fatalities and wounded respectively of that aggregated regimental data. Both 8 RAR and 9 RAR served only 1 operational deployment to Vietnam, while the other 7 battalions of the regiment served 2. The broad comparative data contained in Table 7 clearly reflects that the Vietnam War was a particularly nasty ground conflict.

The data from WWII probably needs to be uplifted to include the 30,560 men and women captured by the enemy and incarcerated, many of whom were executed by the opposing Axis forces or died from horrific deprivations as prisoners of war. That would increase the total casualty rate for that conflict to 8.2%.

Table 8 provides more comparative detail regarding the casualty statistics of the 9 battalions of the Royal Australian Regiment when deployed to Vietnam.

Table 8.

CASUALTY DATA FOR THE 9 INFANTRY BATTALIONS OF THE ROYAL AUSTRALIAN REGIMENT DEPLOYED TO VIETNAM

Battalion	Killed	Wounded	TOTAL	Battalion	Killed	Wounded	TOTAL
1 RAR	50	411	461	6 RAR	61	148	209
2 RAR	32	182	214	7 RAR	33	220	253
3 RAR	28	120	148	8 RAR	18	107	125
4 RAR	23	138	161	9 RAR	35	150	185
5 RAR	50	281	331	All RAR	330	1,757	2,087

Publically available ADF data suggests that some 3,906 enemy were killed by Australian servicemen during the 10-year period of Australia's active military involvement in the Vietnam War. However, that number is seriously understated. Our enemy were almost fanatical in terms of their seemingly driven obsession for the retrieval of their wounded comrades and bodies of their dead from the battlefield. The majority of 8 RAR's contacts with the enemy were at night, which is probably why many of those fire-fights were protracted events with often frustratingly inconclusive outcomes the next morning — extensive, bloody drag trails on the ground, but no bodies.

From an 8 RAR and an Assault Pioneer Platoon perspective, these post-contact congealed blood pools and variable blood spoors — which were often discovered next morning after night-time ambush engagements with the enemy — attest to many more deaths, or serious injuries to our enemy than officially recorded by body count alone. Often deceased and badly wounded enemy soldiers were discovered the very next day harboured-up in villages or hamlets near the previous night's ambush site. 1 ATF didn't ever officially regard these casualties as numerically attributable to the previous night's contact.

The way in which the Assault Pioneer Platoon was operationally tasked in Vietnam, was characterised by a range of distinct and often very different types of activities. Sometimes, these activities or roles quietly merged into one another. The operational tasking of the other diverse elements of Support Company and that of the 12 platoons of the 4 rifle companies, was similarly varied from time to time.

For example, C Company occasionally spent time in fire support bases and night defensive positions, as did the Assault Pioneer Platoon and other support elements of the battalion. C Company also established a very important long-term static site — Night Defensive Position Isa — in the Long Hai Hills, 13.8km south of Nui Dat. Some rifle company platoons destroyed discovered enemy bunker systems. The Assault Pioneer Platoon destroyed plenty of them.

It has occurred to me that many of you reading this book may not know what a bunker or bunker system was, in the context of the Vietnam War. They were nothing like the above-ground reinforced concrete structures, so common during WWII. Basically, they were ground level dug-in weapons firing pits of assorted sizes. These bunker systems were usually connected by crawl trenches, all of which were covered with overhead protection of logs, dirt, and foliage to provide camouflage. They were very hard to detect until you were almost on top of them. Walking into, or assaulting an enemy-inhabited bunker system was extremely dangerous, with a high likelihood of friendly casualties. Bunker systems were sited and constructed so as to provide beneficial enfilading and intersecting firing lines for our enemy. They could always see us well before we became aware of them.

Initially, the overall operational focus of the battalion was on what might be broadly described as reconnaissance-in-force, and search and destroy activities, with most operations generally aimed at locating, confronting, and killing as many enemy as possible. In other words, the classic infantry role. These particularly aggressive day-time tasking activities were, from time to time, interspersed with ambushing, and the cordon and search of selected civilian centres. Of course, night-time ambushing was expected routine tasking for most 8 RAR elements, even when they were temporarily based at fire support bases or night defensive positions.

Early operations of the battalion were typified by the establishment or taking over the defence of fire support bases whenever the operational activities of the battalion were located beyond the effective range of supporting artillery gunfire from Nui Dat — effectively a distance of about 11km. At these static sites, the six 105mm artillery guns from 161 Field Battery were air lifted in from Nui Dat by US Army Chinook helicopters and augmented by battalion mortar support.

Night defensive positions such as Isa, and Kylie, were maintained and defended for lengthy periods of time, usually by elements of Support Company, spasmodically by the Assault Pioneer Platoon, and occasionally by other rifle company elements. Night defensive positions were established to protect specific and important military projects within the province. For example, Isa, which was located well south of Nui Dat, was put in place to provide protection and security for engineering activities associated with the Long Hai Hills quarry, while Kylie was established to support road building activities along Route 2 in the far north of the province, close to the Long Khanh provincial border.

While some of the early operational tasking of the Assault Pioneer Platoon centred on either establishing or defending fire support bases or smaller night defensive positions, the only static sites that the battalion actually built from inception — through the physical efforts of its Assault Pioneer Platoon and other Support Company elements — were Bond, and Peggy. The Assault Pioneer Platoon certainly improved Fire Support Base Pat, and Night Defensive Positions Isa, and Kylie. The Assault Pioneer Platoon was also based at Fire Support Base Lei Loi — a high value asset of the US Army 4th Battalion, 9th Infantry Regiment — and Fire Support Bases Discovery, and Matthew, for brief periods of time.

In conjunction with its leading role of establishing and defending fire support bases and night defensive positions, members of the Assault Pioneer Platoon were also the battalion's first-call field engineers, specialising in light engineering, demolition of enemy bunker systems, mine warfare, and booby trap mitigation tasks. The platoon was also used extensively in a number of other important roles such as a 'ready reaction force' deployable at very short notice — around 30 minutes or less — from a fire support base or a night defensive position to support any other battalion element under fire from the enemy, day and night-time ambushing in adjacent areas, and a range of relatively specific, targeted roles in areas near to these static sites.

After very busy, exhausting, and extremely varied tasking during Operations Atherton, and Keperra (mid-December 1969— late February 1970), the Assault Pioneer Platoon spent almost its entire time during Operations Hammersley, and Hamilton (late February—late March) defending and improving Fire Support Base Pat, and Night Defensive Position Isa. During this time, the platoon conducted many night-time ambushes in vicinities adjacent to those static positions, particularly areas near to Night Defensive Position Isa.

It was around this time when the Task Force operational strategy for confronting and engaging with the enemy changed from one of reconnaissance-in-force, and search and destroy — actively seeking out the enemy — to one of pacification, an operational approach characterised by the ambushing of routes into villages and towns. In other words, bringing the enemy closer to us, rather than us to them.

The aim of this new operational strategy was to deny the enemy access to food, recruits, intelligence, and hard currency, as well as presence and visibility within civilian centres. This new role was interspersed with the cordon and search of large towns or villages that were known to be sympathetic to the enemy, and other extraneous related operational activities. Another reason why the Task Force decided on this change in strategy was to avoid the elevated risk of likely, significant friendly casualties in assaulting heavily-defended enemy bunker systems.

While the Assault Pioneer Platoon was frequently based at static sites for varying periods of time, it also often operated quite independently outside of those sites. Sporadically, the platoon was attached to B, C, and D Companies — more usually D Company — as a fourth rifle company platoon.

On 4 October, the battalion came out of operations and began a one company operational cycle right through until it ceased field operations in Vietnam later that month. During this period, the Assault Pioneer Platoon was deployed on a number of day-time TAOR patrols and singular night-time ambushes, generally no more than about 5km or so from Nui Dat. We found this operational mode very difficult to adapt to.

Although we knew that we were probably not going to be tasked again on another ambush the next evening, and perhaps not even over the next few days, we were always really careful not to drink too much alcohol that night at Nui Dat. We all recognised that we needed to be in first-class physical shape whenever we were again called upon to leave Nui Dat for operational tasking. Often, we were on immediate, 'ready reaction' standby, which meant that drinking alcohol was off limits on those evenings anyway.

It appeared that the battalion had largely ceased its military operations in Vietnam after 4 October, but that wasn't the case. Most operational elements of the battalion were pretty much fully engaged on this sort of irregular, singular night-time ambushing, interspersed with occasional day-time TAOR patrols around the near vicinity of Nui Dat.

This type of very short, sharp, and quite varied operational activity was difficult to become accustomed to, and eventually it became quite unsettling for us. As our remaining tenure in Vietnam diminished exponentially, we were mostly worried about the platoon getting through this 'short-time' period unscathed. If the platoon were to have suffered fatalities, or even casualties during those last few weeks of our time in Vietnam, it would have been nothing short of catastrophic. Fortunately, that didn't happen.

On 25 October, the battalion ceased all military operations. During its last week in Vietnam, the Assault Pioneer Platoon cleaned up its lines at Nui Dat, disposed of obsolete ammunition and other ordinance items, and readied itself to leave Nui Dat for its return to Australia on HMAS *Sydney* on 31 October.

For reasons that I never understood, when deployed out from Nui Dat, we often operated in the far north of the province — very near to the Long Khanh provincial border (and even over it on at least 2 occasions) — in dense jungle, rubber, or amidst other uninspiring and difficult to negotiate terrains. We were usually by ourselves in either platoon, or more often half-platoon strength. It was rare for us to operate in close concert with other 8 RAR field elements.

John Dolgan, one of my platoon mates, once described our particular operational role after March as that of a reconnaissance — 'recon' — platoon. While I'm not sure if that US Army jargon description of the role of the Assault Pioneer Platoon is entirely accurate, there were some very real role similarities in its tasking from time to time.

On those many days and nights, and sometimes weeks when we operated outside of Nui Dat and fire support bases or night defensive positions, we moved slowly and very quietly through areas deemed likely to be inhabited by the enemy and, after a late afternoon meal and brew, laid down an ambush for the night. Landmarks such as creek crossings or track intersections were targeted, as were a range of other landscape features considered as likely transit routes by the enemy into local towns and villages for logistical re-supply and other support needs.

When out in the field, a typical day for us started with '*stand to*' where, for about 30 minutes before dawn, every member of the ambush party was on full alert. After that, we quickly dismantled the ambush and quietly prepared a small meal and brew for breakfast. Weapons were cleaned and equipment readied for the coming day's exertions, the details of which were outlined to us by our section commanders in a short, almost whispered 'O Group' meeting.

These early morning 'O Groups' were extremely important, and we eagerly looked forward to them. They gave us a focus for our upcoming day's activities and provided us with an overview of the wider battalion operational activity on the ground. Personally, it was always very useful to know how our platoon tasking for the day ahead actually fitted into the overall operational tactics of the battalion, and more broadly, to the overall strategy of the Task Force.

For example, we might have been required to move to a certain position as a blocking force to potentially engage enemy driven our way by other elements of the battalion. Or we might have been asked to perform the reverse function. On other early occasions, we were asked to move to a position where TFHQ intelligence suggested a likely enemy presence in a defended position, such as a bunker system. During the first couple of months, we were extensively engaged in demolishing substantial numbers of discovered enemy bunkers.

It was quite varied operational tasking that involved moving very slowly and quietly — with many short breaks — always maintaining our security as much as possible. Generally, we didn't tend to move all that far on any given day. It was probably somewhere between 3-4km. For the most part, I reckon it was towards the lower end of that scale.

Each day, about 75 minutes before darkness enveloped us, we quietly prepared a small meal and brew for dinner before moving into the construction of that night's particular ambush. As dusk quickly turned into night, with all of us in the prone position on the ground, there was always a 30-minute period of '*stand to*' observed by everyone in the ambush party.

The practice of pre-dawn and pre-dusk '*stand to*' was a constant for us, no matter whether we were in fire support bases, night defensive positions, or night-time ambush settings. For reasons I've mentioned previously, members of the Assault Pioneer Platoon weren't often required to observe '*stand to*' when based at Nui Dat. Platoons of the 4 rifle companies and other elements of the battalion weren't so fortunate.

Generally, we spent between 4-6 weeks — and sometimes even much longer — away from Nui Dat on each operation. Often, new operations commenced or overlapped without a break. There were a number of occasions when we didn't see Nui Dat for very long periods of time, other than briefly. See Appendix 7.

Planned operational tenure was quite varied and often subject to change, depending on the operational situation out in the field and the gathering of real-time intelligence of enemy movements by TFHQ. During those lengthy periods, we existed on rations food only and lived what I'd say was a very tough and rough life.

Without any doubt whatsoever, the worst aspect of our time out in the field was the need for continual security. Day after day, as we slowly and quietly moved forward, we hardly ever spoke to one another. On those rare and fleeting moments that we did communicate, it was only in the form of soft whispers and rudimentary sign language. At night when we were hunkered down in ambushes, we didn't talk amongst ourselves either, other than for a few brief whispers when — deployed in half-platoon strength — sentries on each of our 2 M60 machine guns and rear protection group were changed, typically at around 10pm and 2am. When we were in full platoon mode, those times would have been somewhat different, with slightly shorter periods of sentry duty on each of the 3 M60 machine guns.

The early morning 'O Groups' and the 15 minutes or so that we spent late each evening and early the next morning setting up and dismantling night-time ambushes, were the only opportunities we had to quietly talk amongst ourselves. Even then, we only ever spoke to those next to us, in very quiet, soft tones.

For much of the time during the day, we were probably at least 15m apart, sometimes a lot more, depending on the terrain and other prevailing ground

Chapter 23 — Operational Tasking

conditions. We rarely moved forward in a centre line formation, as depicted in the wonderful 2019 Australian produced movie 'Danger Close' (The Battle of Long Tan). Most of the time we were in single file, or 2 or 3 adjacent obliquely-staggered files, about 30m apart. The 2 forward scouts of each section were always much further forward of the main platoon body than that, probably around 40-50m or thereabouts. The formation adopted was determined, in large part, by the manpower resource on hand at any one time, and the terrain. In any formation, quiet conversation between us would have been almost impossible anyway.

As we moved ever so slowly forward, each and every one of us was intently concentrating. We were continuously scanning our surrounds for signs of previous enemy traffic and anything else that might indicate danger or the need to investigate further. Our hearing was acutely attuned and alert for any sound that might seem out of place in the ambient environment. The concentration required to do this, hour after hour, day after day, sometimes week after week, placed enormous strain on our mental resilience. During numerous medical specialist consultations, I've attempted to explain what it was really like for us, mentally, when we were out in the field. However, I feel that I just haven't been able to convey this information accurately — because it's almost impossible to describe.

However, what I do know is this. Late each afternoon as we prepared and set up a night-time ambush, we were always pretty much mentally and physically exhausted from the day's exertions. Not a good place to be, I would suggest. But as I describe later, as soon as we had put an ambush in place and night fell, we always felt far more secure and were able to relax somewhat, unless of course, it was our turn as a rostered sentry on one of the M60 machine guns and in charge of the handheld electrical initiators for the offensive arrays of M18 Claymore anti-personnel directional mines.

After days of not really communicating amongst ourselves, the debilitating climatic conditions, exacerbated by the endless concentration and the physical demands placed on us by the heavy weight loads we were carrying, significantly impacted our stress levels. This was further aggravated by what I can only describe as 'unconscious boredom'.

As each new day began, there was always a vague thought in the back of our minds that we might walk into an inhabited enemy bunker system, or engage in some other sort of enemy contact. We never knew what was about to confront us at any given moment. Although we tried very hard to intently concentrate on what we were doing — eyes slowly moving left to right and back again, as we quietly and ever so slowly moved forward, alert for any sound, looking for sign of any enemy presence — it was impossible to maintain that level of intense concentration for extended periods of time.

The longer the time between contact with the enemy, or change in our operational tasking, the harder it became to maintain those necessary levels of concentration and focus. A kind of detached boredom began to infiltrate our minds, alongside those ever-present stress levels. Not surprisingly, this cocktail of complex emotions and mental challenges tended to make us far less alert than what we should have been. This was a classic Catch 22 conundrum. All members of my platoon, including myself, would have refused to accept that proposition, had it been put to us back then. However, many years later, I know that I'm right.

Now to add some clarity to this scenario of our time away from Nui Dat, the Assault Pioneer Platoon was often deployed in and out of fire support bases or night defensive positions. So, there were breaks — some lengthy and others quite short — from this seemingly endless daily routine of near silence. Many of the other rifle platoons of the battalion weren't so lucky.

Each night we harboured-up in ambush constructs. We didn't move. We just lay on the ground, waiting for the enemy to move into the chosen killing ground before springing the ambush. We were well and truly in the driver's seat, so to speak. For the most part, we felt far more secure when laying on the ground in a night-time ambush. That is, of course, until an ambush was sprung. Whenever that occurred, all hell broke loose. M18 Claymore anti-personnel directional mines were electronically detonated, followed by concentrated M60 machine gun and rifle fire into the designated killing ground, and M79 grenade launcher illumination flares over it.

However, on some nights there was little or no moon and heavy, low cloud cover. On those nights, it was so dark that we couldn't see the backs of our hands, or our weapons…even if they were placed right in front of our faces. The luminescent features of our wrist watches stood out, almost like naval navigation beacons, in stark contrast to the darkness enveloping and seemingly consuming us. Unless the enemy approaching the ambush killing ground on those nights was using torches, there was simply no way that we were ever going to see them. Occasionally, and I have no idea how they were able to do so, the enemy didn't use torches at night.

Night-time ambushing under these extreme conditions was highly stressful because every single sound, benign or otherwise, could herald imminent danger. Simply changing sentries on the M60 machine guns was extremely risky and usually only accomplished by the reliance on using elaborate guidelines of lengths of green cord carefully put in place during the ambush set up. All men participating in an ambush on these sorts of nights were acutely aware of the positional framework put in place. Or, at least they should have been!

On those nights, we prayed for dawn to emerge from the obsidian blackness into which we were intently peering. I can't fully describe this impenetrable darkness and the feeling of abject helplessness that almost overwhelmed us during these times. Frankly, it was nothing short of frightening. Sadly, a number of innocent feral pigs and other ambient nocturnal wildlife lost their lives on some of those nights. One of my veteran mates once told me that his battalion — 3 RAR — had a very high 'kill count' in this regard.

The latent boredom and associated degraded mental alertness that often accompanied many of our day-time activities, never transferred to a night-time ambush. Each ambush in place had a ground position, which made it quite different from those of previous ones. They were never the same because each one was also dependent on TFHQ or BHQ intelligence, the landscape, and our proximity to civilian population centres.

On one occasion, after several weeks of exhausting and sustained operational activity, I decided to take off my boots to see how my feet were coping with the continual lack of ventilation, constant moisture, and general absence of care. It was very early in the morning, just after dawn. We were in a densely vegetated and heavily-treed flat area. While it was still quite dim and gloomy, it was already becoming very hot. '*Stand to*' had just finished and a thin steamy mist was rising in spiralling tendrils from the ground. We'd already dismantled the previous night's ambush and most of us were either quietly fixing up a quick breakfast, cleaning our weapons, or as in my case, examining our feet.

After quickly looking at the poor condition of the sole of one foot, I instinctively glanced up and peered over a large fallen tree trunk, providing me with a fair degree of security and cover. I almost had a heart attack! About 80m away, and moving towards our position, were 2 armed Viet Cong guerrilla insurgents. And here was I, with no boot on one foot. I was never mentally unbalanced enough to remove both boots at the same time.

I quickly gained my section commander's attention and, as we instantly galvanised into a 'confront and engage' mode, I struggled to get my boot back on. I was cursing myself. Anyway, we must have made some sort of noise because these 2 enemy soldiers fled at speed. That was a very wise decision on their part. Even though we attempted to run them down for a minute or so, it ended up being a complete waste of time.

Moving quickly with a loose, untied boot, and my heart pounding out of my chest, wasn't my idea of fun. After this incident, I never again removed my boots during field operations, and only briefly within the confines of a fire support base or night defensive position, no matter how long the duration. I'd well and truly learned my lesson. As I've already mentioned, on one infamous occasion, I rarely took take my boots off, or changed my clothes, for more than 7 weeks!

At another time, we were moving though semi-dense jungle when suddenly my platoon commander — 2LT Phillips — realised that we were smack bang in the middle of a Viet Cong bunker system. No one else in our platoon was aware of this...I certainly wasn't. As a member of the lead section — No.1 Section — I'd just walked right by without noticing it. Thank God this particular bunker system was uninhabited, or my platoon would probably have suffered heavy casualties that day. This just goes to show how that insidious latent boredom syndrome could have seriously brought us undone at any time.

Our platoon commander is probably a luckier man than most of us. There was a later horrendous moment when — PHQ were off to one side of our forward line of movement — he walked into a trip wire at just above ankle height. Fortunately, he had the presence of mind to freeze, not daring to increase or ease the pressure being applied to the wire. After he motioned to the men nearest him to get down, one of my platoon mates, who I'm almost certain was the platoon signaller Paul Jansen, very carefully traced the trip wire to a spent flare, obviously used in a previous friendly ambush at this site, which was still attached to an adjacent tree. Obviously, the inert trip wire had been mistakenly left behind.

Viet Cong trip wire activated booby traps were commonly known to initiate M16 anti-personnel mines, reclaimed by them from the notorious Australian built barrier minefield. It ran from the permanently defended Fire Support Base Horseshoe near Dat Do, south-east to the coast. No wonder my platoon commander froze mid-step, completely terrified for his life, but still with the presence of mind and operational responsibility to make sure that all of his men were laying prone on the ground whilst the predicament was sorted.

The professional way in which Mr Phillips reacted during these incidents came as no surprise to me. While I also regarded our former platoon commander, 2LT Ken Jones, as a highly professional soldier, I felt far more comfortable under the leadership of Mr Phillips.

These diverse incidents serve to reiterate the fact that when out in the field, anything could happen at any given moment. A lapse in alertness and concentration could result in casualties, or worse still, cost lives. And that was something we certainly didn't want to happen to anyone in our platoon. The aggregated psychological effects of consistently elevated stress and concentration levels, exacerbated by not knowing what might happen in the very next moment, is known amongst the collective ex-service community in Australia as the 'malevolent environment'.

Many Australian men and women who served in Vietnam — particularly infantry soldiers — suffer from what is known as Post-traumatic Stress Disorder (PTSD), or Gross Anxiety Disorder. They're both debilitating mental conditions that can usually be attributed to a particular combat incident — or incidents — commonly referred to within the veteran community as 'stressors'.

For example, coming under enemy fire would meet DVA's definition of what is accepted by them as a 'stressor,' as would participating in the interment of dead enemy.

On the other hand, many Australian infantry soldiers may have spent their entire time in Vietnam without ever having to engage with the enemy in combat. Because of their particular roles within the battalion, they may never have fired their personal weapons at all. Conversely, some may have been involved in a large number of contacts with the enemy, or only very few. It was that type of conflict...all so varied and unpredictable. Exposure to this so-called malevolent environment wasn't just confined to infantry and other men out in the field. Potentially, both 1 ATF at Nui Dat, and 1 ALSG at Vung Tau, were susceptible to enemy attack.

The well documented Battle of Long Tan, almost certainly prevented a major enemy ground assault on the emerging I ATF Nui Dat base. Men permanently based at Nui Dat and Vung Tau, although ensconced in very secure areas after late 1966, may well have suffered mental anguish due to their perception of never-ending uncertainty regarding their personal safety. Who knows? And who are we to judge anyway?

As human beings, each of us are quite different in terms of the way we think and rationalise our thought processes, synthesise data, and react to stress. We all have discrete psyches and uniquely different emotional triggers. As far as I'm concerned, any soldier, sailor, airman, servicewoman, civilian doctor, nursing and medical staff, Australian Embassy staff in Saigon, journalists, entertainers, and members of Qantas' Skippy Squadron — who served or spent time in Vietnam — could quite easily suffer from PTSD or Gross Anxiety Disorder, because of the impact that this insidious malevolent environment may have had on them.

The Australian Government, under the leadership of former Prime Minister Tony Abbott, announced that surviving civilian doctors, nurses, and medical staff from the more than 440 of those who served in Vietnam under the auspices of SEATO, were eligible to 'apply' to DVA for a Gold Card (free hospital and medical treatment), commencing 1 July 2020. These magnificent people comprised the medical teams raised by hospitals around Australia and during their time in Vietnam — October 1964 until December 1972 — they delivered superior medical services and wonderful aid to allied soldiers and impoverished Vietnamese civilians, particularly in Bien Hoa Province just north of Saigon, and north-north-west of Phuoc Tuy Province.

While many Australian Vietnam veterans are badly psychologically affected in their later life because of the impacts of their exposure to this malevolent environment, DVA doesn't accept this as a condition for accepting PTSD or Gross Anxiety Disorder as 'war caused' disabilities. This is because it technically fails to meet its prescribed test of being deemed as an accompanying 'stressor.' Perhaps the government's announcement to properly recognise those civilian doctors, nurses, and medical staff, by offering them potentially free hospital and medical treatment eligibility for the DVA Gold Card, might just herald a change in this thinking.

Whenever we returned to Nui Dat, even if it was only for a day, several days, or even longer, it will come as no great surprise to know that we attempted to relax and de-stress by means of the only 'release' readily available to us. And that, of course, was alcohol...which we drank to excess in the company boozer. Our first night back at Nui Dat after an operation almost always ended up with most of us getting very drunk. Other than the occasional distractions provided by enthusiastic bar girls in Vung Tau, alcohol pretty much became our only release mechanism. It's no wonder so many Vietnam veterans returned to Australia as well-seasoned drinkers, if not totally addicted to alcohol. I was one of them.

THE ENEMY

The enemy that confronted 8 RAR soldiers out in the field in Vietnam, manifested in a number of distinct but intrinsically connected forms. The most professional, finest trained, and better-equipped enemy soldiers were the North Vietnam Army (NVA) units. The NVA supported the Viet Cong with weapons, training, and variously, with troops and advisors. The most common enemy that 8 RAR came in contact with, were various Viet Cong provincial and local forces elements.

For example, there was a significant strength — said to comprise about 1,200 men and women — unit known as NVA 274 Main Force Regiment. It operated to the north-west of Nui Dat, along the borders with Bien Hoa and Long Khanh Provinces, aside the junction with Route 2. This unit, at full strength, approached something twice the size of a 1 ATF infantry battalion.

There were also 2 other units, each comprising of between 350-500 people, known as D440 and D445 Local Force Battalions. D440, an Engineer Battalion, often operated jointly with 274 Main Force Regiment in the north of the province, while D445 Battalion operated mainly in the south-east from Dat Do and Long Dien to the Long Hai Hills.

There were also several district-based Local Force units such as C23 Xuyen Moc District Company (strength of between 30-40), C25 Long Dat District Company (110 strong), and C41 Chan Duc District Company (110 strong). The lowest level of numerous enemy enclaves (up to 10 strong) were found in the many villages and hamlets throughout the province. Even though they were more closely aligned with the North Vietnamese Main Force units,

D440, D445 Local force Battalions, and the myriad of local chapters of smaller pockets of insurgents were collectively known as the Viet Cong.

Well before my time in Vietnam, D445 Local Force Battalion was a significant element of the large enemy force that 'massed' — as it's now known — in force to launch a ground attack on Nui Dat. This attack was foiled by the outcome of the Battle of Long Tan on 18 August 1966. Although significantly degraded in that famous battle, D445 Local Force Battalion had well and truly re-established itself as a potent enemy force when 8 RAR arrived in Phuoc Tuy Province in late 1969.

Many of the local Viet Cong guerrilla insurgents were men — and women — who lived in and around the numerous small towns, villages, and hamlets. By day, they were seemingly law-abiding citizens, just eking out a subsistence living on the land. By night, they were often murderous enemy. All of these various enemy elements within Phuoc Tuy Province were associated in some way, and operated under loosely connected, but still common military command and control of the National Liberation Front (NLF).

8 RAR had many contacts with D445 Local Force Battalion, and in those engagements, the enemy always fought hard and proved to be a very clever, resilient, and difficult adversary. D445 Local Force Battalion was comprised of brave and tenacious soldiers who always fought arduously to recover their dead and wounded from the battlefield. Many of the Task Force strategies and 8 RAR field tactics were aimed at engaging D445 Local Force Battalion and degrading the strength of this well trained, highly organised military unit.

Viet Cong provincial elements often inhabited heavily fortified and cunningly concealed bunker systems, many of which were originally constructed during the French occupation of the country. These elaborate bunker systems — which were always located in jungle areas — were well hidden from view from the air, because of the jungle canopy cover. They had been maintained and indeed, even extended by the Viet Cong over many years.

The jungle areas were dotted with these bunker systems. Typically, the Viet Cong would regularly move between them to avoid detection. Generally, if they were discovered in one bunker system, they'd fight tenaciously until they could withdraw — usually after nightfall — and move to another bunker system.

There was far more movement by the enemy at night, so unless Australian soldiers discovered an inhabited bunker system or came across enemy soldiers — or on the few occasions when the Viet Cong decided to actually engage Australian soldiers in force during the day — the chances of coming into contact with either the Main Force, Local Force, or Viet Cong enemy, other than at night, wasn't very high. Soldiers from 8 RAR did have plenty of daytime enemy contacts, usually with Viet Cong forces. However, most enemy contacts by far, especially the larger ones, were in the evening.

At night, the Viet Cong would often move in well-armed groups as large as 100 or more. Groups of 30-60 were common, as were groups between 20-30. The reason for this was because they needed to enter towns and villages to obtain food and clothing, other supplies, and even secreted ammunition...all under the cover of darkness. They also entered these local population centres to gain visibility and profile, promote propaganda, and collect subjugated and illegal taxes imposed on the residents by local chapters of the Viet Cong political structures. And, of course, they also visited these towns and villages for sexual liaisons and to execute 'Choi Hanhs': former Viet Cong soldiers who'd defected to the so-called democratic South Vietnam.

NVA main force units and Viet Cong provincial forces were often armed with Russian manufactured 50cal heavy machine guns and RPD 7.62mm machine guns, as well as 61mm and 82mm mortars, along with a wide range of other Russian and Chinese manufactured armaments. However, the most common personal weapon carried by the collective Viet Cong were both Russian and Chinese manufactured Kalashnikov AK 47 fully-automatic assault rifles. This low-cost, simple and reliable rifle, fired either Russian manufactured 7.62mm x 39mm (7.62mm short) rounds, or Chicom type 56 rimless rounds — in either short bursts or as single shots — from a bottom-fed forwardly-curved 20-round magazine. Some models of this extremely effective enemy rifle featured 30-round magazines. Although a wonderful weapon, the significantly shorter projectile and much lower muzzle velocity — 715m/s — didn't provide as much stopping power as that of a NATO 7.62mm round. To illustrate this feature further, the NATO 7.62mm projectile weighed 9.5gm whereas the AK 47 7.62mm projectile weighed significantly less at 7.9gm.

The Viet Cong also routinely carried large numbers of RPGs which, when in contact with allied soldiers, were invariably fired either directly at oncoming APCs or into trees, thereby creating a dangerous and very effective fragmentation impact on allied infantry soldiers.

Due to extensive and consistent enemy movement at night, in and around towns and villages during the early part of the battalion's time in Vietnam in late March 1970, the nature of 8 RAR operations changed to one of pacification. The main feature of this new tactic was intensive night-time and even day-time ambushing of likely transit routes leading into civilian population centres.

Australian soldiers in the field were confronted by an enemy that was generally supported by most of the local population. If not overtly supportive of the Viet Cong, many of the locals were simply too frightened to do anything else and just got on with their lives. Despite common misconceptions, Australian soldiers didn't confront an inferior enemy in Vietnam. While they had air, artillery, armour, and other mechanised support — and significantly greater overall firepower — they faced an enemy who was extremely well-armed with personal weapons.

Collectively, the enemy we faced in Vietnam was experienced, intelligent, organised, well trained, well-armed, resolute, and very vicious. The guerrilla tactics adopted by the Viet Cong, where they often remained within the dense jungle areas or retreated to their well-concealed bunker systems, or blended into the routine life of numerous civilian centres, nullified the range of supporting firepower available to 8 RAR. Unless cornered, or in numbers and situated in a vastly superior ground position, the Viet Cong wasn't usually inclined to hang around and fight it out. But when they did, they fought very well indeed. The Viet Cong was a worthy enemy.

FIRST DAYS IN VIETNAM

The day after our arrival at Nui Dat, an education and demonstration exercise was conducted in all company areas. Its purpose was to emphasise the maintenance and safety of weapons, given the prevailing climate and the Rules of Engagement we'd be operating under when out in the field.

We were exposed to an impressive firepower demonstration which included 105mm artillery guns, 9 Squadron Bushranger helicopter gunships, along with US Army Cobra helicopter gunships and USAF F4 Phantom jets. This was a very useful exercise and an important introduction to some aspects of operational support available to us as ground troops. Finally, all elements of the battalion were familiarised with enemy mine warfare and booby traps. We also attended lectures focused on air support, street, and house-to-house fighting, and 'Dustoff' — medical evacuation from the field — procedures.

During these 10 days or so of pre-operational climate acclimatisation, a squad of Assault Pioneer Platoon soldiers, led by its sergeant Monty White, performed a one-day TAOR patrol in an area adjacent to Nui Dat. Somehow — I mustn't have been hiding well that day — I ended up as a member of this squad, which was the size of an understrength half-platoon. My recollection is that there were about 10 of us on this patrol. I also ended up carrying one of the platoon's M60 machine guns on this TAOR. This was the first of many shitty days for me in Vietnam. I was never able to find out exactly why we conducted this TAOR patrol when, within a few days, we were scheduled to deploy from Nui Dat on our first major and lengthy operation.

Anyway, I found this patrol physically exhausting, as White set a cracking pace. That was fine for him…he was as lean as an anorexic racing greyhound, and wasn't carrying a 10.5kg M60 machine gun with 4.5 100-round belts — 13.8kg — of ammunition for it either! Like White, I'd only been in Vietnam for a few days and found the prevailing heat and humidity to be nothing short of horrendous. This was another horrible day in the army for me.

Much of the ground we covered that day was over dried paddy bunds, their often narrow and unstable side verges making it difficult for us to traverse along them. We frequently came across villagers — mainly females — working in sub-dry rice paddy fields. I have to say that my first contact with these locals was interesting. For the most part, they simply ignored us and didn't appear to be at all friendly. I had no idea what to make of them and found myself somewhat overawed by the experience. On the other hand, it was evident to me that they were quite accustomed to seeing allied soldiers.

They were dressed in identical manner; loose calf-length black lightweight trousers, half-sleeve voluminous white blouses, and broad-brimmed white conical straw type hats, often seen in news documentaries and movies focused on Asia. The fact that I was absolutely exhausted halfway through this TAOR didn't allow me to appreciate my initial exposure to the basic subsistence farming lifestyle of southern Vietnam. I wasn't having a good day!

Suddenly, Sergeant White discovered what he claimed to be a foreign made hand grenade of some sort. I managed to have a good closeup look at this so-called enemy ordinance item and it didn't seem to be anything like a hand grenade. It looked like a baseball-sized benign lump of shapeless shrapnel. Nevertheless, White was convinced that this device was lethal and, after getting clearance from BHQ, laid down a charge of C4 plastic explosive that on detonation, completely destroyed it.

Was I impressed by any of this 'gung-ho' activity on Monty's part? No, I wasn't. Why would the platoon sergeant be carrying C4 plastic explosive, along with fuses, primers, and detonators, on a routine TAOR patrol? This was a very interesting start to my 12-month sojourn in Vietnam. As far as I was concerned — not that I shared this personal view with any other member of our TAOR patrol that afternoon — I felt that White had completely gone 'over the top' in terms of how he dealt with this supposed threat to our safety. More to the point, I thought he was a complete idiot, just trying to 'big-note' himself. I wasn't alone in this view either, which I discovered some days later when a few of us involved in that TAOR patrol quietly chatted amongst ourselves.

When we safely returned to Nui Dat late that afternoon, I was so tired that I couldn't even be bothered drinking more than a couple of beers in the support company boozer. Sheer exhaustion saw me asleep in my tent at around 8:30pm. My quiet thoughts as I drifted off to sleep — besieged by the legions of voracious mosquitoes ravaging my bed space netting barrier and consumed by the suffocating climatic ambiance — were pretty much the same as those I'd pondered over during transportation by truck from Mangalore Airfield to Puckapunyal, some 9 months earlier:

'This is bad, really bad!!!'

OPERATION ATHERTON
10 December 1969 – 10 January 1970

This operation, the battalion's first, was one of reconnaissance-in-force and day and night ambushing in the far north-west of the province. In other words, one of seeking out the enemy. The ground area for this operation was generally west of Route 2 and extended from the De Courtenay rubber — which straddled the northern provincial border abutting Long Khanh Province — south, down to the Xa Binh Ba rubber, and west to the provincial border abutting Bien Hoa Province. While large parts of this predominantly inhospitable landscape were dense jungle and other challenging afforestation, areas closely adjacent to Route 2 were cultivated with numerous small rubber copses, tracts of coffee, pepper, and other minor agricultural crops.

TFHQ intelligence suggested that the civilians in this operational area weren't generally supportive of forces and largely ignored allied military-imposed curfew timings. That information did nothing to abate the tensions felt by every member of the Assault Pioneer Platoon during the hours leading up to its first operational deployment in Vietnam.

The initial strategic aim of this operation was to engage the D440 Local Force Battalion and degrade it as much as possible — by destroying their prized bunker systems — and driving elements of that enemy battalion towards established 8 RAR ambush positions. Emphasis was placed on ambushing possible enemy transit routes between likely bunker systems and civilian population centres. BHQ intelligence had indicated that the battalion might also encounter elements of NVA 274 Main Force Regiment and perhaps even its associated C21 and C24 Viet Cong support elements. There was also some intelligence suggesting that even though the local C41 Chau Duc Viet Cong Company had seemingly been dormant for some time, it had reformed and may have become active in this northern part of the province.

However, as this operation unfolded it became apparent to BHQ that the NVA 274 Main Force Regiment was far more active in the area than its intelligence had earlier suggested. So, a far more important and strategic aim for this operation emerged; to disrupt the efforts of the NVA 274 Main Force Regiment in its attempts to actively re-establish its presence and authority in the northern Song So area, west of Route 2.

Because much of this operation was to be conducted out of effective range of supporting artillery fire from Nui Dat, a fire support base needed to be put in place to provide that essential fire support for battalion elements out in the field.

Early on the morning of 10 December, C Company — along with 1 section of three 105mm artillery guns from 161 Field Battery, and 1 section of 3 tracked self-propelled 155mm artillery guns from the US Army A Battery, 2nd Battalion, 35th Field Artillery Regiment — deployed from Nui Dat by road and established a temporary fire support base at the Duc Than Military Post, to support the wider deployment of the battalion into the area of operation (AO Ashgrove). The Duc Than Military Post was 10km north of Nui Dat on the eastern aspect of Route 2. D Company, transported in APCs from C Squadron, 3 Cavalry Regiment, deployed from Nui Dat at the same time into an adjoining area of operation (AO Romeo).

Very early that same morning, after clearing by a light fire team — Bushranger gunships — from 9 Squadron, A Company was flown in by Iroquois helicopters — also from 9 squadron — and secured a predetermined site for a yet to be established fire support base. This site, 2.6km west of Route 2, was right on the northern edge of the Ap Cu Bi rubber — 15.6km due north of Nui Dat, 5.6km north of the Duc Thanh Military Post, and 3km south-west of the later well-known Night Defensive Position Kylie. As soon as this site was secured by A Company, other elements of the battalion, including the Assault Pioneer Platoon, were deployed from Nui Dat by US Army Chinook helicopters to establish, and put in place defensive systems for what was to become Fire Support Base Peggy (Peggy).

'Operation Atherton' platoon field insertion by US Army Chinook helicopter.

B Company deployed early the next morning, with C Company relocating from its overnight holding position at the Duc Than Military Post. At the same time, the three 105mm guns of 161 Battery positioned at the Duc Than Military Post, and the battery's remaining three 105mm guns back at Nui Dat, were relocated to Peggy. The section of three 155mm guns of the US Army A Battery, 2nd Battalion, 35th Field Artillery Regiment at the Duc Than Military

Post, then relocated back to Nui Dat.

As soon as the emerging fire support base was firmly established, with defended perimeter defences in place, A Company was deployed on reconnaissance-in-force and night-time ambushing activities in the areas of operation around Peggy, in line with the operational tasking of the other 3 rifle companies.

Peggy was a large fire support base compared to others that the Assault Pioneer Platoon later either helped establish, improve, or spend time in. Some of those fire support bases were significantly smaller and, because artillery guns weren't generally part of their offensive armament or defence systems, are probably more accurately described as night defensive positions. Although APCs sometimes harboured at night within their defensive perimeters, night defensive positions usually only had a section of three 81mm mortar tubes for its heavy defence, and as fire support for 8 RAR elements in the field. By way of contrast, fire support bases usually had a full artillery battery of six 105mm guns, as well as — sometimes — a full mortar platoon complement of six 81mm mortar tubes as battalion fire support.

Unlike other fire support bases and night defensive positions that we spent time in, large parts of Peggy were sited within a wild rubber plantation — known as the Ap Cu Bi Rubber — which at least offered a degree of respite, if not from the unrelenting heat and humidity, from the baking sun. Climatically, it was well into the dry season.

The 6 artillery 105mm guns of 161 Battery were air lifted into Peggy by US Army Chinook helicopters and sited in open gun emplacements, protected by built-up defensive semi-circular bunds of soil, very adjacent to the main part of the fire support base and behind its perimeter defences. Mortar tubes of the battalion's Mortar Platoon were sited in an adjacent area. These earthmoving tasks were quickly achieved by engineers using a D4 bulldozer. Also sharing Peggy with us at that time were a number of other battalion elements, as well as a range of supporting attachments including Task Force elements from the Engineer and Armoured Corps etc. Peggy was a pretty busy place for the first few days or so, while it was quickly established.

The role of the Assault Pioneer Platoon at Peggy was to put in place a defensive perimeter, defend the fire support base, be ready to deploy from it within 30 minutes in support of other elements of the battalion, and to conduct day-time reconnaissance-in-force and night-time ambushing in the adjacent areas.

Our main task during the first few days at Peggy, assisted by elements of Anti-Tank and Tracker Platoon, was to dig-in BHQ and our own personal positions. Simultaneously, men from both platoons rolled out and fixed in place substantial barbed-wire barriers around the entire perimeter of the emerging fire support base. For 3 or 4 days, all of us in the Assault Pioneer Platoon were physically worked into the ground. It was very tough and extremely tiring manual work that involved a lot of digging and earthmoving. This really made me curse those in the army hierarchy who'd condemned me to this kind of manual servitude as a member of the 8 RAR Assault Pioneer Platoon.

One recollection I have of those first few days at Peggy was the sheer amount of water I drank. The volume of water I consumed each day was nothing short of incredible. Being within an emerging large fire support base, there was plenty of drinking water available. Liberal quantities were transported in by helicopters from either Vung Tau or Nui Dat several times each day. The genesis of my later preoccupation about not having enough water to drink out in the field, quite clearly began during the early days of my time spent at Peggy.

Emerging dug-in Command Post at Fire Support Base Peggy.
Peter McCann is sitting centre on the sandbag roof. On the far right is Peter Wood.
Allan Small is sitting on the other chair facing away, legs resting on the roof. The 3 men to the author's right are Des McGrath, Steve Kaliczinsky, and Peter Cousins.

When Peggy was fully established, it was surrounded by a double barrier of concertina circular barbed-wire — each about 2m high, separated by an inner — third — barrier about a metre high — of the same type of wire. The distance between the inner and outer barriers was about 20m. At regular intervals around this defensive perimeter, machine gun posts, augmented by banks of M18 Claymore anti-personnel directional mines, were put in place and manned day and night on a rotational basis by available men within the fire support base.

Early on, there were relatively large numbers of soldiers based at Peggy, so there was no shortage of men to singularly man these gun points throughout the day. However, at night when the alert levels were raised significantly,

Chapter 23 — Operational Tasking

at least 2 soldiers manned each gun point. Whenever we were domiciled at Peggy, we always seemed to be manning more than our fair share of these gun points. I have no idea if that was actually the case, but this is how it seemed to be at the time. In any event, we didn't get too much sleep during our time at Peggy. Even during the early build stage of this emerging fire support base, my platoon was also tasked on spasmodic night-time ambushing in locales adjacent to Peggy.

For example, the Assault Pioneer Platoon conducted 4 night-time ambushes — on 12, 13, 14, and 20 December — in concert with a section of 3 APCs on 2 of those occasions. By way of contrast, during the second 2 weeks of this operation, we were extensively engaged on day-time reconnaissance-in-force activities, demolishing bunker systems, and night-time ambushing. We only spent 2 nights back at Peggy during that time.

Whilst Peggy was under construction, a number of listening — or forward observation — posts were put in place about 50m out in front of her defensive perimeter. Assault Pioneer Platoon soldiers were individually rotated through 1 of these listening posts on a 2-hourly roster during daylight hours. This particular listening post was sited down a gently sloping embankment where lush and fronded vegetation abounded. Its position was set back amongst this vegetation, making it extremely well camouflaged. The lateral line of sight from this semi-concealed position was probably something like 150°.

On 18 December, Allan Small, the M60 machine gunner from No.1 Section of the platoon — who was manning a perimeter sentry point at the time — fired at an enemy soldier he observed about 100m outside the perimeter defences of Peggy. It was thought that this enemy soldier had been wounded, but a subsequent sweep of the area by elements from the Assault Pioneer Platoon, after a clearing fire mission of 10 mortar rounds, was inconclusive. No drag marks or blood trails were found.

A few days later — around mid-afternoon on yet another stinking hot and humid day — I was manning the listening post. Mosquitoes were droning around everywhere and just about driving me crazy. I was absolutely bored shitless and not particularly happy about being well out in front of Peggy's defensive systems by myself. I was totally pissed off!

While doing another routine visual left-to-right sweep of the area in front of me — with high-magnification binoculars — I almost had a heart attack. Over to my near right, much lower than my ground position, about 75m away, a person wearing nondescript clothing, but very clearly armed with a rifle of some sort, was slowly and tentatively half-emerging from the dense jungle undergrowth. With my heart pounding, I took careful aim at this enemy soldier with my SLR rifle and fired one round at him. I was a good marksman, so I don't know how I managed to miss him at that 'drop-dead' distance. Nevertheless,

I must have missed because he just seemed to vanish into thin air. From my elevated position, if I'd killed or badly wounded him, I would have been able to see his body lying on the ground. For a few seconds afterwards, I just sat, shaking all over.

Well, with that one shot, all hell seemed to break loose back at Peggy! As I scrambled back behind the defensive perimeter into my platoon area, muttering about the incident to whomever was manning the nearby M60 machine gun point — I think it was Des McGrath — the area that I'd just vacated became saturated with raking machine gun fire for about 30 seconds.

Within a very short space of time, less than 5 minutes I'd say, my platoon section was deployed from Peggy. Now, with the relative safety of numbers — 8 or 9 of us — we conducted an extensive search of the immediate and adjacent areas but found no significant blood trails or any other indication of enemy presence. We gave an abandoned, rudimentary low-level derelict hut particularly careful attention, and found nothing of any real importance inside it.

Given my professed expertise with the SLR rifle, I was still inwardly seething about how I didn't manage to kill, or at least wound this enemy soldier. All that aside, this was my first encounter with an enemy, and I found the one-on-one surprising personal nature of it, very unsettling indeed. Strangely, it was only after this incident, and not during it, that I felt anxious and nervous. Anyone who says that they were never scared during their time in Vietnam is simply not telling the truth.

Other events that gravely affected my mental health during my time in this Godforsaken country, include a friendly fire incident on 12 January, a cordon and search of the Ap Bac hamlet of Hoa Long on 19 April, and my role in the interment of 2 dead enemy soldiers on 29 May. I wasn't overly excited about the positioning of a 12-man night-time ambush that my platoon conducted on 15 April either. I'll elaborate later on each of these happenings and others — both operationally, and when in Vung Tau.

During its reconnaissance-in-force patrols, B Company located several large enemy bunker systems. Accordingly, on the morning of 26 December, the Assault Pioneer Platoon was deployed from Peggy by Iroquois helicopters to the near vicinity of those bunker systems. We then slowly trekked into their location and destroyed them using dynamite and C4 plastic explosives. We returned to Peggy on foot the next morning after a night-time ambush of a likely enemy transit path near the former bunker systems. We only had 1 day back at Peggy before deploying again on 28 December.

After conducting night-time ambushes on 28 and 29 December, the Assault Pioneer Platoon — after re-supplying at Peggy — deployed the very next day towards the locale of another massive bunker system discovered by

Chapter 23 — Operational Tasking

B Company. Destruction of this bunker system was the main reason for the platoon's deployment from Peggy some days earlier, but it was interrupted for some obscure reason. Our extremely slow rate of movement was directly attributable to the difficult terrain, and the huge weight of rations, water, ammunition, and explosives that we were carrying. See Appendix 5.

This bunker system complex, which we were tasked with destroying, was extensive and located in a very inaccessible area of dense jungle and heavy ground vegetation. Insertion by helicopter simply wasn't possible, which is why we moved to the target locale on foot. It was an exhausting trek through very difficult wet, dense, and almost impenetrable jungle terrain. I can clearly remember the arduous time we had carrying all of the explosives to this bunker system, and knew the difficulty and danger we'd face in placing the complicated explosive materials, which when later detonated, would ultimately destroy this huge enemy resource.

As we ever so slowly moved to the location of this bunker system, always maintaining our operational security, most members of my platoon were carrying 5 or more sandbags crammed full of TNT, plus slabs of C4 plastic explosive. Liberal quantities of primers, detonators, detonation cord, and fuses were carried by others, well away from the explosives. And all of this was in addition to our usual carry load of weapons, ammunition, water, and rations. Because we were going to be away from Peggy for quite a few days, the weight load that each of us carried on this mission was simply astonishing. As I've already mentioned, our rate of forward progress was measured and very slow indeed.

During my time with the Assault Pioneer Platoon, I'd managed to acquire the nickname of 'Stumbles'. This very light-hearted — and well accepted by me — nickname reflected the belief that if anyone in our platoon was going to have an accident, or trip and fall over, it was probably going to be me. Being the tallest man in my platoon meant that I sometimes struggled to negotiate many of the environmental obstacles that shorter men found relatively easy. For example, dense, thorny, bamboo thickets alongside creek lines were nothing short of a nightmare for me.

We were still slowly trekking through very dense jungle terrain, as we neared the map grid reference location of the bunker systems that we were tasked with destroying. Then we came to a creek line which was about 8m wide, with extremely deep, wet, slippery, and almost vertical earthen sidewalls, covered with an array of creepers and thick vine tendrils. After a quiet and careful reconnoitre some 150m left and right of the creek line, we established that there wasn't a footbridge or any other way of easily crossing over it. We had no option other than to descend into the chasm as best we could, traverse this watercourse of indeterminable depth, and then climb up the other side...

all while carrying an incredible weight load. The distance from the top of the bank to the water below was about 6m. The main problem for all of us, was that we only had one free hand to assist us in our short climb down, and then up the other side. The other hand was gripping our personal weapon. I really don't know how Des McGrath and Allan Small, my section's machine gun group, managed their crossing of this creek line without any real apparent problem.

Fred Vincent, Steve Kaliczinsky, and Peter Wood, completed this extremely difficult transition across the creek, quickly followed by Ron Goubareff and the gun group. Then it was my turn. As I started my descent, I looked across to the ground level edge of the far bank and saw Ron Goubareff standing there, looking back and grinning at me. I quietly snarled at him:

'What are you looking at, you prick?'

His whispered response was:

'Waiting to watch you fall into the creek!'

About halfway down my descent of the near side creek wall, with my feet sort of wedged into some tenuous foothold, I released the thick vine tendril that I'd been holding on to, then reached down and grasped another lower one to support my weight. As I let my weight draw on this lower vine, I immediately felt it detach from the sodden earthen sidewall. Well, that was it...there was no way I could recover. I plummeted downwards, completely submerging under the turbid, chest-deep water, before emerging, quite unhurt, but completely covered in slime, mud, and other assorted crud. My mud-encrusted and drenched SLR rifle and M79 grenade launcher looked like they would never work again.

The climb to the top of the far side of the bank was generally uneventful, except for — still grinning — Ron Goubareff's whispered comment that went something like:

'That was fantastic Stumbles! Can you do that for me again on our way back?'

My rather similarly vulgar but much terser response to Goubareff was exactly what he would have expected. Goubareff really was a great guy, and we were quite friendly...but he really managed to totally piss me off on this occasion.

Eventually we all managed to get across this difficult creek line and after reaching the location of the bunker system, defensively deployed and then put in place a variety of explosive charges. This particular operational tasking took us a couple of days to complete and we spent the nights of 30 and 31 December hunkered-down in ambushes. The huge bunker system was

Chapter 23 — Operational Tasking

eventually detonated and destroyed by us on 1 January 1970.

Instead of returning to Peggy, we were then deployed from that location on day-time reconnaissance-in-force activities, demolition of more discovered bunker systems, and night-time ambushing until 7 January. During these ambushes, the Assault Pioneer Platoon often had the supporting firepower of a section of APCs.

On 2 January, our platoon destroyed 15 very large and connected bunkers in one system, and then immediately re-deployed to another location and demolished further discovered bunker systems. One system we destroyed that day comprised of over 58 bunkers. On the subsequent ambush later that night, the platoon welcomed the company of a troop of 3 Centurion tanks in close support. That was very comforting, I can tell you.

Over the next 2 days our platoon destroyed many more bunker systems and ambushed on both nights with the close support of a section of APCs. A very badly wounded Viet Cong soldier was captured by the platoon on 4 January, and later handed over to BHQ for medical assistance and interrogation. On 5 January, the platoon destroyed further discovered bunker systems and ambushed that night, again with a section of APCs in close support.

On 6 January, the platoon was re-deployed in support of D Company elements and later conducted what had become an almost routine night-time ambush. Late on the morning of 7 January, a very weary — and I mean utterly exhausted — Assault Pioneer Platoon returned to Peggy. Physically spent as we all were, we began to relax somewhat, knowing that we were relativity safe within Peggy's secure perimeter. But...this feeling of security didn't last long at all.

At 7:10pm the following night — 8 January — a small composite ambush party comprising of elements from Mortar Platoon and Tracker Section of Anti-Tank and Tracker Platoon — which had deployed some time earlier that afternoon from Peggy — was engaged by a sizeable aggressive enemy force. This night-time engagement confrontation continued for about 9 hours. As soon as it became apparent that this enemy contact had developed into a large-scale fire-fight against a determined, hostile, well-armed enemy force — estimated at something well over 40 strong — BHQ deployed the entire Assault Pioneer Platoon from Peggy, along with a section of APCs to reinforce the ambush party under enemy attack.

Deploying, or any sort of movement at night, was highly unusual — and a very rare occurrence during my time in Vietnam — because doing so significantly compromised the security and safety of those affected men. However, I'm certain that none of us gave that likelihood any thought that night. While we were still exhausted from our previous weeks of almost non-stop physical exertions, we were now running on adrenalin and keen to meet up with our Support Company mates under heavy enemy fire, and help them out of a potentially ugly situation.

It was a pitch-black new moon night. The APC drivers found it very difficult to navigate and traverse the often steep, slippery, and wet terrain, whilst transporting my platoon to the ambush party which — by all reports from the commander of the APC that I was encased in — was continuing to receive very heavy fire from the enemy. My best guess is that our reinforcement party departed Peggy sometime around 9:15pm. There was certainly a lengthy delay while the reinforcement strength requirement, and the optimum route to the ambush site, was determined by BHQ.

At one point, as we slowly moved towards the designated ambush site, the APC that I was encased in, careered down a precipitous embankment and came to a thunderous halt at the bottom of some sort of crater. It nearly knocked those of us inside the cabin almost senseless. I was so badly confused and shaken up from this abrupt collision that it took quite some time to pull myself together. Des McGrath badly injured his knee that night, and has since told me that it still gives him grief to this day. Some of us were likely suffering concussion from this accident as well...I guess we'll never really know.

After what seemed to take ages — but wasn't really — we established ground contact with the Mortar and Anti-Tank and Tracker Platoons ambush party at around 9:45pm. The incoming small arms and occasional RPG fire from the enemy at that time was simply unrelenting. I can still remember the sound of enemy rounds pinging off the APC's armour plating like heavy weather hail, as we joined up with the ambush party inside its defensive perimeter.

Because of the incredible amount of sustained enemy fire that was now being directed at the newly-arrived APCs, the overall commander of the 3 tracks wasn't prepared to lower the rear doors to allow us to egress in support of our mates. So, as soon as the small rear hatches were — reluctantly — opened instead, we scrambled out and quickly deployed in support of the ambush party.

That was a frightening moment for us, I can tell you — we were completely exposed for a short time. It wasn't an experience that I'm keen to repeat. In more recent times, I've discussed what transpired on that night in great depth with both John Dolgan and Robin Jagger, 2 of my platoon mates. Their recall of this horrible moment is identical to mine.

Quite some time after the arrival of my platoon and the section of APCs, as well as the provision of supporting aerial fire by USAF Shadow aircraft augmenting the Mortar and Anti-Tank and Tracker Platoons ambush party position, the enemy gradually withdrew from this engagement. But I have to say that it did take some time. With the advent of significant reinforcements, the enemy were now seriously outnumbered in terms of comparative firepower, so they had no reason to hang around. Nevertheless, they strongly persisted in a nasty fire-fight that lasted over 9 hours…and continued well into the early morning hours of 9 January.

At one point during this engagement, I fired a high-explosive round from my M79 grenade launcher at what seemed to be the torchlight of an enemy soldier who was far too close for comfort. That was a bad error of judgement on my part. The round detonated against the trunk of a tree about 20m in front of me, and we could hear some of the resultant shrapnel blow back over our ground position. Fortunately, no friendly soldier was hit. The lesson I learned from this incident was that the M79 grenade launcher is completely ineffective in heavily-treed areas and especially at night when there's no clear visibility.

This was almost a pitch-black night in a heavily wild, rubber forested area. During this engagement, muted torchlights, depicting movement of the enemy very close to our defensive perimeter, were visible for hours after the battle had seemingly concluded. At dawn the next morning, a sweep of the area found no bodies. However, there were many blood trails and numerous bloody congealed drag marks of presumably recovered dead or wounded enemy bodies. I've already alluded to the almost demoralising effect these 'abated' battlefield enemy casualties outcomes had on the morale of the platoon and, indeed, the battalion.

The recorded history of 161 Field Battery RNZA tells of this engagement, and refers to it as the 'Battle of the Ap Cu Bi Rubber'. A forward artillery observer of 161 Field Battery — though I only vaguely remember him — was in the same APC that transported my section to the battle site that evening. He ended up severely bruised and badly shaken-up like the rest of us in that track, when according to him: '*it vertically dropped some 10m into a creek bed during its stealthy 'no lights' approach to the 8 RAR ambush party under heavy fire from the enemy.*'[41]

This was a very significant engagement with the enemy for several reasons. Firstly, it persisted for some 9 hours or more, which was highly unusual. I can only surmise that the enemy took significant casualties that night and were determined to retrieve the bodies of their dead and wounded comrades from the battlefield. Other than that, there was no real advantage for them to stay engaged in contact with us for as long as they did. Once the infantry reinforcements — and a section of APCs — arrived at the battleground, they surely must have known that it was 'game over' for them.

Secondly, given the very poor visibility that night, the amount of friendly ammunition expended in this fire fight was extraordinarily high. Around 1,000

---

[41] Newman, LT S. D. *Vietnam Gunners – 161 Battery RNZA, South Vietnam, 1965-71*. 1988. Moana Press. Page 100.

50cal and 30cal rounds were fired by APCs. Some 1,500 rounds were fired by M60 machine guns, and over 1,500 rounds by SLR and M16 Armalite rifles. And, not forgetting the one M79 grenade launcher 40mm high-explosive round fired by me. USAF air support in the form of a Shadow gunship fired over 48,000 rounds in direct support from its four 7.62mm mini guns during this lengthy engagement with the enemy.

The Assault Pioneer Platoon returned to Peggy sometime just after dawn on the morning of 9 January. On 10 January, around 4am, a small composite ambush party comprising of a section of men from each of the Assault Pioneer and Mortar Platoons — around 15 men in total — engaged 3 enemy soldiers with M18 Claymore anti-personnel directional mines, M60 machine gun, and rifle fire. A sweep of the area at first light failed to reveal signs of enemy casualties.

As I've previously mentioned, the Viet Cong were almost fanatical in retrieving the bodies of their dead and extracting their wounded comrades from the battlefield. In many 8 RAR night-time ambush contacts with the enemy, it was extremely frustrating the next morning to discover that there were no bodies found to conclusively reflect the success of those ambushes. Nevertheless, blood trails and drag marks always indicated that considerable collateral damage had been inflicted on them.

At the end of the day — I know this may seem insensitive to some — one of the primary operational performance measures for the battalion was the confirmed number of enemy soldiers killed. That was always the officially recorded body count. After the Battle of Long Tan in 1966, the body count of dead enemy was confirmed at 245. However, some less constrained counting has put that number as high as 800.

Throughout the morning of 10 January, the entire battalion gradually returned to Nui Dat for a rotation of all elements through a 40-hour R&C break at 1 ALSG at Vung Tau, for local TAOR patrols adjacent to Nui Dat, and rotational ready reaction standby preparedness within Nui Dat itself. As 8 RAR vacated Peggy, it was taken over by 6 RAR and used by that battalion until 27 February, at which time it was dismantled and closed.

UNDER FRIENDLY FIRE
12 January 1970

Any Australian infantry soldier who served in Vietnam will tell you that one or more operational incidents or experiences from those now very distant times is indelibly etched into the deep recesses of his subconscious mind. While he may or may not dwell on those reflections obsessively, they will, in most cases, have had a significant and very adverse impact on his subliminal psyche and

Chapter 23 — Operational Tasking

ultimately on his underlying mental health. These devastating manifestations, far more often than not, will have emerged many years later in a variety of ugly forms. The specific incident that I'm about to describe was the defining moment of my time in Vietnam as an infantry soldier, and this is why I'm devoting so many words to it.

It was late morning on 10 January 1970 when the Assault Pioneer Platoon returned to Nui Dat after a frenetic and utterly exhausting 32 days of operational tasking — Operation Atherton — for a few days of rest. Fat chance of that… because 2 nights later, on 12 January, I became a member of the 14-man night-time ambush party at a location about 5km from Nui Dat.

I've been able to confidently confirm the exact date of this ambush by reference to detail contained in a personal letter written by one of my platoon mates, Robin Jagger, to his then girlfriend — now wife. He was a key member of this ambush party — see later — and quite incredibly, his wife has kept this letter, along with many others for all these decades. Simply amazing. Anyway, going back a bit.

Once we settled back into our lines at Nui Dat and after stripping, cleaning, oiling, reassembling our personal weapons and restocking our rifle oiled magazines with new ammunition, showering, and donning our first clean greens in many weeks, we got well and truly stuck into a monumental late afternoon and evening drinking session, accompanied by an associated BBQ and prawn fest — the belated 8 RAR Christmas Party — at the Support Company mess and boozer. Similar hedonistic activities would also have been underway at other battalion company venues.

We were all in very high spirits; happy to be back at Nui Dat in relative safety, with the knowledge that our platoon suffered no battlefield casualties during Operation Atherton. Even as physically exhausted as we all were, we certainly gave the alcohol a hell of a lot more than a soft nudge. In fact, we were literally pouring the ice-cold amber fluid straight down our seemingly unquenchable, parched throats. And we also knew that the platoon was scheduled to stand down within a few days and deploy to Vung Tau for a scheduled 40-hour R&C break. I'll talk much more about these rare and almost fleeting withdrawals from operations later in the story.

Around 2:30pm on the next afternoon — 11 January — as I was laying naked on my sagging army issue bed in my shared tent, mosquito net enveloping me, drenched in sweat, suffering from an indescribably awful hangover and almost comatose from the prevailing heat and humidity, I was rudely roused by my section commander — Corporal Fred Vincent — who informed me that I was to be a member of the singular 14-man night-time ambush party that was going to be out in the field late afternoon the next day — 12 January.

The men selected for this ambush party comprised all 9 members of No.1

Section — my section of the platoon. The other 5 members came variously from No.2 and No.3 Sections. Two of those other members were machine gunners. One was a lance-corporal and the other 2 were riflemen, one of whom was tasked with the vital role of 'signaller' for that night. Those platoon role types will make sense as this part of the story unfolds.

At the time, I had no idea whatsoever as to why we were being sent out from Nui Dat on this ambush, the timing of which didn't seem to fit in with any of my logical thinking. Neither the platoon commander, nor the platoon sergeant were going to be members of this ambush party...and that was highly unusual. There should have been at least one of them with us that night. And where was the designated platoon signaller, Paul Jansen? WTF!!!

I was a 'grunt' with a lot of civilian and some really cunning army smarts, but unfortunately I'd somehow managed to find myself well and truly ensconced in an infantry platoon whose operational taskings were sometimes heavily focused on earthmoving, the explosive demolition of enemy operational infrastructure (dug-in bunker systems), and the de-activation of anti-personnel mines and booby traps whenever Engineers weren't available for the task. It was a military career path aspired to by very few in the battalion, and certainly not by many others in the Australian Army I'd suggest. It was also not one that I was overly excited about.

However, all that aside, what I did know with absolute certainty were 2 indisputable facts. Firstly, the platoon was about to proceed on a 40-hour R&C break in Vung Tau in several days' time. Secondly, the entire battalion was going to be out in the field again — Operation Keperra — on 23 January.

So the timing of this night-time ambush didn't sit well with me at all. The fact that it was so close after our return to Nui Dat was a real conundrum. Frankly, after the almost nonstop physical ordeals endured by the platoon during Operation Atherton, all of us were pretty much physically spent and very mentally tired. We all needed more than a few days of respite from operational tasking. Did I ever share these concerns with anyone else? Probably not — I really can't remember — other than perhaps in general chat amongst my section mates the next morning, as we assiduously prepared our weapons and equipment for the upcoming ambush.

As very well trained and highly conditioned infantry soldiers, we never seriously questioned our operational tasking. We always did whatever we were ordered to do, without any complaint. At the same time there were several men, like myself, who always wanted to know exactly what we were going to be doing whenever we were out in the field and, importantly, how that was going to contribute to the benefit of the battalion and perhaps even to the wider 1 ATF. While there were several 'mushrooms' in my platoon, I wasn't one of them.

Chapter 23 — Operational Tasking

In far more recent times, I've learned that the commander of our half-platoon ambush party that night, Corporal Fred Vincent — commander of No.1 Section — had been given a disciplinary penalty for some sort of trouble he got into in the Support Company mess or boozer on the evening of 10 January. Commanding this ambush was the price that he, and the rest of us accompanying him that night, had to pay for his personal misdemeanour, whatever that may have been. Vincent has never told me what his petty crime was.

I have to say that just because a very experienced section commander — my section commander — may have 'fucked up', sending him and 13 other men out on a one-off, last-minute ambush in a highly dangerous and unpredictable war zone as a penalty, seems to be a very poor example of military discipline to me...and a command decision that wasn't all that well thought through at the time. Had this ambush ended up more badly for us than it eventually did, I have no doubt that there may well have been some very ugly ramifications for Support Company Headquarters (SCHQ) and BHQ.

As strange as it seemed to me that night — and it certainly was — we were tasked with ambushing a foot crossing of a minor creek tributary of the relatively significant Song (River) Dinh. TFHQ Intelligence had ascertained it was frequently being used by the enemy on their route east from the Nui Dinh Mountains, west of Route 2, into the relatively large town of Hoa Long — whose residents were long known to be sympathetic to the enemy — and return for logistical re-supply or for a range of other nefarious activities.

The ambush on this night was situated about 4.5km west-north-west of Hoa Long, in the vicinity of the 'Three-Sisters' feature abutting the near approaches to the Nui Dinh Mountains, and about 5km west-south-west of Nui Dat. Hoa Long was approximately 4km south of Nui Dat. The prevailing landscape was flat, lightly vegetated, interspersed with tracts of patchy, seasonally dry, non-commercial rice paddy fields, and sparsely afforested in parts with an amazing proliferation of small, low-height spindly trees and ground shrubbery of dubious genus. On a positive note though, in terms of any later artillery support from Nui Dat, we were going to be in an almost perfect ground position if heavy gunfire support were ever needed to be called in. From my cynical view, this was about the only positive feature of the ambush with which I could identify. I wasn't a happy man at all!

At around 4pm in the afternoon, an army truck dropped the 14 of us off on the western verge of Route 2, about 3km due east of the chosen ambush site. We stealthily trekked to that designated locale (map grid reference) using the vast amount of low to medium height vegetation and abundant spindly trees as cover to hopefully conceal our presence and direction of movement.

Because it was only a singular ambush, we weren't carrying backpacks or overly large amounts of water, only about 2L per man on average. However, given my obsession regarding personal hydration — which I described earlier — I carried 6L of water with me that night. Leopards never lose their spots, do they? Well, in my military world, back then they certainly didn't, particularly when it concerned my personal wellbeing!

Due to our complement of 3 — this was highly unusual — M60 machine guns, we were collectively carrying a considerable amount of very heavy ammunition for those weapons. Each 100-round belt of M60 machine gun 7.62mm ammunition weighed 2.95kg and we were probably carrying as many as 36 of those belts, as well as something like 24 M18 Claymore anti-personnel mines, each weighing 1.6kg. And, other than the three M60 machine gunners, we were also carrying our personal rifles — SLR or M16 Armalite — plus at least one M79 40mm grenade launcher (not me that night — so almost certainly Mick O'Shea) and plenty of ammunition for all of those weapons. In total, it was a very serious shit-load of collective lethal dead weight that we lugged across the tundra on this late afternoon of 12 January.

The going was so easy — it was the height of the dry season after all — that we were able to traverse the generally flat and predominantly stable terrain quite quickly compared to our otherwise slow, methodical, and deliberate operational speed of forward movement when negotiating more difficult, less hospitable, and more seasonally adversely affected terrains. At the same time, were we to have been noticed by any meandering local resident — not that I think we were — he or she would have concluded that we weren't in their general vicinity for a constitutional stroll or an evening BBQ with a few quiet beers.

The focus of our ambush that night was the east-west foot crossing of a north-south running creek line, about 8m wide at ground level with steep banks dropping down some 5m to a relatively slow-flowing watercourse of indeterminate depth. As I could vaguely see a few gravelly patches along the bottom side verges of the creek line, it didn't appear to be any more than maybe 1.5m deep. Then again, I was no hydrologist. I quietly thought to myself that during the long, arduous, and testing wet season that soon lay ahead of us, this seemingly benign watercourse may well become a raging, bank-bursting torrent. As it was, an old — and I mean very old — solid, weathered, roughly hewn, well-trodden, but relatively stable 0.4m wide log footbridge of sorts, traversed the creek line. The eastern bank of the creek line was higher — 1m — or maybe a little more than that of the western bank.

We quickly prepared and devoured a very light evening rudimentary snack and brew — we had a decent lunch at the Support Company mess back at Nui Dat some 4 hours earlier — and then focused our minds on the setting up of this ambush.

The ambush we put in place that night was based on the premise that it would

Chapter 23 – Operational Tasking

be preferable to initiate contact with any enemy — in other words, springing the ambush — on the higher eastern bank of the creek line. This reasoning was based on the likelihood that any enemy returning to their bunkers or secreted hides in the Nui Dinh Mountains, west of our ambush location, in the early hours of the next morning back along the same track — which they'd safely used when they previously entered Hoa Long sometime earlier — would be far less alert and unsuspecting of any later ambush along that route. Our overriding and quite reasonable, but not necessarily correct assumption, was that our potential target enemy that night was already ensconced in Hoa Long.

A command group of 2 men comprising of the ambush commander and the signaller, was put in place on the western bank of the creek line. They were positioned about 5m north of the footbridge, facing west, and looking towards the relatively nearby Nui Dinh Mountains. A rear protection group of 4 men — including an M60 machine gun — was also positioned on the western bank of the creek line, north of, but closely adjacent to the command group. South of the footbridge, on the elevated eastern bank of the creek line, facing east-northeast and looking towards Nui Dat, obliquely right to the slightly nearer town of Hoa Long, 2 adjacent killing groups each comprised of 4 men were positioned. Both killing groups included an M60 machine gun. Serially connected banks of M18 Claymore anti-personnel directional mines were set up about 12m out in front of the command and rear protection group, and both killing groups. I thought it was a well-constructed ambush.

Corporal Fred Vincent was in overall command of the ambush party, as well as in direct command of the signaller and the rear protection group of 4 men on the western side of the creek line. Robin Jagger was the signaller. Lance-corporals Ron Goubareff and Jeff (JJ) Smith were in command of the two 4-man killing groups on the higher eastern side of the creek line.

The closest man in the rear protection group to the command group was Allan Small, who was serving his M60 machine gun. I was also a member of the rear protection group along with Des McGrath and Peter Wood. I was positioned at the most northern limit of this 4-man group with Peter Wood laying on the ground directly to my left side, and Des McGrath, the No.2 on the M60 machine gun, to his left. Corporal Fred Vincent was the closest man to the creek crossing with the signaller, Robin Jagger, lying between him and Allan Small. I was about 12m north of the footbridge.

Based on TFHQ intelligence reports, BHQ had concluded there was some possibility that enemy elements might attempt to enter Hoa Long during that early evening from the Nui Dinh Mountains, west of our ground position and across the well-used creek crossing that we were ambushing that night. This is undoubtedly why our rear protection group had an M60 machine gun as an integral part of its armament capability. I don't recall the actual positioning of the men laying on the ground on the eastern bank of the creek line, but it would have been very similar to those of us laying on the western bank — probably slightly more spread out, given that there were 8 of them, including two M60 machine guns.

Turning around, raising my head, and looking back east from my prone position on the ground, I could occasionally glimpse— through the low-hanging ratty tree foliage — the very faint flickering glimmer of dim distant lights emanating from Nui Dat some 5km away. The south-western reaches of Nui Dat were on a flat, cleared landscape — where the Task Force's artillery resources were well dug-in — and which gently rose north-west to a heavily afforested, but relatively low height plateau. This is where other 1 ATF elements, including 8 RAR, were based. So, this spasmodic visual spotting of dull, flickering lights emanating from Nui Dat, wasn't at all surprising to me.

It was so eerily quiet and still. There wasn't even a semblance of any wafting, semi-cooling breeze. Frankly, it was suffocatingly hot, humid, and disgustingly oppressive. Thankfully, there was no rain. We were yet to appreciate the horrendous ordeals that afternoon and early morning precipitation deluges would later impose on our lives out in the field.

As was always the case with any night-time or day-time ambush, once it was put in place, all of us were ever vigilant, laying prone on the ground, waiting for any enemy to enter the primary killing ground on the track east of the creek line, or perhaps even the secondary killing ground on the track west of the creek line.

Expectations were that if either of these 2 events occurred, it was, more likely than not, to be the primary killing ground sometime between the hours of 2am and 4:30am the next morning, or much less likely, the secondary killing ground sometime between the hours of 8pm and 11pm that evening.

It was one night short of a new moon, which made our night vision less than optimal. Fortunately, as there was no cloud cover whatsoever, our view of the surrounds, particularly the near approaches to the crossing of the creek line from either side, was more than reasonable. That said, it still wasn't an ideal scenario for a night-time ambush. Nevertheless, in my view, if any enemy were to have attempted to cross the creek line across the narrow footbridge from either the west or the east that night, they, and quite possibly ourselves, were very likely going to be involved in a shit-load of trouble.

As time passed ever so slowly — 'tic-toc, tic-toc' — no one near me was able to catch even a few minutes of rostered half-sleep. It seemed to me that each of the 6 men laying on the ground on the western bank of the creek line, were all very alert and just waiting for something to happen, or they were otherwise restless, unsettled, and almost gasping for breath in the suffocating and stiflingly climatic ambience that was engulfing and slowly consuming all

Chapter 23 — Operational Tasking

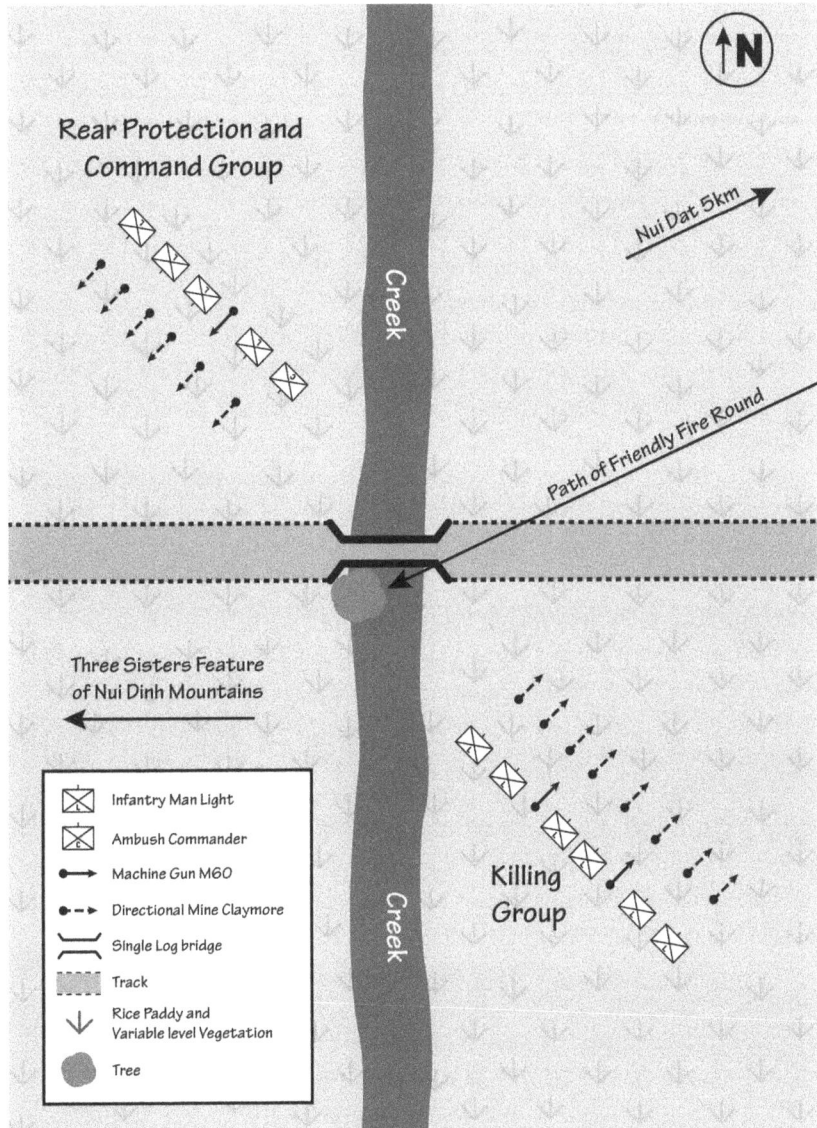

Graphical representation of 'Friendly Fire Incident' on 12 January 1970.

of us. I imagine there would have been an identical climatic cloak enveloping the 8 men lying in wait on the eastern bank as well.

At 11:30pm or thereabouts, those of us in the rear protection group relaxed somewhat, as it now seemed clear that the 8 men comprising of the 2 killing groups lying on the eastern bank of the creek line, were now much more likely to encounter any enemy in the approaching early morning hours of the next day, than we were.

Then…it all began to go horribly wrong! Just before midnight, we heard 3 guns from one of the three 6-gun 105mm artillery batteries at Nui Dat some 5km away, suddenly fire. About 10 seconds later, this salvo of gunfire passed directly overhead with the rounds landing and detonating about 1km west-south-west of our ground position. The three 15kg high-explosive rounds sounded like rushing express trains as they passed overhead.

Now, this was highly unusual because artillery fire wasn't normally directed over a friendly ground position, unless it was called in by them, as supporting fire in an enemy contact situation. I can still remember hearing someone in the rear protection group quietly whisper '*What the fuck was that?*' Knowing who was with me in the rear protection group that night, I'm certain this dry, laconic, and somewhat quizzical but guarded comment came from none other than my very good friend and M60 machine gunner, Allan Small.

Again, a brief time later — maybe 7 or 8 minutes — we heard three 105mm artillery guns fire from Nui Dat, as they despatched a second salvo. These three 15kg high-explosive rounds again passed directly over our ground position, landed, and detonated about 100m out in front of the 6 men comprising of the command and rear protection groups laying on the western bank of the creek line. These high-explosive rounds had a potential killing radius on flat, low vegetated ground — which precisely describes our ground position that night — of between 35-70m. That was getting far too close for comfort!

I sensed that all of us in the ambush party who were lying on the western bank of the creek line were very unsettled by the consistent direction of this artillery gunfire — directly over our ground position — and the extreme closeness of the fall of shot from these second salvo rounds. I imagine that each of the men laying prone on the eastern bank would have been just as concerned.

We weren't in contact with the enemy, and I knew that the ambush commander, Corporal Fred Vincent, hadn't called for any harassment or interdiction artillery fire. It was so horribly still, quiet, hot, and humid that night, I would have clearly heard a whisper over a 15m distance. As it was, Vincent and the signaller, Robin Jagger, were laying on the ground no more than about 7m to my left side. Collectively, the 6 of us laying on the west bank of the creek line weren't all that far apart. More importantly, I hadn't heard the unmistakable sounds of any other friendly contact with the enemy in our near vicinity. I didn't know the reason for this artillery gunfire emanating from Nui Dat.

After those 2 salvos of gunfire, I can tell you that I was really worried. Those of us in the rear protection group were very quietly whispering amongst ourselves about what might be going on back at Nui Dat. I can't imagine that we would have been all that complimentary. Anyway, we didn't have too long to worry about that, as a very short time later, three 105mm artillery guns back at Nui Dat again despatched their high-explosive payloads in a third salvo of gunfire.

When I anxiously peered forward, looking west, to see where and how close to us the rounds from this third salvo were going to land and detonate, I heard the first two 15kg high-explosive rounds pass directly over our ground position. I had no idea where or how close they landed and detonated, because there was a thunderous explosion, ear deafening noise, indescribable brilliant orange and white light, and a physical awareness of intense heat, accompanied by waves of body-numbing, concussing air pressures. I was forcibly and violently thrown back further west from where I was lying for several metres at least, as were the other 3 members of the rear protection group and the 2 men in the adjacent command group.

As it turned out, the third round from this third salvo of gunfire had landed directly amongst us, slamming into a huge tree — a base trunk diameter of around 0.75m — rising out of the western side bank of the creek line and pretty much in the exact centre of our ambush party ground alignment! This tree, which had largely taken the bulk of the impact of this 105mm high-explosive artillery round, was about 1m south of the footbridge that traversed the creek line.

For some reason or other, I must have half-turned around looking back east towards Nui Dat, as this third round hit the tree and detonated. I say that because momentarily, I was blinded by incandescent white brightness, intermingled with orange brilliance arising from this catastrophic explosion. This errant 105mm high-explosive round had slammed into the tree at a velocity of 450m/s — at a height just above the ground level of the western bank, and slightly below the height of the ground level of the eastern bank — equidistant between the groups of 14 men lying prone on the ground on each bank of the creek line.

The noise, brightness, concussing forces, and radiant heat from this explosive detonation are memories that are indelibly etched into my cerebrum. I'll never ever forget what happened that night. I simply can't. To me, these decades later, it's still very much 'as clear as crystal' in my mind. There's nothing ephemeral or vague about my recall of this event, I can assure you.

In discussing this incident in more recent times with Fred Vincent — the ambush commander that night — it seems that our party was extremely lucky not to have suffered significant casualties when this round landed right amongst us.

As the round struck the tree and detonated — about 12m to the left of my ground position — most of the resultant shrapnel dispersion either blew down into the sloping side wall of the western bank of the creek line, into the water, or back into the sloping side wall of the slightly higher eastern bank of the creek line. Any residual shrapnel that did blow forward over the western bank was largely contained by the tree itself, the footbridge, and probably by the very large number of medium-height spindly trees along that side of the creek line. The fact that those of us positioned on the western or lower bank of the creek line were lying down — mostly — in the prone position when the round landed amongst us, undoubtedly contributed to the amazing fact that there were no casualties. Without any doubt whatsoever, we were all very lucky men indeed.

Vincent's recall of this incident, as conveyed to me on 13 March 2007 in a personal email statement, is as follows:

> *'...When the round landed amongst us, the signaller and I were laying on our backs and the next thing we were flying in the air, and I could see the rest of the members* (the 4 men comprising the rear protection group) *doing the same.'*
>
> *The reason I believe no one got seriously injured or killed* (that night) *was that when the round came down it clipped the side of the large tree, about two feet* (600mm) *above the ground, and detonated and the blast and shrapnel continued down into the ground. It also helped that both killer groups were above* (the level of) *the detonation. I believed at that time that if the round had not hit the tree, all the ambush group would have been killed or injured...'*

While Vincent's recall of detail is only marginally at odds with mine, the differences aren't significantly material to the telling of this part of my story. And frankly, after all these years, who really cares anyway?

Although very dazed and somewhat disorientated, I was still very much aware of what had actually happened. A second before the detonation of the errant 105mm high-explosive artillery round right on our ground position, I can remember someone in our ambush party on the eastern bank of the creek line loudly yelling out, *'Drop short'*. That's probably why I was in a half-turned position when the round landed amongst us.

I've thought long and hard about who made that comment of abject despair and have concluded that it could only have been Lance-corporal Ron Goubareff, a seasoned veteran from an earlier infantry deployment to Vietnam with 1 RAR (circa 1965-66). Lance-corporal Jeff (JJ) Smith has confirmed this with me in more recent times.

My first thoughts and physical sensations immediately following the explosion were that my upper back between my shoulder blades, but slightly lower, hurt very badly. Although we couldn't hear each other talk — because of the subsequent deadening to our hearing, caused by the explosive noise of the detonation and the accompanying waves of concussing air pressures — Des McGrath quickly checked me out for any shrapnel wounds and reassured me, by way of rudimentary sign language and loudly shouting revolting obscenities into my ear, that despite my protestations otherwise, I wasn't dead and probably not even wounded. My nagging back pain, which persisted intermittently for the rest of my time in Vietnam, was likely nothing more than a psychosomatic reaction to the frightening, horrific experience. However, this personal physical or mental ailment has never resolved. I have just learned to live with it. Not one of my treating doctors over subsequent decades has been able to diagnose this medical issue.

It's worth thinking about just what our veteran infantry ancestors of previous major conflicts — particularly those men involved in the Great War — must have undergone during extended periods of days, nights, weeks, and even months of constant and unrelenting enemy artillery bombardment. It would have been nothing short of horrendous. My one close call was bad enough, and it has certainly allowed me to sort of understand what it must have been like for those many brave men back then. However, at least those men were ensconced in very deeply-dug narrow trench networks, parallel to incoming enemy fire, not just lying prone on the open ground as we were that night.

After the second salvo of 105mm artillery gunfire right over our ground position, Vincent contacted BHQ back at Nui Dat on the field radio to voice his extreme concern as to the direction of gunfire and the increasing closeness of its fall of shot, relative to our ground position. As he was talking with BHQ, a round from the third salvo of gunfire landed and detonated, smack bang in the middle of our ambush party ground position. Then, in probably less than 30 seconds or so, several things happened.

Firstly, Vincent audibly and very loudly established that there were no casualties amongst us. At the time, I thought this was nothing short of amazing... and that remains my view today. Had that round landed and detonated 1.5m north, 1m west, 10m east, or about 0.5m higher than it did, some, or even all 14 men in the ambush party that night would have been killed or very badly wounded. At the very least, it would have been a nasty outcome for many of the men who participated in this ambush. Think about those metrics...pretty mind numbing I reckon! Clearly, the margins for error or just plain bad luck, were minuscule when you consider that the high-explosive round was fired from an artillery gun some 5km away. Nevertheless, without any doubt whatsoever, we were a very lucky bunch of guys indeed.

Secondly, Vincent immediately called in a 'check fire' to BHQ. We could all hear his voice because he was literally screaming into the signaller's radio handpiece. And it was then that events may have taken a nastier turn. According to Vincent, BHQ didn't initially believe that our ambush party was receiving friendly fire over its ground position — as it had no notification of any 1 ATF artillery fire mission that night in the general vicinity of our ambush party — and said that we were probably receiving enemy fire. WTF!!!

In his written statement to me on 13 March 2007, Vincent also says:

> '...*I finally got through to the BN CP* (Battalion Command Post) *and requested a check fire. The CP didn't believe we were receiving friendly fire as they had no notification that the arty* (artillery) *was firing and* (said that) *that we were* (probably) *receiving enemy fire...*'

Fortunately for us, the commander of an 8 RAR Anti-Tank and Tracker Platoon ambush party, Corporal Arthur (Archie) Mears — also deployed that night as a disciplinary penalty for a misdemeanour on 10 January, probably in concert with Vincent — situated about 3km north of our ground position, informed BHQ by field radio that a cross bearing compass reading taken by him, clearly indicated that it was in fact the guns of 161 Battery at Nui Dat who were firing over our ambush party ground position. Vincent and several other men in our party, including myself, had already visually ascertained this by observing the distant red flashes as the rounds left the barrels of the guns — at a muzzle velocity (presumably at maximum charge) of 450m/s — during the second salvo of gunfire. As I've already mentioned, the 105mm artillery guns of 161 Battery were located in the cleared south-west corner of Nui Dat and the gunfire flashes from its guns could be visually spotted at night from our ambush ground position, even from some 5km away.

Whenever an artillery fire mission was underway, and a 'check fire' was called by anyone other than a forward observer artillery party officer — formally attached to an infantry unit in the field — there was a very short time frame for the party calling in the 'check fire' to identify itself, prove its 'bona fides', and confirm its exact ground position to BHQ, with absolutely no ambiguity whatsoever. The reason for this rather rigid protocol was that our enemy in Vietnam had been known to sometimes use allied forces radio frequencies to call in a 'check fire' when allied forces artillery or mortar rounds were impacting their ground position. All of us in the ambush party that night were very much aware that if BHQ wasn't convinced that the 'check fire' called for by Vincent was from a friendly element, its standard operating procedure was — on orders from TFHQ — to initiate an even more intensive artillery bombardment of the map grid reference ground position associated with the calling of the 'check fire'.

To this day, I can clearly recall Vincent talking loudly, frantically, and animatedly to BHQ, providing them with exact map grid references for our ground position and line of sight bearings back at Nui Dat, even though he'd forgotten to bring his compass with him that night and was relying on his

Chapter 23 — Operational Tasking

excellent map reading skills. As he continued to desperately argue with BHQ over his call for a 'check fire', a fourth salvo of 105mm artillery gunfire was despatched from Nui Dat, yet again, directly over our ground position. This time the 3 high-explosive 15kg rounds landed and detonated well west-south-west of us.

After discussing this incident in depth in more recent times with MAJ John D Thornton Retd, who served in Vietnam as an artillery observer party officer with another infantry battalion — 4 RAR, circa 1968-69 — I now understand more clearly what may have occurred at Nui Dat that night.

The battery commander, or artillery duty officer in BHQ, would have heard Vincent's call for a 'check fire' on the infantry network and relayed that call onto the artillery network at TFHQ. They would have then contacted 161 Battery and temporarily imposed the 'check fire' whilst quickly examining which known troop placements or troop movements might be at risk. Thankfully, the 'check fire' that was temporarily put in place by TFHQ held, and the artillery fire from 161 Battery (as it did indeed turn out to be) ceased after that fourth round of gunfire.

There was no way that any of us were in a fit and proper mental state to continue with this night-time ambush and, if any enemy were to have passed our way sometime later during those early morning hours, I don't really know what would have happened. It may well have been an absolute disaster for us, because our minds were no longer focused on engaging with any enemy from that time onwards. To be perfectly honest, it's something I still don't really want to think about.

To his credit, Vincent recognised this and immediately aborted the offensive nature of the ambush, while leaving the banks of M18 Claymore anti-personnel directional mines in place as defensive systems only. The offensive nature of our ambush construct was largely dismantled by around 1:30am and we spent the remainder of that night in a closed down — sentry alert — mode, eagerly awaiting the onset of dawn, at which time prior arrangements had been made to transport us back to Nui Dat.

It was a very long 5 hours for us to endure, and not one of us could get more than a few minutes, if any, of rostered sleep. In fact, I'm pretty sure that each and every one of us were wide awake for the remainder of the night. I certainly was. And we weren't talking amongst ourselves either, not even in quiet whispers. Frankly, I don't reckon that any of us could believe, or even comprehend what had just occurred those few hours earlier. I can tell you this though, we all realised how unbelievingly lucky we were to have not suffered significant casualties.

Just after a very early and brief '*stand to*' at pre-dawn on the morning of 13 January, Robin Jagger — the signaller — fossicked around on the western bank of the creek line and, amid the morning gloom and ever-present rising ground mist, found a sizeable lump of residual shrapnel embedded in our 'saviour' tree, as well as a 1kg piece of jagged shrapnel laying close-by on the ground. Well, there you go! No more to say, I reckon.

Shortly after that, we deactivated and retrieved the banks of M18 Claymore anti-personnel directional mines that we'd deployed the previous evening and very quickly walked the 3km back to the western verge of Route 2. It was still dark and gloomy as we trekked away from this disaster site. Here we rendezvoused with our army truck transport, which safely returned us to Nui Dat. As we boarded the truck, we were a very quiet, solemn, and pretty relieved bunch of guys. We were safely back in our lines at Nui Dat at around 7:30am and eating breakfast in the Support Company mess not long after that.

One very remarkable thing that those of us who participated in the ambush that night remember very well, all these years later, is that there was no panic amongst us. Or, if there was, it was all personally internalised. Although everyone involved in the ambush party would have been frightened — I can tell you that I certainly was — not one man lost his composure or nerve. Everybody just seemed to hug the ground and get what had to be done, done.

Immediately following our return to Nui Dat, Vincent formally met with the commander of 161 Battery to discuss the serious incident that took place some 7 or so hours earlier. As far as I can now recall, it seems that those discussions from a formal point of view were inconclusive. The feedback from that meeting, which was later provided to us by Vincent, was very vague and almost muted. Basically, he told us that 161 Battery had been conducting a routine, random harassment and interdiction fire mission at the time of the incident, and they weren't aware that our half-platoon element was ambushing in the general area that night. Shit! How could that have happened? Seriously, someone back at BHQ had 'fucked up' in a big way!

In his personal email statement on 13 March 2007, Vincent basically confirmed this with me. He also clarified, in far more detail, the content of his conversation that morning with the commander of 161 Battery. As interesting and mind-numbing as that detail is to me, and it certainly is that, for a number of reasons I have chosen not to include most of it in my story.

Leaving aside the issue of the direction of that totally unexpected harassment and interdiction artillery fire, what occurred that night was probably nothing more than the result of a simple mistake made by a member of one of 161 Battery's 105mm artillery gun crews, in either the laying — aiming and elevation — of the offending gun, or in preparing — number of charge bags — its round propellant. Given the consistent direction of this friendly artillery gunfire over 4 salvos — 12 rounds in total — it seems pretty clear to me that one of the battery's gunners, when preparing the ammunition for the third salvo of gunfire, short loaded the round fired by that gun, by one or more charge bags. Of course, we'll never know. And the recorded history of 161 Battery RNZA doesn't even mention this incident. Frankly, I would have been astonished if it did!

Remembering that these night-time harassment and interdiction artillery fire missions were conducted in dimly-lit, near darkness at Nui Dat, it's amazing that this sort of thing didn't happen more often. Perhaps it did? Anyway, shit sometimes happens, as it surely did on the night of 12 January 1970.

There's no way that I can, or ever will denigrate the wonderful gunners of 161 Battery because of this one, very nasty incident. As I've already said, bad things happen in all military conflicts and this was just another one of those occasions. From my perspective, during the entire time that 8 RAR was in Vietnam, 161 Battery consistently provided marvelous and reliable artillery support to the battalion. I'm also aware that a few other 8 RAR veterans have a less favourable view of 161 Battery. Well, that's up to them.

Over these many years since, I've often thought back to how all of us who engaged in this disastrous ambush that night, dealt with its impacts the following day. Almost unbelievably, I have to say that my very clear recollections are that we unceremoniously 'shit-canned' 161 Battery for a time, largely forgot about it almost straight away, and drank a lot of beer back at Nui Dat the night after the incident. Only a few days later, we proceeded on a 40-hour R&C break at Vung Tau, and were back out of Nui Dat again in full operational mode not too long after this wonderful, hedonistic interlude. That might be very difficult for others to comprehend, but this is exactly how it was at that time.

Was there any debriefing or counselling offered to any of the men involved in this disastrous night-time ambush? No, there wasn't. Alcohol was the only professional help available to us at that time. And I can tell you that there was plenty of that medication stacked up for us in the Support Company boozer refrigerators. Were any of us complaining about the type, nature, and quantity of our medication? Of course not.

If I have any ongoing criticism in relation to what happened that night, it's this. As far as I can tell — and I've exhaustively researched this incident — 8 RAR unit records don't mention it, not even in passing. I simply can't understand how that can be the case. This friendly fire incident did occur. The facts are indisputable. The platoon mates whom I've spoken to regarding this event, decades later, have almost identical recall to mine, as to exactly what occurred that night.

Those platoon mates that I've been able to contact in relation to this incident are Fred Vincent — the ambush commander — Peter Cousins, John Dolgan, Robin Jagger, Des McGrath, Allan Small, Jeff (JJ) Smith, and Peter Wood. As I've already mentioned, Fred Vincent and I have exchanged correspondence and the only excerpt from his writings, pertaining to his meeting with the commander of 161 Battery, that I'm prepared to disclose, is this:

> *'... He then asked me what I wanted to do about this and if I wanted to name the round that fell short so action could be taken against the gunner. I made the decision not to take action as no one was hurt. I now know that this action was a mistake...'*

Steve Kaliczinsky and Mick O'Shea both passed away many years ago, and I've been unable to contact Ron Goubareff, Ray Salmon, or John Floyd, who were also members of the ambush party on that infamous night.

LTCOL Graham Walker Retd, the 8 RAR Adjutant at that time — and later commanding officer of A Company — remembers well the occurrence of this incident. My platoon commander, LTCOL Peter Phillips Retd, who took over the command of the platoon some months after the incident, also recalls its telling by the party members.

I suppose if our ambush party had suffered casualties that night, there would have to have been a full-scale investigation into what had occurred, and that would have resulted in a formal record of the incident. Anecdotally, a lack of formal record keeping in relation to friendly fire incidents, where there were no casualties, was a relatively common occurrence for those times. And, during conversations that I've had with him in more recent times, Capt. Robert A Hall Retd[42], A Company, 8 RAR, has confirmed this fact with me. Hall is a respected and highly regarded University of New South Wales (UNSW) academic, military researcher, historian, and noted author. He encouraged me to tell my rather long story.

Against this background, the impacts of that night-time ambush may have significantly affected the long-term mental health of some of those men who participated. Although I don't intend debating here the efficacy of DVA, I must at least make the point that in my view, poor operational record keeping of those times may have led to difficulties many years later for some Vietnam veterans who may have been unable to substantiate whether an incident or event, crucial to their benefit claim, actually did take place. Without hard documentary evidence, military researchers engaged by DVA have often concluded that an event cited by a veteran that's relevant to his claim, didn't happen. In those cases, the veteran's benefit claim has been invariably refused by DVA.

I'm not saying that platoon mates of mine who, along with myself, experienced extreme fright, perhaps even sheer terror, and who were extremely lucky not to have been killed or badly wounded during the very incident I

---

[42] Hall, Robert A. *Combat Battalion*. Allen and Unwin. Sydney. 2000.

describe, have had their DVA compensation claims, if any, impacted due to adverse findings by military researchers. I simply don't know if that's the case at all.

All I'm saying is that for a military researcher — engaged by DVA — to conclude that a stated event or incident didn't occur because details of it aren't contained in the operational records of a particular unit, is utterly wrong and unconscionable. There are always other more laborious and expensive ways to confirm, or otherwise, the happening of a stated event or incident. Since the early 1990's the rigour and probity of many investigations undertaken by these military researchers on behalf of DVA, has been strongly contested by several Vietnam veterans' groups.

It was very pleasing indeed to see that around late 2014, DVA significantly revamped its contractual relationship with a notable peak body overarching a number of these military researchers. It remains to be seen if there's an eventual change in the disallowance rate by DVA of veterans' disability claims made under the Veterans' Entitlement Act (VEA), or indeed, any considerable number of previously denied claims made under that legislation being subsequently granted.

OPERATION KEPERRA
23 January 1970 – 14 February 1970

Operation Keperra, which had 2 quite distinct and vastly separate phases, began on 23 January, only 11 days after the disastrous night-time ambush incident.

CORDON AND SEARCH OF CIVILIAN RESIDENTIAL CENTRES

The first, very short part of this operation was the cordon and search, in the south-east region of the province, of the comparatively densely populated village of Xuyen Moc, some 22km east of Nui Dat, and the much smaller nearby rural hamlet of Ap Nui Nhon, located on Route 23 near Dat Do. Xuyen Moc, with 2,000 residents, straddled Route 23 at its junction with Route 329. Ap Nui Nhon was home to about 120 families.

Intelligence suggested that enemy units active in this general area were D440 Engineer and D445 Mobile Battalions, along with the C41 Chau Duc Company, the C70 Xuyen Moc, and C610 Ba Ria District Units. It was also thought that these enemy units were readying themselves for more aggressive activities around the Hoa Long area to coincide with Vietnamese Lunar New Year (Tet), which in 1970 (Year of the Dog) was celebrated on 16 February. Tet is normally honoured over a broad 3-day period that occurs variously each year between mid-January and mid-February.

Because Tet was so incredibly important to the Vietnamese people as a religious and cultural festivity, it was also a time when the enemy often used to intensify its operations in most parts of the country. Each year, Tet was always a very dangerous time for allied forces soldiers in Vietnam. For example, the well organised NVA Tet Offensive in 1968 was horrific in terms of US Army, NVA, and civilian casualties. This significantly impacted ATF military operations around Bien Hoa at that time.

Late on the afternoon of 23 January, elements of the battalion were deployed by road — either in trucks or APCs — to lie up positions west of Ap Nui Nhon. The roles of the Assault Pioneer Platoon during the cordon and search of these 2 civilian residential areas were to move into each centre in the early hours of the morning, around 3am, and sweep for anti-personnel and land mines, establish — erect — and protect the interrogation compounds and associated latrines, search designated areas and be ready to deploy in support of other elements of the battalion or elsewhere on other tasks at short notice, and otherwise protect deployed BHQ elements. The cordons were extensive and totally secure. There was no escape avenue for any of the residents.

The subsequent searches and associated interrogations of targeted residents took place on 24 January. Collectively, 1,110 people were screened (873 at Xuyen Moc). Seven people at Xuyen Moc, and 3 people at Ap Nui Nhon — whose names were on the local police 'blacklist' — were detained for further interrogation by allied South Vietnamese Regional Forces soldiers. I have no idea what the outcomes of those interrogations were, other than to hear that one detainee at Ap Nui Nhon was later identified as a senior Viet Cong intelligence officer.

Late — around 5:30pm — on the afternoon of 24 January, about 4 or 5 of us somehow ended up inside the home of an elderly male resident of Xuyen Moc. It turned out that this seemingly friendly old man, and his 'very' extensive and over-friendly family, had an old clunky refrigerator mostly stacked with 330ml bottles of cold Vietnamese beer. We couldn't believe it! The fact that he had a working refrigerator was remarkable enough in itself. Although I didn't see it at the time, he must have had a diesel-powered generator somewhere near his home.

This elderly man may have been the town's resident 'Godfather', or perhaps his advanced age provided him with some sort of special status. His comparatively upmarket lifestyle, in what was quite clearly a significantly degraded provincial agricultural economy, was completely out of place for what we considered to be 'usual' for most residents of Xuyen Moc. We exhaustively searched the home for items such as weapons, substantial amounts of rice, documents, money etc. We found nothing of any importance, which was quite astonishing given his apparent comparative wealth.

Unconscionably, we loitered in this old man's home for well over an hour, seriously drinking bottle after bottle of his very cold, locally produced, high quality beer — Biere 33; more colloquially known as 'Ba Muoi Ba' (33) — for which he charged us an extortionate price. For an old man, he certainly had a head for business.

He was also a very lucky man given that out in the field as we were, some of us carried MPC (Military Payment Certificates) currency — mentioned later in the story — as well as larger amounts of local currency. Why, I have no idea! We'd just returned from a R&C break in Vung Tau and fortunately for him, we were still relatively new to his country, so gave some credence to the niceties usually expected to be observed by civilised people. We therefore begrudgingly paid his grossly inflated price for the beer, without too much argument on our part. The price was still extraordinarily cheap in terms of $A currency, so it wasn't too much of an issue for us.

The long French occupation of Vietnam enhanced the local culture in many ways, including the manufacture of bread — crispy Saigon rolls for example — and the brewing of very good beer. I can personally attest to the high quality of the local beer that was still being produced some 16 years after the French finally withdrew from Vietnam after the signing of the Geneva Accords on 21 July 1954. This followed their catastrophic defeat by the Viet Minh at the Battle of Dien Bien Phu on 7 May 1954. It's well worth noting that some 90,000 French soldiers died in Vietnam.

Alcohol — beer in particular — was an essential commodity for us. Whenever we could get it, we almost always paid whatever the asking price was. This was mostly because we were very well paid compared to men in the US Army, so we didn't really care too much about the price anyway. Having said that, if this interaction with local Vietnamese residents had occurred a few months later, I have no doubt that we would have consumed all of the old man's beer and simply walked away without paying him…opting instead to leave him with the good old Aussie '2-finger salute' as a tip.

Eventually, we were discovered by other members of our platoon who'd been tasked with finding us. It's all a bit vague now, but I seem to recall that we were well and truly in some seriously deep shit with our platoon commander for a time. Strangely, I don't think any of us were formally charged over this gross lapse in operational professionalism. We may have ended up with some form of extra duty punishment for a few days. I just don't remember.

Against that background, at this time we were out in the field within the precinct of a large civilian centre by South Vietnamese provincial standards, the inhabitants of which were well known to have strong sympathies for our enemy. We weren't in a friendly locale, so we really should have known better.

After all, we openly prided ourselves on being highly trained, professional soldiers. While some of us were drinking beers at a fast rate that early evening, other elements of the Assault Pioneer Platoon were still deployed on house searches and night-time ambushing around Xuyen Moc.

Thankfully — charged or not — it all seemed to blow over quite quickly. But I do know that several of my platoon mates were very angry with our irresponsible behaviour. Personally, I reckon they were just pissed-off because they missed out on the beer!

THE NUI DINH MOUNTAINS

The Battalion returned to Nui Dat by road on the early afternoon of 25 January and prepared for immediate deployment into the Nui Dinh Mountains, about 6km west-south-west of Nui Dat, for reconnaissance-in-force and ambushing operations. This rather significant landscape feature was predominantly a steep and difficult undulating terrain, rising to 504m, and significantly covered in very dense jungle. From an infantry point of view, it was a hard slog, I can tell you.

I don't know if anyone still absorbing my story has read the wonderful book 'Matterhorn'.[43] This rather large tome is about US marines operating in the central highlands of Vietnam, just south of the DMZ. What really struck a chord with me, as I devoured this captivating factually-based fictional story, were the problems that the marines experienced when they assaulted enemy positions dug-in at much higher altitude on a steeply rising mountainside (Matterhorn). From an infantry perspective, this is generally not a good idea. In saying that, I take you back to my infantry corps training where the mindset of '*gun right... to the high ground*' was a mantra drilled into us repeatedly. In any infantry engagement with the enemy, holding the high ground was always a very significant advantage.

The Nui Dinhs and its near environs had been identified as an area from which the D67 Engineer Battalion and D41 Chau Duc guerrilla units openly operated, infiltrating villages and towns along routes 2 and 15. This operation was a joint allied one, with 8 RAR tasked with conducting operations on the eastern side of this mountain feature, whilst the US Army 1-16 Mechanised Battalion, 2nd Brigade, 1st Infantry Division (Big Red One) focused its activities on the western slopes. The operational activities of both battalions were designed to prevent any Viet Cong offensive against Ba Ria and the surrounding districts during Tet. See later.

On 27 January, after preliminary clearing by a light aerial fire team —

---
[43] Marlantes, Karl. *Matterhorn*. Atlantic Monthly Press. USA. 2010.

Bushranger gunships from 9 Squadron — the Assault Pioneer Platoon was inserted by 9 Squadron Iroquois helicopters to a landing zone (LZ) on top of a hill known as Nui Thi, a significantly elevated plateau feature of the Nui Dinhs. We immediately secured this LZ for a subsequent fly-in of a section of mortars, as well as elements from both A and C Companies.

For several weeks the Assault Pioneer Platoon, along with A and C Companies, conducted routine reconnaissance-in-force, or search and destroy activities, in conjunction with day and night-time ambushing around the general Nui Dinhs area. The aim of these activities was to drive enemy from their sanctuary in this relatively low-rising but formidable mountain range, down to the foothills and into variable blocking ambush positions put in place by B and D Companies.

Platoon strength night-time ambushes were conducted on 27, 28, 29, and 30 January. These ambushes were unproductive. However, at 4:40pm on the afternoon of 31 January, as our platoon was warily crossing a track, we encountered 3 enemy soldiers at very close range. The forward elements of the platoon immediately engaged the enemy, but the results of this brief contact were inconclusive.

Unless field elements of 8 RAR assaulted a heavily defended bunker system, our enemy usually preferred to flee and fight another day. They didn't often hang around to fight during the day-time. On the other hand, many battalion night-time contacts with the enemy were often extremely fierce and protracted engagements, due to their almost manic obsession for recovering wounded or dead comrades from the battlefield.

During the second half of this operation, the Assault Pioneer Platoon relocated west, out of the Nui Dinhs, and down onto adjacent, quite unremarkable flat landscapes. From 1 February until 14 February, dual half-platoon ambushes — variously comprising of between 12-14 men — were put in place every night following a mix of day-time ambushing and low-level reconnaissance-in-force patrolling.

At 1:30am on 11 February, a platoon ambush party of 14 men killed 2 enemy soldiers at very close range in a fierce engagement — the enemy strength wasn't able to be estimated — that extended for well over an hour. The platoon had been ambushing parts of this track spasmodically during the day-time and on most nights, for quite a while. Generally, this track meandered through relatively flat and wet terrain, notable for its horrendous infestation of mosquitoes and ticks, interspersed with dried rice paddy fields and thick, thorny bamboo thickets that inundated the numerous minor creek lines.

It was during this time when our platoon was deployed operationally in and around the Nui Dinhs, that I was medically evacuated back to Nui Dat for the removal of a badly impacted wisdom tooth (which I've previously mentioned).

I was only away from the platoon for 2 days.

On 14 February, the Assault Pioneer Platoon returned to Nui Dat to make ready for its tasking during Operation Hammersley — which had already commenced several days earlier with the deployment of C Company to the Long Hai Hills, south of Nui Dat — with its deployment to Fire Support Base Pat.

OPERATION HAMMERSLEY
10 February 1970 – 9 March 1970

Operation Hammersley, conducted in the deep south of the province, was a significant operation in that while previously successful reconnaissance-in-force and ambushing tactics were still employed, much of the operation was conducted in a more classic military approach, with infantry soldiers supported by APCs, tanks, and Iroquois helicopters over difficult, open, and rocky landscapes. A major feature of this testing landscape was the infamous Long Hai Hills and the associated ever-present threat of enemy pilfered M16 anti-personnel and larger land mines.

The battalion's initial focus for this operation was to establish a static defensive position, Night Defensive Position Isa, at the foothills of a rugged, low-rising mountain chain known as the Long Hai Hills. This was in order to protect adjacent quarry operations being undertaken by 17 Construction Squadron, RAE (Royal Australian Engineers), in support of a civil aid road building project, and other tasking aimed at degrading the strength of D445 Local Force Battalion that was known to be very active in the general area. Elements of that enemy unit were also known to regularly seek sanctuary in the Long Hai Hills, as opposed to their relatively open operational area around the large provincial south-eastern district of Xuyen Moc. Isa's defences were augmented by a section of 81mm mortars, 3 Centurion tanks, and a troop of APCs, with C Company providing the initial infantry support.

BHQ deployed to Night Defensive Position Isa on 16 February and remained there until the end of Operation Hammersley. Isa was 14.2km due south of Nui Dat, 9.3km south-east of Ba Ria, and 250m east of Route 44.

After 2 days back at Nui Dat, on 16 February, the Assault Pioneer Platoon and other elements of Support Company deployed to, and took over, the defensive responsibility from 5 RAR, for Fire Support Base Pat — located about 300m west of Route 328, 24.7km north of Nui Dat, and 17km east-north-east of Duc Thanh and Route 2.

The main roles of the platoon for the next 3 weeks were the defence and improvement of the fire support base, numerous adjacent TAOR patrols, and some spasmodic night-time ambushing. Personally, I felt that much of this time was wasted on almost mindless, shit-boring operational activity. At least night-time ambushing had some positives in that it completely focused our minds away from extraneous distractions such as thirst, heat, and humidity.

Fire Support Base Pat, originally established by 5 RAR on 30 December 1969, will always be remembered by the various inhabitants based there for its unbelievable infestation of mosquitoes. Unless you were domiciled there, it would be impossible to imagine how bad it really was. Although not a place as utterly miserable as Fire Support Base Bond — described later — it came a very close second in my view. Pat's only redeeming feature was its relatively pliable red soil, compared to the rock-hard grey shale terra of Fire Support Base Bond. But then again, rock-hard flaky shale doesn't transform into glue when it gets wet, does it! The living conditions within both fire support bases gave rise to nothing but abject misery for the men who were based there from time to time. Still on a sombre note, Night Defensive Position Isa wasn't all that much better. Night Defensive Position Kylie — see later — was somewhat more sufferable.

On 20 February, while the Assault Pioneer Platoon was based at Fire Support Base Pat, there was a brief engagement with the enemy during a forward sentry's roster change. Two enemy opened fire with AK47 assault rifles at an optimistic range of around 170m. Both sentries returned fire. A section of the Assault Pioneer Platoon conducted a sweep through the immediate area and although sighting one rapidly retreating distant enemy soldier, found little else of note.

Although Operation Hammersley was highly successful from an operational point of view, it remains infamous in the annals of 8 RAR history. On 28 February, 8 men from No.1 Platoon, A Company, were killed — along with an Engineer — and 15 others were very badly wounded in 2, contiguously-connected M16 anti-personnel mine incidents. This day is commemorated annually by 8 RAR veterans as 'Long Hai' Day.

OPERATION HAMILTON
3 March 1970 – 24 March 1970

Operation Hamilton was based in the Xuyen Moc district, in the south-east of the province. Its aim was to locate and destroy elements of the elusive D445 Local Force Battalion. At the beginning of this operation, the Assault Pioneer Platoon was still ensconced at Fire Support Base Pat and remained there until 11 March, at which time it was redeployed to Night Defensive Position Isa — which had been established about 4 weeks earlier by C Company. The Assault Pioneer Platoon was assisted in this defensive task by one section from Mortar Platoon, and for much of the time by elements of Anti-Tank and Tracker

Platoon. Not one of us was sorry to leave Fire Support Base Pat, which was closed shortly after our departure. I remember it clearly because it really was a shit-hole. And I mean that!

This period of operational activity for the Assault Pioneer Platoon was also relatively uneventful, with its associated relative boredom only interrupted by occasional day-time TAOR patrols and some night-time ambushing. Our rather mundane operational tasking during Operations Hammersley and Hamilton, was in direct contrast to our exhausting but interesting and ever-changing activities undertaken during Operations Atherton and Keperra.

On 24 March, Operation Hamilton concluded and over the next 2 weeks, most 8 RAR elements were rotated through 40-hour periods of R&C rest at Vung Tau, local TAOR patrolling around Nui Dat, and ready reaction standby. Unlike the rest of the battalion, the Assault Pioneer Platoon remained out in the field at Night Defensive Position Isa for much of this time. The platoon's only real break from operations was a short 3-day withdrawal back to Nui Dat, to enable its soldiers to avail themselves of a break at Vung Tau.

OPERATION PHOI HOP
7 April 1970 – 19 April 1970

This operation was significant for the Assault Pioneer Platoon because it was around this time when 2LT Ken Jones — our platoon commander — was replaced by 2LT Peter Phillips. I spoke about this change of platoon leadership earlier.

The strategic aim of Operation Phoi Hop was to deny the enemy infiltration into the towns or villages in the Long Le and Duc Thanh districts, particularly the towns of Hoa Long, Ap Soui Nghe, Binh Ba, Duc My, and Duc Trung. Our tactical focus was the initial ambushing of likely enemy routes into those civilian centres, followed by the cordon and search of the Ap Bac hamlet of Hoa Long on 19 April.

On 15 April, the Assault Pioneer Platoon, in a 12-man night-time ambush just south of Hoa Long, observed an enemy force of unknown size moving across its front and fired on them. I can still remember this ambush almost as if it was yesterday.

Firstly, we were a small night-time ambush party, though we did possess two M60 machine guns. Secondly, we were on very open, flat terrain, with no canopy or any real ground cover whatsoever. The chosen killing ground that night was a likely 3-cornered track intersection, one arm of which led into the town of Hoa Long. The ambush ground position was strategically aligned alongside, but some distance back from,what appeared to be a more frequented track. Anyway, as directed by our new platoon commander — Mr Phillips —

Chapter 23 – Operational Tasking

we set up this ambush on the grey, sandy, shale-type ground surface, targeting what I thought was the least likely track on which to encounter any enemy later that night.

Our position on the ground was slightly — 300mm at most I'd say — lower than the level of this chosen track. From where we were positioned, any ground cover in the form of dense bamboo thickets, was well to our rear. To me, this didn't look anything like an ideal ambush ground position. However, I guess the similarity of the overall adjacent landscape probably made the choice of killing ground a reasonable, but still highly risky option in my view.

As we quickly set up this ambush in rapidly fading light, it seemed to me that given the prevailing reasonable moonlight — with no cloud cover whatsoever — and our exposed ground position, we may potentially be in some serious shit if we engaged in an extended and aggressive fire fight with any enemy later that evening or the next early morning. Other than a relatively small ridge in front of us, we had no real protective land feature of any kind. Have you ever heard of the terms 'sitting ducks' and 'a turkey shoot'? Well, I'll leave that interesting thought with you.

During my entire time in Vietnam, this night-time ambush's construction was the only one that I felt extremely nervous and apprehensive about. I spent much of my time quietly muttering to no one in particular during its set up, and I wasn't alone in being unhappy about it either.

Being a very low-resourced night-time ambush party, we had to adapt and use our manpower to maximum efficiency. What my rapidly ageing cerebrum tells me is that we had a centrally positioned headquarters group of 2 — the platoon commander, and the signaller — 2 adjacent left and right killing groups of 4, and a rear protection group of 2. It was a very lean ambush party indeed, particularly the rear protection group of only 2 men. I'd love to know what they were thinking that evening! I was a member of the left side killing group, positioned about 1m from my section commander. I again reiterate…this was far from an ideal night-time ambush layout in my view.

As we waited in expectation of any enemy entering our chosen killing ground, I remained very apprehensive and extremely alert. I could clearly see all members of our 2 killing groups, the command group spread out to my right, plus our 2-man rear protection party some 15m behind us, almost perfectly silhouetted by the light of the quarter moon beaming down onto the whitish shale on which we were laying.

I thought to myself, '*If I can see this well — and I'm not a bat — what will any enemy see?*' Quite a lot I'd suggest! However, as there were several infantry soldiers more experienced than me in this ambush party, I eventually concluded that I was probably being overcautious. Besides, there was absolutely nothing I could do about my 'predicament' anyway. After a while I settled down and waited for what — if anything — might unfold for us. As it turned out, the waiting didn't last too long at all.

At around 8.40pm, the ambush was sprung by the right-side killing group which engaged 5 enemy soldiers wide of the killing ground, at a distance of about 70m with M18 Claymore anti-personnel directional mines and M60 machine gun and rifle fire. The sound of the Claymores detonating, and that of subsequent concentrated machine gun and rifle fire into and past the killing ground, certainly threw me into action. My heart was racing at breakneck speed.

As soon as the ambush was sprung, my initial role that night was to provide illumination from my M79 grenade launcher. I probably fired, in quick succession, about 10 or so rounds of that ammunition type up and well out ahead of the right-side killing group, and then joined the rest of the platoon in saturating that area of the killing ground with several magazines of rounds from my SLR rifle.

For what appeared to be some serious amount of time, the enemy returned very heavy fire and then they just seemed to lose interest and faded away. As it was, this engagement with the enemy still lasted about 10 minutes. Thankfully, we suffered no casualties that night.

Next morning, at first light, we searched the area and found several heavy drag marks, which were always an indication of recovered, badly wounded, or deceased enemy soldiers. However, given the absence of any extensive blood trails, the overall results from this ambush were deemed to be inconclusive. This was often the case with night-time engagements with the enemy. Having said that, the body count metric wasn't an accurate measure of the effectiveness of Australian soldiers in Vietnam, as I've stated previously. This night-time ambush was notable for other reasons as well.

Sometime during the night, I managed to lose the working components of an army issue wristwatch I was wearing. Next morning, I discovered that the wrist band and the back casing of the watch were the only remaining pieces. After casually mentioning this to my section commander, we conducted a full sweep of the ambush site, looking for the operating components of my watch. I simply couldn't believe that we were bothering to do this!

The next time we were back at Nui Dat, I was amazed by the fuss surrounding my watch. This minuscule loss of government assets generated a proliferation of completely meaningless paperwork. I mean it wasn't as if I'd lost my rifle or anything nearly as important as that. Anyway, I spent countless hours filling out unintelligible forms, which I'm sure would have eventually engendered a raging erection for one of the battalion's anally-retentive bean counters. And…I was even ordered to return the wrist band and watch casing because it was considered crucial evidence in support of the written detail contained within the array of forms that I'd earlier submitted to the Support Company Quartermaster.

Moving on now. As there had been a few contacts with the enemy by C and D Companies in the same general area as my platoon's ambush on 15 April — near the large town of Hoa Long — over previous nights, the general suspicion that the Viet Cong were moving in and out of the town at night, was pretty well confirmed by our platoon's contact. It came as no surprise to be told that we would form part of a battalion-sized cordon and search of the Ap Bac hamlet of Hoa Long, a few days later.

THE CORDON AND SEARCH OF HOA LONG (AP BAC)
18 April 1970 – 19 April 1970

Given the number of recent night-time enemy contacts in the vicinity of the unfriendly town of Hoa Long, and acting on TFHQ intelligence, BHQ decided to use all available elements of the battalion to cordon off and search the clearly defined western residential area of Hoa Long, a hamlet known as Ap Bac. A local allied South Vietnamese Regional Forces unit was co-opted to assist the battalion in providing interpreter services during the interrogation of any citizens suspected of nefarious activities. Hoa Long had an overall population of around 5,400 with some 2,000 persons residing in its hamlet of Ap Bac.

The cordon and search of Ap Bac was put in place on the night of 18 April. Elements of 8 RAR participating in this cordon and search were tactically inserted around the wider Hoa Long area by 6:15pm that evening. The Assault Pioneer Platoon entered the hamlet in the early morning hours of 19 April and commencing at 3am, began construction of the holding compound to be used once the sun rose, and the screening of residents could commence. As a result of this tactical initiative, some 576 residents were screened with 18 detained for further interrogation by allied South Vietnamese Regional Forces. I'm not aware of any outcomes from these interrogations.

As best as I can recall, this particular cordon and search was fairly uneventful from an operational point of view. However, in later years, I've come to realise that it had a profound effect on me during my later time in Vietnam, and in my subsequent life.

The cordon and search of Ap Bac involved most operational 8 RAR elements. It was a seriously large event. When the 2,000 or so residents of that hamlet arose from their slumber next morning, they found themselves effectively surrounded. There was no way out of the cordon, so that meant no escape for them.

Early on the morning of 19 April, before they really knew what was happening, all of the adult residents of Ap Bac were assembled into a number of tightly guarded groups and moved into a large, loosely enclosed compound constructed by the Assault Pioneer Platoon some hours earlier. This rectangular compound, which was about 100m long and 75m wide, contained a few trench latrines surrounded by hessian cloth for privacy. Separate latrines for both males and females were situated apart from one another, but near the 4 corners and about halfway along each of the longer perimeters of the compound.

After helping put in place the compound barriers and the necessary latrines, my initial role that day was to participate in guarding 1 of the 4 corners. Other guard points were put in place midway between each compound corner. Machine gun groups from my platoon and other elements of Support Company manned these defensive key guard points.

There were several of us at our allocated guard positions working in frequent rotation on this absolutely shit-boring task. I mean it wasn't as if the loosely incarcerated residents were going to attempt a mass breakout anyway. Why would they? More to the point, how could they? And, even if they were to do so, there was nowhere for them to go. But…what if they did initiate a breakout of sorts? I had no intention of shooting unarmed civilians and children. As I'd been in Vietnam for about 5 months by this time, I was probably somewhat crazy. However, I wasn't that crazy. Then again, perhaps I was? Some of my platoon mates reckon this was the case…and I know for sure that some of them were definitely a bit loopy.

Around mid-morning, a very elderly woman ambled over to one of the female latrines, about 15m in from my location. Naturally, we all thought she was going in to conduct her personal business. We were very wrong indeed!

She walked over very close to the barrier directly opposite us, turned around, dropped her black trousers, squatted down, revealing her wrinkly, skinny ass in the process, and defecated. I couldn't believe what I was witnessing. We had just been 'shat-on' by an aged, female villager! Clearly, she had no regard for us whatsoever and displayed that in such an emphatic way that I've never forgotten it.

I was truly gob-smacked. My observations are that as a race, the Vietnamese people are generally quite prudish. This overt public display of a natural bodily function, particularly by an elderly female, was nothing short of astonishing. Her look of utter contempt for us as she waddled away, without even wiping her backside, was almost frightening.

That awful experience aside, the cordon and search of Ap Bac was fast becoming a boring and utterly tiresome task for me. It was a very hot and extremely humid day. There was little or no shade in the open areas, and the hamlet's confines were dry and dusty — literally screaming for an afternoon downpour which strangely for that time of the year, never materialised. It didn't take me too long to lose compete interest in what we were supposed to

Chapter 23 — Operational Tasking

be doing in Ap Bac. Despite my best lateral thinking, I couldn't find a way to extract myself from this awful task. There was nowhere to hide, or otherwise go unnoticed.

Around early afternoon, my heat-addled brain was rescued from its rapidly developing — and likely permanent — metamorphous into mush, when my section commander approached our sentry group with a relief squad. He ordered myself and 2 other men to report to the engineer officer co-ordinating the search of residences within Ap Bac. Thank God for that! Anything to relieve the boredom and take my mind off the baking heat and overpowering humidity. It was such a climatically oppressive day that even when doing nothing of a strenuous nature, my trousers and shirt were literally saturated, and I was visually dripping with perspiration. In fact, I was most likely melting. This was just another one of my really 'fun' days in Vietnam.

For the next few hours, 3 of us — individually rotated from time to time — routinely searched a number of private residences — generally hovels with brushed, hard dirt floors — not even approaching minimalist Australian standards of those times — for weapons, abnormally large caches of rice, large sums of money, or anything else that looked to be of a suspicious nature. Mostly, we found nothing of any significant importance. The occupants were generally sullen, mute, and just stared blankly at us. They weren't co-operative and clearly not at all friendly.

Upon entering a house, one of us kept armed guard on the occupants while the other 2 men conducted the search. Sometimes 2 of us kept guard on the occupants. It all depended on our collective view as to which level of security was appropriate. Some occupants were openly more hostile than others and until we searched, we had no idea what we might find. We rotated these tasks house by house. In saying that, over that late afternoon there were numerous changes in the personnel composition of my 'team', including myself.

Now the fact that the 3 of us in this particular search party were generally members of the Assault Pioneer Platoon, was highly unusual. Ordinarily, all cordon and search investigative parties in these operational instances included an engineer, experienced in booby trap and anti-personnel mine deactivation. I can only surmise that as this cordon and search of Ap Bac was a battalion-sized operation, members of the Assault Pioneer Platoon were deployed in their specialised role as the 'first-call' engineer resource for the battalion. Anyway, that's how it was for me and my various 2 other platoon mates that afternoon.

Other than once instance, which I'll now describe, I can honestly say that during these searches of private property we didn't inflict any damage on, or otherwise degrade the meagre assets and possessions of any resident of the hamlet. Quite late in the day, around 4:30pm, 3 of us entered another house to begin a routine search. I was performing the default role of armed guard on this occasion.

For some inexplicable reason, I immediately sensed that we were inside a very hostile house, in fact, enemy territory. I don't know if it was the looks of sheer hatred being directed our way by the young, attractive female occupant of this house, and her husband, or what it was. I just felt very uneasy and became extremely alert. I remember looking at this woman and her husband, mentally pleading with them, *'don't do anything stupid'*.

The very last thing I wanted to do was kill unarmed civilians. I knew that I probably wouldn't have done that anyway, but you never really know what can happen in a difficult moment, particularly if you feel physically threatened. At the end of the day, we were, after all, in a highly dangerous and utterly confused war zone…and we were always acutely aware of that.

We quickly agreed that only 1 man should search this house, as clearly 2 guards were needed. One man searched the place from top to bottom and found nothing. Just as he was about to conclude his search, he picked up what seemed to be an innocuous-looking large wicker sewing basket. The reaction of the female occupant of the house was a dead give-away. Obviously, she didn't want us to look inside that basket. Keeping herself and her husband at bay with my SLR rifle, and with my heart seriously pounding, our investigating platoon mate discovered an extremely large quantity of high denomination notes of local currency, secretly stashed in the base of the basket. Quite clearly, this woman and probably her husband as well, engaged in the illegal collection of taxes extorted by the Viet Cong political structures on the local population of the wider Hoa Long community.

As we forcibly escorted this audibly distressed couple to the interrogation holding area, the young woman went completely crazy. On that oppressively hot and revoltingly humid late April afternoon — it was about 4:30pm — this woman tested my personal resolve to almost my last 1,000th percentile breaking point. Her physical assault on me, which I described earlier, placed me in such a confused and tortured mental state that I still don't know how I was able to retain my composure, innate sense of right and wrong, and not shoot and kill her on the spot!

If she's still alive today, she would have no idea how lucky she was back on that horrendous April afternoon. Honestly, she was only half a millimetre of trigger finger pressure away from having her almost skeletal frame — torso centre mass — being torn asunder by a 9.5gm lump of 7.62mm lead, travelling at 840m/s. It would have blown her apart, and probably her husband as well, who was standing right behind her during the entirety of this horrible confrontation. And more importantly I guess, she would have no idea about the fact that I often think of this very unpleasant moment in my past life, and her in particular.

Clearly, I don't know what ended up happening to this young woman, or her husband. At the time, I didn't care for one moment what might have become of them. However, over the following weeks and months, as my mind often wandered during many hours of silent operational activity, I began to think a lot more about the elderly female I spoke of earlier, and this young woman. I kept asking myself, *'How could an attractive young woman like this support the Viet Cong and extort her fellow community residents out of their meagre incomes?'*

Although I was unable to rationalise it then, I now more fully appreciate the nature of this so-called 'American War' in Vietnam. My experiences at Ap Bac revealed that the divide between the so-called Communist North Vietnam, and the so-called democratic South Vietnam, wasn't as clear-cut as I'd been led to believe. Quite clearly there were staunch supporters of the NLF in South Vietnam. Many years later, I began to realise that the Vietnam War wasn't about communist expansion at all. It was only ever about nationalism.

The extraordinary behaviour of the elderly female in the holding compound at Ap Bac has remained an indelible part of my recall of Vietnam experiences. Who knows what war time tragedies may have befallen her and her extended family. As for the young woman and her husband, whom we handed over to the interrogation holding centre, I still often wonder if her life turned out as she had planned.

I've also never forgotten the fact that we didn't hand all of the money we found in the woman's house that afternoon, into the interrogation holding centre at Ap Bac. How we weren't caught out amazes me, because I'm aware of others in my battalion — and indeed some within my platoon — who did exactly the same thing that day. And several of them were caught, charged, reprimanded, and severely punished. I can surmise that it was probably prudent of us to only give a modest haircut to the proceeds of extortion, which we handed into the military authorities.

Stealing a portion of that money isn't something I'm proud of, but in Vietnam at that time, I think it would be fair to say that many of us weren't an exact reflection of our true selves. However, I will say, as modest as that folding material haircut may have been, it later funded a very substantial amount of beer for myself and my mates during our next visit to Vung Tau for a 40-hour R&C break.

OPERATION NUDGEE
20 April 1970 – 11 June 1970

Operation Phoi Hop rolled over into Operation Nudgee, which then merged into Operations Concrete 1 (with 7 RAR) and Concrete 2 (as part of the wider

1 ATF). Something like 99 days of continuous deployment into the field with only a 3-day break at Nui Dat and 2 days R&C leave in Vung Tau, was a long and exhausting time for all members of the platoon.

The first part of this operation involved working closely with the other 2 Australian infantry battalions based at Nui Dat — 6 RAR and 7 RAR — and associated supporting field elements, on an intensive reconnaissance and an ambush Task Force tactical plan, code named 'Operation Concrete'. The aim of this operation was to seek out and degrade HQ D445 Local Force Battalion and its base areas around the district of Xuyen Moc in the east of the province. This phase of the operation focused on the civilian population centres of Dat Do, Hoi My, and Ap Nui Nhon.

There were also several days when three 8 RAR rifle companies, (B, C, and D) operated in the north-east of the province, and in conjunction with the US 2nd Brigade 25th Division, conducted reconnaissance-in-force and related ambush activities aimed at destroying elements of D440 Local Force Battalion.

For the latter part of this operation, 8 RAR resumed its highly successful night-time ambushing of villages and hamlets, generally in half-platoon strength. Again, this plan was to deny the enemy infiltration into the villages of Hoa Long, Ap Soui Nghe, Duc My, Binh Ba, and Long Dien etc, as well as movement in areas generally west of Route 2 and mostly north of Nui Dat.

One night, towards the end of this operation, the Assault Pioneer Platoon ambushed the Task Force rubbish dump adjacent to the south of Nui Dat. Intelligence was received, suggesting that the enemy was scavenging for food around this area. If this intelligence was proven to be correct, it would clearly indicate that 1 ATF military operations in the province were causing significant logistical problems for the enemy. This night-time ambush though was uneventful.

Although the Assault Pioneer Platoon did spend a few days at Nui Dat during this period, there was one occasion when — probably just like other elements of the battalion — the Assault Pioneer Platoon was away from Nui Dat and engaged on quite varied operational activities for around 7 weeks. This was a very long time to exist merely on rations. On many of those nights we bunkered down in ambush patterns. We'd had almost no rest whatsoever for this entire operational period. When we returned to Nui Dat, we were exhausted and mentally fragile.

Early on the morning of 20 April 1970, Support Company elements of the battalion — including the Assault Pioneer Platoon — moved from Nui Dat by APCs to establish Fire Support Base Bond, some 19km east-south-east of Nui Dat, 7km north of the South China Sea, 4.4km south-west of Xuyen Moc, and 300m from the intersection of Routes 23 and 328. BHQ followed later that morning. The deployment of the fire support base was completed by midday.

Chapter 23 — Operational Tasking

For the next week, the Assault Pioneer Platoon dug-in the command post and established the defensive perimeter systems for the fire support base, as well as conducting numerous day and night-time ambushes adjacent to the fire support base.

Interestingly, during this first phase of Operation Nudgee — as it was known by 8 RAR — whilst each of the 3 infantry battalions based at Nui Dat were concurrently deployed, TFHQ was also deployed into the field, to Fire Support Base Bond. This was the only occasion that this occurred during 8 RAR's time in Vietnam.

I have very clear memories of Fire Support Base Bond...and they're not good ones. It was an awful place, located in a landscape that was forgettable in every sense of the word. The rock-hard grey shale soil, along with almost a complete lack of ground vegetation or shade cover of any type, has been indelibly forged in my memory. At Bond, it was like being immersed into an amalgam of a sauna, a salt mine, and a cement pit. Bond is a place that I don't remember with any fondness at all. Thank God we only spent a little over a week at this site. If there is hell on earth, I have no doubt whatsoever that it's located very near to the former location of Fire Support Base Bond in the south-east coastal area of Phuoc Tuy Province in Vietnam. Actually, no, that's not quite accurate. Fire Support Base Bond was a living hell on earth.

On 25 April, the Assault Pioneer Platoon deployed from Fire Support Base Bond and spent the next 7 days conducting day-time reconnaissance tasking and night-time ambushing, before returning to Nui Dat on 3 May. Sadly, this welcome time away from Fire Support Base Bond provided us with no great relief either, thanks to the requirement of always having to wear metal helmets (2.27kg) and flak Kevlar jackets (3.17kg) — a precursor to military and police body armour — as protection from enemy pilfered M16 anti-personnel mines; and the constant physical aggravation caused by the infestation of large and aggressive sandflies and ticks.

On 8 May, after 40-hours of R&C at Vung Tau, and several days of rest back at Nui Dat, the Assault Pioneer Platoon was redeployed by 9 Squadron Iroquois helicopters back to Night Defensive Position Isa. Like most static positions away from Nui Dat, Isa was a stark and basic place. But I can say with absolute certainty that it didn't even come close to the abject nothingness and associated misery of Fire Support Base Bond, which was vacated on 27 April.

The Assault Pioneer Platoon remained at Night Defensive Position Isa until 12 June, at which time it was redeployed by Iroquois helicopters from 9 Squadron to Night Defensive Position Kylie in the far north of the province. During this time, as well as defending both night defensive positions, the platoon conducted numerous day-time TAOR patrols and half-platoon night-time ambushes in locales adjacent to them.

On 29 May, at around 10pm, a 15-man Assault Pioneer Platoon party, ambushing in open paddy fields about 1km south of Night Defensive Position Isa, engaged an enemy force estimated at more than 30 strong. They appeared to have come from the nearby village of Lo Voi. After a very intense fire fight that continued for more than 3 hours, and which necessitated an ammunition re-supply by a section of APCs, the enemy withdrew east into the Long Hai Hills, leaving 2 bodies behind. It was later established that this enemy party — thought to be an element of D445 Local Force Battalion — had harboured-up in Lo Voi for the previous 24 hours, after killing 2 allied Provincial Forces (PF) soldiers in the village.

A sweep of the area early next morning revealed 8 heavy blood trails and 14 drag marks, heading east towards Lo Voi. A search of Lo Voi that afternoon resulted in the capture of 4 badly wounded enemy soldiers and the detention of 11 civilians. This very successful ambush had clearly resulted in significant collateral damage to our Viet Cong enemy, and far more were killed than what the official records attest to.

At the time of this night-time ambush, I was located with the remainder of the Assault Pioneer Platoon on an elevated, rocky land feature, adjacent to the base of the Long Hai Hills. This wasn't far from Night Defensive Position Isa and about 1km from the ambush site. That evening, we could quite clearly hear the M18 Claymore anti-personnel directional mines as they detonated, and the extended period of exchanges of gunfire emanating during this contact.

Bob Simpson's deep, resonating voice, accompanied by John Dolgan's softer tone, could clearly be heard yelling, '*Grenade!*' as they threw several M26 high-explosive hand grenades into the ambush killing ground position.

At first light next morning, my element of the Assault Pioneer Platoon re-joined the platoon ambush party at the ambush site, and the entire platoon spent a fair amount of time searching the killing ground and its near environs for abandoned weapons, ammunition, related material, and anything else of useful military intelligence. I certainly didn't find anything even remotely valuable. However, there was one very significant item recovered at the site and that was a custom-crafted wooden box containing precision Swiss-made medical instruments. If I could have done so, I would have pilfered those items without any question whatsoever. Who knows where they eventually ended up.

Around noon, just as the prevailing hot temperature and extreme humidity were about to render me comatose, Peter Wood and I, oversighted by Lance-corporal Ron Goubareff — my section second in command — were given the grisly task of digging graves and burying the bodies of these 2 enemy soldiers. I have to say that the graves we scraped that day with our entrenching tools — dug is too strong a word — wouldn't have come anywhere close to satisfying

Chapter 23 – Operational Tasking

those who strictly adhere to all aspects of the Geneva Convention. We just made sure that the scrapes were deep enough for the bodies to be interred, and covered with about 30cm of loose, sandy soil. Quite frankly, neither of us had the time or the proper tools — and certainly not the desire — to do anything else.

I didn't want to be a component of this burial party at all, and the memory of it has never left me. Some 10 hours after they were killed, the bodies of these 2 enemy were already beginning to break down and decompose. It was oppressively hot. The stench of their flesh, even then, was becoming overpowering. It had to be a hurried burial because the bodies would have rapidly decomposed even further, due to the oppressive climatic conditions. This in turn would have created a health hazard for us, if they were left exposed to the elements. After we completed this task, I became violently ill and vomited copiously.

What occurred to me many years later, was the detached way in which the 3 of us dealt with these battlefield deaths and their burials. Whilst there was absolutely no disrespect shown by us towards the deceased enemy, there certainly wasn't any compassion for them either. One was quite a young man, but even so, we didn't really care about them. They were, after all, the enemy. At the end of the day, they were trying to kill us, and we ended up killing them. I suppose that is, and always has been, the nature of war.

There was one day and night, on 6 June, when the platoon was suddenly tasked with defending a significant US Army resource, Fire Support Base Lei Loi, situated some distance north of Nui Dat. While our major day-time attention focused on Alan Small's encounter with a largish green snake of unknown species — that had made itself comfortable amongst all of his personal equipment — we were tasked with another night-time ambush. Because Lei Loi was a very well-equipped US Army resource, a number of us were able to pilfer a range of small, attractive items. We were redeployed back to Night Defensive Position Isa the very next day, again by Iroquois helicopters from 9 Squadron.

OPERATION CUNG CHUNG 1
12 June 1970 – 28 June 1970

By the time this operation began, each of the three 1 ATF infantry battalions were responsible for, or focusing on their operational activities in a discrete ground area of Phuoc Tuy Province. The objective was to deny the enemy infiltration into civilian centres and to protect engineer elements at Night Defensive Position Kylie, along the northern reaches of Route 2.

The specific operational focus for 8 RAR was on Route 2 around the districts of Duc Thanh, Long Le, Long Dien, the larger towns of Hoa Long and Dat Do, and the smaller villages of Ap Suoi Nghe, Duc My, Binh Ba, and Duc Trang.

Each of the four 8 RAR rifle companies were responsible for a specific zone within that broad area of operational responsibility. During this time, a 'virtual' fifth rifle company, comprising of both Anti-Tank and Tracker, and Assault Pioneer platoons was formed. They deployed to Night Defensive Position Kylie — basically an engineer base established 200m west of Route 2 — about 17km north of Nui Dat, and about 3km north-east of the site of the former Fire Support Base Peggy.

Kylie (aka Fire Support Base Jane) was established to support road building operations by 1 Field Engineers, RAE, in the north of the province. Our role was to protect and defend that base as well as undertaking reconnaissance and ambushing in the adjacent areas, close to the provincial boundary abutting Long Khanh Province. Lei Loi — the former fire support base of the 4th Division, US 9th Infantry Division — located just east of Route 2 and about 9km north of Nui Dat, was retained as an operational base for BHQ and the supporting artillery guns of 161 Battery.

At this time, the battalion was now diversely spread from the Long Hai Hills in the far south of the province to the provincial border in the far north. At the same time, it was protecting 2 static bases outside of Nui Dat — Night Defensive Position Kylie and Fire Support Base Le Loi — as well as Fire Support Base Matthew for a very short period of time.

During this 17-day period, the Assault Pioneer Platoon deployed from Night Defensive Position Kylie for a total of 7 days for reconnaissance-in-force and night-time ambushing activities. Operation Cung Chung 1, rolled over into Operation Petrie.

OPERATION PETRIE
29 June 1970 – 13 July 1970

During Operation Petrie, the battalion conducted reconnaissance and ambushing, aimed at locating and degrading D440 Local Force Battalion, primarily in the far north of the province where Night Defensive Position Kylie was located.

Intelligence had been received suggesting that significant elements of D440 Local Force Battalion were located west of Night Defensive Position Kylie, and towards Bien Hoa Province. Reactive battalion tactics were to put in place as wide a cordon from platoon and half-platoon night-time ambushes as possible, supported by APCs and tanks. Once these blocks — or ambushes — of likely escape routes were in place, a massive air and artillery bombardment of the surrounded area was affected, with the aim of driving enemy into these 8 RAR night-time ambush locations. Some 2,000 artillery rounds — both 105mm and 155mm — and a number of 8in naval rounds, together with 48 high-explosive Hi-Drag bombs — each weighing 227kg — comprised this bombardment. They were dropped by USAF Phantom aircraft.

As this strategy was put in place, elements of the Assault Pioneer and Anti-Tank and Tracker Platoons operated well north of Night Defensive Position Kylie in the Long Khanh Province, just to the south of the large US Army base 'Blackhorse'. At the same time, other elements of the Assault Pioneer and Anti-Tank and Tracker Platoons were located well south of Night Defensive Position Kylie, just to the east of Route 2 and about 6km north of Nui Dat. Elements of my platoon were probably operating the furthest distance from Nui Dat — around 25km out.

During this short but very intense operation, the Assault Pioneer Platoon — in its 2 separate half-platoon units — conducted reconnaissance-in-force activities during the day, and ambushed likely landscape features every night. The northern located elements of the Assault Pioneer Platoon often ambushed at night during this period, assisted by the massive firepower support of Centurion tanks.

OPERATION DECADE
23 July 1970 – 2 August 1970

This very short operation was designed to temporarily relieve 7 RAR of its operational responsibilities, and for 8 RAR to continue the village interdiction role in the south-east of Phuoc Tuy Province. This particular tasking had been going on for several months. Specifically, the battalion employed saturation night-time ambushing in platoon and half-platoon strengths, between the Long Hai Hills and its close population centres.

For this short period of time, elements of Support Company — including the Assault Pioneer Platoon — re-occupied Night Defensive Position Isa, about 15km south of Nui Dat on the south-western reaches of the Long Hai Hills. In conjunction with Anti-Tank and Tracker Platoon, and in line with overall battalion tactics for this operation, they conducted numerous platoon and half-platoon night-time ambushes in the general vicinity of Isa.

OPERATIONS CUNG CHUNG 2 AND CUNG CHUNG 3
3 August 1970 – 25 October 1970

The end of Operation Decade and the beginning of Operations Cung Chung 2, and Cung Chung 3, merged into each other with the Assault Pioneer Platoon still effectively based at Night Defensive Position Isa. On 25 August, the Assault Pioneer Platoon vacated Night Defensive Position Isa, handing it over to 7 RAR.

Following the highly successful and legendary 8 Platoon C Company ambush on the nights of 11 and 12 August, indications again pointed to significant enemy movement into, around, and out of Hoa Long. Accordingly, on the night of the 26 August, A, C, and D Companies established an 'L' shaped ambush to the west of Hoa Long. A and C Companies were located on the eastern side of the 'L', and D Company, along with the Assault Pioneer Platoon, occupied the southern sector.

On 27 August, B Company deployed north to its interception position in the Chau Pha Valley. The Assault Pioneer Platoon was relocated to Night Defensive Position Kylie in the far north of the province, where it remained for several weeks defending the site and conducting numerous night-time ambushes in the near vicinity. On 13 September, Night Defensive Position Kylie was closed and the Assault Pioneer Platoon returned to Nui Dat where it was engaged on spasmodic local TAOR night-time ambushing from that time onwards.

On 4 October, the entire battalion came out of operations and from that time until it ceased all operational activity in Vietnam on 25 October, rotational night-time ambushing was put in place in and around Hoa Long — the town we loved to hate — and in other areas reasonably adjacent to Nui Dat. During this period, only one company at a time was committed to these fairly limited operations. The Assault Pioneer Platoon came under the effective control of B Company for those final few weeks of our time in this nasty country.

OPERATIONAL INTERACTION WITH THE LOCAL PEOPLE

Generally, we had very little to do with the local people and apart from our limited time in Vung Tau, we did our utmost to avoid them as much as possible. Unless we were operationally located in and around large towns, hamlets, or other civilian centres — cordon and search tasking — the only real contact we seemed to have with the locals was largely confined to workers in rubber plantations or rice paddy fields. These workers, who were predominantly female, weren't friendly.

Whenever we did come into contact, we tried our best to disregard them, but at the same time our concentration and alert levels significantly increased. We took the view that it was very good field craft to treat all mature-age civilians with a great deal of suspicion. I also formed the view that Vietnamese children were exactly that... just children.

One afternoon, we stopped for a brief rest in the de Courtenay rubber

Chapter 23 — Operational Tasking

plantation in the far north of the province and I tried to chat with a stunningly-beautiful slender young woman. She was one of many variously-aged women working at maintaining the trees. This young woman's sheer beauty completely captivated me. I would have done almost anything to engage her in an extended one-on-one personal interaction. While some of my platoon mates were lewdly suggesting that I only had a carnal interest in this young woman, that was only partially true. At this time in my relatively short life, I'd never come across a more attractive young woman. I was besotted with her.

Somehow — by way of rudimentary sign language — I indicated that I would like her to show me the process of scoring the rubber trees to enable the sap, or raw rubber, to seep into the ceramic bowls that were attached to the trunks of the rubber trees — about 1.5m above ground level.

She seemed very flattered that I was showing interest in her work and after demonstrating how to diagonally score the trunk of a tree, passed me her razor-sharp implement and gestured for me to try it. Well, did I stuff that up in a big way! My embarrassing attempts to emulate her expert work simply resulted in almost ring-barking the tree.

Once she saw what I'd done to her rubber tree, she went off her brain! Our emerging love match disintegrated instantly and I can still remember her wailing and the tears in her eyes, as our platoon slowly moved on past her. Naturally, I didn't mean to fatally wound her rubber tree, but I don't think she would have viewed this damage as an accident, even though it honestly was. I really regret possibly killing her tree.

During the cordon and search of the Hoa Long hamlet of Ap Bac, we were in very close contact with the local people for about 36 hours; an experience I didn't enjoy at all. There were also times when we were in and around towns such as Xuyen Moc, Ap Nui Non, Ap Soui Nghe, and Binh Ba, that we had no alternative but to interact with some of the residents. While not as overtly hostile as those who lived at Ap Bac, and the wider population centre of Hoa Long, these locals didn't go out of their way to make any interaction pleasant. The fact that we couldn't communicate with them properly was always a major difficulty for us. But, as my time in Vietnam went on, I slowly formed the view that the local people didn't like us much at all. Clearly, we were certainly not winning their 'hearts and minds'.

The only interesting contact with local people from my point of view was with children, and this occurred mostly when we were in Vung Tau or near any town or hamlet. The Vietnamese youngsters were just like young children back home in Australia, but with greater street smarts. Most of the time they tried every trick in the book to get us to give them cans of food, chewing gum, lollies, and of course cigarettes. And, as friendly as they seemed to be, most of them were very adept in the worldwide game of ripping-off tourists who, in effect, we were to them.

For the most part, we didn't have much contact with local people when we were out in the field. Whenever we did, we were generally respectful of them, but always very cautious and alert. Of course, how we interacted with the locals on those rare times in Vung Tau on our 40-hour R&C breaks, is another story altogether.

CHIEU HOI ATTACHMENTS

The Chieu Hoi Program fostered by 1 ATF, was an 'open arms' policy where selected former enemy soldiers — who'd been captured or defected from the Viet Cong — were, after a proper period of indoctrination and re-training, attached to allied units as 'Hoi Chanhs'. The role of a Hoi Chanh was to provide allied units with expert 'on the ground' intelligence, so to speak.

For a brief period of time the Assault Pioneer Platoon was graced with the dubious presence of a Hoi Chanh whom we named 'Nigel Nog'. Because we always had difficulty with Vietnamese names, we tended to give any native person the generic gender names of 'Nigel Nog' or 'Nancy Nog'. Keep in mind, this allocated surname 'Nog' was highly insulting to the Vietnamese race.

Our Nigel Nog was a complete and utter waste of space, and a total oxygen thief as far as I was concerned. I don't recall him doing anything that was even remotely of any assistance for the platoon. We couldn't effectively communicate with him anyway, so the whole Chieu Hoi concept was totally lost on me.

Late one afternoon out in the field, as we were brewing up and heating a meal before setting up an ambush for the night, Nigel spent about 30 minutes wallowing in a waist-deep creek line, wearing only his iridescent red boxer shorts — where he stole those from, I don't even want to think about — garnering freshwater mussels. As soon as he emerged from the water with his floppy green hat full to the brim with these delicacies, I immediately became Nigel's new best friend. I then proceeded to forcibly take from him, cook, and eat everything he collected. He quite happily handed over his mollusc treats as soon as I indicated that I wanted them. Not quite sure if that was because he liked me, or because he was terrified of me. It was probably the latter. I didn't really care anyway. My main concern at that time was consuming a half-decent evening meal for a change: tasty freshwater mussels and curried rice.

Because Nigel had no money whatsoever, we would buy all of his beer and cigarettes at Nui Dat. Although he was a chain-smoker, he wasn't a big drinker, so it didn't cost us too much. In some ways, I guess Nigel may have thought that he was part of our platoon. Well, sad to say...that was never, ever the case.

Chapter 23 — Operational Tasking

And we never trusted him. How could we?

Out in the field we always made Nigel assume positions where the likelihood of him being the first one killed — if we were to engage the enemy in any contact — was very high. For example, when moving with APCs, No.1 Section — my section — of the platoon was always on the lead track, so we made Nigel sit up at the very front, totally exposed. He was with us for about 6 weeks. Sometime after he left us, we heard that he'd been killed in a contact with the enemy while attached to another 1 ATF infantry platoon. We were never able to confirm his reported demise, but I don't think anyone in our platoon cared a toss about even trying to find out. At the time, I certainly didn't.

On much later reflection though, the way in which we all treated Nigel was nothing short of appalling. He was a human being after all, and probably a decent one at that. We never really got to know him...not that any of us seriously tried. The language and cultural barriers were just far too difficult for us to overcome. And, at that time, we didn't regard any Vietnamese native — friend or foe — as worthy of even belonging to the human race.

What our behaviour at that time reflected was a significant degradation in our core life values. In other words, what we were doing as soldiers, the extreme stresses that we were continuously under, the primitive way in which we lived out in the field, and our day-to-day personal strategies for survival, all contributed to us almost reverting back to an 'animal state' — merely survival of the fittest, and no real rules which needed to be observed. After 6 months in Vietnam, we weren't very nice people.

After returning to Australia, many of us had great difficulty in adjusting to civilian life with its orderly framework, underpinned by all its civilised rules and niceties. It took me quite some time, I can tell you. Some Vietnam veterans have never adjusted. All these many years later, it's very easy for me to see why this is the case for those veterans.

CHAPTER 24

VUNG TAU

1ST AUSTRALIAN LOGISTIC SUPPORT GROUP (1 ALSG)

Back in 1970, the largest provincial civilian centre within Phuoc Tuy Province was the coastal port city of Vung Tau. It was located 35km south of Nui Dat at the most southern limit of Route 15, which intersected just north of Vung Tau with Route 2, at the provincial capital of Ba Ria. The significant military support elements comprising 1 ALSG were based at Vung Tau and sited in a strategically located and very heavily defended position on the eastern peninsular coast, adjacent to this vibrant city.

The role of 1 ALSG was to provide whatever logistical support necessary to keep 1 ATF at Nui Dat fully operational. It also provided spasmodic short-term rest facilities for Australian and New Zealand soldiers serving in Vietnam. At any one time, some 3,000 servicemen and servicewomen based at Vung Tau — comprising a range of diverse elements — were engaged in supporting about 5,000 combat field and other support soldiers based at Nui Dat.

REST IN COUNTRY (R&C)

At varying times, all 8 RAR elements were provided with R&C leave in Vung Tau. Typically, most soldiers who completed a full 12-month tour of Vietnam were able to avail themselves of 2 — or 3 if they were extremely fortunate — periods of R&C leave. I somehow managed to enjoy 3 such breaks, whereas the bulk of my platoon mates only had 2. It sometimes pays to be adept in that rare military art of 'not being noticed'. Putting this into context, for an infantry battalion deployed on active service to Vietnam for 12 months, the provision of 2 such periods of '*stand down*' from operational tasking wasn't particularly generous.

Essentially, R&C was a 2-day withdrawal from operational activities, highlighted by a 40-hour leave pass and free sojourn — accommodation and mess facilities — at the Peter Badcoe Club, located within the secure confines of 1 ALSG. While we were able to remain within the club precinct for our entire duration on R&C, most of us spent our time at downtown Vung Tau for all sorts of reasons: the ready availability of uninhibited and hedonistic sex being the main one, I'd suggest.

Typically, we'd arrive by army truck at the club at 1 ALSG at around 10am on day 1, and return to Nui Day early on day 3. That gave us 2 nights and about a day-and-a-half to do whatever we wanted in Vung Tau.

PETER BADCOE CLUB

The Peter Badcoe Club was more-or-less something like a very large, basic 2-star country motel/resort, with the added advantage of being completely free of charge, including 3 square meals a day. Shared — 6 beds as I recall — fairly spacious cabin type accommodation was quite adequate. The quantity and standard of food available at the mess each day was extraordinarily good... it was the army after all.

The venue had a good-sized swimming pool and a number of sailing options available at the adjacent, secure Back Beach area. The club also had a well-patronised bar where copious quantities of very cheap alcohol could be — and were — leisurely consumed over many long hours. As a facility, the Peter Badcoe Club was pretty good. It provided a relatively modern and safe environment for soldiers to rest, relax, and unwind after long and difficult periods of operational activity. Australian and New Zealand soldiers looked forward to these rare breaks and made the most of them.

However, the majority of men taking advantage of their R&C break ventured into Vung Tau to take in the sights and sounds of this small but vibrant Asian city — which was coping as best as it could with the various exigencies resulting from ongoing internal conflict and occupation of the country by allied soldiers from lands quite foreign to its residents. At night, most of the married soldiers returned to the club for another extended drinking session, dinner at the mess, and a good night's sleep in a real bed — something we'd all been deprived of for many weeks, even months in some cases. Many of the rest of us preferred to stay overnight in downtown Vung Tau, in the company of one or more of the many bar girls living and working in the city.

CURRENCY

During our time in Vietnam, we used a particular type of currency known as Military Payment Certificates (MPC) — which I've mentioned previously. The various notes resembled Monopoly game money. This substitute currency was of the same face value as $US and freely negotiable within 1 ATF and 1 ALSG. Although highly illegal, it was widely used by us as negotiable tender in Vung Tau and other parts of inhabited Vietnam.

This substitute currency was put in place by the US military to deny the

Military Payment Certificate (MPC).

North Vietnamese access to hard $US currency. From time-to-time, the series number, and even the design of MPC currency changed. Once that occurred, the old issue notes became completely worthless. Potentially, it was very risky for the Vietnamese — both north (covertly) and south — to deal in MPC currency. As allied forces soldiers in Vietnam, we were easily able to exchange cancelled MPC currency for any new MPC currency at par value.

Strangely, those cagey Vietnamese Vung Tau bar proprietors — more often than not mature females — always seemed to know when MPC currency was about to be changed. Obviously, there was graft money being made somewhere by US Army personnel. Nothing much has changed over the years, has it? At that juncture, they wouldn't transact business — bar girls and alcohol — in MPC currency, or even exchange MPC currency for the local currency. That meant we had to resort to financial exchange transactions at the official (low) conversion rate available at the 1 ALSG pay office...not that I was ever caught out by an MPC currency change anyway.

Currency notes, denominated in both Piastres and Dong, were issued from 1953 for the State of Vietnam. These hybrid currency notes, an oddity harking back to the former French occupation, were in common use throughout Phuoc Tuy Province circa 1969-70, and were commonly and collectively referred to by the local population as 'pee'.

Although we were all aware that it was a serious offence to transact or negotiate MPC currency exchanges outside of 1 ATF or 1 ALSG pay offices, not one of us gave a rat's arse about those rules and regulations. The black market MPC currency exchange rate in the Vung Tau bars was something around 450:1 — and sometimes even more — whereas the official exchange rate within 1 ATF and 1 ALSG pay offices was something around 118:1. Like all of my platoon mates, I illegally exchanged MPC currency in Vung Tau bars for local currency — Piastres/Dong (pee) — at the vastly higher rate. I don't ever recall anyone in our platoon getting caught by the allied military police when doing this. On 3 May 1978, this hybrid currency was formally renamed as the 'Dong' by the Vietnamese Government, and remains so today.

In Vung Tau bars, $US could be exchanged for Piastres/Dong (pee) at a rate of something well in excess of 1,000:1. There was one memorable occasion during my second visit to Vung Tau when I managed to firstly exchange MPC currency into local currency at a really good rate, as well as trade about 6 cartons (24 boxes of matches per carton) of Australian waterproof 'Greenlight' matches with a US Army soldier for a very large sum of $US. I quickly followed this up with a highly illegal exchange in one of the bars of those $US into local currency. I made a massive profit in each transaction which totally funded — with plenty of change left over — my alcohol and carnal expenses during that period of my R&C.

I'm sure that my lovely mother had no idea why I was endlessly asking her to send me cartons of Greenlight matches! The almost fanatical attraction of these particular matches to US Army servicemen was that they were water resistant — not waterproof — and came packed individually in small boxes, unlike the low-grade tear-off strip matches only available to them.

And, after my first R&C in Vung Tau, my mother, at my request, would also regularly send me bars of scented soap. I would later selectively gift the soap to bar girls in Vung Tau and much more often, to attractive female villagers I came across from time to time. Frankly, the reaction from any recipient of this largesse was simply amazing. There's no way I can properly describe their obvious joy and happiness. It might just say something about the abject poverty of their life at that time. And more to the point I guess, it made me feel really good about myself for a short while.

The exchange rate of MPC and $US into notional $A was around 1.00:1.23. Expressed in another way, it cost $A0.81 to buy $US1.00. We were being paid in MPC currency and at that very beneficial exchange rate, we were doing rather nicely, thank you very much. In fact, we were literally drowning in cash! Strangely, US Army soldiers seemed to be very poorly paid compared to us, and by a substantial margin. And didn't the bar girls and bar managers know it! Too right, they did.

Illegally trading in $US was a much more serious offence than trading in MPC currency. However, the prospect of obtaining hard currency in the form of $US was like an intoxicating drug to the local Vietnamese, and the massive profits to be made by allied soldiers, like myself, significantly outweighed the risk of being caught. However, we exercised a great deal of caution when negotiating these highly illegal financial transaction trades. Not only did we have to keep our eyes peeled for any allied military police, but we also had to make sure that the various Vietnamese currency dealers — with whom we were trading — didn't rip us off either.

I always observed my strict rules of not undertaking a currency exchange if I was seriously drunk, and I always counted the local currency before handing over any $US or MPC currency. And…I simply never accepted notes that had been folded in half. While all the bar proprietors and bar girls smiled warmly as they eagerly supplied us with alcoholic drinks, followed by even more of the same, their main focus was to extract as much cash out of us as possible.

In Vung Tau there was a street which, colloquially, was known as the 'street of a thousand bars'. While that nomenclature is quite obviously a gross exaggeration, its broad description is completely accurate in terms of how allied soldiers in Vietnam perceived Vung Tau to be. Did we like Vung Tau? Yes, we certainly did!

DOWNTOWN

Compared to the numerous small towns, villages, and hamlets we came across during our operational activity, Vung Tau was by far the largest urban centre. Unlike most other civilian focal points of the province, Vung Tau was a regional metropolis of sorts, with its inhabitants desperate to make money and otherwise survive. Back in 1970, while Vung Tau was an exciting and vibrant place to be, it was also extremely dangerous: a very primitive city in a very third world country. The availability of electricity was patchy, the provision of potable water was unreliable, and basic services such as sewage were often non-existent. We never drank water that wasn't from an imported, bottled source. When it rained, which was most of the time when I was there, the gutters of the city streets became wide, fast-running torrents.

The general height of the footpath gutters was 250mm or maybe even higher. Many inhabitants — both male and female — openly urinated and

Chapter 24 — Vung Tau

defecated in the streets. Did any of this ever concern most of us? Not for one minute. All we really cared about was getting drunk and getting laid.

My best researched guess is that the population of Vung Tau back in 1970 was something in the order of 35,000. It certainly would have been no more than that. Nevertheless, it was a densely populated, bustling, and busy place. While the commercial business district of Vung Tau was tightly contained, it's associated overpopulated and relatively primitive residential and light industrial areas extended well beyond the business and commercial precinct.

Vung Tau was, at one time, a major commercial shipping port and it had also once boasted an extensive fishing industry. However, during the Vietnam conflict, its large and very deep harbour was used almost extensively by the US Army and Australian military forces. It was long recognised that if allied military forces ever needed to exit southern Vietnam quickly and easily, then Vung Tau harbour provided one of those escape routes.

During the Vietnam War many counties other than the USA, Australia, and New Zealand, provided support to the government of South Vietnam. In Vung Tau a monument was erected by the South Vietnamese Government to recognise the collective support of these many countries. This monument, reflected in the image shown below, was called 'The Flags' for obvious reasons, and it was a common meeting point for allied forces soldiers.

'The Flags' at Vung Tau.

While not all of these countries participated militarily as an ally of the South Vietnamese Government during this conflict, a surprising number did. The following mortality data is very enlightening:

Table 9.

ALLIED FORCES FATALITIES IN VIETNAM

Country	Fatalities
USA	58,315
South Korea	5,099
Australia	521
Thailand	351
New Zealand	37
Taiwan	25
Phillipines	9

I find it extraordinary that 5,099 South Koreans and 351 Thais died in combat in Vietnam. In all of the post conflict public debate surrounding the Vietnam War, those numbers are never mentioned. While I was broadly aware of the South Korean commitment to the allied forces war effort in Vietnam — Corps Tactical Zone 1 — just south of the DMZ, I never knew that it was so intense. As for the Thai involvement, I now feel very ashamed about the universal lack of recognition for their veterans as well. I make this same observation about the veterans of all those other countries whose soldiers also served and did their very best in Vietnam.

During more than 6 decades of occupation in Vietnam — which ceased shortly after the catastrophic defeat of its military forces by the Viet Minh at the Battle of Dien Bien Phu in 1954 — the French imposed many aspects of its culture on larger regional centres such as Vung Tau and indeed in smaller residential hubs as well. As a result, many of the larger buildings in Vung Tau had strong overtones of 1950's European architecture.

Vung Tau – Downtown.

Chapter 24 — Vung Tau

Vung Tau – Downtown. *Note the very high gutters.*

Vung Tau – Downtown.

Vung Tau – Downtown.

Being an Asian city, it was surprising to discover fresh, crispy bread rolls, freely available early each morning and throughout the day. The Vietnamese had obviously been taught how to bake bread by the French, and handed this skill down to subsequent generations. That's probably why so many of the small, independent, family-owned bakeries that operate in Australia today are run by people of Vietnamese heritage.

Communication was always the most difficult problem that Allied soldiers had to somehow try and overcome when interacting with local people. Understandably, most Vietnamese people didn't understand or speak more than a handful of English words. Similarly, very few of us had made any effort whatsoever to learn the Vietnamese language, other than expertly mastering several highly insulting phrases and a few words with explicit sexual connotations.

Many of the Vung Tau residents spoke passable French, so anyone who'd studied that language at school had some advantage over the rest of us. Several of my platoon mates spoke a very poor version of French. In other words, they weren't fluent at all, but understood enough of it — or at least pretended they did — to make them useful, savvy guys to be around when frequenting the bars of Vung Tau. My reasonable proficiency in very basic Latin didn't 'cut the

Chapter 24 — Vung Tau

mustard' at all in Vung Tau.

Vung Tau wasn't a secure city. It was strongly rumoured that our Viet Cong enemy may have also used the city for a variety of purposes. While our Rules of Engagement provided relative certainty for us when we were out in the field, it was impossible to know who was friendly — or otherwise — in residential settings, particularly in large civilian centres like Vung Tau. Because of this, the local South Vietnamese military and allied commanders jointly put in place a strictly-policed curfew that ran from 10pm each night until 6am the following morning.

Within that curfew period, Australian and New Zealand allied forces soldiers had to be back at the Peter Badcoe Club at 1 ALSG (elsewhere for US Army soldiers) or suitably ensconced for the night in the company of one or more of the local bar girls. Any allied forces soldier wandering around the streets of Vung Tau during this curfew period ran the very real risk of being shot and killed by the vicious local police known as the 'White Mice' — due to the distinctive colour of their uniform.

These White Mice police were utterly ruthless and we did our best to avoid them. I only had one run-in with them, and it was nothing short of frightening. Fortunately, as my 2 platoon mates and I (on that occasion) were not in possession of any marijuana — cannabis — or any other drug, it was all sorted fairly quickly. However, having a loaded and cocked pistol held to my head isn't something I ever want to relive. Strangely, these White Mice police were supposedly the good guys. In my considered view, they were nothing more than brutal, opportunistic thugs.

Downtown Vung Tau was a seething mass of abject poverty and surging activity. Most of the business and residential precincts absolutely stank. The putrid smell of rotting food market slops, and overburdened open sewage drains and gutters, permeated everywhere. Droves of young street urchins hunted in packs. Their only focus seemed to be on trying to steal wrist watches and wallets from, or otherwise ripping off, unsuspecting allied soldiers who were seemingly regarded by nearly all of the locals as 'fair game'.

Many of the open food markets were astonishing in terms of the variety of fresh produce and other food types being sold, amid the relative filth in which these commercial activities seemed to take place. As unhygienic as they appeared to me, the locals were avid customers, so I guess there couldn't have been too many issues regarding the safety of the food being sold or traded. I did observe that bartering was a favourite pastime of market customers and proprietors.

Street cart vendors sold wonderful pork and salad crispy bread rolls, affectionately known by us as 'heppo' rolls — the notion being that anyone eating them could contract hepatitis, given the total lack of refrigeration or hygiene standards of their mobile food carts. While most of my mates avoided these delicious rolls, I ate plenty of them…and never ended up contracting hepatitis or any gastric affliction. I was probably pretty lucky. The crispy bread rolls being sold to allied forces soldiers back in those times were almost identical to the 'Saigon' bread rolls sold today in wider Australia, by the many Vietnamese bread and pastry vendors.

Vung Tau Market.

Vung Tau Market.

Chapter 24 – Vung Tau

Vung Tau Market.

Vung Tau – Street food vendor preparing a 'heppo' roll.
Note the lack of any refrigeration.

Vung Tau – Street food vendor preparing a 'heppo' roll.
Bob Blackmore looking on.

We were advised not to roam around the city alone — certainly not at night — and to remain within the main commercial areas as much as possible. We were also told to keep a watchful eye out for each other, especially when we were drinking alcohol. Our final piece of advice was that if we sought an overnight sexual liaison, to try and negotiate arrangements with bar girls who lived together. That way, we'd always have a mate to back us up if things ever turned nasty.

As interesting and as culturally different as Vietnam was, compared to Australia, our main reason for visiting downtown Vung Tau was to drink massive amounts of alcohol and to have as much sex as possible from the smorgasbord of completely uninhibited young — and even somewhat older — women who were freely available at relatively low cost.

US ARMY SOLDIERS

During my time in Vietnam, the Assault Pioneer Platoon never operated militarily in close conjunction with US Army soldiers. I don't remember any operational US Army unit in or near Phuoc Tuy Province, other than the 1st Infantry Division — the 'Big Red One' — which was based at the large US Army base Black Horse, in Long Khanh Province, directly abutting the northern

Phuoc Tuy Province border. However, at certain times, other platoons of the battalion did operate interactively with elements of this US Army infantry division, particularly as it degraded its Black Horse presence over time, exiting Vietnam through the port city of Vung Tau.

There were always large numbers of US Army soldiers in Vung Tau at the same time as Australian and New Zealand soldiers. They frequented Vung Tau for the same reasons we did, and naturally enough, we came across quite a few of them. My recollections of them as a class of people are 'kind'. Many of them were African-American and seemed to be very young indeed. Large numbers of their non-commissioned officer and other ranks men were only 19 or 20 years of age.

I generally found US Army soldiers to be quiet, unpretentious, and not out to make trouble for anyone, least of all themselves. While we were required to wear civilian clothing when in Vung Tau, the US Army soldiers always remained in uniform. I guess that may have tempered their public behaviour somewhat.

Allied forces soldiers of common language countries always tend to gravitate towards each other, and we were certainly no different. We were curious about them, as they were about us. During idle chat over numerous beers or Bacardi rums and Coke, we soon learned that their preparation and training prior to arriving in Vietnam was totally different and vastly inferior to ours. While a lot of their training was based around physical fitness and weapons proficiency, it wasn't too operationally focused. So, while they may have been supremely fit, as were we, I believe that they were far less prepared for the rigours of Vietnam in terms of being able to confront a well-trained, determined, and very vicious enemy.

It was common to find US Army soldiers in Vietnam who'd only been in the military for 4 or 5 months. What sort of operational training could they have possibly received in that brief period of time? Not a lot I'd suggest. And they were already wearing ribbons for this, and badges for that...it seemed to me that you could probably receive a decoration for almost anything in the US Army.

We were never able to become friends or mates with our US Army comrades, as Australians tend to do so easily among themselves. There was simply no time for those sorts of relationships to develop, and the almost universal, reserved nature of the US Army soldiers I met, would have made that almost impossible anyway.

So, while my personal interactions with US Army soldiers weren't of a combat nature, I have to say that the way they're often so poorly portrayed in movies — as loud-mouthed, 'gung-ho', high risk soldiers — isn't something to which I can subscribe. To me, they seemed to be decent human beings who just like us, were doing their duty and trying to survive in a shitty country. My overall memories of US Army soldiers in Vung Tau are very positive.

However, while I can't be certain about this, I did form the vague view that they thought Australians were totally crazy — something akin to the more radical elements of the French Foreign Legion.

DRINKING - ALCOHOL

As mentioned, one of our 2 main pastimes when loitering in downtown Vung Tau was drinking as much alcohol as possible within the many bars that festooned the city. Most of these bars were relatively small with quite elongated and very narrow shopfront entrances.

For example, upon entering a typical bar, there would be a long pedestrian corridor running sort of centrally along its entire forward vertical length. On one side of the corridor there would be small tables abutting the wall, with as many chairs as possible crammed into that space. On the other side of the corridor there was much wider seating in blocks for perhaps 6 of us, sitting side by side and across from one another.

Towards the back of the wider side of the corridor there was always a large, well-stocked, refrigerated bar — ice or power — I don't remember which. At the end of this corridor and beyond the bar there were toilets of doubtful hygienic quality, usually just foot stalls — a hole in the floor and a tub of water and ladle close by. Talk about a balancing act whenever you needed it for some serious toileting. As far as I could tell, there was no reliable sewage sanitation system of any sort in Vung Tau. No wonder the place absolutely stank. And thank God it rained a lot in Vietnam!

One bar in Vung Tau achieved notoriety among allied forces soldiers, and increased patronage, because its owner installed a western-style seated, porcelain toilet. That was all very well and good, however you still had to use the water ladle after you finished your business. There was no flushing system in place. And because it was far more comfortable in comparison to the usual 'starting blocks' toilets, some of us — when really drunk — often fell asleep 'on the throne'. I can personally tell you that being roughly woken from that slumber by a very angry female (always) bar person wasn't nice. Seriously, if you fell asleep or passed out on their 'shitter' they became really angry.

The main form of alcohol freely available to us in the bars of Vung Tau was beer — US and Vietnamese varieties — and a wide range of mixed spirit drinks. Although still extremely cheap, alcohol in Vung Tau was relatively expensive compared to the price we paid at Nui Dat and the 1 ALSG Peter Badcoe Club. The most common spirit consumed in Vung Tau was Bacardi rum and Coke. I drank a lot of it. Away from Nui Dat it was always my preferred alcoholic drink because of its lower overall volume and relatively high alcohol content.

So, on a 40-hour R&C break in Vung Tau, we'd arrive by truck at 1 ALSG around mid-morning and be seated in a downtown bar, getting well and truly stuck into the alcohol by around noon. For many of us, our drinking continued unabated until we left 1 ALSG for Nui Dat, some 2 days later. It's amazing how much alcohol a man can consume in a 40-hour binge if he tries really hard. And believe me, many of us tried very, very hard!

Naturally, this excessive drinking sometimes resulted in arguments, punch-ups and other unseemly behaviour. As a general rule, the bar proprietors put up with our poor behaviour because we were, after all, well-heeled, cash paying customers. Occasionally, when things got too out of hand, the proprietors seemed to have a magical way of quickly summoning Australian or New Zealand military police who, once they arrived on the scene, sorted us out in no time. The military police were usually only 'called on' to help the locals when a bar was getting trashed — furniture and fittings being destroyed. This wasn't a common occurrence.

However, on one occasion I observed Australian and New Zealand military police at their worst, bludgeoning drunken troublemakers into senselessness before dragging them away under arrest. While I recognise the need for military police in all service arms, their almost universal enthusiasm for a very physical approach in resolving situations involving alcohol, troubled me. I didn't think too much of the army military police.

The military police and my very good mate Mick O'Shea, most certainly weren't friends. One time in Vung Tau Mick had his head bashed-in by one of them. As he was eventually dragged away — almost senseless — from a semi-trashed bar, there was a substantial amount of military police collateral damage all over the place. Mick was a tough sort of guy and he was always in your face, causing grief. But he was our mate, my mate, and we all loved him.

I can't recall what happened to Mick after his excellent display of bar room fighting on that occasion, but I'm led to believe that unless you actually killed or seriously injured someone, or the bar owner made a formal complaint, an overnight sleep in the cells at 1 ALSG was the usual outcome. Because of the physical beating that the military police gave Mick on that occasion, I'm sure they weren't too keen to make an issue of it by charging him with an offence. But I don't really know. Mick passed away many years ago, so I can't seek clarification on this anyway.

GIRLS AND SEX

It seemed to me that downtown Vung Tau was inundated with many hundreds of girls touting their bodies for a price. Before leaving Nui Dat around mid-

January 1970 for our first 40-hour R&C break, the Assault Pioneer Platoon was paraded before Captain Richard Green, the battalion's Medical Officer. Capt. Green's short, stern oral presentation, centred on his view of the apparent endemic extent of social diseases rife among the bar girls of Vung Tau. He advised measures that we should take to avoid contracting any, or all of these horrible afflictions.

His advice was basically to either abstain from sex altogether — not really an option that most of us even remotely considered — or use the condoms made freely available to us by the army. Even to this day, I can't forget the closing remarks of his highly entertaining presentation to us. His final words were something like:

'If you do go with these disease-ridden women, put two condoms on your penis and one over your head, and — you will still catch the jack!'

I liked Capt. Green a hell of a lot.

Vung Tau - My Favourite Bar.

The bars where we gathered to drink were also thinly disguised shopfronts for sex workers ostensibly employed by the proprietors as 'bar girl' companions. Their key role was to try and extract as much cash out of us as possible by urging us to purchase overpriced alcohol, and to buy them small glasses of non-alcoholic Saigon Tea — also at exorbitant prices — for their companionship

Chapter 24 – Vung Tau

and 'conversation', before transacting any business of a sexual nature. Saigon Tea was touted as whisky-based, but in reality, it was nothing more than lightly coloured water.

Almost universally throughout Vung Tau, and in many other parts of South Vietnam, Australians were referred to by the locals as Uc-Dai-Loi — pronounced '*ook-day-loy*' — which loosely translated to mean 'great continent' or 'big rat' (kangaroo), depending on who you want to believe. If the bar girls liked you, then you were Uc-Dai-Loi No.1, as opposed to being Uc-Dai-Loi No.10, if they didn't. If you were buying them a lot of Saigon Tea drinks and paying for plenty of sex, then you were always Uc-Dai-Loi No.1. More likely 'No.1 cash cow'.

The pressure they applied to extract cash from us was simply enormous. And if they sensed that someone was a tight-arse and simply wasting their time, they would gather around the culprit in a group and sing the 'Cheap Charlie' (Char-lee) song — in very poor enunciated English — the words of which are set out in Appendix 8.

Bar girls were highly skilled in playing the common chance games of 'Noughts and Crosses' — otherwise known as 'Tic-tac-toe' — and 'Gin-rummy'. Playing these simple games might seem innocuous enough, but after alcohol has dulled one's senses, any lapse in concentration was costly. Each game was played for very high stakes. Bar girls stood to win a costly Saigon Tea. On the other hand, if we won a game, our negotiated and agreed prize was almost always something of a sexual nature.

On most occasions we lost these wagers and ended up being fleeced out of a lot of money. While alcohol was without any doubt the main reason for this, the bar girls always had an unfair advantage that we never seemed to catch onto. If we did, we were probably too drunk to care. When playing 'Gin-rummy', the bar girls used to make sure that we were seated with our backs to the narrow traffic corridor. Their girlfriends would casually walk by and tell them, in Vietnamese, what cards we were holding. They were cheating all the time. As for 'Noughts and Crosses', it's only the person who goes first that has any chance of winning a game. If you play second, you can always avoid losing — in other words, drawing — a game, if you concentrate. Most early games in a typical 'Tic-tac-toe' session ended as draws. However, the bar girls simply played game after game with us, waiting for our lapses in concentration, which naturally became more frequent the longer we played and the more alcohol we drank.

The bar girls made a financial killing out of us. But to be fair to them, on those occasions when they lost a wager, they mostly honoured their side of the agreement. I know this is pretty gross telling, but that's exactly how it was back then.

Many of the Vung Tau bar girls that I encountered were widows of South Vietnamese soldiers. Others were opportunistic young women chasing some very easy money. As far as I could ascertain, once Vietnamese women married, their extended families no longer provided financial support, even if it was possible for them to do so. And after their husbands were killed in action there was no government social security safety net for them to fall back on. In fact, there was no financial support available to them whatsoever. So, given the times, selling their bodies for sex was a popular, highly profitable, and in many cases, necessary profession for the many widows of this very nasty war.

For each R&C break we only had about 40-hours to drink and sexually extend ourselves to exhaustion. Most of us — including me — accomplished that without even trying. During each of the 3 short periods of time I spent in Vung Tau, I behaved appallingly — just like many Australian soldiers — in trying to unwind and relax after lengthy periods of unrelenting, exhausting and dangerous operational activity. But, being honest with myself, my behaviour back in those times was sometimes really ordinary. On reflection, it's a part of my life that I'm not at all proud of.

Over the aggregated period of 6 days and nights I spent in Vung Tau, there was only one occasion when I returned to sleep at 1 ALSG...and that was only because I ran out of money — another story I'll reveal later. Every other night, I was ensconced with a more than enthusiastic bar girl. And during the day-time, it was usual for us to transact any number of short-time sexual encounters. It was common for a mate to say to his drinking comrades:

'I'm just going upstairs with this girl. I'll be back in 15 minutes.'

We thought the price for these personal services was exorbitantly high at $US10 ($A8.00) for oral or short-time sex. An overnight arrangement usually cost around $A16. In reality, given our funding largesse compared to that of US Army soldiers, it was extraordinarily cheap. In 2023 prices, an all-night arrangement cost around $A125.

We didn't care about the price anyway and quite happily paid whatever the going rate was asked for these sexual interactions — which was sometimes as high as $A24, depending on how classy the girl was, and how drunk we were. The bar girls of Vung Tau were quick to take advantage of a drunken man, but at the same time, provided a debauched sexual smorgasbord that most of us eagerly devoured.

One of the bar girls I gravitated to, on 2 separate occasions, was a very attractive, but not particularly beautiful woman named Minh. However, she was stunning in so many other ways: short, slightly curly — unusual for a Vietnamese woman — very shiny black hair; anorexically thin; and amazingly friendly. She never stopped smiling, laughing, or trying to communicate and interact with me. Over our long hours together on those 2 separate occasions, initially at the Binh Minh Bar and then later back at her apartment — a small, rudimentary, minuscule, second level bed-sit type room with communal public toileting facilities — holes in the ground with no privacy whatsoever on the central ground level enclosed quadrangle — Minh was somehow able to convey to me that she was a 28-year-old widow with 2 children, who were being cared for by a girlfriend whilst she spent time with me.

I don't pretend for one moment that Minh actually enjoyed having sex with me. After all, for her it was nothing more than a business arrangement and I fully realised that. However, I do know that I liked her a lot and intuitively knew that she was entirely relaxed with me. During our 2 nights together, months apart, and even though we couldn't really communicate, we shared lots of laughs. I'm sure she formed the view that I was a decent sort of guy. In other words, I was going to pay her our agreed fee and probably more — not beat her up, rob her, or subject her to any deviant sexual practices. From my point of view, she was a delightful person of the opposite sex with whom I was, for 2 nights only, able to relax and somewhat forget about the real reason that I was in Vietnam.

What I particularly liked about this lovely woman was the way she looked after me. During those nights she made sure that I was relaxed and provided me with some of her wonderful home-cooked meals, which I very generously paid for. Her apartment — owned, rented, or loaned — was a complete, minuscule slum, by even the worst Australian standards of the 1970's. Nevertheless, it was Minh's castle for those 2 nights and I completely respected that. I have never ever forgotten her...and nor should I. All these years later, I'm pleased that on both of those sexual interludes I paid her far more than I was obliged to.

On another occasion, I spent a night with a woman who turned out to be very interesting. All she wanted to do was have sex. I know this is every young man's dream...but for a sex worker, very strange! Anyway, being with a girl whose sexual drive was that strong, was terrific — up to a point. That night I didn't get much sleep, but even worse, early the next morning — it had now become a nightmare for me — she was into it again.

This bar girl was very different for a number of reasons. She wasn't a typical Vietnamese woman stereotype. She was unusually tall and not anorexically slim. Racially, she appeared to be more Chinese than Vietnamese. Her facial features strongly suggested that. Although she wasn't fluent by any measure, she understood more than a few words of English, along with a smattering of basic grammatical rules. I thought this was nothing short of sensational and probably the only reason why I decided to spend this night with her.

Apart from my inability to match her exceedingly high sexual appetite, I had a wonderful time with her. We sort of chatted for hours. I think she more or less understood what I was saying and to a limited extent, she conveyed her thoughts and responses to me. I recall us having a lot of laughs together. Seriously, being able to — sort of — communicate with someone of the opposite sex in Vietnam, was almost like winning the lottery!

Next morning, there was a young boy — around 2-years-of-age — in bed with us! I don't recall ever seeing him during the night and I have no idea where he came from. He just appeared. This child had dark brown hair, blue eyes, and very moderated Asian facial features. Clearly, this boy — her son, obviously — had either a white American, Australian, or New Zealand father. After she provided me with a basic fish broth and rice breakfast, I had great difficulty leaving her. She seemed almost desperate and pleaded with me to stay.

When I tried to pay her for our business arrangement she got very angry, refused to take the money, and started crying. Talk about being in a tricky situation. In the end I insisted that she accept the 'very' generous amount of money I proffered, and left her with tears in her eyes. She was sobbing and wailing uncontrollably. I've never forgotten that.

I think I realised that this woman was troubled and possibly traumatised about what may eventually become of her — probably a mixed-race woman herself — and her mixed-race son. It was apparent to me that she was looking for any opportunity to cement a dependent relationship with an allied forces soldier. There were numerous instances of Australian soldiers marrying Vietnamese women, and then being locked into legally enforceable long-term financial obligation arrangements. Back in those days, I may well have been addicted to alcohol and sex, but I wasn't that stupid!

War is a very nasty business and always results in civilian collateral damage, particularly for women. The future life prospects in Vietnam for this lovely woman and her son were going to be challenging, and I knew that. I just hope that their lives have at least been reasonably happy.

Prostitution and war have always co-existed. Vietnam was no different. Quite apart from my sexual interactions with several of them, my experiences with the bar girls of Vung Tau were exceptionally positive. They never robbed me, or set me up for a mugging by local thugs. The women with whom I formed passing relationships with, were friendly and seemed quite happy — almost enthusiastic — to complete their part of our business arrangements. My memories of those girls, and times, are pleasant ones.

Although this may seem strange, it has always troubled me to think about how the Vietnamese women I associated with, fared after the end of this awful conflict. At 21, while I was young and inexperienced in life, I was still very much aware that the long-term life prospects of these basically decent women weren't good, should South Vietnam ever fall to the North Vietnamese — which it did after the Paris Peace Accords of 27 January 1973 were breached by them in 1975.

It's simply not right to regard them as collateral damage or low-value by-products of a very nasty war. They were, after all, real people with expectations, optimism, dreams, and hopes for their futures. As far as I could tell, most of them were generally not in the sex industry by choice, but rather by necessity. For the most part, they were good women whom I respected. Certainly, these 2 lovely women were in that category.

In the late 1970's, I discovered that after the fall of Saigon — now Ho Chi Minh City — in 1975, many bar girls in areas formerly under the control of South Vietnamese and allied forces — such as Vung Tau — were rounded up by the North Vietnamese as the new Vietnamese Government, and interned for many years in indoctrination camps for education and punishment. I know that many of these women wouldn't have survived under that harsh regime.

NEAR DEATH EXPERIENCE IN VUNG TAU

In Vung Tau one night just before 10pm, with the evening curfew about to be imposed and both of us almost completely out of any currency type, Mick O'Shea and I drunkenly lurched down to the local taxi rank near The Flags feature, to hire a Lambretta taxi to take us a short distance — maybe 1.5km — back to 1 ALSG.

These 3-wheeled Italian-made 550cc scooters were fitted with micro-bus cabin bodies, and we could usually cram 5 or 6 of us into one of them. The taxi drivers were rat cunning, and as they knew that the last 1 ALSG transport vehicle had already departed The Flags that night, O'Shea and I were in deep shit and fair game for extortion.

The fare these guys were asking us to pay for a 5-minute taxi ride was ludicrous. We argued for ages, trying to negotiate a price we were prepared to pay, and more to the point, one that we could actually pay. As I said, we were both pretty much flat broke.

Then, seemingly out of nowhere, 2 ARVN soldiers turned up on Honda motorcycles and gestured for us to mount their vehicles as pillion passengers. ARVN soldiers were our local South Vietnamese allies so, without any hesitation, O'Shea and I jumped on the back of each bike. As we sped off, we energetically gave the assembled throng of Lambretta taxi drivers the well-known Australian 'one finger salute', along with cries of '*Fuck you!*'. O'Shea and I naturally assumed that we were getting a free lift back to 1 ALSG. Well... how wrong were we!

It was a very moonlit night and after a minute or so, I noticed that we were travelling in the wrong direction. I may have been drinking steadily for the last 12 hours, but I wasn't that drunk. Well, perhaps I was...because I could hardly talk or stand upright. Anyway, we were quite clearly heading towards the Vung Tau docks, an area totally prohibited to us at any time of the day or night.

Within a few minutes, our motorcycles came to a halt and the drivers anxiously gestured for us to get off the vehicles, which we reluctantly and very slowly did. That was a bad mistake on our part. As soon as we got off, both bikes sped away, leaving us alone on a wharf at the infamous Vung Tau docks. So, there O'Shea and I were, by ourselves, unarmed and totally defenceless. As drunk as we both were, we knew that we were in a very dangerous place. We had no idea what to do next.

After a few minutes, I noticed — quite remarkable given my alcohol-induced blurred vision — a number of adult males slowly emerging from the shadows of the almost derelict sheds near us. From their appearance, these guys were either local thugs or perhaps even enemy soldiers in civilian clothing. I had no idea who they were. Anyway, they were obviously bad guys, as they were carrying chains and steel rods, and several of them were armed with machetes. On a minor positive note, I didn't observe that they were carrying any more lethal military weapons.

Through slurred communication, O'Shea and I drunkenly agreed that things looked very grim for us. So we decided that if we were to be killed by these thugs, we'd at least go down fighting — not that it was going to be much of a fight anyway, given our grossly drunken condition. Anyway, having made this decision, we assumed the classic back-to-back defensive position and waited to be assaulted by these thugs, killed, and then disposed of in the Vung Tau harbour.

I'm led to believe that God sometimes works in mysterious ways. In saying that, I must declare...even after my many years of solid Catholic-based Christian upbringing, I'm an avowed atheist. I don't believe in any God, or the afterlife. However, if there were to be a God, then he surely worked His miracle for O'Shea and I at this very precarious time.

All of a sudden, a dozen or so motorcycles — also ridden by ARVN soldiers — appeared on the wharf near us. These guys were quite heavily armed — 9mm pistols and a number of M16 Armalite rifles — and anxiously insistent that we mount the pillion seats behind 2 of them. We needed no encouragement to do so. Within a few minutes O'Shea and I were dropped off at 1 ALSG, where we both expected to be well and truly in the shit for breaking curfew — and charged accordingly.

I don't think the guard detachment at the front gate believed our story. I mean, how could they? We were so drunk, and on top of that, we both managed to give our ARVN saviours the Australian 'one finger salute', along with cries

Chapter 24 – Vung Tau

of '*Fuck you!*' as they drove off…and they were supposedly the good-guys!

Why we weren't charged for breaking curfew that night, I'll never know. However, I do know this. O'Shea and I were extremely lucky to be alive. Right then and there, we resolved to be inseparable mates, and from that moment on we really were like brothers. We were already good friends anyway, but this ugly event just cemented our mateship into an indelibly bonded one.

Over the many decades since this incident, I've often tried to understand why O'Shea and I were placed in this potentially fatal predicament by supposedly friendly allied forces soldiers. And why were our lives likely saved by soldiers from the same allied forces cohort, some few minutes later? There are no reasonable explanations that I can conclude. Even after all these years, I battle to come to terms with what nearly happened to both of us that night.

As was usually the case with young men of those times, O'Shea and I lost contact with each other after returning to Australia. I was greatly saddened to discover many years later that he passed away in 1975 in tragic circumstances in Kalgoorlie, Western Australia, at the youthful age of 27. In 2005, his widow Lynley, amazingly established contact with me and we stayed in touch for a time. She's a wonderful lady and we both honour his fine memory. He was a good soldier and — while more often than not, a complete pain in the arse — he was a wonderful mate. I've not forgotten him.

CHAPTER 25

BEHAVING BADLY

During our time in Vietnam, one of the prescripts that 8 RAR soldiers were supposed to observe and nurture, was that of a so-called 'hearts and minds' tactic. This formed part of a wider overall 1 ATF pacification strategy.

I guess the rationale behind this officially promulgated initiative was that if we could win-over the hearts and minds of the local populace, they'd be less likely to support enemy insurgents within Phuoc Tuy Province. Theoretically, this would in turn provide far more beneficial outcomes for 8 RAR military operations. It was an admirable policy but, as far as I can now recall, no one in my platoon — at the base operational level of private — ever took much notice of it.

Even before our arrival in Vietnam, enemy soldiers, civilians, and even allied South Vietnamese soldiers, were routinely referred to by us as 'Nogs', 'Slopes', 'Slope-heads', 'Gooks', 'Charlie', 'Victor Charlie', 'VC', 'Nigel', 'Nancy', etc. None of these personal descriptors were respectful of our enemy, the general Vietnamese race, or our South Vietnamese military allies. Did we care? Not for one moment. As far as we were concerned the life status of the collective Vietnamese race was something lower than that of shark shit.

During the cordon and search of several large towns or villages, our behaviour was occasionally quite appalling. While it's impossible to accurately describe this sort of inappropriate behaviour, it usually manifested itself in total lack of respect and privacy for the inhabitants — women in particular — and in some rare cases, disregard for property value and ownership.

Whenever we were out in the field and close to inhabited or commercial areas, we'd occasionally come across civilians. Mostly, these civilians were females and young children. As I mentioned earlier, generally we just ignored them. Sometimes we threw them almost inedible scraps of food from our meagre rations. We also found it amusing to toss them a can of food that we knew they wouldn't be able to open, or food that was probably close to rancid. They begged us to open the cans for them. Did we ever oblige? Only sometimes. On the other hand, we used to routinely hand out cigarettes and chewing gum to the young kids, and scented bars of soap to the females. Our generally unpredictable and quite erratic behaviour must have been very disconcerting for them. On our part, it was pretty disgusting.

Chapter 25 — Behaving Badly

One afternoon, as we were slowly moving through the very northern and non-commercial reaches of the Binh Ba rubber plantation, a young boy of around 13-years-of-age and a girl — whose age I guesstimate to be around 9 or 10 — emerged from seemingly nowhere. So much for our operational security! Between them, these very young and clearly malnourished children were dragging — on some sort of wheeled trolley — 2 large and seemingly heavy polythene containers — similar in many respects to a large 1960's Australian esky — packed with residual ice and numerous small 10oz (300ml) bottles of Coke soft drink. We couldn't believe it! Where did they come from? And given the appalling heat and humidity that particular day, how had the ice stayed frozen?

Their aim that afternoon was to transact business at the rate of something like $A0.05 for each small bottle of soft drink. Many of us were prepared to pay this bargain price and the majority of platoon members purchased 2 bottles each. As we consumed these treats, the children's hands were continually stretched out, trying to get the bottles back from us, even before we had finished drinking the contents.

I noticed that the bottles had embossed French markings on them, and it soon dawned on me that they were extremely valuable. With the demise of the French in Vietnam in 1954, the technology and the wherewithal to manufacture replacement bottles would have simply disappeared from the country. To the Vietnamese people, these empty Coke bottles were just as valuable as $US... or perhaps even gold!

In one of my more insane moments in Vietnam, whilst we were avidly drinking these refreshments, I urged all those near to me — maybe 6 or 7 of us — to slam down the contents and then smash the bottles, rather than return them to the children. Some of us, including myself, did exactly that. The reaction of these 2 kids was instantaneous. They were completely and utterly devastated. It seemed to me that in their minds we'd totally destroyed the economic lives of their parents. Both children burst into tears and ran away, leaving the trolley and near empty containers behind.

At that time, we all laughed and thought it was ridiculously funny. I think I laughed more than most. However, reflecting on it many years later, I realised what we'd actually done on that revolting hot and steamy afternoon. I have to say that this atrocious act — which I personally instigated — continues to haunt me to this day. As a mature adult, I simply cannot understand how we could possibly have done what we did to those young children. Of my occasional recurring dreams surrounding this time in Vietnam, my abysmal behaviour that day is a constant regret.

Towards the end our time in this country, again in a non-commercial rubber plantation late one afternoon, a young boy and his sister — presumably

— confronted us. The boy, who was probably no older than 14, was very keen to transact a sexual business arrangement with his sister. She looked to be no more than about 10 or 11, if that. As we were brewing-up for coffee and a cigarette, I noticed that one member of our platoon showed great interest in further exploring this proffered sexual transaction. I never observed any inappropriate relations or any later signs to suggest that this may have occurred, but I've always had my suspicions…both then, and now. Had I observed this platoon member doing anything untoward to that young girl, I know that while I probably wouldn't have shot him, he would have solidly received the butt of my SLR rifle to his face, much more than several times over. And I sincerely mean that! This particular platoon member and I were never all that friendly and when I later confronted him about this particular matter, he very aggressively told me to:

'Fuck off and always watch your back!'

For the rest of my time in Vietnam, as far as I was reasonably able to do so, I made sure that this man and I were never alone. I wasn't too concerned about him when out in the field, but Nui Dat was always going to be the most likely problem venue for me. Anyway, nothing ever came of it, so perhaps I imagined a potentially adverse personal event coming my way. For those of you who think I may be grossly and quite wrongly maligning an innocent platoon member, my answer to both of these propositions is no…I'm certainly not!

Vietnam was an utterly awful country back in 1970 and after seemingly endless months of operational deployment there, many 1 ATF soldiers were not of sound mine. I include many in my platoon — along with myself — in that large cohort.

During those 3 R&C breaks in Vung Tau — collectively 6 days and nights — my behaviour was often quite appalling. Most of us drank ourselves into an extended alcoholic-induced stupor on each of these 40-hour withdrawals from hostile operations. At times, we physically fought amongst ourselves and occasionally with US Army soldiers. And, in a few instances during these fleeting periods of time, some of us had little or no regard for property, ownership of commercial enterprises, or for the personal well-being of Vung Tau residents.

While many of us eagerly befriended the bar girls, some of us occasionally treated these women pretty badly. To put it mildly we had in some respects, almost become feral animals. While I always respected the bar girls whom I interacted with, there was one shameful incident — quite late in my time in Vietnam — when I behaved extraordinarily badly towards 2 of these sex-workers. I vividly recall this ugly incident and I still can't explain how I was

Chapter 25 — Behaving Badly

able to do what I did that day.

Late one afternoon, I was running out of funds and it just wasn't feasible to go back to the 1 ALSG pay office, withdraw more funds from my paybook account, and return to Vung Tau. I also knew that the paymaster wouldn't be receptive to a drunken soldier rocking up to ask him to open his pay office for a one-off cash withdrawal. So I had a major funding problem.

Another platoon mate was in the same predicament. We decided there was no alternative other than to reluctantly return to the security of the Peter Badcoe Club for the night. Well, that was our initial plan anyway. However, as we rapidly depleted the remainder of our meagre cash holdings on even more alcohol, we began to develop a more sinister scheme.

We figured that by late afternoon, many of the bar girls would have accumulated a fair amount of cash from their numerous day-time sexual encounters. Even though they would have regularly and prudently divested themselves of these cash holdings throughout the day, we reasoned — correctly as it turned out — that they'd be carrying more than enough cash to keep both of us topped-up with alcohol for the remainder of the afternoon and evening. Perhaps there might even be surplus cash to allow us to enter into overnight business arrangements with other bar girls?

So, my platoon mate and I quietly negotiated a foursome arrangement with 2 exceedingly enthusiastic, attractive and — as usual — almost anorexic bar girls, and proceeded upstairs with them to a small private room. Once there, we put our cunning plan into action. While there was no sex involved, we restrained — but didn't physically assault — the 2 women and forcibly garnered all the cash they'd accumulated during the latter part of the day. It wasn't an overly large amount but it certainly solved our immediate funding problem.

We then casually sauntered downstairs whilst the women upstairs screamed like rabid banshees behind us. Once out of the bar, we bolted like a pair of startled gazelles. After a very rapid sprint we ended up at another bar — an awfully long distance away — where we spent out ill-gotten gains on even more alcohol. I don't think we gave a second's thought to our poor victims back in the bar where we had previously enjoyed ourselves for most of the day.

I have to say…besides our reprehensible behaviour on this occasion, what my platoon mate and I did that afternoon in Vung Tau was stupid and extremely risky. We were alone, neither of us spoke a word of Vietnamese, and our understanding of the geography of the Vung Tau CBD was rudimentary at best. The fact that we weren't tracked down by the dreaded South Vietnamese White Mice Police — thank God that didn't happen — or allied forces military police, still amazes me.

The particularly nasty act of robbing those bar girls was extremely out of character for me, and I must admit that it was yet another low point of my time in Vietnam. Even now, I occasionally think about what we did to those 2 unsuspecting young women and wonder how they fared later in life. Yes, they were sex workers...but first and foremost, they were human beings. We certainly didn't treat them with the same respect that one should afford all women, totally irrespective of their line of work. If I could reverse that awful moment in my life, I'd do so without any hesitation.

When the build-up of Australia's commitment to its war effort in Vietnam was fully in place, there were 3 infantry battalions operating out of 1 ATF at Nui Dat, at any given time. Each battalion was replaced annually on a staggered basis. 8 RAR was the first infantry battalion not to be replaced. This was the earliest tangible indication that the Australian Government — in concert with its US allies — was rethinking its position on its military commitment to the Vietnam conflict.

As Australian infantry battalions were replaced, their lines — or designated unit areas — within Nui Dat were taken over in their entirety by the new battalion. In our case, as we were the first battalion not going to be replaced by another Australian infantry battalion, we were told that our lines would be taken over by allied South Vietnamese ARVN soldiers — our allies. I have no idea whether this eventuated or not. But at the time, this was what we were led to believe. Our collective view of ARVN soldiers as a dependable, trustworthy, and useful military resource, was pretty much in line with our view of the wider Vietnamese population. We didn't hold them in high regard at all.

So during our last few days at Nui Dat, as we cleaned up our lines and otherwise made ready to leave this awful country, a number of us discussed placing M26 high-explosive fragmentation hand grenades — safety pins removed with the spring-loaded release arming mechanisms only restrained by rubber bands — under the floorboards of our tents. Our rationale for this very enthusiastic and deadly serious debate was that the rubber bands would rot within a few weeks and the grenades would eventually detonate...hopefully killing or maiming a few ARVN soldiers.

At the end of the day, common sense and wise judgment prevailed and we never put this awful plan into effect. But I have to say, the fact that we enthusiastically spoke at length about it for a time and came remarkably close to actually carrying it out, was a clear indication that our thinking of the time was far from what was expected of normal, functioning individuals. It's just as well we were leaving Vietnam. On the other hand, it was probably just as unfortunate for Australia that we were returning to its orderly communities, underpinned by prescribed behavioural norms.

Did Australian soldiers of previous military conflicts, and Australian soldiers of later military conflicts, behave any differently to us? The answer to that question is an emphatic 'no'! In fact, my military historical research suggests to me that the behaviour of our military cohort was quite restrained compared to that of long-ago deployments.

Nevertheless, all said and done, we'd gradually turned into different versions of ourselves in comparison to who we were when we arrived in Vietnam some 12 months prior: a direct result of what we did as infantry soldiers, the impacts of associated operational stressors, and the conditions under which we lived at Nui Dat and during operational activities. To put it mildly, we didn't give a toss about the South Vietnamese people — military or civilian. To us, they were simply low value and affordable items of collateral attrition.

The strange thing is this. If back in those times we were actually confronted with the inappropriateness of our behaviours, we would have reacted quite indignantly. As far as we were concerned, we were behaving quite normally. But the reality is that our behaviour wasn't 'normal' at all. The true and sad fact is that by the end of our 12 months in Vietnam, we were incapable of recognising behaviour that was uncivilised or otherwise totally inappropriate in the eyes of the Vietnamese people.

In terms of winning the hearts and minds of the local Vietnamese people we were, in my view, abject failures. We never really gave that 1ATF strategy and related 8 RAR tactics any proper consideration whatsoever. Was I one of those hard-core offenders? Yes, I most certainly was.

In our interaction with Vietnamese civilians, we often resorted to their language expletive 'didi mau' — literally meaning 'go away'. This was pretty much the equivalent of 'fuck off!' In Vietnamese society, this was a highly offensive insult and one that we often used without impunity whenever interacting with civilians.

CHAPTER 26

'THE VIETNAM GAME'

A VERY DEEP MUSING BY TERRY LUCAS

As I was accumulating material for this book, I contacted as many former members of my platoon as I could. This wasn't only in order to clarify unclear recollections on my part, but also to capture more accurately the operational sense of our collective infantry experiences in Vietnam and what they meant to each of us, not only as a strongly bonded group of young men, but as individuals as well. Hopefully my story conveys this wide range of recollections that are often impossible to portray in written form.

During the extensive research process, one of my former platoon mates — Terry Lucas — provided me with an immensely powerful metaphoric work that he'd written. With his permission, I've included his work — unedited by me in any way — in my story.

The reason I chose to do so is this. Terry's article is one individual's perspective of his time in Vietnam as an infantry soldier. It may or may not be exactly how I remember my time in Vietnam, though I reckon he has it pretty much correct in the broader sense. His profound and deeply cynical work is so poignant in the way it metaphorically describes what he believes infantry soldiers were exposed to during their time in Vietnam. And, at its very end, he subtly touches on the poor regard that the general Australian community held for its Vietnam veterans in the late 1960's and early 1970's.

'The Vietnam Game'

'... In order to provide you with some understanding of what infantry soldiers experienced in Vietnam, I invite you to use your imagination and play this game — this Vietnam Game.

Firstly, to play this game you have to be young, fit and in the prime of your life. You have to be amongst the best physical specimens in your entire population and you have to be unlucky enough to have been born on a particular date, in a particular month of a particular year. You must be prepared to put aside all of your dreams and aspirations and put at risk everything you have, including your life. Or you may be one of

Chapter 26 – 'The Vietnam Game'

those brave souls that believe you can make a difference in which case you would volunteer to play the game.

This is an outdoor game played by individuals. It can be a team sport but the reliance you must have on your fellow team members is all consuming. When played as a team sport, and it usually is, the individual will lose all self-identity for the benefit of the team.

The setting for this game is a large park which you have never seen before. A park full of trees, bushes, animals, rocks, ponds, creeks, knee deep mud, leeches, mosquitoes, defoliant spray and foul odors of rotting vegetation and animal faeces.

As an individual in this park, you will be left completely on your own. As a team member you will have the company of others, however, you will learn to only speak in whispers or communicate with sign language. You will have no contact with anyone outside the park, except for the occasional letter. Once inside the park there is no escape, no way out and the purpose of the game is this.

You have to stop and then take all their money from any person who visits the park, provided always that the person has blue eyes. You are not to stop or harass anybody with any other colour eyes.

In the park you will find workers, those people who clean and maintain the park for the visitors. You are not to harass the workers either, even if you think they have blue eyes. You should be aware that contact with the workers although inevitable is very dangerous, no matter what colour eyes they have.

In order to play the game, you will be provided with some clothes, a green shirt, green pants and a green hat and a pair of boots. The purpose of this uniform is to allow all blue eyed visitors to recognise you. The blue eyed visitors on the other hand may wear whatever clothing they choose. You will also be provided with a steel bar that weighs 4.5kg. You must carry this bar with you at all times as it is used to frighten, stop, and beat any blue eyed visitor. You will also receive a backpack in which you will carry your tins of food, normally enough to last three weeks. You will also carry in your backpack snares and nets to trap the blue eyed visitors plus all other essential items. Your backpack when loaded will weigh approximately 40kg. You will receive three litres of drinking water and when you have used it you will need to find your own water in the park. None of the food you have been given is ever to be heated before it is eaten.

Each game lasts for twelve months and is broken into twelve three week periods. During the active three week period you must be on the lookout for blue eyed visitors twenty four hours a day, seven days a week. At the end of each three week active period, you will be given time to rest in a safe area. You will use this time to prepare for the next active period. At this time, you may change your clothes for the first time in three weeks, have a shower, sleep on a bed in a tent, be given a fresh supply of tinned food and water. You will also be given a hot meal or two. You are still not allowed to leave the park.

During the three week active period you will be constantly on the move, walking up to 7.0km each day. The reason for this is simple. The blue eyed visitors know you are in the park. They know you want their money and they don't want you to have it. The blue eyed visitors have plans to hurt you and therefore, you must be on the move and be very clever if you are to catch a blue eyed visitor and not be caught yourself.

You must hide in places that no one will ever think to look. You must see everyone who enters the park and most importantly you must learn to recognise the blue eyed visitors a long time before they see you. I know it's hard to tell the colour of peoples' eyes until you are very close to them, but you will learn or you will pay a dreadful price.

The game rules state that if you stop and harass a person who does not have blue eyes that person is allowed to hit you as hard as possible with a baseball bat. The person is also allowed to tell everyone that enters the park that you are there and where you were last seen. This could result in a large group of blue eyed visitors chasing after you and if they catch you they would all be allowed to hit you with a baseball bat.

If you do stop a blue eyed visitor you must make sure to take all his or her money. The blue eyed visitor will not give you the money willingly. Unfortunately for you, you are not a thief at heart. The idea of beating another person with a steel bar is abhorrent to you, but if you don't beat the blue eyed visitor and take the money then you will be beaten with a baseball bat. Not every blue eyed visitor to the park has money. This is unfortunate but true.

If you catch a blue eyed visitor who has no money on the day you must let them go, without hurting them, and you must hope that they don't return later in the day with their friends to beat you for catching them.

The park will become your home. You will learn where to hide, where to get water, where you can rest and where you feel some degree of safety.

Chapter 26 – 'The Vietnam Game'

But remember the workers in the park; they also see the park as their home. They have all worked there for many years. They are friends with the blue eyed visitors and they don't like you. You are an outsider, a thief from another place. The workers may from time to time be friendly toward you, but never trust them. They will tell the blue eyed visitors where you are, because if they don't the blue eyed visitors will beat them with a baseball bat.

There are always many visitors to the park early in the morning and again late in the afternoon. These are the best times to catch a blue eyed visitor or to be caught by a blue eyed visitor. Be careful! Make sure to set your traps only for the blue eyed visitor, because if you catch a brown eyed or green eyed visitor, all your work will be wasted, and you will also receive a beating.

You may not like living in the park. After all, you have to live like one of the animals. You have no bed, no house, no family and very little food and water. You sleep on the ground and it doesn't matter whether it's hot and humid, raining or not. The park is all you know or have known so you make the best of it. There is no escape for you. The visitors may come and go as they please. They are allowed to do anything and everything to avoid you or beat you and whenever they feel like doing so they can leave the park and go home to their families.

After you have survived two or three of these three week active periods you may find that some of your senses and values have changed, particularly if you have taken some beatings and you have not made any money. You must resist the temptation to become less human than you already have. The temptation to catch, beat and rob every visitor to the park will be enormous. You must resist. If you catch beat and rob non blue eyed visitors you will be punished severely by the people who allowed you to enter the park.

As time passes, seven, eight or nine of these three week active periods will have been completed. Your time in the park is almost over. You may start to relax just a little. You may even start to count the money you have been able to steal from the blue eyed visitors but, be warned, this is a dangerous time. You will now be very tired and although you are now more aware and better skilled than at the beginning of the game you have to remember that fresh, well rested, and fit blue eyed visitors are entering the park every day. If you are not ready they will catch and beat you.

Some people who play the Vietnam Game have to leave the park before they finish the twelve three week periods. They have been beaten so often they cannot go on. Others stay for the full time. Unfortunately, all who play this game end up with the same result.

They are branded as thieves. They didn't intend to become thieves; they don't think of themselves as thieves. They simply see themselves as people who went into the park to play the game.

At the end of any game, you have a winner and a loser. At the end of the Vietnam Game, you would expect the person with the most money to be the winner. That is not how this game works.

The innocent and successful players of this game will not be seen as winners but rather as some lower form of life who stole from the blue eyed visitors.

… This is not a very nice game and I don't suggest that anyone should ever play it again…'

Terry Lucas at Nui Dat.

PART 6

RETURNING TO AUSTRALIA

CHAPTER 27

THE VOYAGE HOME

On the early morning of 31 October 1970, the main body of 8 RAR — comprising 459 officers and other ranks — was transported by US Army Chinook helicopters from Nui Dat to HMAS *Sydney*, anchored 1.3km offshore in Vung Tau harbour. The advance party of 65 men flew back to Australia on 5 November, followed by the rear party of 65 men on 11 November.

The total size of the battalion when it departed Vietnam was 158 men less than when it arrived some 12 months earlier. The churn effect of staggered National Service intakes that fed into the battalion over the previous 18 months or so, was the main reason for this. It resulted in large numbers of 8 RAR reinforcement members continuing their deployments to Vietnam with postings to the 2 remaining infantry battalions (2 RAR and 7 RAR) and 1 ALSG elements.

8 RAR was the first Australian infantry battalion deployed to Vietnam that wasn't replaced by another battalion at the conclusion of its deployment. While complete Australian military withdrawal from the Vietnam conflict occurred in 1973, objectively it might be argued that operational withdrawal commenced in late 1970 when 8 RAR returned to Australia. As Bruce Picken states in his wonderful book:

> '... *the first Australian withdrawal from Vietnam occurred on 18 May 1970 with the end of radar operations at Fire Support Base Horseshoe Hill* (the Horseshoe). *The following day, all radars, and sound-ranging sections from 131st Divisional Locating Battery Detachment were closed and withdrawn to Australia in July and October 1970 respectively...*'[44]

The 131st Divisional Locating Battery Detachment RAA — known more colloquially as '131 Div Loc Battery' — provided a real-time mortar radar-locating capability to the Task Force. They were capable of providing the Task Force with map coordinates of the firing positions of enemy mortars within 5 minutes or less, thereby enabling return fire onto those ground coordinates. I have no idea why this valuable resource was withdrawn from operational service well before the complete withdrawal of Australian soldiers from Nui Dat, and its eventual closure in December 1972.

---

[44] Picken, Bruce. *Fire Support Bases, Vietnam*. Big Sky Publishing. 2012. Page 506.

Chapter 27 — The Voyage Home

I remember the Chinook helicopter flight from Nui Dat to HMAS *Sydney*. I think all of us were relieved that we were leaving a country which we'd grown to pathologically hate! None of us said much on this short 20-minute flight, not that conversation would have been easy, given the engine and dual-rotor noise of these large troop and material carriers. Our relief that we were leaving this Godforsaken country alive, would have been clearly reflected in our quiet and sullen demeanours.

There were a number of sailors positioned on the flight deck of *Sydney* to help us disembark and otherwise reacquaint us with our new home for the next 12 days. One of the most startling observations I made at that time — and one that I've never forgotten — was how pale and overweight the sailors looked compared to us. However, they were probably quite normal in a physical sense and not overweight at all. The fact of the matter was that all of us were extremely lean. Many of us were grossly underweight and gaunt-looking and — like myself — almost skeletal in some cases. Our faces were well-tanned and weathered from exposure to the harsh elements. Compared to us, the sailors were perspiring profusely, an indication as to how well we'd adapted to the appalling climate of Vietnam. While we had become inured amongst ourselves as to how we looked and stank, we must have seemed to be a very haggard and ragged sight to the sailors aboard *Sydney*.

Our brief relocation between Nui Dat and the ship, saw us leave a very hostile environment — where we could rarely relax or let down our guard — and finally retreat to the relative safety aboard *Sydney*. After 12 months in Vietnam, we were a physically tired and mentally exhausted group of young men when we disembarked onto the flight deck...and I'm certain that the sailors recognised that. While they were well aware that we'd all been through a very rough time, they weren't exactly sure how we were going to react once we began to unwind on the ship. Those underlying concerns on their part were well founded, as I talk about later.

When *Sydney* departed the harbour later that morning, I recalled those wonderful words from the song 'I Was Born Under a Wand'rin Star' sung by Lee Marvin in the highly popular western movie, 'Paint your Wagon', released in the USA in October 1969.

'... I never seen a sight that didn't look better looking back...'[45]

I'd watched this classic comedy a few weeks earlier at the open-air movie theatre at Nui Dat and those few words in the feature song, well and truly resonated with me.

---

[45] Originally written and scored by Alan Jay Lerner and Frederick Loewe in 1951 for a stage musical of the same name as the movie.

On our return voyage home to Australia, *Sydney* was escorted as far as Singapore by HMAS *Vendetta*, another very heavily-armed Daring Class destroyer like HMAS *Duchess* some 12 months prior. While I was undertaking research for my book, it was interesting to discover that the Captain of the *Vendetta* at that time was Admiral Mike Hudson Ret'd, a man very well known to me. We worked together during the early years of the new millennium as Directors of the Australian Veterans' Children's Assistance Trust (AVCAT) based in Sydney.

Our voyage home was uneventful and although physically relaxing, it was a time of mental and emotional turmoil for many of us. We had far too much free time on our hands to think and dwell over recent dark memories and, more importantly, concerns about our future directions in life after we berthed in Brisbane.

I didn't have a clue whether I even wanted to return to my guaranteed job with the ATO. For a brief time prior to my discharge, I contemplated signing on for further service with the army. I have never shared that fact with anyone, let alone my family. I was very unsettled and I knew it. My platoon mates — many of whom were also National Servicemen — were similarly tormented about their looming re-integration back into society and the civilian workforce. Many of them didn't really have proper jobs to return to, so it must have been very unnerving for them.

The Regular soldiers in my platoon were besieged by a completely different set of worries that I never fully understood. From talking with them, my best guess is that they were mostly confused about the relevance of their future careers in a non-operational environment, and the relentless boredom of service life back in Australian-based army establishments.

On our voyage back to Australia — *Sydney's* 17th — we were all tormented to varying degrees by memories of what we'd done, taken part in, and experienced in Vietnam. What was really interesting was the fact that we weren't talking extensively amongst ourselves about those experiences, whether good or bad. In some respects, it was almost as if we'd never been to Vietnam. For much of the time we just lazed around, doing nothing much at all. Rarely did we interact intelligently or in any meaningful way, other than during the frenetic daily 4pm beer ration. I've often thought over the years about how strange and almost surreal this voyage back home to Australia actually was.

Some of us were aware that the political landscape had changed significantly since we left Australia for Vietnam some 12 months previously. We were conscious that public opinion, community agitation, and public disobedience in some instances, for an end to conscription and for a complete withdrawal of Australian troops from Vietnam, had almost reached a crescendo back home.

We had also been alerted to disconcerting and ultimately accurate rumours that the Returned and Services League (RSL) wasn't generally accepting of Vietnam veterans as legitimate returned service members. We also knew that this wasn't official RSL policy, but there was anecdotal scuttlebutt that strongly suggested many RSL Sub-Branches were adopting this indefensible and reprehensible position, particularly in relation to membership eligibility of Vietnam veterans and even entry into their licenced premises. To say that we felt extremely disheartened by that revelation is probably an understatement at best.

All said and done, many of us were confused and very apprehensive about our imminent return home. As we neared Australia, several of my platoon mates said that they were going to miss Vietnam, without ever taking that comment any further in discussion. While I didn't — for one moment — ever share that view…I could certainly understand it.

As to be expected, we weren't required to undertake any formal military training on the voyage home. I don't remember doing any physical exercise other than jogging or walking a few laps around the flight deck — 213m long — of the ship, something I did 3 or 4 times a day (most days) even if it was only to try and deal with the day-to-day ennui.

I mentioned earlier that we all had far too much free time on our hands which, on reflection, wasn't a good thing. Although many of us were required to help with the daily logistical duties onboard the ship, it wasn't onerous work by any means. Unbelievably, I again ended up peeling potatoes in one of the galleys for a few hours each day. And even more unbelievably, I managed to reclaim my unique sleeping position under one of the ship's lifeboats, where I managed to sleep reasonably comfortably, if not well, each night.

All of us were completely obsessed with the daily beer ration at 4pm. By now alcohol had, for many of us, become an important constant in our lives and although I didn't fully recognise it then, booze played a major factor in my day-to-day life…and remained that way for many years.

Unlike the relatively trouble-free issue of daily beer rations onboard *Sydney* some 12 months earlier, there were now many arguments each afternoon, and far too much aggression associated with the process. The problem was that most of us couldn't get enough beer on any given day. The ship's prescribed beer ration of one 750ml can ($A0.20) per day, per man, was grossly insufficient for most of us. Former non-drinkers were now confirmed drinkers, which significantly exacerbated the problem. It was now extremely difficult to get more than one can of beer each afternoon. Was I one of those soldiers desperate for more alcohol than what was available? Too right I was!

As a well-meaning physical release mechanism for us during our voyage home, inter-service boxing competitions were arranged. This initiative seemed to work quite well for a day or so, and huge crowds gathered to urge on their respective men. However, these contests became violent. Most combatants from each service arm weren't acquainted with — or accepting of — the 'Marquis of Queensberry' rules of boxing, preferring instead to aggressively batter their opponents into senselessness even when the contest was effectively over. Incompetent refereeing also magnified the problem. Some contests were sickening to watch. This inter-service boxing was eventually abandoned due to the extent of injuries being sustained by many of the combatants, and the 'bad blood' which developed between the men from both services. Halfway through our voyage home, it was clear to me that the soldiers and sailors aboard *Sydney* were clearly not the same 'brothers in arms' as we'd been on our travel to Vietnam a year previously.

Several days before we were due to berth in Brisbane, a sergeant whom I'd never seen before, ordered me to have a No.1 haircut at the ship's barbershop. Why he'd even conjure up this order remains a complete mystery to me. We were all sporting short haircuts as it was. Because of the heat and humidity, long hair wasn't popular in Vietnam. As many of us were going to effectively be out of the army in a few days' time, I didn't think that this inane order was a proper one. So, my natural reaction was, '*Sergeant, go and fuck yourself!*'

He threatened me with being charged for insubordination and for disobeying a lawful command. Really! How were those charges ever going to be formally heard before a competent authority? What could they possibly do to us? What penalty could really be applied? Effectively, many of us weren't going to be under military control, as distinct from military orders, within a few days. I clearly remember laughing at this sergeant and walking away with the Aussie 'two finger salute'. However, he didn't deserve to be treated so disrespectfully and unfairly by me, or anyone else. He was simply doing what he was told to do, and that was having the battalion's soldiers squared away in terms of haircuts. This minor breakdown in military discipline was expected as tensions onboard escalated dramatically, the closer we neared Brisbane.

We were aware that once berthed in Brisbane, we were going to be saying farewell to a way of life that we'd become accustomed to. More importantly, we were going to lose the intimate interaction with, and companionship of, many guys who'd become close mates under extremely adverse conditions. It was an incredibly stressful time for us and we didn't need any army bullshit like 'last minute haircuts' to test our solidarity. Needless to say, not one of us had a haircut.

As the ship veered toward the North Queensland coast, we stopped for a brief time offshore from Cairns, to allow officials from the Australian Customs and Quarantine Services to board *Sydney*. Prior to this, we'd spent many hours over recent days cleaning all of our personal equipment — especially our boots — making sure that any trace of the glue-like red dirt that permeated much of

Chapter 27 – The Voyage Home

the Vietnamese landscape was removed. While absolutely shit-boring work, it did give us something to do.

These government inspections were routine and uneventful, but there were a few reported incidents of soldiers being asked to pay customs duty on a number of items. The difficulty here of course was that these goods had been purchased very cheaply in the US Army PX stores — at Nui Dat or in Vung Tau — and the requisite Australian customs duty that was now being levied, was extremely high in relation to those purchase prices. In some cases, the customs duty exceeded the original purchase price. There were several reported instances of soldiers dumping hard goods over the side of the ship to avoid paying this excessive duty tax.

Several guys on the ship decided to smuggle quantities of cannabis back into Australia. I did this as well, because of the potential substantial cash profit I'd be able to make upon resale in Australia. In fact, on my last 40-hour R&C break in Vung Tau, I managed to acquire about 1kg —a guess — of tightly-compressed dried cannabis, which I carried with me from Nui Dat to *Sydney*. For obvious reasons, I never shared this fact with any of my platoon mates.

However, at the end of the day, I decided that the trafficking of cannabis into Australia was far too risky, not because of any moral reasoning on my part, but because I was acutely aware that the penalties for being caught with illegal drugs in my possession in those days, were extremely harsh. I wasn't too keen on serving any custodial sentence after 12 months of abject misery in Vietnam.

Back in those days, cannabis was considered by the authorities in Australia to be an extremely dangerous drug of addiction. So, I managed to trade my cannabis stash with a guy I knew from another company, in exchange for a sizeable sum of money and 6 extra cans of beer, over the 12 days that it took *Sydney* to steam back to Brisbane. In more reasoned times, I know that I made the right decision. The guys who successfully imported cannabis back into Australia — and there were more than a few — would have made very tidy profits indeed. I don't recall any soldier on the ship being discovered with cannabis in his possession. Good luck to those men!

Early on the morning of 12 November, *Sydney* entered the Brisbane River and at around 8am, berthed at Hamilton Wharf where families, media, and never-ending masses of military and civilian officials had gathered to meet and greet soldiers from the returning battalion. As 8 RAR was a Queensland-raised and based unit, many of its Regular soldiers were from Brisbane. The crowd that greeted us at the wharf that morning was simply massive. It was a very emotional time for all of those guys who had family there to greet them. Were we envious of those guys? Yes, we certainly were.

After we disembarked from *Sydney*, those of us without family members present, were warmly welcomed by support elements of the army and the ever-present Salvation Army. I remember drinking several mugs of steaming hot tea provided by those magnificent Salvos as I meandered amongst the packed crowd, chatting to my platoon mates, several mates from other platoons, and absorbing all the emotion that was coursing around the wharf.

At that very moment, did I feel special? Yes, I did. Did that feeling of euphoria, tempered by the relief of being safely back in Australia, last for a long time? No, it didn't. In fact, it lasted less than 24 hours.

PART 7

HOME SWEET HOME

CHAPTER 28

WELCOME HOME

An hour or so after our emotional 'welcome home' at Hamilton Wharf, we were marshalled into some sort of order and transported by army buses into the Brisbane CBD where we formed-up in parade order for a march through the city.

8 RAR had been awarded the prestigious honour of 'Freedom of the City' by the Lord Mayor of the Brisbane City Council, an award gratefully received by the battalion. All of us — including men like me who couldn't march properly — were excited about this upcoming public recognition of the battalion by the people of Brisbane.

The march commenced at 11am and it was a very emotional event. We proceeded down Elizabeth Street and along George Street. I remember the vast crowds of people who lined the footpaths cheering us on. At some point in the march, an elderly man tried to share a jug of beer with us as we marched past him. It was a lovely gesture by a patriotic digger. About halfway through the march — and for reasons totally unknown to us at the time — we came to a complete stop. This was unusual given the associated road closures and marshalling arrangements that had been put in place by the Brisbane City Council. After a few minutes, the march resumed and we eventually ended up on Henschel Street at the southern end of the city near the Brisbane River, close to where the Roma Street transport hub is now located.

As we milled around after the march, word filtered back to us that the stoppage was caused by a few university students and a number of anti-conscription and anti-Vietnam War protestors who laid across the road, impeding our route for a time. I have no idea if this was actually true or not. However at the time, it certainly seemed plausible to us. A protest of some sort during the march was exactly what we'd been warned about, were half expecting, and typified the appalling way Vietnam veterans were often treated when they returned to Australia. Whilst not wanting to believe all of those rumours, by this time, we knew that they were quite possibly accurate.

Shortly after the march concluded, we were transported by army buses back to our home base at Enoggera Barracks. We weren't there long at all, just time enough to hand in our rifles and bayonets; partake of the free BBQ food and beer on offer; sign for our pay books; a cash advance; and airline, train, or

Chapter 28 – Welcome Home

bus tickets for transport later that day back to our home cities or towns.

My charter airline flight to Adelaide didn't depart Brisbane until 6:30pm that evening. So, to pass the time, I did exactly what anyone who knew me at that time would have expected me to do. I headed straight into downtown Brisbane with the firm intention of having a big drink of beer.

A number of us met up at Lennon's Hotel, which was one of our favourite drinking haunts whenever we were based at Enoggera. There would have been at least 30 or more of us congregated at that locale. Others whom I remember drinking with that afternoon were Mick O'Shea, Des McGrath, Allan Small, Peter Wood, Steve Middlemo (Mortar Platoon) and Bob Blackmore (C Company). I also knew a number of other men with us, as many were from Support Company. The staff at Lennon's Hotel clearly remembered our valued past patronage and provided us with free beer for the early part of the afternoon. It was a fabulous time and we ended up getting nicely primed by 4:30pm, at which time I shared a taxi to Brisbane Airport to catch my flight to Adelaide.

The charter flight out of Brisbane that evening was transporting men back to Adelaide and Perth. For some, it was going to be a big journey. The flight was more-or-less full and not long after our departure, one of the flight attendants announced that the army Colonel seated at the back of the plane would be picking up the tab for beer consumed by soldiers on this first flight leg — about 3 hours — from Brisbane to Adelaide. With a hearty 3 cheers for the Colonel, we well and truly got stuck right into the good stuff.

On our approach to Adelaide Airport at about 9pm local time, a flight attendant came across to Mick O'Shea and I, and asked us to help her rescue — from the forward toilet — the soldier who'd been seated next to us. Shit! I only vaguely knew this guy from Admin Company.

Naturally, O'Shea and I would do anything to please a pretty girl, and this young flight attendant was incredibly attractive. She used a pass-key to unlock the toilet door. There he was. He'd either passed out, gone to sleep, or died while sitting on the toilet. It was a bit hard to tell. O'Shea and I concluded that on balance, he wasn't dead…just inebriated. The flight attendant was beside herself until O'Shea and I were able to extract him from the toilet seat, pull up his trousers, dress him half-decently, drag him back into the cabin, and strap him into his allocated seat next to us.

After landing at Adelaide airport, the flight attendant begged — almost pleading — O'Shea and I to help get him off the aircraft. We really didn't have a choice because we couldn't leave him with her in that state. Besides, he was one of us. I've never forgotten that flight attendant. She loved us and hated us, all at the same time. She gave both O'Shea and I a big hug and kiss as we stepped out of the aircraft with this drunken mate between us, onto the disembarkation staircase.

Once we reached the tarmac, we helped manoeuvre him — he could hardly stand upright, let alone walk — over to where his many family members were gathered. They had a huge welcoming banner for him, so it wasn't hard to spot them. Mick and I were happy to get rid of him, and wished he and his family well. I have a faint recollection that he was married and that his wife — who was there to meet him — was none too pleased with his grossly intoxicated condition.

Then, it was time to meet my own large family group. That was a very emotional time for me. O'Shea, who was travelling on to Perth later that night, and then back east to Kalgoorlie next morning, felt a bit out of place. He made his escape within minutes, leaving me to my parents, uncles and aunts, and numerous other McCann family members. To be perfectly honest, I don't remember too much about this part of my homecoming at all. Emotion, exacerbated by the alcohol I'd already consumed that day, was becoming far too exhausting for me.

Back at my parents' house there was even more drinking to be done. A very boozy party was in full swing. However, after a few hours of trying to be nice to everyone, I was becoming increasingly overwhelmed by it all. Years later, my parents told me that I became progressively withdrawn and even off-hand to some of those well-meaning people who'd gathered to welcome me home.

And they were probably right. I was completely unable to comprehend how close family members and neighbours that I'd known all my life, could expect me to sit back with a beer in hand and intelligently respond to questions like, '*What was your time in Vietnam like?*' I was tired, emotionally drained, and nicely drunk. I felt out of place among all these really tiresome people. I didn't want to talk about Vietnam at all. What I really wanted to do was either go to sleep, or be back with my army mates. Already, in the space of a few hours, adjusting to civilian life was fast becoming exceedingly difficult for me.

My observant and very astute father recognised the signs of inebriation and anxiety that I was displaying and before anyone knew what was really happening, he adroitly manoeuvred me out of the lounge room and down to my former bedroom at the end of the house. Here I crashed and slept for a solid 10 hours. I was back home safely amongst family and friends but that didn't mean the demons of Vietnam had gone away. They were buried in the deep recesses of my mind, waiting to emerge, as they eventually did in all of their nasty forms in later years of my life.

The next morning, as I was helping my father take armfuls of post-party trash down to the backyard carbon polluting incinerator at our home, I heard a very loud bang after something in the incinerator exploded. I loudly yelled '*down*' and dropped prone to the ground and lay there for a brief time before — embarrassingly — getting to my feet, brushing my clothes off, and saying '*sorry about that*' to my father. He was simply astonished — that's the only word I can conjure — and at that moment in time, he fully realised that I had issues I needed to deal with. Although we never discussed this incident, he became a far more concerned parent than he'd ever been prior to my deployment.

There's one thing that I still deeply regret not doing on my first day back in Australia, and that was finding the time and technological wherewithal, to telephone my girlfriend in Canberra. I was completely overwhelmed by the euphoria of being home among family and friends. That, together with tiredness and poor judgment, blurred my good manners. It may well have been an intuition that our relationship was over. Nevertheless, she didn't deserve that from me at all. She was a lovely woman and I formally apologise to her for that gross lapse in common decency on my part.

CHAPTER 29

DISCHARGE FROM THE ARMY

About 10 days or so after arriving home from Vietnam, I received a letter from the army ordering me to report to Keswick Barracks in the Adelaide CBD, at some future date and time. I duly reported to the barracks on that day and met up with a number of other 8 RAR men — all 15th Intake National Servicemen — most of whom I either didn't know, or only vaguely knew. It was a hideously hot, sweltering day. While there were 2 other National Servicemen — Robin Jagger and Mark Smith — from Adelaide in my platoon, I don't recall meeting up with either of them on this day. Very strange indeed.

The duty officer informed us that going forward we were required to report to Keswick Barracks each day for duty, in full greens dress, until our interim discharge from the army. A number of us wanted to know why we had to report for duty at all and asked him what we'd be doing on those days. He was unable to answer these questions or deal with this sort of reasonable contestability.

He was being confronted by a group of National Service conscripts who'd recently returned from active service in Vietnam, who had about 10 weeks left to serve before their National Service obligations expired. We were no longer a usable army resource, so any form of training would be a complete waste of time. And what exactly would we be training for? My criticism of the army back then was that it hadn't given any thought whatsoever as to how to deal with National Servicemen Vietnam veterans in our situation — a brief period of time yet to serve — following our return home. It wouldn't have been the same problem for those National Servicemen who didn't deploy to Vietnam.

After conferring behind closed doors with his hierarchy at the barracks, this duty officer advised us that we would now be regarded as being on long-term paid leave. So, it did seem that reason and common sense prevailed. To my way of thinking, this was a first for the administrative arm of the army. In my view, back in 1969-1970, common sense resolution of administrative problems wasn't an army strong point.

During the first week of January 1971, I received a letter from the army ordering me to again report to Keswick Barracks on 18 January for my interim discharge from the army. I duly reported on that day, dressed in neat, casual, civilian attire.

After filling out some meaningless forms, a quartermaster store corporal asked me to return my webbed belt and bayonet toggle, as distinct from my identical, highly-polished, black ceremonial items. I was gob-smacked! I told him that I couldn't do this because those very items were in my steel trunk which was being transported back to Australia by the army. He then informed me that as I couldn't produce those items, there would be a deduction from my final separation payment to compensate the army for this loss of official government property. I reacted badly to that and put on quite a scene for a time. Finally, he assured me that as it was the army who ordered me to store those items in my steel trunk, I wouldn't have to pay for them.

Eventually an officer — a Major representing the Keswick Barracks Headquarters Central Command Commandant — individually interviewed us for this formal, interim, discharge process. As I stood at '*Attention*' — even while wearing civilian attire — in front of him, he said to me:

'Private McCann, I suppose that there is no point in me asking you if you would like to sign on for a further term of military service, is there?'

My immediate response was:

'No Sir, no point at all.'

After that polite verbal exchange, he looked at me for a time, signed my interim discharge paper — effective from 29 January — rose and shook my hand, and wished me well in my future life as a civilian. Apart from my platoon commander, 2LT Peter Phillips and Capt. Green — the 8 RAR medical officer obsessed with venereal disease — this Major was the only other army officer I really liked.

I was now almost out of the army and a civilian once more. I was both elated and confused. Over the next few weeks I received a number of what were supposedly final pay cheques, the values of which I never even came close to reconciling. The attached statements were incomprehensible. But, as my rough figuring indicated that the aggregate values of these cheques were generally in my favour, I never bothered to query them. I simply kept banking cheque after cheque. The statement attached to one of these cheques reflected a deduction for non-returned army equipment. Those quartermaster store functionaries at Keswick Barracks turned out to be first-class arseholes after all!

Some months later, when I was again living and working in Canberra, I received my formal discharge certificate — effective from 29 January 1971 — dated 15 March 1971. At that time I also received a formal notification stating that I was now a member of the Army Reserve for a 3-year period ending on 29 January 1974.

Although I should have been aware of this legislated post National Service discharge obligation, I was absolutely astounded. It seemed perfectly clear to me that I could now be 'called-up' again in time of war or in case of national emergency. In other words, for the next 3 years I was still ostensibly at the beck and call of the army. There was simply nothing I could do about this. I eventually concluded that it was better for my confused mental state at the time, to just accept reality, noting that the chances of being recalled for further active military service in the early 1970's were pretty close to zero.

CHAPTER 30

RETURN TO CIVILIAN LIFE

INTEGRATION

The average Australian citizen of the late 1960's and early 1970's probably thought that National Servicemen returning home from Vietnam and re-entering civilian society and the workforce, would find that relatively straightforward. Well, that was far from the case for many of them. Those same challenges would have also confronted National Servicemen who didn't serve in Vietnam.

My experiences on returning to Australia and disengaging from the army, are that there was never any debriefing or counselling of any kind offered to National Serviceman Vietnam veterans. We were just expected to exit the army and slide seamlessly back into our former civilian lives and jobs. It seemed to me that as far as the army was concerned, now that we were back home in Australia with Vietnam well behind us, there was no apparent reason why we'd have any difficulty doing that.

Besides my shocking facial acne condition, a painful lower left rib resulting from the drunken punch-up with a platoon mate during my last days in Vietnam, and a problematic right knee — which became arthritic in later life — I was in pretty good physical condition.

However, my mental health wasn't in such great shape. Although it wasn't apparent to me at that time, it was seriously compromised due to my active service in Vietnam. The effects of this were destined to emerge much later in my life in a number of ugly forms, and intermittently torment me through many of my more recent years.

The immediate problem I had to deal with was that of alcohol. I was astute enough to recognise this addiction and have been fortunate to be able to — for the most part — manage it throughout my subsequent life. Nevertheless, I've never been able to completely rid myself of this addiction and it has remained an ongoing irritation. Before entering the army, I was the same as most young men of that era. I regularly enjoyed a few quiet beers and on some occasions, overindulged. However, routinely drinking to excess was something of a rarity for me back in those wonderful halcyon days in Adelaide and Canberra, before I was deployed to Vietnam.

After returning home, there was a period of about 9 weeks when I was on full pay, leading up to my interim discharge from the army on 18 January 1971. So, what did I do each day? Apart from having a lot of sex with a somewhat older but really lovely woman who lived in a spacious and superior apartment at Brighton Beach, just north of the Esplanade Hotel, I either drank beer during the day with my newfound 8 RAR mates in the Adelaide CBD or red wine with her at night.

During this very confused time in my life, I paid — air travel — for my girlfriend from Canberra to come to Adelaide to be with me for a week. The fact that I'd been unashamedly cheating on her during my time in Vietnam and, even more so since arriving back in Adelaide, didn't bother me at all. I don't think she ever knew about any of this, but even if she did, I don't think I'd have been too concerned anyway. I had only been back in Australia for a few weeks and was already rapidly losing focus on reality and, to some extent, the accepted normal standards of civilised behaviour. Basically, I was having extreme difficulty in adjusting to civilian life. At that point in time, I wasn't a very nice person as all.

In early January, my father kept asking me about my plans after my upcoming interim discharge from the army. I was unable to answer him intelligently because I hadn't actually given that any thought at all. I hadn't even bothered to contact my former employer — the ATO. Eventually, my father and I had an almighty row one evening over my aimless and seemingly endless drinking and, during this very unpleasant exchange, he completely lost his temper and heavily slapped me in the face. I have to say that I was shocked by this. I was 22 years of age and my father, until that very moment, had never once laid a hand on me in anger.

As I stood there looking back at him, I sensed his complete regret at what he'd just done, along with his despair and total unease regarding how I might react to this physical assault. There was no way I was going to respond in the manner that he may have been expecting and dreading. He was, after all, my father. I didn't escalate this confrontation any further. I simply told him that I was sorry for the grief I'd been causing himself and my mother — or words to that effect — and retired to bed. We never spoke about this incident again and we didn't need to. Both of us were out of line that night, and each of us knew it.

Over the next few weeks, as we continued to drink together on Saturdays in the front bar of the Brighton Hotel, we spoke candidly. My father strongly suggested that it might be in my best interests to resume employment with the ATO as soon as possible. These rather difficult and emotional discussions between us eventually prompted me to contact the ATO and arrange to resume my employment with the agency back in Canberra.

So, much to the relief of my parents, a few days before the effective date of

Chapter 30 – Return to Civilian Life

my formal discharge from the army, I bade them farewell, returned to Canberra — with all my worldly possessions crammed into my new Holden Kingswood car — and resumed my career with the ATO on Monday 1 February. I was very apprehensive about this because I still wasn't even certain that I wanted to return to that workplace. I was a confused and very unstable young man.

Shortly after arriving in Canberra, I returned to house-share with a group of guys I lived with before entering the army back in 1969. We were still good mates and it seemed that none of us had changed all that much over the intervening 2 years. This wasn't true of course, but it seemed that way at the time. I resumed playing rugby union, and moderated — but never eliminated — drinking from my life, whilst I tried very hard to carve out a decent career with the ATO. My relationship with my girlfriend totally disintegrated and on very good terms, we went our separate ways.

Sometime in September of that year, one of my house mates got married and I attended his wedding. The reception — Italian/Greek-style mix — was a terrific event. Late that evening I noticed a very attractive and diminutive young woman with shiny, very long — almost waist-length — black hair, sitting alone while most of the other guests danced and partied. I was overcome by her stunning good looks, her slender figure, and general aura of what I'd describe as 'rare niceness'. After asking her if I could sit down at her table — to which she didn't object — I was even more captivated by her lovely Spanish accent. I don't think she liked me very much that night — I wasn't exactly sober — but obviously she was far too polite to tell me to go away. However, we must have struck some sort of chord between us that night because 8 months later, on 13 May 1972, this beautiful Spanish lady and I were married and have remained together ever since.

WITHDRAWAL

So, some 18 months after returning home from Vietnam, I was again living in Canberra, married to a lovely woman, and working for the ATO. Outwardly, and even within myself, my life seemed to be idyllic. However that wasn't the case at all. Without actually realising it, I'd managed to mentally detach myself from my Vietnam experiences and in that process, had become almost obsessively reclusive about that part of my life. This unhealthy detachment from past reality was to continue for many decades.

Apart from several treating medical specialists, I've never discussed any aspect of my time in Vietnam with anyone, other than my brother-in-law — also a Vietnam veteran — in anything other than vague terms. Whilst our operational experiences are amazingly similar, our conversations regarding Vietnam have been rare and not overly-focused on operational activities. We get on well.

My wife has never once asked me about my time in Vietnam and I've never initiated any discussion about it with her either. Until they became mature adults, neither of my 2 children showed any interest in understanding that difficult part of my life. This was largely my wrongdoing because I simply haven't wanted to talk about it with anyone. I know that many Vietnam veterans are the same as me.

During the first 30 years of my life, after returning from Vietnam, I only ever marched on ANZAC Day on one occasion. And that was with my father and brother-in-law in Adelaide in 1976. There were several very good reasons for this withdrawal from, or denial of, my service in Vietnam as an infantry soldier.

When I returned home from Vietnam in late November 1970, public opinion and community agitation for an end to conscription, and for a complete withdrawal of Australian soldiers from Vietnam, was very much in the media. This adverse community view that tainted all Vietnam veterans, remained firmly in the public arena until well after the end of conscription, and the final withdrawal of Australian troops from Vietnam in 1972. Vietnam veterans were not 'flavour of the month' back in the early 1970's. It didn't seem to me to be such a clever idea to overtly identify as one.

Those rumours we heard on the voyage home from Vietnam on HMAS *Sydney*, suggesting that the RSL wasn't generally accepting of Vietnam veterans as legitimate returned service members, while not universally true, were certainly accurate in terms of the way some of its sub-branches operated. Many Vietnam veterans were treated as pariahs and even today, some still refuse to join the RSL. While my experiences with the RSL weren't as negative as others, I didn't actually become an RSL service member until the early 2000's.

As previously noted, because of the appalling living conditions and other deprivations that infantry soldiers were continually exposed to out in the field in Vietnam, I arrived home with an almost skeletal physique and an acute case of disfiguring facial acne. My lovely wife overlooked that disfigurement, however, as a young man, I was very self-conscious about it. I developed an even more reticent and reserved nature which I believe, to a large degree, had a negative impact on my career with the ATO.

Public speaking has never been easy for me and wherever possible, I always took the opportunity to blend into the workplace background. That being said, you may recall that I'd honed this skill to near perfection during my time in the army. Although I've always been quietly and strongly assertive, I was never able to confidently display that character trait in large public forums. Quite frankly, the thought of having to make a presentation to a large group of peers, or worse still 'the public', usually terrified me.

That aside, my 37-year career with the ATO was a highly successful one and, for the most part, hugely enjoyable. The fact that I so quickly attained such a relatively senior level within that agency astounds me. At the same time, I remain firmly of the view that because of my shy and reserved nature, and by living my life as a semi-reclusive man rather than as a proud Vietnam veteran, I was never able to display my full potential within the ATO.

For decades, my family and my work were my only focus. And, of course, I always had my very good friend 'alcohol' to fall back on whenever I felt the need to escape reality and re-set.

AWAKENING

For many years I managed to function seemingly as a very normal person. To any casual observer there would have been no outward signs to suggest that I was dealing with alcohol addiction, or that my repressed demons from my time in Vietnam may have been slowly emerging. I rarely missed a day's work and my workplace sick leave credits accumulated astronomically. Moreover, I never did anything outrageous that some people addicted to alcohol do from time to time. Pretty much all of my drinking was done within my own home. While I was always more of a consistent drinker — by that I mean every evening over a number of hours — rather than an intermittent binge drinker, alcohol was clearly a major factor in my life.

Although my wife, and occasionally my children sometimes commented on my drinking, I was always able to positively rationalise this behaviour in my own mind: I was a high-income earner — so I could easily afford to drink — and I rarely, if ever, became aggressive. I was what was known as a 'passive drunk'. More importantly, I always functioned very effectively at work. I never drove my vehicle after drinking and I never drank during the day when I was working. Even at workplace lunches, I'd only drink club soda. However, after 7:30pm or thereabouts, in the confines of my home, it was a completely different story.

At my absolute worst, I was probably consuming 2 casks — 8L (11 x 750ml bottles) — of red wine, plus a case of full-strength beer — 12 x long-necks (750mm) — each week. Fortunately, for much of the last 15 years of my ATO career I was routinely working interstate for several (or more) days of many weeks, which significantly limited my alcohol intake on those occasions.

When working interstate, I rarely drank alcohol for quite obvious reasons. As a relatively senior 'man from Canberra' I just couldn't risk an alcohol related incident. Strangely, those periods of irregular abstinence never once tested or concerned me. When I wasn't drinking, I was just not drinking. It was that simple. Of course, when waiting for an airline flight connection on my return back home to Canberra, I was always back to my old self.

Back in Canberra, on winter Saturday afternoons, it became routine for me to drink 5 (or more) long-necks of beer while watching the AFL on television. Other than the odd breakout over and above these alcoholic intakes — on one infamous New Year's Eve gathering I managed to imbibe the entire contents of a 4L cask of red wine by myself — I was convinced that I was never out of control...and I really mean that. I just thought that I was nicely relaxed most nights when I went to bed. I never woke up late and I can't remember ever suffering from a hangover. Frankly, I don't understand it at all. I'm quite certain that if I woke some mornings feeling like absolute shit, that may have made me think more about what I was doing to my body.

One Friday evening in March 1996, on my way back home to Canberra after another week-long business trip to Brisbane, I was relaxing alone in the — now defunct — Ansett Golden Wing Lounge at Sydney Airport, awaiting a delayed connecting flight to Canberra. I was, of course, drinking plenty of the free, expensive, high-quality red wine and Cognac on offer. It was about 8:30pm and I was totally absorbed with my private thoughts.

Suddenly, I had a brain explosion — better known in more recent times as a 'light bulb moment'. It dawned on me that I couldn't recall the last day I didn't partake of alcohol when in Canberra. To this very day, I remember the profound and lasting effect that moment of self-realisation had on me. Frankly, it bothered me. In fact, it bothered me a lot. With my heart racing and my cerebrum in overdrive, I resolved then and there not to have another drop of alcohol until Christmas Day that year — some 9 months later.

In all honesty, my resolve didn't last that long. However, I didn't drink alcohol until late November of that year, a period of over 8 months. Once I'd made up my mind, I found it relatively easy to forgo the booze. I didn't miss its sedating effect, I slept better, I was far more alert, more vibrant, and much more at ease with myself and my life. While I'm not certain about this, I'm pretty sure that my lovely wife would have liked me a lot more than she did previously.

This was a significant and cathartic life-changing time for me. The almost endorphin-like exhilaration during the first few weeks was very similar to what I experienced when I successfully gave up smoking cigarettes in September 1986. Interestingly, my wife never commented — not even once — on my lengthy period of alcohol abstinence. As to why, I have no idea. I've never raised this issue with her because I haven't seen any real reason to do so.

Since November 1996, my drinking has abated significantly. Of course, I still drink: not every day, but more often than not, I still do. However, I don't consume anywhere near the volume that I used to, and am now reasonably comfortable with my alcohol addiction. And, let's be honest, that's what it is

Chapter 30 – Return to Civilian Life

— an addiction. Although we've never discussed it, my wife now seems to be much more accepting of my vastly reduced, more controlled consumption of alcohol and continues to support me as she always has.

It was around this time, late 1996, that I began to feel more relaxed about my military background and operational experiences as a former infantry soldier and Vietnam veteran. Since then, I've marched on ANZAC Day 5 times. Most years, I don't march…it very much depends on how I'm feeling on the morning of each ANZAC Day. I often plan to march and arise from bed early, but it doesn't eventuate. My wife and children weren't all that interested in attending these events, not that I've ever asked them to. However, in more recent years, my wife has criticised me for not marching. I know that had I asked her to attend and watch me march on ANZAC Day for all those lost years, she would have done so. I'm also certain that she's far more aware of the demons that still eat away in the recesses of my mind, than I give her credit for.

It isn't wise to underestimate my wife, as she's a very astute woman. I'm also convinced that she's somewhat clairvoyant! She can certainly read my mind. But that's another story altogether and one which has become part of family legend. Suffice to say that whenever I do something that I know is going to really piss her off, I always confess to the petty crime — or venial sin — before she finds out.

On ANZAC Day in 2007, I marched with several of my former platoon mates at Bateman's Bay, NSW, and met up with some more of them over the next few days at nearby Merimbula. My wife accompanied me on this trip and I'm sure that she thoroughly enjoyed herself. Meeting up with those men and their wives was terrific for me and we had a wonderful time together. In 2013, my son asked if he could march with me in Canberra. We did so, and it too was a great experience. We did it again in 2015. I have no doubt in my mind whatsoever that March 1996 was a defining moment in my life. Since that time, I've been far more at peace with myself and I'm sure this has had a very positive effect on my family.

Around the middle of 1998, I transferred to a different, more challenging, and much more public focused senior position within the ATO — one that I really liked. Responsible for the service delivery of a major government policy program, I spent a lot of time working interstate in Adelaide, Brisbane (again) — in particular — and Melbourne. I was extremely busy and content, both at work and at home. Then, disaster struck.

Late one Tuesday afternoon in July 2000, I travelled by air from Melbourne to Brisbane for several meetings scheduled over the next few days. My taxi had just left the precinct of Brisbane Airport at around 8:30pm when the driver ran a red light at the intersection of the East-West Arterial and Nudge Road in the suburb of Hendra. I was sitting in the back seat of the taxi, behind the driver, scanning my diary meeting schedule when I heard a piercing scream from my female co-worker seated in the front passenger seat. Glancing up and over to my left, I saw a B-Double truck seemingly about to enter the taxi through both left side doors.

The impact of the B-Double truck on the taxi was nothing short of catastrophic. My co-worker and I were both very badly injured. I spent 12 days in the Royal Brisbane Hospital with multiple rib fractures — some more than once — a badly bruised spleen, and a punctured left lung. I wasn't a well man at all. My co-worker — a young Graduate trainee — recovered from her injuries much more quickly than I did.

On returning to Canberra, I immediately proceeded on paid sick leave. Because of the excruciating trauma and pain from my collective 17 rib fractures — along with the array of associated torn cartilages — I could barely walk unaided for about 4 weeks. I was also unable to lay prone in bed for the best part of 3 months. The left side of my ribcage had been effectively shattered. I spent most of this recovery time reposing in a recliner chair in the downstairs family area of my home. I dozed in this chair every night until the end of October 2000. This was a terrible time in my life. On a positive note though, my consumption of alcohol within my home at this time was significantly curtailed.

Because I was so physically incapacitated, there was nothing I could do each day other than watch television, read books, and reflect. All of this time to think was the very worst thing for me. I was in pain, largely immobile, and utterly bored. Even though my body slowly healed, my mind was in turmoil. My sleep pattern was very poor and I began to obsess about my time in Vietnam.

By January 2001, I was more-or-less back at work full-time. However, I struggled with the day-to-day physical demands of the workplace. Working interstate was no longer a viable option for me, so this significantly impacted my ability to actually do my job. My ribs — or more likely my cartilages at that time — were still extremely painful. I had to be careful how I lifted anything heavy, or rose from, or lowered to a seated position. I found that a full day at work utterly exhausted me. Even though I was able to physically lay prone in my bed by this time, my sleep pattern had deteriorated even further. I would have been lucky to get a few hours of sleep each night — and that was broken at best. My dreams and thoughts as I tossed and turned in bed every night, were sometimes vaguely focused on my time in Vietnam, but not necessarily on operational aspects. On some nights, it almost seemed like I was back in those awful times.

Towards the middle of the second half of 2001, I again proceeded on long-term paid sick leave and my employment with the ATO was eventually

Chapter 30 – Return to Civilian Life

terminated — medical retirement — in March 2003 on psychological grounds directly related to my military service in Vietnam.

Since then, I've managed to get order and focus back into my life. My physical injuries from that vehicle accident have healed and though my sleep pattern remains abysmally poor — every morning without fail I'm up, out of bed and showered by 5:30am — I don't obsess about my experiences in Vietnam to quite the same extent. Yet, there are many nights where it still seems like I'm back in that hostile environment. Whenever I'm subconsciously engrossed in a confused — and now long past — Vietnam moment, I often suddenly wake up startled, sweating profusely, and wonder where I am for a time. Whenever this occurs, I always get out of bed — often as early as 3am — and spend the remainder of the early morning hours either working on my computer or reading.

I've managed to keep my drinking very much under control, so it's no longer a major issue, other than for the occasional breakout…and my wife is very alert to those! The only important things that matter in my life right now are my wife, my children, my grand-children, and my health.

CHAPTER 31

8 RAR REUNIONS

8 RAR arrived back in Australia on 12 November 1970. Because significantly more than half its complement was comprised of National Servicemen, the Assault Pioneer Platoon basically disbanded on that very same day. While all of its members proceeded on leave, the Regular soldiers in the platoon later returned to Enoggera Barracks in Brisbane — or to other postings — for ongoing military service. Short-time National Servicemen like myself — only a few weeks left to serve — were destined to eke out their remaining periods of service life on paid leave in their home cities and towns, as they awaited their formal discharge from the army. A number of National Servicemen with longer periods of time still to serve — for example, my platoon mate Terry Lucas — were posted to a range of various units in Australia.

Very few of us exchanged addresses or other contact details as we left Brisbane that day. Guys just seemed to bid each other farewell with vague references such as, '*Look me up at the Mentone RSL Club some time*'. On reflection, it was strange that a group of guys who'd been through so much together wouldn't make some sort of minimal effort to maintain contact. Anyway, that's not how it was…and none of that can be changed now. Mind you, the technological options to facilitate that ongoing contact hadn't even emerged at that time.

Perhaps the Regular soldiers weren't too bothered about ongoing personal contact, as the nature of their service life had probably inured them to a continuous churn of workmates. And I guess that most National Servicemen — like myself — were so relieved to be home and almost out of the army, that the thought probably never entered their heads anyway. I know that was in fact the case with me. To be perfectly honest, I never really gave it a moment's consideration.

While many of the Regular soldiers of the Assault Pioneer Platoon resided in Brisbane, its National Service complement seemed to mainly come from other major cities and regional towns. I was its only member who originated from Canberra. Other than one guy — Peter Wood from Goulburn — there was no one from my platoon living close by with whom I could maintain an ongoing friendship in civilian life. Although I'm certain there would have been some former 8 RAR men also living in Canberra at that time, I was unaware of who they were.

Chapter 31 — 8 RAR Reunions

After some years, Peter Wood relocated to Canberra. He and I have seen a bit of each other in later years and that's fantastic. However, as we're both quiet and reserved men, we've never managed to establish the sort of bonded relationship that we should have, given the experiences we shared in Vietnam. This is very strange. Wood was one of the forward scouts in my section, so I knew him very well. When operationally out in the field, I trusted him implicitly and relied on his judgement and operational instincts without question. He was a very good infantry soldier.

Around 1999, as part of my coming to terms with my status as a Vietnam veteran, I joined the 8 RAR Association and have remained a financial member ever since. When the association publicised the fact that it was convening its 2nd National Reunion at Coolangatta, Queensland, in February 2005, the vague thought entered my head that perhaps my wife and I might attend.

In August 2004, I received an 8 RAR Association broadcast email from a woman living in Kalgoorlie, Western Australia. She was trying to contact anyone who'd served in Vietnam in 1969-70 with her late husband Mick O'Shea. Well, you could have almost knocked me over with a feather! As you know, O'Shea was a member of our platoon and one of my best mates in Vietnam. Although I was vaguely aware that he'd passed away many years previously, it never entered my head that perhaps his widow might be interested in contacting guys that he served with.

After reading and re-reading her email enquiry many times — over several weeks — I decided to contact her. Following my extremely cautious introductory response, we corresponded regularly by email and I began to feel very keen to meet her. She confirmed that her late husband passed away in 1975. She also indicated that she and her second husband — Don Scarlett — were going to make a huge effort to travel from Kalgoorlie, Western Australia, by private vehicle to attend the 8 RAR Reunion in Queensland. After a long period of considered thought and discussion with my wife, I decided to also attend the reunion.

I was very apprehensive about meeting up with guys that I had served with in Vietnam for a number of reasons. I guess the main one was — apart from Peter Wood — that it had been 35 years since I last saw any of them. What were we going to talk about? Would they be as I remembered them? Would I be as they remembered me? Would there be any problems between any of us? This dilemma array confronting me at that time may seem to be minor. But, to me, it wasn't.

I was also very wary about the amount of peer-induced compulsory drinking that might be the order of the day during those 8 days and nights at Coolangatta. I was worried about how my wife might deal with army and veteran-focused interactions, which would more than likely dominate her time there as well. All sorts of inane thoughts kept running through my mind in the weeks and days leading up to the reunion. Anyway, in the end, we did make the trip and attended the reunion.

As it turned out, there were 10 other men — and some wives — from my platoon who also attended. They were John Dolgan, Terry Lucas, Dave Matheson, Dennis McNab, Bob O'Callaghan, JJ Smith, Joe Stepien, Fred Vincent, Peter Wood, and Bob Whylie. As you're aware, Fred Vincent was my former section commander in Vietnam, and Peter Wood, John Dolgan, and I were also members of No.1 Section of the 8 RAR Assault Pioneer Platoon.

My initial meeting with my platoon mates — and some partners — was cathartic. I was extremely nervous, apprehensive, and maybe even terrified. I'm sure that my wife was as well. And I was absolutely accurate in my sense that alcohol would be a major feature of the reunion, as we always seemed to be hunkered down in one of the many bars within the Twin Towns RSL Club at Tweed Heads, adjacent to Coolangatta. However my concerns about attending the reunion, and my wife's likely adverse reaction to it, were totally unfounded. I had a marvellous time and I'd like to think that she mostly enjoyed her time there as well.

The consumption of alcohol wasn't overtly encouraged — some men imbibed huge quantities. On the other hand, no one was pressured to drink anything other than water...and I drank plenty of that. With the help of my lovely wife, I managed to keep myself pretty much under control for most of the time. The fact that I'd forgotten to bring prescribed medication for a reflux condition with me, ensured that I was very careful about how much alcohol I consumed each day.

After meeting, we spent the first few hours checking each other out and then we all began to relax, almost as if we'd been seeing each other on and off for years. It was quite amazing. Most of the wives joined in, and much of the non-stop banter was very humorous. I don't recall anyone publicly discussing any operational incident from Vietnam.

However, I did speak privately (and in some detail) with Fred Vincent about the friendly fire ambush I described earlier in my story. He was able to further clarify certain parts of that incident for me. This event has been constantly in the subliminal background of my mind ever since it occurred.

Our last day together as an 8 RAR Assault Pioneer Platoon veteran group was nothing short of euphoric. After being together for 8 days, we were well and truly in touch with each other and it seemed to me that it was such a shame that we'd never before managed to come together like this.

On reflection, attending this reunion was good for me for several reasons. While each of us had lived vastly different lives since our return to Australia, I became acutely aware of the fact that each and every one of my former platoon mates had also been mentally scarred by his time in Vietnam. I realised that I wasn't alone. And while I knew that many Vietnam veterans were severely mentally damaged because of their military service, I began to wonder if my problems in life were any different to those experienced by men with whom I'd actually served in Vietnam. The short answer to that question is no. My problems were pretty much the same as theirs. The only variable seemed to be one of degree.

And then of course, there's the lovely Lynley Scarlett (Mick O'Shea's widow). While Lynley is now married to Don Scarlett — a very nice man — she remains tormented by her need to know more about Mick's time in Vietnam. I think I privately provided a lot of that detail to her. I'm certain that the references I've made to Mick in my story will reinforce that as well. I like to think that Lynley found the reunion worthwhile.

While her efforts to extract detailed information from his former platoon mates — regarding her late husband's activities in Vietnam — may not have been as successful as she hoped they would be, the exigencies and vagueness of time are not at all helpful. At the very least, Lynley will have formed a view about some of the men that Mick was intimately associated with for 12 months of his life in a very nasty environment. On balance, I'd say it must have been a very positive experience for her. My wife found the reunion very worthwhile as well.

Subsequently, the 8 RAR Association held reunions in Adelaide (2010), Ettalong NSW (2013), and Canberra (2016). While I did attend the Adelaide and Canberra events, I consciously decided not to attend the gathering at Ettalong. This was mainly because at that time in my life, I experienced a major lapse back into the seductive embraces of 'Madam Alcohol', so I didn't want her to become even more alluring than she already was. Although Adelaide and Canberra were both enjoyable experiences for me, they didn't even come close to replicating the wonderful array of emotions I experienced in Coolangatta.

The Welcome Home Parade in Sydney in 1987 was a cathartic experience for those thousands of Vietnam veterans who attended the event. While I now regret not attending, the 8 RAR reunion at Coolangatta in 2005 provided me with that same feeling of euphoria. It was another truly defining moment in my life.

PART 8

REFLECTION

CHAPTER 32

PERSONAL INTROSPECTION

When I was conscripted for 2 years of compulsory military service with the Australian Army back in early 1969, there were 2 commonly held — but diametrically opposed — community attitudes to this government imposition on the lives of a select number of unlucky 20-year-old men.

One was the emerging civil unrest and agitation by a relatively small but cogent cohort, against the compulsory and selective nature of National Service, and a very much larger cohort actively objecting to Australia's military involvement in the Vietnam War. On the other hand, there was a widely held community view that 2 years in the army would do no one any harm...simply making men out of boys.

My family has a proud record of military service in both the Great War and WWII. So, while not at all happy about being conscripted into the Australian Army, it never once entered my head to actively object to, or publicly protest, my upcoming 2-year period of compulsory military service. And, later during my recruit training at Puckapunyal, I raised no objection when asked by Capt. Ghost what my views would be if I were to be posted on operational service to Vietnam.

From the time I enlisted in the army on 30 January 1969, I made the conscious decision to serve my country as best I could. I was also determined to make the very most of what lay ahead of me and to try to enjoy what promised to be a range of different and quite unique life experiences.

Vietnam circa 1969-70, was an awful place. It was impossible to spend a lengthy time in that horrible and hostile environment and not be affected by it in some way. For example, I've come across a number of veterans who didn't fire a shot in anger, or ever come under enemy fire, but who are nevertheless very unwell and mentally disturbed men. I guess it's all about how one's brain absorbs and synthesises real time data. It's what I like to call 'head space'. Every individual is completely different. This was somewhat typified by my 'probably' irrational obsession regarding personal hydration whenever I was out in the field. If I was ever subjected to a deficiency of that basic life-supporting commodity — other than for a brief period of time — I reckon I would have completely lost my composure.

When I returned home from Vietnam, I was certainly a man in comparison to the 'boy' who enlisted in the army some 93 weeks earlier. I was also a vastly different person to the happy-go-lucky young guy that I once was.

As I've stated numerous times, I was — to a variable extent — addicted to alcohol. This addiction has continued to impact many aspects of my subsequent life. Although my father was often fond of saying, '*every man is in charge of his own destiny*', I don't absolve the ADF — and by extension, the government — from their responsibility for this drinking culture that developed within most, if not all ADF units serving in Vietnam. And while the ADF may not have actively or formerly promoted large-scale drinking within its ranks, it must have been aware of the alcohol abuse that was eagerly embraced by large numbers of its soldiers in Vietnam.

When we returned home there was never any debriefing or counselling, either offered by, or available from, the Australian Army. What was the thinking within the ADF at that time? Whatever it was, the health and welfare of those many thousands of National Servicemen and Regular soldiers was not high on its agenda. While I'm no longer overtly critical of the ADF, my residual anger is with the government of that time and its highly paid advisors.

In today's contemporary ADF, debriefing and counselling — call it what you like — is a mandatory part of a soldier's transition from operational service to peacetime service or civilian life. That's a very good thing. Even so, soldiers returning from relatively recent ADF operational deployments seem to be experiencing many of the problems and difficulties that typify those of so many Vietnam veterans. A large number of those veterans have been granted a range of compensation disability pensions by DVA.

Like the rest of the National Service complement of my battalion, I transitioned from operational service in a very hostile and dangerous war zone, to a safe and normal civilian life relatively quickly. That being said, I found this transition was very hard to cope with.

The difficulties I experienced were as basic as unconsciously asking my almost puritanical mother at the dinner table to '*pass the fucking butter*' — what I call inured infantry 'grunt' speak — to being unable to properly focus on returning to an ordered society as a functioning civilian. Underpinning these difficulties were the influences of alcohol addiction, and the then repressed underlying mental stresses, directly related to my military service experiences.

For most of my married life, I've been a very difficult person to live with. While never destabilising my long-term marriage to breaking point, there have been a number of times when that was likely to have occurred, However, without my wife ever showing me that she was aware of the torment that was gradually eating away inside me, she has continued to support me all these many years. For that I'm eternally grateful. Most other women may well have just walked away. Had she done that, I don't think I'd be here today telling my story.

One of her consistent criticisms of me is that I'm selfish and intolerant of others. And she's right. I'm not a gregarious person and my day-to-day preoccupations have generally tended to focus on me, at the expense of others, even family members. When my 2 children were growing up, the standards of behaviour, education, and sporting achievement I imposed on them were — in hindsight — entirely inappropriate. I was too harsh a parent. And, although I seemed to maintain a good paternal relationship with my daughter, it took many years for me to develop a similar one with my son. Thankfully, that has now been well and truly established. I like to think that he and I are now very good mates. In fact, I know that's the case.

My generally shy and retiring nature, which insidiously manifested itself in my underlying psyche from the time I was discharged from the army, made it difficult for me to establish and foster the social relationships that my wife and I, as a loving married couple, might otherwise have made. I don't make friends easily and I always react badly to any personal criticism — particularly if I feel that it's unwarranted. I'm extremely uncomfortable in the company of large numbers of strangers or when placed in unfamiliar environments or otherwise stressful situations.

On the other hand, I'm entirely at ease in my own company. Solitude has never concerned me. Because of this, my wife has immersed herself in a range of external social activities and I have managed to develop a range of external interest pursuits as well. At the same time, we have our relatively quiet, but still busy life together, and shared friends and interests, mainly focused on our adult children and 4 grandchildren.

Like most long-term marriages, mine has survived difficult and turbulent moments. But I have to say achieving that — especially on the part of my wife — has been made significantly more difficult and much more complicated due to the mental impacts of my experiences in Vietnam. All said and done, compared to many Vietnam veterans, I'm a very lucky man and I know that. My wife, Elvira (Elvi) is a saint!

CHAPTER 33

VIETNAM

When my army training commenced, I was a raw and relatively inexperienced young man. Before I really knew it, I became a highly-trained and well-armed infantry soldier who served as a member of an 8 RAR infantry platoon.

Even though the army trained me well for this role, I had no meaningful appreciation — in terms of any wider political sense — as to why we were actually in Vietnam. What were we trying to achieve in concert with our allies? I was vaguely aware of some issues regarding the so-called partition of Vietnam into north and south sectors after the Geneva Agreement of 1954, which ultimately led to France's complete withdrawal from Vietnam. But that was about as far as it went.

To be perfectly honest, during our time in Vietnam, most of us had no real idea what the war was even remotely about. Only a few of us were even slightly aware of the 'Domino Theory'. While I was across that line of thought and had some sort of notion that what we were trying to do was to stem the 'apparent' surging tide of Communist expansionism in South-east Asia, I never for one minute thought that the Vietnam conflict may have been one that was deeply steeped in Nationalism which, in reality, it was. The Vietnam War was never ever about Communism.

As far as I can recall, the army made no real effort to provide its other ranks soldiers with any overview of the political situation in Vietnam. Nor did it advise the potential outcomes that an adverse consequence of this conflict may have on neighbouring Asian democracies, and perhaps even the wider western world. I believe this would have been very useful information. The only literature we were provided was a small, extremely basic — and almost useless — 'Australian Military Forces Pocketbook', full of bland statements about South Vietnam which we were left to individually read at our leisure. See Appendix 2.

The cordon and search of the Ap Bac hamlet of the town of Hoa Long in April 1970 obsessively occupied my mind in a very confused way for the remainder of my time in Vietnam. My unhappy experiences during that operational tasking have remained some of my enduring memories. To this day, I remember them as 'clear as crystal'.

Servicemen and servicewomen of today are so much more informed. And so they should be. While exponential advances in communications technology, particularly the availability of the internet and email while serving overseas in operational areas, has contributed to that. I'm also certain that the modern ADF prepares its soldiers for operational service in an educative sense, far better than it did in the late 1960's.

I arrived in Vietnam as an extremely fit and highly-trained infantry soldier, but I was anxious about what lay ahead of me. At the same time, I was determined to do what was going to be asked of me, to the very best of my ability. As far as I'm concerned, I did that, and did it very well, as did all of my platoon mates. However, many things I did and experienced during my time in Vietnam changed me as a person forever and indelibly forged in my mind a range of views about that country, its people, and indeed the modern prosecution of the art of war.

Vietnam's relentless and never-ending heat, humidity, and seasonal torrential rain, are some of my most vivid memories. The fine red dirt and the red glue-like mud, mosquitoes, and other environmental challenges that we encountered out in the field simply need to be experienced to be believed.

In more recent years, I've spent time in Singapore, which is about 1,063km closer to the equator than Phuoc Tuy Province. Although Singapore is also a very hot and wet country, it doesn't even come anywhere close to the debilitating climatic conditions I experienced in Vietnam. However, it's fair to say that being a tourist in Singapore, and an infantry soldier in Vietnam, is probably a totally meaningless comparison anyway.

The amount of time we spent out in the field on operations and the associated deprivations we encountered day after day, sometimes crosses my mind. Not for one minute am I saying that we, as infantry soldiers, did it any tougher than our veteran forebears or veterans of today's more recent ADF deployments. The only point I'm making is that the life of an Australian infantry soldier in Vietnam was extremely harsh, and it was over an extended period of time. We had very few breaks to rest and recover before again proceeding out into the field on further operational tasking. When I finished my 12-month deployment, I was completely exhausted, physically and mentally, and pretty much spent as a proper and reliable infantry resource.

As our time in Vietnam progressively passed, I became exposed to more of the rural commercial activities, as well as the less densely populated areas of the province. I realised that the economy of Phuoc Tuy Province might have once been comparatively robust. Although its economy was largely agricultural and marine based, the French, through their former colonial investment programs, had left their indelible footprint across the province in a number of very positive ways.

For example, the Binh Ba and the De Courtenay rubber plantations were very large commercial operations which quite amazingly seemed to be able

Chapter 33 – Vietnam

to survive, and I imagine, eke out a profit during the many years of hostilities in the province. I have no idea as to the extent of collateral damage wreaked by Australian soldiers on these organisations but I imagine that it would have been significant; no doubt with substantial compensation paid by the Australian Government to the proprietors of each of those commercial entities.

There was also evidence of a number of other light agricultural industries such as rice mills and timber sawmills. The production of copious amounts of rice and other high-yield agricultural commodities like cinnamon, coffee, pepper, various spices, and a range of vegetables — during times of peace — would have been highly profitable enterprises for the economy of the province.

Given that Vietnam was very much an embryonic, emerging third world country back then, the French had built roads, river crossing bridges, and other significant infrastructure throughout Phuoc Tuy Province. And for those times, it was all of a very high quality. In and around Vung Tau the French built some marvellous buildings and created a huge, once vibrant, deep water commercial port that the allied military forces valued so highly and used extensively throughout the Vietnam War.

However, against that positive view of what once might have been a prosperous province, what I observed in the various hamlets, villages, and towns we came across from time to time — and even in the major metropolis of Vung Tau — was extreme and abject poverty. Part of the reason for this was the nature of the war within the province and the fact that allied soldiers were, in effect, occupying that part of the country. It certainly would have been a much happier place for the locals if the so-called 'American War' hadn't touched their lives to the extent that it did.

Although Phuoc Tuy Province had a population of around 160,000 in the late 1960's, it didn't seem to be densely populated, other than in Vung Tau and in a small number of scattered civilian centres. Large tracts of the provincial landscape were extremely inhospitable and many parts of it were totally uninhabitable. To be perfectly honest, as relatively resource-wealthy as Phuoc Tuy Province may have been in its peacetime ambience prior to the war, it's a part of the world that I'm not keen to revisit any time soon.

Apart from the bar girls and staff of Vung Tau and the hordes of young children who seemed to be almost everywhere whenever we operated close to a civilian area, the Vietnamese people I encountered were generally not friendly. Although some of that ill feeling against Australian soldiers can be attributed to ingrained sympathies for the Viet Cong, I believe that the overriding reason for this general indifference — and at times almost insolence — towards us, was nothing more than a reflection of their total disillusionment with, and abject despair about, their dangerous, fractured and economically degraded lives. Quite frankly, we were a major part of their problem.

CHAPTER 34

CONSCRIPTION

I have very mixed views on the concept of military conscription. However, those views need to be measured against community attitudes and government policy, which have changed vastly over the last 5 decades.

In 1965, conscription was re-introduced in Australia without too much public debate, criticism, or fanfare. Back in those days communications were not as they are now, so it's difficult to compare community views over such a lengthy period of time. The community of today is much better educated, informed, and far more politically aware because of the astronomical advances in education and communications technology.

Under Prime Minister Menzies, Australia committed militarily to the Vietnam War in staunch support of its ally, the USA. Because of this cosy political arrangement, conscription was absolutely necessary for Australia to be able to properly prosecute its military involvement in that conflict. Without it, the army wouldn't have been able to increase the number of its infantry battalions from 3 to 9, as well as increasing the vast array of field and other supporting units, which ultimately enabled the deployment of those 9 infantry battalions to Vietnam on a staggered 12-month rotational basis. For the most part, 3 battalions were on the ground in Vietnam at any one time.

In the 1960's, many veterans of WWII were in their 40's and 50's and almost universally shared a widely held view that military service would be good for the country's 20-year-old men. My father was one of those veterans who strongly supported military conscription. I can't recall anyone in my wider family who openly opposed it.

However, I'm also certain that the community back in those days never considered for one moment that such large numbers of conscripted National Servicemen would ever be sent to Vietnam and die there in the numbers they did. Of approximately 60,000 Australian soldiers, sailors, airman, and servicewomen who served in Vietnam, some 19,450 were National Servicemen. Of the 521 Australian servicemen who died in Vietnam, 210 were National Servicemen.

Over the 8 years that the 2nd iteration of National Service — or conscription — was in place in Australia, community attitudes changed markedly. By 1970, public agitation against this, by then, hugely unpopular government policy,

Chapter 34 – Conscription

as well as Australia's military involvement in the Vietnam conflict — largely orchestrated and led by university students and concerned mothers — had reached a crescendo in terms of regular, well-organised public demonstrations and in some few cases, instances of civil disobedience.

I must ask myself this question. Did being in the Australian Army for 2 years as a conscripted soldier make a man out of me, as my close and extended family expected? Well, the answer to that question is that I don't really know. Leaving aside my service in Vietnam, I have to say that exposure over a lengthy period of time to army discipline, process, way of life, and the inevitable bonding of men within particular units must by virtue of its all-encompassing regimented and close-knit nature, change a person in many ways.

I also have a view that a person's core life values will have determined the extent of that change, and whether that change has been for the better or worse. Having said that, I have no doubt that for most National Servicemen, that change would have been positive and beneficial. No 20-year-old man, irrespective of his service record, can undergo 2 years of service in the Australian Army and not re-enter society as a completely different person and — in most cases — a better or more adult version of their prior selves. So, I guess that I do subscribe to the former commonly accepted community mindset that the army, '*will make a man out of him.*'

Had my 2-year period of National Service been confined to service in Australian-based army establishments — irrespective of the corps unit to which I may have been posted to — I would have been very unhappy. I wasn't at all comfortable about my private life, and my importantly — to me — emerging career with the ATO, being interfered with. And, if there wasn't going to be new, significant life experiences accruing to me out of all this, then were there any real positives? I couldn't see them.

Even taking into consideration the free full board, accommodation, and clothing provided to me by the army, I was still being paid substantially less than what I would have been if I remained working with the ATO. While some generous employers did make up that financial difference, this wasn't the case for the then Commonwealth Government. It seemed to me that 2 years of potential boredom, frustration, and pecuniary disadvantage while serving time in Australia would have been a very long ordeal for me. I don't think I would have coped at all well with that.

So, as far back as when I was undertaking recruit training at Puckapunyal, many of us thought that going to Vietnam would be a far preferable experience than the other alternative — rightly or wrongly — mundane existence back in Australia. We thought that Vietnam would be something quite different and exciting. Well, wasn't that the sad truth!

There's no doubt whatsoever in my mind that when I was formally discharged from the army on 29 January 1971, I was a completely different person to who I was before being 'press-ganged' into the army some 2 years previously. Whether I became a more improved or better person, I'm not so sure about. And whether my time in the army or my 12 months in Vietnam generated changes in my maturity and persona, I can only speculate. I was however, without any doubt whatsoever, a very confused young man.

When I really think long and hard about this, my considered view is that while serving in the army probably would have been really good for me in terms of becoming an adult and honing my already inured core life values, what significantly changed me as a person wasn't conscription, or National Service 'per se'. It was my operational military service in Vietnam and the associated myriad of life changing experiences that I was exposed to, once immersed in that war theatre.

As for the actual concept of conscription, while accepting that it was probably essential for the viable military involvement of Australia in the Vietnam War, it was a very unfair government policy because of its selective nature and the very arbitrary way in which it was applied. How morally right and defensible was it for the ADF's quite massive intrusion into the lives of a relatively small cohort of young men, (63,735 out of 804,286 registrants) by the secret — for the most part — mechanism of randomly selected birth-dated marbles drawn out of some obscure barrel?

Contemporary military conscription schemes of other modern countries, and some not so modern countries, tend to include all specifically aged young men — and women in some instances — not just a small selective sample from a somewhat older age profile, as was the case here in Australia. And those comparative schemes were — and still are in many cases — usually based on shorter service periods of either 12 months or more rarely, 18 months.

After my discharge from the army — and re-integration back into society and the civilian workforce — it seemed that the checks and balances that had been legislatively put in place to ensure that there was no employment or job-based disadvantage to former National Servicemen, weren't working as well as they should have.

While the relevant legislation guaranteed my job with the ATO, there was no real protection to realistically and effectively look after my workplace interests and career prospects while I was absent for 2 years on compulsory military service. For example, when I re-joined the agency on 1 February 1971, I found that I'd lost significant ground in terms of status and rank and much more importantly, in terms of salary. My career had stagnated, whereas many of my peers had blossomed. For quite some time, I'm certain that I was a major problem for the ATO. I was a round peg in a square hole, in a board game which the ATO and I had no idea how to conclude.

Chapter 34 – Conscription

Nevertheless, over a 15-month period, I was able to get my career with the ATO back on track and in parity with my workplace peers. But I have to say, I had to achieve all of this by myself with little, if any, consideration by the ATO in terms of the disruption that compulsory military service had on my career. It didn't take me long to realise that my military service was a promotional negative and I quickly removed that reference from my job application résumés.

The experiences of many other National Servicemen re-entering the civilian workforce were far more unpleasant than mine. I've heard countless stories of unscrupulous employers paying only lip-service to the job retention aspects of the relevant legislation. Many of those adversely affected National Servicemen just couldn't be bothered to judiciously take on those recalcitrant employers. It was all too hard for them.

When I was returning home to Australia aboard *Sydney*, I wasn't even sure that I wanted to return to my former employment with the ATO. I wasn't at all well prepared to re-enter society and the civilian workforce. That I ultimately made the right decision — as it turned out — to re-join the ATO, was largely the result of my own common sense, augmented by the measured and compelling advice of my father. Although I really struggled for a time once back at the ATO, I eventually came to realise that I was one of the lucky former National Servicemen.

Many of my 8 RAR National Service mates returning home with me aboard *Sydney* were just as confused as I was. Several of them felt that they were just unable to go back to their former jobs and told me that they weren't inclined to take on shifty employers who ignored the relevant legislation. For many National Servicemen, re-integration back into society and re-entry back into the civilian workforce was very traumatic and for some, it was nothing short of impossible.

While I've not done any associated research on this, my sense is that veterans from the Great War and veterans from WWII weren't treated anywhere near as badly by their former employers. I'm unable to comment on the comparative experiences of veterans of the Korean War because of the absence of reliable data, or even compelling hearsay. No wonder that conflict is still known as the 'Forgotten War'.

So, after all of that, I have to say that I don't support military conscription in any form, unless it were to be imposed in times of dire national threat. If my grandchildren were to ever be compelled to enlist in the military for any other reason, I'd be one of those protesters doing all that I could to stop that from happening.

CHAPTER 35

THE AUSTRALIAN ARMY

When I think about the Australian Army and try to relate that military machine to the contemporary ADF of today, what seems to strike me most of all are 2 things.

The first is how the army that I remember seemed to be unconcerned about the post deployment health of its soldiers compared to today's ADF. And secondly, how the ADF of today has become so politicised.

When I entered the army I was very much aware that the next 2 years of my life were now largely out of my control. I was also aware that there was no honourable way for me to extricate myself from the awful predicament now facing me. And, as I was to quickly learn during those first few days of recruit training at Puckapunyal, I had no rights or avenues of complaint that were of any practical use.

So, what did young National Servicemen like me do back in those days? We simply got on with our job of soldiering and, I guess, made the best of what some might describe as a 'bad lot'. That's just how it was back in those days. Once National Servicemen were well and truly ensconced in the army and caught up in that 'system', there wasn't much point at all in complaining about the unfairness of conscription. While many of us may not have liked being in the army, there was no easy way out, so we just got on with it.

The Australian Army circa 1969-1970, seemed to be an uncomplicated, well-structured, and relatively efficient organisation. By the time I entered its ranks, it was well-experienced in absorbing and integrating National Servicemen into its mainline unit structures, particularly infantry battalions. As a measure of the army's success in achieving that, I can categorically say that during my time with 8 RAR — both in Australia and in Vietnam — I never observed any happening or event that specifically focused on who was a National Serviceman or who was a Regular soldier. Importantly, when I was in Vietnam, being a National Serviceman was simply never an issue at all.

When you consider that the collective posted strength of 8 RAR throughout 1969-70 was comprised of National Serviceman and Regular soldiers in about equal proportions, this was a highly commendable outcome for the battalion. I imagine that the integration of National Servicemen and Regular soldiers in other operational units in Vietnam and army establishments based in Australia, would have been just as successful.

When I arrived in Vietnam, not only were we very fit and extremely well-trained infantry soldiers, our personal weapons were cutting-edge military technology of the time. We also had a whole raft of direct and indirect support elements available to us, which were second to none. In other words, we were 'state of the art' Australian infantry soldiers for those times.

The Vietnam War was the first conflict in modern times where helicopters played such an important and significant role. Wounded or ill soldiers were generally able to be quickly air-lifted by helicopter out of a 'hot' (or other) zone for treatment and care at superior Australian and US Army medical facilities in Vung Tau or — sometimes — even at Nui Dat. In other words, I believe that the army could have done no more to look after its soldiers during their operational service in Vietnam.

In more recent ADF deployments, veterans returning home to Australia have been routinely given proper debriefing and provided with professional counselling. This care of its servicemen and servicewomen now extends to their separation from the ADF and integration back into society and the civilian workforce. That's a very good thing, but such a great pity that the government back in 1962-1975 wasn't as proactive in looking after the mental health of its soldiers returning home to Australia after their operational service in Vietnam.

It's fair to conclude that the mental health of Vietnam veterans has been significantly and adversely affected by their operational service. DVA wouldn't contest that view. It has estimated that as of 30 June 2022, there were 36,700 Australian Vietnam veterans still alive, reflecting an annual average mortality rate over a 6-year period to 30 June 2017 of 867.[46] The average annual mortality rate for the last 5 years is 1,120. This would suggest, as expected, an inexorably increasing mortality rate over time.

As of 30 June 2022, there were 30,419 Vietnam veterans — 82.9% of the estimated surviving population — receiving some quantum of DVA Disability Compensation. Of that number, 18,478 — 60.7% — were being

Table 10.

ESTIMATED NUMBER OF SURVIVING AUSTRALIAN VIETNAM VETERANS

Date	Number	Deaths
30 June 2012	46,800	900
30 June 2013	46,000	800
30 June 2014	45,100	900
30 June 2015	44,200	900
30 June 2016	43,400	800
30 June 2017	42,500	900
30 June 2018	41,500	1,100
30 June 2019	40,400	1,100
30 June 2020	39,300	1,100
30 June 2021	38,000	1,300
30 June 2022	36,700	1,300

---

[46] DVA Annual Reports 2000-2022, Various Tables.

compensated at the Special Rate, the highest possible amount.[47]

Considering that some 60,000 Australian servicemen and servicewomen served in Vietnam, this data is very compelling and clearly indicates that had the ADF paid more attention to the physical and mental health of its Vietnam veterans all those many years ago, then I have no doubt that their overall health today would be much better than it actually is. While the government has consistently tried to talk down the results of government-funded studies into the health of Vietnam veterans, those results clearly show that fighting the war in Vietnam has had a dramatic adverse effect on the overall health of those who fought in it.

Over the last several decades, the ADF has been engaged in a number of deployments: Iraq, Afghanistan, Timor-Leste, and the Solomon Islands for example. With so many Australian men and women deployed to various trouble spots of the world, the likelihood of casualties, even fatalities, is high. The fact that Australian casualties on these deployments have been — in comparative terms — relatively few, is testament to the training, leadership, and overall professionalism of the modern ADF.

However, whenever there has been an operational casualty, it seems to me that the context and proper focus of that was often overtaken by politicians almost tripping over themselves to make as much political capital as possible out of the event. Invariably, a death or serious injury to a deployed service person becomes the subject of numerous official media releases and television interviews with the Minister for Defence and the Chief of the Defence Force. Other politicians often seem to get in on the act as well and the message they put out to the community is, *'isn't this awful!'* Today, operational fatalities arising out of any sort of firefight with enemy combatants, no matter how minor, always end up as the subject of an official media release.

Does all this send the right message to our serving men and women? Apart from 2 periods of National Service, life in the ADF is, and always has been, a chosen career path — but one that is often tempered with danger. There's always the possibility that servicemen and servicewomen may well lose their lives or suffer serious wounds in the line of their service. That's the very nature of service life.

Australia's servicemen and servicewomen are trained to defend their country and its wider external interests, depending on government foreign policy of the day. In that role, they may well be placed in harm's way and some might even suffer injury or death. However, it must be noted that these servicemen and servicewomen were acutely aware of the personal risks attached to service life when they enlisted, and were actually doing what they

---

[47] DVA Annual Report 2020-22, Pensioner Summary, VEA 1986, Table 11.

wanted to do in life when they were either killed or wounded.

As MAJ John D Thornton Retd, who provided me with invaluable technical advice in relation to the artillery component of this book — 'under friendly fire' segment — once conveyed to me in a personal email:

> '... *All of us who were there* (Vietnam), *Regular soldiers and National Servicemen alike, wanted to go looking for a fight and play big boys' games with big boys' toys...*'

It's worth thinking about Thornton's poignant comment because it's so very true. I can relate to it entirely. My very clear recollection of my time in Vietnam is that no member of my platoon was ever, not even once, averse to being sent out into the field on operations, irrespective of what our variable deployable numbers might have been. We were always raring to go. In other words — while this may confound some readers — we really did want to go out and confront the enemy.

Thornton, who later served with the British military forces in Germany, also tells of a marvellously droll British response to a complaint about anything that ever went wrong and caused discomfort or injury, even on a training field exercise:

> '...*Well, if you can't take a joke, you shouldn't have joined...*'

It seems to me that since the early 1970's and particularly in recent years, the ADF has, in some respects, lost its way. I have no doubt whatsoever that the main reason for this has been its insidious politicisation. While minimisation of operational casualties is an admirable key performance indicator, it really is no more than that. Getting the right job done right, the first time, is far more important.

I'm very much aware that there will be some readers who won't agree with my conceivably inflammatory views about the politicisation of the ADF. Well, that's not really my problem. It is, after all, my personal view — and I'm entitled to that.

CHAPTER 36

AGENT ORANGE

Since as far back as the early 1970s, Australian Vietnam veterans lobbied hard for proper recognition by the government, and it took until the Welcome Home Parade in 1987 for that to occur. Vietnam veterans have never stopped pursuing government, on behalf of themselves, their children, and their grandchildren, over their 'perceived' exposure to Agent Orange and other herbicides and chemicals during their time in Vietnam.

Over the early years, I've often been asked by family and friends if I was ever exposed to Agent Orange, or if I ever saw it sprayed during my time in Vietnam. Generally, I've always tended to respond to those questions in a vague sort of way. I don't think I've ever seriously put my mind to that specific question until I started to write this part of my story.

I won't explore this issue in any great depth. Others have done that far better than I could ever do, particularly Peter Yule.[48] Nevertheless, as it's a record of my experiences in the army and of my time in Vietnam in particular, it's appropriate that I record my broad recollections regarding the spraying of herbicides, insecticides, and other chemicals in Vietnam.

In his paper, 'Agent Orange — A History of Deception (New Zealand Vietnam Veterans and the McLeod Report)' — presented to the Health Select Committee of the New Zealand Parliament in the early 2000's, Lachlan Irvine, an Australian Vietnam veteran himself and a recognised expert on this issue, says that:

> '... From 1965 to 1970, some 362,360 US gallons (1,449,440 litres) of herbicides and chemicals were sprayed in Phuoc Tuy Province as part of Operation Ranch Hand. Of that herbicidal and chemical volume, some 202,910 US gallons (811,640 litres) was Agent Orange.'

At various times Australian soldiers also operated in other provinces, particularly Bien Hoa Province, and occasionally in Long Khanh Province, where even more significant amounts of herbicides and chemicals — again including Agent Orange — were sprayed. See Appendix 9. Irvine also says in

---

[48] Yule, Peter. *The Long Shadow*. New South Publishing, University of New South Wales Press Ltd, University of New South Wales. 2020.

his paper that:

> *'...The most heavily sprayed part of South Vietnam was the Rung Sat special zone, a vast expanse of mangrove swamps, which forms the western boundary of Phuoc Tuy Province...'*

Irvine also suggests that Vung Tau:

> *'...Received 7,350 US gallons (29,400 litres) of Agent Orange in separate spraying...'*

As an integral part of research for my story, I contacted as many of my former platoon mates as I could to clarify a range of unclear recollections. One evening, as I was quietly chatting on the phone with Terry Lucas, he said to me:

'Do you remember seeing or hearing the sounds of birds when we were in Vietnam together?'

As I sat in my study, phone glued to my right ear, I was absolutely stunned. Seriously, I reckon I would have been able to hear a feather drop to the floor at that very moment. After thinking about his question for quite some time, my quiet response to Terry was:

'Terry, no I don't!'

I've often thought about this conversation...and the title of my book arose from it. Unlike most land-based animals — including humans — birds are a very fragile life form, easily impacted by human-induced environmental change. Birds don't remain in locales that aren't conducive to the quiet enjoyment of their lives, or that don't facilitate their natural breeding urges. They simply go elsewhere. Gunfire and chemical insecticide and pesticide spraying were an anathema for bird life.

Within Nui Dat itself, there was spraying of some kind always going on — to keep the never-ending vegetative growth around the main dirt road thoroughfares and unit lines scattered throughout the large 1 ATF base under control, and to inhibit the ever-present legions of ravenous mosquitos. This sort of housekeeping spraying must have been almost constant, because I always noticed it taking place on each rare occasion that we were back at Nui Dat. We never knew what these herbicides, insecticides, and chemicals were, probably because we never asked. To be perfectly honest, I don't think anyone really gave it another thought at the time either. I know I didn't.

The 13km perimeter of Nui Dat was very heavily defended. The major defence system in place was a protected, deep, continuous-wired and mined area, largely devoid of any serious vegetation whatsoever. In other words, it had to have been significantly defoliated by something, and I can only conclude that Agent Orange or some other herbicide or chemical was used to achieve and maintain that near moonscape-like vista.

In addition, throughout Phuoc Tuy Province itself, there were numerous defoliated areas. In some cases, they resembled huge swathes seemingly gouged out of otherwise lush vegetation. I'm not referring to 1 ATF land clearing operations where army engineers — protected by infantry soldiers — used D9 dozers to cut down huge corridors of trees, creating so-called 'fire trails'. I'm talking about vast tracts of desolate and featureless land that appeared totally out of place, given the prevailing landscape. At the time, we didn't give these stark and surreal vistas a second thought, other than to recognise them for what they were, and to be aware that we needed to move around them and not across them, to maintain our operational security.

While I don't recall having any chemicals or herbicides — or anything else — sprayed over me out in the field or back at Nui Dat, this may not have been the case for others. I just don't remember it happening to me. Having said that, within Nui Dat the numerous water storage containers generally weren't appropriately covered.

Also, whenever we were out in the field, we used to collect and drink water from a range of naturally occurring catchments. I can only conclude that I, and most other Australian, New Zealand, and other allied soldiers deployed operationally in Vietnam, would have constantly ingested Agent Orange and other herbicides and chemicals in variable diluted concentrations during our entire tours of duty.

Irvine also says in his paper that:

'...A study...found a marked elevation of dioxin in blood samples taken from residents of the Vietnamese city of Bien Hoa (25km north of Saigon) more than 30 years after the last herbicide flight...'

Irvine further goes on to say that several recent studies:

'...provide the clearest proof yet that dioxin in Agent Orange stays in the environment, pollutes the food chain and contaminates humans regardless of whether or not they were directly sprayed...'

Having regard to my personal observations and the very compelling data and arguments put forward by Yule and Irvine, there's no doubt in my mind whatsoever that Australian soldiers in Vietnam were exposed — directly and indirectly — to a wide range of noxious herbicides, insecticides, and chemicals, probably including Agent Orange.

EPILOGUE

For those readers who have persevered and absorbed the wide-ranging content of my very personal story, I thank you sincerely. I hope that you found it an interesting, informative read and perhaps even an enlightening source of information.

This memoir is a large work and I certainly hope that it adds to the public record data base of Australia's military involvement in the Vietnam War. If it were to only do that, I'd be content.

APPENDIX 1

PERSONAL ITEMS

Item 1.

Item 2.

Item 3.

Item 4.

Item 1: The indispensable, all-purpose, lightweight aluminium mug that I carried while in Vietnam. In fact I carried 2 of them. The handle of the mug collapsed and folded under the base, and a water bottle could be inserted into it.

The whole combined unit was then crammed into a soft carry holder attached to the standard webbing belt, thereby consolidating and facilitating the storage need. The practical or usable volume of the mug was around 650ml. I used it every day for heating canned rations meals, cooking par-boiled and dried rice, boiling water for coffee and tea, and even for shaving and cleaning teeth.

Item 2: The KFS — knife, fork and spoon — set was made from aluminium and only weighed a few grams at most. I discarded the knife and fork early on, and relied upon the spoon as my universal eating utensil.

Item 3: 'Fred' was the P38 can opener, a vital implement that was included with each day's ration pack, per man. Most of the men who served in Vietnam probably took a number of these back home to Australia. My wife occasionally uses this implement, many of which rest peacefully in our kitchen utility drawer. Sadly, ring-pull technology has rendered them pretty much obsolete these days.

Item 4: I've spoken at length about the wonderful GP boots provided to us. Our US allies were very envious as their standard issue footwear was canvas-based and nowhere near as durable, given the climate conditions of Vietnam.

APPENDIX 2

AUSTRALIAN MILITARY FORCES 'GUIDE' TO SOUTH VIETNAM

Chapter 1 – The War in South Vietnam

Chapter 2 – History

Chapter 3 – Geography

Chapter 4 – Government and Administrative Structure

Chapter 5 – The People

Chapter 6 – The Armed Services

Chapter 7 – The Viet Cong

Chapter 8 – Vietnamese Language Guide

Chapter 9 – Useful Information

Chapter 10 – Security

APPENDIX 3

CLIMATE DATA FOR VUNG TAU PHUOC TUY PROVINCE VIETNAM

AUGUST 2013 - JULY 2018: AGGREGATED MONTHLY AVERAGES

MONTH	TEMP MAX (C)	TEMP MIN (C)	RAINFALL(mm)
August	34	29	505
September	33	29	504
October	33	28	451
November	33	28	137
December	31	27	74
January	31	26	4
February	31	26	5
March	31	27	5
April	33	29	44
May	34	31	307
June	34	30	452
July	33	29	506
			Total: 3,064

Data courtesy of: www.worldweatheronline.com

Around 96% of southern Vietnam's average annual rainfall falls during the 7-month wet season from May to November. According to the meteorological source on which I've relied, there are no significant variations from the long-term average monthly rainfall norms, as reflected in the above table.

Over this 5-year period, average relative humidity — a key indicator of personal comfort — was consistently high at about 85%. More importantly, the average dew point was similarly consistent and disgustingly high at 23°C. Collectively, high dew point and humidity levels invariably result in extremely oppressive conditions. While the actual temperature is also a significant contributing factor, it isn't anywhere near as important as those 2 other measures.

While the maximum day-time temperature in Vietnam occasionally exceeded 34°C, the night-time temperature was never lower than about 28°C. This explains why my recall of climatic conditions during my 12 months in Vietnam is so utterly negative. Welcome to my Vietnam!

Appendix 3 — Climate Data for Vung Tau, Phuoc Tuy Province Vietnam

It's also worth noting that all of these fairly recent meteorological observations were recorded in a coastal peninsular locale, impacted by subtle, cooling sea breezes for much of the time. The inland temperatures, humidity, and precipitation levels within the wider environs of Phuoc Tuy Province, would have been somewhat higher than the levels reflected in this data, as has always been the case in Australia.

For example, in Sydney for the greater part of the year, the temperatures and humidity levels are always significantly higher inland, when compared to those of the coastal areas. In terms of daily summertime maximum temperatures, that difference can often be as high as 7°C. While I'm not suggesting that the climatic difference in inland Phuoc Tuy Province would have been of that magnitude, there would have been at the very least, some quantum of adverse measurable change.

Significantly, the rainfall and humidity trend lines recorded in Vung Tau over this 5-year period hardly ever moved from a long-established norm, clearly illustrating that back in 1969-1970, the men of 8 RAR had little, if any, respite from the oppressive nature of the climate of southern Vietnam.

I've spoken to a number of Vietnamese people now living in Canberra and their very clear recollections from their former lives — pre 1988 — back in Bien Hoa Province, north of Ho Chi Minh City (formerly Saigon), are that the temperature was the same every day of the year — a maximum of 38°C during the day and a minimum of 30°C at night. Those metrics are pretty close to the average recorded meteorological observations contained in the above table.

While these people didn't know what the average humidity or dew point levels were back then, they conveyed to me that it was always sticky and unpleasant and that they had grown up amid that debilitating, testing climate... and utterly abhorred it. From those common themed comments, I've concluded that they were talking about an average humidity level of (say) 85% and quite possibly as high as 90% on many days each year. As far as they were concerned, the only climatic seasonal variable that they were consciously aware of, was the rainfall. Otherwise, for them it was always just plain disgusting. No argument from me on that score.

APPENDIX 4

OPERATIONAL RATIONS

The following table reflects the typical maximum daily food resources that I packed and carried when engaged on operational activities in Vietnam:

1 x 160gm (5.65oz) can of either:
- Diced ham and egg
- Corned beef hash
- Beef steak
- Ham slices
- Tuna
- Turkey loaf
- Luncheon Meat.

1 x 250gm (8.75oz) can of either:
- Apple sauce
- Apricots
- Peaches
- Pears
- Fruit salad.

2 x 80gm (2.75oz) pack of cheese and crackers.

Very liberal quantities of par-boiled and freeze-dried rice, curry powder, soup powders, salt and pepper, other condiments, and plenty of coffee and tea making materials and occasional 'Jack' rations.

And, for a fairly brief period of time (around 2 months or so):

1 x 340gm (12.0oz) can of either:
- Spaghetti and ground meat (usual)
- Spaghetti and meatballs
- Ham and beans
- Meatballs and beans
- Beef and onions
- Beef and vegetables
- Steak and potatoes
- Sausages and beans.

APPENDIX 5

EQUIPMENT AND ASSOCIATED WEIGHTS

The typical aggregate weight load carried on day 1 of an operation — with a planned 5-day resupply in the field — by an 8 RAR Assault Pioneer Platoon soldier in Vietnam, is reflected in the data contained in the following lists:

SUMMARY VERSION

ITEM	Kg
Clothing and boots	4.00
Packs and webbing	7.00
SLR Rifle & magazine (1 x 20 rounds)	5.27
SLR Rifle magazines (8 x 20 rounds)	5.84
M60 Machine gun ammunition belts (2 x 100 rounds)	5.90
Machete	0.70
Bayonet	0.50
M18 Claymore mines x 2	5.20
M26 Hand grenades x 2	0.90
M8 Smoke grenades x 2	1.36
M72 LAW Rocket launcher x 1	2.95
Contents of backpacks and bum packs	20.00
Water (4L)	4.00
Entrenching tool	1.73
Other	2.50
Rounding	*(0.85)*
Total Weight	67.00

The 2 men who comprised each of the platoon's M60 machine gun groups, those men who carried the platoon's M79 grenade launchers, and the platoon signaller, would have carried more than 67kg of weight.

I usually carried more weight than anyone else in the platoon because of my obsession regarding personal hydration — water — and the fact that I very often — almost always — also carried our section's M79 grenade launcher and all of its heavy ammunition.

DETAILED VERSION
WEIGHT CARRIED ON DAY 1 OF AN OPERATION
(This data reflects a planned 5-day resupply)

List A: Clothing and Personal Items

ITEM	Kg	COMMENT
Trousers	0.71	
Shirt	0.40	
GP boots	1.50	
Netting - loose weave (1m)	0.15	
Floppy hat	0.20	
Towelling sweat rag (0.75m)	0.15	
Other	0.89	
Sub Total A	4.00	

List B: Webbing and Equipment

ITEM	Kg	COMMENT
Backpack (empty)	1.73	Also See List C
Bum pack (empty)	0.37	Also See List C
Webbing shoulder harness	0.38	
Webbing belt	0.34	
Machete scabbard	0.25	
Bayonet frog	0.15	
Ammunition pouches x 2	0.63	
Water bottles (empty) & carriers x 4	2.24	Also See List E
Aluminium mugs x 2	0.47	
KFS set	0.30	
Rounding	*0.14*	
Sub Total B	7.00	

List C: Contents of Backpacks and Bum Packs

ITEM	Kg	COMMENT
Rations (5 days)	4.50	
Assorted 'jack rations'	1.00	
SLR Rifle magazines (4 x 20 rounds)	2.92	
Can openers 'Freds' x 4	0.15	
Rifle cleaning kit	0.35	

Appendix 5 — Equipment and Associated Weights

ITEM	Kg	COMMENT
Bottles of weapons cleaning oil x 8	0.72	
Army issue torch + spare batteries	0.55	
Pencil torches + spare batteries	0.30	
Scissors x 2	0.35	
Army issue waterproof maps & protractor	0.30	
Army issue compass	0.29	
Camouflage grease paint - tins x 2	0.20	
Sewing kit (Housewife)	0.15	
Bottles of insect & tick repellent x 6	0.72	
Personal toiletries	0.30	
Boot cleaning materials	0.40	
Black electrical tape rolls x 8	0.56	
Cigarettes	0.40	
Letter writing materials	0.15	
Bedding 'silk'	0.45	
Green army general purpose cord - 20m	0.25	
Slabs of C4 plastic explosive x 6	3.42	Cooking heat
Entrenching tool	1.73	
Rounding	*(0.16)*	
Sub Total C	20.00	

List D: Weapons and Armaments

ITEM	Kg	COMMENT
SLR Rifle & (1 x 20 round magazine)	5.27	
Shell dressing (taped to rifle butt)	0.08	
SLR Rifle magazines (8 x 20 rounds)	5.84	
M26 Hand grenades x 2	0.90	
M8 Smoke grenades x 2	1.36	
Machete	0.70	
Bayonet	0.50	
M72 LAW rocket x 1	2.95	
M18 Claymore mines x 2	5.20	
Belts of M60 ammunition x 2	5.90	
Rounding	*0.30*	
Sub Total D	29.00	

List E: Water and Other

ITEM		Kg	COMMENT
Water (4L)		4.00	Also See Lists B, F and G
Other		2.50	
Rounding		*0.50*	
	Sub Total E	7.00	

	TOTAL WEIGHT	67.00	

Much of this data has been gleaned from information made publicly available by the Pension and Advocacy Team of the Sunshine Coast Sub-Branch of the Vietnam Veterans Association of Australia.

List F: *My Estimated Personal Adjustments to Standard Platoon Carried Weights (On Day 1 of any operation – 5 Day resupply)*

ADDITIONAL WEIGHT	Kg	LESS WEIGHT	Kg
SLR Rifle magazines (4 x 20 rounds)	2.92	M72 LAW rocket x 1	2.95
Water (4L) bottles & carriers	6.24	M26 Hand grenades x 2	0.90
Knives x 2 (15cm & 12cm blades)	0.70	Bayonet & frog	0.65
Other	1.00	Rations (1 day)	0.90
Rounding	*0.14*	*Rounding*	*0.60*
TOTAL	11.00		6.00

List G: *My Estimated Personal Adjustments to Standard Platoon Carried Weights (When I carried the Section's M79 Grenade Launcher)*

ADDITIONAL WEIGHT	Kg	LESS WEIGHT	Kg
M79 Grenade launcher & HE x 1	2.93	Belts of M60 ammunition x 2	5.80
M79 ammunition (60 HE & Illum)	13.50	M18 Claymore mines x 2	5.20
Water (2L) bottles & carriers	3.12		
Rounding	*0.45*		
TOTAL	20.00		11.00

Appendix 5 — Equipment and Associated Weights

This data clearly demonstrates that while each member of the Assault Pioneer Platoon mixed and matched what he carried, the basic weight carry load for all of us on the first day of an operation was around 67kg. When the first resupply was scheduled for 7 days out, it became a lot trickier because of the need to carry extra rations. I only carried rations for 5 days on those few occasions.

Overall, members of the machine gun groups and those men who carried the M79 grenade launchers, would have been carrying a minimum of at least another net 12-14kg of weight, compared to other members of the platoon.

And the vital radio communications 25/77 set, along with its basic battery and accessories carried by the platoon signaller, weighed a whopping 12.4kg. Spare batteries (3+) for the radio each weighed 1.15kg.

MATERIALS CARRIED BY THE PLATOON FOR ENEMY BUNKER DEMOLITION TASKS

The previous lists, and indeed the content of my story more generally, don't include — or explain in any detail — the very large collective weight of the explosives, primers, detonators, detonation cord, fuses, hundreds of rolls of black electrical tape etc used by the Assault Pioneer Platoon when it was tasked with demolishing enemy bunker systems. This was often a feature of the platoon's operational tasking during the period 10 December 1969 until late March 1970.

Many of these bunker systems were in very hard to access areas and, while the platoon may have been dropped off by Iroquois helicopters — sometimes — or by APCs — occasionally — as close as possible to those locations, we usually had to walk quite some distance, carrying with us all of the necessary demolition materials. In doing so, more than half of the members of the platoon had to lug several fully-laden sandbags with them, each containing around 6kg or more of explosives.

While much of this detail is now not so clear in my mind, from what I do seem to recall, the collective weight of the pyrotechnic materials carried by the platoon for the demolition of a reasonably-sized bunker system was extraordinarily large, something like 200kg.

Now, not all members of the platoon were loaded up with this extra weight. The men comprising PHQ, forward scouts, and the M60 machine gun groups, were exempt from this 'pack horse' duty, as were several others such as section commanders, etc. Having said that, I do clearly recall my section commander — Corporal Fred Vincent — always carrying plenty of primers, detonators, detonation cord, and fuses on these occasions. This meant that for obvious reasons, he wasn't carrying any hard explosives. Vincent had no aspirations whatsoever in becoming 'Guy Fawkes the 2nd'!

Anyway, it doesn't take too much math to figure out that there were only around 16 or less poor sods like me carrying this additional 200kg (12.5kg per man) of weight — which gets back to my recall of 2 crammed sandbags of explosives, per man. A slab of C4 plastic explosive weighed 570gm. The TNT that we also used was slightly heavier per slab and much bulkier in shape.

When the platoon was engaged on the demolition of multiple enemy bunker systems, resupplies of explosives and associated initiators were delivered to it by either Iroquois helicopters or APCs.

APPENDIX 6

ASSAULT PIONEER PLATOON DEMOGRAPHICS ENHANCED

NAME		RANK #1	AGE #2	SERVICE Type #3	TIME WITH PLATOON IN VIETNAM
Ken Jones		2 LT	23	R	28 Nov 69 - 1 Apr 70
Peter Phillips		2 LT	21	R	5 Apr 70 - 5 Nov 70
Cliff Grant		Sgt	36	R	17 Nov 69 - 1 Nov 70
Monty White		Sgt	28	R	17 Nov 69 - 28 Jun 70
Ron Goubareff		Cpl	24	R	19 Nov 69 - 12 Nov 70
Bob O'Callaghan		Cpl	25	R	17 Nov 69 - 12 Nov 70
Fred Vincent		Cpl	25	R	19 Nov 69 - 12 Nov 70
John Dolgan		LCpl	19	R	17 Nov 69 - 12 Nov 70
Dave Matheson		LCpl	23	NS	17 Nov 69 - 12 Nov 70
Jeff (JJ) Smith	# 4	LCpl	23	R	17 Nov 69 - 11 Jun 70
Bob Whiley		LCpl	33	R	17 Nov 69 - 12 Nov 70
Peter Cousins		Pte	23	NS	17 Nov 69 - 12 Nov 70
Mick Domarecki	# 8	Pte	24	R	22 Jul 70 - 3 Oct 70
John Floyd	# 4	Pte	22	R	17 Nov 69 - 4 Jun 70
Robin Jagger		Pte	21	NS	17 Nov 69 - 12 Nov 70
Paul Jansen		Pte	21	NS	17 Nov 69 - 12 Nov 70
Steve Kaliczinsky		Pte	22	R	17 Nov 69 - 12 Nov 70
Arthur Koo	# 5	Pte	22	NS	17 Nov 69 - 4 July 70
Bill Leebody	# 6	Pte	25	NS/V	15 Jul 70 - 12 Nov 70
Des Lock		Pte	22	NS	17 Nov 69 - 21 May 70
Terry Lucas		Pte	21	NS	3 Jul 70 - 12 Nov 70
Les Lupuljev		Pte	22	R	17 Nov 69 - 12 Nov 70
Peter McCann		Pte	21	NS	17 Nov 69 - 12 Nov 70
Adrian (Peter) McCormick		Pte	21	NS	25 Mar 70 - 12 Nov 70
Des McGrath		Pte	22	NS	17 Nov 69 - 12 Nov 70
Denis McNab		Pte	23	NS	25 Mar 70 - 12 Nov 70
Tony Marlborough	# 7	Pte	20	NS/V	17 Nov 69 - 25 Mar 70
Mick O'Shea		Pte	21	NS	17 Nov 69 - 12 Nov 70
Tom Parrott		Pte	22	NS	17 Nov 69 - 25 Mar 70
Ray Salmon		Pte	20	R	17 Nov 69 - 12 Nov 70
Bob Simpson		Pte	22	NS	17 Nov 69 - 2 Jul 70
Allan Small		Pte	22	NS	17 Nov 69 - 5 Nov 70
Geoff Smith	# 8	Pte	21	NS	7 Aug 70 - 3 Oct 70
Mark Smith		Pte	21	NS	17 Nov 69 - 10 Nov 70
Josef Stepien	# 8	Pte	21	NS	22 Jul 70 - 3 Oct 70
Brian Taylor		Pte	21	NS	17 Nov 69 - 12 Nov 70
Arthur Walsh	# 8	Pte	19	NS/V	22 Jul 70 - 3 Oct 70
Peter Wood		Pte	22	NS	17 Nov 69 - 12 Nov 70

#1 Rank depicted in this table is on the day of return to Australia, or on the day posted out of, or removed from the platoon.

#2 Age is on 10 December 1969 — the first day of the battalion's initial operation in Vietnam — or the age on the day a member was posted into the platoon after that date.

#3 Service type was either Regular, National Service, or National Service Volunteer.

#4 John Floyd and Jeff (JJ) Smith were 9th Intake National Servicemen who both signed on for a further (3rd) year term to facilitate a deployment to Vietnam with 8 RAR, thereby becoming Regular soldiers.

#5 Arthur Koo was bitten by a scorpion and after 10 days as an in-patient at 1 AFH in 1 ALSG, he was seconded on 5 July 1970 — probably because of his engineering background — to 1 ACAU within 1 ATF. While he remained on the platoon's posted strength, he never re-joined it, or the battalion, and returned to Australia on 10 November 1970 courtesy of a Qantas 'Skippy Squadron' flight out of Tan Son Nhut Airport, Saigon.

#6 Bill Leebody was posted into the platoon from D Company quite late in the tour, sometime around mid-July 1970. Because of his date of birth, he was also quite clearly a National Service Volunteer.

#7 Tony Marlborough, because of his age (20) on the first day — 10 December 1969 — of the battalion's initial operation in Vietnam, must have also been a National Service Volunteer. That would be correct as the DVA Vietnam Veterans' Nominal Role reflects that he departed Vietnam on 25 March 1970.

#8 Because their periods of National Service or Regular service obligations extended significantly beyond the date of 8 RAR's return to Australia, 4 platoon reinforcements were posted out of 8 RAR to other operational units in Vietnam on 4 October 1970. They didn't return to Australia with the battalion. Those platoon members were:

Appendix 6 — Assault Pioneer Platoon Demographics Enhanced

Mick Domarecki	2 RAR until 1 June 1971
Geoff Smith	HQ 1 ATF until 15 Jul 1971
Josef Stepien	2 RAR until 1 Jun 1971
Arthur Walsh	7 RAR until 4 March 1971

KNOWN PLATOON MORTALITY AFTER RETURN TO AUSTRALIA

NAME	DATE OF DEATH			AGE
Steve Kaliczinsky	23	Oct	1972	25
Mick O'Shea	27	Jul	1975	27
Bob Simpson	05	May	2006	58
Bill Leebody	26	Mar	2010	64
Cliff Grant	16	Dec	2016	83
Bob Whiley	25	Oct	2022	85
Peter Phillips	25	Jan	2023	74

APPENDIX 7

ASSAULT PIONEER PLATOON ACTIVITY MATRIX (DAYS)

MONTH	HMAS *Sydney*	NUI DAT	BATTALION OPERATIONS	VUNG TAU R&C	TOTAL DAYS
Nov 69	11	3	-	-	14
Dec 69	-	10	21	-	31
Jan 70	-	11	18	2	31
Feb 70	-	1	27	-	28
Mar 70	-	7	24	-	31
Apr 70	-	5	25	-	30
May 70	-	7	28	2	31
Jun 70	-	-	30	-	30
Jul 70	-	9	22	-	31
Aug 70	-	-	31	-	31
Sep 70	-	13	15	* 2	30
Oct 70	-	16	15	-	31
Nov 70	12	-	-	-	12
Totals	23	76	256	6	361

* Not all members of the platoon were able to avail themselves of 3 periods of R&C leave. And not all members proceeded on R&R leave, which was generally of a 5-day period or 7 days if that leave was taken back in Australia.

APPENDIX 8

ENHANCING VIETNAMESE CULTURE

THE CHEAP CHARLIE (CHAR-LEE) SONG[49]

Verse 1 Uc-dai-loi, Cheap Charlie He no buy me Saigon tea Saigon tea costs many Pee Uc-dai-loi, he Cheap Charlie	**Verse 4** Uc-dai-loi, Cheap Charlie Make me give him one for free Mamma-san go crook at me Uc-dai-loi, he Cheap Charlie.
Verse 2 Uc-dai-loi, Cheap Charlie He no give me MPC MPC costs many Pee Uc-dai-loi, he Cheap Charlie	**Verse 5** Uc-dai-loi, Cheap Charlie He give baby-san to me Baby-san costs many Pee Uc-dai-loi, he Cheap Charlie.
Verse 3 Uc-dai-loi, Cheap Charlie He no go to bed with me Bed with me costs many Pee Uc-dai-loi, he Cheap Charlie.	**Verse 6** Uc-dai-loi, Cheap Charlie He go home across the sea He leave baby-san with me Uc-dai-loi, he Cheap Charlie.

A few basic meanings of some of the words in this song, which was often sung with great passion by the Vung Tau bar girl prostitutes to the tune of 'knick knack paddy whack, give the dog a bone' are set our below:

- Charlie - pronounced 'char-lee'.

- Cheap Charlie - a 'round-eye' who was stingy or unwilling to spend money.

- Uc-dai-loi - a Vietnamese term for an Australian (pronounced 'ook day loy') purportedly meaning 'big rat' because there is no word in the Vietnamese language vocabulary for 'kangaroo'.

- Saigon Tea - served to bar girl prostitutes ostensibly as whisky and Coke — at inflated prices when a 'round eye' was paying. It was never alcoholic and was usually just diluted, tepid green tea.

- Round eye - Vietnamese term for a non-Asian.

---

[49] International War Veterans Poetry Archive.

- MPC - Military Payment Certificates that replicated US dollars at face value.
- P - Piastre - the alternative unit of currency in south Vietnam during the so-called American War. It was almost worthless. The official currency, also worthless, was the 'Dong'.
- Mamma-san - female bar/brothel owner.
- Baby-san - baby.

So, there you have it. Australia's wonderful, and probably only contribution to Vietnamese culture during the Vietnam War! At least the French built wonderful architectural edifices, along with a wide range of other economically beneficial social infrastructure, as well as imparting their knowledge to the Vietnamese on how to brew beer, bake bread, and make butter.

APPENDIX 9

US HERBICIDE MISSIONS DELIVERED IN SOUTH VIETNAM

An extract from Lachlan Irvine's paper: *Agent Orange - A History of Deception* (New Zealand Vietnam Veterans and the McLeod Report).

US GALLONS — 4 LITRES — OF HERBICIDE SPRAYED BY TYPE

Province	Missions	Year	Agent Orange	Agent Blue	Agent White	Total
Long Khanh	480	1965-70	983,562	16,745	612,356	1,612,663
Biah Duong	246	1965-70	395,835	40,510	373,973	810,318
Hua Nghia	54	1965-70	483,215	10,345	51,273	544,833
Bien Hoa	237	1965-70	425,037	8,950	386,985	820,972
Phuoc Tuy	113	1965-70	202,910	2,700	156,750	362,360
Gia Dinh	229	1966-70	532,685	43,400	225,485	810,570
Totals	1359		3,532,685	122,650	1,806,822	6,768,538

Abbreviations

DISTANCE
cm	Centimetre
click	Kilometre
ft	Foot
in	Inches
km	Kilometre
m	Metre
mm	Millimetre
nm	Nautical mile

SPEED
kts	Knots
km/h	Kilometres per hour
m/s	Metres per second
rpm	Rounds per minute/Revolutions per minute

WEIGHTS AND MEASURES
gm	Grams/Grains
kg	Kilograms
L	Litres
lb	Pounds
ml	Millilitres
mg	Milligrams
M	Million
oz	Ounces
tn	Tonnes/Tons

POWER/ENERGY/TEMPERATURE
00C	Degrees Celsius
00F	Degrees Fahrenheit
cal	Calories
hp	Horsepower
j	Joules
kj	Kilojoules
ke	Kinetic Energy

MILITARY
1 ACAU	1st Australian Civil Affairs Unit
1 ATF	1st Australian Task Force
1 AFH	1st Australian Field Hospital

Abbreviations

1 ALSG	1st Australian Logistical Support Group
1 ARU	1st Australian Reinforcement Unit
AAAGV	Australian Army Assistance Group Vietnam
AATTV	Australian Army Training Team Vietnam
ADF	Australian Defence Force
ADFA	Australian Defence Force Academy
AO	Area of Operation
APC	Armoured Personnel Carrier
ARVN	Army of the Republic of Vietnam
BCP	Battery Commander's Party
BHQ	Battalion Headquarters
CHQ	Company Headquarters
CMF	Citizens Military Forces
D&E	Defence and Employment Platoon
DDG	Guided Missile Destroyer
DFC	Distinguished Flying Cross
DI	Drill Instructor
DLNS	Department of Labour and National Service
DMZ	Demilitarised Zone
DUSTOFF	Medical Evacuation
DVA	Department of Veterans' Affairs
FOP	Forward Observer Parties
GAF	Government Aircraft Factories
GOPHER	Soft Drink
GP	General Purpose
IED	Improvised Explosive Device
JTC	Jungle Warfare Training Centre
LINES	Living Quarters
LZ	Landing Zone
MAA	Master-at-Arms
MACV	Military Assistance Council Vietnam
MEDEVAC	Medical Evacuation
MPC	Military Payment Certificate
NLF	National Liberation Front
NVA	North Vietnam Army
OCS	Officer Cadet School
PF	Provincial Forces
PHQ	Platoon Headquarters
PT	Physical Training
PTI	Physical Training Instructor
PTSD	Post Traumatic Stress Disorder

PX	Post Exchange Store
R&C	Rest in Country
R&R	Rest and Recuperation
RAA	Royal Australian Artillery
RAAC	Royal Australian Armoured Corps
RAAF	Royal Australian Air Force
RAE	Royal Australian Engineers
RAN	Royal Australian Navy
RAP	Regimental Aid Post
RAR	Royal Australian Regiment
RBT	Recruit Training Battalion
RHA	Rolled Homogenous Armour
RMC	Royal Military College
RN	Royal Navy
RNZA	Royal New Zealand Army/Royal New Zealand Artillery
RPG	Rocket Propelled Grenade
RSM	Regimental Sergeant Major
RTB	Recruit Training Battalion
SASR	Special Air Service Regiment
SCHQ	Support Company Headquarters
TAOR	Tactical Area of Responsibility
TB	Training Battalion
TFHQ	Task Force Headquarters
USAF	United States Air Force
USMC	United States Marine Corps
USN	United States Navy
VEA	Veterans' Entitlements Act

Bibliography

3 Field Battery Asn. au (Web).

5 RAR Assn. au. (Web).

Australia's Navy in Vietnam
Royal Australian Navy Operations 1965-72, Sea Power Centre, Department of Defence.

Australian War Memorial
War Diaries, Sub Class 7/8, 8 Battalion, The Royal Australian Regiment.

Carroll, John R
Out of Sight, Out of Mind. The Royal Australian Navy in Vietnam 1965-72.

Clunies-Ross, Adrian AO MBE (Ed)
The Grey Eight in Vietnam (The History of Eighth Battalion, The Royal Australian Regiment, November 1969 – November 1970.

Denham, Neil
Artillery imagery.

Defence, Australia
RAN Imagery and related statistics.

Department of Veterans Affairs
Annual Reports 2011-12 and 2020-22.
Map imagery of Phuoc Tuy Province.

Department of Veterans Affairs and the Australian Institute of Health and Welfare
Dapsone Exposure and Australian Vietnam Service: Mortality and Cancer Incidence Study. September 2007.

Dapin, Mark
The Nashos' War 2014.

Eather, Steve
Target Charlie, Aerospace Publications. 1993.

Edwards, Peter
A Nation at War: Australian Politics, Society, and Diplomacy during the Vietnam War 1965–1975, the Official History of Australia's Involvement in Southeast Asian Conflicts 1948–1975, vol. 6 (Appendix).

Fairchild, Fred
A summary of operations by the Royal Australian Regiment in the Vietnam War 1965-1972.

Hall, Robert A
Combat Battalion, the Eight Battalion in Vietnam. Allen and Unwin 2000.

HQ IATF. org/phuoctuy. (Web).
International War Veterans Poetry Archives.

Irvine, Lachlan
Agent Orange. A History of Deception. New Zealand Vietnam veterans and the McLeod Report (A paper).

Lockhart, Greg
The Minefield: An Australian Tragedy in Vietnam. Allen and Unwin 2007.

Lucas, Terry
The Vietnam Game (A personal reflective article).

Marshall, Ern
Australia's Involvement in Vietnam (Web).

Lee Marvin, Alan J. Lerner & Frederick Loewe
The song 'Wand'rin Star' from the movie 'Paint your Wagon.'

Navy News
Volume 49 No. 15, 'Towing the line' (a special feature) by John Perryman. 24 August 2006.

Newman, Lt S D: (Retd)
Vietnam Gunners – 161 Battery RNZA, South Vietnam, 1965-71, 1988, Moana Press.

Nott, Rodney MBE RFD RAN (Retd)
Northbound for Vietnam (An article).

Nott, Rodney MBE RFD RAN (Retd) and Payne Noel OAM
The Vung Tau Ferry (HMAS Sydney) and Escort Ships (Vietnam 1965-1972).

Odgers, George
Mission Vietnam (Royal Australian Air Force Operations 1964-1972).

Picken, Bruce:
Fire Support Bases, Vietnam. 2012.

Possums (From Vietnam 1965-1971 and East Timor and beyond)
161 Recce Flight and 161 Independent Recce Flight (Web).

Ross, Andrew Dr
Mine Warfare. 1st Australian Task Force's Struggle for South Vietnam.

Ross, Brian
Australia's Military Involvement in the Vietnam War 1995 (A paper).

Ryerson, Michael USMC:
The man in the doorway (a poem 1986).

The Australian Army
Australian Military Forces Pocketbook on South Vietnam. (7610 – 66 – 023 - 3281).

Victor Company Originals
Royal New Zealand Infantry Regiment, Vietnam, 1967 (Web).

Vietnam Veterans Association of Australia (VVAA) Sunshine Coast Sub-Branch
Pension and Advocacy Team Weights Chart.

Vietnam Veterans' Federation of Australia (VVFA)
Letter of 6 September 2006 to members addressing the government published results of studies into the health of Vietnam veterans.

Wilson, Stewart
Military Aircraft of Australia. Aerospace Publications. 1994

Wikipedia - Various.

www.ingramcontent.com/pod-product-compliance
Lightning Source LLC
Chambersburg PA
CBHW062030290426
44109CB00026B/2581